A LINGUISTIC HISTORY OF RUSSIA

A Linguistic History of Russia to the End of the Eighteenth Century

A. P. VLASTO

CLARENDON PRESS · OXFORD
1988

01 9815660 X

Oxford University Press, Walton Street, Oxford OX2 6DP

Oxford New York Toronto
Delhi Bombay Calcutta Madras Karachi
Petaling Jaya Singapore Hong Kong Tokyo
Nairobi Dar es Salaam Cape Town
Melbourne Auckland

and associated companies in
Berlin Ibadan

Oxford is a trade mark of Oxford University Press

Published in the United States
by Oxford University Press, New York

First published 1986
Paperback edition first published 1988

British Library Cataloguing in Publication Data

Vlasto, A. P. (Alexis Peter), 1915–
A linguistic history of Russia to the
end of the eighteenth century.
1. Russian language, to 1800
I. Title
491.77'009
ISBN 0-19-815662-6

Library of Congress Cataloging in Publication Data

Data available
Vlasto, A. P.
A linguistic history of Russia to the end of the
eighteenth century.
Bibliography: p.
1. Russian language—To 1300—Grammar, Historical.
2. Russian language—1300–1700—Grammar, Historical.
3. Russian language—18th century—Grammar, Historical.
I. Title.
PG2101.V55 1985 491.75 84-25497
ISBN 0-19-815662-6

Printed in Great Britain
at Oxford University Printing House, Oxford
by David Stanford
Printer to the University

CL DS

600328383

328383

FOREWORD

This book contains the essential matter of a Russian historical grammar but its purpose is rather wider—to illustrate and interpret the various kinds of written language current in Russia from the beginnings of literacy down to the establishment of the modern 'received standard' literary language at the beginning of the nineteenth century.

This history is not intelligible—and literary appreciation, for that matter, is often impeded—without a constant scrutiny of Church Slavonic. The interaction of the Russian vernacular and Church Slavonic is therefore the subject of Chapter 1 (the formal aspect) and the concluding Chapter 7 (the stylistic aspect), and throughout the other chapters the points at which they differed are everywhere clearly indicated.

The student reading a Russian text of any period should thus be enabled to recognize and appreciate in its historical context the amalgam which written Russian usually was and still is.

If only for reasons of length it was not practicable to continue this history in detail beyond the establishment of the 'classical' standard, though more recent features receive incidental mention in appropriate places. Moreover, the critical century before Pushkin's lifetime, of first importance in establishing the nineteenth-century standard, could not be treated in all respects as fully as it deserves.

The reader should particularly note the following points:

(i) A considerable proportion of the illustrative examples has been taken from the documents and excerpts given in Obnorski and Barkhudarov (reprinted in Lehr-Spławiński and Witkowski; see Bibliography) since this is still the best selection available; some indispensable items cannot be found elsewhere.

(ii) Every such example is dated as accurately as possible but in several important cases the date has to be conventional rather than actual. In particular, quotations from the *Russian Primary Chronicle* are given for easy reference under their year of entry (e.g. *s.a.* 945) on the understanding that the linguistic forms are unlikely to be older than the date of compilation of the original 'edition' (i.e. *c.*1100) and could have been altered thereafter at any time down to the date of the earliest extant copy. In this connection consult the Remarks in Table I (pp. 24 ff.) on each text.

(iii) To ease the technical difficulties of production the use of obsolete letters and special symbols has been kept to a minimum. They are, of course, employed whenever necessary to the philological argument; if not, they are replaced by modern equivalents, in particular я for ᴀ and ꙗ. Old Church Slavonic is given in the generally accepted Latin transcription. Texts of the eighteenth century and later are given in modern orthography unless there is a special reason to preserve the contemporary form.

(iv) Much of the dating in Chapter 5 (Vocabulary) is uncertain since a comprehensive historical dictionary of Russian does not yet exist.

(v) Cross-references are given in the form 2.27 = Chapter 2, §27. References of the form 'text no. 4' are to the texts listed in Table I.

Selwyn College   *Midsummer 1983*
Cambridge

CONTENTS

TABLES, DIAGRAM, MAPS   xii

ABBREVIATIONS   xiii

SELECT BIBLIOGRAPHY   xvi

1. PRELIMINARIES   1

I. PREHISTORY OF RUSSIAN: EAST SLAV IN RELATION TO COMMON SLAVONIC AND OLD CHURCH SLAVONIC §§1–32

1–2 the Slav languages; 3–5 expansion of the Slavs; 6 the East Slavs; 7–9 writing; 10–13 Christianity; OCS and the Cyrillic alphabet in Russia. *OCS and ESl. compared*: 14 palatalization; 15–17 palatalization of velars; 18 palatalization of labials; 19 palatalization of dentals; 20 palatalization of consonant groups; 21 nasal vowels; 22–3 functional diphthongs (C*a*SC, C*e*SC); 24–5 initial VSC; 26–9 other initial vowels; 30 other differences in vocalism; 31 morphological differences; 32 summary.

II. EARLY EAST SLAV DOCUMENTS §§33–8

Table I: The principal early documents; 34–7 linguistic analysis of the documents; 38 periodization.

III. ALPHABET AND ORTHOGRAPHY §§39–44

Table II: The Cyrillic alphabet; 39–40 the Cyrillic alphabet in Russia; 41–4 revisions of orthography.

2. PHONOLOGY   42

1–2 principle of open syllables; 3–4 early ESl. vowels; 5–6 early ESl. consonants (Table III); 7–8 vowel length; 9 ESl. *(j)ä* < *ę*; 10 ESl. *ě* (ѣ); 11 the jers (ь, ъ); 12–13 weak jers; 14 strong jers. *Immediate consequences of the loss of the weak jers*: 15–16 new consonant pairs (hard/soft); 17 status of ы; 18 closed syllables; 19–22 new consonant clusters; 23 diphthongs; 24–6 assimilations; 27 long consonants; 28 dissimilations; 29–30 irregularities; 31 Slavonicisms; 32 false analogies; 33 jer + *j*. *Further consonant changes mainly subsequent to the loss of jers*: 34 new phoneme /f/; 35 devoicing of final consonants; 36 the velars; 37 *š/ž*; 38 *c'* and *č'*; 39 *š'/ž'*; 40–1 special history of /g/. *Further adjustments in the vowel system*: 42–4 sequence C'*o* (C*ë*); 45–6 exceptions and irregularities; 47 *polnoglásie*; 48 sequences

CONTENTS

Cъ/ьSC and CSъ/ьC; 49–50 'secondary *polnoglásie*'; 51–2 summary;
Table IV: Modern Russian consonantal phonemes.

3. MORPHOLOGY   81

NOMINAL DECLENSION   §§1–36

1–3 introductory. *Feminine nouns*: Table V; 4–7 commentary to
Table V. *Masculine and neuter nouns*: Table VI; 8 neuters; 9–13
changes in masc. pl. (9–10 nom./acc., 11 gen., 12–13 loc., dat., instr.);
14–17 ŭ-stems; 18 ĭ-stems; 19 irregularities in neuters. *Consonant
stems*: Table VII; 20–2 masculines; 23–4 feminines; 25–7 neuters; 28
summary. 29 velar stems; 30 vocative case; 31–2 dual; 33–4 masc. pl.
in -á; 35 masc. pl. in -ья; 36 indeclinable nouns.

THE ADJECTIVE   §§37–53

37 introductory; Table VIII: Declension of the long adjective; 38–40
masc. sing.; 41 fem. sing.; 42 pl. forms; 43 personal possessive
adjectives; 44–7 other types of adjective; 48–9 survival of the short
forms; 50 adjectives as nouns. *Comparison of adjectives*: Table IX;
51–2 comparative; 53 superlative.

THE PRONOUN   §§54–70

54–8 personal pronouns, 1st and 2nd persons (Table X); 59–60
pronoun of the 3rd person (Table XI); 61 demonstrative pronouns
(Table XII); 62–3 interrogative pronouns and adjectives; 64 relative
pronouns; 65 possessive adjectives; 66 various pronominal adjectives;
67 definite article; 68–9 adverbs; Table XIII: Conspectus of pronominal and adverbial series; 70 commentary to Table XIII.

NUMERALS   §§71–86

71–5 one to nine; 76 ten; 77 teens; 78 decades; 79 hundreds; 80
thousand; 81 fractions; 82 higher numerals; 83 ordinals; 84 collectives; 85–6 multiplicative and distributive expressions.

THE VERB   §§87–140

87 introductory; Table XIV: The verbs of position; 88–94 the athematic verbs. *Regular verbs*: 95–8 present tense; 99–100 imperfect tense;
101–2 aorist tense; 103–5 the perfect tenses; 106 pluperfect tense;
107 future-perfect tense; 108–11 the future tenses; 112–13 imperative;
114 infinitive; 115 supine; 116 conditional; 117 participles; 118 present
participle active (p.p.a.) (Table XV); 119–20 present gerund; 121–2
native and ChSl. forms; 123 continuous tenses with the p.p.a.; 124–5
past participle active; 126 the perfect participle in -*l*; 127 present
participle passive; 128–31 past participle passive; 132 the participles
of быть; 133–4 the passive voice; 135–6 the verbal noun; Table XVI:
Summary of the modern verbal paradigm; 137–8 verbs with various
anomalies; 139–40 verbs of motion.

CONTENTS

4. SYNTAX   188

TYPES OF SENTENCE (MAIN CLAUSE) §§1–11

1–2 nominal; 3 negative; 4 interrogative; 5–10 passive constructions; 11 impersonal sentences.

TYPES OF SUBORDINATE CLAUSE §§12–33

12–17 relative; 18 temporal; 19 locative; 20 causal; 21 manner and comparison; 22 final; 23–7 conditional; 28 concessive; 29 consecutive; 30 generalizing; 31 subordinate clauses with participles and gerunds; 32 indirect speech; 33 indirect questions.

WORD ORDER §§34–9

USE OF CASES §§40–54

40 apposition. *Genitive*: 41–2 animacy; 43 verbs constructed with gen.; 44 gen. of possession; 45 gen. of time and comparison. *Dative*: 46 dat. of direction; 47 dat. of possession; 48 dat. and infinitive; 49 dat. absolute; 50 verbs constructed with dat. *Instrumental*: 51 various; 52 predicative instr. *Locative*: 53 various. *Nominative*: 54 nom. and infinitive.

PREPOSITIONS (INCLUDING VERBAL PREFIXES) (SELECTED) §§55–69

55 вы-; 56 въз-; 57 за; 58 меж-; 59 на; 60 низ-; 61 о; 62 пере-/пре-; 63 пред; 64 по; 65 про, с; 66 через; 67–9 various points.

SYNTAX OF ADJECTIVES §§70–2

SYNTAX OF NUMERALS §§73–8

CO-ORDINATING CONJUNCTIONS §§79–82

79 да; 80 но; 81 а; 82 то, ино.

ASPECT AND TENSE §§83–97

83–7 aspect—general considerations; 88–9 imperfect and aorist; 90 prefixation; 91 imperfective suffixes; 92–3 unpaired verbs; 94 perfective-iteratives; 95 verbs of motion; 96 summary; 97 usage of *pf/impf* in *RP*.

5. VOCABULARY   251

1 introduction; 2–3 Balto-Slav; 4 Iranian; 5 Gothic; 6 other Germanic; 7–10 Turkic; 11 Baltic; 12 Finnic; 13 Scandinavian; 14 Greek; 15–16 Church Slavonic; 17 ChSl. prefixes; 18 ChSl. suffixes; 19 identification of Slavonicisms; 20–2 the period of the Tatar yoke; 23 the 'Second South Slav Influence'; 24 Baltic trade; 25–8 medieval learning; 29–31 Polish; 32–4 the reign of Peter the Great; 35 the early 18th c.; 36–7 the arts; 38 the impact of French; 39–43 the period 1730–60

(Kantemír, Trediakóvsky, Lomonósov, Sumarókov); 44–7 the later
18th c.; 48 summary.

6. DIALECTS: THE BASIS OF THE MODERN STANDARD LANGUAGE   300

1–5 introductory; diagrammatic layout of dialect areas; 6–7 contrast
of N. and S. dialects; Table XVII: Diagnostic features of the main
dialect areas (modern state); 8–11 consonants; 12–13 vowels; 14–16
unstressed vowels (reduction); 17–18 other phonetic features; 19–22
morphological features; 23 postposited 'article'; 24–6 other features;
27 vocalic characteristics of N. dialects; 28 vocalic characteristics of
S. dialects; 29–32 яканье; 33–5 аканье; 36–43 general theory of the
evolution of unstressed vowels; 44 absence of ёканье; 45 treatment
of ѣ; 46 Moscow standard; 47 summary; 48–52 Moscow dialect (Table
XVIII); 53–4 the modern standard; 55–6 false orthography; 57 ChSl.
pronunciation; 58 foreign loan-words; 59–60 history of stress; 61 two
important dialects: 62 Nóvgorod dialect; 63 Pskov dialect; Table
XIX: Evolution of East Slav; 64–8 Ukrainian and White Russian
compared with Great Russian; Table XX: Distinguishing features of
Ukrainian and White Russian.

7. SPOKEN LANGUAGE AND WRITTEN LANGUAGES   344

A. THE KIEVAN PERIOD TO c.1250   §§1–14

1–3 introduction; 4–5 Church Slavonic; 6–7 literary genres; 8–11
historical narrative; 12–13 other Kievan literature; 14 summary.

B. THE PERIOD OF FRAGMENTATION c.1200–1400 §§15–16

C. THE MUSCOVY PERIOD c.1350–1600   §§17–24

17–18 Muscovite bilingualism; 19–20 the 'Second South Slav Influence'; 21–2 various writers; 23 West Russian chancellery language;
24 Muscovite administrative language.

D. THE MUSCOVY PERIOD: THE SEVENTEENTH CENTURY   §§25–35

25 the Western current; 26–8 grammatical writings; 29–30 'secular'
ChSl.; 31 Kotoshíkhin; 32 history and biography; 33–4 anonymous
prose and poetry; 35 Avvakúm.

E. THE EIGHTEENTH CENTURY AND BEYOND   §§36–59

36–40 the first quarter of the century (the reign of Peter the Great);
41–6 the pioneers of a new literature and literary language, c.1730–60
(Kantemír, Trediakóvsky, Lomonósov, Sumarókov); 47–8 poetry in
the later 18th and early 19th c.; 49–56 prose in the later 18th and
early 19th c. (Fonvízin, Novikóv, Karamzín); 57–9 conclusion.

CONTENTS

APPENDIX.   ILLUSTRATIONS OF THE *POLNOGLÁSIE* AND   395
             NON-*POLNOGLÁSIE*   (CHURCH   SLAVONIC)
             FORMS IN RUSSIAN WORD-GROUPS

REGISTER OF RUSSIAN WORDS TREATED IN CHAPTER 5   403

TABLES, DIAGRAM, MAPS

I.	The principal early documents	24
II.	The Cyrillic alphabet	35
III.	Early ESl. consonantal phonemes	45
IV.	Modern Russian consonantal phonemes	79
V.	Feminine noun declensions	83
VI.	Masculine and neuter noun declensions	87
VII.	Consonant-stem nouns (early ESl. state)	97
VIII.	Declension of the long adjective	110
IX.	Declension of the comparative	119
X.	Pronouns of the first and second persons	123
XI.	Pronoun of the third person	125
XII.	Demonstrative pronouns	128
XIII.	Conspectus of pronominal and adverbial series	136
XIV.	The verbs of position	150
XV.	The present participle active	170
XVI.	Summary of the modern verbal paradigm	184
XVII.	Diagnostic features of the main dialect areas (modern state)	304
XVIII.	Characteristics of Moscow language	325
XIX.	The evolution of East Slav: diagrammatic summary	336
XX.	Distinguishing features of Ukrainian and White Russian (Belorussian)	338

DIAGRAM

Diagrammatic layout of dialect areas	302

MAPS

1.	East Slav dialects	*facing p.* 302
2.	Early East Slav settlement	*facing p.* 303

xii

ABBREVIATIONS

A(cc).	accusative	dial.	dialect(al)
adj(s).	adjective(s)	dim.	diminutive
adv.	adverb	doc(s).	document(s)
Af. Nik.	Afanási Nikítin	*Dom.*	*Domostrój*
Ags.	Anglo-Saxon	Dost.	Dostoiévsky
anim.	animate	du.	dual
aor.	aorist	*dur*	durative
Ar.	Arabic		
Arch. Ev.	Архáнгельское	ed.	edited (by)
	евáнгелие	edn.	edition
Ass.	*Codex*	Eng.	English
	Assemanianus	EO	Евгений Онегин
AV	Authorized Version	ESl.	East Slav(onic)
	(Bible)	Est.	Estonian
Avv.	Avvakúm		
		f(em).	feminine
Blg.	Bulgarian	fig.	figurative
BSl.	Balto-Slav	Fr.	French
		fut.	future
C.	Central	fut.-perf.	future-perfect
C	consonant		
C′	palatalized	G(en).	genitive
	consonant	Ger.	German (modern)
ChSl.	Church Slavonic	ger.	gerund
coll.	colloquial	Gk.	Greek
comp.	comparative	Glag.	Glagolitic
conj.	conjugation	Gmc.	Germanic
cons.	consonant	Goth.	Gothic
cpd(s).	compound(s)		
CSl.	Common	*Hyp.*	*Hypatian Chronicle*
	Slav(on)ic		
Cyr.	Cyrillic	IE	Indo-European
Cz.	Czech	imperat.	imperative
		imperf.	imperfect
Dan. Zat.	Daniíl Zatóchnik	*impf*	imperfective
D(at).	dative	inan.	inanimate
dat. abs.	dative absolute	inf.	infinitive
decl.	declension	I(nstr).	instrumental

ABBREVIATIONS

intr.	intransitive	part.	participle
It(al).	Italian	pass.	passive
		past p.a.	past participle active
Kar.	Karamzín		
Kot.	Kotoshíkhin	pers.	person
		Pers.	Persian
Lat.	Latin	*pf*	perfective
Lerm.	Lérmontov	*pf-it*	perfective-iterative
lit.	literary	pl.	plural
Lith.	Lithuanian	PN	place-name
L(oc).	Locative	Pol.	Polish
Lom.	Lomonósov	Pos.	Pososhkóv
		p.p.a.	present participle active
Mar.	*Codex Marianus*		
m(asc).	masculine	p.p.p.	past participle passive
MHG	Middle High German	pred.	predicative
mod.	modern	pres.	present (tense)
		pres. p.p.	present participle passive
N.	North		
N	nasal (consonant)	pret.	preterite
NBG	see Table I, no. 16	*Ps. Sin.*	*Psalterium sinaiticum*
neg.	negative		
n(eut).	neuter		
N(om).	nominative	R.	Russian, river
Novg.	Nóvgorod	rec.	recorded
Novg. Chr.	*First Novgorod Chronicle* (Synodal copy)	repr.	reprinted
		RP	Русская Правда (text no. 2)
NR	North Russian	*RPC*	*Russian Primary Chronicle* (text no. 10)
OB	Obnorski and Barkhudarov (see Bibliography)		
		S.	South
obs.	obsolete	S	sonant (*r* or *l*)
OCS	Old Church Slavonic	*s.a.*	*sub anno* (chronicle entries)
OE	Old English	*Savv.*	*Savvina Kniga*
OFr.	Old French	Scand.	Scandinavian
OHG	Old High German	SCr.	Serbo-Croat
OPr.	Old Prussian	s(in)g.	singular
Ostr.	Ostromir's *Gospel Book* (text no. 5)	Skr.	Sanskrit
		Sl.	Slav(onic)

ABBREVIATIONS

SPR	*Slavistische Drukken en Herdrukken* (Hague)	V	vowel
		V̄	long vowel
		V(oc).	vocative
		Vl. Mon.	Vladímir Monomákh
SR	*Slavonic Review* (London)		
SR	South Russian	WhR.	White Russian (Belorussian)
SSl.	South Slav(onic)		
sup.	superlative	*WSJ*	*Wiener Slavistisches Jahrbuch*
Supr.	*Codex Suprasliensis*		
		WSl.	West Slav(onic)
Tat.	Tatar		
tr.	translation, translated	*ZslPh*	*Zeitschrift für slavische Philologie* (Leipzig)
trans.	transitive		
Turg.	Turgénev		
		Zogr.	*Codex Zographensis*
Ukr.	Ukrainian		
ult.	ultimately (from)		

SYMBOLS

< derived from
> proceeding to, becoming
* hypothetical or reconstructed form (e.g. IE or CSl.)
† obsolete word
/ / phoneme
[ ] phonetic transcription

SELECT BIBLIOGRAPHY

B. Unbegaun, *Bibliographical Guide to the Russian Language* (Oxford, 1953) gives more or less complete coverage of the subject up to 1953.

Artsikhovski, A. V., *et al.*, Новгородские грамоты на бересте, 3 vols. (1953–63).

Auty, R., and Nandriş, G., *Handbook of Old Church Slavonic*, 2 vols. (London, 1959–60).

Avanesov, R. I., Очерки русской диалектологии (1949).

—— Русское литературное произношение (2nd edn., 1954).

—— and Borkovski, V. I., Палеографический и лингвистический анализ новгородских берестяных грамот (1955).

—— and Ivanov, V. V., Историческая грамматика русского языка: морфология — глагол (1982).

—— and Orlova, V. G., Русская диалектология (2nd edn., 1965).

Bielfeldt, H. H., *Altslawische Grammatik* (Halle, 1961).

Boeck, W., *et al.*, *Geschichte der russischen Literatursprache* (Düsseldorf, 1974).

Borkovski, V. I., Синтаксис древнерусских грамот (L'vov, 1949).

—— and Kuznetsov, P. S., Историческая грамматика русского языка (1963).

Borras, F. M., and Christian, R. F., *Russian Syntax* (Oxford, 1959).

Bulakhovski, L. A., Исторический комментарий к русскому литературному языку (Kiev, 1950).

Cherepnin, A., Русская палеография (1956).

Chernykh, P. Ja., Историческая грамматика русского языка (1952).

—— Очерки русской исторической лексикологии (1956).

—— Язык Уложения 1649 года (1953).

Cocron, F., *La Langue russe dans la seconde moitié du XVIIme siècle* (Paris, 1962).

Comrie, B., *The Languages of the Soviet Union* (Cambridge, 1981).

—— and Stone, G., *The Russian Language since the Revolution* (Oxford, 1978).

Dal', V., Толковый словарь живого великорусского языка (1st edn., 1863–6; 3rd edn., 1903–9).

Efimov, A. I., История русского литературного языка (1963).

Entwistle, W. J., and Morison, W. A., *Russian and the Slavonic Languages* (London, 1949).

Filin, F. P., Истоки и судьбы русского литературного языка (1981).

—— Образование языка восточных славян (1962).

Filin, F. P., Происхождение русского, украинского и белорусского языков (1972).

Gardiner, S. C., *German Loanwords in Russian, 1550–1690* (Oxford, 1965).

Gilliou, J.-Y., *Grammaire du vieux-russe* (Paris, 1972).

Gorshkov, A. I., История русского литературного языка (1969).

Gorshkova, K. V., Историческая диалектология русского языка (1972).

—— and Khaburgaev, G. A., Историческая грамматика русского языка (1981).

Hüttl-Worth, G., *Foreign Words in Russian, 1550–1800* (Berkeley, Cal., 1963).

Isserlin, E. M., Лексика русского литературного языка XVII в. (1971).

Ivanov, V. V., Историческая фонология русского языка (1968).

Jones, D., and Ward, D., *The Phonetics of Russian* (Cambridge, 1969).

Kiparsky, V., *Der Wortakzent der russischen Schriftsprache* (Heidelberg, 1962).

—— *Russische historische Grammatik,* 3 vols. (Heidelberg, 1963–75).

Kochman, S., *Polsko-rosyjskie stosunki językowe od XVI do XVII w.* (Opole, 1975).

Kotkov, S. I., Московская деловая и бытовая письменность XVII в. (1968).

—— Московская речь в начальный период становления русского национального языка (1974).

Kovtun, L. S., Лексикография в московской Руси XVI–начала XVII в. (1975).

Kuzakov, V. K., Очерки развития естественнонаучных и технических представлений на Руси в X–XVII вв. (1976).

Kuznetsov, P. S., Очерки исторической морфологии русского языка (1959).

Larin, B. A., Лекции по истории русского литературного языка (1975).

—— Русско-английский словарь-дневник Р. Джемса (1959).

Lehr-Spławiński, T., and Witkowski, W., *Wybór tekstów do historii języka rosyjskiego* (Warsaw, 1965).

Levin, V. D., Очерк стилистики русского литературного языка конца XVIII–начала XIX вв. (лексика) (1964).

Likhachëv, D. S., Культура Руси времени Андрея Рублева и Епифания Премудрого (1962).

Lomtev, T. P., Грамматика белорусского языка (1956).

—— Очерки по историческому синтаксису русского языка (1956).

Lunt, H. G., *Old Church Slavic Grammar* (6th edn., The Hague, 1974).

Martel, A., *Lomonosov et la langue littéraire russe* (Paris, 1933).

Matthews, W. K., *Russian Historical Grammar* (London, 1960).

Obnorski, S. P., Очерки по истории русского литературного языка старшего периода (1946).

—— and Barkhudarov, S. G., Хрестоматия по истории русского языка, 3 vols. (1938–48). (The references given in Table I are to vol. 1.)

Orlova, V. G., История аффрикат в русском языке (1959).

Panzer, B., *Der genetische Aufbau des Russischen* (Heidelberg, 1978).

Samilov, M., *The Phoneme* Jat' *in Slavic* (*SPR* 32) (The Hague, 1964).

Schooneveld, C. H. van, *A Semantic Analysis of the Old Russian Finite Preterite System* (The Hague, 1959).

Selishchev, A. M., Старославянский язык (1951).

Shevelov, G., *A Historical Phonology of the Ukrainian Language* (Heidelberg, 1979).

—— *A Prehistory of Slavic* (Heidelberg, 1964).

Shvedova, N. Ju. (ed.), Грамматика современного русского литературного языка (1970).

Словарь академии российской (СПб. 1789–94; 2nd edn. 1806–22).

Словарь русских народных говоров (1965–).

Словарь русского языка XI–XVII вв. (1975–).

Словарь современного русского литературного языка, 17 vols. (1948–65).

Slovník jazyka staroslověnského (Prague, 1966–).

Sobik, M. E., *Polnisch-russische Beziehungen im Spiegel des russischen Wortschatzes des 17–18 Jhdts.* (Meisenheim, 1969).

Sobolevski, A. I., Лекции по истории русского языка (4th edn., 1907).

Sreznevski, I. I., Материалы для словаря древнерусского языка (1893–1909; repr. 1958).

Stang, C. S., *Die westrussische Kanzleisprache des Grossfürstentums Litauen* (Oslo, 1935).

Stetsenko, A. N., Исторический синтаксис русского языка (1972).

Talev, I., *Some Problems of the Second South Slav Influence* (*Slavistische Beiträge* 67) (Munich, 1973).

Thörnqvist, C., *Studien über die nordischen Lehnwörter im Russischen* (Stockholm, 1948).

Tobolova, M. P., and Uspenski, V. A., Российская Грамматика А. А. Барсова (1981).

Ulukhanov, I. S., О языке древней Руси (1972).

Unbegaun, B., *La Langue russe au XVIᵐᵉ siècle* (Paris, 1935).

—— *Russian Surnames* (Oxford, 1972).

—— (ed.), H. W. Ludolf, *Grammatica russica* (Oxford, 1959).

Uspenski, V. A., Архаическая система церковнославянского произношения (1968).

Vaillant, A., *Grammaire comparée des langues slaves,* 5 vols. (Paris, 1950–77).

SELECT BIBLIOGRAPHY

Vaillant, A., *Manuel du vieux slave,* 2 vols. (Paris, 1948).

Vasmer, M., *Russisches etymologisches Wörterbuch* (Heidelberg, 1953–8).

Veenker, W., *Die Frage des finnougrischen Substrats in der russischen Sprache* (Bloomington, Ind., 1967).

Vinogradov, V. V., Очерки по истории русского литературного языка XVII–XIX вв. (1934; repr. Leyden, 1950).

Vinokur, G. O., Русский язык: исторический очерк (1945).

Ward, D., *The Russian Language Today* (London, 1965).

Yakubinski, L. P., История древнерусского языка (1953).

1

PRELIMINARIES

I. PREHISTORY OF RUSSIAN: EAST SLAV IN RELATION TO COMMON SLAVONIC AND OLD CHURCH SLAVONIC

1 The Slav (Slavic or Slavonic) languages form a well-defined branch of the Indo-European (IE) family of languages. They are most closely related to the Baltic branch, of which Lithuanian and Latvian are still spoken along the eastern coastlands of the Baltic Sea. Opinion is still divided as to their precise relationship—whether Baltic and Slav diverged from a common ancestor (Proto-Balto-Slav), or whether their many similarities can be adequately explained by a long period of contiguity and mutual influence. About the long geographical contiguity there is no doubt: it has been a fact since at least the beginning of the second millennium BC. However that may be, the separate evolution of the Proto-Slav language in directions different from Baltic began at the very latest at the beginning of the Christian era and in all probability much earlier.

2 Apart from a few personal and place-names, there is no record of any form of the Slav language before the middle of the 9th c. AD; the earliest surviving manuscripts of Slav texts scarcely antedate AD 1000. The elaboration of a written Slav language is traditionally ascribed to two bilingual Greek missionaries, Constantine (Cyril) and Methodios, who devised an alphabet about the year 863 and began translating the Scriptures and Orthodox liturgical texts into the Macedonian Slav dialect spoken about Salonika, of which city they were natives. The work was continued by them in Central Europe—Moravia, Slovakia, and Pannonia (W. Hungary), where somewhat different Slav dialects were spoken—and carried on after 885 by their pupils and successors in yet other Slav-populated lands, above all in Bulgaria. This written language, intended at the outset for ecclesiastical use, was bound to be somewhat artificial, being under the strong influence of Greek in its vocabulary and syntax. It is usually known as Old Church Slavonic (OCS). It is the earliest,

1

and hence philologically the most important, extant form of any Slav language and, provided certain specifically South Slav (SSl.) features are abstracted, provides the best evidence for the reconstruction of late Common Slavonic (CSl.), that is, the language of the Slavs in the early centuries AD before it began appreciably to split up into the modern separate languages. The fortunes of OCS in the 10th–11th c. show that at that time the various local forms of the Slav language had not yet diverged to the point of mutual unintelligibility, since OCS served as a written medium, or literary norm, for several Slav peoples remote from one another. But in each mission field OCS tended to take on some colouring of the local dialect.

3   The expansion of the Slavs during the early Christian centuries had brought them from a compact area north of the Carpathians (parts of present-day Poland and Ukraine) to NW Europe (as far as the R. Elbe), Central Europe (modern Czechoslovakia and Hungary), the Balkans, and the more westerly part of Russia. It was inevitable that over such an immense area the small differences within CSl. would soon be magnified, and new ones added to them, by loss of contact between different parts of the Slav world, by new conditions of life, by mixing with other peoples. In the 9th–11th centuries contact between northern and southern forms of Slav speech was much reduced, if not completely ended, by the intrusion of a belt of alien languages, namely the extension of High German (Bavarian) speech eastwards into Austria and beyond, the irruption of the Finno-Ugrian Magyars into Hungary (from the closing years of the 9th c.), and the consolidation of speakers of Balkan Latin in the plains of Romania on the lower Danube. As a result there are now, both geographically and linguistically speaking, three groups of Slav languages:

1. South or Balkan Slav (SSl.), consisting of (from west to east): Slovene, Serbo-Croat[1] (SCr.), and Bulgarian (Blg.). (Macedonian as now understood and codified in a literary language is a medieval product of Serbian–Bulgarian mixing.)

2. West Slav (WSl.): Czech (in Bohemia) and Slovak, joined by the transitional dialects of Moravia; Polish (Pol.); Upper and Lower Sorbian (sometimes called Lusatian after the district of Lusatia/Lausitz), now relict enclaves in German-speaking lands.

[1] Serbian is the Orthodox, Croat the Roman Catholic variant of the modern language of Yugoslavia (Slovenia and Macedonia apart).

3. East Slav (ESl.) in the USSR, now comprising Russian, Ukrainian, and White Russian (Belorussian).

4   The migrations of the Slavs cannot be reconstructed with any precision. It cannot be shown—indeed it is improbable—that the *SSl. language group* descends from a single CSl. dialect spoken by one more or less compact group before the migrations began. Slovene and SCr. are relatively closely related; Bulgarian differs considerably and has had an idiosyncratic development in recent times (since *c.*AD 1100). The Macedonian dialect on which OCS was based, belonging to the East Balkan (Blg.), not West Balkan (Slovene–SCr.) type of language, must be considered rather conservative for the time when it was codified (9th–10th c.).

The *Czechoslovak type* can be properly grouped with Polish (and the other extinct Lechitic languages of N. Germany) but has certain features of the West Balkan type probably acquired during several centuries of mixing and contact in the migration period in the general area of present-day Hungary.

The *ESl. type* would appear to descend from a relatively uniform continuum of dialects and retained such relative linguistic unity down to about the beginning of the 13th c. when large political changes brought about a gradual split (6.64 ff.).

The basic linguistic features which differentiate the three groups had accumulated during the centuries of expansion—mainly in the 6th–10th c. AD—by the end of which we can no longer speak of CSl. In the case of ESl. some of the characteristic features are shared with SSl., some with WSl., and a few are developments peculiar to it.

5   The combined evidence of archaeology and comparative philology has confirmed—as far as these different disciplines allow[2]—that the 'original area' (прарóдина) in which the Slavs lived and their language developed extended in the CSl. period from the foothills of the Carpathian chain northwards as far as the basin of the R. Pripet (Припять) and eastwards to the R. Dnepr in the vicinity of Kiev. A precise and complete geographical definition of the whole area at any given date is virtually impossible. North and east of these river boundaries other languages were spoken:

(*a*) In the Pripet basin and in all the middle and upper Dnepr

---

[2] Archaeology can only bear witness to a certain uniformity of *material culture* over a given area, philology to a *linguistic* one. Neither provides direct evidence of *ethnic* uniformity.

valley—*Baltic* dialects. Topographical study (especially hydro-nyms[3]) has shown that the Baltic-speaking area originally extended much further east and rather further south than today (Map no. 1).

(*b*) In C. and N. Russia—*Finno-Ugrian* dialects. This group of languages apparently had its focus in the Urál region, whence its speakers over a long period gradually spread over the Russian plains westwards as far as Finland and Estonia. A large part of the older toponymy of C. and N. Russia is Finno-Ugrian, e.g. Вόлогда, Вы́чегда with Finnic initial stress; Lake Il'men', earlier Йл(ь)мѣрь < Finnic *Ilm(a)järv(i)*; Lake Ládoga; R. Lóvat'.

Thus, when the East Slavs penetrated further into Russia in the early centuries AD—after the collapse of the 'Gothic empire' in the Ukraine towards the end of the 4th c.—they mixed with, or brushed aside, Baltic and Finnic peoples of a cultural level similar to (Balts) or more primitive than (Finno-Ugrians) their own. The first phase of this expansion (say, AD 500–700) brought them close to the Gulf of Finland in the north[4] and to the region of Moscow in the east. The *Russian Primary Chronicle* (Повесть временных лет) gives the names and approximate locations of these ESl. 'tribes' as still known with tolerable accuracy in the 11th c. (Map no. 2).

6   The recorded history of the East Slavs hardly begins before the 9th c. In the course of that century Scandinavian (principally Swedish) rule was imposed on some of the main Slav settlements, finally including Kiev on the lower Dnepr, in the interests of the long-distance trade with the Byzantine Empire. Scandinavian trade relations with the Islamic world had started earlier by the Volga route but, although Slavs no doubt took some part in this, the route itself lay largely outside their settled territories.

We are indebted to Greek sources for the earliest notices of the rise of Kiev as a political centre, of growing interest to Constantinople in view of Greek commercial establishments on the coasts of the Black Sea, the need for protection against aggression from the steppe peoples, and Byzantine rivalry with the Islamic world. By the 10th c. relations with Kiev were close and continuous enough for formal treaties (commercial and military) to be negotiated. The

[3] The fundamental study is V. N. Toporov and O. N. Trubachëv, Лингвистический анализ гидронимов верхнего Поднепровья (Moscow, 1962).

[4] Stáraja Ládoga, the Scandinavian base for the Volga trade route, near the south shore of Lake Ládoga, shows certain (archaeological) traces of Slavs in its population from *c.*AD 800, so their arrival in the north should be put a century or so before this.

texts of three such treaties (at least in part) are recorded in the *Primary Chronicle* and, though more or less remote from their original linguistic form (since the *Chronicle* only took shape in the 11th c., and no copy survives earlier than the late 14th c.), are the first important material from the ESl. world (Table I below, no. 1).

7 Anthropologists give no clear answer to the question, 'at what stage in its development does a people feel an imperative need to record its own language in written form?' All we can say is that it may vary widely, depending partly on social organization and partly on relations with other peoples. Poetry, religious and legal texts can be transmitted orally without difficulty for many centuries (e.g. Iceland); conversely, a complicated palace economy may lead to an early development of written records of a limited kind (Knossós, Mycenae). In some cases writing is first practised in a foreign language and the system only gradually adapted to the native tongue (Japan).

Words for 'write' and 'read' (though not to be conceived in narrow modern terms) are present in CSl., i.e. almost certainly before AD 500, but there is commonly a period of knowing about writing by others, of contact with literate peoples, before practising it oneself. The Slav words (in Russian form) писáть, читáть, кнúга, бýква no doubt belong to this stage of development. The semantic shift of CSl. *pĭsati (IE root *poik'-/peik'-/pik'-) from 'scratch, make (decorative) marks on' to 'write, make symbolic marks on' is paralleled in Iranian[5] and may therefore possibly date from the period of close contacts with Iranian peoples on the steppes (Scythians and Sarmatians—not, however, themselves literate in the light of available evidence) between *c.*700 BC and AD 200, when Iranian influence on the religious vocabulary of the Slavs is also visible (5.4). Words for 'read' are exceedingly various: читáть derives from a CSl. root signifying 'reckon, count'.

The etymology of CSl. (pl.) *kŭn'igy is obscure. If it should prove to be native it could have a meaning parallel to Ger. *(Buch)stabe,* i.e. the material on which magic formulae and the like were inscribed, but it is generally held to be of Asiatic origin.[6] At all events *kŭn'igy* came to mean 'written signs', from which only later was extracted a singular (Russian) кнúга, a 'text',

---

[5] Also in Gk. γράφω and Lat. *scrībō* from other roots.
[6] See I. G. Dobrodomov in Русская речь, 1971/5.

a 'book'. Бу́ква (in its earliest form *buky*, pl. *bukŭve*) is certainly the youngest of the four: it was borrowed by some C. European Slav dialect from Germanic (5.6), was used in the early OCS texts, and was thence propagated to other areas.

8   Despite the general diffusion of these terms there is no good evidence for any native Slav system of writing, in the full sense of the term, prior to the 9th c. AD. The alphabets that came to be used by the East Slavs were those devised in the 9th–10th c. (Glagolitic and Cyrillic) for the C. European and Balkan Slavs. These alphabets were imported into Russia from Bulgaria, and principally the Greek-style Cyrillic; Glagolitic, the original alphabet of SS Cyril and Methodios, was known to some ecclesiastics in early Russia, who were able to transliterate from it into Cyrillic, but was never a competitor for ordinary use.

The only other literate people of importance impinging on the ESl. world was the Khazars (5.7(4)), whose merchant class, if no other, employed the Hebrew and Arabic alphabets. But the Khazar influence on early ESl. culture did not apparently go beyond a few loan-words.

It is to be observed that Mediterranean culture had no part in Slav knowledge or adoption of writing and its terminology until the missionary work of the 9th c. introduced a profound change. This is supported by the fact that Latin words entered CSl. in Roman Imperial times only via other languages (Gothic and other Gmc. languages, 5.5–6). Trade links between Kiev and the Byzantine Empire from the later 9th c. stimulated, if they did not themselves initiate, the use of writing and led, as in Bulgaria from the 8th c. onwards, to some knowledge of the Greek language and its alphabet. On the one hand Gk. (neut. pl.) γράμματα is adopted as (fem. sg.) гра́мота 'letters, written text'; on the other, the new need for keeping written official records, diplomatic and commercial, is confirmed in the Treaty of 945: . . . ношаху сли печати злати. а гостье сребрени. нынѣ же оувѣдѣлъ есть кнѧзь нашь. посылати грамоту . . . и гостье да приносѧть грамоту пишючe сице . . . 'envoys [to Constantinople] have [hitherto] been provided with gold seals and merchants with silver ones; but now our prince has determined that a written document be sent . . . and merchants are to bring with them a document running as follows . . .'.

9   Clearly the change comes in the early 10th c. The beginnings may perhaps be put back to 860 when the Rus' (Русь)—Scandinavian-led Slavs—mounted a large-scale naval attack on Constantinople itself and acquired much plunder but failed to penetrate the city walls. The raid came out of the blue and it is likely to be true, if rhetorically exaggerated,[7] that little or nothing was then known of the Rus' in the City. Greek diplomacy took immediate steps to deal with this new menace. An embassy was sent to the ruler of Khazaria, centred on the lower Volga and N. Caucasian region, to concert defensive measures. On this embassy served the brothers Constantine and Methodios who were a few years later to be sent as missionaries to the Slavs of Moravia and to invent for them the so-called Glagolitic alphabet, which represented the repertoire of Slav sounds with very adequate precision. But also a direct missionary approach is said to have been made to Kiev, which may have had some initial success but had come to a standstill before the end of the century. Greek missionaries in Kiev, for however short a time, imply a working church, literate clergy, and (at that time) Greek service-books.

10   Little advance was possible as long as the Viking dynasts (Varangians) remained pagan, recruiting their armies from still-pagan Scandinavia. We have to wait till the reign of Olga (945–62) for the first Christian ruler at Kiev. But a church seems to have continued to function for a small Christian community there throughout the early 10th c. As important to Russia at this stage, however, were close contacts with Bulgaria, which entered its period of greatest cultural development with the accession of Symeon in 893. Of all the Slav peoples the Bulgarians lived closest to the Imperial City and Greek culture; indeed, they inhabited lands which had been before the incursions of the Slavs and Bulgars[8] part of the Roman Empire. Their literate culture was based partly on the Glagolitic alphabet received from Cyrillo-Methodian pupils in 885 and then from 893 predominantly on the Cyrillic alphabet, deliberately modelled on the Greek, with which they had been long familiar. Moreover, when the Imperial Chancellery required clerks who knew and could write the Slav language it naturally had recourse to Bulgarians.

Thus the East Slavs derived their writing early in the 10th c. from

---

[7] Patriarch Photios, *Homilies* nos. 3 and 4.

[8] The Bulgars were a Turkic tribe who imposed their rule on a large sedentary Slav population and soon adopted their language.

Bulgaria; the part played by Constantinople was much smaller. The increasing importance of Christianity at Kiev, leading to the formal conversion of Prince Vladímir and the whole realm in 988–9, ensured that the practice of writing in Russia would thenceforward be carried on *in the medium of OCS*, the Blg. written language with already established cultural prestige, and *according to the orthographic conventions of the (East Bulgarian) Cyrillic alphabet*. This point is of fundamental importance for the subsequent history of Russian.

11   For lack of evidence it is impossible to determine how soon the Cyrillic alphabet spread in Russia beyond its primary ecclesiastical and other formal uses, that is to say, was used to record the everyday language of the country for one practical purpose or another. Nothing survives from the 10th c.[9]

Extensive excavations at Nóvgorod carried out from 1951 (published from 1953) brought to light many hundreds of texts written, to be precise incised, with a stylus on bast. These берестяны́е гра́моты are predominantly secular (private and commercial letters, etc.) and colloquial in language. However, the earliest strata examined,[10] of the late 10th and early 11th c., produced none. That the active merchant class of Nóvgorod, engaged in a valuable and expanding commerce in fur and fish, early kept some sort of written records can be taken for granted, but the recovered documents do not suggest general literacy before the middle of the 11th c.[11]

It should be noted that the Scandinavians contributed virtually nothing in this field; altogether they introduced few cultural innovations. In the case of writing, the runic script, generally believed to have been invented much further south, in contact with the Latin alphabet, reached Scandinavia about the 4th c. AD, but it had remained an epigraphic script for limited purposes and we have no reason to suppose that the Slavs found any use for it.

12   The conversion of Vladímir led to an immediate influx of Greek priests and missionaries and the presence in Kiev of a large Greek

---

[9] Except a single word scratched on a pot, now dated *c.*950–75, of uncertain interpretation.

[10] As each level of wooden paving, etc., sank into the soft ground another was built on top. The sequence can be followed down to the 15th c. and fairly precise dating is possible by the method of tree-ring patterns. The excavations found no trace of a settlement (in that particular area of Nóvgorod) earlier than *c.*950.

[11] As far as accounts are concerned, the all-important numerals can always be shown and the only other essential is a few conventional symbols for commodities. Thus records of a purely *quantitative* kind do not necessarily require an *alphabet*.

entourage for his imperial bride, the Princess Anna. From then on close relations with both the political and ecclesiastical powers in Constantinople were assured. This Greek participation, necessary for the development of the Church, did not, and apparently did not attempt to, dislodge OCS from its position as the written language of those Russians who were already Christians; the Greeks had the long experience of Bulgaria behind them. Literate Bulgarians resident in Kiev no doubt taught Russians a 'correct' pronunciation of OCS, no longer corresponding exactly to the then spoken norm of Bulgarian nor, of course, to that of ESl. There is always a strong tendency to maintain a 'sacred' language unchanged but this is least comfortable and necessary in pronunciation; the living sounds of the native speech are almost certain to creep in. In all countries where OCS was used, permanently or temporarily (Bohemia, Croatia, Serbia, Bulgaria, Russia), this happened at an early date, so that by the end of the 11th c. it is necessary to operate, philologically speaking, not with a unitary OCS but with the regional variants, e.g. Serbian Church Slavonic, Russian Church Slavonic (ChSl.). This situation is already clearly present in the earliest surviving manuscript of the ESl. world—Ostromir's *Gospel Book*, copied in 1056–7 (below, Table I, text no. 5).

13   The suitability of OCS to serve as the written and learned language for the ESl. world rests on the fact that the basic repertoire of phonemes (both consonants and vowels) in each dialect was largely the same and that differences of a *grammatical* kind were, *at the time of its introduction*, neither numerous nor profound. Differences of a *syntactical* kind (sentence organization in general, conjunctions) are bound to be present between a written language and a spoken vernacular and could be readily accepted. Differences in the *lexical* field were considerable: not only did OCS have a certain component of SSl. vocabulary, unfamiliar or missing in ESl., but—what was more important—it offered *en bloc*, ready-made, a large abstract and intellectual vocabulary to complement the predominantly concrete lexicon of everyday ESl. speech. But, be it noted, the early translators had been careful, in translating from Greek, to use *Slav* material for this (there were comparatively few Greek loan-words) so that at least the components and structure of a new word were usually intelligible to an East Slav even if the precise sense had to be learnt (5.16). But the two shared, of course, an extensive CSl. vocabulary, especially in the most usual words. It is appropriate therefore to review the differences in phonology and morphology between these two Slav dialects.

Old Church Slavonic and East Slav Compared

PHONOLOGY

14 *Palatalization*

A more or less strong tendency to palatalize consonants in certain contexts has been characteristic of the development of both CSl. and certain Slav languages in the historical period. If consistently carried through this will result in a form of 'intra-syllabic harmony': all syllables will consist either of phonetically front elements or of phonetically back elements, but not a mixture of the two (C + back vowels, C′ (palatalized consonant) + front vowels). The most important CSl. changes were:

15   (*a*) The *First Palatalization of velars* (early centuries AD), whereby *k, g, x* + front vowel > CSl. *č′*, (*dž′* >) *ž′*, *š′*:

(*ĕ*) **kel-*: CSl. **č′elo* 'brow' (R. чело́);
  sg. voc. **bog-ĕ* > *bož′e* (бо́же);
  Gmc. **helmaz* (Goth. *hilms*) > **xelmŭ* > **š′elmŭ* (OCS *šlĕmŭ*);
(*ē*) **kēs-*: CSl. **č′ēsŭ* > **č′asŭ* (час);
(*i*) adj. suffix *-ĭn-*: mod. R. грех/гре́шный, бок/побо́чный, смех/смешно́й, прилега́ть/приле́жный;
(*ī*) **gʷī-w-* (Lat. *uīuus*): CSl. **ž′iw-*[12] (OCS and R. жив-).

Similar, and probably more or less simultaneous, was the palatalization of velars before *j*:

pres. sg. 1 in *-jǫ*: mod. R. пла́кать/пла́чу; (**lŭg-*) лгать/лжу; паха́ть/пашу́;
fem. nouns in *-jā*: **dux-jā* > душа́ (cf. дух < *duxŭ*).

After these operations velars can only stand before back vowels (syllables ка, ко, ку, кы, къ) and the products of their palatalization *č′*, *ž′*, *š′* are soon established as *new phonemes*. These palatalizations are *permanent* in all Slav languages and therefore *identical in OCS and ESl.*

---

[12] Opinions differ as to whether **ž′iw-* or **ž′iv-* is the more correct representation; *w* will be preferred to *v* henceforward. See also 2.34.

16   (*b*) The *Second Palatalization of velars* (not long after the First, probably 6th–7th c. AD). The diphthong *ai* (including *oi*) had moved to *ē* (*ě*) and in some contexts *ī*; before these *new front vowels* we get:

$$k, g, x + ě, ī > c', dz'/z', š'/s'.$$

The reflexes of this palatalization were not identical throughout Slav. Part of WSl. (Lechitic) maintained *dz'* and all WSl. had *x'* > *š'* (Pol. *sz*). OCS also maintained *dz'* on principle: the Glagolitic alphabet had separate symbols for [dz] and [z]. Examples:

*kaina > **kēna* > *c'ěna* 'value, price' (= Gk. ποινή);
?Gmc. **haira-* > *s'ěr-*: R. се́рый but Pol. *szary* 'grey';
*gail- (Lith. *gailùs*, Ger. *geil*): OCS *dz'ělo* (R. ChSl. зѣло́) 'very'.

This palatalization produces changes in the final stem consonant in declension, viz.

  (i) sg. DL of fem. *ā*-stems: (*rǫka, noga, muxa*) OCS *rǫc'ě*, *nodz'ě* (ESl. *noz'ě*), *mus'ě*;

  (ii) sg. and pl. loc. of masc. *o*-stems: (*věkŭ, rogŭ*) OCS *věc'ě/věc'ěxŭ, rodz'ě/rodz'ěxŭ* (ESl. *roz'ě/roz'ěxŭ*);

  (iii) pl. nom. of masc. *o*-stems: (*rogŭ, duxŭ*) OCS *rodz'i, dus'i*; early ESl. вьлци 'wolves', Чѣси 'Czechs';

and in the imperatives and iterative stems of certain verbs:

  (iv) **rek-ti* 'say': OCS imperat. *rĭc'i, rĭc'ěte*; **strig-ti* 'shave': *stridz'i, stridz'ěte.*

The *Second Palatalization* is *permanent* in OCS (ChSl.). In ESl. dialects ancestral to Russian it is permanent if part of the root (R. се́рый, цена́ above); it is later removed in most other contexts (2.36). The Ukr. and WhR. areas have been more conservative in this respect. It was possibly never completely carried through in the northernmost ESl. dialects (Nóvgorod area), since we find Novg. кеп for standard цеп (цѣпъ) *et sim.*

Here also we may note that initial *kw-, gw-* (*kv-, gv-*) are subject to the Second Palatalization in SSl. and ESl. but not in WSl., and there are similar hesitations in the Nóvgorod area:

*kwait- 'flower': CSl. **kwětŭ*; OCS *cvětŭ*, R. цвет, but Pol. *kwiat*, Cz. *květ*;

*gwaizda 'star': CSl. **gwězda*; OCS *zvězda*, R. звезда́, but Pol. *gwiazda*, Cz. *hvězda*;

Nóvgorod квет, квёлый, and квели́ть (recorded in the Слово о полку Игореве, text no. 14): ESl. цвели́ть, Pol. *kwilić*.

There was therefore here a point of divergence between ChSl. and later Russian.

17 (c) The *Third Palatalization of velars* is generally considered to have overlapped or immediately followed on the Second.[13] Unlike the first two this is a *progressive* palatalization:

$$\breve{\iota} + k, g, x > c', (d)z', s' \text{ (WSl. } \check{s}').$$

The front nasal *ę* < *ĭn* also exerts this palatalization. The phenomenon is irregular, more consistent in Balkan Slav, including OCS, than elsewhere. Not all the irregularities have been satisfactorily accounted for but, generally speaking, the palatalization does not take place (i) if the velar is followed by a high back vowel: *kŭnędzĭ* but fem. *kŭnęgyn'i* (R. князь, княги́ня); *lĭgŭkŭ* (лёгкий); *tixŭ* (тих); *kŭn'igy* (кни́га); (ii) if the velar is followed by another consonant: *mĭgla* (мгла), *klik-nǫti* but *-klicati* (вос-кли́кнуть, -клица́ние). Examples:

ăwĭkā: OCS and ESl. *ovĭc'a* 'sheep' (mod. R. овца́)
ătĭkŭ:[14] *otĭc'ĭ* 'father' (оте́ц)
wĭxŭ:[14] *vĭs'ĭ* 'all' (весь)
lĭkă (neut.): *lic'e* 'face' (лицо́: but ChSl. лик < *lĭkŭ* (masc.))
mēs-in-kŭ:[14] *měsęc'ĭ* 'moon' (ме́сяц).

The common Russian diminutive suffix -*ĭk*- > -ец, -ца, -цо́/-це is thus regular, but most if not all nouns in -ица are borrowed from OCS: страни́ца, столи́ца, десни́ца, колесни́ца, деви́ца (native дѣвъка > де́вочка, де́вушка), and there is a no doubt younger formation in -ика (брусни́ка). The suffixes -их, -иха only appear in this form.

The incidence of this palatalization is therefore *somewhat less in ESl. than in ChSl.* and is again sporadically absent in NW dialect, especially in the word *wĭx-*:[15] forms such as вьхемо (= pl. dat. всем), вхоу же тоу землю (*c.*1200, text no. 15) occur in Nóvgorod texts right down to the 15th c. (e.g. *NBG*, nos. 359, 439). Shevelov has also drawn attention to the fact that Gmc. (Scandinavian) -*ing*

---

[13] Three stages can be detected in Gk. toponymy: pre-palatalization Ἀβαρῖκος; half-way Γαρδίϰι (implying [k']), full palatalization (7th–8th c.) Γαρδίτσα.

[14] Since -*ĭkŭ*, etc., in sg. masc. nom. *does* give -*ĭc'ĭ*, etc., this raises the question as to whether the termination was in fact -*ŭ* at the relevant time.

[15] Original stem *wĭs*- with *s* > *x* in CSl. after *ĭ* (3.58(7)); Lith. has *vìsas*.

in a pl. toponym from *büring-* 'cottage' appears several times in the Novg. area as Буреги but further south as Бурези.

18 (*d*) Palatalization of the *labials* before *j* produced in CSl. the complex consonant groups *pl'*, *bl'*, *wl'* (*vl'*), *ml'*. This palatalization is *common to OCS and ESl.* and permanent in the latter. It was later lost in Bulgarian (such forms occasionally occur in later Blg. ChSl. texts) and WSl., except in roots with initial labial. Examples:

> *zem-jā:* (OCS and) ESl. земля́ (Pol. *ziemiu*);
> *kap-jā:* ка́пля;
> pres. sg. 1 *-jǫ:* R. люби́ть/люблю́, терпе́ть/терплю́;
> pres. tense in *-j-:* дрема́ть/дремлю́, дре́млет.

Preserved everywhere:

> Goth. *biuþs, biudis* > CSl. *bl'udo* 'plate' (R. блю́до);
> *pi(e)u-:* CSl. *pl'ewati* (R. плева́ть/плю́нуть 'spit'; cognate with Eng. *spew*).

19 (*e*) The *dentals* were palatalized before *j* at a very late stage and the reflexes are different in the three major divisions of Slav and even within them. The following correspondences are representative:

CSl.	OCS	ESl.		Pol.	SCr.[16]
t+j	*št'*	*č'*		*c'*	*t'*
d+j	*žd'*	(*dž'* >) *ž'*[17]		*dz'*	*d'*

No new phonemes appeared in ESl. The Bulgarian–Macedonian (OCS) reflexes are eccentric (perhaps the end-product of the palatalization of *tt + j*, etc.) but stable and accorded partial special representation in the alphabets.[18] Both groups tended early towards depalatalization: Bulgarian has now [št], [žd]. There is here a *strong contrast between OCS and ESl. phonology*:

CSl.	OCS (ChSl.)	ESl. (R.)	
svĕt-jā	*svĕšta*	свеча́	'candle'
med-jā	*mežda*	межа́	'boundary'

[16] The SCr. reflexes have remained nearest to plain palatalized dentals, but are usually slightly assibilated: [t$^{š'}$], [d$^{ž'}$]; the special signs ħ, ђ were finally regularized in the 19th c.

[17] As *g+j* > *ž'* also, false derivation can result, e.g. *pud-* > пуди́ть > пужа́ть > new back-formation пуга́ть (with derivatives, e.g. испу́г).

[18] Cyrillic Щ may be based on *š+t* but the two components are often written side by side (шт), as жд always was (the two shapes not combining easily).

In derivation ChSl. words will show the alternations *t/št*, *d/žd*, but native R. words *t/č'*, *d/ž'*:

ChSl.	*Russian*
сопровождáть 'accompany'	провожáть/проводи́ть *pf* 'see off'
pf убѣди́ть 'persuade, convince'/ *impf* убѣждáть; убѣждéние 'conviction'	—
хождéние (игýмена Дании́ла) 'journey'; расхождéние 'discrepancy'	хожéние (Афанáсия Ники́тина) 'journey'; похóжий 'similar'
рождествó (Христóво) 'Christmas'; урождённый 'native'; *pf* породи́ть/*impf* порождáть 'give rise to'	рожáть 'bear'; урожáй 'harvest'; урожéнец 'native'
pf возбуди́ть/*impf* возбуждáть 'arouse' (fig.), p.p.p. возбуждённый	*pf* разбуди́ть 'rouse', p.p.p. разбýженный
тождествó 'identity'	тожествó 'identity'

(both are in use)

мéжду 'between' (du. loc. of *mežda*)	смéжный 'contiguous'; межевáть 'survey (land)'; промежýток 'interval'
трепетáть 'tremble'; pres. трепещý, трепéщет	—
еженóщный 'nightly' (нощь 'night' is frequent in 'high style' down to the 18th c.)	ночнóй 'nocturnal'; переночевáть 'pass the night (somewhere)'
питáть 'nourish, feed'/пи́ща 'food' (*pīt-jā*)	—
pf обрати́ться/*impf* обращáться 'turn'; *pf* разврати́ть/*impf* развращáть 'corrupt'; (see also Appendix, no. 16)	переворóт 'turning-point'; ворóчаться 'toss and turn'
pf просвети́ть/*impf* просвещáть 'illumine' (early ESl. 'baptize'); просвещéние (18th c.) 'enlightenment, education'	просвéчивать 'pass through' (of light)
надéжда 'hope' (the Slavonicism has prevailed as a basic theological term)	надёжный 'reliable'; *pf* обнадёжить 'instil hope' (the noun надёжа is now only dial.)

The prevalence of mixed groups deriving from the colloquial and literary (ChSl.) strata is highly characteristic of Russian vocabulary (5.23 and Appendix).

20 (*f*) The reflexes of the groups *sk/zg* and *st/zd* when subject to palatalization were rather variable since complicated and liable to simplification, but the following contrasts are usual:

		OCS	*Russian*
sk+j, st+j		*št' (št)*	*š'č'*
zg+j, zd+j		*žd' (žd)*	*(ž'dž' >) ž̄'*

Examples:

pres. sg. 1	**isk-jǫ*	*ištǫ*	ищý [iš'č'u]
	*pust-jǫ	*puštǫ*	пущý [puš'č'u]
	gvozd-	*pri-gvožden* (p.p.p.)	—
	*jĕzd-jǫ		éзжу [jež̄'u]

See further 2.39.

Differences in the Treatment of Vowels

21 (*a*) The two *nasal vowels* of CSl.—*ę* (front) and *ǫ* (back)—reverted to oral vowels very early in ESl. They had arisen at a late stage of CSl. as one of the processes of producing open syllables (2.1), from VNC initially and internally and from -V̄N, -Vns, -Vnt finally (but not -Vn, which gave -V): **žĭm-ti* 'press' and **žĭn-ti* 'reap' > *žęti*; **pont-i-* > *pǫtĭ* 'way' (R. путь); fem. sg. acc. **rankām* > *rǫkǫ* (R. рýку); OCS *pętĭ* 'five', R. пять. The ESl. reflexes *ę* > *ä* (2.9) and *ǫ* > *u* (also *jǫ* > **jų̄* > *ju*) suggest a quality for the nasals of approximately *ą̄, ų̄* just before their disappearance.

OCS was established in the 9th–10th c. when the nasals were still present in most Slav dialects (they persisted particularly late in most of the Blg. area). ChSl. preserved them on principle, though never consistently in practice, in contrast to the ESl. vernacular. The moment of their disappearance in ESl. speech is generally put in the early 10th c., that is, just before Blg. manuscripts with a more or less regular use of nasals arrived in Kiev in any considerable quantity. The evidence of ESl. toponyms as given in Constantine Porphyrogenitos' compilation *De administrando imperio* (mid 10th c.) gives a *terminus post quem non*, especially (ch. 9) Βερούτζη [verutsi] which surely represents an ESl. p.p.a. вьруч- < *vĭrǫtj*- 'seething' (name of one of the rapids on the Dnepr below Kiev). The Greek could have shown a nasal here, indirectly but unequivocally, if it had still been present.[19]

Early ESl. loans to Baltic and Finnic show the presence of nasals (2.7) but they cannot be dated sufficiently exactly to be useful. More important is the earliest stratum of loans from Scandinavian: варяг, Судъ 'Bosporus' (obs.), and якорь (plausibly 9th c. loans) show the normal development of nasals from *vāring-, sund* (= Eng. *sound*), *ankari*, whereas the name Игорь (Ingvar) does not: the first prominent bearer of this name in Russia died in 945. By the middle of the 11th c. it is abundantly clear that for a Russian the nasals were *learnt letters* (*sounds* only in so far as some Bulgarians may still have used them) and that their correct employment depended on the knowledge of the scribe and the accuracy of the manuscript from which he was copying. The scribe of *Ostr.* displays very imperfect knowledge, alternating between OCS and native forms, e.g.

	right (OCS)	wrong (ESl.)
rǫk-	порѫчи	пороучение
jęz-	ѩзыкъ	ꙗзыкъ
fem. sg. acc. -*ǫ*	водѫ	водоу
pres. sg. 1 -*(j)ǫ*	рекѫ, г(лаго)лѭ	молю
pres. pl. 3 -*ǫt-*	могѫть	въвьргоуть
p.p.a. -*ǫ-tj-*	продаѩщиимъ	въстьрьзающе

In чѭждаахѫсѧ the first nasal is a wrong guess, the other two correct; there was never any nasal in морѧ, лѭбите (for sg. gen. морꙗ; любите). The distribution of faults, including some more or less consistent ESl. features, suggests (as was often the case) that he was writing from dictation. The wording of the colophon does not exclude this.

22   (*b*) The 'functional diphthongs' (often called 'liquid diphthongs') of form C*a*SC (C*o*SC), C*e*SC[20] were removed at a late stage of CSl.

---

[19] In the same passage Νεασήτ [neasit] < *nejęsyt(ĭ)* 'pelican(?)' agrees but is less good evidence since the transcription may have been influenced by toponyms in Νεα-, e.g. Νεάπολις.

[20] In the long process towards a virtually strict structure of open syllables old diphthongs, e.g. [ai], [au] (vowel+semi-vowel) were removed first, then functional diphthongs with nasals (§21 above), e.g. C*a*NC, finally those with sonants (or liquids), e.g. C*a*SC. They were all diphthongs in virtue of carrying distinctions in pitch.

with different reflexes in all three groups; ESl. has the form known as полногласие (pleophony), the rest inversion (less properly metathesis),[21] thus:

CSl.	SSl. (including OCS)[22]	Pol.[22]	ESl.
*CarC	CrāC	CroC	CoroC
*CalC	ClāC	CloC	ColoC
*CerC	CrēC (CrěC)	CreC	CereC
*CelC	ClēC (ClěC)	CleC	ColoC[23]

Examples:

CSl.	SSl. (including OCS)	Pol. (mod.)	ESl. (mod. R.)
*gard-	OCS gradŭ; SCr. grâd	gród [grut]	го́род
*wals-	vlasŭ; vlâs	włos	во́лос
*berg-	brěgŭ; brêg	brzeg [bžek]	бе́рег
*melk-	mlěko; mléko	mleko	молоко́

Note. There are CSl. roots of the form CrāC, etc., which will remain on principle the same in *all* Slav languages, e.g. R. гла́дить, пла́кать, страда́ть, прав-, слаб-; след, грех, кре́пкий, слепо́й (all with ѣ).

23 Whatever the precise process of the inversion, about which opinions differ, the phonetic development in ESl. is of the most commonplace: the insertion of an at first obscure vowel in contact with a strengthened or otherwise altered sonant, viz. *gardŭ > *garrdŭ or *gaṛdŭ > *garədŭ.[24] The process is everywhere active c. AD 750–850,[25] and is complete in OCS (mid 9th c.) and in ESl. by the time of (almost certainly a good deal before) the earliest evidence, which consistently shows identical vowels either side of the sonant (2.47(1))—colophon of Ostr. (1057): володимир(ъ), новѣгородѣ; РП (shortly after 1054): Персѣгъ; 1073 Anthology (text no. 6): полонъ 'booty', воротитъ са, норовъмь.

[21] As terms of linguistics *inversion* is used of contiguous sounds, *metathesis* of non-contiguous, e.g. R. Фрол < Gk. Φλῶρος (Lat. *Florus*).

[22] The Czechoslovak dialects here go with SSl.

[23] By simultaneous velarization of the [ł], so that there is no distinction between *pelti > R. полоть 'weed' (Pol. pleć) and *kolti > R. колоть 'cleave'. CełoC will appear after soft š', ž', č': Gmc. helm- > R. шелом (ошеломи́ть 'stun'); *ž'elb- > R. жёлоб/жо́лоб 'gutter', pl. желоба́. Се́лезень 'drake' is probably of different formation. Irrelevant is pan-Slav zelen- 'green' with suffix -en-.

[24] Cf. Dutch *Delft, Alkmaar*, pronounced approximately [déləft], [ałək-] with a very strong velar [ł].

[25] The earliest stratum of Slav toponyms in Greece (7th–8th c.) is pre-inversion: Γαρδίκι, Βάλτουκα < *Baltŭkă (*baltă = болото), Βεργουβίτσα < *berg-.

The earliest ESl. loans to Finnic (*c*.600–800) appear to be pre-*polnoglásie* but Finnic phonetics may have blurred the picture: **daltă* (R. долотó) > *taltta*, **kalkalŭ* (кóлокол) > *kalkkale*, **kar-stā* (корóста) > *karsta*, **wertenă* (веретенó) > *värttinä*, **paltĭnă* (полотнó) > *palttina*.

ESl. received the name of Charlemagne (d. 814) from more westerly Slavs; a basic **karl-jĭ* underwent regular treatment in each language: Cz. *král*, Pol. *król* [krul], ESl. корóль 'king'.

The striking contrast OCS *gradŭ*/ESl. гóрод was *rigorously maintained* as a touchstone of ChSl. *vis-à-vis* the vernacular even when other distinctions (e.g. the nasals) were blurred.[26] As a result Russian vocabulary is full of doublets and mixed groups by borrowing from ChSl. A conspectus is given in the Appendix.

24   *Initial VSC (where V = a/o, e and S = r/l)*

In this similar phonetic situation only inversion occurs but the ESl. reflexes vary according to earlier *pitch* distinctions.

(*a*) Rising pitch (long vowel everywhere):

CSl.	OCS	Pol.	ESl.
*ár-dlă 'plough'	*ralo*	*radło*	рáло
*álk- 'thirst'	*lakati*[27]		лáк-омый

(*b*) Falling pitch (long vowel only in SSl.):

*âlk-ŭtĭ 'elbow'	*lakŭtĭ*	*łokieć*	локъть
*ârst- 'grow'	*rast-*	*rosnąć*	рост-
*âld- 'boat'	*ladĭja*	*Łódź*	лодья, лóдка

Reliable examples of *er*C-/*el*C- are rare but here probably belong:

*élbędĭ **ólbọdĭ* } 'swan'				лéбедь (for
		SCr. *łăbūd*	*łabędź*	лéбядь, 6.56)

*êrb- **ôrb-* } 'child'[28]		*rabŭ*	*robić, robota*	реб-ёнок
*êrm- 'strap'				рем-éнь

---

[26] It has been observed that *polnoglásie* was admitted into strictly ChSl. texts when dividing a word at the end of a line, e.g. го//родъ was preferred to гра//дъ—a purely orthographic convention of no general import.

[27] But also exceptionally *alkati*, whence Russian Slavonicism áлкать. There are some variations also in loans from Latin: *arca* (via Gmc.?) > OCS *raka*, but *altare* > *altarĭ* (*oltarĭ*).

[28] 'Young person in a dependent state' (physically or socially), hence 'child, slave, orphan' (Lat. *orbus*, Gk. ὀϱφανος).

Note. CSl. roots in *ra-*, *ro-*, etc. will on principle be the same everywhere, e.g. R. рад, род.

25 On these criteria we can distinguish:

ChSl.	Russian
рáвный 'equal'	*рóвный* 'even'
(наравнé, сравнéние 'comparison', рáвенство 'equation')	(ровнятьcя, врóвень c + instr.)
вóзраст 'age'	*рост* 'height'
óтрасль 'branch'	*вóдоросль* 'aquatic plant'

In the case of *rab-/rob-* there has been much confusion. OCS *rabŭ*, f. *rabá/rabýnja* 'servant, slave' and the derivatives *rabóta* 'labour' (> 'work' in general), *rabótati* passed into ESl., particularly the last two which have become fully colloquial. Conversely WSl. *rob* spread, no doubt from Bohemia (Prague was a centre of the slave trade in the 9th–11th c.), in the specific sense 'slave' and is not infrequent in SSl. texts. Ukr. робúти, робóта may be native or Pol. loans. Пáробок (пáрубок) 'lad' is clearly native ESl. but has not survived in the literary language: паропци (*RPC s.a.* 1096, Поучéние Мономáха); а паробки да девочки ходят наги до семи лѣт (c.1470, Af. Nik.).

The CSl. prefix **ắrz-* 'apart' becomes regularly ESl. роз- but here áканье spelling (6.52 ff.) eventually intervenes. Native роз- is preserved under stress (about a dozen in all): рóспуск, рóзыск, рóсчерк, pret. рóздал, but otherwise the spelling is always раз-/рас- in conformity with the pronunciation. Whereas разорéние, разграблéние, etc. are clearly Slavonicisms (also páзве < развѣ), размазня 'waffle' and a host of verbs in раз-/рас- are equally clearly native. Unstressed роз-/рос- commonly appears down to the 17th c. except in obviously ChSl. words. ChSl. páзный and its derivatives (páзница, cpds. in разно-) have virtually ousted native рóзный, but the adverbs врозь, пóрознь remain and there are two verbs рóзнить 'separate, differ' and páзниться 'differ'. In разрóзненный 'odd' both variants are associated. The native noun рóзница survives in the phrase торговáть в рóзницу 'retail'.

Other Initial Vowels

26 Initial vowels tended to be avoided in late CSl. since, in the period of uniform open syllables, there would be hiatus with the preceding word of the utterance: a prothetic *j-* or *w-* *(v-)* is usual but not universal.[29] Exceptions are only small auxiliary (usually enclitic) words, including а, и, and у. As between OCS (ChSl.) and ESl. there are the following contrasts:

27   (*a*) OCS *a-* (sometimes *ja-*)/ESl. *ja-*:

*ĕg'h- (Lat. *ĕg-o*) 'I'	*azŭ*	язъ (> я)
*āg- 'berry'	*agoda/jagoda*	я́года
(cf. Lat. *agnus*) 'lamb'	*agnę, agnĭcĭ*	ягн-ёнок
OHG *ahor(n)* 'sycamore'	*avor(ovŭ)*	я́вор
*āw- 'show'	*aviti/javiti*	яви́ть

All Russian words beginning with a- are on principle foreign loans, either Slavonicisms (апре́ль) or more recent loan-words (айва́ 'quince', арба́ '(Tatar) cart', ата́ка, etc.).

28   (*b*) Conversely, OCS *ju-*/ESl. *u-*:

(cf. Lat. *iuuenis*) 'young'	*junŭ, junostĭ,*	early ESl. унъ, etc.[30]
	júnoša	
[etymology uncertain]	*jugŭ* 'south'	early ESl. угъ[31]
*jus- 'juice, broth'	*juxa*	R. уха́
Lat. (via Gk.) Julian-		Улья́н(ов)
Justin-		Усти́н(ов)

We may also include the following with nasal prefix:

	ChSl.	early ESl.
*ǫ-rod-	*juródŭ* 'simpleton'[32]	урод-ивъ[32]
*ǫ-dol-	*judólĭ* 'vale'	удолье[33]

Сою́з 'union' is a Slavonicism (**sŭ-ǫz-*; cf. OCS *ǫza, ǫže* 'bond'); the corresponding native noun is связь (**sŭ-(w)ęz-ĭ*). У́тро 'morning' is the invariable form in ESl. from a prototype in *ju-* (Pol., SCr. *jutro*).

---

[29] See G. Y. Shevelov, *A Prehistory of Slavic*, pp. 235 ff.

[30] Уности его ради (*RPC s.a.* 1093).

[31] Къ угу (*RPC s.a.* 1096). It is improbable that R. у́жин 'lunch' belongs here; it is more likely to be connected with у-жа́ть/у-жина́ть 'reap'. The recurrent hydronym юг in N. Russia is from Finnic (Finnish *joki* 'river'), e.g. in У́стюг < устье юга.

[32] Adj. юро́дивый 'foolish' (but pure in the eyes of God); cf. Eng. *silly*, originally 'holy' (Ger. *selig*). Уро́дливый 'deformed' and its congeners appear to have prefix у-.

[33] Яко по удольемъ крови (dat.) тещи (*RPC s.a.* 1019), 'so that the valleys ran with blood'.

That the contrast was alive for early Russian writers is shown by occasional bogus Slavonicisms by hypercorrection, e.g. ютѣшитель (12th c.), югльхъ (for ǫgl-).

29 (c) Whereas initial *ā-* in CSl. widely took prothetic *j-*, initial *ă-* (> *o-*) was normally unaffected; *orĭlŭ* 'eagle', *orati* 'plough' (Lat. *ăr-āre*), *olow-* 'tin, lead' (R. орёл, орáть, óлово). Hence a strong tendency in ESl. to substitute олтáрь, Ондрéй, Олексáндръ for the virtually non-existent initial *a-* in such loans as *altar, Andrew, Alexander*.

But certain ESl. words in *o-* correspond to CSl. *(j)e-*. The phenomenon is full of apparent irregularities; the following are typical:

OCS (ChSl.)	Polish	Russian
(j)esenĭ 'autumn'	*jesień*	óсень
(j)ezero 'lake'	*jezioro*	óзеро
(j)ed- in *(j)edinŭ, (j)edŭva*	*jeden*	одúн

The correspondence had some vitality, as witness relatively late loans into ESl. such as

Gk. Ἰωσήφ > OCS *(J)esifŭ/Josifŭ*[34]	R. Óсип
Scand. *Hĕlgi, Helga* (de-aspirated)	early ESl. Ольгъ, Ольга (2.46(6))
Gk. Ἑλένη [ɛlɛni] > OCS *(J)elena*	R. Олéна > Алёна
Gk. Εὐστάθιος (vulgar Εὐστάφος) 'Eustace'	R. Остáп

But ель 'fir', есть 'be', емý, егó, and others retained initial [je-]. Conversely, initial *o-* is found sporadically elsewhere: R. óльхá 'alder' and also Pol. *olcha, olsza*; Gk. toponym Ὄζερος [ózeros] in Epirus; R. ещё (dial. also ощó, óще), SCr. *jŏš*, Blg. *ošte* but Pol. *jeszcze*.

Vaillant has suggested that ESl. tended to generalize the variant which would arise after a hard (non-palatalized) consonant, e.g. in free position *jezero* (phonetically close to *jăzero*; cf. Lith. variation *ēžeras/āžeras* according to dialect) but *w ăzerĕ* > *ozerĕ*. This may indeed be a contributory factor. It follows from the above that forms with initial e- in Russian are Slavonicisms (provided that there are parallel forms in o-). The most important living ones are derivatives of 'one':

---

[34] There was no sequence [jo] in CSl. native words; *Josifŭ* is a learned transcription.

ChSl.: еди́ный, едини́ца, еди́нственный, etc.
Russian: одино́кий, одна́ко, одина́ковый, etc.

A modern dictionary records about fifty such words with ChSl. e-. Some ecclesiastical terms and Christian names have exclusively e-: ева́нгелие, е́ресь, епи́скоп; Елизаве́та, Евге́ний.[35]

Early ESl. texts show a considerable mixture of ChSl. and ESl. forms. There is a clear preference for един- in *RPC* but езеро/озеро are used more or less indifferently (в Ылмерь озеро, около езера Илмеря); native одва́ occasionally appears (одва одолѣша грьци, *s.a.* 941), though in this case едва́ became standard.[36]

30   *Other Differences in Vocalism*

(*a*) ESl. sequences Съ/ьSC and jer + *j*: there were differences here at least in orthography. For the details see 2.48 and 2.33.

(*b*) ESl. dialectal а́канье, я́канье, and ёканье were at least partly present in the initial period (see Chapter 6) and were strictly excluded from ChSl. texts (exception, 2.43).

31 MORPHOLOGY

Morphological differences between OCS (ChSl.) and ESl. will be discussed in Chapter 3 and may simply be listed here, viz.

  (i) OCS -*ę*/ESl. -ѣ in certain case-endings (Table V);
  (ii) OCS -*omĭ*/-*emĭ* but ESl. -*ŭmĭ*/-*ĭmĭ* in the masc. and neut. sg. instr. of nouns (Table VI);
  (iii) Present tense sg. 3 and pl. 3 OCS -*tŭ*/ESl. -*tĭ* (3.97(d));
  (iv) OCS uncontracted/ESl. contracted forms in the 'long' adjective (3.39) and the imperfect tense (3.99);
  (v) Contrast in the formation of the active present participle (gerund) in the sg. masc. nom. (3.118).

32   In sum, imported OCS and the ESl. vernacular differed in hardly more than a dozen features of phonology and morphology, some of which were quite trivial and only very imperfectly maintained in Russian ChSl. from the outset. A Russian could easily make these transpositions. For him OCS was not so much a foreign language as a more cultivated form of his own language

---

[35] The surname Есе́нин is not from ChSl. е́сень 'autumn' but from Есе́ня, a familiar form of Éсип/Óсип 'Joseph'.

[36] Одва́ still occurs in 17th c. texts and exists in contemporary dialects.

(словѣньскъ языкъ) bearing the authority and prestige of its use as the medium of the new Christian religion. He did not need to keep the two forms strictly apart but did so according to more or less simple rules of thumb as the matter demanded.

II. EARLY EAST SLAV DOCUMENTS

33 The principal early documents for the study of Russian are given in Table I (a more extensive list is given by Kiparsky, *Russische historische Grammatik,* vol. i, pp. 30 ff.).

34 These texts may be categorized as to language broadly as follows:

(i) OCS (East Blg. (Presláv) rather than Macedonian (Ohrid) type): nos. 1?, 5, 6, 8;

(ii) Russian ChSl.: nos. 3, 4, 7, 11, 13, 17, 24 (all original Russian works are included in this category);

(iii) mixed language: nos. 9, 10, 12, 14, 19;

(iv) ESl.: nos. 2, 15, 16, 18, 21, 22, 23;

and as to source (omitting nos. 11, 14, 20, 21):

(*a*) Kiev: nos. 1, 4, 6, 7, 10 (including 9), 12;

(*b*) Nóvgorod (not necessarily written there): nos. 2, 3, 5, 8, 15, 16, 19;

(*c*) other centres (not necessarily reflecting local features): nos. 13 (Galicia), 17 (Rostóv), 18 (Smolénsk), 22 (Rıazán'), 23 (Chernígov), 24 (Pólotsk).

No single text can be classed unequivocally as (*a*)(iv)—Kiev vernacular—which is unfortunate for historical study. The nearest approaches are to be found in parts of no. 9 (Monomákh's autobiography) and in certain (but not all) reported speeches in no. 10.

No. 12 is particularly important. It represents, we must suppose, the elegant style of princely documents at Kiev and a typical 'free association' of ChSl. and ESl. elements. Native are (as always) personal and place names (володимирь, всеволодъ); certain legal and administrative terms (вира,[37] продажа, осеньнее полюдие). Slavonicisms are used in the more abstract vocabulary (кнажение, perhaps also състоить са and изоостанеть са[38]) and cliché phrases

[37] This may be a Scandinavian loan-word (5.13) but *vis-à-vis* ChSl. it counts as native.

[38] A *hapax legomenon*; probably a calque of Gk. ἐκλείπεσθαι 'pass over, die'.

TABLE I. The Principal Early Documents

No.	Title	Date	Contents	Remarks
1	Treaties between Kiev and Constantinople [OB no. 30 (ii)]	911, 944, 971	Diplomatic texts included in the *Primary Chronicle* (no. 10) *s.a.* 912, 945, 972.	The original linguistic form cannot be certainly determined (probably OCS, translated from a Gk. master copy).
2	*The Law Code of the Rus'* (Русская Правда) [OB no. 17]. Abbr.: *RP*	1020?	ESl. customary law (with some intrusive Scandinavian and Christian elements), reputedly committed to writing by command of Jaroslàv in Nóvgorod, before he became sole ruler in Kiev (1036).	There are shorter and longer forms of the text, which despite its obsolescence continued to be revised and added to until well into the 13th c. The earliest surviving copy is part of a Nóvgorod Kórmchaja (legal code) dated 1282; it is the so-called 'long text' (пространная редакция). 'Up-dating' started soon after Jaroslàv's death (1054), as art. 2 shows (added by his sons), and the later the part the more probable that there will be Slavonicisms in the language. The earliest nucleus of the whole gives *a remarkably pure text of early ESl. language.*
3	*Sermon* of Luke Zhidjata, Bishop of Nóvgorod (Поучéние Лукú) [OB no. 47]	c.1034?	Probably the sermon given by him at his installation as second bishop of Nóvgorod.	ChSl. Earliest MS dates from 14th c.

4	Hilarion's *Sermon on the (Mosaic) Law and Grace* (Слово о законѣ и благодати) [OB no. 45]	1040s	Court sermon on an important occasion, praising Vladímir's Christianization of Russia.	The earliest surviving copy of this popular text is of the 16th c. only; the orthography has been much altered but the text is probably fairly reliable in other respects. Good example of the early cultivation of OCS on Russian soil.
5	Ostromir's *Gospel Book* (Остромйрово Евáнгелие) [OB no. 1]. Abbr.: *Ostr.*	1056–7	*Áprakos*-gospel, i.e. not the continuous text of the four gospels but only those passages to be read as lessons in the liturgy.[39]	Original. Copied for the Governor of Nóvgorod, Ostromir-Joseph, by a Deacon Gregory,[40] probably a native of Nóvgorod. He used apparently a Blg. MS of the type of *Savina Kniga* (Presláv revision of the original *Áprakos*) and, to judge by the correctness of the OCS (especially the jers), a MS considerably older than mid 11th c. But there are several more or less regular concessions to ESl. pronunciation, one of them more specifically Novgorodian.

[39] There are several varieties of *Áprakos*; this is a 'short' *Áprakos*. For definitions see A. Vlasto, *The Entry of the Slavs into Christendom*, p. 64.
[40] The first twenty-four folia are in a different hand.

TABLE I (*cont.*)

No.	Title	Date	Contents	Remarks
6	Svjatosláv's *First Anthology* (Сборник/ Изборник Святосла́ва) [OB no. 4]	1073	Collection of favourite excerpts from Christian literature on devotional and learned themes.	Original. Copied from a Blg. compilation for the Grand Prince of Kiev. Typical of the Orthodox texts in OCS entering Russia.
7	Svjatosláv's *Second Anthology* [OB no. 5]	1076	Similar, but some excerpts are new translations (direct from Greek) and some appear to be original compositions.	Original. The excerpts vary from more or less strict OCS to R. ChSl. with sporadic concessions to the vernacular.
8	*Nóvgorod Minéi* (Новгоро́дские служе́бные мине́и) [OB no. 6]	1095–7	Fragments of services for saints' days (month by month) with marginal scribblings by several scribes.	Original. Deviations from strict OCS similar to those in no. 5.
9	Vladímir Monomákh's *Admonition* (Поуче́ние Монома́ха) [OB no. 30, pp. 122–6]	c.1100–25	An original composition intended for the edification of his sons, in two contrasting parts: a moral disquisition in ChSl. and an autobiographical sketch in more or less vernacular language.	Inserted in the *Primary Chronicle* arbitrarily *s.a.* 1096. Text probably fairly faithful to the original in its essentials.

10	The *Russian Primary Chronicle* (Повесть временныхъ лѣтъ) [OB no. 30]. Abbr.: *RPC*	completed *c*.1113	Typical annals compiled from various learned and popular sources. The introduction gives the past history of the Slavs and the annals proper a record of events down to the end of the 11th c. Mixed language, varying with the matter.	The material was edited in the Cave Monastery (Киево-печёрская лавра) in the course of the 11th c. The primary text led to: (1) a version of 1116 by Sylvester of Vydubitsa monastery (not extant) which was passed on and survives in the *Laurentian Chronicle* of 1377 (Súzdal' area)—the form quoted in this book; (2) another version made for Mstisláv (see no. 12) in 1118, passed on into other chronicles, notably the *Hypatian Chronicle* of *c*.1425 [OB no. 41]. The original state of the *Primary Chronicle* is therefore not exactly reconstructible.
11	Abbot Daniel's *Pilgrimage to the Holy Land* (Хожде́ние игу́мена Дании́ла) [OB no. 48]	*c*.1106–8	Travel diary basically in ChSl.	Earliest extant MSS date from the later 15th c. only and are considerably modernized.
12	Mstisláv's *Deed of gift* (Гра́мота вел. кн. Мстисла́ва Володи́мировича) [OB no. 8]	*c* 1130	Deed of gift to St George's monastery at Nóvgorod (Юрьев монастырь), founded *c*.1119.	Original. The earliest surviving secular document.

TABLE I (*cont.*)

No.	Title	Date	Contents	Remarks
13	The *Galician Gospel Book* (Га́лицкое четвероева́нгелие)	1144	The complete text of all four gospels.	Original. The text shows some local linguistic features (early Ukrainian).
14	The *Tale* (or *Lay*) *of Igor's Campaign* (Сло́во о полку́ Йгореве) [OB no. 51]	c.1185?	Semi-poetic account of a disastrous expedition of Igor against the Cumans (По́ловцы). The authenticity of the *whole* text is still questionable but the vocabulary at least points to an early nucleus.	The unique MS was destroyed in the conflagration of Moscow in 1812. Discovered in 1795, the MS was thought at the time to date from the 16th c. More or less inefficient copies of this difficult text were made in the 1790s, containing much guesswork and probably a good deal of retouching. The text is therefore of low value for the history of Russian except from a lexical point of view.
15	Varlaam's *Deed of gift* [OB no. 11]	c.1200	Deed of gift to Khutyn' monastery at Nóvgorod.	Original (probably now destroyed). Local Nóvgorod language with a few Slavonicisms.
16	The earlier documents on bast from Nóvgorod (Новгоро́дские берестяны́е гра́моты). Abbr.: *NBG*	12th c.	Domestic and commercial letters, etc., often fragmentary and beyond restoration.	Original. Recovered during excavations at Nóvgorod since 1951. Local language. About 60 out of over 400 are fairly complete and usable. The majority date from the 13th–14th c.

28

17	The *Life of St Nifont* (Житиé Нифонта) [OB no. 12]	1219	Typical hagiographical text, tr. from Greek, perhaps in Rostóv.	Original. No earlier tr. known. R. ChSl.
18	The *Treaty* between Smolensk, Riga, and Gotland [OB no. 13]	1229	Treaty between Prince Mstisláv of Smolensk, German Riga, and Swedish Gotland regulating legal and commercial matters (since the routes were often unsafe because of war).	Original. There were parallel German and Latin versions. Local language with some Germanisms.
19	The *First Nóvgorod Chronicle* (Synodal copy—Syn. no. 786) [OB no. 24]	later 13th c. onwards	Annals, especially of local history.	Original. Near-contemporary MS. Language variable according to matter but many entries predominantly vernacular.

Further works in OCS (ChSl.) of interest for the history of Russian might be cited, e.g. Putjáta's *Minéi* (now thought to antedate *Ostr.*), the *Dobrílo Gospels* (a пóлный áпракос of 1164), Mstisláv's *Gospel Book* (*c*.1115–17; original; OB no. 7 quotes part of the colophon), the Юрьевский Апракос (*c*.1118–28), etc., but there are no, or no reliable, editions. Other compositions and translations of the 11th c. are occasionally useful even if now extant only in later copies, e.g. Josephus' *Jewish Wars* (ed. N. A. Meshcherski, 1958) and the stories of Boris and Gleb. It has been estimated that only about 10 per cent of the manuscripts now surviving in Russia written before *c*.1400 (and not all written *in* Russia) belong to the period before *c*.1200; the majority are unpublished ChSl. works.

29

TABLE I (*cont.*)

To the above texts of considerable extent should be added the following short inscriptions, which contain certain points of interest:

No.	Title	Date	Contents	Remarks
20	Signature of Anna, daughter of Jaroslav the Wise, wife of King Henry I of France [OB no. 2]	Latin document dated 1063	АНА РЪИНА	The Cyrillic letters more probably represent OFr. *reine* (three syllables) than Lat. *regina*, hence *e* > ъ.
21	The *Tmutorokán' Stone*	1068	OB no. 3	Preserved in the Hermitage Museum. Authenticity questionable.
22	Inscription from (Old) Riazán'	*c.*1100	НОВОЕ/ВᴺН [ВИНО?] ДОБРИЛО/ПО СЛАЛЪ/КНАЗЮ/ БОГОУНКА	On a large vessel discovered in 1948.
23	Inscription on a goblet	*c.*1150	OB no. 9	Vessel made for Prince Vladímir Davídovich of Chernígov (d. 1151), now in the Hermitage Museum.
24	Inscription on a cross	1161	OB no. 10	Cross made for Princess Euphrosyne of Pólotsk.

Several graffiti in the Sofia Cathedral at Kiev date from before 1068.

30

(се азъ; въ д[ь]нь пришествия своего). Much of the vocabulary is neutral, that is, common to both languages. The syntax is notably well organized, clearly modelled on ChSl. (e.g. the conjunction донелѣже).

The same association is even more obvious in no. 15: the phonology and vocabulary of the main text are local Novgorodian (рьль, вольмина); ChSl. are the set formulae аще кто дияволомь на[уч]енъ . . ., въ сь вѣкъ и въ будущии.

35 From the above emerge clearly two things:

1. Though the Grand Prince's secretaries evolved a more or less consistent conventional style for their documents it was not necessarily used elsewhere. Kievan Russia never became a strongly centralized 'state' as did the later Muscovite one. At this stage of cultural evolution regional variation is to be expected.

2. Legal and administrative documents were, as such, outside the range of ChSl. both for theoretical and practical reasons. This remained true from Русская Правда down to the time of Peter the Great at least (in the 18th–19th c. legal and administrative language was considerably Slavonicized). An exception may be made for *diplomatic* documents where a higher style was usually considered appropriate.

36 It will have been observed that *poetry* is virtually unrepresented in the above early texts; on this see further Chapter 7. In the genre of literary *prose* there is a large corpus of historical chronicles. It is precisely here that ChSl. and the vernacular meet on the most intimate terms. Annals were compiled in monasteries or at least by the clergy (e.g. in the Sofia Cathedral at Nóvgorod) but for all that were a secular rather than an ecclesiastical genre. There is no uniform style; the language varies according to subject-matter (7.8 ff.).

37 Thus there was felt to be no barrier, in principle or practice, to a mixed language *in certain genres of writing*. OCS was, however, essentially a fixed, written literary language; it incorporated only superficial vernacular features, thus becoming 'Russian Church Slavonic'. It was the vernacular which benefited from coexistence with ChSl., above all in vocabulary. Slavonicisms (loan-words from ChSl.) were absorbed from the outset into ESl. writing and (more gradually) speech, since all education came through religious texts and religious texts were constantly heard in church. The process

of absorption is constant throughout the centuries, but complicated and not always easy to follow. A few typical examples must suffice here:

1. OCS *brěgŭ* and ESl. берегъ might be at first treated as exact synonyms, even if this was not quite strictly true.[41] In the long run native бéрег sufficed, брег being relegated to poetic use (5.46).

2. The field of ESl. городъ was not identical with that of OCS *gradŭ*: the sense город 'fort, township with defensive walls' was not typical of OCS; *gradŭ* 'city' was not present in ESl. usage. Here differentiation was possible and survives to a limited extent (toponyms of the type Ленин-град; contrast горожáнин/ граждани́н).

3. The pair OCS *strana*, ESl. сторонá covered a wide semantic area—'direction, side, region'; each sense might occur in either form, but eventually Russian was enriched by crystallizing out the doublet (ChSl.) странá 'country'/R. сторонá 'side', carrying on the distinction into their derivatives.

In all cases 1–3 there is frequent alternation in *RPC* but it is impossible to establish with certainty, in view of the numerous recopyings, what was the original choice (if no stylistic differentiation is apparent). Thus: и высѣдше на брѣгъ, отринуша людье от берега (*s.a.* 1016); и ста Володимѣръ на сей сторонѣ, а печенѣзи на оной, и не смяху си на ону страну, ни они на сю страну (*s.a.* 992).

4. Native вы- was preferred to ChSl. из- in the literal, spatial sense (выходи́ть (из) 'go out', вы́тащить (из) *pf* 'drag out'), contrasting with both ChSl. and native из- in other more metaphorical senses (ChSl. изъяви́ть *pf* 'manifest', исходи́ть (из) 'proceed from'; R. износи́ть *pf* 'wear out') (4.55).

5. Пред- as a verbal prefix was a total loan from the learned language, there being no native cpds. in *перед-, at first confined to existing ChSl. words but later acclimatized as a Russian prefix (4.63).

6. ChSl. пре- and R. пере- have been specialized in different uses, the former (as usual) being normally abstract and metaphorical (преступи́ть *pf* 'transgress'), the latter more concrete and literal (переступи́ть *pf* 'step over, cross') (4.62).

The following diagram illustrates the situation:

---

[41] SCr. *brêg*, no doubt continuing Balkan usage, does not mean the same as R. бéрег.

Pure OCS	R. ChSl.	Mixed language	Written R.	Spoken R.
religious texts; theoretical rather than real in Russia	religious texts and the higher literary genres	mixture according to matter, rarely half-and-half	always contains some (fully acclimatized) ChSl. elements	intake of some ChSl. words

————————————strong current———— ———————→

←————————————weak current————————————

38 *Periodization*

For convenience of study and clear terminology it is customary to divide the history of any language into *periods*, as far as possible on linguistic criteria alone. In the case of Russian these coincide well enough with the larger political periods. It is sufficient to distinguish:

Linguistic

1. *Early East Slav* to *c.*1250, with subdivisions:
   (*a*) pre-Christian and pre-literate (to mid 10th c.);
   (*b*) Christian and literate: introduction of OCS, cultural dependence on Constantinople.

2. *Middle or Muscovite Russian, c.*1250–1700, with subdivisions:
   (*a*) transitional, *c.*1250–1400;
   (*b*) High Muscovy, 15th–16th c.;
   (*c*) the 17th c. (beginnings of strong Western influence).

One more or less standard *administrative language and*

Political

The 'Kiev period' (Kievan Russia), including the decline of Kiev and the rise of the new centre down to the Mongol conquest (1240). Centres: Kiev, Nóvgorod.

The period of political fragmentation covers the 12th–14th c. The 'Muscovy period': creation of the Muscovite Empire from *c.*1300; translation of the Metropolitanate to Moscow (Metr. Peter, 1328); end of the 'Tatar yoke' (1480). Centre: Moscow.

style (делово́й язы́к) for the whole Empire (from *c.*1500). *ChSl. as the principal language of literature.* A period of *deliberate bilingualism.* By the accession of Peter the Great (1689) the modern standard has by and large been reached in linguistic *forms* but not in linguistic *usage.*

During periods (*a*) and (*b*) the Ukr. and WhR. areas were not part of the Muscovite Empire and ceased to share Great Russian linguistic innovations: crystallization of Ukr. and WhR. as distinct languages.

3. *Modern Russian,* from *c.*1700, with subdivisions:

- (*a*) the 18th c. (transitional) —search for a new literary standard;
- (*b*) the 19th c.—the modern literary standard established;
- (*c*) Russian since 1917 (the Soviet period).

Westernization of the educated class from Peter the Great (1689–1725). Russian literature as a part of European literature. Centres: St Petersburg, Moscow.

III. ALPHABET AND ORTHOGRAPHY

39 The East Blg. 'Cyrillic' alphabet was designed to preserve as many Gk. letters as possible (in their formal, or uncial, shapes) with the same or similar values. For sounds unrepresented in Greek recourse was had to the earlier Glagolitic alphabet (§8 above) or to fresh invention. The total repertoire of signs used in Russia is given below, together with their (ChSl.) names and numerical values. The cursive forms (not given) have naturally varied a good deal; in the case of д and т two widely different forms are still current as free alternatives.

TABLE II. The Cyrillic Alphabet

Letter	Numerical value	Name	Letter	Numerical value	Name
а	1	аз(ъ)[12]	ф	500	ферт(ъ)[12]
Б[1]	—	бу́ки[12]	х	600	хер(ъ)
в[1]	2	ве́ди (вѣди)	ψ†[5]	700	пси
г	3	глаго́л(ь)	ω†[6]	800	от(ъ) (ѡтъ)
д	4	добро́	ц[8]	900	цы
е[2]	5	есть	ч[8]	90	червь
ж	—	живе́те (-ѣте)	ш	—	ша
ꙃ, s, ᶼ†[3]	6	(д)зело́ (зѣло)	щ	—	ща
з (ᴣ)[3]	7	земля́	ъ	—	ер(ъ)
и[4]	8	и́же			(твёрдый
й[4]	—	и кра́ткое[12]			знак)
ѳ†[5]	9	фита́	ы (ъı)[9]	—	еры́
ι, i, ï†[4]	10	(ижеи)	ь	—	ерь (мя́гкий
к	20	ка́ко			знак)
л	30	лю́ди	ѣ†	(900)	ять (see 3.94
м	40	мысле́те (-ѣте)			fn.)
н[4]	50	наш(ь)	э[2]	—	э оборо́тное
ѯ†[5]	60	кси	ю	—	ю
о[6]	70	он(ъ)	я (ꙗ†)[10]	—	я
п	80	поко́й	ѥ†[2]	—	—
р	100	рцы (рци)	ѧ†[10]	(900)	юс ма́лый
с	200	сло́во	ꙗ†[10]	—	—
т	300	тве́рдо	ѫ†[10]	—	юс большо́й
у (оу, ꙋ)[7]	(400)	ук(ъ)	ѭ†[10]	—	—
			ѵ†[5]	400	и́жица[12]

The dagger indicates a now obsolete letter. Superior figures refer to the numbered paragraphs of commentary in the text.

40 *Commentary to Table II*

1. By the 9th c. AD Greek no longer had the sound [b] (except after [m]); the Slav alphabets therefore introduced a symbol for this phoneme—a modified *beta*—between Gk. α and β, presumably following Lat. *a, b, c,* . . . or perhaps Semitic *aleph, beth,* . . . As a new symbol it had *no numerical value* in the Cyrillic codification in order that strict correspondence with the Byzantine numerical

conventions should not be disrupted. Similarly with the other inserted special Slav letter ж.

2. The loop of e was in the early centuries sometimes open (є), sometimes closed (e). East Blg. scribes had invented ѥ to make a complete series of iotated vowels (ꙗ, ю, etc.) but it was never an indispensable symbol in OCS (ChSl.). Later rules for the use of e/ѥ were arbitrary and variable: in the earlier centuries ѥ was commonly used after vowels (знаниѥ) and as an initial (ѥмоу), often as a sign of [je], i.e. that the preceding consonant is fully palatalized (занѥ = [za-n-je]; but село, etc.). ESl. phonetic evolution did not produce a need for any new symbol except for the minor distinction e/э; for the latter see §43 below.

3. Some Slav dialects, including OCS, needed to distinguish between [z] and [dz] (the latter not then present in Greek), but not East Blg. nor ESl. The two signs were retained for their numerical values. Зело (sѣло) = [dz] was little used outside accurate ChSl. in Russia; however, the shape s was favoured by Trediakóvsky for all z's (§43 below).

4. Gk. η and ι *(ēta, iota)* had coalesced long before the 9th c. AD, together with υ *(ípsilon)* and the diphthongs ει and οι, in [i]. The early Cyrillic alphabet retained both in transcription and for their numerical values (hence the names и (в)осьмери́чное, і десятери́чное), but they had no distinct phonetic function. In Russia their use was dictated by arbitrary scribal conventions. I originally had no superscript dot, as in Greek, but almost all ESl. manuscripts show one dot (i) or two (ï). The latter went early out of favour but was revived for a time during the Second South Slav Influence (§42 below). i was retained down to 1917 for the position before another vowel (знаніе).[42] Russian orthography did not distinguish between, e.g., disyllabic (pl.) мои and monosyllabic (sg.) мóи for a long time after the appearance of the new diphthongs [ai], [ei], [oi], etc. (2.23).[43] Eventually the modification й was affected to the diphthong, but not consistently before c.1735. The position of the bars in и [i] and н [n] has been variable: in the early stages the Gk. forms H and N respectively were quite usual, i.e. the reverse of the modern.

5. The Gk. symbols θ, ξ, ψ, and ν (и́жица) were retained principally for their numerical values, being either irrelevant or

---

[42] It was also used to distinguish миръ 'peace' from мiръ 'world'.
[43] Originally both were disyllabic, [mo/jĭ] and [mo/jĭ] respectively.

redundant to an adequate representation of Slav phonology. They were used to a limited extent by more learned scribes in transcriptions (Алеѯей, Ѳома) and occasionally to save space (ѱати for п(ь)сати). ѵ was occasionally used for ю in the 11th–12th c.: вьсѵ (1092).

6. The doublet о/ѡ was taken over automatically from the Gk. alphabet, though the phonetic distinction [ŏ]/[ō] had long been lost in Greek and never existed in Slav. ѡ was moderately useful to indicate an initial o, since space was rarely left between words, and was almost universal in the special abbreviation ⁓ѡ = от(ъ); hence the name of the letter.

7. оу is once again a mere reproduction of Greek habits: ου = [u], υ = [i] (cf. Fr. ou = [u], u = [ü]). оу, or its ligature form ȣ, is almost universal in early ESl. orthography but in course of time the first element was dropped—not officially till the reform under Peter the Great (§43 below). The earliest examples of simple у are found in the 13th c. In the Muscovite period various conventions were in vogue for employing оу, ȣ, or у—all quite artificial.

8. The shapes have slightly changed, the earliest notation being ч (for ц) and Үᴛ (for ч).

9. In ESl. usage there were only scribal preferences between ъı and ъи; Deacon Gregory uses exclusively ъı in Ostr. and this was generally more usual. The alteration to ы comes later (§42 below).

10. The four nasal signs ᴀ, ꙗ, ꙗ̑, ꙗ̈ were required in the most accurate OCS orthography. Otherwise ѫ and ѭ were little used in Russia, being replaced by their oral equivalents оу, ю. The Second South Slav Influence was responsible for a considerable reintroduction of ѫ (§42 below). ᴀ remained moderately useful as long as ä had not (in most contexts) merged with ja (2.9), but even then ᴀ and ꙗ were widely used as alternatives. The modern form я is a combination of the two. By the 17th c. either я or ᴀ was written indifferently but ꙗ had become wholly ChSl.

11. The need for [j] (which had no separate representation in the early alphabets) was covered fairly efficiently by the Blg. ꙗ, ѥ, ю (later я, е, ю), and after the 13th c. also by ь; ji was too rare to worry about (2.51(2), note (b)). For jo see 2.42 ff.

12. The names survive in: áзбука 'alphabet'; (стоя́ть) фе́ртом 'with one's hands on one's hips'; от аза́ до и́жицы 'from A to Z'; (по)хе́рить 'to cross out'. й is alternatively called и с кра́ткой or

и с крáтким. The whole sequence of names was established fairly early in the OCS tradition from an acrostic poem (see A. Vaillant, *Textes vieux-slaves,* pt. 1 (Paris, 1968), pp. 68–70).

41 *Revisions of the Orthography*

These fit in exactly enough with the linguistic periods defined above:

    1. *Kiev Period*

All the signs listed above with the exception of э were used in accordance with the notes.

42   2. *Muscovy Period*

From the end of the 14th c. Russian orthography was affected by the *Second South Slav Influence* (the *First* being the original introduction of OCS and the Cyrillic alphabet). Learned men from the Orthodox Balkans (Bulgaria and Serbia) attempted to 'improve' the Church Slavonic then used in Russia, both grammatically and orthographically. Grammatically the improvements had some justification, but orthographically they were misconceived. Manuscripts of the 15th–16th c. (the fashion was waning in the 17th c.) have an archaizing appearance and moreover are usually formidably scarred with signs of abbreviation, 'decorative' Greek breathings and accents. There was a recrudescence of ï, ѕ, ѳ, and ѫ (to a lesser extent also ѩ and ѭ). While they might be correctly used in the high-style literature for which the reform was primarily intended, by the time they filtered down into everyday writing they were as often as not wrong and always irrelevant. We find, for example, ѫзыкъ for языкъ (correct original form ѩзыкъ) in accordance with contemporary Blg. usage, which had practically abandoned ѩ and ѭ and followed the arbitrary rule of ѫ after hard and а after soft consonants. But in fact Balkan scholars such as Metropolitan Kiprian did not so much restore 'classical' standards of OCS as introduce their own contemporary usage (there was a more or less uniform Bulgarian–Serbian style during the 14th c. exemplified in John Alexander's *New Testament* (1355–6)). Thus ъı was now modified to ы,[44] which has remained, illogical but harmless. Ѵжица (v), until then only a numerical

---

[44] The sign ъ had become early obsolete in Serbian. Another sign of this in ChSl. was a great increase in spellings of the type влъна for OCS влъна (R. вълна > волнá; 2.48).

symbol, was introduced into a number of ecclesiastical words (мѵрь 'myrrh'; Кѵрилъ 'Cyril'). Uniotated vowels were commonly written after a vowel in defiance of Russian phonology (добраа, всеа). Outside this fashion we may note that ѥ finally disappeared in the Muscovy period since е now always implied [je] or ['e]. е prevails over є, and reversed э occasionally appears without specific value.

43 3. *Modern Period*

(*a*) *Eighteenth Century*. Peter the Great's reform of the alphabet (1708–10) created a new *secular script* (гражда́нский шрифт, vulgarly гражда́нка), simplified in the *forms* of the symbols and slightly in their *number*. For ecclesiastical texts in ChSl. the older orthography remained unchanged, thus making a permanent break between religious and secular writing. The reform was made in the interests of *printing*; it was not a thoroughgoing 'scientific' reform. In the new alphabet oy (ȣ), ꙗ, ѧ, ѡ, and ѕ finally disappear, replaced (as they were already to a considerable extent) by у, я, о and з; i, ѳ and ѣ were retained though redundant, as was also final ъ.

During the 18th c. й[45] came into regular use to clarify the diphthongs ай, etc., and э[46] for the non-iotated (hard) *e*, required more and more in foreign loan-words with initial *e*—эпо́ха, экипа́ж, элеме́нт. It was not extended to internal positions: ше, же, це remained an adequate though inaccurate representation of these now hard syllables (2.37–8).

In the earlier 18th c. ѳ was still much in fashion for ф and by extension for devoiced в: противѳъ, ѳ(ъ)сякому; also for new foreign [f]: ѳ(ъ)регатъ, аѳицероѳъ (= офицеровъ).

At the very end of the 18th c. ё was proposed (allegedly by Karamzín) to indicate ['o] in alternation with ['e]: село́/сёла. A need for this was felt by most theoreticians; nevertheless it has continued to be disregarded in printing and writing except in special circumstances (elementary reading primers, philological works, cases of ambiguity). Among ostensibly more 'scientific' proposals for further reform we may note Trediakóvsky's elaborate Разговор

[45] й originated as a way of indicating [j] in the Kiev schools in the 17th c. and passed into Russian usage via such works as Smotrítsky's *Grammar* (7.26).
[46] э was apparently invented in White Russia as early as the 16th c., where there was a precocious use of many European words in the chancellery language.

. . . об ортографии (1748),[47] in which he advocated s for з; i for и in all positions; E (= [je]) initially and after vowels, otherwise e (there is thus no need for э); шч for щ,[48] consistent notation of й; iô for [′o]. He also used ѳ himself without specifically recommending it. He retained ѣ since his pronunciation of it conformed to the ChSl. standard as a close diphthongal [ie] (2.10). Though more professional in their argument, Trediakóvsky's proposals were just as half-hearted as Peter's reform. They differ in direction because Trediakóvsky is (1) making some capital out of the Latin alphabet (both want a break with ChSl.); (2) considering literary rather than utilitarian ends. Thus he recognized that ъ could be dispensed with but was not bold enough to say so. He further made an approach to 'phonetic spelling' ('писать по звону'), e.g. упадок(ъ) but упатка, сладость but слаткий,[49] but his argument in this matter is confused and partial: he does not include *лоп/лба, perhaps because of the danger of homonymy (рот/род, лук/луг).

No one took any notice of Trediakóvsky's treatise.

44 (b) *Nineteenth Century and Soviet Period.* Changes in the 19th c. were minimal. The Soviet reform (1917–18) finally removed the otiose letters ѣ, i, ѳ, ѵ, ъ: занятіе > занятие, лѣсъ > лес, Ѳома > Фома. Final ъ, which had been silent since at latest 1200, had retained some usefulness down to Peter's time as an indicator of the end of a word. It is now only retained (internally) to preserve the correct syllabic separation of certain prefixes, e.g. подъём, изъявить, разъехаться, объедаться, sounding [pad/jom] not [pa/d′om], etc., though it is doubtful if this is always strictly observed.[50] Съел 'ate' ([sjɛł] or [s′jɛł]) must always be distinct from сел 'sat' [s′ɛł]. In the early Soviet period an apostrophe was suggested for this limited use but ъ has prevailed.

These changes did not give rise to any serious ambiguities, though it is occasionally advantageous to distinguish pl. все (< всѣ) from neut. sg. все [f′s′o] (if so, всё is always available), and a few other similar cases.

[47] Published according to his system as Разговоръ . . . об ортографіи.
[48] The spelling сч rather than шч for щ is in fact fairly common throughout the 18th c. Trediakóvsky evidently wished to safeguard the 'high style' pronunciation [šč] as against the 'vulgar' [š′] (2.39).
[49] This principle has been adopted in SCr. orthography.
[50] The prefix was nevertheless subject to palatalization in Classical pronunciation: [v′jɛxət′]. This is still common with с- and в- but not with об-, от-, над-, под-, раз-. Initial и passes over to the hard variant after such prefixes, e.g. разыскáть, подытóжить, безымя́нный.

The mobile stress of Russian, as has fortunately always been recognized, makes it inadvisable to attempt anything other than an 'etymological' representation of unstressed vowels: нагá, pl. нóги; гóръд, pl. гърадá would be no improvement on the approximation to the actual sounds which is inherent in virtually all writing systems.

2

PHONOLOGY

1 The sound system of late CSl., ancestral to all the Slav languages, can be reconstructed by comparative methods in which the evidence of the OCS texts is of primary importance. All writing systems are approximations; scarcely any fail to be ambiguous at one point or another. Certain imprecisions in the OCS evidence on minor points apart, by the 9th–10th c. AD CSl. was a language almost entirely of *open syllables* (V, CV, CCV, etc.). Thus the reputed first translation by St Cyril,[1] recorded in his newly invented alphabet (Glagolitic), appears in Cyrillic transcription as follows (John 1: 1–3; text of *Codex Assemanianus*): и/ско/ни[2] бѣ сло/во и сло/во бѣ оу Бо/га и Бо/гъ бѣ сло/во. се бѣ и/ско/ни оу Бо/га. Вь/сѣ тѣ/мъ бы/ша и бе/жне/го[2] ни/че/со/же не бы/стъ е/же бы/стъ.

2   The open-syllable structure inherited by ESl. was soon to be lost but is still dominant in a 12th c. text such as the following (*Novgorod Chronicle* (Synodal text), *s.a.* 1143): въ лѣ[то] 6651 сто/ꙗ/ше в[ь]/сѧ о/се/ни/на дъ/жде/ва от го/[спо]/жи/на д[ь]/ни до ко/ро/чю/на, те/пло[3] дъ/жгь, и бы во/да ве/ли/ка ве/ль/ми въ Во/л[ъ]/хо/ве и в[ь]/сю/де, се/но и дръ/ва ра/зне/се, о/зе/ро мо/ро/зи въ но/щь и ра/стьр/за[4] вѣ/тръ и в[ъ]/не/се в[ъ] Во/л[ъ]/хо/во[5] и по/ло/ми мо/стъ.

By that date many of the jers (ъ, ь) were either very weak or had ceased to be pronounced; those in brackets are already omitted in the text. Всѧ, дни, etc. did not lead to closed syllables but such are almost certainly present in the new monosyllables вѣтръ, мостъ (the final jer already being silent).

Despite the gradual dissolution of the open-syllable principle Russian syllabication still demands that syllables be open *in the*

---

[1] *Vita Constantini,* cap. 14.
[2] As the regressive palatalization shows ([z-n'e] > [ž'n'e]) proclitic elements were fully integrated phonetically into the sense-group (< из кони, без него).
[3] For те/плъ.   [4] On -стьр- *et sim.* see §48 below.   [5] For Волховъ.

measure of the possible. Correct are: о́/стров (not *ос/тров, *ост/ров), ну/жда́, лю/блю́, е́/хать. However, structural units (prefixes, some suffixes) are now normally treated as inseparable elements: раз/нес- (cf. above), пред/у/пре/ди́ть (not *пре/ду-).

East Slav Vowels (Early State)

3   By late CSl. times the CSl. repertoire of corresponding short and long vowels, *ă, ĕ, ĭ, ŭ*, had lost its symmetry by the development of differences of timbre. By *c.*AD 1000 ESl. had the following repertoire:

CSl.	ă	ā	ĕ	ē	ĭ	ī	ŭ	ū
ESl.	ŏ	ā	ĕ	ē	'ə	ī	ə	y
Cyrillic	о	а	е	ѣ	ь	и	ъ	ы

Commentary

1. *ă* > *ŏ* was virtually universal in Slav *c.*8th c. AD (6.36).

2. *ĭ, ŭ* had become lower, more central vowels of the type [ə]; ь < *ĭ* must have been a little higher and more fronted than ъ < *ŭ*. There is, of course, no direct evidence of the timbre of these jers. Henceforward they will be transcribed, where appropriate, as *ə*, *'ə* (*ə* with palatal on-glide, but not yet exerting full palatalization on the preceding consonant (§16 below)).

3. *ē* and *ĕ* were both rather open vowels of the type [ɛ] in late CSl. In OCS *ē* was very open indeed since the well-designed Glagolitic alphabet made one symbol do duty for both *(j)ē* and *jā*. There were regional variations: by *c.*AD 900 the new Cyrillic alphabet of E. Bulgaria separated *(j)ē* as ѣ and *jā* as ꙗ.[6]

In ESl., *ē* and *ĕ* may scarcely have differed except in length for a time but a difference in timbre (aperture) soon developed, as given on the diagram below.

4. The exact quality of early ESl. /o/ is not quite clear but it must have been relatively open since average foreign *o* was heard as nearer to [u]: Gk. ὄξος > у́ксус 'vinegar'; Scand. *þjónn* > ти(в)у́н (5.13). It is entered as [ɔ] on the diagram. Transcriptions below will use *o* unless there is special reason to specify [ɔ].

5. *ū* had become a high central vowel, by unrounding, of type [ɨ]; its central or back-central position is confirmed by лы, кы, etc.

---

[6] The open quality of ѣ is confirmed in early Romanian loans from Slav such as *veac* < вѣк[ъ].

[ɫy, ky]. In the context of Russian it will be transcribed *y*. A new [ū] arose from the diphthong *au*.

6. ESl. *a* seems always to have been approximately central; consequently other /a/ are not represented on the diagram. It may be noted, however, that the average /a/ of Ukr. and WhR. is a little further back, i.e. nearer the [ɑ] of Eng. *father*, uncharacteristic of the R. dialects as a whole.

4   To the above must be added the late CSl. nasals (1.21), front *ę* and back *ǫ*, of varying timbre according to region and time. The ESl. reflexes were [æ] and [u], both long. The former will be transcribed, where appropriate, *(j)ä*. The ESl. developments start from the following repertoire of vowel phonemes:

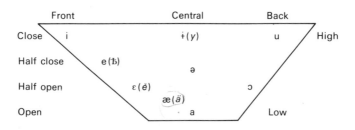

It will be observed that both the *high close* vowels and the *low open* ones were inherited by ESl. as *long* by nature; *short* by nature were those at the middle level: e, ь, ъ, o.

East Slav Consonants (Early State)

5   Successive processes of palatalization during the CSl. period had produced the pairs *n/n'* (*nitĭ* 'thread'/*n'iwa* 'field'), *l/l'* (*wola* 'ox' sg. gen./*wol'a* 'will'), *r/r'* (*mora* 'plague' sg. gen./*mor'a* 'sea' sg. gen.), *s/s'* (*wĭsĭ* 'village'/*wĭs'ĭ* 'all'), *z/z'* (voiced correlative), and the unpaired *š'*, *ž'*, *č'*, *c'*.[7] The earliest ESl. repertoire appears as in Table III.

[7] Sources: *n'* < *n* + *j*; *l'* < *l* + *j*, also labial + *j* > *pl'*, etc. (1.18); *r'* < *r* + *j*; *s'*, *z'*—Second and Third Palatalization of velars (1.16–17); *š'*, *ž'*—First Palatalization of velars (1.15), *x*, *g* + *j*, *z* + *j*; *č'*—First Palatalization, *k* + *j*; *c'*—Second and Third Palatalizations; *č'*, *ž'* < *t*, *d* + *j* also, in ESl. only (1.19).

TABLE III. Early East Slav Consonantal Phonemes

			Velar	Dental and alveolar	Labial (bilabial)	Palatal and palatalized
Stops	Plosive	unvoiced	k	t	p	
		voiced	g	d	b	
Fricatives	Spirant	unvoiced	x			
		voiced			(v)[4]	
	Sibilant	unvoiced		s		s', $š'$[1]
		voiced		z		z', $ž'$[1]
	Affricate	unvoiced				c', $č'$[6]
		voiced				
	Nasals			n	m	n'
	'Liquids'		$ł$[2]	r[3]		l', r'
	Semi-vowels				w[4]	j[5]

Superior figures refer to the numbered paragraphs of commentary in the text.

6 *Commentary to Table III*

1. $š'$, $ž'$ are classed as palato-alveolar (or post-alveolar) fricatives.

2. *l* is classed as a lateral non-fricative. A velar type [ł] before back vowels is assumed for ESl. (transcribed henceforward as (Polish) *ł*). A 'middle' [l] should perhaps be assumed at first before front vowels until merged with [l'] (§16 below); 'middle' [l] is not characteristic of later Russian.[8]

3. ESl. *r* is rolled, never flapped or uvular.

4. *w* ⪖ *v* (voiced labio-dental fricative) appears to have been general in Slav not later than the 9th c. AD. The change appears to have been retarded in ESl.; see further §34 below.

5. No alphabetic sign; incorporated in the vowel symbol (-ая = [aja], -ую = [uju]). All initial /e/ have a prothetic [j]: есть [jes't'].

6. The voiced correlates *dz'*, *dž'* were simplified to *z'*, *ž'* in ESl.; *dz'* was known from OCS but was not a part of the native repertoire.

7. For long $\bar{š}'$, $\bar{ž}'$ see §39 below.

[8] [l] for [ł] is recorded sparingly in modern NR dialects; [l'] is always retained. European 'middle' [l] is normally heard as nearer to [l'] and so transcribed (параллéль).

Development of the Vowel System

7　　As little correlation remained between short and long vowels in
ESl., significant length was soon lost. Orthography gives no clue
to the chronology. V. Kiparsky[9] has shown that ESl. vowel length
was perceptible to the Finnic tribes in their early mixing with the
expanding Slavs. Loan-words into Finnic reflect differences in
vowel length rather than timbre, this being the distinction which
the receiving dialects made. The loans can scarcely be earlier than
*c.*AD 600, the majority perhaps about AD 800. Examples:

> *ā:* лāд-ити > Finnish *laat-ia*[10] 'arrange'
> *ă:* пăпъ (R. поп) > *pappi* 'priest'
> *ē:* мѣрā (мéра) > *määrä* 'amount, degree'
> 　　хлѣвъ (хлев) > *läävä* 'byre'
> *ě:* печь > *pätsi* 'oven'
> *ī:* свитā > *viitta* 'robe'
> *ĭ* (ь): вьрстā (верстá) > *virsta* (measure of distance)
> 　　пăлтьнă (полотнó) > *palttina* 'linen'
> *ū:* лужā > *luosa* (Est. *loos*) 'puddle'
> 　　гумьнă (гумнó) > *kuomina* 'threshing-floor'[11]
> *ŭ* (ъ): търгъ (торг) > *turku* 'market-place'
> 　　лъжькā (лóжка) > *lusikka* 'spoon'
> *у* (ы): мылă (мы́ло) > (Karelian) *muila* 'soap'.

In contrast, demonstrably later loans only reflect length, if at all,
as a complement of *stress*; they reflect *timbre* as nearly as the
receiving system allows:

> ESl. поп(ъ) > Finnish *poppa* 'wizard'
> 　　погост(ъ) > *pokosta* 'village' (or *pogosta*)
> 　　вѣсть > *viesti* 'news'.

8　　It is probable therefore that significant vowel length had largely
disappeared in ESl., with few exceptions, by *c.*950, and certainly
by the time of the earliest written records (11th c.). и/ы, of the
same range but distinguished as front/central, are no *longer*, nor

---

[9] *Russische historische Grammatik*, vol. i, pp. 76 ff.

[10] The examples are mostly from Finnish, in which long vowels are indicated by
doubling. Slav voiced plosives are regularly heard as nearer Finnic 'single' and
unvoiced plosives as nearer Finnic 'double' consonants.

[11] In some Finnic dialects *uu*. A distinction of length is also made in the still
extant Slav nasals but this is an effect of the position of the stress: **sǫdŭ* (R. суд;
cf. Pol. *sąd*) > *suunta*; **sǫdĭjī* (R. судья́; Pol. *sędzia*) > *suntio*.

ь/ъ (both central) *shorter*—at least at first—than the front/back pair e/o.

Note. A former contrast of vowel length used for morphological purposes is still visible in certain derived verbs (frequentatives), which CSl. developed in the 'lengthened zero-grade' of the old IE ablaut series, e.g.

o-grade	e-grade	zero-grade	lengthened zero-grade
(раз-)дóр 'strife'	(раз-)дерý	(разо-)дрáть *(dĭr- < dr̥-)*	(раз-)дирáть *(dīr-)*
столъ? 'table'	стелю́ (постéль 'bedclothes', deverbative noun)	стлать *(stĭl-)*	-стилáть настúл (recent deverbative noun) *(stīl-)*
утóк(ъ)? 'weft'		ткать, ткнуть *(tŭk-)*	(спо-)тыкáть(-ся) *(tūk-)*

and similarly, by extension:

	normal grade	lengthened grade
o/a (= ä/ā)	(рас-)смотрéть	(рас-)смáтривать
	(у-)говорúть	(у-)говáривать

The correspondence e/ě (= ě/ē) is no longer perceptible in mod. R. orthography and pronunciation (cf. OCS *(po-)greti, -grebǫ/(po-)grěbajǫ*). The correspondence o/a has remained sufficiently alive to be applied to quite modern derivatives, e.g. (благорóдный >) облагорóдить *pf* 'ennoble' > облагорáживать *impf* (19th c.; earlier облагорóживать).[12]

9 The unstable members of the system were [æ] (*ä*) and *ě* (ħ), both front vowels without symmetrical correlates among the back vowels.

1. CSl. *ę* > ESl. *ä* (soon, if not at once, exerting full palatalization). As can be seen from the table (p. 44) it was close to *(j)a*. The difference could be phonemic, e.g. in *mati* 'mother'/ *mäti* < *męti* inf. 'crumple', but was not morphologically important and conflation starts very early (*'ä* > *ja*): the bad orthography of

---

[12] The o/a relation is only maintained if the latter is stressed: догарáть (*pf* догорѣть) has been replaced by догорáть; -ложúть/-лагáть appears to be the only exception.

the *Nóvgorod Minéi* (1095–7; text no. 8) already shows видѧ for видѧ (pres. ger.), кнѧзь for кънѧзь, тѧ for та (acc. of ты), and others; телѧ neut. (noun type no. 28; see Table VII) and волѧ fem. (type 6; see Table V) are soon confused in spelling.

However, the sound [æ] was protected and perhaps retained if followed by another 'soft' (palatalized) phoneme: *pęt-*: пя́тый [p'at-] but пять [p'ät']. So начать [-č'ät'], понять [-n'ät'], and many verbs in -лять, -рять; and, after depalatalization of *š'* (§37 below), we get the contrast:

ча́ша 'cup' [č'aša]   ча́ща 'thicket' [č'äš'a]
(**kjās-?*)   (**čęst-* < **kimst-*)

Thus *ä* early ceased to be a separate phoneme and became the *positional variant* of *a* between 'soft' phonemes, irrespective of its origin. In words such as пять it may well be that the [ä] has been stable throughout the history of Russian.[13] The presence of this variant in early ESl. accounts for the continued wide use of the symbol ѧ (correct in пѧть, soon merely traditional in пѧтый), whereas ѫ < *ǫ* was superfluous (1.40 (10) and n. 13 below).

10   2. The phoneme ѣ (*jat'*) is unstable everywhere in Slav.[14] Early raising of ѣ to a more close [e] is evident in ESl. in the contrast between the earlier and later Finnic loans: *määrä* [ɛ]/*viesti* [e] (§7 above); the same can be shown for successive loans into Baltic. A somewhat artificial distinction [e]/[ɛ] has been adopted on the diagram on p. 44, which was surely one phase of a changing situation. The evidence of ChSl. is not very helpful: whereas variant spellings such as в'сѣкъ/вьсѩкъ in *Ostr.* point to the older very open ѣ,[15] this was surely artificial. Not infrequent confusions of the

---

[13] It is widely held that in ESl. *ǫ* > *u* but *jǫ* > *jü*, i.e. a slightly fronted *u* (*not* Ger. *ü*), parallel to the pair *a*/*ä*. Such fronting is perceptible as a positional variant between 'soft' phonemes today: любо́вь [l'ub-] but люби́мый [l'üb'-]; юг 'south' [juk] but Ю́рий 'George' [jür'-]; so чуть [č'üt'], ключ [kl'üč'], лю́ди [l'üd'i]. But it is doubtful whether this *ü* had phonemic status: *jǫ* occurred chiefly finally (pres. sg. 1 *-jǫ*; fem. sg. instr. *-ojǫ*, etc.) and in pres. pl. 3 (зна́ютъ, пи́шутъ, ме́лютъ) where the *-t'* was early depalatalized (3.97 (*d*)). It thus had much less support in the system than [ä], especially as the latter was distinct from all varieties of /e/.

[14] Consult M. Samilov, *The Phoneme Jat'* (The Hague, 1964).

[15] This pronunciation appears to have survived in пря́мо < OCS *prěmo* (**per-mo*, adverb of the type ми́-мо) unless due to attraction to ка́мо/та́мо (3.70 (7)); cf. OCS *prěko* in the Slavonicism прекосло́вить 'contradict'. The adj. прямо́й is secondary to the adverb. Blg. has preserved the open pronunciation under stress before hard consonants: мля́ко, бряг (*mlěko, brěg*).

type лете for лѣтѣ, contemporary with *Ostr.*, if reflections of the Kiev vernacular of the 11th c., may point to a minimal difference in timbre but some residual distinction of length. Early raising (narrowing) is characteristic of the North. The final raising of ѣ to [i] is characteristic of Nóvgorod dialect (тьрьпиние = терпѣние in *Novg. Minéi*, 1095–7) and over most of the North, with slightly varying conditions; лѣсъ is typically pronounced [l'is]. The diphthongal stage [ie] is also represented (6.12).[16]

Elsewhere ѣ conflated with *e*, i.e. there was no raising. This position is evident in the Smolénsk Treaty of 1229 (text no. 18; West dialect), where e/ѣ are used at random (ь also intervening): sg. loc. берьзѣ/березѣ/березе/бѣрезѣ/берьзе (also gen. бѣрѣга!); смольнеска/смольньска/смольнѣскь (loc.!)/смолѣнеске/смольнѣскѣ.

Moscow (Central dialect) also conflated ѣ/e, but relatively late (*c.*15th c.). The symbol ѣ is virtually missing in Ivan Grozny's colloquial correspondence with Vasili (1570s). By the 18th c. the distinction was merely orthographic (etymological). If theoreticians of the time claimed that there was, or ought to be, a distinction (Trediakóvsky, Lomonósov)[17] this was by then a purely artificial, literary one due to the traditional ChSl. pronunciation current in the 'high style' (6.57). It had become a matter of education to know 'correct' orthography, following ChSl. norms, and it so remained till the abolition of the symbol ѣ in 1917. Probably the relative correctness in the use of ѣ in Muscovite texts after the 15th c. is aimed at signalling that the /e/ in question does not represent ['o] (§42 ff. below). This applies mainly to stressed ѣ, naturally. In unstressed syllables ѣ was widely ignored, even in ChSl. texts: вѣра, врѣмѧ were usually maintained but средá, пре- (unstressed prefix) gradually became the normal orthography.[18]

The practice of Kotoshíkhin can be taken as typical of a man of education in the 17th c.: stressed ѣ is by and large correct, but unstressed (especially final) ѣ is often ignored (въ томъ дѣле, в мѣсте, о измѣне). Only scribes at the lowest level ignore the symbol ѣ altogether (some wholly colloquial 17th c. texts).

In modern standard Russian, based on the conflation of ѣ/e in

---

[16] In parts of the Ukr. area also stressed ѣ > [ie] or [i], unstressed ѣ > [e].

[17] So also Sumarókov: 'ѣ всѣгда нѣсколько въ i вшибается'.

[18] Unstressed ѣ might be maintained to preserve morphological parallels, e.g. fem. sg. DL -ѣ (stressed or unstressed).

Moscow dialect, the pronunciation of stressed ѣ and e, if not otherwise modified (§42 below), is now contextual only and regulated by the following consonant: *open* [ε] (Fr. *è*) before *hard*, *close* [e] (Fr. *é*) before *soft* (palatalized), e.g. мépа (мѣра) [m'εrə] but мépe (мѣрѣ) [m'er'ε], śто [εtə] but śти [et'i], Лéна [l'εnə] but Лéнин [l'en'in]. Final *e* is generally rather open but may be reduced.

THE JERS

11 The state of an open-syllable language reached by late CSl. times did not last long. Certain jers, already central vowels of the type [ə], began to drop out. There was a transitional stage during which they might properly be called 'ultra-short' (сверхкрáткие, *ultrabrèves*) without implying a three-length vowel system.[19] This applies to virtually all Slav dialects. In the OCS texts there is an evident attempt to maintain the purity of the 'classical' norm, already at variance with spoken usage. But the not infrequent orthographical contrasts such as *dŭva* m./*dĭvě* f. (e.g. in *Zogr.* and *Mar.*) must indicate (for the 11th c.) either an assimilation of the jer to the articulation of the following syllable (hard/soft) or, which is more probable, the further stage of an assimilation in the articulation of a new consonant group, the jer being already absent: [dva]/[d'v'ε].[20]

A parallel change takes place in ESl. The jers were very common vowels. If there was a succession of syllables with a jer as vowel, stress tended to introduce variations in length and quality between them. Jers can therefore be divided into 'weak' and 'strong'. Broadly speaking jers were 'weak'

    (i) in *final* position;
    (ii) if *isolated* (disregarding final jers), all other vowels in the word being 'normal';
    (iii) as *alternate* jers of a series in successive syllables.

12 Fairly precise chronological limits can be given for the whole process of the elimination of weak jers in ESl., but the exact

---

[19] A phenomenon of great rarity but exemplified in modern Estonian (short, long, ultra-long).

[20] A few etymologically wrong jers were perpetuated in ESl. from such assimilations, e.g. *tĭnŭk-* (Pol. *cienki*) > *tŭnŭk-* (R. тóнкий); Lat. *disc-us* > *dĭska, dŭska* (доскá); *wĭdăwa* (Lat. *uidua,* Eng. *widow*) > *vŭdova* (вдовá); *dŭbrĭ* > *dĭbrĭ* (дебрь); probably *mŭdĭl-* > *mĭdĭl-* (мéдленный).

order of elimination is not wholly clear, since orthography was conservative. The earliest reliable examples of missing jers belong to category (ii).

The transcriptions of Russian toponyms in *De administrando imperio* (1.21; mid 10th c.) suggest that the jers were intact at that time:

> Μιλινίσκα [miliniska] = Смольньска
> Βερούτζη [verutsi] = Вьруч-
> 'Οστροβουνι- [ostrovuni-] = островън-.

Finnic loan-words, probably earlier than mid 10th c., are rather ambiguous evidence by reason of Finnic phonetics (see §7 above):

> *ăkŭnă* (окъно > окно́) > *akkuna*
> *lŭž'ĭkā* (лъжька > ло́жка) > *lusikka*.

De administrando imperio also gives

> Νεασήτ [neasit] = неѧсытъ/ь
> -πραχ [-prax] = -прахъ.

The Emperor received these words at second hand or worse. It is certain that there were Bulgarian interpreters in the imperial chancellery and -πραχ is clearly in Blg. (OCS) form, not ESl.[21] Greek, however, does not admit final *t* or *x*: therefore the words were presented to him as having these final consonants. A Bulgarian might well so pronounce as early as 950 since weak jers began to fall out in his vernacular earlier than in ESl. These transcriptions are thus not the best evidence for the precocious lapse of *final* jers in ESl. As final jers were scrupulously maintained in writing, ESl. texts give no direct pointer to the time when they ceased to form a syllable.

13   In category (ii) reliable examples of omission date from mid 11th c. onwards: книгамъ (*Ostr.*); кназю (кън-) (text no. 22); (text no. 12) кто for къто; кназь and кнѧжение; всеволодъ (вьсе-). These are all *pretonic* jers, i.e. in the syllable preceding the main or a subsidiary stress. Other isolated jers are still present: по́чьнеть, ру́сьску). In such a carefully written text as no. 12 this strongly suggests that pretonic jers were the weakest type of internal jer.[22]

---

[21] Often held to represent ESl. *porogŭ* 'threshold' but more probably **poroxŭ* < **porsŭ* = Scand. *fors* 'waterfall'; cf. *Helsingfors* and N. English toponyms of Scand. origin such as *High Force*.

[22] Similarly in Eng. *police* > [pə'li:s] > [pli:s]; Fr. *revenir* [Rəv'niR].

Other common words early written without a pretonic jer are что, где (frequently but wrongly гдѣ), and мног-. Evidence for the dropping of isolated post-tonic jers comes only later: утъка > у́тка (and other words with suffix -ък-, -ьк-), холодьно > хо́лодно (and numerous adj. in -ьн- and -ьск-). It must be borne in mind that the process is gradual and operates according to categories of words rather than *en masse*. All the above pretonic jers, for example, could easily be dropped in speech since they were not supported by any morphological pattern and also led to no new consonant groups of insuperable difficulty.

Surviving texts—by no means ideally distributed—suggest that the process started at latest in the mid 11th c. and was complete in the South by *c.*1200 but in the more backward North by *c.*1250 or even later. The vacillating orthography of the 1229 Treaty shows strikingly in its spelling that the weak jers were no longer present in that dialect by that date.[23] ChSl. texts are not irrelevant here: though many, naturally, are deliberately conservative the *Dobrilo Gospels* of 1164 show many of the new forms.[24]

14 *The 'Strong' Jers*

If all the vowels in a word were jers at least one jer had to be 'strengthened' to the status of a normal vowel *pari passu* with the elimination of the others in order to maintain the viability of the word. This so-called 'vocalization' can be expressed in the rule that a jer in a *new closed syllable* was strengthened. In all Slav languages such strong jers were vocalized, with different reflexes in different areas. In ESl. the two jers remained distinct under all conditions, ь preserving its palatal on-glide. In strong positions we get:

$$ъ [ə] > o$$
$$ь ['ə] > \begin{cases} o \text{ before } hard \\ e \text{ before } soft \end{cases} \text{consonants, i.e.} \begin{cases} C'oC \\ C'eC' \end{cases}$$

In the latter case it is usually assumed that there was a first stage *'ə > 'e* and a second *'e > 'o* in appropriate contexts, but the time interval need not have been appreciable. Examples:

---

[23] Spellings such as дьнетъ, отидето (for final -тъ) in this text do not imply a final syllable with a jer or any other vowel. Many Northern texts show e/o in place of a lost final jer; see 6.62 (4).

[24] The jers in *Ostr.* are exceptionally correct but this may be due as much to the excellence of the manuscript from which it was copied as to the spoken practice of the scribe in 1056–7.

съвъ > съв > сон [son] 'dream'
дьнь > дьн҄ь [d'ən'] > день [d'en'] 'day'
вьсь > вьс҄ь > весь [v'es'] 'all'
льнъ > льн > лён [l'on] 'flax'
плъть > плът҄ь > плоть [płot'] 'flesh'
шьвъ > шьв > шов [š'ov] 'seam' (later [šof]).

The second stage is that of new closed syllables. By extension, in any sequence of jers there will be an alternation of *weak* and *strong* (the latter here given the stress-mark `) reckoning backwards from the end of the word or word-group:[25]

тѣнъка > тонка́   вѣшьли > вошли́
кусъкъ > кусо́к   жьньць > жнец
тѣмьно > темно́   къ мьнѣ > ко мне.

The jer is always treated as strong in the sequences Съ/ьSC and CSъ/ьC, irrespective of other considerations: see §48 below.

Immediate Consequences of the Loss of the Weak Jers

15   1. *All consonants,* with the exception of the velars (after which no ь could stand) and the old products of palatalization *š'*, *ž'*, *č'*, *c'* (after which no ь could stand), now appeared as *paired phonemes:* otherwise expressed, to the existing pairs *n/n'*, *r/r'*, *ł/l'*, *s/s'*, *z/z'* (§5 above) *dental* and *labial* pairs were added. This is especially important in final position:

n/n' { данъ 'given' > дан [dan]
      { дань 'tribute' > дан҄ь [dan']

t/t' { плътъ 'raft' > плот [płot]
      { плъть 'flesh' > плот҄ь [płot']

v/v'[26] { кровъ 'roof' > кров [krov]
          { кръвь 'blood' > кров҄ь [krov']

The frequency of *s'*, *z'*, hitherto low, was increased.

16   2. Consonants followed by a *front vowel* in early ESl. (perhaps in late CSl.) received a slight palatal articulation (automatic positional variants) and are sometimes referred to as 'semi-soft' (полумягкие). In the case of the *dentals* and *labials* there were two variants of *one* phoneme, but in the case of *n, l, r, s, z* three variants and *two* phonemes:

[25] So in spoken French *jè ne tè le donnerai pas* [ʒən təl dɔnʀe 'pa].
[26] See further §34 below.

'hard' syllable (back vowel, no palatalization)	'semi-soft' syllable (front vowel)	'soft' syllable (full palatalization)
ta, to, tu	*te, ti*	—
na, no, nu	*ne, ni*	*n'a, n'i*
ła, ło, łu	*le, li*	*l'a, l'u*
sádŭ	*sełó*	*vĭs'egó*

The semi-soft (partially palatalized) positional variants were now finally eliminated by merging with the fully palatalized, establishing binary oppositions throughout:

> нить [n'it'] with [n'] as in (original) нива [n'iva]
> лѣс(ъ) [l'ɛs] with [l'] as in воля [l'a].

In the important case of the jers the changes can be resumed as follows:

semi-soft: $*m\breve{i}$ > early ESl. $m\breve{b}$ > $m'ə$ > $\begin{cases} \text{weak } m' \\ \text{strong } m'e/m'o \text{ (§14)} \end{cases}$

hard: $*m\breve{u}$ > early ESl. $m\breve{ъ}$ > $mə$ > $\begin{cases} \text{weak } m \\ \text{strong } mo \end{cases}$

This change was thus certainly well established before the elimination of the weak jers. The denasalization of $ę > \ddot{a} >$ '*a* (§9 (1) above) must be seen as part of this process. Contrasting *final* pairs *t/t'*, etc., complete and regularize the whole development.

17　　3. The phonetic shape of a word is henceforward controlled by the consonants. It follows that ы (*y*) lost its independent status and became a positional variant of и (*i*): мил(ъ) [m'ił] v. мыл(ъ) [muł]; both *[m'уł] and *[mił] are impossible. This change is also essentially pre-literate, proceeding directly from (2) above (10th–11th c.): in нити dat. [niti]/ныти infin. [nyti] ы is still phonemic; with respect to new [n'it'i] it ceases to be so.

This automatic positional adjustment is later reflected in such spellings as в ызбу (< *v iz-*) and recognized orthographically in modern сыскáть *et sim.* (< *s-isk-*).

18　　4. From being a language of open syllables Russian became a language with many closed syllables and many monosyllables, as exemplified in сон, дан, кровь, весь (above) and the more complicated смерть, трость, взгляд. Of the numerous new consonant clusters which appeared not all were acceptable. The morphology of the word and the position of the cluster will decide whether adjustments are needed, not all of which can be reduced to rules. As examples of *ad hoc* simplifications of difficult cases may be cited:

гърньчаръ > гончáр 'potter'
Тьхвѣрь > Тверь (Finnic toponym)
Пльсковъ > Псков (Ger. *Pleskau* preserves the earlier shape)
Дьбряньскъ > Брянск
дъхорь > хорь 'polecat' (cf. Pol. *tchórz*)
сьрдьце > сéрдце [s'ɛrcə] 'heart' ⎱
сълньце > сóлнце [soncə] 'sun' ⎰ with conservative orthography
стьлалъ > стлал [sɫaɫ] 'spread', homonymous with сълалъ > слал 'sent'
чувьство > чýвство [č'ustvə] 'feeling'

19   5. (i) There is virtually no limitation on new *initial binary clusters*: мнóго, кнѝга, кто, птѝца, рвать, где, взять, пшенѝца, жму, лбу (loc. sg.), лжец, хмель, ртуть. According to J. D. O'Connor (*Phonetics* (1973), p. 231) there are 289 initial clusters in Russian of which 188 binary. The corresponding figures for English are 50/44.

Particular cases:

(ii) The cluster жд now arose in the common words ждать (< жьдати) and каждый (ко-жьд-; 3.66 (iv)). This rather common OCS cluster (1.19) had hitherto been avoided in the writing, and presumably in the pronunciation, of ChSl., being replaced by native ж (*ž'* or perhaps *ẓ̌'*; §39 below), e.g. побѣженъ in *Novg. Minéi*. Henceforward it becomes acceptable and reasserts its status in all Slavonicisms (modern побеждён; see also 7.20).

(iii) New native срок (< съ-рокъ) and others underpin ChSl. срам, среда, зрак, etc., though these alien clusters were not actively avoided, except at the vernacular level, where we find страм for срам, and standard встрет- from въ(з)-с-рѣт-; so also аже бы миръ не ръздрушенъ былъ (1229); изд Ростова (17th c.).[27]

(iv) The groups *tl, dl,* which had been eliminated in both E. and S. Slav, are accepted on their reappearance:

[27] OCS *sr-/zr-* from inversion (1.22) only; in other contexts more or less regularly avoided, being brought into line with CSl. *sr/zr > str/zdr: vŭz-rad- > vŭzdradovati sę*; Gk. Ἰσραήλ > *izdrailŭ*. But OCS kept *s(ŭ)rětenie* (= встреча) as if an inversion (verb *sŭrěsti/sŭręštǫ*).

old: вед-лъ > велъ [v'oł]; мы-дло > мы́ло 'soap'

new: сѣдьло > седло́ [s'e/dło] 'saddle'; метьла > метла́ [m'e/tła] 'besom';
initially для (< дѣля), длина́ 'length' (< дьл-).

(v) The clusters *-stn-/-zdn-* are reduced to *-sn-/-zn-* in all but
learned words (without change of orthography):

vernacular: по́здно [pozn-], ме́стный [m'ɛsn-], ле́стница [l'es'n'-],
пра́здник [prazn-] (Slavonicism);

learned: коры́стный 'mercenary' [-stn-]. 'Received standard' pronunciation also simplified *-stk- > -sk-,* e.g. in неве́стка, but this is now
rare.

20   6. *Final clusters*. There was much hesitation over various new
clusters in absolute *final* position.[28] Generally speaking:

(i) *r, l* + C and *s, z* + C are acceptable: смерть, твёрд, горб,
торг, борщ, серп, верх, мёрз, морж, чернь, корм; долг, столб,
сельдь, полз, полк, холм; мост, -езд, воск, визг; new foreign
suffices -изм, -ист from the 18th c.

(ii) C + *l', n'* are acceptable but C + *ł, n* usually avoided:

     (*a*) рубль, кремль, кора́бль, мысль, жизнь; *but* угль
        (gen. у́гля) > у́голь, огнь (gen. огня́) > ого́нь,
        сте́бель (gen. сте́бля).

     (*b*) узлъ (gen. узла́) 'knot' > у́зел; углъ (gen. угла́)
        'corner' > у́гол; сукно́ 'cloth', pl. gen. су́кон; весло́
        'oar', pl. gen. вёсел; Па́вел, gen. Па́вла 'Paul' (Gk.
        Παῦλος [pavl-]); за́мысел 'intention' (cf. мысль
        above); and regularly in the pret. masc. (examples
        from the 13th c.): пеклъ, умерлъ, ослѣплъ, моглъ
        > пёк, у́мер, осле́п, мог.[29]

(iii) Two plosives are not acceptable but there is usually a
potentially strong jer to break the cluster, e.g. ошибъка, pl. gen.
ошибъкъ > оши́бка, оши́бок.

(iv) C + *r, r'* is variable:

     (*a*) Днепр, Днестр, смотр (supported by смотреть),
        осётр 'sturgeon'; but more commonly

     (*b*) вѣтръ > ве́тер 'wind' (gen. ве́тра); сестра́, ведро́,
        ребро́: pl. gen. сестёр, вёдер, рёбер.

[28] O'Connor (§19 (5)(i) above) gives 142 final clusters, of which 112 are binary
(Eng. 130/75).

[29] Solutions of the form у́мерел, мо́гол are found in dialect.

21   Such spellings as огънь, сестъръ, хытъръ, остъръ occur quite commonly shortly after the fall of the jers and clearly indicate some trouble in pronunciation. Building on the pattern produced automatically by the fall of the jers in сон/сна, кусóк/кускá, жúдок/жидкá, мúрен/мúрна, etc., the spoken language freely inserted an analogical o/e (commonly called 'mobile' o/e) into the difficult clusters, as exemplified above. Once the rhythm was established it was extended in parallel morphological situations to clusters which were on principle acceptable. Thus, though there is no bar on -рг, -лг, -ск, the pl. gen. of кочергá, úволга, доскá are кочерёг, úволог (or úволг), досóк. This also preserves an equal number of syllables throughout the declension (pl. instr. apart).

22   Exceptions to the above will often be Slavonicisms, to which the vernacular preferences did not apply, e.g. sg. masc. nom. храбр, мудр, щедр; pl. gen. букв, жертв, молúтв, бездн; Прóмысл 'Providence' (native прóмысел 'business'); жезл 'wand'; ноя́брь, декáбрь; хитр (native хитёр). The high-style writers of the 18th c. continued to favour the ChSl. forms: сестр not сестёр, огнь not огóнь, остр not остёр. But the greatly increased intake of foreign loan-words from the 17th c., some of which had unusual final clusters, led to a more fluid situation, much hesitation over the best form of such loans, and the present-day lack of uniformity in their treatment. The procedure of inserting a 'mobile' o/e continued to be active in the genuinely colloquial stratum, e.g. мáрка 'stamp', pl. gen. мáрок.

23   7. *Reappearance of diphthongs.* These can only be of the type V + *j*, a following jer being lost: *mojь* > мой; *lьjь* > лей (imperative of лить); трéбуй (from трéбовать); молодóй; слýчай.

24   8. *Assimilations*

(i) Consonants newly in contact normally assimilate regressively. Orthography reproduced this sporadically in the Muscovite period (voicing rather earlier than devoicing) but only a few words, morphologically isolated, have incorporated it permanently. Examples:

> къде > где 'where' (гдѣ recorded 1219)
> истъба > избá 'cottage'
> чьбанъ > жбан 'jug'
> съдоровъ > здорóв 'well'
> сватьба > свáдьба 'wedding'.

(NB: [v] *does not voice* a preceding consonant, whether in old or new clusters, hence [svad'bə], [tvoj], [kvart'irə].)

Зделает(ъ), лотка, уско, ношка, жерепцѣ (*NBG*, no. 43), -тца for -тся, з золотом, бес трав, etc. are frequently written down to the end of the 17th с. Otherwise etymological spelling has prevailed:

> лодъка > лóдка [łotka] 'boat'
> коробъка > корóбка [karopka] 'basket'.

25　　(ii) Assimilation in the majority of contexts includes *regressive palatalization*:

> *bĭkel-*:　бьчела > пчелá [p'č'eła] 'bee'
> 　　　　　сьдѣсь > здесь [z'd'es'] 'here'
> 　　　　　възати > взять [v'z'ät'] 'take'.

Извóзчик 'driver' is pronounced, and sometimes written, извóщик.

Palatalization does not regularly pass back through *r'* (cf. the old clusters [pr'i, tr'i]), nor can it affect the velars: [kn'äz', xm'el']. Conversely, *r* is not nowadays affected by a following soft consonant: the classical standard distinguished between [s'm'er't'] with preceding front vowel and [pórt'it'] with preceding back vowel. These are, of course, cases of contact without assimilation. There is much individual variation in the treatment of such groups; normative dictionaries do not agree among themselves.

Note. More extreme regressive palatalizations (not provoked by loss of jers) are usually Slavonicisms, OCS having carried through the principle with great consistency: мысль, мы́слить but размышля́ть, мышлéние; умертви́ть *pf* 'mortify'/умерщвля́ть; изощри́ть *pf* 'refine'/изощря́ть (but native обостри́ть *pf*/обостря́ть); вожделéние 'desire' (*vŭz-žel-*); иждивéние (*iz-živ-*) 'maintenance'. However, шлю (*sŭl-jǫ*), pres. of слать, belongs to the colloquial stratum.

26　　(iii) Similarly, *regressive depalatalization* is general:

> коньць, gen. коньца > конéц, концá [kan'ɛc, kanca]
> правьда > прáвда 'truth' [pravdə]
> тъщьно > тóшно 'sick' [tošnə]
> тьмьн- > тёмный 'dark' [t'omn-]

and so numerous adjectives in -ьн-.

With adjectives in -ьск- the depalatalization was much retarded

(16th c. or later) as we have (excluding Slavonicisms) жéнский, деревéнский, etc., not *-ёнск- (§42 ff. below).[30]

But [l′] is always preserved: сúльный, céльский, тóлько, though ь is frequently omitted in Muscovite texts.

27 9. *Long Consonants*

The elimination of jers produced identical consonants in contact, actual or by assimilation. The syllabic structure of CSl. did not allow any 'double' consonants (otherwise called 'strong', 'long', or 'emphatic'), as, say, in Italian, and in general the Slav languages have continued to eschew them.[31] Spellings such as и Смолиньска (*RPC s.a.* 1096) and и своего гор[о]да Смольнеска (1229) (both из с-) confirm this for early ESl. In the period following the fall of the jers we find русьск- > руск- [rusk-], which has *remained the pronunciation down to the present*, but the more 'correct' orthography русск- was finally restored.[32] The majority of written double consonants in Russian are merely orthographic, whether in native (расскáз, искýсство) or foreign words (суббóта, баллáда, мácca, грýппа, параллéль, эффéкт, граммáтика (earliest form граматикия)). A long consonant is, however, obligatory to avoid ambiguity, especially with the prefixes в-, с- (sometimes also as prepositions):

воз [vos] 'load' but ввоз [v̄os] 'import'
судúть [sud′-] 'judge' v. ссудúть [šud′-] 'lend'
садúть [sad′-] (various senses) v. ссадúть [šad′-] 'dismount' (trans.)
    (ссадиша и с[ъ] колъ (*RPC s.a.* 1097) 'lifted him off the cart');
верх [v′ɛrx] 'top'[33]: вверх [v̄′ɛrx] 'upwards'.

Similarly sometimes with от-, над-, под-: отопúть v. оттопúть; пóданный v. пóдданный. But if no serious ambiguity arises it is doubtful whether the best speakers pronounce a long consonant, e.g. in отдáть (there is no *одáть), оттýда, восстановúть, сзáди,

[30] Polish has retained [-n′sk-]; some R. dialects have [-n′s′k-]. See also Table XX (24).

[31] OCS consistently reduced double to single consonants in spelling and surely also in pronunciation: *bezakonije* (*bez-z-*), *raširiti* (*raz-š-*), *vŭšĭdŭ* (*vŭz-š-*), but to avoid occasional ambiguities, as in the last example (prefix *vŭ-* or *vŭz-*?), later enlarged the prefix where necessary to *bezŭ-, razŭ-, vŭzŭ-, otŭ-*, etc. Double consonants are still strictly taboo in SCr.

[32] The verb развáть/разúнуть *pf* 'open wide' (usually with рот) has preserved the earlier pronunciation and spelling.

[33] Or [v′er′x]; see §45 (4) below.

ввиду́, and generally with the prefixes раз-, из- before c (рассе́янный, исся́кнуть). Long *š/ž* arise but are not always well maintained: расширя́ть, бесшу́мн- [-šy-, -šu-], изжа́рить [-ža-], изжо́га [ižogə *or* ižogə], мы с жено́й [žynoj]. [c̄] is correct in reflexive infinitives: боя́ться [bajac̄ə]. Many speakers make a perceptible hiatus in such cases as к кому́, к го́роду (where dissimilation was formerly usual, §28 below), and подда́ть [pod-d-], if to be distinguished from пода́ть. Universal literacy has no doubt tended to favour long consonants (spelling pronunciation). Outside prefixes doubled *nn* is the only frequent case but it is difficult to be certain to what extent [ñ] was pronounced in earlier times. Nowadays there is much variation, with [ñ] common immediately after the stress: вое́нный [vajɛñ-], дли́нный [d′l′iñ-], стра́нный [strañ-] as opposed to ка́менный [kam′ən-] *et sim.*[34] In the p.p.p. the -нн- is recent and artificial (3.129 (3)) and was disregarded in good pronunciation until the present century; it is still lacking in Ukr. (ку́плений). For long consonants by assimilation (N. dial.) and in Ukr. and WhR. see Table XVII (10) and Table XX (18).

28   10. *Dissimilations*

These are much rarer and chiefly affect velars:

льгъко > легко́ [l′exko] (and ле́гкий [l′oxkəj])
къто > кто [xto]
чьто > что [što][35]
мякъко > *мя́кко [m′axkə], now with the erroneous spelling мягк- (after легк-) which has produced masc. мя́гок [m′agək].

The spelling што is recorded from 1164 and хто from the 14th c.; ни х каким *et sim.* is quite common in the 17th c. but in modern times [kto] has reappeared.

The group -чьн- regularly passed to [šn] in Moscow dialect and thence into standard pronunciation from the 17th c. but learned words usually maintain [č′n]: ночно́й [našnoj], доста́точно 'enough' [-təšnə], коне́чно 'of course' [kan′ɛšnə], but коне́чный 'final' [-č′n-], ли́чный 'personal' [l′ič′n-]. *Dom.* already spells

---

[34] Pol. *stranny* has [ñ] but Cz. *stranný* has [n].

[35] The group [č′t] is not avoided, at least in more learned words, e.g. мечта́ 'dream', but the hypercorrections in the recent loans по́чта (1669, from older Pol. *poszta*) and ма́чта (1696, originally машта) point to spoken [št] as in почти́ 'almost' [pašt′i].

обышный, пшенишный. The coll. дотóшный 'meticulous' (so spelt) clearly derives from доточн-.

11. Exceptions to the General Rules for the Treatment of Weak Jers

29 (i) Stem levelling for morphological symmetry was general from the 16th c.: жьньць, gen. жьньца > жнец, *женца, reformed as жнецá 'reaper'.

Смольнѣскъ, gen. Смольньска > Смольнеск, Смоленьска, reformed as Смолéн(ь)ск, -а. Forms such as Рылеск(ъ), Брянеск(ъ) are found as late as the 17th c.; the variation is perhaps dialectal.

Дъскá > (with assimilation) цка,[36] but pl. gen. дъскъ > дос(о)к, whence доск- throughout.

tǐnǔkǐ, fem. *tǐnǔka* > *тнок, тонкá, reformed as тóнок, тонкá (so тёмен/темнá and others).

In рóпот, шёпот < *rǔpǐtǐ, š'ǐpǐtǐ* the onomatopoeic structure provoked the retention of both jers. The expected forms ръпътъ > рпот (1307) and ръпъту > ропту (c.1500) show that the adjustments were slow.

In дъчи/oblique stem дъчер- 'daughter' the latter led to NA дчерь in the 13th–14th c. but the word is eventually reformed as дочь/oblique stem дóчер-, no doubt following мать/мáтер-; the jer was not restored in пáдчерица 'stepdaughter'.

Чьсть, gen. чьсти 'honour', leads to честь/чти (with simplification of cluster), reformed as честь/чéсти (similarly месть 'vengeance').

30 (ii) Jers may be preserved to avoid difficult consonant clusters, e.g. in

крьстити > крестúть 'baptize' (supported by крест), but кстить occurs in dialect;
стьбль, gen. стьбля > стéбель (with 'mobile' e)/стéбля 'stem';
стькло > стеклó 'glass' (earlier скло, шкло, and still склянка);
tǐstja > тёща 'mother-in-law' [t'oš'a], supported by тесть 'father-in-law' < *tǐstǐ*;
пьстр- > пестр- generalized (пёстрый);[37]
кузнéц, gen. кузнецá but normally конéц/концá, etc.

[36] The form цка is not infrequent in Muscovite texts and became the technical term for the board on which icons are painted.
[37] The limits of the tolerable vary widely in Slav: Polish accepts *chrzcić* [xšc'ic'], *źdźbło* (from parallel neut. *stǐblo*), *szkło*; Czech has *pstrý*.

31 (iii) *Slavonicisms*. In reciting and singing ChSl. all the jers had to be maintained as syllable-forming vowels.[38] Whether weak or strong they were pronounced o/e. This habit was called sarcastically хомония from the aorist pl. 1 suffix -хомъ (pronounced -хомо), frequent in prayers, etc., but already extinct in spoken Russian. This ecclesiastical pronunciation accounts for

> собо́р 'cathedral' < съборъ (native сбор 'collection')
> восто́к 'east' < въстокъ (R. dial. всток)

and numerous words with the prefixes во-, воз-, со-, e.g. воцари́ться, во́зраст, возобнови́ть, собы́тие, сове́т, сопоста́вить. The forms во-, воз-, со- are of course sometimes produced in native words by the normal rules (as in со мной, во мне), e.g. созва́ть *pf*/созыва́ть (but also созыва́ть).

32 (iv) *False analogies*. The rhythm рот/рта 'mouth' (< ръ́тъ/ръта) leads to ров/рва 'ditch' (*rovŭ*/*rova*), and similarly лён/льна 'flax' (< льнъ/льна) to лёд/льда 'ice' (*ledŭ*/*leda*; cf. Tmutorokan' stone (1086): мѣрилъ мо[ре] по леду).

Честь/чти (§29 above) leads to шесть/шти 'six', eventually rejected for correct шести́. Occasionally there is fluctuation: мъхъ gen. мъха 'moss' > мох, мха, but now usually мо́ха and pl. usually мхи.

33 12. *Jer + j*

OCS orthography suggests that the jers had a special quality before [j], perhaps positionally short *ĭ, ў̆* but spelt with the symbols for long *ī, ȳ*, viz. *myjǫ, sǫdija; novyi, iskrennii; molenie*. Such spellings naturally occur abundantly in early ESl. texts and are perpetuated in many Slavonicisms, notably in the verbal nouns in -ние (-*nĭje*) (3.135) and in the long adj. sg. nom. endings -ый/-ий (3.38). They are to be found even in vernacular documents such as the 1229 Treaty: (у)биють, Роусию instr., соудиями, держания; Varlaam's Deed of Gift (text no. 15): челядию; and, of course, Mstislav's Deed (text no. 12): княжение, полюдие, пришьст-вия. There is no good evidence that such jers differed in their quality and development in the majority of ESl. dialects (there

---

[38] Revision of the music or underlay to eliminate weak jers (from the Russian point of view) was only attempted in the 17th c. (Patriarch Nikon's reforms).

are special treatments in the peripheral Ukr. and WhR. areas).
We get:

*warbĭjĭ, gen. *warbĭja: OCS врабий but R. воробе́й, воробья́ 'sparrow';
*aulĭjĭ, gen. *aulĭja: R. у́лей, у́лья 'beehive';
pres. sg. 1 bĭjǫ: OCS бинѫ, R. бью;
pitĭje: OCS питие, R. питьё;
novŭ-jĭ, sinĭ-jĭ: R. но́вой, си́ней (widespread Muscovite spelling rejected
   in the lit. norm);
žiznĭjǫ, instr.: ChSl. жизнию, R. жи́знью (recorded in the 12th c. though
   the word was a Slavonicism, 5.6).

Learned names of Greek origin have remained in ChSl. form, e.g.
Васи́лий, Евге́ний.

As the nouns in -ние (and -тие) were by and large literary, the
Russian form is relatively rare, e.g. жа́лованье 'salary'; литьё
'casting', враньё 'lying', and others of this type were outside the
range of ChSl. vocabulary. A few doublets have resulted, notably
ChSl. житие́ 'Saint's life' (literary genre) and бытие́ 'existence'
(also прибы́тие 'arrival') but R. житьё-бытьё '(mode of) life';
ChSl. Мари́я but colloquial Ма́рья (and other names of this shape).
However, orthography fluctuated even in the 19th c.: Herzen writes
увлече́нье, сча́стие, the opposite of the modern norm увлече́ние,
сча́стье.

Further Consonant Changes Mainly Subsequent to the Loss of the Jers

34   1. Assimilatory devoicing produced f at internal boundaries and
initially:

$$лав(ъ)ка > [łafka]$$
sg. neut. NA   в(ь)се > [f's'o]
$$в(ъ)тор- > [ftor-]$$

We have therefore the stages $w > v > f$. OCS clearly had v, not w,
but f is an alien sound which, if preserved, had to be transliterated as
Gk. φ:

Φίλιππος > Филипъ 'Philip'
Φαρισαίος > Фарисе́й 'Pharisee'
Φεβρουάριος > февра́ль 'February'.

Early ESl. had only w. The earliest vernacular loans render Gk.
φ as p, the nearest unvoiced labial:

Φίλιππος > Пилип(ъ) 'Philip'
Ἰωσήφ > Óсип 'Joseph'
Στέφανος > Степáн[39] 'Stephen'

just as Gmc. *fulk- had been taken over by CSl. as пълкъ > полк (5.5, c.3rd c. AD?). These names point to the early Christian period, i.e. 10th–11th c. A word such as фофудь(я) in *RPC* (s.a. 912)—a kind of costly stuff—cannot be classed as learned (ecclesiastical), but it must be remembered that a high proportion of the Kievan traders in Constantinople were *f*-possessing Scandinavians (Varangians).

The adoption of foreign *f* eventually gave this consonant phonemic status in Russian (влáга/флáга) though it remains a very rare contrast in native words (дровá/дрофá). Though /f/ is now present in most Slav languages, in some it is still only a rather unstable member of the system.

The change *w* > *v* was not universal in ESl.; some dialects continued to have only or mainly [w] (see 6.9). In those in which /f/ was developed the new pair *v*/*f* automatically produced the further contrasting pair *v'*/*f'*:

лавъка > [ɫafka] (elsewhere [ɫawka])
вься > [f's'a] (elsewhere [ws'a]).

Assimilation is rarely indicated in Muscovite spelling because the symbol ф was itself rare: фпрокъ (1501), пофторяючи (16th c.). Except in such assimilated groups (where ф is not written) initial *f* cannot be native in Russian, apart from a few onomatopoeic words such as фы́ркать 'neigh'.

Dialects which did not develop *f* as a normal phoneme often have *xw* in its place (i.e. labial *spirant* = velar *spirant* + nearest *labial*):

дрофá 'bustard' (typical steppe bird), S. dial. дрохвá [draxwa];
Gk. Φλῶρος > Фрол, S. and W. dial. Хрол (with simplification of group).
Similarly Хомá, Хóдор.[40]

---

[39] Similarly SCr. *Stèpān*, later also *Stèvān* (*Stèfān* is only learned). A similar difference of age can be seen in Blg. Тóдор, (later) R. Фёдор < Θεόδωρος ([t] = nearest plosive, [f] = nearest spirant to non-existent [θ]). Despite the fact that Gk. δ was already pronounced [ð] (voiced variant of [θ]), it never appears in OCS or ESl. as [v]; cf. Cockney *nuffin(k), bruvver* for *nothing, brother* [θ, ð].

[40] The reverse is also found (i.e. in an *f*-using dialect): фóрост for хвóрост 'brushwood', фатáть for хватáть 'seize'; cf. SCr. *hvála,* coll. *fála.* The spelling ко Тфери, межю Тферью (*c.*1300) points to [txw-] before the simplification of this initial group (§18 above), rather than to a progressive assimilation [tv] > [tf].

35 2. The devoicing (§24 above) which started internally was extended to *final consonants*. This is not a necessary consequence of the loss of final jers: SCr. assimilates internally, and incorporates it in the orthography, but there is no final devoicing: *Sȓb(in)*, adj. *sȓpski*; *rédak*, f. *rétka*; *zub* [zub] *not* [zup]. Ukrainian also does not normally devoice final voiced consonants. In ESl. texts final devoicing is rarely shown; there are rare examples from the 13th c. (Конратъ for *Konrad*? (1229); отинуть = отнюдь (1296)) but it may not have been generalized till a good deal later. There is occasional, but not serious, homonymy:

лук 'onion' } [łuk] but oblique cases { лу́ка etc.
луг 'meadow' }   { лу́га

под 'hearth' } [pot] but oblique cases { по́да etc.
пот 'sweat' }   { по́та

Final groups assimilate as expected: по́езд [pojɛst], pl. gen. надёжд [nad'ɛšt], мозг [mosk].

Devoicing produced final *f/f'*:

ров, gen. рва [rof, rva] 'ditch'
кровь, gen. кро́ви [krof', krov'i] 'blood'
masc. pl. gen. столо́в [-of].

'Non-*f*' areas preserve [row], [krow], [stałow]. Final *f/f'* may not have been generalized before the 17th c. In documents of Peter the Great's time spellings such as аѳицероѳъ = офицеров become common and *f* is freely admitted, including finally, in foreign loan-words, e.g. верфь 'dock'.

It is possible that the spelling трут 'tinder' perpetuates devoicing: the CSl. form would appear to be *trǫdǔ*.

36 3. The velars *k, g, x*[41] could only stand before back vowels: **ke, *ki*, etc. had been eliminated by CSl. palatalizations (1.15 ff.). Such syllables, foreign to native phonology, had to be used frequently in OCS in transcribing Greek (largely biblical) vocabulary, in which there was no such limitation, e.g. кѣсарь, евангелие, хѣровимъ, Георгий, кивотъ, китъ, архистратиге (*Novg. Minéi*), декабра (*Ostr.*).[42] The earliest rendering of Cyril (Κύριλλος [ki-]) in ESl. was *Kurilǔ*, or with traditional palatalization *Čuril(o)*.

---

[41] The sources of *x* are various in Slav, including *ĭ, ŭ, r, k + s* (**wĭrs- >* вьрх-). Consult Shevelov, *Prehistory of Slavic*, pp. 127 ff.

[42] In Greek of that time *k* and *x* were slightly palatalized before front vowels; *g* was already [ɣ] before back and moving to [j] before front vowels (as today); thus Геѡргий is the learned, ecclesiastical form, but Юрий taken directly from spoken Γεώργιος [jörjos].

There was an early tendency in some parts of ESl. to restore the unity of noun stems ending in a velar, e.g. in fem. sg. DL руцѣ > рукѣ; masc. sg. loc. волцѣ > волкѣ, восцѣ > воскѣ (на воскѣ 1073); пасцѣ (or пастѣ) > пасхѣ 'Easter'.[43] Similarly in adjs. in -ьск- restorations are relatively common from an early date: небесьскимъ, въ русьскѣи сторонѣ велицѣи (both 12th c.; note contrast in велицѣи), but others are very rare before the 13th c.: великии, киихъ (12th c.).

It is possible that the Second Palatalization did not, or did not fully, take place in some extreme N. dialects, in which case dat. Дъмъкѣ (*Novg. Minéi* 1096) may be local pronunciation rather than an early restoration (1.16).

These factors were grounds for a general shift in the spoken language, already active in the 12th c. but not complete till the 14th c.: Кыевъ > Ки́ев, хытрыи > хи́трый, гыбель > ги́бель. These velars are slightly fronted (palatalized) but the conditions for the rise of paired phonemes *k/k'*, etc., were lacking (кь, etc., did not exist in any context) and they have remained positional variants.

By the time of the mass borrowing of foreign words, ке, ки, etc. could be taken over freely: генера́л, гипс 'gypsum', киби́тка (5.22), кило-.

Standard Russian has accepted the normalization ткать 'weave', pres. тку, ткёт (similarly скать), but not печь 'bake', пеку́, печёт (пекёт is frequent in dialect). Кы, etc., are not now a regular feature of any dialect but may appear in local loan-words, e.g. in the Far North and in contact with Turkic languages.

37   4. *The consonants* ш/ж, ч, ц. For sources see §5 above.

(i) Early orthography wrote indifferently ша/шя [š'a], жу/жю [ž'u], etc.; сижю́, пожя́ловал, пи́шют are still found in the 17th c. The pair *š'/ž'*, as very generally in Slav, was early depalatalized. The change started in the 12th and was complete by the late 14th c. (later or not at all in a few N. dialects). The best evidence is the spelling шы/жы, since all other vowels are ambiguous:

---

[43] Though transcribed пасха the word was apparently usually pronounced па́ска, as in spoken Greek (τὸ Πάσχα, neut. indecl.). The group *sc'* was commonly simplified to *st'/st* in later OCS (and R. ChSl.); hence such forms as pl. nom. рустии < русьск-, which are doubtfully native.

слышышь (1300); кнѧжылъ (1372); жывота (1389).

Orthography has been capricious in maintaining the spelling ши/жи, so that we have today ша, ше [šɛ], ши [šy], шо, шу, and an otiose jer in pres. sg. 2 пишешь and fem. nouns such as ложь [łoš], молодёжь [-d'oš].[44]

The new hardness of *š/ž* is also shown by the passage of e > ё before them (§42 ff. below): ежь 'hedgehog' > ёж [još], идёшь [id'oš]. Different stages of the process are illustrated by дешёв(ая), with *ё* after still soft [š'], but дёшево (with [š]). A few dialects have evolved *š/š'*, etc., as for other consonants, in conformity with the following vowel: [ša], [šu] but [š'e], [š'i].

38 (ii) The sound ц (*c'*) also lost its palatal component but at a distinctly later date than *š'/ž'*. Hardened [c] was the norm at Moscow by the late 16th c.; manuscripts of the *Domostrój* from that time show отецъ, концы, and others. The process was no doubt initiated a century or so earlier: с Троицына дни (Af. Nik.). But general hardening was just late enough to miss the change e > ё: the suffix -ец(ь) never appears as *-ёц (купéц, отéц, немéцкий).

Unlike ши/жи the spelling цы was generalized in native words (купцы́, цыплёнок), but early borrowings from W. Europe, e.g. на́ция, kept the alternative ци alive, though good pronunciation was, at least until recently, [ná:cyjə]. Hence the modern variation цыга́н 'gypsy', цы́нга 'scurvy' but цирк 'circus', ци́ркуль 'compasses', цифр 'cypher' (all with [cy-]).

The sound ч (*č'*) has remained soft in standard Russian.[45] However, these two isolated phonemes were subject to confusion. In much of the North *č'* fused with *c'* as [c'] (цóканье, 6.10), which may later harden to [c]; less commonly *c'* and *č'* fuse in [č'] (чóканье) > [č] (rare). The phenomenon is usually ascribed to the Finnic substrate in the population of the North since few, if any, Finnic languages have both /č/ and /c/.

39 (iii) *The phonemes š̄'/ž̄' (long)*. Normal processes of palatalization (1.20) produced sk + front vowel, *sk + j, st + j > š'č'*;

---

[44] Masc. nouns dropped the jer: ножь > нож [noš].
[45] WhR. has *hard č, c, š, ž* but has a new [c'] < [t'] (14th–15th c.; Table XX (17)). Ukr. has hardened [c] before original *e, i* (as all other consonants) but otherwise [c'] (кінець, місяць); its [č] is *hard*, as in Pol. Orthographic convention in Russian now has меч m. but ночь f. (as with ш/ж).

zg + front vowel, $zg + j$, $zd + j > \check{z}'d\check{z}' > \overset{\vee}{\check{z}}'$.[46] Also from some assimilations: и Щернигова (*RPC s.a.* 1096) < *iz-č-*; с(ъ)частье [š'č'ä-].

These have remained, with some regional variations. The original reflex *š'č'* is chiefly Northern; it passed to $\overset{\vee}{\check{s}}'$ (parallel to $\overset{\vee}{\check{z}}'$) in Central dialects, including Moscow, whence it became until recently the standard. This pronunciation is well represented in, e.g., the Muscovite Kotoshíkhin: деншик(ъ) for денщик ([-š'ik], not [-šyk]). Modern examples: щит [š'it], счёт [š'ot].[47]

Original ESl. *š'č'* was an adequate equivalent of OCS [*št'*] (1.19) and adopted its symbol щ. Thus no difference is made between ESl. *isk-jǫ > ищý and the Slavonicism трепетáть/pres. трепещý (< *-t-jǫ*). ChSl. maintained the pronunciation [š'č'] in face of 'vulgar' [$\overset{\vee}{\check{s}}'$].

There was no parallel convenient symbol for [$\check{z}'$]. Early spellings vary and it is not always clear what they represent. Дъжгъ (< *zd* + *j*) 'rain' is frequent in the north-west (Nóvgorod, Pskov), but дъжчь in the south-west (Galicia, 1144); the latter may be [ž'dž'], for Ukrainian now has (hardened) [ždž] in, e.g., їжджу (Table XX (16)). Modern orthography has дождь/дождя́ [do$\overset{\vee}{\check{s}}$', daž'a], (при-)езжáю [-jež'äju] (< *zd* + *j*), визжать [v'iž'ät'] (< визг), but дрóжжи 'yeast' (*zg* + *j*). Af. Nikítin (15th c.) spells indifferently выежжаеть, выещають, выежають. Вóжжи 'reins' would appear to be spurious, as the root is surely *vod-*.

As the frequency of $\check{z}'$ is very low in Russian compared with *š'* (including *š'č'*) not all speakers maintain it well but substitute *ž* or *ž̌*, e.g. in éзжу [ježu *or* ježu] for [jež'u], жужжáть [žužat'] for [žuž'ät'], жжёт [žot] for [ž'ot]. Some S. dialects have wholly merged *š'*/*ž̌'* with *š*/*ž*: ящик [jašyk]. It is fairly probable that in avoiding OCS *žd'* (1.19) ESl. replaced it by [$\check{z}'$] rather than [ž'], though the spelling is always побѣженъ, etc. Well-entrenched Slavonicisms are frequently, if not always, pronounced with [$\check{z}'$], e.g. Рождествó 'Christmas', but побеждён and the like with [žd'].

It cannot be said that $\check{z}'$ is obligatory in any Russian word today. Where *š'č'* prevails, *š'*/*ž̌'* are clearly obsolescent.

---

[46] The (fairly recent) confusions that can arise from an awareness of a double relationship are illustrated by: *blěsk(ŭ), blĭsk-* > блещ-, блищ- > new false back-formations блестѣть, блистáть; **pust-* > пустúть > пущáть > new back-formation пускáть (with derivatives in -пуск, e.g. óтпуск).

[47] In final position $\overset{\vee}{\check{s}}'$ is usually simplified to *š'*: товáрищ [tavar'iš'], борщ [borš' *or* borš'č'].

40 *Special History of* /g/

The velar 'box' was asymmetrical in late CSl. and early ESl. It is therefore possible for *g* to be shifted to become the voiced counterpart of *x*:

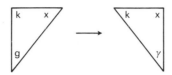

The change is motivated by morphological alternations: since ESl. lost *dž* (and *dz*) the alternation *g/ž'* was no longer parallel to *k/č'*, but an alternation *γ/ž'* will be parallel to *x/š'*.

This shift of *g* is characteristic of the Czechoslovak area (*gora* > *hora*) and in ESl. of Ukr. (*g* > *γ* > *h*, pharyngeal fricative), WhR. (*γ* or *h*), and most S. Russian dialects (*γ*), to which it spread from the WhR. area.[48] The chronology is not entirely clear but there is probably no connection between the WSl. and ESl. phenomena. The Ukr. change is usually held to be unlikely before the loss of the jers, i.e. *c.*1200, but forms such as осподь, осподаря (*c.*1150, Chernígov, text no. 15), suggesting an initial 'breathing' [h] for [g], may point to local earlier change.[49]

Though the evidence afforded by the Cyrillic alphabet is poor it would seem that it early became a widespread, if not universal, habit to pronounce [g] as [γ]/[h] in ChSl. Adaptation to ESl. phonology has been noted as frequent. In the North and Centre, where *g* remained a velar plosive, this may have prevailed in ChSl. also. In these areas [γ] developed only exceptionally by dissimilation,[50] for example:

[48] Before front vowels some S. dialects have the end-product [j] as in Gk.: могúла [majiłə], генерáл [jen'erał]; cf. Gk. γάλα [γala] but γεμάτο, γινομένο [jem-, jin-]. S. dial. ерáнь 'geranium' is a more or less standard form.

[49] Absence of *g* is practically confined to this word-group. Af. Nikítin, a man of Tver' (N. dial.), still writes в оспожино говейно in the 1470s, and also княини.

[50] There are some small areas of -ого > [-оγо/-оho] in the North; see 3.40 for this termination.

къдѣ > где [ɣd'ɛ]

adverbs in -гда: тогда́ [toɣda];

sg. gen. дёгтя [d'oxt'ə] whence nom. дёготь 'tar' [d'oɣət'] (similarly ко́готь/ко́гтя 'claw' and но́готь/но́гтя 'nail');

лёгкий, мя́гкий (§28 above), masc. pred. лёгок, мя́гок [l'og- *or* l'oɣ-, m'ag- *or* m'aɣ-].

All the above were standard literary pronunciation in the 19th c. but are now obsolescent. In the 17th c. the Ukr. pronunciation of the Kiev schools reinforced, if it did not reintroduce,[51] the pronunciation [ɣ]/[h] in ChSl., which then spread to Moscow: Бог, gen. Бо́га [box, boɣə], Госпо́д- [ɣospod-], благо- [bɫaɣo-]. The fashion extended in elegant usage without becoming universal for all *g*'s. Lomonósov still recommended it in his *Grammar* (1755); Ба́rsov's *Grammar*, written in the 1780s, indicates that pl. gen. ног, pret. мог as [nox, mox] were quite usual in Moscow at that time, and they remained so for another generation or more; [nok, mok] were 'readmitted' as alternative pronunciations in the second edition of the *Academy Dictionary* (1806–22).[52] The fashion then died out, especially with the obsolescence of 18th c. 'high-style' literature which maintained ChSl. norms of pronunciation. Богát- [baɣat-] might be heard in the 19th c. but disappeared after 1917.

41 It should be noted that the transcription and pronunciation of *foreign h* (of various kinds), especially initially, as *g* rather than *x*—Га́мбург, геро́й, гармо́ния—was not a part of the Ukr. fashion but had started much earlier in the western borderlands, heavily engaged in the Baltic trade. The convention must have spread from the WhR. area in which *ɣ* < *g* was established by the 14th c. and кг was adopted to represent a plosive [g]. Thus, in the Smolénsk Treaty of 1229 we already find *Hendrik* > Гиндрик(ъ) and (less certainly) *Johann* > Ягант(ъ). Similarly *Herzog* > герцик is frequent in Galician texts of the 13th c. Nóvgorod also rendered Finnic /h/ as *g* from the 14th c. In the late 16th c. transliteration of English *h* shows fluctuation between *x* (predominating), *g*, and occasionally nil (Унтинтонъ = *Huntingdon*)[53]; *x* and *g* may well represent the same pronunciation [ɣ]. Very recent loans normally have *x*: хокке́й 'hockey'.

[51] Giles Fletcher's transcription (1588) '*hospody* or *aspody*' presumably reflects the then Moscow norm.

[52] 17th c. Moscow orthography often has торхъ, pl. gen. денех(ъ), *et sim.*, but never *денек(ъ), etc.

[53] See L. Iivainen in *Scandoslavica* 16 (1970).

Further Adjustments in the Vowel System

42 *The Sequence C'o (Cë)*

In late CSl. and OCS *o* could not stand after palatal(ized) consonants: we have regularly *jo* > *je*, etc., as exemplified in the 'hard' and 'soft' declensions. As the early Slav alphabets had no separate symbol for *j* the representation of *jo* and, to a lesser degree, *'o* in ESl. caused difficulty. There is some controversy as to when they first developed there. The sequence *jo* is relatively rare (mod. моё, ёрзать, мытьё, подъём); the common case is *'o*.

Late CSl. *ē* and *ě* were clearly both open vowels whose nature Shevelov indicates by the notation $_e\tilde{a}$, i.e. acoustically not far removed from [jä] but the on-glide is a form of /e/ (not a diphthong [ea]).

The corresponding back vowels would thus be of the form $_o\tilde{a}$. The system therefore contained at the time no simple *e* and *o*. In the dialect which formed the basis of OCS the pair of short vowels was somewhat raised to *e/o*; the long *ē* remained open and very close to [ja] (§10 above). In the E. Blg. dialect *ē* was less open; the Cyrillic alphabet provided the new symbol ѣ. ChSl. orthography in Russia therefore gave representation to *ŏ*, *ā* and *ě*, ѣ but these did not necessarily correspond to the native vowels. The evidence of ESl. dialects (6.37) points strongly to the early development of *'o* < $_e\tilde{a}$ but this is not universally accepted. Many see it as a phenomenon following the loss of the weak jers (1200 onwards). It is not controversial that *some* cases of *'o* belong to that period, but it must always be borne in mind that in the early literate centuries there was little impulse to show a vernacular feature which contradicted the norms and tradition of ChSl. pronunciation and orthography.

43 The sole context in which *'o* could be reflected in the traditional orthography was in the position following the old palatal consonants *š'/ž'*, *č'* (and *š'č'*, *ž̌'*):[54] the syllables шо, жо, etc. represent unambiguously [š'o], [ž'o], etc. Such spellings occur sporadically from the late 11th c., even in purely ChSl. texts: пущонъ, осужонъ, блажонъ, чоловѣка, чотыремъ, бывшомъ; жена, but occasionally жона, in the 1076 *Anthology* (text no. 7). This is clear proof that *'o* then existed in some contexts in some R. dialects at

---

[54] Theoretically after any of the inherited palatal(ized) consonants, therefore also possibly after *n'*, *l'*, *s'*, *z'*, and certainly *j*.

least. It should be specially noted that *o* in such positions remained on principle in Ukrainian, whether stressed or not: жона́(тий), пшоно́, чоти́ри (see further 6.38).[55]

At least three stages can be distinguished:

(i) automatic *'e* > *'o*, irrespective of stress, in all sequences C′*e*C where C′ is an old fully palatal(ized) consonant: *ž'oná, č'otýre, š'č'oká, jomú, š'órŭtŭ*. To these are added all C*e*C (i.e. C*e*O*C) as soon as the semi-soft first consonant (§16 above) becomes fully palatalized: *n'osú, n'ósŭ, m'ódŭ*. These developments lie between the establishment of *polnoglásie* and the elimination of the weak jers, i.e. 9th–11th c.

(ii) 'strong' ь [′ə] > *'o* (12th c.): осьлъ > осёл, льнъ > лён.

(iii) *'e* > *'o* before *new* hard consonants, depalatalized after the fall of the jers: ежь > ёж, несешь > несёш(ь), растеть > растёт, конемь > конём, дешево > дёшево (§37 above), тьмьн- > тёмн- (§26 above).

(iv) It is not clear to which stratum final *'o* belongs. Though many instances come within the scope of (i) (suffix *-tĭje, -nĭje* > -тьё, -ньё; *moje* > моё; *xoroš'é* > хорошо́) Ukrainian does not have it in such contexts: плече́ = R. плечо́; пече́ = печёт. It would be risky to exclude the possibility of considerable later analogical levelling, e.g. хорошо́ after добро́.

The 'law' ceases to operate *c.*1500; see the case of ц, §38 above.

44 There was a fundamental distinction here, however, between N. and S. dialects. Those of the North, which made the early change *ă* > *o,* and therefore *'e* > *'o* (6.36 ff.), have retained by and large *all* the above stages. Unstressed жёна́, сёло́, вёсна́ is widespread though no longer universal; post-tonic cases are also present but rarer (бу́дём). Spellings such as днов(ъ), рубло́в(ъ), беро́сто, Потра́, ному́ (= ему́), но́бом, за́ мором are abundant in Nóvgorod and other northern documents.

The S. dialects, in contrast, lacked *unstressed o* (see а́канье, 6.33 ff.) and consequently unstressed *'o* also; only *stressed 'o* was present. This limitation was introduced to the speech of Moscow and eventually to the standard language. There thus arose the frequent declensional contrasts село́/pl. сёла, сёл; жена́/pl. жёны, жён (not the original plural stress); весёлый but pred. ве́сел,

---

[55] There are many irregularities in modern standard Ukr., e.g. пшоно́ but пшени́ця, чоти́ри but четве́ртий. For a full discussion see Shevelov, *Historical Phonology of the Ukrainian Language* (1979), pp. 143 ff.

весела́; тёмный but pred. темна́/темно́. Без, being on principle an unstressed proclitic, never appears as *бёз, and this is carried over into бе́здна, бе́столочь. The same applies to не.[56]

Real and Apparent Exceptions

45 1. In dialects where ѣ remained distinct from e during the relevant centuries ѣ does not pass to 'o: лѣсъ > лес [l'ɛs], мѣсто > ме́сто [m'ɛstə]. This is the case of the standard language.

2. ѣ > ë by analogy in: (звѣзда) звезда́/звёзды pl. 'star' (= жена́/жёны); (гнѣздо) гнездо́/гнёзда pl. 'nest' (= село́/сёла); (сѣдьло) седло́/сёдла pl. 'saddle'; (при-, из-)обрёл (*rět-, §19 (iii) above) after (по-)брёл (*bred-, 3.139).

3. 'o may appear before *soft* consonants by analogy with other forms in declension and conjugation: на берёзе after берёза; землёю after рукою; pres. pl. 2 несёте after pl. 1 несём; тётя after тётка. ë remains before velars in щёки *et sim.* (< щёкы), supported by gen. щёк.

4. A palatalized pronunciation of *r* was preserved in CerC (< CьrC, §48 below) except before dentals: верх, серп, четве́рг, перв- but четвёртый, мёрзнуть, pl. зёрна, твёрдый, напёрсток 'thimble' (as opposed to now archaic перст 'finger').[57]

46 5. As 'o was absent from ChSl., Slavonicisms show e before *hard* consonants. These are numerous. There is often contrast with fully colloquial senses or derivatives:

ChSl.	Vernacular
не́бо 'sky' (pl. небеса́ 'Heaven')	нёбо 'palate'
Лев 'Leo' (лев (льва) 'lion')	familiar hypocoristic Лёва
крест 'cross', adj. кре́стный (e.g. кре́стное зна́мение 'sign of the cross')	перекрёсток 'crossroads'; adj. крёстный (e.g. крёстный сын 'godson')
пеще́ра 'cave'	dial. and toponym Печо́ра
adj. соверше́нный 'complete'	p.p.p. с(о)вершённый 'completed'
вселе́нная 'universe' (calque of Gk. οἰκουμένη)	p.p.p. вселённ(ая) from всели́ть *pf* 'colonize'

[56] Unstressed 'o does not appear in any word of the standard language. Names such as Шостако́вич are of Pol. origin.

[57] The spelling перьв-, верьх(ъ) was not uncommon in the 17th and even in the 19th c. Modern pronunciation is often [p'ɛrv-], etc., with depalatalized [r], but not, of course, *[p'orv-].

ChSl.	*Vernacular*
падёж '(grammatical) case'	падёж 'murrain'
рубёж, мятёж	грабёж, чертёж
учёбник 'textbook'	учёба 'study'

Adjectives in -ьн- are frequently Slavonicisms: ежеднёвный, прилёжный, любёзный, душёвный (душовной, 15th c., has not survived), though late depalatalization of the consonant cluster is also possible in some cases, as regularly with the adjs. in -ьск- (жёнский, деревёнский, §26 above).

6. Foreign loans from *c.*1500 are not affected: аптёка, лёнта, тёма, прёсса, газёта. For the early loan Олег (5.13; 1.29) one must suppose Ôлег(ъ) (cf. fem. Ôльга), Олёг being a misapprehension of the 19th c.

47 *Polnoglásie*

1. The genesis of this sequence has been give in 1.22–3. ESl. orthography consistently shows two identical vowels either side of the sonant: -город, волод- (1057). Shevelov, among others, takes the view that this became at once the phonetic reality ('vowel harmony' on either side of a sonant). If we were to posit a longer stage *gorŭdŭ, *porŭgŭ (§14 above), we should get in due course гóрод, порóг by the normal rules of the jers; but this is clearly chronologically too late.[58] Moreover, the oblique cases *gorŭda, etc., should give *gorda, etc.; there is no reliable evidence whatever of such a development. The 1229 Treaty has once и[з] своего горда Смольнеска, surely a mere error; all other *polnoglásie* forms are normal within the limits of the orthography: золъта, сторону, холъп-/холоп-, вълък-/волок-, пьрьд-/перьд-/пьред-. After the 13th c. the vowels cease to be equal, by the intervention of vowel reduction (6.14) and áканье leading to modern [górət], [parók].

2. *False and Concealed* polnoglásie

A few words have been attracted to this model, notably:
CSl. *sĭrebră 'silver' > серебрó (OCS sĭ/ŭrebro and commonly ChSl. srĕbro by the same attraction.

---

[58] Ukr. at first sight upholds this view, having город, горох, мороз, etc. with apparently regular *o* < *ŭ* before a lost jer. Against this there is порir (gen. порогу), implying *porogŭ* before the fall of the final jer (as in *nosŭ* > ніс, Table XX (2)) and other similar cases. Later analogies have certainly intervened. The question remains open.

CSl. *č'ĭlăvĕkŭ 'person' > человéк. The etymology is uncertain but all other Slav languages have čło- (čo-) < č'ĭto-. Человéк could have been influenced by челó 'forehead'. Alternatively, čel- is original and čĭl- an allegro form.

R. дерéвня 'countryside, village' may descend from *dĭrw-, influenced by дéрево (*derw-); cf. Lith. dirvà 'cultivated land', a sense found for дерéвня too as late as Dom. (16th c.).

R. твóрóг 'curds' should be *тварог (cf. Pol. twaróg). Conversely, парóм 'ferry' is an áканье spelling and pronunciation for *пором (SSl. pram; 6.55).

R. муравéй 'ant' is altered from ESl. *моровей (ChSl. mravii) by attraction to муравá 'sward, turf'.

Early моромор(ъ) is a Russianization of learned мрáморъ 'marble' < Lat. marmor or a Gk. form. Conversely, ChSl. скомрахъ is an artificial Slavonicism for the vernacular word скоморóх, of uncertain etymology.

Polnoglásie is often introduced into the Turkic PN Astrakhan' (Асторохань). See also каракáтица, 6.55.

48 3. 'Secondary polnoglásie' and Allied Matters

(i) In the sequence Съ/ьSC we have an analogue of polnoglásie with a jer in place of ă/e. The ĭr, ĭl, ŭr, ŭl is referable to a primitive sonant r̥, l̥. The latter phonemes reappear in reflexes of Съ/ьSC in some Slav languages, including (to all appearances) OCS.[59]

There is no sign of a new r̥, l̥ in ESl. except perhaps as a transitory phenomenon; the jer was maintained and treated invariably as 'strong':

CSl.	OCS	ESl.	R.
*dĭlg- 'long'	dlŭg- (= dl̥g-)	dŭlg-	долг-
*dŭlgŭ 'debt'[60]	dlŭgŭ	dŭlgŭ	долг
*wĭlkŭ 'wolf'	vlŭkŭ (= vl̥kŭ)	wŭlkŭ	волк
*gŭrdlă 'throat'	grŭlo (= gr̥lo)	gŭrlo	гóрло
*mĭrt- 'death'	sŭmrŭtĭ	sŭmĭrtĭ	смерть
*pŭlkŭ 'army'[61]	plŭkŭ	pŭlkŭ	пŭлкŭ

(ii) In the sequence CSъ/ьC most ESl. proceeds as in (i); some

---

[59] W. Balkan (SCr. and Slovene) and Czechoslovak areas: (ĭr) SCr. smr̥t, Cz. smrt; (ĭl) SCr. vûk < vl̥k, Cz. vlk; Slovene Trst 'Trieste' < Lat. (or local Romance) Tergeste/Tirgeste.

[60] Loan-word from Gmc. (5.5).

[61] Loan-word from Gmc. (5.5).

other languages develop *r̦*, *l̦* but *not including OCS*. In Russian the jer is treated as strong and generalized:

CSl.	OCS	ESl.	R.
*krŭw- 'blood'	krŭvĭ[62]	krŭwĭ	кровь, gen. кро́ви; adj. крова́вый
*krĭst- 'cross'	krĭstŭ	krĭstŭ	крест (Slavonicism)
*blŭs-[63] 'flea'	—	blŭxa	блоха́
*slĭz- 'tear'	slĭza	slĭza	слеза́
*plŭt- 'flesh'	plŭtĭ[64]	plŭtĭ	плоть

(iii) Comparison of the above reveals one of the few imprecisions of OCS (and thence ChSl.) orthography: the shape of *plŭkŭ* and *plŭtĭ* is the same. That there was a real difference, and important to the users of OCS, is shown by the fact that in later texts the jer in CSъ/ьC is sometimes vocalized (кровь), but in Cъ/ьSC never. Neither of the Classical alphabets (nor for that matter Semitic) suggested a procedure to indicate *r̦*, *l̦*. If these phonemes were not already present in the original Macedonian (SW Bulgarian) dialect of OCS, they were introduced in the earliest areas of its use, viz. Moravia, Slovakia, and Pannonia, all of which had or have them now. OCS noted these sonants as *rŭ, lŭ* (the distinction *rŭ/rĭ, lŭ/lĭ* being lost early); this thus became the correct spelling in ChSl. and no doubt pronunciation followed spelling.

The ChSl. forms are irrelevant to ESl. phonology but there is a not unexpected confusion in orthography: ESl. scribes tended to introduce their own variant into ChSl. *Ostr.* is rarely correct, showing either ESl. мьртвы, въвьргуть (OCS въвръг̰тъ), цьркъвь, тържникомъ or a compromise съдрьжаще, съврьша, почрьпальника (*rĭ* long extinct in OCS).

49 (iv) Certain ESl. dialects, notably that of Nóvgorod (which provides most of the early material), treat Cъ/ьSC in a parallel manner to *polnoglásie* proper, i.e. develop CĭrĭC, CŭrŭC, CŭlŭC. Such forms already appear in *Ostr.* and make it highly probable that Deacon Gregory, who copied all but the first twenty-four pages, was a Novgorodian:

[62] SCr. *kȓv*.
[63] *blŭs-* > *blŭx-* by the 'iurk rule' (§36 above).
[64] SCr. *pŭt* (< *pl̦t-*), now nearly obs.

почьрьпатъ for чьрп- (OCS чрѫп-)
въстьрьгнете for -стьрг- (стрѣг-)
мьрътв- for мьртв- (мрѫтв-)
вьрътоградъ for вьрт- (врѫт-).

They are also to be found in the 1076 *Anthology* (*ispŭlŭnĭ*) and the *Nóvgorod Minéi* (1095–7; пьрьва, гърѫдыню, жьрьтву).

In the *First Novgorod Chronicle* secondary *polnoglásie* amounts to about a tenth of all *polnoglásie* occurrences. They are also fairly common in the *NBG*, e.g. молови ему 'tell him'.

Formerly secondary *polnoglásie* was dismissed as another 'compromise' spelling but two things contradict this:

(*a*) Early musical manuscripts show that both jers were a phonetic reality, being allotted separate notes.

(*b*) It has persisted, in modified form (with the vowels e/o of normal *polnoglásie*) down to the present day in the Nóvgorod area and further afield within its radiation.[65]

Typical cases are:

Standard	Novgorod
вьрхъ > верх	вьрьхъ > верёх (new stress)
кърмъ > корм	къръмъ > кóром

CołoC < CŭłŭC is much less usual: some words, e.g. волк, толст-, never appear with secondary *polnoglásie*. Moreover, it is worth considering whether secondary *polnoglásie* was not a general ESl. phenomenon up to a stage *vĭr′əxŭ, *kŭrəmŭ (which restored open-syllable structure), later lost except in the more conservative North. In other words, secondary *polnoglásie* may have been contemporaneous with *polnoglásie* proper, not a later analogical development. Established CĭrĭC, etc., in the 11th c. excludes any explanation as a 'second' *polnoglásie, after* the fall of the jers, e.g. кърмъ > корм > кором. See also Shevelov, *Prehistory of Slavic*, pp. 468–9.

50 (v) Few secondary *polnoglásie* forms have entered the standard language. Пóлон, дóлог (pred. of пóлный, дóлгий) are more probably due to rhythmic analogy. True cases are words of obviously popular origin: пóсолонь 'sunwise' (east to west), сýдорога 'cramp' (cf. дёргать 'tweak'), бéстолочь 'confusion' (cf.

---

[65] e.g. in the Far North (Двинские грамоты, 15th c.): чéтвереть, óдерень (< дёрн).

бестолко́вый), верёвка 'string' (< вервь), су́меречный 'twilight' (cf. су́мерки pl.); perhaps ожере́лье 'necklace' (which agrees with the N. dial. words жерело́ 'arm of a delta' (*RPC, ad init.*) and жерегло́, the Pskov name for the strait in the middle of Lake Peipus).[66]

The toponymy of the Nо́vgorod region provides a number of examples: Вере́бье (ве́рба 'willow'), Столобёнки (столб), and Торожка́, Торожку́ (but usually Торжо́к) in Novg. chronicles.

Summary of Sound Changes

51 1. Table IV opposite shows that the consonant phonemes have increased from 24 to 34 (35).

2. The nine or ten vowel phonemes of early ESl. (§4 above) have been reduced to the five basic vowels. The main positional variants are: i/y, e/ɛ, a/ä, and the reduced [ə]. Except in the North the number of distinct *unstressed* vowels is always less.

Graphically the vowels make five pairs, the upper line being 'hard' (uniotated), the lower 'soft' (iotated), indicating that the preceding consonant is palatalized. For a language with many consonant pairs this is the most economical notation.[67]

Uniotated	а	э[a]	ы	о	у
Iotated	я	e	и[b]	ё[c]	ю

Notes

(*a*) Uniotated *e* arose internally in the syllables ше, же, це, but э is reserved for initial position (1.43). In foreign loan-words there has been much hesitation between *e* and *'e*, and normative dictionaries do not always agree with one another. In апте́ка, темп, теа́тр, for example, [t'ɛ] is standard, in пастерна́к, протез [tɛ].[68] The foreign prefixes де-, дез- (< *dis-*) and ре- are usually rendered [dɛ], [dɛz], [rɛ].

(*b*) A strongly iotated *i* is required (initially only) in им, ими, их ([jim] . . .) since *j*- is the stem; otherwise име́ть, из ([im'et', iz]).

[66] For the form жерегло́ see also 6.63 (6); жерело́ < *gĭrło,* an ablaut form of *gŭrło* (го́рло); cf. *žĭrati* (жрать) 'devour'.

[67] Cf. SCr. which notes its only four consonant pairs with special consonant symbols: *n'*—њ (н + ь), *l'*—љ (л + ь), *t'*—ћ, *d'*—ђ (1.19); ь and ъ are no longer needed but j is added.

[68] Spellings such as тэма are found in the 19th c. but did not become standard.

TABLE IV. Modern Russian Consonantal Phonemes

		Velar plosives	Velar spirants	Dental plosives	Labial plosives	Labial spirants (labio-dental fricatives)	Sibilants (alveolar fricatives)	Sibilants (palato-alveolar fricatives)	Affricates	Nasals	Liquids	Semi-vowels
Early ESl.	unvoiced	k	x	t	p	(v)²	s s'	š'³	c' č'	n n'	l l'	j
	voiced	g		d	b		z z'	ž'³		m	r r'	w²
Mod. Russian	unvoiced	k¹	x̣¹	t t'	p p'	f f	s s'	š š̌'	c č'	m m'	l l'	
	voiced	g¹	(ɣ)¹	d d'	b b'	v v'	z z'	ž ž'		n n'	r r'⁴	ĵ⁵

¹ Subject to positional (non-phonematic) palatalization; [ɣ] is now only marginal to the system.
² §34 above.
³ Early š' č' and ž' can only be questionably reckoned as phonemic (§39 above).
⁴ Russian is notable in preserving the symmetrical pair r/r' in all positions.
⁵ No alphabetic symbol, except in so far as it is represented by й: май [maj].

(*c*) Not normally distinguished graphically from *e*.

(*d*) [ə] has no symbol, being a reduction of various unstressed vowels (6.14). Cf. the phonemic value of the early ESl. jers (§3 above).

(*e*) Stressed vowels are automatically somewhat lengthened but there is no longer any significant contrast of vowel length (§7 above).

(*f*) The iotated vowels also indicate the presence of [j] between vowels: -ая, -ое, -ую [aja, oje, uju].

52 Though the evolution of the jers greatly changed the structure of Russian words, the phonetic changes taken as a whole did not bear on sensitive areas of morphology. There was thus no breakdown of the declensions as in the passage from Latin to Romance; the losses in the paradigm of the verb are otherwise motivated.

3

MORPHOLOGY

Nominal Declension

1 The Slav languages have been remarkably conservative in the morphology of the noun. None of the seven cases of CSl. has been lost except partly the vocative (§30 below). The Bulgarian–Macedonian region alone is aberrant in having almost completely rejected declension. Of the eight well-defined IE cases gen. and abl. had become conflated in CSl. times: some of the gen. endings are historically abl. and 'ablative' prepositions such as от 'from', из 'out of', and с 'off' all take the gen.

2 ESl. inherited from CSl. nominal paradigms in which form and gender were already closely coupled. The gender of a Russian noun is not obvious from the form of the *sg. nom.* only in the following categories:[1]

(i) Masc. *jo*-stems (Type 19) конь = fem. *ĭ*-stems (Type 10) кость.

(ii) Nouns of 'common' gender—masc. or fem. according to context—belonging to the colloquial vocabulary, with a large variety of suffixes, e.g. пья́ница 'drunkard', зева́ка 'idler', бродя́га 'tramp', забулды́га 'profligate', обжо́ра 'glutton', непосе́да 'fidget', со́ня 'sleepyhead' (со́ня f. 'dormouse'), тихо́ня 'prig', пройдо́ха 'rascal', пла́кса 'cry-baby'. Сирота́ 'orphan' (an old abstract) and неве́жда 'ignoramus' are from ChSl.

(iii) Hypocoristics of *masc.* Christian names: Са́ша (Алекса́ндр), Ко́ля (Никола́й), and the earlier pagan types such as Добры́ня, Гостя́та (representing cpd. names with first component Добро-, Гости-). It has been suggested that the former were originally neuters of Type 28 but there is no record of their being treated as other than fem. (§27 below). Here too a number of Gk. and biblical names (via Gk.) adopted into Slav, e.g. Θωμα (mod. R. Фома́) 'Thomas', Илья́ 'Elias', Никита 'Nicetas' (Νικήτας).

[1] Cf. Gk. ὁ ἄνθρωπος, ἡ νῆσος, τὸ νέφος; Lat. *dominus* m., *nurus* f., *tempus* n.; Ger. *der Esel, die Gabel, das Rätsel*.

(iv) A few survivals of a no doubt much larger number of CSl. *masc.* in -a, either simple, e.g. слуга́ 'servant', ста́роста 'headman', ChSl. ю́ноша 'youth'[2] (cf. Lat. *nauta*), or more usually cpds., e.g. воево́да 'war leader', вельмо́жа 'magnate', предте́ча 'Forerunner' (John the Baptist), cpds. of -би́йца (уби́йца 'murderer', братоуби́йца 'fratricide'), -пи́йца (кровопи́йца 'blood-sucker'), -де́ля (древоде́ля 'wood-carver'), -но́ша (вестоно́ша 'messenger') (cf. Lat. *agricola*). The cpd. type was considerably extended in OCS and most such Russian words are of ChSl. origin.

(v) Neuters in -я (Types 26 and 28): see below.

(vi) There are very few recent additions to masc. nouns in -a, and those are from Polish, e.g. колле́га 'colleague'. Pol. -*ista* m. (*flecista, pejzażysta*) was not copied (R. -ист, international suffix), nor -*ca* m. (*mówca, dozorca*).

3 For convenience the declensions are arranged according to the ancient system of thematic vowels which CSl. developments had already greatly obscured. The characteristic vowel is best seen in the pl. dat. (early ESl.):

m. and n. *o*-stem: стол-о-мъ, сел-о-мъ (Types 12, 14)
m. and n. *jo*-stem: кон-е-мъ, пол-е-мъ (Types 17, 18) (*jo* > *je* in CSl.)
masc. *ŭ*-stem: дом-ъ-мъ (ъ < *ŭ*) (Type 20)
m. and f. *ĭ*-stem: пут-ь-мъ, кост-ь-мъ (ь < *ĭ*) (Types 21, 9)
fem. *ā*-stem: рук-а-мъ (Types 2, 3)
fem. *jā*-stem: дол-ꙗ-мъ (Type 6)
various consonant stems: re-formed; see §§20 ff. below.

Note. The order of cases here used is that most convenient for the examination of historical change; it has no other significance.

FEMININE NOUNS

Commentary to Table V

4 1. The fem. declensions have been very stable. The main change has been the conflation of Types 2 and 6 (cf. masc. nouns Types 12 and 17 below), which had become partly independent as a result of CSl. phonetic processes. In the sg. GDL several analogical levellings were possible, all represented in dialect:

(*a*) The *jā*-stems conform to the *ā*-stems. This is the procedure of standard Russian (Type 7 = Type 4). The tendency is

---

[2] All these appear to be personified abstract fem. nouns, as also судья́ 'judge' (originally fem. in -*ī*: судьи, §7 (v) below).

TABLE V. Feminine Noun Declensions

	ā-stem ('hard')				jā-stem ('soft')			ǐ-stem		
	1	2	3	4	5	6	7	8	9	10
	OCS (ChSl.)	Early ESl.	Velar stem	Modern	OCS (ChSl.)	Early ESl.	Modern	OCS (ChSl.)	Early ESl.	Modern
Sg. N	*měr-a*[1]	мѣр-а	рук-а	мер-а	*dol-ja*[1]	дол-я[2]	дол-я[3]	*kost-ǐ*	кост-ь	кост-ь
A	-ǫ	-у	-у	-у	-jǫ	-ю	-ю	-ǐ	-ь	-ь
G	-y	-ы	-ы	-ы	-jě	-ѣ	-и	-i	-и	-и
L	-ě	-ѣ	руцѣ	-е	-(j)i	-и	-е	-i	-и	-и
D	-ě	-ѣ	руцѣ	-е	-(j)i	-и	-е	-i	-и	-и
I	-ojǫ	-ою	рук-ою	-ой	-jejǫ	-ею	-ей	-ijǫ	-ью	-ью
V	-o	-o[4]	-o	—	-je	-e	-e	-i	-и	—
Du. NAV *měr-ě*	*měr-ě*	мѣр-ѣ[4]	руцѣ	—	*dol-(j)i*	дол-и	—	*kost-i*	кост-и	—
GL	-u	-у	рук-у	—	-ju	-ю	—	-iju	-ью	—
DI	-ama	-ама	-ама	—	-jama	-яма	—	-ǐma	-ьма̀	—
Pl. NV *měr-y*	*měr-y*	мѣр-ы[4]	рук-ы	мер-ы	*dol-ję*	дол-ѣ	дол-и	*kost-i*	кост-и	кост-и
A	-y	-ы	-ы	N or G[5]	-ję	-ѣ	N or G[5]	-i	-и	-и
G	-ǔ	-ъ	-ъ	мер	-jǐ (-i)	-ь	дол-ей[6]	-ǐjǐ[7]	-ии	-ей
L	-axǔ	-ахъ	-ахъ	мер-ах	-jaxǔ	-яхъ	-ях	-ǐxǔ	-ьхъ	-ях
D	-amǔ	-амъ	-амъ	мер-ам	-jamǔ	-ямъ	-ям	-ǐmǔ	-ьмъ	-ям
I	-ami	-ами	-ами	-ами	-jami	-ями	-ями	-ǐmi	-ьмѝ	-ями

Note. No account is here taken of stress. Forms 'boxed' in broken lines are specifically treated in §4 (1) (GDL sg.), §4 (2) (NA pl.), and §29 (palatalized velar stems).

[1] The *syllabication* is, as always (2.2), *měl/ra, dol/ja,* etc. The stems are *měr-, dolj-*.

[2] Here also early межа/межа, душа/душа, etc. (2.37).

[3] Similarly шея, стая. Nouns in -ия, nearly all of foreign origin (áрмия, нáция), make sg. LD in -ии and pl. gen. in -ий, following the learned neut. type in -ие (§135 below).

[4] Voc. distinct only in sg., where -o < *ā* (cf. Gk. νύμφᾱ, nom. νύμφη (η = *ā*).

[5] For animate/inanimate see 4.41 ff.

[6] Variable between -ъ and -ей; see §5 (ii) below.

[7] Normally written -ii.

observable from the earliest texts, even if ChSl.: въ пустынѣ
(1096), въ вѣтъсѣ одежѣ (1095), dat. госпожѣ (1095), dat.
землѣ (1215).
(*b*) GDL all -ѣ: rare.
(*c*) GDL all -ы/-и: characteristic of NW dialect (Nóvgorod),
where the process is as much phonological as analogical
since (under certain conditions) ѣ > и (6.12): из земли́, к
земли́, в земли́; (hard) на óной страны́.
(*d*) Gen. -ѣ, DL -ы/и (the reverse of (*a*)): rare.

2. In the pl. NA the *jā*-stem ending -ѣ undergoes the double
influence of Types 2 and 9 and the form is eliminated by the 16th
c. The reverse analogy is not found.

3. After these changes Type 7 is an automatic variant of Type
4, 'soft' (palatalized) v. 'hard' stems.

5   *Other Changes*

(i) The disyllabic ending sg. instr. -ою/-ею was shortened
colloquially to -ой/-ей, the longer form remaining as a formal or
poetic variant down to the present day. In the *ĭ*-stems -ию was
probably always an artificial (ChSl.) spelling (2.33) representing
an actual -ью. The stressed ending -éй (землёй) is analogical to
женóй, рукóй (2.45 (3)).

(ii) With the fall of the weak jers the pl. gen. appears as the
bare noun stem, but a vowel ('mobile' o/e) may be introduced in
certain now final groups of consonants: сестр(ъ) > сестёр, земль
> земéль; see further 2.20–2. Nouns in -ня with a preceding
consonant show from the 16th c. a tendency to substitute a 'hard'
-н; this is now the rule: бáшня 'tower', pl. gen. бáшен; пéсня
'song', пéсен; сóтня 'hundred', сóтен.

Further, the pl. gen. of the *jā*-stems was strongly attracted
to that of the *ĭ*-stems (all 'soft' stems show the same tendency,
§§8, 11 below). In the 16th c. the pl. gen. is still свѣч(ь) as opposed
to (*ĭ*-stem) рѣчéй. The present standard forms are rather arbitrary
and there is still some hesitation: ня́ня 'nurse', ня́ней but пу́ля
'bullet', пуль; статья́ 'article', статéй but струя́ 'stream', струй;
ды́ня 'melon', дынь; сáжéнь 'fathom' makes сáжен or сажéнéй;
пусты́ня 'desert', пусты́нь; затéя 'plot', затéй.

(iii) The *ĭ*-stem declension (Type 9) remains quite distinct,
being a large class of predominantly inanimate nouns in which the

identity of sg. and pl. NA did not cause syntactical ambiguity.[3]
Virtually the only recent recruits to it are abstracts in -ость/-есть.
The pl. LDI have conformed to the *jā*-stems. There are examples
from the 16th c. (въ тѣхъ записяхъ (1508), на ихъ лошадяхъ
(1546)), but written styles of the 17th c. still have predominantly
the pl. рѣчи, рѣчей, рѣчехъ, рѣчемъ, рѣчьми (with e < ь). The
instr. moved relatively late; a few have retained the earlier form:
лошадьми́, детьми́,[4] and some obsolescent combinations, e.g.
лечь костьми́ 'fall in battle', бить плетьми́ 'flog' (otherwise
костя́ми, плетя́ми).

6   (iv) About twenty *ĭ*-stem nouns have sg. loc. in -и́ (in contrast
to unstressed GD -и). Including adverbialized forms these are:
вдали́, втиши́; на груди́, в грязи́, в двери́, в кости́, в крови́, на
мели́ 'aground', в ночи́, на печи́, в пыли́, на рыси́ 'at a trot', в
сети́, в степи́, в связи́ с + instr. 'in connection with', в тени́, в/
на цепи́, в чести́; also на Руси́, which is conventionally stressed
on all final -и (but Ру́сью). This is a reflex of earlier pitch contrasts:
cf. masc. sg. loc. in -ý (§17 below). Here also come the adverbs
вблизи́, взаперти́, внутри́, впереди́; назади́, of which the noun
is no longer current except possibly in dialect.

7   (v) CSl. possessed a well-known IE type of fem. in -*ī* (represented also in the declension of the comparative (Table IX) and
the active participles (§§118, 124 below). In ESl. the sg. nom. had
been regularized as -я by the 16th c.; the rest of the declension was
identical. Here belong: судья́ (masc.!), боги́ня, княги́ня, святы́ня,
пусты́ня, рабы́ня, тверды́ня, ми́лостыня 'alms'.[5] It is doubtful
whether any of these except княги́ня, ба́рыня 'mistress' (<
боярыни), and простыня́ 'sheet' (if it formally belongs) were in
colloquial use; the majority are clearly Slavonicisms, including
ethnics such as грекини 'a Greek woman'.

    (vi) In Type 3 the modification of the stem consonant is elimi-
nated as in the corresponding masculines (§29 below).

    (vii) The only notable formal difference in ChSl. is sg. gen. and
pl. NA of Type 5 in -*ję* (ESl. -ѣ). No explanation of the difference
is wholly satisfactory. Spellings in Russian texts (frequent) such

---

[3] Many old athematics were reformed in CSl. in this declension, e.g. ночь (cf.
Lat. *nox, noct-is*), соль (cf. Gk. ἅλς, ἅλ-ος).
[4] Дети is a formally genderless *plurale tantum* linked to singulative f. *dětĭ and
n. дитя́ (§27 below).
[5] Here also come мать and дочь, early ESl. мати, дъчи (§23 below). Polish has
preserved a few fems. in -*ī*: *pani* 'lady'; *bogini* 'goddess'.

as sg. gen. душѧ and denasalized as душя/душа are therefore Slavonicisms.

(viii) It should be noted that, whereas ночь and вещь remain soft stems, молодёжь and вошь, etc., adapt to the depalatalization of *š* and *ž* (2.37): [məɫad'óš, voš], sg. gen. молодёжи, вши [məɫad'óžy, fšy]. The retention of final -ь distinguishes them graphically from masculines such as нож [noš].

MASCULINE AND NEUTER NOUNS

Commentary to Table VI

8   *Neuter*

1. The neuter declensions Types 14 and 18 maintain their distinctive sg. NA and pl. NA. Otherwise, apart from some differences of detail, their history is subsumed under that of masculines below.

2. Type 14 maintains its pl. gen.: селъ > сёл. The soft Type 18, of which there are few, maintained the corresponding поль until *c.*1700 but soon after came into line with the majority of soft stems of whatever gender with modern standard полей (§11 (*a*) below).

Masculine

9   The masculine declensions have been drastically remodelled in the *plural*.

1. The pl. NA tend to conflate from the 13th c. in favour of the *pl. acc.* The earliest examples are in ChSl. texts but no doubt indicate the change in ESl.:

> nom. for acc.: идѣмъ въ . . . гради (1215);
> acc. for nom.: чины расставлени быша (1219).

The impulse comes from (*a*) the fact that pl. NA were identical in all fem. and neut. declensions; and perhaps (*b*) the replacement in Type 13 of волци/волкы by волки/волки (§29 below).

Here too mistakes appear before the levelling:

> correct: одва одолѣша греци (*RPC s.a.* 941);
> wrong: пересѣчены быша грекы (ibid. 915).

The distinction in Type 17 кони/конѣ survives a little better, but конѣ is eliminated in the 16th c.

10   2. The original pl. nom. survived into the 16th c. in a few traditional formulae, e.g. на то послуси . . . (послух, Type 13)

TABLE VI. Masculine and Neuter Noun Declensions

	11 *o*-stem ('hard') OCS (ChSl.)	12 Early ESl. masc.	13 Early ESl. velar stem	14 Early ESl. neuter	15 Modern masc.	16 *jo*-stem ('soft') OCS (ChSl.)	17 Early ESl. masc.	18 Early ESl. neuter	19 Modern masc.	20 *ŭ*-stem Early ESl. (masc. only)	21 *ĭ*-stem Early ESl. (masc. only)
Sg. N	*stol-ŭ*[1]	стол-ъ	рог-ъ[2]	сел-о	стол	*konj-ĭ*[1]	конь-ъ[3]	пол-е[4]	конь	дом-ъ	пут-ь
A	*-ŭ*	-ъ	-ъ	-о	N or G[5]	*-ĭ*	-ь	-е	N or G[5]	-ъ	-ь
G	*-a*	-а	-а	-а	стол-а	*-a*	-ꙗ	-ꙗ	кон-я	-у[7]	-и
L	*-ě*	-ѣ	розъ	-ѣ	-е	*-i*	-и	-и	-е	-у[7]	-и
D	*-u*	-у	рог-у	-у	-у	*-u*	-ю	-ю	-ю	-ови	-и
I	*-omĭ*[6]	-ъмь[6]	-ъмь[6]	-ъмь[6]	-ом[6]	*-emĭ*	-ьмь[6]	-ьмь[6]	-ем[6]	-ъмь[6]	-ьмь[6]
V	*-e*	-е	роже	(-о)	—	*-u*	-ю	(-е)	—	-у	-и
Du. NAV	*stol-a*	-а	рог-а	сел-ѣ	—	*konj-a*	кон-ѣ	пол-и	—	дом-ы	пут-и
GL	*-u*	-у	-у	-у	—	*-u*	-ю	-ю	—	-ову	-ью
DI	*-oma*	-ома	-ъма	-ома	—	*-ema*	-ема	-ема	—	-ъма	-ьма
Pl. NV	*stol-i*[1]	-и	рог-ы / розꙑ	сел-а	стол-ы	*konj-i*	кон-и	пол-я	кон-и	дом-ове	пут-ие[8]
A	*-y*	-ы	-ы	-а	N or G[5]	*-ę*	-ѣ	-а	N or G[5]	-ы	-и
G	*-ъ*	-ъ	-ъ	-ъ	стол-ов	*-ĭ*	-ь	-ь	кон-ей[9]	-овъ	-ии[8]
L	*-ěxŭ*	-ѣхъ	розохъ	-ѣхъ	-ах	*-ixŭ*	-ихъ	-ихъ	-ях	-ъхъ	-ьхъ
D	*-omŭ*	-омъ	рог-омъ	-омъ	-ам	*-emŭ*	-емъ	-емъ	-ям	-ъмъ	-ьмъ
I	*-y*	-ы	-ы	-ы	-ами	*-i*	-и	-и	-ями	-ъми	-ьми

Note. No account is here taken of stress (stressed sg. instr. -ем > -ём). Forms 'boxed' in broken lines are specifically treated in §§9–10 (NA pl.) and §29 (palatalized velar stems).

[1] The syllabication is, as always (2.2), *sto/lŭ, ko/nji*, etc.

[2] So also волкъ/волцѣ, мѣхъ/мѣсѣ.

[3] Similarly stems in *-j-* (*krajĭ* > край) and stems in originally soft ж, ш, ц (ножь, отьць > нож, отéц).

[4] Type знание (of ChSl. origin, §135 below) retains sg. loc. знании, pl. gen. знаний, in contrast to modern пóле, полéй.

[5] For animate/inanimate see 4.41 ff.

[6] 1.31 (morphological difference); 6.11 (depalatalization of labial).

[7] This distinction is due to a CSl. pitch contrast, cf. SCr. dat. *grâdu* (falling pitch), loc. *grádu* (rising pitch, from an earlier stressed final *-ú*).

[8] Representing *-ije, -iji*.

[9] See §11 below.

'the witnesses thereto . . .'; and for less clear reasons in бѣси, че́рти 'demons', сосѣди (сусѣди) 'neighbours', and холо́пи 'serfs' (also холо́пы).

The old nom. form has persisted in сосе́ди and че́рти but the whole plural has moved to Type 19: gen. сосе́дей, черте́й, whereas the sg. declension has remained 'hard': сосе́д, -a, чорт (чёрт), -a. In the case of Type 17 the pl. nom. кони could be said to have survived, though the important thing was the parallel to new NA столы́/сто́лы in Type 12.

11   3. *Plural Genitive*

(*a*) That of Types 12 and 13 (столъ > стол), identical with the sg. nom. and consisting of the bare stem with the fall of the final jer, was abandoned soon after in favour of -ов borrowed from the *ŭ*-stems (Type 20). The process started very early, probably in pre-literary times, and occurs in early ChSl. texts: бѣ бо въпрашалъ волъхвовъ и кудесникъ (*RPC s.a.* 912; old and new). In the 'soft' stems (Type 17) there was long hesitation between the parallel -ев and the pl. gen. of the m. and f. *ĭ*-stems -ей. The modern repartition is, with few exceptions:

(i) stems in -*j*- take -ев: крае́в, сара́ев, воробьёв;

(ii) stems in (hardened) -ц- take -ов: отцо́в, ме́сяцев (formerly often written -ов even if unstressed);

(iii) all others, including stems in soft ч, щ and hardened ж, ш, take -ей: коне́й, ноже́й, калаче́й, това́рищей. Down to the 16th–17th c. -ев was more widely used: монастыревъ (12th c.); иже ма сихъ дневъ допровади (12th c.); ножев(ъ), царевичев(ъ), рублев(ъ); also commonly with nouns in -тель (приятелев(ъ)). Some N. dialects in which ц remained soft or persisted as soft longer than elsewhere (2.38) have retained -ей in (ii): зайцей, пальцей (standard за́йцев, па́льцев).

(*b*) The 'suffixless' pl. gen. survived largely in contexts after numerals or the equivalent where the fact that the form was not a sg. nom. was obvious. In the 16th c. 20 алтынъ, 30 аршинъ, 10 возъ 'cartloads', 5 мѣсяц(ь), сколько пудъ were still normal usage. They tend to disappear from *c.*1700; Peter the Great writes both восми фут and по пяти футов. There remain today: (не́сколько) челове́к, (пять) раз 'times'; (пять пар) чуло́к, сапо́г (без сапого́в is not incorrect); certain military terms (even if recent loan-words): мно́го солда́т, 1000 драгу́н; (оди́н из двух) глаз 'eye'; certain ethnics (cf. Type 23): ту́рок, pl. ту́рки, ту́рок; башки́р, pl. gen. башки́р, and others; some geographical terms, e.g. pl. Карпа́ты, Карпа́т 'Carpathians'; Балка́ны, Балка́н 'Balkans' (if not to be considered fem. pl., following го́ры, гор). There is some fluctuation of usage in the latter two categories.[6]

12 4. The pl. LDI were discarded in favour of the fem. endings -ах, -ам, -ами. This was a gradual and complicated process only completed by the early 18th c. Gender distinctions were virtually eliminated in all plurals (adjective §42 below; verbal past tense §104 below). The older forms may be found more or less intact in more formal texts (even if not strongly ChSl.) in the 16th–17th c. but there can be no doubt that substitutions started in speech at a very early date, both in the masc. and the neut., e.g. съ клобука́ми (1271), безако́ниямъ (1271), къ лати́намъ (Type 28) (1284).

One can point to a number of possible morphological catalysts, some of which would not yet have been active in the 13th c.:

(*a*) Original masculines of fem. form (§2(iv) above): слуга́.

(*b*) Early avoidance of stem alteration in Type 13: волцѣхъ > волка́хъ.

(*c*) The spread of the pl. masc. nom. in -á (§§33–4 below), plus the normal pl. neut. NA in -a (specially if stressed, as места́).

(*d*) The homonymy of pl. NA and instr. (столы́) which became syntactically ambiguous in the 17th c. (4.52).

(*e*) Moreover, increasing vowel reduction in unstressed syllables after *c.*1200 (6.14) made the endings of ме́сяцем and зе́млям scarcely distinguishable phonetically.

It must not be assumed that the process of replacement was uniform with respect to (1) all dialects of Russian, (2) all three cases, (3) both genders, (4) all types of noun. Such statistical information as is available suggests that before the 17th c.:

(i) NW dialect (Nóvgorod) was less conservative than Moscow.

(ii) In the masculines the loc. led, followed by dat. and instr., whereas in the neuters the new dat. is commoner in the early stages. In both, the instr. only falls fully into line in the 17th c.

---

[6] ChSl. was somewhat conservative, so that phrases such as отъ востокъ до западъ remained in use as correct (imitation of the Gk. *plural* idiom ἀπὸ ἀνα-τολῶν . . . ἕως δυσμῶν).

(iii) Velar stems and masc. *animates* adopted the new endings relatively early and consistently.

(iv) The soft Type 17 was late in settling down owing to the attraction of the *ĭ*-stems (§18 below). An unstressed dat. -ем is still quite common in Peter the Great's time, though -ям was normal; and we have a progression pl. instr. кони > коньми́ (*ĭ*-stem) > коня́ми rather than a shorter route. But individual words and writers often contradict these generalizations. *Domostrój* (mid 16th c.) has few -ами (зубами, домами, с товарищами); the conservative 1649 *Uloženie* equally few; the Учение и хитрость ратного строения (1647) has a majority in -ами. In Kotoshíkhin (writing in the 1660s) the new dat. and loc. are less common than the old but -ами/-ями preponderate over the old instr. Smotrítsky's *Grammar* (first published in Vilna in 1619 and revised in 1648 in Moscow to take account of some contemporary features), though not dealing primarily with current Russian, accepts -ам, -ах as normal and recommends -ами also (but not -ями). Avvakúm (writing 1672–3) has indifferently в попѣх and в попах in adjacent sentences. The instr. further shows that all syntactical uses cannot be lumped together: the old ending was often maintained after prepositions, where the case was quite clear (a remnant is seen in the phrase с това́рищи 'and Co.', which was still in use in the 19th c.),[7] whereas in predicative use -ами/-ями was becoming obligatory.

The new forms may be considered correct from the time of Peter the Great. Only one old form has survived—in the adverbialized (pl. dat.) подело́м 'according to one's deserts' (cf. *RPC s.a.* 986: въздати комуждо по дѣломъ его).[8]

13   The generalization of one plural pattern to all masc. (and *mutatis mutandis* neut.) nouns facilitated the reinterpretation of Types 12 and 17 as 'hard' and 'soft' variants, as in the feminines. In the sg. loc. (на) кони́ is gradually replaced by (на) конѣ: no other adjustment was required. However, (на) кони́ persists until a very late date, just as fem. (на) земли́ did. The pl. gen. remain distinct: hard -ов/soft -ей.

[7] Pososhkóv still uses the cliché бить батоги [= батогами] *c*.1724. Хожение Ф. Котова в Персию (*c*.1623) has: с кувшины и с пьяли и с чарки и с чаши (note the attraction of the fems. to the masc. form).

[8] Polish, though moving in the same direction as Russian, has kept the pl. dat. in *-om* (as opposed to *-ach, -ami*). Certain 17th c. Russian texts which largely employ dat. -ом were perhaps influenced by this.

14   *Masculine* ŭ-*stems (Type 20)*

This very distinct declension existed in CSl. as a rather small but influential group of masc. nouns with a tendency to expansion. Here belonged for certain: *wĭrxŭ 'top' (cf. Lith. *viršùs*), *wolŭ 'ox', *domŭ 'house' (cf. Lat. *domus*), *medŭ 'honey' (cf. Gk. μέθυ neut. ŭ-stem[9]), *polŭ 'half', *synŭ 'son' (cf. Skr. *sūnúḥ*), *borŭ (original sense uncertain; in Russian бор now = 'coniferous wood'); and with somewhat less certainty: *darŭ 'gift', *ledŭ 'ice', *pirŭ 'feast', *razŭ 'stroke', *sadŭ 'plantation, garden', *sanŭ 'high position, dignity' (5.10), *činŭ 'rank'. The now obsolete олъ 'ale' is also clearly a ŭ-stem with exact correspondences in Lith. *alùs* and Ags. *ealu* (i.e. a 'North European' word—5.2). There are no recognizable 'soft' *ju*-stems.

In the above list *synŭ and the less important *wolŭ were the only *animates*. Even in OCS *synŭ* is partly transferred to Type 11, an acc./gen. *sýna* being preferred (4.41), and often also a dat. *sýnu*.

No Slav language has kept Type 20 separate but during the absorption of its members into the dominant Type 12 it has permanently affected the latter to different degrees in different languages. In ESl.:

15   1. Pl. gen. -ов alone imposed itself as a basic element of Type 12 (see Type 15).

2. Sg. dat. -ови was widely affected in early ESl. to *animates*, especially personal names: Петрови, Игореви, Данилови, Кѣсареви 'the Byzantine Emperor'; other anim. мужеви, коневи, воробьеви (all in *RPC*). Also occasionally to inanimates: огневи, холмови (*RPC*). This dat. is abandoned by the 15th c. in favour of -y.[10]

3. Pl. nom. -ове shows a similar extension to Type 12 *animates* (especially peoples): грекове, угрове (sg. угринъ 'Magyar'), жидове 'Jews', фрязове 'Franks', послове, воробьеве; occasionally to inan.: овощеве (*RPC s.a.* 969), разбоеве (ibid. 996), борове (ibid. 1092), манастыреве (ibid. 1037). This variant ending similarly dies out in the 15th c.[11] A trace is to be seen still, through

---

[9] Neuter ŭ-stems (Lat. *cornu*) are not represented in Slav; *medŭ is transferred to the masc. *without change*.

[10] Sg. dat. -*ovi* is normal in Cz. for *animates* (inan. -*u*) and more or less generalized in Pol. for *all* masc. In ESl. it has persisted in Ukr. and WhR. (Table XX (21)).

[11] Pl. nom. -*ove* is current in Cz. and Pol. for *animates*, in Blg. for *monosyllables* (домовé, боговé), and considerably extended in SCr. (e.g. *grâd*, pl. *gràdovi*, *gràdove*, *gradóvā*, *gradòvima*).

сынове, in the modern hybrid pl. nom. сыновья́ 'sons', etc. (§34 below) and in хозя́ева with *-eva* for *-eve*.

16   4. The sg. gen. -y (unstressed) of Type 20 invaded the *o*-stems in pre-literary times (inanimates only): во́ску, свѣ́ту, льну (11th c.). It continued to extend its range in two contexts:

(*a*) as a *partitive* genitive, for which the starting-point among the original *ŭ*-stem nouns could have been (мно́го) мёду. Further extended to *negative* phrases (нѣ́тъ мёду) and comparison (бо́льше го́ду).

(*b*) adverbial phrases with the models и́з дому and съ ве́рху, perhaps also сра́зу (OCS *sŭrazu* is recorded).

By the 16th c. usage (*a*) had become so widespread that some grammarians consider it possible to speak of a separate 'partitive case' distinct from the gen. However, this position was never quite reached. Statistics gathered by Unbegaun[12] and others show that by then:

(i) *most*, but not all, weighable materials took *exclusively* the gen. in -y, e.g. мёду, во́ску, лу́ку, чеснокý (but always хлѣ́ба, овса́!);

(ii) many other nouns, including even some abstracts, used consistently the gen. in -y without partitive sense: e.g. бе́рег, бой, бор, год, лѣс, мост, полк, торг, час; (нѣт) отвѣ́ту, (без) прика́зу, (нѣт) слѣду.

Conceivably there was some Pol. influence here, at least in the 17th c., since Pol. *inanimates* have in principle sg. gen. in *-u*.

After a summit of popularity in the 16th–17th c. (being widely reflected in делово́й язы́к) the gen. in -y has receded. Present usage has rather imprecise boundaries. It is still available as a 'partitive' *in contrast to the normal* gen. in -a (мно́го наро́ду/вкус наро́да, ча́шка ча́ю/цена́ ча́я), but cannot be said to be obligatory. Petrified adverbial phrases survive in some number, but far fewer in standard literary language than in some dialects: adverbs сбо́ку, све́рху, сни́зу, до́верху, до́низу, сду́ру 'like a fool',[13] сра́зу 'at once', сря́ду (= подря́д); phrases брать с бо́ю 'take by storm', (умере́ть) с го́лоду (= от го́лода), и́з дому, и́зо рту, (нам) не до сме́ху 'no laughing matter', ни ра́зу не, ни слу́ху ни ду́ху (нет

---

[12] *La Langue russe au XVIᵉ siècle. La flexion des noms* (Paris, 1935).

[13] Positing a now non-existent m. *дур 'fool' (replaced by дура́к), current f. ду́ра.

o + loc.) 'nothing has been heard of', с чáсу на час and час óт часу 'from hour to hour', ни шáгу (дáльше), (смеáться) без ýдержу 'uncontrollably', без тóлку 'senselessly', óтроду не (видáл), без рóду и плéмени 'without kith or kin', (упускáть) из виду 'lose sight of', с бóру по сóсенке 'at random', ни склáду ни лáду 'neither rhyme nor reason'.

17 5. The sg. loc. in -ý (stressed) enjoyed similar popularity in the 16th–17th c.[14] It was very general as a true locative, i.e. after в and на, was the exclusive loc. form of бéрег, бор, круг, лѣс, мост, стан, сад, óстров, дом, and others, and usual with place-names in -ск (в Пóлоцку). At its widest use it was not limited either by the stress pattern of the noun (в спúску, в Мцéнску) or by the preposition (при кнáзи при Борúсу (1369), о кормý), or by the exclusion of animates (на быкý).

It is, like the gen. in -y, absent from ChSl. This procedure has also receded in standard Russian since the 18th c. The forms that remain exclude *animates*, are confined to the locative prepositions в and на, and (with few exceptions) require the stress contrast sg. dat. лéсу/loc. (в) лесý. The accepted locatives in -ý are now a somewhat arbitrary collection, often tied to a particular sense of the noun: хлеб на корню́ 'standing corn' (otherwise кóрне); в дóме (despite й-stem дом!) but рабóта на домý 'at home'; в рáде слýчаев 'in a number of cases' but в трéтьем рядý 'in the third row'; во вторóм часý 'between 1 and 2', but в чáсе; в хóде 'in the course of' but в ходý 'current'; в XIX вéке but на моём векý 'in my lifetime'; в/на родý but врóде áтого 'something of the kind'; сдéлан на гончáрном крýге 'thrown' but в кругý любúтелей; в цветý but в цвéте лет/сил.[15]

Apart from the above there are about fifty in obligatory literary use, including such adverbialized combinations as нарядý с + instr., навесý 'by weight', внизý, вверхý/наверхý, сон наявý 'day-dream'.[16]

A list is given below; many more are to be found in special vocabularies and country speech (на парý 'fallow', в стогý 'rick'). It has been applied to a number of recent foreign loan-words: на балý, на бортý, в грунтý 'in the open ground', на плацý 'on (the)

[14] Sg. loc. in -*u* is generalized to *all masculines* in SCr.
[15] A good example of the idiomatic specialization of alternatives is дух: gen. не хватáет дýха/дýху and example in §16 above; loc. на духý 'at confession' (как на духý 'frankly') but быть (не) в дýхе 'be in a good/bad mood'.
[16] A noun *яв no longer exists; cf. Pol. *wyjść na jaw*.

parade (ground)', в порту́, на посту́ 'on sentry duty', в шкафу́.[17]
Полк, пруд, and сук now contradict the stress rule: полк, -а́, в
полку́. -у́ has been transferred to the Slavonicism в плену́ from
earlier native в полону́.

18 *The ĭ-stems (Type 21)*

The original members were not very numerous:[18]

(i) personal animates: гость, зять, тесть (< тьсть), де́верь,
тать 'thief'; also ChSl. Госпо́дь;

(ii) other animates: го́лубь, гусь, зверь, ле́бедь (for ле́бядь,
6.56), моль 'moth', лось 'elk', медве́дь, рысь 'lynx', червь 'worm',
probably also вепрь 'wild boar';

(iii) inanimates: ого́нь (< огнь, cf. Lat. *ignis,* Lith. *ugnìs*),
путь, жёлудь (жо́лудь) 'acorn', у́голь (< угль).

(iv) the *plurale tantum* лю́ди (early ESl. pl. nom. людие; the
sg. люд is a later back-formation).

This declension lost its separate identity by conflation with the
jo-stems (Type 17). Путь alone has retained the majority of its *ĭ*-
stem forms. The pl. nom. путие had vanished by the 16th c. in
favour of pl. NA пути́ (as in the fem. *ĭ*-stems); so also людие >
лю́ди. The pl. DIL adopt, as all other masculines, the fem. endings.

The rest follow one of two possibilities:

(*a*) remain *ĭ*-stems but become *fem.*: so моль, рысь (sometimes
masc. in dialect). Ле́бедь is masc. in standard language but widely
fem. in dialect (gen. ле́беди). Горта́нь 'throat' and тень 'shadow'
have long been fem. *ĭ*-stems and not well authenticated as masc.
in ESl. though comparative evidence would seem to require it.
(Pol. *gęś* is fem. and SCr. *zvìjer* of either gender.) Other possible

---

[17] Бег, бе́рег, бок, бор, быт, воз, глаз, гроб (also в гро́бе), жар, клей, корм,
край, лад, лёд (на льду), лес, лёт (на лету́ 'in flight'), лоб (на лбу), луч, мел,
мех, мозг, мост, мыс, нос, паз, пах, пир, по́вод (на поводу́ 'on a leash'), под,
пол 'floor', пот (but biblical phrase в по́те лица́), пух, пыл, рай, рот (во рту),
сад, снег, сок, счёт (на счету́), таз, торг, тыл, у́гол (в углу́ 'in the corner', на углу́
'on the corner', but math. в угле́ 'in the angle'), хмель (во хмелю́ 'intoxicated'), ход
(на ходу́ 'in motion', but в хо́де), чад, шаг (на ка́ждом шагу́). Also a few
geographical names: Росто́в на Дону́, в Крыму́, в Клину́.

[18] Other ancient *ĭ*-stems can be detected, which had already been reformed in
CSl. with various suffixes, e.g. IE *owĭs* 'sheep' makes masc. *owĭnŭ* > OCS (ChSl.)
ове́н 'Aries' (zodiac) (replaced in ESl. by the loan-word бара́н), fem. *owĭka* >
овца́. *Neut.* *ĭ*-stems (none in CSl.) can be detected in *sĭrdĭ-ko* > се́рдце and *mari*
> мо́ре (cf. Lat. *mare* < *mari*).

masc. > fem. are: боль 'pain', печа́ть 'seal', пе́чень 'liver', сте́пень 'degree'.

(*b*) join the *jo*-stems: all the rest.[19] The process is gradual and is obscured by the fact that the *jo*-stems widely adopted forms of the *ǐ*-stems before the obsolescence of the latter and their eventual reorganization as the 'soft' variant of the *o*-stems. The *ǐ*-stem declension is fairly well preserved down to the 14th c. Thereafter the *sing.* moves over to the *jo*-stems, whereas the *plur.* lags behind. In particular a pl. instr. such as гостьми́ was still current in the 17th c. and as an archaism in the 18th c.

Hesitations between (*a*) and (*b*) are not uncommon. In Czech, Ukrainian, and some R. dialects путь is *fem.*, in WhR. and some R. dialects a masc. *jo*-stem (WhR. пуць, пуця). Ivan Grozny writes без путя.

19 *Irregularities in Neuter Nouns (Types 14 and 18)*

1. The stability of the neuter was never seriously undermined in ESl. by any morphological or phonological changes.[20] Gender distinctions are somewhat blurred in many S. dialects (Table XVII (19)) (also WhR.: Table XX (22)), whence no doubt came a certain popularity of pl. NA -ы, gen. -ов for neuters, found from the 15th c. but mostly in the 17th–18th c., e.g. блюды in *Domostrój*. The last examples are probably to be found in Krylóv and Gribojédov (мы с ва́ми не ребя́ты; в э́ти ле́ты in *Горе от ума*), indicating their presence in the colloquial of Moscow down to the early 19th c.

A few masc.-type pl. gen. have been accepted as the literary standard, e.g. пла́тье 'dress', пла́тьев, подмасте́рьев 'apprentices' (originally neut. collective, now treated as masc. animate).

2. Nouns in unstressed -ко usually had pl. NA in -ка down to the 17th c. Thereafter -ки has been preferred in general, probably by confusion with feminines in -ка, indistinguishable by then in pronunciation (6.24):

я́блоко 'apple': pl. nom. я́блоки (formerly я́блока), gen. я́блок; дре́вко '(flag)staff': дре́вки, дре́вков (Slavonicism);

---

[19] One noun, те́терев 'black-cock', has been transferred to the *o*-stems. Till c.1600 the sing. is те́теревь, -ви. The pl. is now тетерева́ (§33 below), -о́в or -е́й, -а́м, etc.

[20] It was lost in Lith. (neut. > masc.) and in the passage from spoken Latin to Romance.

вѣко 'eyelid' (вѣко): вѣки, век (in form this could be an old dual: cf. §32 below);

местéчко 'spot': местéчки, местéчек.

Also stressed очкó (various senses): pl. очкú, -óв 'spectacles'; but вóйско 'army': pl. войскá, войск 'troops'. Former animate diminutives in -ишко are now written -ишка and treated as fem.: сынúшка 'sonny'.

The mixture óблако 'cloud' (Slavonicism), pl. nom. облакá, gen. облакóв arose from a change of gender in Russian; cf. ChSl. óблак m., Pol. *obłok*, SCr. *ȍblāk*. Оболок exists in dialect.

CONSONANT STEMS

Various old types, in process of dissolution as separate declensions as early as CSl., preserved a few special features in early ESl.

Commentary to Table VII

20   *Type 22*

The essential peculiarities are sg. gen. -e and pl. nom. -e. Several different sub-types can be distinguished: CSl. **kamy* (< *kamōn-s*), stem *kamĕn-* (cf. Lat. *homō, homin-is*); **korę* (< *korēn-s*), stem *korĕn-*.

Here belong: грéбень 'comb', день 'day' (original nom. unknown), кáмень 'stone', кóрень 'root', кремéнь 'flint', мишéнь 'target' (5.21), олéнь 'deer', пéрстень 'ring', плáмень 'flame', плетéнь 'hurdle', ревéнь 'rhubarb' (5.21), ремéнь 'strap', сажéнь 'fathom', стéпень 'degree', стрéмень 'stirrup', шéршень 'hornet' (**sĭršę*), ячмéнь 'barley' (original form obscure), ясень 'ash'.

The original sg. nom. was discarded early in favour of the acc.

Of the above, мишéнь, сажéнь, and стéпень (probably a Slavonicism) became *fem.* ĭ-stems by the 17th c.; плáмень and стрéмень were transferred to the neuters (Type 26) as плáмя, стрéмя. The rest, while at first preserving the two cases in -e, were attracted to the masc. ĭ-stems and so with them ended up as *jo*-stems (Type 17), and in the majority of cases the -e- of the sg. NA was reinterpreted as 'mobile', so that we have кáмень, кáмня, etc. (but олéнь/олéня, ревéнь/ревеня́, ячмéнь/ячменя́, ясень/ясеня).

In the 16th c. the declension was still essentially that of путь. Then forms such as отъ синего каменя (1532) began to appear.

TABLE VII. Consonant-Stem Nouns (Early ESl. State)

	Masculine		Feminine		Neuter		
	22 n-stem	23 nouns of origin	24 r-stem	25 ū- (w-) stem	26 n-stem	27 s-stem	28 (n)t-stem
Sg. N	кам-ы	киевлян-инъ	мат-и	свекр-ы	им-я	слов-о	тел-я
A	камен-ь		матер-ь	свекръв-ь	им-я	слов-о	тел-я
G		(sing. as	-е	-е	имен-е	словес-е	телят-е
L	-е (-и)	Type 15)	-е (-и)	-е (-и)	-е (-и)	-е (-и)	-е (-и)
D	-и		-и	-и	-и	-и	-и
I	-ьмь		-ию (-ью)	-ию (-ью)	-ьмь	-ьмь	-ьмь
V	(-и)		мат-и	свекр-ы		—	тел-я
Du. NAV	камен-и	—	матер-и	свекръв-и	имен-ѣ (-и)	словес-ѣ (-и)	телят-ѣ (-и)
GL	-у	—	-у	-у	-у	-у	-у
DI	-ьма	—	-ьма	-ама	-ьма	-ьма	-ьма
Pl. NV	камен-е	киевлян-е	матер-и	свекръв-и	имен-а	словес-а	телят-а
A	-и	-ы	-и	-и	-а	-а	-а
G	-ъ	-ъ	-ъ	-ъ	-ъ	-ъ	-ъ
L	-ьхъ	-ъхъ	-ьхъ	-ахъ	-ьхъ	-ьхъ	-ьхъ
D	-ьмъ	-ъмъ	-ьмъ	-амъ	-ьмъ	-ьмъ	-ьмъ
I	-ьми	-ы	-ьми	-ами	-ы	-ы	-ы

Notes

1. These declensions no longer fully represent their (theoretical) CSl. form: the pl. LDI have all been reformed in masc. and neut. with ĭ-stem -ь- and in Type 25 with ā-stem -a-. Not all cases are recorded. Vocative scarcely required except in fem.
2. The ChSl. declensions differ only essentially in the nasals of sg. NA imę, fem. sg. instr. -iǫ, Type 28 stem telęt-.

Genitives such as дни, из камени, до корени are still found in the 18th c.

День was fully integrated to the *jo*-stem type пень/пня but the old pl. gen. дён (< *dīnŭ*) lingered into the 19th c. and is still correct in пóлдень 'noon', pl. gen. полдён. Пополýдни 'p.m.' preserves the old loc.

Кáмень and кóрень commonly had the neut. collective plurals камéнье, корéнье (по каменью (Avv.)), which were reformed as plurals (§35 below) камéнья 'precious stones', корéнья 'root vegetables' in these special senses, side by side with the new normalized кáмни, кóрни.

21   In Type 22 may also be put:

(i) A few CSl. *t*-stems visible in лóкоть 'elbow' (early sg. gen. лóкте), нóготь 'nail', дёготь 'pitch' (5.11), кóготь 'claw', and perhaps кóпоть 'soot' (now fem.). They show practically no consonant-stem forms in ESl.

(ii) Nouns in -тель and -арь. Only the pl. nom. in -e remains in OCS and ChSl. No doubt usually a Slavonicism in Russian, as indeed the suffixes are also (5.6 and 18). On this model pl. nom. болгаре, козаре 'Khazars' are usual in *RPC*.

22   The masc. nouns of origin (Type 23) are essentially the same as Type 22, but here the *plural* is the basic part. Only in this group was the characteristic pl. nom. in -e[21] and pl. gen. in -ъ (without -ов) preserved. The singulars are regular *o*-stem nouns (Type 15) with the singulative suffix -ин.

The original suffix was -*ēn*- (-*ĕn*-), generally reformed as -*jĕn*- > -*jan*-. The N. Russian tribe *Slovĕne* preserved the original form of this native name (still not interpreted with any plausibility) which later became словяне and by learned fancy славяне (6.56).

Here belong:

(i) the still extensible category of ethnics (англичáнин, рúмлянин, etc.);[22]

(ii) similar words of social and other distinctions:

---

[21] Dialect variations in pl. nom. -ан-а (North) and -ан-ы (South) are clearly recent.

[22] In family names the stress is always penultimate: Гречанúнов, Турчанúнов (the forms гречанин, турчанин are no longer used as ethnics). Рахмáнинов has suffix -ин-, not -анин-.

pl. nom.	pl. gen.	sg. nom.	
крестья́не	крестья́н	крестья́нин	'peasant'
меща́не	меща́н	мещани́н	'bourgeois' (5.30 (7))
миря́не	миря́н	миря́нин	'layman'
южа́не	южа́н	южа́нин	'southerner'

and, by extension:

боя́ре	боя́р	боя́рин	'boyar'
тата́ре, now only тата́ры	тата́р	тата́р(ин)	'Tatar'

and some others.

Notes

(i) A singulative -ин (not -янин) may be combined with a Type 17 (collective) plural: in the Muscovite period there were many of the form тверѝтинъ 'inhabitant of Tver'', pl. тверичѝ, and нѣмчинъ, pl. нѣмцы. Москвичѝ 'Muscovites' had sg. москви́тинъ, later learned москвитя́нин, finally the back-formed москви́ч.

(ii) Certain early texts show the original consonant-stem forms of the pl. DL, e.g. *RPC, ad init.*: полемъ же жившемъ особѣ (dat. absolute, 4.49) and дѳржати почаша родъ ихъ княженьѳ в поляхъ, а въ деревляхъ свое . . . A later normalization has поляномъ же жившимъ особѣ. Instr. полями is also recorded. These forms represent *poljan-mй, -хй, -mi* from pl. nom. *poljane*, and are clearly obsolescent in the 11th c.[23]

23 *Type 24: r-stems*

Here belong only мать 'mother' and дочь 'daughter', early ESl. ма́ти and дъчи́ (ChSl. дъщи). In the sg. nom. IE *mātēr, **dhŭg(h)ətēr* > CSl. *mātē, *dŭktē (final consonants being lost) > мати, дъчи, probably by attraction to the fem. nouns in -*ī* (§7 (v) above). ChSl. continued to use nom. мати, acc. матерь; the latter also tended to oust the nom. (as in all these consonant stems): Бо́жия Ма́терь is common. Similarly with дъщи.

In ESl. the original nom. and acc. are sparingly represented in dialect and Ukrainian has also preserved nom. мати. The standard

---

[23] Similar forms are authenticated also in the W. Balkans (SCr., Slovene) and above all in the Czech PN (loc.) *Doljas, Pol(j)as* with original -*sй* unchanged to analogical -*хй* (§58 (7) below).

language preferred a compromise producing NA мать, дочь in conformity with Type 10. The new forms are establishing themselves in the 16th c.:

> (nom.) язъ Отаөья Семенова дочь (1525)
> (acc.) отпустилъ дочь (1503)

but Ivan Grozny still writes (1574), in a colloquial context, дóчерь свою далъ.

The plurals early join the ĭ-stem declension: матерéй, матерями, etc., but дочь has preserved the older instr. дочерьмú (neither дочерями nor матерьмú is standard).[24] The sg. gen. -e is early given up in favour of ĭ-stem -и.

24   *Type 25: ū-stems*

(*a*) Fem. only. The sg. nom. has -ы < -ū but -ъв- < -ŭw- (-ŭų-) before the vowel endings. The type was expanding in late CSl., taking in Gmc. feminines in -ō-. Original members are: свекры 'mother-in-law' (cf. Lat. *socrūs*); the now obsolete *ятры (*jętry) 'daughter-in-law' and *зълы 'sister-in-law' (husband's sister); кры 'blood' (cf. Lat. *crū-entus, crū-dēlis*); *ǫty (ESl. утовь) 'duck'. Early additions: любы 'love', цьркы,[25] *тыкы 'gourd', *смокы 'fig', букы[26] 'letter, writing', *redĭky 'radish',[27] *žely 'tortoise', and others not represented in ESl.

Few of the theoretical sg. nom. are recorded in ESl., as with the masc. of Type 22. Even in OCS acc. *krŭvĭ* is normal as nom., though nom. *kry* has survived in Slovene *kri* and is recorded from early Polish.

(*b*) Two adaptations were available:

(i) NA свекрóвь, etc., with transference to the ĭ-stems (sg. gen. -e > -i very early): so also ятровь (now only dial.), *золовь > dim. золóвка, кровь, любóвь, цéрковь, морковь 'carrot(s)' (presumed < *mŭrky/mŭrxy, which may be Gmc.—5.6).

> The nom. свекры survives in some S. dialects: любы and цьркы (церки) must be considered Slavonicisms. The hybrid nom. церкви persists into the 14th c.

---

[24] The pl. instr. of дочь is in the nature of things much commoner than that of мать.

[25] From Gmc. *kĭr(ĭ)kō-* (< Gk.).

[26] From Gmc. *bōkō-*.

[27] From Lat. *rādīc-* via Gmc.

(ii) Transference to the fem. *ā*-stems (Type 4), using the oblique stem: тыꙑква, смоꙵква (Slavonicism), буꙵква (originally a Slavonicism). Реꙵдька, уꙵтка, and probably боꙵчка 'barrel' (< *bŭčĭ < Lat. *buttis*?) merely adopt a diminutive suffix. Here also probably Москваꙵ: acc. Моꙵсковь, gen. Моск(ъ)ве are attested (but not *Москꙑ), at first for the river, then for the town.[28] The name is no doubt Finnic.

This solution is commoner in dialect, where цеꙵрква, свекроꙵва, морквáꙵ, золваꙵ[29] are widespread.

Further, one or two words have become masc. Theoretical *žĭrny* > OCS. *pl. žrŭnŭvi* 'hand-mill' (the usual form) but R. жёрнов 'mill-stone' (pl. now жерноваꙵ, but probably not a dual, §33 below).

(*c*) The plurals, where used, follow the *ī*-stems, except for церкваꙵх, etc. (no doubt influenced by ChSl.; dial. often церквяꙵх, etc.).

A distinction is now made between abstract любоꙵвь, gen. любвиꙵ and personal name Любоꙵвь, Любоꙵви (instr. in both cases любоꙵвью).

25 *Type 26: n-stems (neut.)*

This small group is well preserved in Russian with its sg. NA in -мя < ?-*mēn*[30] (oblique stem -*men*-; cf. similar but not identical Lat. *sēmĕn* and Gk.neuters in -μα < -*mṇ*): бреꙵмя 'burden', вреꙵмя 'time', выꙵмя 'udder' (*ūd-mēn*-), знаꙵмя 'banner', иꙵмя 'name', плаꙵмя 'flame' (§20 above),[31] плеꙵмя 'tribe, clan', сеꙵмя 'seed', стреꙵмя 'stirrup' (§20 above), теꙵмя 'sinciput, crown'. Also a few dialect words, e.g. голомяꙵ 'stripped tree-trunk' (*gol-mēn*-), соломяꙵ 'strait' (< Finnic *salmi*), шоꙵломяꙵ (a by-form of холм?). The paired plurals (rare in sg.) пис(ь)менаꙵ 'letters' and чисменаꙵ 'figures, numbers' were Slavonicisms and perhaps not original members of the type.

The sg. now conforms (*mutatis mutandis*) to путь: GLD иꙵмени.

In early ESl. and in modern dialects the stem may become имян-, etc., after sg. NA. This is not literary except for the pl. gen. семяꙵн, стремяꙵн (otherwise имён, etc.).

---

[28] На Москвѣ was usual down to the end of the 17th c. With the founding of St Petersburg (в Петербуꙵрге), в Москвеꙵ prevailed.

[29] Cf. SCr. *cȓkva, zȁova*.

[30] See A. Vaillant, *Grammaire comparée*, II/1, §184.

[31] Another form поꙵломя or поꙵлымя is subliterary, corresponding to the Slavonicism плаꙵмя. For бреꙵмя, вреꙵмя see also Appendix.

Téмя has no pl.; зна́мя has penultimate stress in the pl. (знамёна, знамён). This group is widely reformed in dialect either as neut. Type 18: и́мё, gen. и́мя, по и́мю, or Type 14: имено́, pl. имена́ (cf. Cz. *jméno*); or rarely as fem. Type 7 (и́мя, acc. и́мю). The first will occasionally be found (as colloquialisms) in 18th–19th c. texts; Pushkin once wrote до вре́мя.

26   *Type 27: s-stems (neut.)*

A very small group: не́бо 'sky', сло́во 'word' (the only two *clear* CSl. members), and probably те́ло (тѣло) 'body', ко́ло 'wheel'. The type was considerably extended in OCS and ChSl. but not in ESl.

The sg. NA provide the model for dropping the element -ec- throughout; only one native word has generalized it: sg. колесо́, pl. колёса (колеса́ in dialect), no doubt because the word is more frequently used in the pl. But early forms without -ec- are also found, especially pl. ко́ла 'cart, wheeled vehicle' (cf. SCr. *kòla* 'cart, motor car'): въложивше на кола (*RPC s.a.* 1015). This usage is now obsolete but there remain derivatives based on the preposition о́коло 'round' (око́лица, око́льный).

All forms which include -ec- are Slavonicisms: небеса́ 'heavens', чудеса́ 'miracles' (R. pl. нёба < нёбо 'palate', чу́да 'wonders'), with derivatives небе́сный, чуде́сный (R. чу́дный), слове́сный, слове́сность 'literature' (common in 18th and early 19th c. before the generalization of литерату́ра), теле́сный;[32] but native посло́вица 'proverb', нате́льный крест.

ChSl. дрѣво 'tree, wood' forms древе́сный, древеси́на, etc., but the word is not an original *s*-stem; native are only деревя́нный, деревене́ть, etc. Occasional other Slavonicisms by extension of the type will be met with from ди́во 'marvel', дѣло 'deed', и́го 'yoke', о́ко 'eye', у́хо 'ear' (pl. очеса, ушеса; normal ESl. dual > pl. о́чи, у́ши).

27   *Type 28: Neuter animate* nt-*stems*

The only large and extensible group, comprising young living beings. Suffix -ęt- < -ent-. In Russian only the pl. is still current: ребя́та, AG ребя́т. The sg. went out of use in the 17th c.,[33] being

---

[32] Pl. телеса́ in special ironical sense ('corporation') is no doubt also bookish.

[33] The SSl. languages have kept the sg. better. Pol. still has *cielę*, pl. *cielęta* but a new sg. *cielak* is more usual. Lomonósov still accepted the sg. type теля in his *Grammar* (1755) but this already belonged to the 'high style'. Current also in WhR. and Ukr. (Ukr. гуся́, -я́ти).

reformed with another diminutive suffix: телёнок (AG телёнка preferable to NA теля). Дитя́ 'child' (< *dětę*), sg. gen. дитя́те (later дитя́ти) lost ground in the 16th c. (except as a Slavonicism) in favour of дѣти́на, дѣтёныш (дѣти́шть is purely ChSl.), but here the collective pl. was always дѣти.[34]

The collective nature of the pl. is strong, leading to such analogical extensions as внуча́та '(all one's) grandchildren' (sg. внук; there is no *внучёнок) and, by popular etymology, опя́та, масля́та 'species of toadstool' (sg. опёнок < *o-pĭn-йкй* < пень, пия 'tree-stump'; маслёнок). Plurals in -ёнки are subliterary, but in a few cases there has been conflation: бесеня́та 'imps', волченя́та, лисеня́та, чертеня́та.

It is uncertain whether hypocoristics of the type Ва́ся (§2 (iii) above) and Вася́та (< Васи́лий) originally belonged here. At any rate they are treated in all Slav languages as fem.: от Гостя́ты к Васильеви (*NBG*, no. 9, *c*.1200). So SCr. *Mìleta*, acc. *Mìletu*, etc.

28 *Summary*

The net result of all the above changes in declension has been a *great reduction of independent types*. There now remain only:

   (i) *one* masc. declension in two variants (hard/soft);
   (ii) *one* neut. declension in two variants (hard/soft), essentially the same as (i);
   (iii) *two* fem. declensions, in -а/я (variants) and -ь;
   (iv) the anomalous groups in Types 23, 26, 28.

Gender distinctions have practically disappeared in the pl., only the pl. gen. being in part a pointer: -ов/-ев masc., *nil* fem. or neut., -ей 'soft' stem of any gender. *Pluralia tantum* such as дѣти, лю́ди, са́ни 'sledge', щи 'cabbage soup' cannot be said to have a gender, whatever their relationship, if any, to a singular.

29 *Nouns with Roots Ending in a Velar (Types 3, 13)*

In accordance with 1.16 (Second Palatalization) к > ц, г > з, х > с before ѣ in fem. sg. LD, fem. du. NAV, masc. sg. loc., masc. pl. loc., and before -и in masc. pl. nom.

In ESl. there was an early tendency to restore the velars in these

---

[34] In dialects which have retained the sg. it is usually reformed as дитё, gen. дитя́ (cf. и́мя above) or as *fem.* дитя́, дити́.

cases. As the dual went out of use (§31 below) and the masc. pl. nom. was abandoned (§9 (1) above), the restoration must be observed in the locatives and fem. sg. dat.

Restoration depended on the readmission of syllables кѣ, ки, etc. (2.36). There is some evidence for the view that in the most northerly dialect (Nóvgorod), as is often the case in remote and peripheral areas, the Second Palatalization did not take place, or at least not completely and consistently. The earliest 'new' forms come from this area: рабу своему дъмъкѣ (*Novg. Minéi,* text no. 8; 1096): къ лоукѣ and на отрокѣ (*NBG* of *c.*1100). They may therefore be unchanged rather than new forms.

Elsewhere the changes are considerably later but the chronology is not very clear owing to the inhibiting effect of ChSl. on written texts and the maintenance of many clichés. Statistics suggest that ц > к was more precocious than з > г. In the 1220s на волоцѣ, у Ризѣ appear to be still regular at Smolénsk. By *c.*1500 к had been generally restored. In 16th c. texts на дорозѣ, во (многихъ) торзехъ *et sim.* are still common, but a single text of 1529 has both к(ъ) рѣцѣ к(ъ) молозѣ and въ рѣкѣ мологѣ, showing the end of the older situation. The change с > х comes in the same century: моей снохѣ, but still occasionally въ мѣсехъ (1549) (мѣхъ). Many clichés, especially ChSl., remain into the 17th c., e.g. къ руцѣ, о Велицѣ дни 'on Easter Sunday', во иноцѣхъ 'in religion', во всѣхъ его грѣсѣхъ. The older form is preserved in нельзя́ < не льзѣ (loc.?) < *льга (now only льго́та 'privilege'). Russian goes further than any other Slav language in making a complete restoration of the velars; cf. Ukr. and WhR. (Table XX (14)).

30 *Vocative Case*

Only distinct in the sg. masc. and fem. It has been maintained in Ukr. and partly in WhR. but shows early decadence in other ESl. areas. There are mistakes in *Ostr.* likely to be due to the Russian copyist. It ceased to be a living form by the 14th c. It was maintained thereafter only in certain ChSl. words (о́тче, Бо́же, Го́споди, Христе́) and common words of address (господи́не, бра́те, кня́же, влады́ко 'bishop').

The Сло́во о полку Игореве has correctly Братие и дружино!, о Днѣпре Словутицю!, Княже Игорю! Similar formulae remained in oral poetry and were still present in the былины collected in the 19th c.; in fact the voc. is sometimes used for the nom. for metrical reasons, as also in SCr. oral poetry.

Apparent vocatives in Novg. dialect such as Варламе for nom. Варламъ (text no. 15, *c.*1200) are only orthographical. A phrase such as ту лежитъ с[вя]тый Епифание in a ChSl. text (Хождение иг. Даниила, text no. 11) is a Balkanism of the Second South Slav Influence (5.23): SCr. sg. nom. Епифаније.

A certain artificial revival of the vocative is noticeable in diplomatic correspondence of the 16th–17th c. in imitation of Polish.

It should be noted that the voc. was only used if the noun was isolated. The adjective had no voc. forms: a qualified noun always appeared in the nom.: мой брат!

Dual Number

31 The dual was used both for natural pairs and for any two like objects, especially in close conjunction with the number 2: самому ему и подружию его Өеофанѣ и чадомъ ею 'himself and his wife Theophani and their children' (colophon to *Ostr.*; parents are necessarily two).

The correct use of dual forms can best be studied in *RPC*, especially in its more ChSl. portions, e.g. *ad init.* сима же пришодъшема, начаста съставливати писмена . . . и преложиста Апостолъ и Еуангелье (*s.a.* 898, the story of Cyril and Methodios); *s.a.* 1019: Брата моя! аще еста и тѣломъ отошла отсюда но молитвою помозѣта ми . . .; *s.a.* 1022, the story of the single combat (снидѣвѣся сама боротъ . . .); *s.a.* 1071, the story of the two wizards (встаста два волъхва . . .).

Duals can be observed becoming more and more rare in consecutive parts of chronicles, e.g. in the *First Novg. Chron.* during the period 1250–1350.

Incorrect usages appear as early as the 13th c.:

correct: та два была (послѣмь) (1229)
2 гр[и]внѣ безъ 2-ю [= двою] ногату (*c.*1270)
incorrect: помози рабомъ своимъ [pl. dat.] . . . написавшема [du. dat.]
    книгы сия (1219) (both should be dual)
    даю два села (13th c.) (masc. forms for двѣ селѣ).

After the mid 14th c. all examples are probably deliberate archaisms.

32 *Survivals*

A few modern masc. plurals in -á and neut. plurals in -и referring to *natural pairs* would appear to be duals reinterpreted as plurals (the true plural was much less often needed): masc. бока́ 'sides, flanks', рога́ 'horns', рукава́ 'sleeves'; neut. о́чи 'eyes', у́ши 'ears', колѣ́ни 'knees', пле́чи 'shoulders'.[35] The fem. duals руцѣ 'hands' and нозѣ 'feet' were rejected because of their form. Here also (neut.) двѣсти '200' (§79 below). Certain other apparently likely cases may not be survivals in fact: берега́ 'banks' is not recorded before the 16th c. nor глаза́ 'eyes' (replacing о́чи in the vernacular) before *c.*1590. The dual had long been extinct by those dates. Only the *nominative* survived; oblique cases of the dual are extremely rare[36] after the 14th c. except in ChSl. (a common ChSl. cliché was instr. очима '(with my) two eyes'). Such old dual forms had perhaps the best chance of surviving if there was a stress contrast with the sg. gen., e.g. in бока́, рога́ (sg. gen. бо́ка, ро́га). Hence we may tentatively include as duals the combinations 2 часа́, 2 шага́, 2 ряда́ in contrast to the normal sg. gen. не ра́ньше ча́са, с пе́рвого ша́га, по́сле ря́да несча́стий.

Development of the Masculine Plural Nominative in -á

33 The reinterpretation of such duals as бока́, рога́ as *plurals* encouraged the spread of this form. There were other likely convergent factors:

(i) fem. *collectives*, normally taking a pl. adjective or verb and so able to be reinterpreted as plurals, e.g. господа́ 'masters, gentlemen',[37] сторожа́ (= ChSl. стра́жа) 'the guard(s)', Литва́ 'the Lithuanians', бра́тья 'the brothers (brotherhood)', дружи́на 'the (Prince's) military retinue'.

Examples: рѣкоша дружина Игореви . . . (*RPC s.a.* 945); гдѣ суть дружина наша?; а поидутъ на насъ Литва (1386); совокупишася вся братья (*RPC s.a.* 1101); предъ господою (= советом).

---

[35] The true pl. коле́на and the collective pl. коле́нья also exist in special senses; the pl. плеча́ is subliterary. The following descendants of old duals are also found in dialect: neut. муде́ or муди́ 'testicles' (CSl. *mǫdo*), fem. скуле́ 'cheeks' (скула́ now = 'cheek-bone'), брыле́ 'jowls'.

[36] In some N. dialects the fem. pl. DI are confused (see Table XVII (16)) and the prevailing form is often du. -ама rather than -ам or -ами. Dual forms may have survived longer in outlying parts.

[37] Already present in later OCS: без волѧ господы ихъ.

By the 16th c. господа́, господъ, -ахъ, etc. (new pl. *oblique* cases) is already the normal pl. of the singulative господи́н.

(ii) neuters with the stress-pattern сло́во, sg. gen. сло́ва, pl. NA слова́, identical with the masc. in the oblique cases. There were about a dozen such common nouns, but others were added (места́, лета́).

(iii) the gradual generalization of fem. -ax, -ам, -ами to all nouns.

34   The number of masc. pl. in -á recorded up to and including the 16th c. is still small. The formation is virtually unknown in Ukr. and WhR., therefore its inception can hardly be before *c.*1300. Among the earliest new analogical forms are: города́ (1495), мастера́ (1509), луга́ (1529). But го́роды, ма́стеры predominated down to the 17th c. (Pososhkóv, *c.*1724, has both го́роды and города́). Despite its large vernacular vocabulary there is only one in *Dom.*; the more formal *Stoglav* (1551) and *Uloženie* of 1649 each have only one of these 'vulgarisms' (лѣса and лѣсы in the latter). They achieved acceptance only in the 18th c. and above all in the 19th c. when they were freely formed in many technical vocabularies and were particularly affected to foreign loan-words, e.g. борта́, веера́ 'fans', вексселя́ 'bills of exchange', катера́ 'cutters', номера́, паспорта́, профессора́, сорта́, etc., down to contemporary дизеля́ 'diesel engines'. До́мы is still fairly common down to the mid 19th c. At the present time they appear to have suffered a certain loss of popularity, инспе́кторы, тра́кторы being preferred to инспектора́, трактора́. The total in *obligatory* literary use from *native* words is about forty.[38]

The form apparently entered Moscow town dialect from S. dialects, where it is common even in the feminines (степя́, лошадя́). Only one such fem. has any literary standing: зеленя́ 'sprouting corn' (the first signs of growth in the spring) < зе́лень f.

The small group in -ья́ arose from a crossing of the original pl. nom., e.g. кня́зи, with fem. collectives of the type бра́тья (the old collectives кня́жья, etc., were fem. sg.: вся кня́жья ру́сьская).

[38] Бег, век (ве́ки is ChSl. or poetic), ве́ртел, вес (веса́ 'weights' but весы́ 'scales'), ве́чер, воз 'cartload', во́рох, глаз, год (also го́ды in сороковы́е го́ды), го́лос, же́мчуг, за́кром, ко́локол, ко́роб, ку́зов, лес, лог, о́браз (образа́ 'icons' but otherwise о́бразы), о́стров, па́рус, пе́репел, по́вар, по́греб, по́дрез, по́езд, по́яс, при́став, про́вод, рог, снег, стог, сто́рож, счёт (счета́ 'accounts' but счёты 'abacus'), те́рем, те́терев (n. 19 above), цвет (цвета́ 'colours' but цветы́ 'flowers'), and those in §32 above.

They are established as plurals in the 17th c. with the oblique cases following rather slowly (бра́тьями is recorded in 1517 but з братьею, послал свою братью, etc. are still fairly usual in the 17th c.). They comprise: дядья́ (pl. gen. дядьёв), друзья́, князья́, кумовья́ (< кум), мужья́ 'husbands', сват(ов)ья́, сыновья́. The final stress would appear to come from the new plurals in -а́.

35   A small group of masc. plurals in unstressed -ья has come from the neut. collectives in -ье[39] which were giving way to plurals in the 17th c. The *Uloženie* of 1649 has бортное деревье side by side with тѣмъ бортнымъ деревьямъ. Avvakúm still uses под каменьем. Pososhkóv writes both то деревье 'those trees' and стоячие деревья. The collective sense is still strong in перо́ 'feather', pl. пе́рья, less so in крыло́ 'wing', pl. кры́лья. The following masculines are now included: бру́сья, зу́бья,[40] каме́нья (§20 above), кли́нья, кло́чья, коло́сья, ко́лья, ко́мья, коре́нья (§20 above), крю́чья, ли́стья,[41] лоску́тья, лу́бья, пово́дья (< по́вод 'rein'), поло́зья, пру́тья, сту́лья, су́чья, у́голья, хло́пья, шу́рья (< шу́рин).

36 Indeclinable Nouns

Foreign nouns which do not conform in their finals to an appropriate gender are usually left undeclined. This applies particularly to personal names: Дюма́ 'Dumas', Гёте 'Goethe' (cf. Pol. gen. *Goethego*). But there are variations: пальто́ (Fr. *paletot*) and бюро́ (Fr. *bureau*), though capable of being treated as neuters, are in practice indeclinable, and the neuter-shaped ко́фе is masc.

The Adjective

37   One of the prominent agreements between Slav and Baltic—therefore no doubt a BSl. innovation—is the possession of two adjectival paradigms: a *nominal*, indeterminate ('short') and a *pronominal*, determinate ('long'), a compound of the nominal forms with the anaphoric pronoun *jĭ, je, ja* (§59 below). Thus: новъ, ново, нова '(a) new' (cf. Lat. *bonus filius, bona filia, bonum*

---

[39] Those still in use are predominantly end-stressed: бельё 'underwear', сырьё 'raw materials'. This collective type has been particularly favoured in some N. dialects, where комарьё may be said to be the normal pl. of комар 'mosquito'. A few occasionally appear in literature: бабьё '(gaggle of) old women', дурачьё '(pack of) fools'.

[40] Зу́бы '(human) teeth' but зу́бья 'teeth of a saw'.

[41] Листы́ 'sheets, pages' but ли́стья '(plant) leaves' (collective листва́ 'foliage').

donum); новъ-jь, ново-je, нова-ja '(the) new' (already mentioned).
See further 4.70–2.

CSl. had, however, only the *declensional* types m. *novŭ*, n. *novo*, f. *nova* (with 'soft'-stem variants); *ĭ*-stem and *ŭ*-stem adjectives had disappeared or been reformed.[42]

The compound 'long' declension was already subject to a number of adjustments in CSl., especially in the pl. where some juxtapositions were awkward, e.g. masc. sg. instr. **novomĭ-jimĭ > novyimĭ*, pl. loc. **novĕxŭ-jixŭ > novyixŭ*, fem. pl. dat. **novamŭ-jimŭ > novyimŭ* (the gender distinction disappears). The generalized base *novy-* may come from the fem. pl. nom. *novy-ję*.

Commentary to Table VIII

38   1. *Sg. masc. nom./voc.* The original structure of this ending is *-ŭjĭ*, *-ĭjĭ*. The phonetic history of the jers before *j* is not entirely clear (2.33). OCS exhibits the alternative spellings *-yjĭ (-yi)/-ijĭ (-ii)* and *-ŭjĭ (-ŭi)/-ĭjĭ (-ĭi)*, which surely indicate the same sound sequence perhaps not quite identical with either spelling. Early ESl. texts, whether ChSl. or not, have predominantly -ыи/-ии (-ъи/-ьи probably only if copied from an OCS original). It is doubtful that this ever represented the ESl. phonetic reality but this orthography has remained traditional down to the present day. The expected ESl. forms -ой/-ей (i.e. the normal treatment of a strong jer followed by a weak final jer) begin to appear from the mid 14th c., e.g. князь великои (1339), and irrespective of stress. That these were the true native forms is supported by the fact that the *pronunciation* (as far as can be ascertained) has always been *stressed* [oj] as in дорогóй, *unstressed* [əj] as in нóвый and сѝний (*not* [-yj, -ij]), i.e. the normal reductions of unstressed -ой/-ей. Only recently has the *written* form нóвый, сѝний begun to influence pronunciation: велѝкий [v'el'ik'ij] is increasingly heard. Stressed -ой (there are no stressed -ей)[43] early became the regular spelling. There has been considerable variation between the stressed and unstressed models, e.g. standard тóлстый but W. dial. толстóй.[44]

---

[42] Lith. still has many *ŭ*-stem adjectives: *kartùs, saldùs* (so also Gk. ἡδύς 'sweet'); in Slav *ŭ*-stems were given a suffix *-k-* in CSl.: **līgŭkŭ, *saldŭkŭ, *gladŭkŭ, *tĭnŭkŭ, *nizŭkŭ, *blizŭkŭ, *rĕdŭkŭ, *kartŭkŭ* (R. корóткий). *ĭ*-stems are visible in *velikŭ < *welĭ*, with a number of active forms in OCS but not in ESl. (*velĭmi*, prefix *vele-*). Similarly **kolĭ, *tolĭ >* колик-, толик- (Table XIII).

[43] Except **третéй in сам-третéй, пол-третья́ (§§81, 83 below); standard (ChSl.) трéтий.

[44] See also A. Vaillant, *Grammaire comparée*, II/2, §299.

TABLE VIII. Declension of the Long Adjective

	Hard			Early East Slav	Soft	
	Masc.	Neut.	Fem.	Masc.	Neut.	Fem.
Sg. NV	нов-ыи (-ои) N or G	нов-ое	нов-ая	син-ии (-еи) N or G	син-ее	син-яя
A	N or G	-ое	-ую	N or G	-ее	-юю
G	-ого		-ыѣ (-оѣ)	-его		-иѣ (-еѣ)
L	-омь[1]		-ѣи (-ои)	-емь[1]		-еи
D	-ому		-ѣи (-ои)	-ему		-еи
I	-ымь[1]		-ою	-имь[1]		-ею
Du. NAV	нов-ая	нов-ѣи	нов-ѣи	син-яя	син-ии	син-ии
GL		-ою (-ую)			-ею (-юю)	
DI		-ыма			-има	
Pl. NV	нов-ии	нов-ая	нов-ыѣ	син-ии	син-яя	син-ѣѣ
A	-ыѣ	-ая	-ыѣ	-ѣѣ	-яя	-ѣѣ
G		-ыхъ			-ихъ	
L		-ыхъ			-ихъ	
D		-ымъ			-имъ	
I		-ыми			-ими	

Church Slavonic

	Hard			Soft		
	Masc.	Neut.	Fem.	Masc.	Neut.	Fem.
Sg. NV	nov-yĭ (-ŭĭ)	nov-oje	nov-aja	sin-ĭi (-ĭĭ)	sin-jeje	sin-jaja
A	N or G	-oje	-ǫjǫ	N or G	-jeje	-jǫjǫ
G	-ago (-aago)		-yję	-jago (-jaago)		-jęję
L	-ěmĭ (-ějemĭ)		-ěi	-imĭ (-iimĭ)		-ii
D	-umu (-uumu)		-ěi	-jumu (-juumu)		-ii
I	-ymĭ (-yimĭ)		-ǫjǫ	-imĭ (-iimĭ)		-jǫjǫ
Du. NAV	nov-aja	nov-ěi	nov-ěi	sin-jaja	sin-ii	sin-ii
GL		-uju			-juju	
DI		-yma (-yima)			-ima (-iima)	
Pl. NV	nov-ii	nov-aja	nov-yję	sin-ii	sin-jaja	sin-jęję
A	-yję	-aja	-yję	-jęję	-jaja	-jęję
G	-yxŭ (-yixŭ)			-ixŭ (-iixŭ)		
L	-yxŭ (-yixŭ)			-ixŭ (-iixŭ)		
D	-ymŭ (-yimŭ)			-imŭ (-iimŭ)		
I	-ymi (-yimi)			-imi (-iimi)		

[1] Early depalatalized (6.11); cf. Table VI, n. 6.

111

No vocative forms are found in ESl.; OCS (ChSl.) has occasionally, in the sg. masc. only, безумие!, буе!, Фарисею слѣпе!, but already more often the long form: отьче праведьный!

39 2. *Sg. masc. gen./dat.* The contraction of *-ajego, -ujemu* can be followed in OCS (frequent) *-aago, -uumu,* no doubt representing [āgo] [ūmu], later *-ago, -umu.* The ESl. forms -ого, -ому cannot be phonetic contractions; they are borrowed from pronominal -ого, -ому (вьсякому, etc.). The ChSl. spelling -аго is usual in early ESl. texts and remained as a Slavonicism in Russian spelling down to 1876 if stressed (святаго > свято́го) and down to 1917 if unstressed (но́ваго > но́вого). It has become petrified in a few surnames of ecclesiastical origin, e.g. Жива́го, where it is pronounced as written. Native -ого is rare before the 13th c.: новгородского (1149), великого (1151), but already normal in the 1229 Treaty (text no. 18): изъ гочкого бѣрѣга, смольнеского князя, латинеского человѣка. Conversely, ChSl. -уму is rare from the start compared with -ому: славьному (1073).

40 3. *Pronunciation of* -ого/-его. Spellings revealing the modern pronunciation with *-v-* occur from the 15th c.: великово (1432), третьево (1436), брата молодшево (1439), правово (1445), друго́во (1473). Somewhat later we find вели́кова (1553). A purely phonetic explanation is improbable. Most S. dialects with [g] > [ɣ] (Table XVII (1)) have [-oɣa]/[-oɣə], [ɣ] being stable.[45] A few NW dialects (Onéga–Oló́nets area) which also have [g] > [ɣ] in some contexts show a further weakening of the spirant in intervocalic position, with recorded pronunciations [-oho] or [-oo]. With strong labialization of a final *stressed* o, the latter could clearly lead to [-owó] > [-ovó],[46] e.g. in кого́, того́. But the earliest examples are all unstressed; moreover, some N. dialects have pronominal [togó] or [toɣó] but adjectival -ова. As these areas do not have а́канье (6.33 ff.), the final -a is genuine. We must suppose therefore at least a strong interference from the *possessive adjectives* in -ов, in universal use till recent times (§43 below). The prototype of [-ovo] is to be sought in the combinations Ива́нова сы́на, Петро́ва до́ма, Ду́хова дня *et sim.*

The phenomenon is certainly of N. dial. origin in standard

---

[45] Likewise Ukr. has the normal evolution [-ogo] > [-oɣo] or [-oho].

[46] Cf. spoken SCr. over large areas where *x* is weak or dropped, e.g. *kȕhār* > *kȕvār* 'cook', *ȕho* > *ȕo* or *ȕvo* 'ear'; *mȕhi* > *mȕvi* 'flies', *bȕha* > *bȕva* 'flea'. These also show that the development of an intervocalic *v* to remove hiatus is not dependent on a following *o*.

Russian, which has maintained the traditional spelling -ого except in a few personal names, e.g. Дурновó, Суховó (where the stress is not that of the adj. дурнóго, сухóго).

41   4. *Sg. fem.* All the forms except the NA have been reformed on pronominal models.

Gen. The ending -ыя/-ия (< -*yję*/-*iję* for -*jęję*) is always a Slavonicism and often written -ые/-ие: изъ московские земли (1497), безъ лишние волокиты (17th c.).[47] The pronominal endings -оѣ/-еѣ (cf. тоѣ, сеѣ, Table XII) are used concurrently and are attracted to the LD -ои/-еи from the 15th c.; -ой/-ей finally prevailed in the 17th c. There is an early example of -оѣ in the *Arch. Ev.* (1092).

Loc./dat. -ѣи is similarly supplanted by pronominal -ои (-ой).

Instr. -ою is again pronominal (ChSl. -*ǫjǫ*) and was reduced to -ой recently, as in the nouns. The presence of -ою in *Ostr.* suggests that it was already the normal native form in the 11th c.

42   5. Dual forms disappear early in the adjective. Even in ChSl. style святыхъ апостолъ Петра и Павла is more usual than святую (or wrongly святою) апостолу . . .

6. *Pl. nom./acc.* The adjectives here conform to the nouns in preferring the pl. acc. (§9 above). Confusion begins in the 13th c. and is frequent in the 14th c. With the general confusion of unstressed ѣ and е we get masc. and fem. NA -ые; -ыя is a Slavonicism (< -*yję*) and was revived for no good reason in the 18th c. for the neut. and fem. (this anomaly was suppressed in 1917). The neut. -ая survived well into the 15th c.; after its decadence there were no longer any gender distinctions in the pl. Злая дела in Avvakúm is a deliberate ChSl. archaism.

A hybrid masc. -ыи/-ии occurs sporadically down to the 16th c.: люди добрыи (1501). It was not entirely abandoned by 18th and early 19th c. grammarians.

7. *Other pl. forms.* The contracted forms -ых(ъ), etc. (also sg. masc./neut. instr. -ым(ь) and du. -ыма) are normal by the 13th c. (always so in the 1229 Treaty), but the uncontracted remain as Slavonicisms. It was not simple contraction but rather adjustment to a generalized base добры-, since intervocalic *j* does not normally fall in Russian. Early ChSl. texts (*Ostr.* and *Novg. Minéi*) have about half and half contracted and uncontracted forms.

---

[47] When written -ыѣ/-иѣ it is presumably a cross between native -оѣ/-еѣ and ChSl. -ыя/-ия.

8. The declension of the adjectival participles follows the above changes (§§117 ff. below).

Types of Adjective

43   1. *Personal possessive.* Down to the 17th c. the normal formula was of the type Петро́в дом 'Peter's house', се́стрин сын '(my) sister's son'. The gen. of possession had to be used only when there was a qualification: сын твое́й сестры́. There were two formations:

(*a*) in -ов/-ев from masculines and -ин/-ын from feminines (or masc. in -а/-я);

(*b*) in -jĭ, from masculines.

Being bound by nature to particular persons these adjectives had only the 'short' paradigm.[48] With the decadence of the oblique cases of the 'short' paradigm (§48 below) their nominal were replaced by pronominal endings.

Except in popular speech the whole category became nearly obsolete in the 18th c., only a few 'family' terms remaining in cultivated and domestic usage: се́стрин, ба́бушкин '(my) grand-mother's', дя́дин 'Uncle's' (also from hypocoristics: Ко́лин, Та́нин 'Nicholas's', 'Tatjana's').

Meanwhile type (*a*) had petrified in family names, being either patronymics or the name or nickname of the grandfather.[49] Алекса́ндр Серге́ев сын Пу́шкина = A., son of Sergej, grand-son of 'Пушка'. Their declension is therefore now mixed: the 'long' pronominal forms have prevailed in the masc. sg. instr. (Пу́шкиным), all the fem. except the sg. NA (oblique cases Пу́шкиной), and all the pl. except the nom. (Пу́шкиных, etc.).

These possessive adjs. likewise became widely fossilized as place-names and are so used from the earliest texts: Кыевъ (sc. город), loc. Кыевѣ (1057), the 'short' form being normal as in Нов(ъ)городъ, loc. Новѣгородѣ (4.53). There was thus no devi-ation from a noun in the sg. (no pl. forms are needed), except sometimes for a 'long' instr. (под Кыевымъ).

Type (*b*) in -jĭ required palatalization of the stem: а от смерти Ярославли до смерти Святополчи лѣтъ 60 (*RPC s.a.* 852); Мьстиславъ Володимирь сынъ (text no. 12); княжь 'the

---

[48] Long forms are occasionally found for wives: Всеволожая (1097), Мьстиславляя (1122).

[49] See B. Unbegaun, *Russian Surnames*, section I, and V. K. Chichagov, Из истории русских имен, отчеств и фамилий (1959).

Prince's'; митрополичь 'the Metropolitan's'; and perhaps Царь-градъ (or Царьгородъ) 'Constantinople (the Emperor's city)'.

The formation might be unclear or ambiguous; alternatives in -ов/-ев were early preferred: Ивань день > Иванов день. They were obsolescent by the 16th c. and remained into the 17th c. only in a few set formulae, e.g. на патриаршѣ дворѣ. There are some survivals as place-names: Яросла́вль, Влади́мир (earlier Владимирь, sc. город).

Notes

(i) The patronymics developed from these formations—Андре́евич, Ива́нович, Илья́ч (no -ин-!) and their feminines Ива́новна, Арсе́ньевна, etc.—are *nouns*.

(ii) Surnames of gen. form—Дурново́, Черны́х—arose by omission of сын, дочь, дѣти, or similar.

(iii) In bourgeois and peasant society the patronymic became the more polite and formal mode of reference to a person: Ludolf (1696) records поди въ поварну и позови Ивано[в]ну; Avvakúm always refers to his wife as Марковна (we are only told at the beginning that her baptismal name was Anastasia).

(iv) Surnames (фами́лии) in -ович/-евич are of Polish origin and have Polish penultimate stress: Станке́вич, Шостако́вич.

(v) Surnames in -ский (fully adjectival)—Достое́вский, Оболе́нский, Чайко́вский—appear to belong to the western borderlands; the type is very common in Polish. Some, however, are 'seminary' names (ChSl.): Рожде́ственский, Вознесе́нский, Успе́нский.

44 2. The type in -*jĭ* must not be confused with the type in -*ĭjĭ* (-*ii*), e.g. ли́сий, ли́сье, ли́сья 'belonging to or characteristic of foxes'. This type is still current, especially from animals, but the declension is 'long' except for sg. neut./fem. nom., fem. acc., and pl. nom. (во́лчье, во́лчья; во́лчью; во́лчьи). Here also belong Бо́жий (OCS *Božii*), a true possessive from *Bogй*, and тре́тий (§83 below).

45 3. *Adjectives in* -(ь)ск-. A common formation of *general* relationship or possession: монасты́рский 'monastic', же́нский 'female' or 'feminine' (not 'my wife's'), гре́ческий 'Greek'. Such adjs. were also derived from personal possessives: отцов(ъ) > *отцовый > отцо́вский 'paternal' (not 'my father's').

The 'short' declension early became obsolete. Short forms survive only in nominalized place-names, e.g. Смоле́нск.

See also adverbs in -ски (§69 (a) below).

46   4. *Adjectives lacking the determinate ('long') forms.* The most notable is рад, -а 'glad' (so generally in Slav), of uncertain origin. The old pl. masc. nom. ра́ди is still to be found in the 18th c.

Further: гора́зд (a Gothic loan-word, 5.5) 'capable', now subliterary as an adj. (country speech: он гора́зд на всё); there remains the adverb гора́здо, 'very' until the 17th c., thereafter only with comparatives (гора́здо лу́чше 'much better').

47   5. *Indeclinable adjectives.* There was a small number of these in OCS; all seem to be relics of *i*-stem adjectives. The following may occur in ChSl. texts: различь 'different'; свободь 'free'; исплънь 'full'; удобь 'easy'; сугубь 'double'. Normalized with suffix -н- in most cases.[50]

48 *Survival of the Nominal ('Short') Forms*

1. The complete short declension remained in use until about the beginning of the 13th c., at least in writing. Thereafter only the nom. and acc., singular and plural, were usual, the other cases being replaced by 'long' forms or otherwise avoided. In particular the sg. masc. and neut. instr. and sg. fem. LD disappeared early, the latter no doubt because a stem change was sometimes needed (нага, DL назѣ). ChSl. retained longer the short forms still normal in, e.g., *Ostr.* (1057): мъногамъ д[у]шамъ кр[ь]стияньскамъ *et sim.* The pl. NA follow the lead of the nouns and long adjectives in generalizing -ы for all genders: какъ бы сыти были (1493) but незваны (participle) не ѣздять (1515).

By the 16th–17th c. делово́й язы́к, reflecting the colloquial but not without its own conservative procedures, uses the short forms only as predicates or pseudo-predicates (apposition, etc.); the accusatives have all the appearance of a conventional cliché, including word order:

> ея за то казнити живу;
> жена . . . дитя родитъ мертво;
> прислалъ ковшъ золотъ;
> купилъ двѣ кобылы, игреню да гнѣду.

[50] Vaillant is of the opinion that the resultant apparent suffix -ьн- was then isolated and developed to become one of the main adj. suffixes (replacing -н- as in ясный, where there was never any jer).

The dat. is not unrepresented in dat. + inf. constructions: ни нагу ни голодну . . . было ему не ходити (1502). But at late dates they will be ChSl., e.g. in Pososhkóv c.1724: ему подобáет быть трéзву. This type of apposition did not entirely disappear from learned language until well into the 19th c.: Dal' in his great Толкóвый словáрь (1863–6) uses formulae of definition such as: . . . сплошь покрывáться чем-либо падáющим, быть засыпану.

By the 18th c. the pseudo-predicate in such phrases as онъ лежитъ боленъ (1532), та дорога крива лучилась (1515) had in principle gone over to the long form, nom. or pred. instr. (4.52). There thus now remain only the nominatives as *true* predicates.

49 *2. Relics of the Past*

(*a*) Oral poetry preserved, since much dependent on fixed formulae, other cases than the nom.:

он садился на добра коня.

Note. Apocopated forms were much affected by poets in the 18th and more rarely in the 19th c.: мрáчна ночь (for мрáчная; the short predicative form is мрачнá).[51]

(*b*) Petrified adverbial phrases (NB no instr. and no plural):

средь бéла дня 'in broad daylight';
на босý нóгу 'barefoot';
от мáла до велúка 'of all ages';
мáло по-мáлу 'little by little'.

Acc.: зáмертво (повалúться), зáново, зáсветло, нáглухо (закрыть), налéво/напрáво, нáскоро, нáчерно (писáть), нáчисто (отказáться);
Gen.: дóкрасна, дóсыта, úздавна, издалекá, úзредка, úскоса, and the type úзжелта 'yellowish' (úссиня зелёный 'bluish-green'), свысокá, сгорячá, слегкá, снóва, спервá, сполнá, неспростá;
Dat.: помалéньку, попрóсту, пóпусту, пóровну;
Loc.: вполнé, вчернé, наготóве; вкрáтце, вообщé, and наравнé are Slavonicisms.

50 *Adjectives as Nouns*

A frequent process, which only concerns long adjectives in ESl.: рýсский 'a Russian',[52] портнóй 'a tailor'; (modern) кривáя (sc.

---

[51] N. dialect shows *contracted* forms: злā < злая, маленьки дети, в прежни годы. See Table XVII (11).

[52] Of long standing. The singulative noun русин(ъ), from the original collective Русь, had some currency in early centuries (*RP*, art. 1; 1229 Treaty) but did not outlive the Muscovite period. Россиянин (and Росс) are learned inventions of the 18th c.

ли́ния) 'a curve', живо́тное 'an animal'. 'Short' are only a few
words inherited from CSl.: вдова́ 'widow' (the adj. вдо́вый exists),
де́ва (дѣва) 'virgin', and no longer felt as adjectives; and a few
inherited from OCS usage: бла́го 'the good', зло, and добро́. The
latter have, of course, the normal declension of neuter nouns:

> ме́ньшее из двух зол 'the lesser of two evils';
> не плати́ злом за зло.

Some nominalized adjectives have different stress: жарко́е
'roast' (adj. жа́ркое).

An original noun вожа́тай (cf. хода́тай) has been altered by
phonetic confusion to вожа́тый, -ого 'leader' (cf. жена́тый).

Comparison of Adjectives

1. Comparative

51   (*a*) A relatively small number of common adjectives have preserved an archaic CSl. formation in -*jĭs*- > -ьш- with palatalization
of the stem; an adjectival suffix may be dropped. So:

болии, больш- 'more';
хужии, хужьш- 'worse' (stem худ-);
вышии, вышьш- 'higher' ⎱ now reformed ortho- ⎰ высш-
нижии, нижьш- 'lower' ⎰ graphically as ⎱ низш-
глублии, глубльш- 'deeper' (adj. глубок-) (obs.);
мьнии, мьньш- 'less(er)' (modern меньш-);
вячии, вячьш- 'greater'[53] (lost; OCS *vęštii*);
луч(ш)ии, лучьш- 'better' (ESl. innovation; also late OCS *lučĭši/luče*
'more fitting').

(*b*) Most have the more evolved formation in -*ē-jĭs*- > -ѣиш-,
which becomes -*(j)ajš*- regularly after velars and certain palatalized
consonants (cf. §87, B2 below): нов-ѣйш-ий; ближ-айш-ий;
горьч-айш-ий (adj. stem горьк-).

(*c*) Comparison with Table VIII will show that only a few
adjustments were needed (as in the participles) to bring this declension into conformity with all other 'long' adjectives: the oblique
stem in -ѣйш- is generalized in the sg. nom. and gender obliterated
in the pl. nom.:

> новѣ́йший, новѣ́йшее, новѣ́йшая; новѣ́йшие.

---

[53] A CSl. form (SCr. *vèćí*, ChSl. вящ(ьш)ий) but apparently peculiar to NW
dial. (Novg.) in ESl., e.g. *Novg. Chr., s.a.* 1215: ано тамо измано вачьшие
моуж[ь] а мьньшее они розидоша са. Survives in the rare name Вячесла́в
(Wenceslas), borrowed from Czech.

TABLE IX. Declension of the Comparative

	Short			Long		
	Masc.	Neut.	Fem.	Masc.	Neut.	Fem.
Sg. NV	нов-ѣи	нов-ѣе	нов-ѣиши	нов-ѣи	нов-ѣе	нов-ѣишия
A	N or G[2]	-ѣе (-ише)	-ишу	N or G	-ѣе[1]	-ишую
G	-ѣиша		-ѣи	-ишего		-ѣѣ
L	-ѣише		-иши	-ишемь		-ишеи
D	-ишу		-иши	-ишему		-ишеи
I	-ишемь		-ишею	-ишимь		-ишео
Du. NAV	нов-ѣиша	нов-ѣиши	нов-ѣиши	нов-ѣишая	нов-ѣишии	нов-ѣишии
GL	-ишу		-ишу	-ишую		-ишую
DI	-ишема		-ишама	-ишима		-ишима
Pl. NV	нов-ѣише[3]	нов-ѣиша	нов-ѣишѣ	нов-ѣишии	нов-ѣишая	нов-ѣишѣѣ
A	N or G[3]	-иша	-ишѣ	N or G	-ишая	-ишѣѣ
G	-ишь		-ишь		-ишихъ	
L	-ишихъ		-ишахъ		-ишихъ	
D	-ишемь		-ишамъ		-ишимъ	
I	-иши		-ишами		-ишими	

[1] Usually reformed as новѣишее.
[2] Often reformed as новѣишь.
[3] Usually nom. -ѣиши; original acc. -ѣишѣ.

119

The 'short' declension evidently went out of use early in the vernacular (*pari passu* with that of other adj.) and most uses of it are probably Slavonicisms, e.g. желая больша имѣнья (*RPC s.a.* 945).

52 However, except for the *four most usual opposite pairs*, spoken Russian early ceased to decline comparatives (cf. the primacy of the invariable 'gerund' in the p.p.a., §§118 ff. below). By the Muscovy period the forms in -ѣйший/-айший were considered bookish. The surviving eight were all of the simpler type (*a*):

> бо́льший/ме́ньший[54] 'greater/less(er)';
> лу́чший/ху́дший 'better/worse';
> вы́сший/ни́зший 'higher/lower';
> ста́рший/мла́дший[55] 'older (elder)/younger'.

Statistically comparatives (at least in speech) are much more common as *predicates* than as attributes, hence mainly required in the nom. Thus the comparative forms reduced themselves to:

> sg. (nom.) новѣи, новѣе, новѣиши;
> pl. (nom.) новѣиши,[56] новѣиша, новѣишѣ.

The *neuter singular* early prevailed as an invariable predicate: it is so found from the early 13th c.:

> аже капь (f.) льгче будеть (1229);
> не еси богатѣе Давыда (masc. reference).

Formally бо́льше, ме́ньше, лу́чше appear to be *plurals* (neut. sg. бо́лее, ме́нее still available as adverbs);[57] a few fem. sg. forms were common down to the 17th c., but they were not maintained.

The ending -ѣе (-ее) prevails over -ае: свежѣе, ловчѣе (learned свежа́йший etc. remain). 'Incorrect' forms in -ae/-яе, not uncommon in the 17th–18th c., appear to be a N. dial. extension:

> чтоб поскоря́е отказа́ли (1660).

---

[54] The comparative бо́льший contrasts with a new positive большо́й. Меньшо́й, старшо́й (dial. only) are new coll. variants of the *comparative* (меньшо́й replacing ChSl. мла́дший).

[55] Slavonicism; ESl. моло́дший also occurs but failed to survive in Russian: дайта ми дружину свою молотшюю (*RPC s.a.* 1097). The original sense of **mald-* was 'weak, helpless, infant', still seen in OCS (ChSl.) младе́нец 'infant'; the OCS for 'young' was ю́ный (1.28).

[56] Properly новѣише (as a consonant stem) but commonly so even in OCS.

[57] Тем бо́лее (что), тем не ме́нее; otherwise the simple adverb is бо́льше, ме́ньше. The same with normal да́льше 'further' but и так да́лее 'and so on'; and ра́ньше 'earlier', but зара́нее 'in advance'.

In the 18th c. Sumarókov favoured -яе but Lomonósov advocated the standard -ѣе (-ее).

The shortened новѣй, сильней, etc., is now mainly poetic.

Most stems in dentals and velars have type (*a*) comparatives with palatalization: тверд-/твёрже, густ-/гýще, тих-/тише, коротк-/коро́че, жидк-/жи́же, also дешев-/деше́вле. Alternatives are occasionally possible: богат-/бога́че, less often богатéе.

After the above reorganization the attributive comparative is made with бо́лее (ме́нее) + positive: со всё бо́лее ре́дкими исключе́ниями.

53   2. *Superlative*

There were no special *superlative* forms (comparison between *more than two*). The comparative sufficed but might be pointed with the intensive prefix наи-. The form appears to be recent in OCS where it is only applied to *adverbs* (*naivęšte*) but it is CSl. and has remained in most Slav languages. Even if native in ESl. too, it became obviously bookish with the obsolescence of the type нове́йший.[58] By the 17th c. наинове́йший is either a Slavonicism or a Polonism. Лу́чший/ху́дший and ста́рший/мла́дший are still either comparative or superlative according to context. The vernacular superlative with са́мый (§66 (ii) below) is recorded rarely from the 16th c. but may, of course, be considerably older:

> да купилъ бы сандалу доброва самова.

Forms in -ейший/-айший have a limited currency in the higher literary style and officialese: с глубоча́йшим приско́рбием; кратча́йший путь; крупне́йший поэ́т; миле́йшая из подру́г 'her dearest friend'. They are still occasionally used as *comparatives* in the 19th c.:

> вскрича́ла она́ в ещё сильне́йшем испу́ге (Dost.).

The comparative sense is preserved in поздне́йший 'later, subsequent' and дальне́йший (в дальне́йшем).

The intensive prefix прѣ- (not a true superlative) is, of course, always a Slavonicism (4.62 (*d*)): прѣвели́кий 'very great' (cf. прѣмудрость), прекра́сный (fully acclimatized in Russian); cf. Lat. *permagnus,* Gk. περιπληθής.

For the predicative and adverbial superlative Russian uses

---

[58] Dialects show a possibly parallel formation in на- (never literary): стро́го-на́строго 'very strictly'; Ukr. and WhR. still have най-.

(probably has always used) comp. + всех (people) or всего́ (things), already attested in OCS (*mĭnjii vĭsěхŭ* 'least (of all)'): он лу́чше всех, э́то лу́чше всего́.

The Pronoun

PERSONAL PRONOUNS

First and Second Persons and Reflexive

Table X gives the early forms.

54   *Commentary to Table X*

1. *1st pers. sg. nom.* Both язъ (ꙗзъ) and я (ꙗ)[59] are found from the early texts, side by side with ChSl. азъ, e.g. in Mstislav's Deed of Gift (text no. 12):

> се азъ мьстиславъ . . . (formal opening)
> а ꙗзъ далъ роукою своею . . .
> а се ꙗ всеволодъ . . .

Се азъ as a legal formula continued to be used for many centuries. Muscovite делово́й язы́к helped to keep яз alive even into the 17th c. (it is still common in more or less colloquial texts of the 15th–16th c.), perhaps as a compromise between аз and я.

In the 17th c. Avvakúm can still make stylistic play with аз: он . . . начал мне говорить: поп ты, или роспоп? И аз отвещал: аз есмь Аввакум протопоп . . .

55   2. *Sg. acc.* The forms мене, etc., are replaced by меня́, etc. (мене + мя?)[60] during the 15th–16th c.; they appear to be of N. dial. origin. The genitives conform to this (acc. мене, etc., must in fact be gen. forms extended to the personal animate acc. in CSl. times). The enclitic forms мя (мѧ), etc., are syntactically unstressed (whereas мене, etc., are emphatic) and freely used as verbal objects:

> пустилъ же мя а иную поялъ (*NBG*, no. 9, *c.*1100)

and after prepositions:

> . . . ихъ же послахомъ по тя (*RPC s.a.* 945) 'whom I sent to fetch you'; покоривше я под ся (*RPC s.a.* 898) 'having brought them under his rule'.

---

[59] Most Slav languages have alternating *jaz/ja* in the early stages, until the allegro form becomes standard.

[60] Some consider the analogy of animate *jo*-stems more important, e.g. коня́.

TABLE X. Pronouns of the First and Second Persons

Person	Early East Slav			OCS (Church Slavonic)		
	First	Second	Reflexive	First	Second	Reflexive
Sg. N(V)	язъ ог я	ты	—	*azŭ*	*ty*	—
A	мене, мя	тебе, тя	себе, ся	*(mene), mę*	*(tebe), tę*	*(sebe), sę*
G	мене	тебе	себе	*mene*	*tebe*	*sebe*
L	мънѣ	тобѣ	собѣ	*mĭně*	*tebě*	*sebě*
D	мънѣ, ми	тобѣ, ти	собѣ, си	*mĭně, mi*	*tebě, ti*	*sebě, si*
I	мъноюо	тобою	собою	*mŭnojǫ*	*tobojǫ*	*sobojǫ*
Du. N	вѣ	ва		*vě*	*va*	
A	на	ва	[no dual]	*na, ny*	*va, vy*	[no dual]
GL	наю	ваю		*naju*	*vaju*	
DI	нама	вама		*nama, na*	*vama, va*	
Pl. N(V)	мы	вы		*my*	*vy*	
A	насъ, ны	васъ, вы	[no plural]	*nasŭ, ny*	*vasŭ, vy*	[no plural]
G	насъ	васъ		*nasŭ*	*vasŭ*	
L	насъ	васъ		*nasŭ*	*vasŭ*	
D	намъ, ны	вамъ, вы		*namŭ, ny*	*vamŭ, vy*	
I	нами	вами		*nami*	*vami*	

The *second forms* throughout the Table are enclitic only.

123

By the beginning of the 16th c. the enclitics had become rare or archaic (or ChSl.), except for ся with its special function in the verb (§133 below).

56 3. *Sg. dat./loc.* Though мьнѣ is correct, мънѣ predominates in early ESl., following instr. мъною. In any case the pretonic jers disappear early. A form менѣ, paralleled elsewhere in Slav, occurs sporadically in dialects but is likely to be a recent analogical formation to меня.

Тобѣ, собѣ > тебѣ, себѣ in the 14th–15th c. under the influence of AG тебе and no doubt also of ChSl. *tebě/sebě*. Many dialects, in both N. and S. Russia (also Ukr. and WhR.) have retained тобе/ собе; conversely тобе/тобя were widely used as AG (especially in Moscow) in the period c.1400–1650, but then disappear from standard usage.[61]

In regions where e and ѣ were early conflated (Table XVII (5)) the final vowel of AGLD fluctuates.

57 4. *Sg. dat.* ми, ти, си are unstressed enclitics, but unlike мя, etc., never appear after prepositions. They did not survive the 15th c. in the living language; си was always rather rare.[62] Certain ChSl. clichés last longer, e.g. как ми Бог поможет (16th c.).

5. The *dual* forms disappear early outside ChSl. usage: аще на пустити . . . аще ли наю погубиши (*RPC s.a.* 1071).

58 6. *Pl. acc./dat.* The enclitic forms ны, вы disappear *pari passu* with those of the sg., perhaps rather earlier. Early examples: (acc.) хочу на вы ити (*RPC s.a.* 964); послю по вы 'I shall send for you' (ibid. 945); (dat.) кто ны поможеть (ibid. 971).

7. *Pl. loc.* Насъ, васъ are the *only forms* to preserve the original loc. ending -*sŭ*, changed in the fem. *ā*- and *jā*-stems to -ахъ/-яхъ by analogy with the phonetically correct -ъхъ, -ьхъ, -ѣхъ < -*ŭsŭ*, -*ĭsŭ*, -*oisŭ* (the 'iurk' rule: after these four sounds s > x in CSl.).

8. *Pl. 2nd pers.* Вы becomes the formula of politeness only in the 18th c. under French influence (5.32 *ad fin.*). There are some examples from the later 17th c.: Поистине, дядюшка, прельщени есте вы (Житие боярыни Морозовой . . ., 7. 32).

---

[61] От тобе, у собе, etc. are still sparingly attested in dialect. Тобя/собя also occur as AG.

[62] It survives in the Slavonicism восвояси 'homewards' (now only used humorously). Short forms мя, etc., dat. ми or ме, etc., occur here and there in dialect but are surely recent allegro forms: this is fairly clear in я те дам! 'I'll give you what for!'

TABLE XI Pronoun of the Third Person

		Early ESl.			OCS (ChSl.)		
		m.	n.	f.	m.	n.	f.
Sg.	N	—	—	—	i (jĭ)[1]	je[1]	ja[1]
	A	и, его	е	ю	i (jĭ)	je	jǫ
	G	его	его	еѣ	jego	jego	jeję
	L	(н)емь	(н)емь	(н)еи (ей)	jemĭ	jemĭ	jei
	D	ему	ему	еи (ей)	jemu	jemu	jei
	I	имь	имь	ею	imĭ	imĭ	jejǫ
Du.	NA	я	и	и	ja	i (ji)	i (ji)
	GL		ею			jeju	
	DI		има			ima	
Pl.	N	—	—	—	i (ji)[1]	ja[1]	ję[1]
	A	ѣ	я	ѣ	ję	ja	ję
	G		ихъ			ixŭ	
	L		(н)ихъ			ixŭ	
	D		имъ			imŭ	
	I		ими			imi	

[1] As nominatives only in the relative pronoun иже (4.12).

Pronoun of the Third Person

Commentary to Table XI

59   1. This anaphoric pronoun lost its *nominatives* from the beginning of the ESl. tradition in favour of the short forms of the demonstrative оный (§61 below): онъ, онó, онá; они́ (онѣ). The nominatives are in any case sparingly used down to the 15th c., the verbal form sufficing unless emphasis was required. Strict reference to the *last* noun of the right gender (as now) does not apply before the 15th c.

The *accusatives*, however, remained in use as unstressed enclitics (cf. мя, etc., above) but finally yield to the AG его, его, еѣ; ихъ, including the *neuter*, both sg. and pl. (the only instance of acc. = gen. outside animates). Examples:

sg. masc. acc.: то ему за платежь оже и били
          то оному вести и по кунамъ   } и = 'him'
but also: оже ли не будеть кто его мьстя (all *RP*, 1282)
fem. acc.: и вда ю за Ярополка (*RPC s.a.* 977). So still кто коли на ню
   возрить (1393)

neut. acc.: велѣлъ есмь бити въ не (1130) (*vŭ-n-je*)

but: понесеть его домовь (1230)

pl. masc. acc.: покоривше я под ся (*RPC s.a.* 898; ChSl.).

2. The sg. fem. gen. еѣ > ее́ > её. The pronunciation ее́ still exists in some dialects.

The sg. LI lose the final palatalization as in nouns and adjectives (6.11): modern нём, им.

60   3. *Epenthetic* н-. This arose from the prepositions **sŭn* (instr.),[63] **kŭn* (dat.), and **wŭn* (acc. and loc.) > съ, къ, въ. Normal syllabication of the word-group (the preposition being proclitic) caused transference of the -*n* to the pronoun: **wŭn jemĭ* (*wŭ/nje/mĭ*) > въ немь. This procedure was early (partly in CSl.) generalized to *all* true prepositions, to the gen., and partly to the prepositions used as verbal prefixes. After prepositions the old sg. acc. will therefore appear as нь (*njĭ*), e.g.

то 40 гр[и]в[е]нъ положити за нь (*RP,* art.1).

With the obsolescence of the enclitics such forms remain only in cpds. such as зане́(же) 'since', поне́же 'inasmuch as' (both neut. e).[64]

In the case of 'impure' prepositions the н- is hardly obligatory before the 19th c.: межю ими (*RPC s.a.* 996), now ме́жду ни́ми; мимо его > ми́мо него́; по́сле него́. Vulgarly the н- is attached also in other syntactical contexts: в по́льзу неё, гора́здо ши́ре него́.[65]

In free position (not bound to a preposition) forms with epenthetic н- are fairly widespread in dialect, e.g. dat. нёму (N. dial.).

---

[63] **sŭn* is seen in the alternative form *sǫ-* (before *consonants*), e.g. *sǫsědŭ* 'neighbour' > сусе́д, common in early ESl. and elsewhere but now only dialectal in Russian (standard сосед < *sŭ-sědŭ*).

[64] They are better preserved in Pol., e.g. *zań, nań, odeń,* etc., which, however, are now used also in reference to *plurals*.

[65] Examples from other contexts: поднима́ть (usual) but also подыма́ть; приня́ть, отня́ть (simple verb яти obsolete: не яша ся по то 'they would not agree to do so' (*Novg. Chr., s.a.* 1215)); Slavonicism предприня́ть but предприя́тие 'undertaking'. A simple verb няти was sometimes extracted from these dominant forms.

Various mistakes naturally occur: ядро́ > *vŭ-n-ědra* (n. 95 below), whence a new noun не́дра pl.; раз-ори́ть 'destroy' but *sŭn-oriti* > deprefixed **noriti* > ронити (R. урони́ть, роня́ть 'let fall'). Cf. Eng. *an adder* < *a nadder* (Ger. *Natter*), *an orange* < *a *norange* (Pers. *naranj*).

61   ESl. inherited a three-member system corresponding to the three persons:

> сь, се, си (ся): 'this' (near me; Lat. *hic*);
> тъ, то, та: 'that' (near you; Lat. *iste*);
> онъ, оно, она: 'that' (distant; Lat. *ille*).

This system is still active in Русская Правда (1282; original 11th c.):

> и сему платити что у него погыбло;
> и проторъ тому же платити;
> а что с нимь погыбло, а того ему желѣти, а оному желѣти своихъ кунъ.

For the forms see Table XII.

As a demonstrative онъ dropped out of its special function, the short nominatives becoming 3rd pers. pronouns (§59 above), the long forms о́ный, etc., remaining as Slavonicisms and in officialese down to the 19th c. Relics are found in a few obsolescent phrases: наме́дни 'the other day' (< loc. ономь дне), об он пол 'on the far side' (cf. и ста Володимеръ об онъ полъ города, *RPC s.a.* 988); во вре́мя о́но 'in days of yore' (Slavonicism; original sense (in the Gospels) 'in those days'). A binary system sufficed in living speech.

With the fall of the jers, сь, тъ are reinforced either as сей, той or as reduplicated сесь, тотъ (< сьсь, тътъ). These were regional solutions, with a considerable variety of forms: masc. sg. nom. той, тый, or тей (after сей), fem. sg. NA тая, тую or та, ту; neut. sg. NA тое or то; masc. pl. nom. тии; *et sim.*:

> пр[о] сеи миръ (Smolensk, 1229);
> тая правда оузяти роусиноу (Smolensk, 1229) (side by side with такова правда, такоу правдоу);
> тотъ Иволтъ *and* тей Иволтъ (Pskov, *c.*1464);
> тое пиво и медъ поимали наши люди (Pskov, *c.*1464).

Forms of той and тот are still used more or less indifferently by Pososhkóv (*c.*1724).

Сесь was always rarer than сей. The word eventually became bookish (officialese or Slavonicism), remaining in a few set phrases: се азъ (§54 above); сего́дня 'today'; сейча́с 'at once'; до сих пор 'up till now'; ни то ни сё 'neither';[66] сию́ мину́ту 'at once' (bookish); and dial. днесь 'today' (< дьнь-сь).[67]

---

[66] Cf. там и сям 'here and there'; так и сяк 'thus and thus'.
[67] Also others on this model: вчера́сь, лони́сь 'last year'.

TABLE XII. Demonstrative Pronouns

	East Slav Masc.	East Slav Neut.	East Slav Fem.	Church Slavonic Masc.	Church Slavonic Neut.	Church Slavonic Fem.	East Slav Masc.	East Slav Neut.	East Slav Fem.
Sg. N	сь, сесь (сей)	се > сё	ся	sĭ	se > sije	si > sija	тъ, тот (той)	то	та
A	N or G	се > сё	сю	sĭ	se	sijǫ	N or G	то	ту
G	сего		сеѣ > сей	sego		seję	того		тоѣ > той
L	сём		сей	semĭ		sei	том(ъ)		той
D	сему́		сей	semu		sei	тому́		той
I	сим		сею > сей	simĭ		sejǫ	тѣм(ъ) (тем)		тою > той
Pl. N	си	ся	сѣ	sí, sii	si(ja)	siję	ти > те	та > те	ты > те
A	сѣ	ся	сѣ	siję	si(ja)	siję	ты > те	та > те	ты > те
G	сихъ			sixŭ			тѣхъ > тех		
L	сихъ			sixŭ			тѣхъ > тех		
D	симъ			simŭ			тѣмъ > тем		
I	сими			simi			тѣми > тѣми		

Notes

1. To the *soft* type of declension belong the possessives мой, etc. (§65 below). To the *hard* type belong онъ, овъ, инъ, the group of какъ, etc. (with some variation in the oblique pl. cases). *Mixed* are весь 'all' (*vіsĭ't*): sg. hard (and masc./neut. sg. instr. *vіsěmі*); and самъ 'self': sg. hard, pl. soft (and sg. instr. самím).

2. Note that the common Muscovite phrase и того 'total' [itavó] produced by back-formation the *noun* итóг 'total', pronounced [itók, itóga], whence the verb подытóжить.

3. As with the adjectives gender distinctions disappeared relatively early in the pl., the NA being all conflated as тѣ (finally те), except in so far as an anim. AG was later required (и тѣхъ прия, *Novg. Chr.*, *s.a.* 1215). The form follows the oblique cases (cf. весь). Similarly, earlier pl. NA си, etc. > later uniform сѣ or си.

While both сей and той (тот) were alive, their respectively soft and hard declensions tended to react on one another: one finds pl. gen. сѣхъ after тѣхъ, тихъ after сихъ, etc.

Сей was replaced in the colloquial by этот (deictic prefix э-), of which there are sporadic examples from the 16th c. onwards: етотъ (1510); до етова году (1673); на етихъ указехъ (17th c.); parallel form ентово (1622). Despite their rarity it is clear that этот must have been accepted in good Moscow speech by the end of the 16th c.: Mark Ridley, the Tsar's physician, gives *c.*1599 its declension side by side with that of literary сей (*se, sea, see*), viz.:

sg.	*etot, eta, eto*	pl.	*eti*
	etovo (etogo)		*etich*
	etomu		*etemi*
	fem. acc. *etu*		

He also quotes *etako*.[68] (SCr. has the parallel formations *èvo* = *voici, èto* = *voilà, èno* (distant), but only as particles.)

The acceptance of этот as the literary norm belongs to the 18th c. While тот retained its pronominal forms тех, etc., этот now makes этих, etc., perhaps under the influence of сихъ, etc., which it replaced.

INTERROGATIVE PRONOUNS

62   There is no distinction of gender, only of animate/inanimate. The stem is **kŭ-/čĭ-* (< IE *kʷo-/kʷi-*). In the paradigms which follow, superior letters refer to the corresponding paragraphs of notes below.

N	къ-то[a] (> кто)[c]	чь-то[a] (что)[c]
A	кого[b]	чьто (что)
G	кого[b]	чего (чесо,[e] чесо́го)
L	комь (> ком)	чемь (чесо́мь) (> чём)
D	кому́	чему́ (чесо́му)
I	цѣмь (> кем)[d]	чимь (> чем)[d] [69]

[68] Dial. этак, этакий, эдакий, etc. The prefix was at first loosely joined; a preposition might intervene: и я с е с тѣм луком поѣду (1590s). Dialects also show эвтот, эстот, энтот, but usually with the appropriate preposition (в эфто, с эстим, на энтот). All forms but этот have remained subliterary (occasional in informal letters: так в евтом дѣлѣ и поступаю, L. Naryshkin to Peter the Great).

[69] An older instr. чи, Pol. *czy* (introducing a question), did not survive as such.

Notes

(*a*) The strengthening suffix -то is almost but not quite universal: OCS has normally ničĭtože 'nothing' but also ničĭže, whence two (ChSl.) verbs уничтожить 'annihilate' and уничижать 'disparage'. So also Pol. *zacz* < *za-čĭ and čakavic SCr. *ča* < *čĭ*.

(*b*) AG кого is regular and universal from CSl. onwards.

(*c*) Кътo and чьтo are among the earliest words to show loss of pretonic jer (2.13).

(*d*) Цѣмь early restores the velar as кѣмь > кем; чимь follows кѣм(ь) as чѣм(ь) from the 14th c.

(*e*) Чесо (properly чьсо) is a unique survival in CSl. of a well-attested IE gen. in -*s*-. This and the late analogical forms чесого, чесому, чесомь must be considered Slavonicisms in ESl.[70]

(*f*) Derivatives are of the types: никто́ 'nobody' (ChSl. usually никтоже); нѣкто 'a certain person'; кто́-то 'a certain person, someone'; кто́-нибудь 'someone, anyone'[71] (generalizing ни; 4.30); кто́-либо 'anyone' (earlier -любо: аже пьрьстъ оутьнеть кыи-любо, *RP*, art. 23).

(*g*) Кто, что from early times stand for indefinites in conditional clauses: аже кто кого ударить батогомь (*RP*, art. 23); оу кого ся избиеть оучанъ (1229); оже ли не боудеть кто его мьстя (*RP*, *ad init.*) ('if anyone', 'if anyone's', 'if no one . . .').

(*h*) Кто almost always takes sg. agreement but a pl. is occasionally necessary: кто же должны́ быть ца́рскими сове́тниками?

(*i*) At the colloquial level ничего́ is used as subject as well as object: ничего́ не меша́ет.

63   INTERROGATIVE ADJECTIVES

The simple adj. from the interrogative stem *kŭ-jĭ > кыи/кой, ко́е, ка́я 'what, which?'[72] is not rare in ChSl. and remained in делово́й язы́к as a *relative* (4.16); the neuter кое was widely used therein as a *conjunction* (потому кое (1576) = потому что). Cpds. of кой retained a certain currency, especially никой: а со мною нѣт ничего, никея книги (Af. Nik., 15th c.); modern ни в ко́ем слу́чае 'on no account'; не́кий (нѣкий, a Slavonicism) 'a certain' (не́кий Ива́нов); and petrified in the cpds. кое-кто́ (кой-кто́) 'a

---

[70] Чьсо is better preserved in Pol. NA *co* < gen. *czso*.

[71] -то indicates ignorance but *no choice* (кто́-то идёт по у́лице), -нибудь (and more literary -либо) *choice* (пошли́те кого́-нибудь).

[72] Best preserved as an *interrogative* in SSl.: SCr. *kòjī*, Blg. кой.

few people', кое-что 'this and that', кое-где 'here and there', кое-
как 'somehow or other'. A few other expressions such as на кой
чёрт 'what the devil!' belong to country speech. It appears also to
be concealed as a short neut. pl. in покамест < *po ka mesta =
'as far as which places (times)'.

64 RELATIVE PRONOUNS

For the use and chronology of кто, что, который, etc. in this
function see 4.12 ff.

As in many languages, the true relative series in *j*- was lost in
the vernacular quite early and replaced by the corresponding
interrogatives in *k*-; the relative етеръ is unknown in ESl. but
occurs in OCS (ChSl.), rarely as a relative, usually in an evolved
sense 'a certain' (= нѣкий), e.g. in *Ostr.*; cf. *RPC s.a.* 1074: аще
который братъ въ етеро прегрѣшенье впадаше . . . ('fell into
any sin'); аще братъ етеръ выидяше из манастыря . . . ('if any
brother . . .' = аще который братъ).

The same applies to когда, какъ (како), колико (> сколько),
and где, which replace егда, яко, елико, and иде(же) (i.e. *jĭde*).
All these became components of ChSl. style at an early date,
though егда remains fairly frequent in less learned texts (like
ChSl. аще). See Table XIII. The only living cpd. of который is
некоторый (нѣ-) 'some, certain'; никоторый has been replaced
by никакой (никоторымъ временемъ его не отстати (1435)).

65 POSSESSIVE ADJECTIVES

Мой, etc., наш (early ESl. нашь), etc., and чей 'whose' (which
is either interrogative or relative[73]) decline according to the 'soft'
variants (Table XII): sg. gen. моего, чьего, etc.; pl. gen. моих,
чьих, etc. Their history calls for no special comment.[74] Свой 'one's
own' has always referred to all persons and numbers as subject.
There may be no expressed subject in more popular usage: своя
рубашка ближе к телу = 'blood is thicker than water'.

In OCS (ChSl.) and literary Russian the possessives of the *3rd
person* are taken from the pronoun: его, её, их книга (immediately
before or after the noun). So ChSl. самому ему и подружию его

---

[73] Чья это книга? 'Whose book is this?' Сосед, чья собака убежала 'the
neighbour whose dog ran away'. Note also neg. ничей 'nobody's'; in games в
ничью = 'a draw' (sc. сторону, партию).

[74] There is a special stress по-моему, etc., 'in my opinion' (dat. моему), perhaps
after по-нашему.

Феофанѣ и чадомъ ею (dual gen.) (*Ostr.*, colophon). Slavonicized orthography distinguished possessive ея from the fem. acc. pronoun ee down to 1917.

The tendency to create adjectives analogical to мой, etc., is widespread (particularly in SSl.)[75] but has been rejected by literary Russian. Such forms as еговый 'his', ейный 'her', ихний 'their' (also ихий, иховый) have clearly long existed in popular speech, especially N. dialects, and may be found in texts of the 16th–17th c. There is an exceptional example in *Stoglav* (1551), §101: еговымъ небрежениемъ. An example from popular language: а буде коны [sic] ихны вамъ надобѣ на обмено [= обменъ] (1578).

The *dative of possession* is used in OCS (ChSl.) and is often to be accounted a Slavonicism in Russian: отецъ ми бысть священникъ Петръ (followed by отецъ мой); имя ей Анастасия (Avvakúm). See 4.47.

VARIOUS

66   (i) Identity is shown by adding же: тот же 'the same' (strengthened тот же самый); similarly тоже, также 'also, likewise'.

(ii) Сам(ъ), само, сама, pl. сами 'self' and the adjective самый 'same, very'. The declension of сам is 'mixed' (Table XII, n. 1): sg. gen. самого (adj. самого), but the fem. sg. acc. is either саму or newer самоё (by rhyme with её).

(iii) Другой 'other' and the more learned иной are pure adjectives. The reciprocal relation is shown by друг друга, instr. друг с другом *et sim.* (singular forms only), with друг invariable (i.e. no gender distinctions). Друг is here clearly the noun.

(iv) Каждый 'each', 'every' derives from къ-жьдо with invariable suffix (masc./neut. кожьдо, fem. кажьдо, masc. sg. gen. когожьдо[76]). There is an occasional ChSl. variant къжьде, perhaps the original form (the suffix is obscure). The declension was, as in many numerals, early transferred to the end of the word, the first pronominal element petrifying as ка- (fem. or analogy of ка-к?). Modern forms are found from the 14th–15th c.: каждому (1398).

(v) Весь 'all' (stem *vĭs'-*) has mixed declension (Table XII, n. 1). Soft oblique forms всих, etc., also occur. The pl. nom. *vĭsi, vĭsja, vĭsě* (ChSl. *vĭsę*) is replaced by genderless в(ь)сѣ by the 16th c.

---

[75] e.g. SCr. *njègov, njȉhov, njèn.*
[76] По голуби [dat.] комуждо 'one pigeon each' (*RPC s.a.* 945).

67   No Slav language except Bulgarian and Macedonian has developed a definite article (один acts as an indefinite one when required). The source of the Blg. innovation (a 'Balkanism' triggered by the presence of an article in Greek, Albanian, and Balkan Romance) can be seen in OCS in the frequent postposition of the demonstrative тъ (less often сь), which with the changes in the jers gives (late OCS) домотъ < домъ тъ 'that house, the house'. The same procedure, certainly unconnected with Balkan developments, turns up in ESl. in N. dialects: домот, рекатa, селото. It did not, however, reach the state of a fully systematized article, since declension nowhere completely broke down (though some confusion of cases is widespread; 6.22). The most typical N. dial. system is

> sg. N: -от (m.), -то (n.), -та (f.);
> sg. A; -от (m.), -то (n.), -ту (f.);
> pl. NA (all genders): -те, -ти, or -ты;
> all oblique cases: -то.

In the more rudimentary systems the affix is always -то.

Avvakúm, who came from the region of Nízhni Nóvgorod and therefore spoke a Vladímir–Vólga dialect, occasionally introduces these forms into the most colloquial parts of his narrative, but quite sporadically and without apparent stylistic intention: Увы мнѣ! Какъ дощеник-отъ в воду-ту не погрязъ со мною? Стало у меня в тѣ поры кости-те щемить и жилы-тѣ тянуть, и сердце зашлось, да и умирать сталъ.

This feature has never entered the spoken or literary standard.

ADVERBS

68   Adverbs are of three main kinds:

1. Basic adverbs of time and space with suffixes *-de, -da,* etc. (See Table XIII).

2. Petrified case-forms of nouns and adjectives, with or without a preposition: see §49 (*b*) above.

Here also дóма 'at home' and вчерá 'yesterday' which may derive from an obsolete sg. instr. or ablative (= gen.).

Forms in the instr. case (all numbers) *without* preposition are particularly numerous, some with differentiating stress: sg. верхóм 'on horseback', бегóм 'at a run', кругóм 'around' (*noun* instr.

вéрхом, бéгом, крýгом); дáром 'in vain'; целикóм 'wholly'; днём 'by day'; нóчью 'at night'; дорóгой 'on the way'; чáстью 'partly'; du. весьмá 'very' and some others, all ChSl.; pl. вельмú 'very', also ChSl. The type in -ы (OCS *maly, pravy*) has not survived in Russian, except for -ски (see below). Note also the popular intensive type давны́м-давнó 'long ago'.

3. Neut. short adjectives—the general living type. CSl. (OCS) used both the neut. sg. acc. *dobro* and loc. (?in some cases instr.) *dobrě*.[77] WSl. has favoured the loc., ESl. the acc., but the loc. is present also in many dialects, at least from a restricted number of adjectives. In early texts forms in -ѣ are usually Slavonicisms, e.g. добрѣ сътворѧ (*NBG*, no. 9, *c.*1200), reproducing a Byzantine epistolary formula (the language is otherwise colloquial). ChSl. tended to enlarge the number of forms in -ѣ.

Adverbs in -o sometimes preserve the original stress while the neut. predicative has an analogical one: adv. мáло, pred. малó (after малá).

69　　(*a*) Adjectives in -ский form an adverb in -ски (presumably pl. instr.) either alone or with prefixed по-: скотьски 'in a bestial manner' (*RPC, ad init.*), дрýжески 'in a friendly manner', мертвéцки пьян 'dead drunk'. The type по-рус(ь)ски would appear to have arisen by a crossing of рус(ь)ски with the dat. formula по-рус(ь)скому; cf. по-нóвому 'in a new way', по-рáзному 'in different ways'.

(*b*) The colloquial type стоймя́ 'upright', плашмя́ 'flat', лежмя́ (= лёжа) must be founded on the du. instr. -ма with a similar development to двѣма > двумя́ (§72 below).

(*c*) An obsolete CSl. sg. loc. in -ĭ is to be traced in such forms as опя́ть 'backwards' > 'again'; прочь (cf. noun прок); (ChSl.) впредь; вдóволь 'enough'; but the formation is not always clear; prep. + fem. noun is certainly commoner, e.g. acc. внутрь (loc. внутрú), поóдаль 'further off', нáземь, вплоть (до), нáискось 'on a slant'.

(*d*) Adverbs and similar auxiliary words are particularly liable to abbreviation in speech: лише > лишь, сквозѣ > сквозь (preposition); similarly нѣту > нет (§90 below), тамо > там, како

---

[77] Not to be confused with the type in -*je*, already obsolescent in OCS: *tače* (= *tako*), *drevlje, prěžde, daleče* (= *daleko*), *pače* (cf. *paky*), and probably *ješte* (etymology uncertain). OCS forms in -*ě* are few: *dobrě, ljutě, mǫdrě, pravě.*

> как. Some of the reductions are recorded from the 14th c. The ordinary phonetic laws do not apply. Посл is probably from *poslědĭ* (type (*c*) above).

(*e*) Тóже and earlier тáже[78] 'also' appear to rest on CSl. *tăd-je* (neut. sg. acc.) and *tō-ge* (neut. sg. instr.) respectively. In other words, in ESl. there has been confusion of two suffixes—the же of identity and an intensive же < *ge* (cf. Gk. γε) which probably also provided the -g- of *ko-g-da, ko-go, et sim*.

(*f*) *Miscellaneous formations*. Of verbal origin are: ведь < pres. sg. 1 вѣдѣ (§93 below) 'I know', чуть 'scarcely' < inf. чути = чýять, and почти́ 'almost', imperat. sg. 2 of почéсть 'reckon' (почти́ сто = 'count as being 100').

The various pronominal and adverbial series are resumed in Table XIII.

70 *Commentary to Table XIII*

1. Col. 7 is a more learned synonym of col. 8.
2. Col. 13: see 4.3 (4).
3. Сиць 'of this kind'; cf. Avvakúm сице начáло 'beginning as follows'.
4. Я́ко: various senses, including conjunction (4.20 *ad fin*.) and adverb 'approximately' (бѣ яко полдень).
5. Only in the phrase так и сяк (cf. там и сям); сяков- also occurs: о сяковых бо Давыдъ глаголаше (*RPC s.a.* 969).
6. Russian has muddled *inako* 'otherwise' with *inače* 'in one way'. Other formations of the latter type are ChSl.: *tače, obače* ('in both ways' > 'however').
7. The series камо originally implied *motion* (= куда́);[79] сѣмо/ сям and там(о) have become *static* and камо has disappeared. (По)всюду has also become *static*. Камо, тамо = 'whither, thither' are to be presumed in камь его хочеть, тамъ дѣжеть (1229).
8. Colloquially also the series докýда, досю́да, дотýда ('how far?').
9. ChSl. rare отнюдуже (e.g. *RPC s.a.* 1054) 'whence'.

---

[78] Ta 'and then' as a conjunction may belong here. It is frequent in the colloquial portion of Vladímir Monomákh's *Admonition* (text no. 9) and survives in Ukr.

[79] The type куда́ originally implied 'by what way?' The final vowel was -*u* (CSl. *kǫdu*), which survives in всю́ду. The same -мо of motion is seen in ми́мо 'past' and пря́мо < *prě-mo* (2.10). SCr. preserves *òvamo, ònamo* = 'hither, thither' and *òvudā, ònudā* = 'this way, that way'.

TABLE XIII. Conspectus of Pronominal and Adverbial Series

	Interrogative	Relative	Demonstrative			Negative
	1	2	3	4	5	6
who?	кто	[иже]	(сей) этот (§61 above)	тот	(онъ, оный) (§61 above)	никто
what?	что	[еже] (4.12)	это	то		ничто
what kind of?	какой (каковой)	[етер] (§64 above)	[сиць, сицев][3]	такой (таковой)		никакой (никоторый)
which of a series?	который					
whose?	чей	чей		(possessive pronouns)		ничей
what?	(кой) (§63 above)					(никой)
how?	как(о)	[яко][4]	(сяк)[5]	так(о)		никак
where?	где (камо)[7]	где [идеже][14]	здесь (*sí-de-sí)	там(о)	ту(т)	нигде
whither?	куда (куды) (камо)[7]	[еда] [ямо]	сюда (сям) [сьмо]	туда (туды)		никуда
whence?	откуда[8]	(See §70 (9))	отсюда	оттуда		ниоткуда
when?	когда	[егда]	теперь[10]	тогда	[оногда]	никогда
how much?	(колико) сколько[11,13]	(елико)	(селико)	(только), столько[11]		нисколько 'not at all'
why? (reason)	почему, отчего	(понеже) (занеже)	поэтому	потому, оттого (что)		
why? (purpose)	зачём				затём (чтобы)	

| | 7[1] | Indefinite | | | Generalizing | Differentiating (isolating) | Negative (impossibility) |
		8[12]	9[12]	10[12]	11	12	13[2]
who?	[нѣкто]	ктó-то	ктó-нибудь/либо	кое-ктó	кáждый 'each' (§66 (iv) above)		нéкого, etc.
what?	[нѣчто]	чтó-то	чтó-нибудь/либо	кое-чтó	(do.)		нéчему, etc.
what kind of?		какóй-то	какóй-нибудь/либо	кое-какóй	вся́кий 'every kind of'		
which of a series?	нѣкоторый '(a) certain, some'					инóй 'other'	
whose?		чéй-то	чéй-нибудь/либо				
what?	[нѣкий] 'a certain'						
how?		кáк-то	кáк-нибудь/либо	кое-кáк	[вся́чески] 'in every way'	инáче[5] 'otherwise'	
where?	(нѣгде)	гдѣ-то	гдѣ-нибудь/либо	кое-гдѣ	вездѣ		нéгде
whither?	(нѣкуда)	кудá-то	кудá-нибудь/либо		(по)всю́ду[7] 'everywhere'		нéкуда[15]
whence?		откýда-то	откýда-нибудь/либо		отовсю́ду 'from all directions'		нéоткуда
when?	нѣкогда	когдá-то	когдá-нибудь/либо	кое-когдá	всегдá	иногдá	нéкогда
how much?	нѣсколько 'some'		скóлько-нибудь 'to any degree'				
why? (reason)		почемý-то	(почемý-нибудь)				нéчему
why? (purpose)							нéзачем

The forms in square brackets are to be considered *Slavonicisms*, those in parentheses antiquated or unusual in modern standard Russian. Superior figures refer to numbered paragraphs of commentary in §70.

137

10. Earliest form то-перво[80] (e.g. *RPC s.a.* 988); much variation in dialect. There is no evidence for *сегда in ESl.

11. Cpds. насколько/настолько 'to what extent' and поскольку (поелику ChSl.) 'inasmuch as'.

12. The differences between cols. 7, 8, 9, and 10 are given in §62 (*f*).

13. The adj. коликъ is the normal early form. The sg. loc. of the root-word *kolĭ* (*ĭ*-stem adj.) has survived in subliterary коли 'if, when'; the sg. gen. in доколѣ (still used by 18th c. poets). Коль, сколь, and кольми are high literary Slavonicisms. The reduction of the vowel and addition of the prefix of approximation (с + acc. 'about') take place in the 15th–16th c. The relative *jelĭ* is not attested in ESl.; there are only the ChSl. cpds. *do-n-eléže* 'until' and *jelě* (> éле) 'hardly, scarcely', now well acclimatized in colloquial (он éле жив; éле-éле 'barely'). Derivatives of *selĭ* and *tolĭ* are also virtually disused: *ot(ŭ)tolě, dotolě*; *ot(ŭ)selě(va), doselě(va)*.

14. ChSl. *ideže* has the cpd. *do-n-ĭdeže* > дондéже 'as long as'.

15. Also нéкамо: уже намъ нѣкамо ся дѣти (*RPC s.a.* 917). Long extinct.

Numerals

71 *Unity*

ESl. одинъ, OCS (ChSl.) *jedinŭ*, is a cpd. of **jed-ĭ* (cf. OCS *jed(ŭ)va*, R. dial. одвá) and the true numeral ин- (cf. инóй 'other', инок 'monk', инорóг 'unicorn'), corresponding to Lat. *ūnus* < **oin-os*. In declension the stem varies between один- and одьн-; the latter was generalized (одногó, etc.). It was no doubt a colloquial allegro form since the same variation is found in OCS (standard *jedinago*, etc., later *Supr.*, etc., *jedĭna, jednojǫ, et sim.*). The modern pl. declension has been attracted to the 'soft' pronouns: одни, одних, etc. The pl. is used: (i) with *pluralia tantum*, одни часы 'a single watch'; hence 'only': в одних трýсиках parallel to в однóй рубáшке 'in nothing but a shirt'; (ii) in the alternatives одни . . . другие 'some . . . others'; (iii) as an adj. 'alone' (extension of (i)): пастухи были не одни. All words in ед- are Slavonicisms, e.g. единица 'unit', единственный 'sole', as opposed to

---

[80] Already present in later OCS *toprĭvo/toprŭvo* (in *Supr.*) and current also in WSl. (Cz. *teprv*, Pol. *dopiero*). Теперь takes over from ныне in the 16th–17th c.

R. одино́чество 'solitude', одина́ково 'alike' (мне всё одина́ково 'it's all the same to me'), etc. (1.29).

72 *Two*

Dual declension:

	m.	*n.*	*f.*
NA	дъва	дъвѣ	дъвѣ
GL	дъву, дъвою		
DI	дъвѣма		

Notes

(i) The jer disappears early, being pretonic.

(ii) DI occasionally д(ъ)вома after the *o*-stem nouns.

(iii) GL д(ъ)ву is the commoner (and original). The form is more and more used for *any* oblique case, to which *plural* markers were eventually attached: dat. двум, GL двух. The process is only completed by the end of the 17th c.: the *Uloženie* of 1649 still uses gen. дву, loc. дву(х), dat. дву(м). An analogical двѣм(ъ) (after двѣма and perhaps тремъ) is also found more rarely. Двум is first recorded in the early 16th c.

(iv) Instr. двѣма survived into the 17th c. but had long been rivalled by двуми́ (after трьми́) and the compromise двума. A form двѣмя, with unclear -я, is recorded from the 15th c. (двѣмя поити нельзя, Af. Nik.) which with the stem дву- gives the modern standard двумя́, only established in the 18th c.

(v) To form compounds either the gen. дву (rarely двою) or (later) двух is used, e.g.:

двою́родный брат 'second cousin' (oldest type)
двуязы́чный 'bilingual' (ChSl.)
двугла́вый орёл 'double-headed eagle' (ChSl.)
двусмы́сленный 'ambiguous' (ChSl.)
двухдне́вный 'lasting two days' (newest type)
двухме́стный 'two-seater' (newest type)

(vi) The neut. NA early becomes д(ъ)ва except in двести (§79 below); the fem. form две has been retained.

(vii) О́ба 'both' originally followed дъва exactly, i.e. oblique cases обо́ю, обѣма, and the NA is still in agreement: masc./neut. о́ба, fem. о́бе. However, the oblique stem became predominantly обѣ- (gen. обѣю 1339) and there was further confusion with the forms of the adjectival обои (§84 below), leading to the variable forms gen. обѣих(ъ)/обо́их(ъ), dat. обѣим(ъ)/обо́им(ъ), etc.

(. . . что имъ къ суду об҄ѣимъ стать (Kot.) 'both of them must appear before the court'). The formalization of об҄о́их, etc., as masc./neut. and об҄е́их, etc., as fem. only was a more or less arbitrary decision of the early 19th c. (N. Grech, 1827).

73 *Three*

The declension was the pl. of an *ĭ*-stem noun:

	m.	*n.*	*f.*
N	трие[81]	три	три
A	три (later N or G)		
G	трии[82]		
L	трьхъ		
D	трьмъ		
I	трьми́		

Notes

(i) Like all such pl. nom. трие[83] is given up early in favour of три, thus removing gender entirely.

(ii) LD трьхъ, трьмъ evolve *regularly* to трёх, трём.

(iii) The theoretical gen. *трей never established itself in face of analogical трёх (after всех, двух, etc.).

(iv) Instr. (regular) треми́ and трема́ (after дв҄ѣма/двума) are used indifferently down to the 17th c. Тремя́, first recorded 1571 on the analogy of дв҄ѣмя́, eventually becomes standard.

(v) The further influence of два can be seen in a sporadic form such as GL тре́ю.

(vi) Cpds. are in (learned) тре- and (more recent) трёх-: треуго́льник 'triangle'; трёхме́сячный 'quarterly'.

74 *Four*

The declension was the plural of a consonant stem (§§20 ff. above):

	m.	*n.*	*f.*
N	четы́ре	четы́ри	четы́ри
A	четы́ри (later N or G)		
G	четыръ		
L	четырьхъ		
D	четырьмъ		
I	четырьми́		

[81] Representing *trĭje* (cf. путие, §18 above).
[82] Representing *trĭjĭ*.
[83] Ярославичи же трие (*RPC s.a.* 1067).

Notes

(i) Here the masc. четы́ре has prevailed for all genders.

(ii) The rest follows the evolution of три: GL четырёх, dat. четырём, instr. четырьмя́ (after considerable currency of DI четыр(ь)ма́).

(iii) An occasional instr. четырью is modelled on пятью.

(iv) Cpds. only in четырёх-; четырёхсторо́нний 'quadrilateral'.

Note on 2–4. The instr. двумя́, трьми́/трсми́, четырьми́ still exist in dialects. Conversely, some N. dialects have generalized the ending -мя of these numerals to all or most *pronouns* (всемя, темя, своимя, etc.).

75 *Five–Nine*

(i) These numerals were fem. *ĭ-stem nouns* in the sg. down to the 16th c.; see further 4.74 ff. The declension has remained that of an *ĭ*-stem with final stress: пяти́, пятью́. A distinction is made in the instr. between normal пятью́ and multiplicative пя́тью (пя́тью пять 'five times five').

(ii) Шесть often made oblique cases шти, as if from *шьсть (2.32).

(iii) The ESl. form of 'seven' is семь, as opposed to ChSl. седмь, and of 'eight' во́семь (influenced by семь), as opposed to ChSl. осмь. For the initial в- see 6.27 (1)(*a*).

76 *Ten*

Де́сять was originally a masc. consonant-stem *noun* in -*t*-, e.g. sg. GL десяте́, pl. nom. десяте́, gen. деся́тъ. At an early date it was assimilated to де́вять and thus confined to the sg. forms, except for the pl. gen. in cpds. (пять-деся́т 'fifty'; §78 below). The sg. loc. also survived for some time in the *teens* side by side with newer десяти́ (§77 below).

77 *Teens*

The structure три на десяте (loc.) 'three onto ten' is peculiar to Slav. At first treated as phrases (gen. одного на десяте *et sim.*), they were soon contracted in speech, certainly from the 14th c.; but examples are few since numerals were usually expressed by their alphabetical signs (Table II). In the early stages the second half was usually -надцати, finally -надцать after the pattern of the nominatives of 5–9. The first half was still either declined correctly or (more often) stood in the gen. as with the cpds. mentioned above (§§72–4):

gen. у двунадцати человѣкъ (1597)
     меньши осминадцати лѣтъ (1649)
dat. по пятинадцати рублевъ.

With final assimilation of the second half to nom. form the declension was transferred entirely to the end of the word and the first half reverted to nom. form, which had always been the case with один-. 'Twelve' has двена́дцать for no clear reason.

The final modern forms are not reached till the 17th c.

78 Decades

(i) Два́дцать 'twenty' is based on the du. два десяти and три́дцать 'thirty' on the pl. три(е) десяте, with the same assimilation to the type 5–9 as in the teens. Stages can be seen in треми десять (1284) and тридесяти (14th c.).

(ii) *Fifty–eighty*. These are cpds. with the pl. gen.: пять десятъ. Declension as a cpd. remained current: в семидесятъ судехъ; во штидесятъ верстахъ. Once again the second half was assimilated to the type 5–9, except in the nom., so that the modern standard has become:

NA   пятьдеся́т
GLD пяти́десяти́
I   пятью́десятью́

The further assimilation пяти́десятью́ is widespread in speech but subliterary.

(iii) *Forty*. The original formula четыре десяте (still used by most Slav languages) was early replaced by the colloquial Nóvgorod term со́рокъ, a standard bag in the fur trade containing forty skins;[84] cf. modern соро́чка 'caul, shirt'.[85] There is an early example in Русская Правда (not later than 1282, probably 11th c.): въ чьеи же вьрви голова лежить, то .п. [80] гр[иве]нъ; паки людинъ, то сорокъ гривенъ.

Со́рок was a normal *o*-stem noun:

[84] Furs continued to be sold in forties down to the 17th c.
[85] Though not unusual in special vocabularies (e.g. Eng. *brace* = 2, *score* = 20; Ger. *Schock* = 60 (a 'shock' was a pile of sixty sheaves)), such words rarely become the *sole* numerical expression.

три сороки белъ (1397);
пять сороков бѣлки (15th c.);
а послан тот сорок в Литву (1584).

It was gradually assimilated to the reduced declension of сто (§79 below), with all oblique cases сорока́ and the noun in the same case: въ сорока́ верста́хъ (17th c.). The dat. по сороку is still sparingly used in the distributive sense.

(iv) *Ninety.* Девять десятъ also appears to be only ChSl. in ESl. usage. As early as 1265 we find an ESl. form девеносто, and about a century later девяносто by assimilation to девять. It too assumed the reduced declension of сто. Its form is far from clear; the first half may be an *ordinal* девено-, suggesting a structural parallel to Goth. *niuntēhund.*

79 *Hundreds*

Сто (съто) was a normal neuter noun and so still in cpds.:

> du. д(ъ)вѣ с(ъ)тѣ > двѣсти '200'
> pl. nom. три, четыре ста '300', '400'
> pl. gen. пять сот (< сътъ) '500'.

In the cpds. there has been attraction to the same case in all oblique cases: gen. двухсо́т, dat. трёмста́м, loc. пяти́ста́х, etc.

However, when used in isolation, сто developed a simple form ста for all oblique cases. The full neut. declension was still common in the 17th c. По́ сту '100 each' is still possible as well as the more usual по́ ста.

80 *Thousand*

The fem. noun ты́сяча is an ex-p.p.a., as OCS тысѧшти/ тысашти (fem. sg. nom.) and the parallel Goth. *þūsundi* show. Reinterpreted as a noun it is always followed by the pl. gen. of the thing counted. An instr. ты́сячью, by assimilation to the type 5–9, may be used if ты́сяча is not qualified by another numeral. The pl. gen. is ты́сяч (incorrectly тысяче́й).

81 *Fractions*

1. There are three primary words:

½: пол(ъ) (masc. *ŭ*-stem, §14 above), later also полови́на;
⅓: треть (fem. *ĭ*-stem);
¼: че́тверть (fem. *ĭ*-stem; often contracted in early texts to четь).

Thereafter a suffix -ина was available. The type is now obsolete except for осьми́на and десяти́на which survived until recently as terms of measurement (осьми́на = ¼ *desjatína*; десяти́на = about 3 acres).

   2. Пол enters into composition in three ways:

     (*a*) По́лдень 'midday', gen. по́лдня or полу́дня.

     (*b*) Полукру́г 'semicircle'; полуо́стров 'peninsula'; полу-све́т 'half-light'; полугра́мотный 'semiliterate'; полуто́н 'semitone'; полушутя́ 'half-joking'. Gen. полукру́га, etc.

     (*c*) With second component in the *gen.*: полбуты́лки 'half-bottle'; полго́да 'six months'; полсло́ва (с полусло́ва but also на полсло́ве); за полцены́ 'at half price'. In the oblique cases the first half usually (but not always) becomes полу- and the second half reverts to the case required:

> получа́сом ра́ньше (from полчаса́ 'half an hour')
> в полубуты́лках

but also:

> на полдоро́ге, на полпути́ 'half-way'
> вполго́лоса 'under one's breath'.

On this model small fractions and various composite numbers were formed before the 18th c.:

> пол(ъ)тре́ти '⅙'
> полполтре́ти '¹⁄₁₂'

and with ordinals (short form):

> пол(ъ) в(ъ)тора > полтора '1½'

(sc. 'half of the second integer').
Examples:

> полътретия десяте гривьнъ '25' (text no. 13)
> въ полудесятѣ рублехъ '9½'
> на полтретьянадцате рубля '12½'
> полсемадесятъ '65'
> въ полутретьѣстѣ рублѣхъ '250'.

Only полтора́[86] '1½' and полтора́ста '150' remain in

---

[86] Полтора́ has fem. полторы́, and nowadays an invariable case-form полу́тора. The type *półtrzecia* (indecl.) is still current in Polish.

modern usage. The Westernization of mathematics under Peter the Great introduced the simpler models:

одна́ шеста́я[87] (sc. часть от до́ля) '⅙'
два с полови́ной '2½'.

82 *Higher Numerals*

Миллио́н comes into use in the 17th c., from which time all large numbers have been on Western models. Тьма '10,000' ('myriad') and various scarcely numerical learned words such as легион disappear.

83 *Ordinals*

The forms were:

	Short	Long
1	пьрв(ъ) (перв)	пе́рвый
2	друг(ъ), в(ъ)тор(ъ)	друго́й, второ́й
3	третьи, трете́й	тре́тий, тре́тье, тре́тья
4	четвёрт(ъ)	четвёртый
5	пят(ъ)	пя́тый
6	шёст(ъ)	шесто́й
7	сём(ъ)	седьмо́й (dial. семо́й and сёмый)
8	? (OCS *osmŭ*)	восьмо́й
9	девя́т(ъ)	девя́тый
10	деся́т(ъ)	деся́тый

Notes

(*a*) The first two are, as in many languages, not numerical.[88] 'Second' in ESl. was друг(ой) and so widely remains in dialect; the original usage is retained in на друго́й день 'the next day' and the marginally literary вдруго́рядь 'a second time, again' (see §85 (i) below). Второ́й is a Slavonicism, generalized from the ecclesiastical calendar, cf. на второ́й день пра́здника and вто́рник 'Tuesday'. It becomes the normal literary word only from the 16th c.

(*b*) The Slavonicism седьмо́й similarly became standard in the 17th c. (ChSl. седьмо́й день; сед(ь)ми́ца 'week'; and other calendrical expressions). The now only dial. семо́й will be found in early texts: до дне семаго (*RPC s.a.* 1066; Ukrainian still has сьо́мий).

---

[87] Две, три, etc., шесты́х (since шеста́я is a nominalized adj.).

[88] Пьр-в- cognate with *per-/*pro- 'in front'; въtop- surely cognate with Gmc. *anþar- (Eng. *other*, Ger. *ander*).

(*c*) The 'short' forms are now obsolete in literary usage except for полтора́ (§81 (2)(*c*) above) and the marginal country expressions сам-друг (not сам-втор!) 'myself and another', сам-трете́й 'the three of us', etc.

(*d*) Ordinals of the *teens* were originally cpd. phrases (§77 above): пьрвъ (пе́рвый) на десяте 'eleventh' (ChSl. also еди́ный на десяте), etc.

By the 16th c. the ordinal component had become indeclinable with a connective vowel -o/e- and the second half took adjectival declension: въ шестонатцатой день. They are gradually brought into line with the cardinals: шестна́дцатый, etc., including 'eleventh' and 'twelfth' (оди́ннадцатый, двена́дцатый).

Examples of пе́рвый на десяте *et sim.* in the 18th c. belong to the artificial high style.

84 *Collectives*

Three types:

(i) Adj. д(ъ)вой, д(ъ)вое, д(ъ)воя (трой, обой).

(ii) From *four* upwards neut. *nouns* че́тверо, gen. че́твера, etc. The sg. declension of (i) (type мой) was little used; there remains only the neut. NA дво́е, тро́е (not обо́е), combined with the oblique pl. cases двои́х, трои́х, etc.[89] Че́тверо, etc., fall into the same pattern: че́тверо, четверы́х, etc. Forms beyond се́меро are now hardly ever found. The original sense of двой, трой was taken over by new derivatives двойно́й 'double', двоя́кий 'twofold' (э́то мо́жно понима́ть двоя́ко 'this can be taken in two ways').

The pl. NA forms двои, etc., survived into the early 19th c.: дво́и, тро́и, че́твери су́тки. The only survivals of the sg. oblique cases are обо́его по́ла 'of both sexes' and adverbs of the type вдвоём '(two) together'.[90] For their use see 4.77 (6).

(iii) Nouns in -ица, e.g. Тро́ица 'Trinity', are of ChSl. origin. The corresponding native type is дво́йка, тро́йка, семёрка (of cards and in other special uses).

85 *Multiplicatives*

(i) A type in -жды (apparently from *-šĭd-i*, a case-form of **šĭdĭ* 'a "go"' of which the modern equivalent is ход 'a move' (e.g.

---

[89] The same paradigm is now followed by the words of vague number, e.g. не́сколько, не́скольких, etc.; мно́го, мно́гих, etc.

[90] Acc. вдво́е, etc., = 'two times': вдво́е бо́льше 'twice as big'.

at chess)) exists for 1–4: однáжды (now only a temporal adverb), двáжды (older двóжды) 'twice', трúжды (now as rare as Eng. *thrice*), четы́режды (only in arithmetic) '4×'; многажды is a Slavonicism. The general colloquial procedure is, however, with раз 'blow, stroke': два рáза, пять раз. Dialects show other nouns in this function, especially ряд:[91] в другой ряд 'a second time' (cf. вдругóрядь, §83 above).

(ii) OCS (ChSl.) formed multiplicatives with *krat-* (CSl. **kart-*): *dŭva kraty* or *dŭvo(e)kraty*, and with the instr. of nouns in *-ica: storicejǫ* 'a hundred times'. Neither is native ESl.[92] which only has such ChSl. derivatives as вторúчный 'secondary', многокрáтный 'repeated, frequent'.

86 *Distributive Expressions*

The procedure has at all times been with the preposition по but the case varies between acc. and dat. Modern usage has: по одномý (or plain noun по я́блоку 'an apple each'); 2–4 with acc.: пó два, пó две, пó три (ChSl. по дъвѣма du. dat.); 5 onwards with dat.: по пятú (including пó ста, по сорокá). The collectives, when unavoidable, are in acc.: пó двое нóжниц 'two pairs of scissors each', по пя́теро, etc. Modern colloquial tends to generalize the acc.: по пять, по сóрок рублéй.

The Verb

87 Apart from five verbs of ancient lineage and antiquated paradigm (§§88 ff. below) all CSl., and therefore all ESl., verbs are *thematic*, i.e. have a vowel ('theme') inserted between the root and the personal endings. The vast majority of Russian verbs fall into the following broad categories:[93]

A. Thematic vowel *-e-* ('First Conjugation'):

1. Consonantal roots: type нес-тú; pres. sg. 1 нес-ý, pl. 2 нес-é-те. A relict type; no new creations in ESl.

2. With infixed *-n-*: type мú-ну-ти; мú-н-ý, мú-н-е-те. The final

---

[91] *Rěd* is similarly used in SCr., but more literary is *pût* (= путь); the latter is apparently not represented in ESl., nor is ESl. раз in SSl.

[92] WSl. has the type in **-kart-*, e.g. Pol. *dwakroć* (adj. *dwukrotny*).

[93] Full categorization requires also inclusion of the infinitive stem. The traditional numeration can be found in H. H. Bielfeldt, *Altslawische Grammatik* (1961), p. 189. Cf. also A. Vaillant, *Grammaire comparée*, III/1, pp. 137 ff.

consonant of the stem in many cases drops before -н-: двѝнути < *dvig-nu-ti, дёрнуть/-дёргивать, вернýть/вертéть; but more recent formations no longer conform, hence погѝбнуть is younger than гѝнуть 'perish'. The infix -н- may be lacking in the preterite: исчéз, -ла (исчéзнуть). The type is productive in a small way, more at dial. than literary level: there are some characteristic subliterary formations such as двиганýть (lit. only двѝнуть, двѝгать), саданýть (< садѝть)[94] 'hit'. The majority of verbs in -нуть are *perfective* with typical 'semelfactive' aspect, e.g. *pf* крѝкнуть 'give a (single) shout', *impf* кричáть 'emit (a series of) shouts'; дýнуть 'give a puff', дýть 'blow (continuously)'.

3. With infixed -j-:

   (α) Primitive vowel stem: *zna-ti, zna-j-ǫ, zna-j-e-te* (R. знáю, знáете). Relict type. So: греть, грéю 'warm'; гнить, гниŏ 'rot'; дуть, дýю 'blow'.

   (β) Secondary vowel stem: *děl-a-ti, děl-a-j-ǫ, děla-j-e-te* (R. дéлаю, дéлаете); *im-ě-ti* (имéть); *dar-ov-a-ti, dar-u-jǫ* (даровáть, дарýю). Highly productive type, largely denominatives and cpd. derived imperfectives (4.91).

   (γ) Consonant stem with palatalization: *pis-a-ti, pišǫ < *pis-jǫ, pišete < *pis-je-te*. (R. писáть, пишý, пѝшете). Not productive. Some have gravitated towards Type 3β as regular: махáть 'wave', машý, мáшет (older) and махáю, махáет (younger).

B. Thematic vowel -i- ('Second Conjugation'):

1. Infinitive in -i-: R. говор-ѝ-ть, говор-ю̏, говор-ѝ-те. Typically denominatives and causatives (вредѝть 'harm', стáвить 'put' ('cause to stand')). Productive.

2. Infinitive in -ě- (-ē-): *gor-ěti, gor-jǫ, gor-i-te* (R. горéть, горю̏, горѝте).

-ѣти/-еть will appear as -ати/-ать after -j- and ancient palatalized consonants, e.g. *derž-á-ti* 'hold', *derž-ú, dérž-i-te*; *stoj-á-ti* 'stand', *stoj-ú, sto(j)-í-te*.

Typically *verbs of state*: сидéть 'be in a sitting position', горéть 'burn' (intr.), as are those of Type A3β, e.g. белéть 'be (or appear) white', умéть 'be able to, know how to' (sg. 3 белéет, умéет). Productive in A3β but not in B2.

---

[94] -анýть is no doubt áканье spelling (6.55) for -онýть as the sequence of derivation appears to be тóпать > тóпот > *impf* топтáть/топотáть (intensive) > *pf* топонýть.

The relationship of some of these categories may be seen in the table of the verbs of position (Table XIV).

ATHEMATIC VERBS

88   The five (irregular) athematic verbs are (pres. sg. 1):

есмь 'I am'	stem: *es- (cf. Lat. s-um, es, es-t)
pf дамь 'I (shall) give'	*dā-d- (< dō-)
имамь 'I have'	*ĭm- (jĭm-)
вѣмь 'I know'	*vēd- (< *woid-)
ѣмь 'I eat'	*ēd-

The type corresponds to the *mi*-verbs in Greek (εἰ-μί 'I am', δί-δω-μι 'I give' (with reduplication)).

89   1. The verb быть 'be' is wholly anomalous. It has a suppletive paradigm from several different aspectual stems: present (durative) *es-, past durative *b(h)ē- (cf. Lat. fiō 'become'), perfective *b(h)ū- (cf. Gk. aor. ἐφῦ 'came into being, grew').

Early ESl. has the following forms (OCS/ChSl. variants in brackets; the dual forms are omitted):

		Pres. dur	Pres. pf (fut.)	Imperf. (past dur)	Aor. (past pf)
Sg.	1	есмь	бу́ду (bǫdǫ)	бѣяхъ, бяхъ (běxŭ)	быхъ
	2	еси́	бу́деши	бяше (bě)	бы
	3	есть (jestŭ)	бу́деть (bǫdetŭ)	бяше (bě)	бы, бысть (bystŭ)
Pl.	1	есмъ	бу́демъ	бяхомъ (běxomŭ)	быхомъ
	2	есте́	бу́дете	бяшете (běste)	бысте
	3	суть (sǫtŭ)	бу́дуть (bǫdǫtŭ)	бяху (běšę)	быша (byšę)

Commentary

90   (*a*) The frequent forms бѣхъ, etc., in early texts belong to ChSl., the anomalous formation (with *aor*. terminations) being supplanted by regular бѣяхъ or contracted бяхъ in ESl. and sometimes in ChSl. Бѣхъ and бяхъ are always clearly a tense of state (*impf*): Вольга [Olga] же бяше въ Кыевѣ . . . воевода бѣ Свѣнелдъ (*RPC s.a.* 945); у Кыева бо бяше перевозъ (ibid., *ad init.*) 'for there was a ferry at Kiev'.

TABLE XIV. The Verbs of Position

	Root	1 Primary verb of action (intr.)[1]	2 Primary verb of state (intr.) Type B2	3 Imperfective of col. 1 (reflexives of col. 4)	4 Causative (trans.)[4] Type B1	5 Derived frequentatives, etc., of col. 4. Type A3β
'stand'	*stā-	pf стать, стáну[2] replaced by встать < вз-стать 'stand up'	impf стоять, стою[3] 'be standing'	в-ставáть, -стаю (earlier -стаяти)	стáвить 'cause to stand, put'	(за-)ставлять, (у-)становить[2]
'sit'	*sĕd- *sŏd-	pf сесть, сяду 'seat oneself'	сидеть < сѣдѣти 'be sitting'	садиться 'seat oneself'	садить 'cause to sit, set' (noun сад 'garden')	-сáживать (ChSl. -саждáть)
'lie'	*lĕg- *lŏg-	pf лечь, лягу 'lie down'	лежáть[3] 'be lying'	ложиться 'lie down'	pf положить 'cause to lie, lay' (noun лог 'lair')	(по-)лагáть
'hang'	? (etymology unknown)	pf (повиснуть) 'become suspended' (no early form recorded)	висеть (висѣти) 'be hanging'	—	pf повесить and impf вешать 'cause to hang, suspend' (весить now only 'weigh', pf свесить, noun весы pl. 'scales')	(вз-)вешивать

[1] All have ancient presents with -n- infix: stā-n-, sĕ-n-d-, le-n-g-.
[2] Стать now only 'become', with impf становиться (the pf was also early статься).
[3] CSl. * stā-(j)ē-ti, *leg-ē-ti.
[4] Perfectives all in по-. *Ложить is obsolete, replaced by the verb класть, кладý. The parallel *становить is only now used reflexively (n. 2) or in cpds. (col. 5).

(*b*) Быхъ is equally clearly a tense of *event* (*pf*): идеже послѣже бысть Кыевъ (*RPC, ad init.*) 'where Kiev later arose'; быша си злая мѣсяца иуля въ 23 (ibid. 1093) 'these terrible things happened on 23 July'.

(*c*) Rare forms were the (ChSl.) *pf imperfect* будяхъ, будяше (4.88 (ii)) and the *fut. participle* бышащ- (*byšęšt-*), a unique relic of the sigmatic future in Slav (**bū-s-jęt-j-*; cf. Lith. fut. *búsiu* 'I shall be'; fut. part. *búsiąs*).

(*d*) In Russian only the inf. быть, perfect был (есмь), and fut. бýду remain in use. With the wide use of nominal sentences of the type он студéнт and the very early dropping of the copula in the perfect (4.1) the present-tense forms became virtually superfluous. The modern literary language, under ChSl. influence, makes limited use of sg. 3 есть and pl. 3 суть:

(i) Бог есть (= существýет) (not normal usage of OCS and earlier ChSl.); *x* есть *y* (mathematical or philosophical identity); мысль изречённая есть ложь (Tyútchev); есть as the positive of нет 'there is not': есть такúе . . . 'there are such people'; есть чем занимáться '(I have) plenty to do' (neg. нéчем занимáться 'there is nothing to do', 4.3 (4)).

(ii) Глáвные рéки Россúи суть: Вóлга, Днепр, Дон . . . (to introduce lists only).

(iii) Other persons of the present survive down to the 16th–17th c. in more or less bookish style, especially the sg. 2 есú (§105 below) and the pl. 1 which had by then acquired several regional forms—есмé (Novg., Pskov; recorded from 13th c.), есмó (SW and some Ukr. dialects; recorded from 14th c.), есмы́ (rare; after pronoun мы), есмя́ (Centre): и орду есмя проѣхали, и сараи есмя проѣхали, и выѣхали есмя в бузанъ (Af. Nik., 15th c., who also has sg. 1 есмú after есú: приѣхалъ есми на Кострому).

(iv) A reduced alternative form of sg. 3 есть—е (surviving in Ukrainian where it tends to replace all forms of the pres. tense)—must be posited for нѣтъ < нѣту < **ne-je-tu-tĭ* (verbal 3rd pers. ending) nearly parallel to Fr. [*il*] *n'y a* [*pas*], and in the negative adverbs of the type нѣкогда (Table XIII, col. 13) < *ne je kogda*, which now act as impersonal verbs: мне нéкогда 'I have no time to . . .'.

(v) The frequentative derivative бывáть (see also §133 (3)) provides *impf* tenses for *pf* быть in certain contexts.

91 2. Дать *pf* has only partly normalized its present-future:

		OCS (ChSl.)	Mod. Russian
Sg.	1	*damĭ (*dād-mĭ)*	дам
	2	*dasi*	дашь
	3	*dastŭ* (ESl. дасть)	даст
Pl.	1	*damŭ*	дади́м
	2	*daste*	дади́те
	3	*dadętŭ* (ESl. дадять)	дадýт

Sg. 1 and sg. and pl. 3 lose their final palatalization; даси is remodelled on the normal sg. 2 in -ши (-шь) (§97 (*c*) below); the pl. has been reformed—pl. 3 дадять > дадут(ь) (after бýдут?) from 14th c. and дади́м, дади́те in the later Muscovy period. (Since the sg. and pl. 1 soon coincided, дади́м is brought in probably from the imperative; дади́те follows.)

The derived *impf* was даѩти, later and colloquial давати; the latter infinitive is now combined with the present of the former: давáть, даю́.

Note. The root зьд- 'build' (Slavonicisms здáние, зóдчий) has in the cpd. *pf* соз(ь)дáть been attracted to дать and now makes *pf* fut. создáм, etc. The corresponding *impf* созидáть has accordingly been largely replaced by создавáть: создаю́, etc.

92 3. The forms connected with 'have' need to be carefully distinguished. Early ESl. has:

(*a*) *pf* ѧти, pres.-fut. иму, имет (**jĭm-ti, jĭm-ǫ*; cf. Lat. *ĕmo, ĕmere* 'buy') 'take, acquire' (act of taking into possession):

мьстисла[въ] . . . въеха въ Новъгородъ . . . и я [aor. sg. 3] Хота Григоревиця (*Novg. Chr., s.a.* 1215).

Now only used with prefixes: вз-я́ть, воз-ьмý; при-н-я́ть, примý (**pri-jĭmu*), etc.

(*b*) *impf* имáти, pres. éмлю, éмлет(ь), also newer имáю, имáет 'take'. The latter now provides the aspectual pair to -ять: принимáть, -нимáю.

The earlier (and ChSl.) present -éмлю is now antiquated or poetic: приéмлю; cf. literary cpd. неприéмлемый 'unacceptable'.

(c) *impf* имѣ́ти, pres. имамь, имать 'possess, have' (verb of state). The athematic present disappears early in favour of the regular имѣ́ю, имѣ́ет.

Sparingly used colloquially for possession (4.2), more in literary language: ро́за имѣ́ет си́льный за́пах. Cf. имѣ́ние 'estate' (lands which one possesses).

93 4. The primary verb вѣмь 'I know' (inf. вѣдѣти) has disappeared in Russian (not in WSl.: Pol. *wiem*, Cz. *vím*) but there remain many derivatives of the root *vĕd-*, e.g. вѣ́дать (Type A3β), по́весть 'story', развѣ́дка 'reconnaissance'.

The earliest texts have not only sg. 1 вѣмь but also вѣдѣ, a unique relic of the old perfect (parallel to Gk. οἶδα 'I know', Lat. *uīdī* 'I saw'), e.g. in Русская Правда: не вѣдѣ у кого есмь купилъ.

Я не вем is still used by Pososhkóv *c.*1724, but surely as a Polonism, by Prokopóvich and others in the 18th c. as an element of Slavonicized 'high style'.

Both вѣмь and вѣдаю = *savoir* have been displaced in modern Russian by знать = *connaître* (cf. the nouns весть 'news'/знáмя 'sign'). Вѣ́дать + instr. 'be in charge of' is the only use of this verb.

Вѣдѣ survives in the adverbial particle ведь (§69 (*f*) above), and the sg. 3 in the Slavonicism Бог вѣсть.

94 5. ѣмь 'I eat' (root *ēd-*; cf. Lat. *ĕdo*). The OCS (ChSl.) spelling is normally *jamĭ*, etc., which frequently occur in all types of language.[95]

The present has been reformed on the same lines as дам, with pl. 1, 2 following maintained pl. 3:

		OCS (ChSl.)	Mod. Russian
Sg.	1	*jamĭ*	ем (not *ём, since ѣ)
	2	*jasi*	ешь
	3	*jastŭ* (ESl. ѣсть)	ест (< есть)
Pl.	1	*jamŭ*	еди́м
	2	*jaste*	еди́те
	3	*jadętŭ*	едя́т (not *едут)

---

[95] The rule was: initial *jē-* > *jā-*, internal *jē* (ѣ) remains; *jē* and *jā* were phonetically very close to one another in late CSl. (2.3 (3)). Hence: *ob-ĕdŭ* (R. обе́д), Slavonicism снѣдь, but Slavonicism я́ства 'victuals' and я́сли pl. 'manger' (*ēd-sl-).

REGULAR VERBS

95 *Present Tense*

		A1	A2	A3α, β	A3γ	B1	B2	OCS (ChSl.)
Sg.	1	нес-у	двин-у	зна-ю	пиш-у	говор-ю	сиж-у	-ǫ/-jǫ
	2	-еши	-еши	-еши	-еши	-иши	сид-иши	-ši
	3	-еть	-еть	-еть	-еть	-ить	-ить	-tŭ
Du.	1	нес-евѣ	двин-евѣ	зна-евѣ	пиш-евѣ	говор-ивѣ	сид-ивѣ	-vě
	2	-ета	-ета	-ета	-ета	-ита	-ита	-ta
	3	-ета	-ета	-ета	-ета	-ита	-ита	-te
Pl.	1	нес-емъ	двин-емъ	зна-емъ	пиш-емъ	говор-имъ	сид-имъ	-mŭ
	2	-ете	-ете	-ете	-ете	-ите	-ите	-te
	3	-уть	-уть	-ють	-уть (-ють)	-ять	-ять	-ǫtŭ/-jǫtŭ, -ętŭ

Commentary

96 (*a*) *Sg. 1.* After the early centuries there remained only two current sg. 1 in -м: дам and ем. We do not find in Russian the partial or complete generalization of this ending in the productive conjugations, characteristic of WSl. and SSl., e.g. SCr. *glȅdām, čìnīm, kùpujēm.* The essential analogy would seem to be:

> *imāš(i)* : contracted *znāš*
> *imā(tŭ)* : contracted *znā*
> whence   *imām(ĭ)* : *znām* (replacing *znaju*).

But Russian did not normally lose intervocalic *-j-* (still unique in Slav with знáешь, знáем) and the form имам(ь) went out of living usage early.

(*b*) *Pl. 1.* The suffix varies in detail throughout Slav (as indeed throughout IE.: Gk. *-men*, Lat. *-mus*). At least *-mo(s)* and *-mŭ(s)* could have been dialectal variants in CSl. ESl. has predominantly *-mŭ* > -м but *-mo* was apparently also present and preserved (improbably created) in Ukr. and WhR. under stress: несе-мó. OCS (ChSl.) likewise had *-mŭ*. As ESl. did not develop a sg. 1 in *-m* there was no confusion; elsewhere this was avoided by sg. 1 *-m*, pl. 1: SCr. *-mo*, Blg. *-me*, Pol. *-my*.[96]

In Russian stressed -ем automatically became -ём: несём, даём.

97 (*c*) *Sg. 2.* There is no form *-sī* (> Slav -ши) in IE, only 'primary' *-sĭ* (> Slav -шь) and 'secondary' *-s* (which disappears in Slav, e.g. in the aor.). But -ши is universal in OCS and all early ESl.

---

[96] *-me* after pl. 2 *-te*?; *-my* after the pronoun *my*?; cf. есмы in §90 (*d*) (iii) above.

documents. Apparent reduction to -шь appears in the 13th c. (посулишь 1229). It cannot be excluded that the native ESl. ending was the theoretical -шь < *-$s\breve{\imath}$.[97]

Despite the depalatalization of $\check{s}'$ (2.37) -шь [-š] has continued to be written to the present day.

(d) *Sg. and pl. 3.* ESl. had regularly -ть, OCS -*tŭ* in both. The ESl. form was widely introduced into ChSl. texts from the outset, e.g. *Ostr.*, which has only five examples of -*tŭ*. Here again ESl. appears to be historically correct (-*tĭ* > -ть) and the OCS -*tŭ* anomalous.

'Hard' -тъ begins to appear in vernacular texts from the late 13th c. Depalatalization of a final dental can scarcely be a purely phonetic process.[98] The influence of ChSl., especially during the 'Second South Slav Influence', may have counted for something in the written language but improbably in the spoken. Nor is depalatalization universal: the S. and W. dialects (including Ukr. and WhR.) have preserved -*t'* (WhR. -*c'*). Since some N. dialects, where -*t* first appears, have sg. 3 -*t* but pl. 3 -*t'* we must suppose a morphological pressure to avoid confusion with the infinitive, which was simultaneously being reduced from -*ti* to -*t'* (§114 below). The confusion arises in B1 verbs not exhibiting mobile stress:[99]

Inf.	Sg. 3	Pl. 3
говори́ти	говори́ть	говоря́ть
говори́ть	говори́т	

Thus говоря́ть could be retained. But in the Central dialects, and therefore in Moscow usage, -*t* was eventually generalized to *all* sg. and pl. 3. It is well attested in Moscow from the 14th c.

In view of the *nil ending* in Slav generally and sporadically in ESl. N. dialects, it is safest to suppose a CSl. reduction -*tĭ* > -*t* (rather than a 'secondary' ending -*t*), which was strengthened in OCS by -*t* > -*tŭ*, like *ot* > *otŭ* in suitable contexts, and a hesitation -*tĭ*/-*t* in ESl. Some late OCS texts, e.g. *Supr.*, have sporadic examples of third persons without -*tŭ*. An example in the colophon of

---

[97] The form -*ši* was generalized from the 2nd Conj., where it is regular (-*i-si* > -*i-xi* > -*i-ši* (§58 (7) above)), but -*si* persisted in the athematic presents (*dasi*, etc.: §§88 ff. above).

[98] Depalatalization of the infinitive in -ть is found sporadically in some Muscovite texts side by side with -ть and -ти and regularly in a few dialects. The examples in Ludolf (1696) are hardly likely to be from such a source but rather inadequacies of his transcription.

[99] Sg. 3 лю́бить is not identical to inf. люби́ть.

Ostr. (да иже горазнѣе сего напише), if not a mere scribal error, may reflect local speech of that time; such forms are in fact quite common in vernacular Nóvgorod texts.[100] SCr. *-nesū* and Cz. *nesou* show, however, that *-t* was present in the pl. 3 until a late date, so probably also in the sg. 3. At all events it is improbable that ESl. -ть was generalized from the athematics, though есть, суть—in so far as they were still used (and they are not vernacular)—had remained 'soft'.[101]

98   (*e*) The *dual* was dropped early in the pres. and all other tenses. There are examples of pl. verbs with du. nouns in the 13th c. The 3rd pers. is only -та in ESl. (ChSl. *-te*), and the 1st pers. sometimes -ва by attraction to -та.

The Inflected Past Tenses

99   1. *Imperfect.* The descriptive past tense (past of the present). Selected paradigms:

		East Slav			OCS (ChSl.)
		A1	A3	B1	
Sg.	1	нес-яхъ	зна-хъ	мол-яхъ	*-ахй*
	2	-яше	-ше	-яше	*-aše*
	3	-яше	-ше	-яше	*-aše*
Du.	1	нес-яховѣ	зна-ховѣ	мол-яховѣ	*-axově*
	2	-яшета	-шета	-яшета	*-ašeta*
	3	-яшета	-шета	-яшета	*-ašete*
Pl.	1	нес-яхомъ	зна-хомъ	мол-яхомъ	*-ахотй*
	2	-яшете	-шете	-яшете	*-ašete*
	3	-яху	-ху	-яху	*-ахǫ*

The above are the normal ESl. *contracted* forms. ChSl. partly maintained OCS *uncontracted* forms несѣахъ, знаахъ, моляахъ (*mol'jaaxй*), which presumably represented in fact a similar incipient contraction to that found in the 'long' adjectives (§39 above).[102]

---

[100] Commoner in sg. 3 than in pl. 3, but there are two examples of the latter in the *Novg. Minéi* (text no. 8).

[101] For a somewhat different view see C. Watkins, *Indogermanische Grammatik*, III/1 (Heidelberg, 1969), pp. 216–19.

[102] Contracted forms increased in late OCS manuscripts; there are few in *Zogr.* and *Mar.*, many in *Savv*. The whole tense was clearly new in late CSl. (OCS), replacing a simpler tense **nes-ŭ, -e, -e* whose sg. 2, 3 were transferred to the aorist.

Ostr. has about ten times as many uncontracted as contracted forms, which may rather represent the proportion in the manuscript from which it was copied rather than the incursion of ESl. norms. ChSl. tends further to unify by replacing хотѣаше by хотяаше *et sim.*

The uncontracted Slavonicisms became more frequent again in the period of the 'Second South Slav Influence', both the tense and the form belonging by then only to high literary style.

100   *Commentary*

(*a*) The -ть of the pres. sg. and pl. 3 is often added to the 3rd persons of the imperf.: бяшеть, бяхуть.

(*b*) In du. 2, 3 and pl. 2 there are alternative forms -ста, -сте.

(*c*) The tense early became obsolescent and was no more than a literary archaism by the 16th c. It has been questioned whether the tense was really alive in ESl. *spoken* language from the very beginning of the records (11th c.). Texts do not give a clear answer since those nearest to the living language, e.g. Русская Правда, do not require the imperfect, the only common 'past' tense being the perfect. However, its use seems natural in the more colloquial parts of Novg. chronicles of the 13th c., e.g.

кадь ржи купляхуть по .ӏ. гр[и]венъ . . . ядяху люди сосновую кору . . . дѣти свое даяхуть одьрень . . . (1215).

It is also sometimes affirmed that the imperfect declined earlier than the aorist. It can only be said that the aorist was better *maintained*, and to a later date, in literary usage.

(*d*) The imperfect was in the nature of things mainly formed from *impf* verbs, but imperfects of *pf* verbs occur in a special sense (4.88).

(*e*) The imperfect was replaced by the *impf* preterite (4.89).

101   2. *Aorist.* The narrative past tense (events).
Paradigms:

		East Slav				OCS (ChSl.)
		A1	A3	B1	B2	
Sg.	1	нес-охъ	зна-хъ	ход-ихъ	вид-ѣхъ	-*хй*
	2	-е	зна	-и	-ѣ	-*е* (nil)
	3	-е	зна	-и	-ѣ	-*е* (nil)

	A1	A3	B1	B2	OCS (ChSl.)
		East Slav			
Du. 1	нес-оховѣ	зна-ховѣ	ход-иховѣ	вид-ѣховѣ	*-хově*
2	-оста	-ста	-иста	-ѣста	*-sta*
3	-оста	-ста	-иста	-ѣста	*-ste*
Pl. 1	нес-охомъ	зна-хомъ	ход-ихомъ	вид-ѣхомъ	*-хотй*
2	-осте	-сте	-исте	-ѣсте	*-ste*
3	-оша	-ша	-иша	-ѣша	*-šę*
	(-шя)	(-шя)	(-шя)	(-шя)	

102 *Commentary*

(*a*) ESl. had eliminated all types of aorist except the sigmatic type given above. Older types still in use in OCS (e.g. asigmatic *padй, pade, pade, padoмй, padete, padǫ*) sometimes appear in ChSl. texts. Fairly common is sigmatic sg. 1 pѣхъ (**rēk-sŭ*), 2, 3 рече, side by side with younger pѣкохъ, etc.; the verb is in any case characteristic of ChSl.

(*b*) -тъ is occasionally added to certain monosyllabic sg. 3 (избитъ = изби). On these and дастъ, быстъ see Vaillant, *Grammaire comparée*, III/1, p. 55 (§366), and C. Watkins, *Indogermanische Grammatik*, III/1, pp. 216–19.

(*c*) ESl. contractions had made sg. 1 and pl. 1 identical with the imperfect in certain verbs (знахъ, знахомъ). The aor. pl. 3 was easily confused with the imperf. sg. 3. These ambiguities were no doubt one of the reasons for the decadence of both tenses in the vernacular.

(*d*) The aorist was principally formed from *pf* verbs but *impf* aorists are not uncommon, representing the result of a composite action: въ томь вечерѣ перевозися Ярославъ съ вои '. . . got his troops across the river' (sc. in several similar operations). See further 4.88.

(*e*) Literary usage maintained the past narrative tense, exactly as French has done,[103] with varying consistency down to the end of the 17th c. and even, as an affectation, beyond. The moment of its extinction in the living language, as stated under the imperfect, is impossible to pin down.

---

[103] *Passé défini* 'je vis', replaced in speech by the *parfait* (*passé composé*) 'j'ai vu'. French, however, has maintained the *imparfait* 'je voyais'.

The Perfect Tenses

103   These form a complete group (aspect)—present (perfect), past (pluperfect) and future (future-perfect)—of compound tenses formed with an active aorist or perfect participle in *-l* (§126 below) and appropriate parts of the auxiliary быть. The participle (short forms only since always a predicate) shows *number* and *gender*, and may be of either aspect.

Selected forms:

	Present	Past	Future			
Sg. 1	есмь	бяхъ	буду	} вйдѣл-ъ,	купйл-ъ	m.
2	есй	бяше	будешь	-а,	-а	f.
3	есть	бяше	будет(ь)	} -о,	-о	n.
Pl. 1	есмъ	бяхомъ	будемъ	} вйдѣл-и,	купйл-и	m.
2	есте́	бяшете	будете	-ы,	-ы	f.
3	суть	бяху	будут(ь)	} -а,	-а	n.
	'I have seen, bought'	'I had seen, bought'	'I shall have seen, bought'			

Commentary

104   (*a*) *Present of the Perfect*: есмь купилъ indicates a present *state* resulting from a past *action*: 'I am [now] one who bought'. Nearly parallel to the Fr. (and antiquated Eng.) *je suis venu* 'I am come'. The perfect aspectual situation, as more vivid, often usurps the place of the plain statement about the past (aorist) in speech. The supersession was complete in Russian, but thereby the perfect forms inevitably forfeited their unique aspectual sense.

(*b*) The two parts of the cpd. are not closely linked and may be separated in various ways in the sentence.

(*c*) Gender distinctions were, as everywhere, early given up in the *plural*, but here the pl. masc. *nom.* naturally prevailed; there is thus a distinction:

adjective: вялъ(ый) 'withered, limp'; pl. вялы (§42 (6) above)
verb: вянуть 'wither'; pret. pl. вяли.

105   (*d*) With the colloquial dropping of the auxiliary есмь, etc. (4.1 (*b*)) the perfect is reduced to a single gender-showing participle. Though it is, on general grounds, likely that the auxiliary was most consistently absent or omitted in the 3rd persons[104] (there normally being an expressed subject) it was certainly facultative in the 1st pers., and presumably also the 2nd pers., in colloquial speech by the 12th c. ChSl. tended to preserve the auxiliary and written traditionalism therefore often inserted it even in otherwise colloquial texts down to late Muscovite times; see the example from Af. Nik. in §90 (*d*)(iii) above.

In literary styles close to ChSl. it was still felt in the 17th c. that the 2nd pers. should be distinguished in view of the awkward identity in the sg. 2 and 3 of both the aorist and imperfect. Hence early grammars, essentially ChSl., recommend a wholly artificial past tense with mixed forms, e.g. aor. спасохъ, спаслъ еси, спасе (Zizáni, 1596; similarly in Smotrítsky, 1648). A Slavonicized style always favoured more copulas, both in present and past; they are naturally frequent in translations from Latin or German in the 16th–17th c., e.g. the calque (он) есть тоѣ надежды = *(er) ist der Hoffnung*.[105] Avvakúm, however, rarely uses any even in relatively 'high' passages: самъ разболѣлся . . . яко и очи опухли . . . и онѣ отвѣщали . . . и я вскричалъ.

Pari passu with the omission of the auxiliary goes the inclusion of the personal pronoun (though never obligatory): я, ты, он дал.

(*e*) The 'long' forms of the *l*-participle have survived in considerable number as *adjectives*, sometimes with stress specialization, e.g.: былóй 'former' ('which has been'), гнилóй 'rotten', зрéлый 'ripe', (за)лежáлый 'shop-soiled' ('which has been lying [too long]'), (по)линялый 'faded', запоздáлый 'belated'; как угорéлая кóшка 'like one possessed'. Устáлый 'tired' is still very close to the verbal form я устáл 'I am tired'.

106　(*f*) The *pluperfect* is properly formed with the *imperfect* бяхъ (occasionally with the *impf aor.* бѣхъ in ChSl.) but there are examples with *pf aor.* быхъ.

With the decadence of both these tenses and before the elimination of the pluperfect altogether, the auxiliary has to be replaced by the new all-purpose preterite, viz. (есмь) былъ видѣлъ,[106] the first auxiliary being normally omitted. Examples:

[104] Absence of the 3rd pers. auxiliary, but not others, is frequent in late OCS, e.g. *Supr.*, and is the position of modern Pol.; SSl. preserves the auxiliary *throughout*, e.g. SCr. *b̀io sam, je, bíli su*.

[105] S. C. Gardiner in *SR* 39/93 (1961). But Novikóv (1769): я сам того мнения.

[106] This is again parallel to the Fr. *passé surcomposé* 'j'ai eu donné' replacing literary 'j'eus donné', with different syntactical use from the *pluperf.* with the imperf. auxiliary (= бяхъ) 'j'avais donné'.

Early ESl.:

у Ярополка же жена грекини бѣ и бяше была черницею (*RPC s.a.* 977) 'Jaropolk's wife was a Greek [intrinsic state] and had [formerly] been a nun';

Святополкъ . . . всю нощь пилъ бѣ съ дружиною своею (ibid. 1016) 'Svjatopolk . . . had been carousing all night with his retinue'.

Muscovite period:

а что селъ и свободъ дьмитриевыхъ, то дали есме былѣ Андрѣю (14th c.) '. . . we had already given them to Andrew' (better tr. 'we have given . . .', just as се далъ at the beginning of a legal document is the equivalent of 'I [hereby] give . . .');

да и назад уж был сходил (1576) 'I had already turned back'.

The sense of unrealized intention can be detected in the later examples, e.g. послал был Крылова, и Кудеяр сам назвался (1576) 'I was going to send Krylov but Kudejar volunteered'. This becomes modern посла́л бы́ло.

(*g*) The pluperfect disappeared in the course of the 17th c. and no doubt earlier in colloquial speech. Dial. formulae of the type земля́ была́ вы́сохла (но опя́ть промо́кла) still exist, though not widespread, but it is difficult to be sure that they are direct descendants of the pluperfect; the *l*-form may be felt as purely adjectival.

107 (*h*) The *future-perfect* is frequent in early legal documents; the following examples show the standard formula (from Русская Правда):

а кто будеть началъ, тому платити . . . 'whoever began [it] must pay . . .';

оже будеть убилъ въ свадѣ или въ пиру явлено . . . 'if he shall have killed [someone] in a brawl or in public at a feast . . .'.[107]

Modern usage still requires the *future* in such contexts: this has to be the *pf* fut. (когда́ приду́ 'when I arrive').

There was no widespread tendency to use the form as a *pf* simple fut. (without perfect reference), as in Polish,[108] but some examples may be taken this way.

(*i*) The future-perfect became obsolescent somewhat earlier than the pluperfect. Thus by the 17th c. the perfect aspect (system

---

[107] So in ChSl.: аще буду Богу угодилъ и приялъ мя будетъ Богъ (*RPC s.a.* 1074).

[108] Mod. Pol. *będę pisał* or *będę pisać* 'I shall write'.

of perfect tenses) with its built-in relative relation had been given up together with the two relative past tenses, imperf. and aor. The (present) perfect becomes a unique generalized *preterite*. Modern Russian has no tenses of *relative* time.

The Future Tenses

108　There were a number of inherited *pf presents* in ESl., e.g. from *pf* дать, пасть, сесть, лечь, стать, купить, which formed a basis for the reinterpretation of *all pf* presents as *pf futures* (4.87). The present often suffices for the (immediate) future, as in most languages: за́втра е́ду в Ло́ндон 'I am going to London tomorrow'.

CSl. apparently had no specific future formations; all the Slav languages have created new types. A (compound) *impf* future came to be formed with various originally modal auxiliaries from which the modal significance gradually drained away. In early ESl. texts we find:

1. *pf* present иму, имет(ь) + inf. and also *impf* present имамь, имать + inf. (§92 above) 'have'. The latter is a *Slavonicism* only and belongs to the literary tradition thoughout:

(*a*)　OCS: не иштѣте чьто имате ѣсти и чьто пити (Matt. 6: 31) 'Take no thought, saying, what shall we eat? or what shall we drink?'
ChSl.: злою смертию умрѣти имаши (1073 *Anthology*, text no. 6) 'you shall die a dreadful death'. Pólotsky still uses it in his learned and artificial ChSl. poetry (17th c.).

(*b*)　си имуть имати дань на насъ (*RPC ad init.*) 'these people will exact tribute from us';
аще бо възмете рать межю собою, погании имуть радоваться и возмуть [*pf* fut.] землю нашу (*RPC s.a.* 1097) '. . . the pagans will be glad and will take away our land';
а хто сю грамоту иметь рушити (1353) 'whoever shall break [the provisions of] this document'.

This formula is perhaps the prevailing one of clear, if slightly modal, futures down to *c.*1450. It has since died out in Russian[109] but is preserved in Ukr. where procedure (3) below did not develop: читатиму 'I shall read' (parallel to Romance *j'aimerai* < coll. Lat. *amāre habeo*).

---

[109] A future with (и)му + *impf* inf. is recorded in some N. dialects along the Volga.

109 2. Formations with хощу/хочу 'wish':

се уже хочемъ померети отъ глада (*RPC s.a.* 997)
предатися хотять людье печенѣгомъ (ibid. 968) (side by side with
предатися имамъ печенѣгомъ).

These are clearly futures of *necessity* ('we are bound to die . . .');
no *wish* is involved.

Despite the sporadic use of the Russianized хочу the formula is
always a Slavonicism. It is more or less modal in OCS but has
become the normal (neutral) SSl. future (SCr. and Blg.).[110] As in
modern SSl. languages the inf. can be of *either aspect*.

3. Formations with -чьну 'begin'. Нач(ь)ну, поч(ь)ну and
уч(ь)ну are all used. The first two appear in early texts, поч(ь)ну
perhaps belonging especially to the North (Novg. dial.). Уч(ь)ну
is characteristic of the Muscovy period; the earliest example is
dated 1405. It is the commonest auxiliary in the *Stogláv* (1551) and
throughout the 17th c. The inf. could be of *either aspect* but is
normally *impf.*[111] The literal sense is, of course, frequent and it is
not always possible to decide whether the formula is to be taken
as a neutral future:

которая ли вьрвь начнеть платити дикую виру . . . (*RP,* art. 4) 'if any
commune begins(?) to pay a communal wergild . . .';
аже начьнеть не знати у кого купилъ (ibid., art. 37) 'if he shall not
recognize whom he bought [it] from . . .'

110 4. The modern буду + inf.[112] appears only at a late date. There
is no reliable example from Central Russia before the 15th c.:
а язъ буду ся отъ нихъ боронить закономъ Божиимъ (1450).
It is still rare throughout the 16th c.

Its formation is similar to that of German *ich werde lesen* (but

[110] The 'wish' future may be accounted one of the conspicuous 'Balkanisms' in
SSl., shared with Greek, Albanian, and Romanian. Greek was probably the
originating language: *impf* θὰ γράφω, *pf* θὰ γράψω (θὰ < θέλω ἵνα 'I wish to').
SCr. has likewise greatly reduced the auxiliary forms: SCr. *ću* < *hoću* (still required
for the literal sense 'I wish'), etc.; Blg. has invariable ще [šte], as in Greek.

[111] Throughout the history of Russian all verbs of beginning, continuing, and
ending require an *impf* infinitive: я на́чал/продолжа́л/ко́нчил чита́ть; all define a
process (reading).

[112] Бу́ду is a *pf* future (entry into state) so is to that extent parallel to иму,
начьну, etc. and стану (type (5) below).

the German is without aspectual limitation), which had become normal in most German dialects by *c*.1300. Before that we also find *werden* + p.p.a. The earliest Czech texts (before 1300) have both of these—*budu* + inf., rarely *budu* + p.p.a.—as well as the strictly speaking fut.-perf. *budu* + *l*-participle.

There is at least a strong possibility that *budu* + inf. is a Germanism in Czech (Prague had a large German population at all times).

Polish also shows *będę* + inf. from its earliest texts; the native *będę* + *l*-participle was at first used very sparingly but became commoner from the 16th c. as an alternative *simple* future (an alternative which still remains today).[113] Polish came under strong Czech influence from *c*.1350.

It must be specially noted that *budu* + inf. is virtually absent from SSl.[114] and completely absent from OCS (ChSl.). The first examples in Muscovite texts are either in documents concerned with Western politics, i.e. with either Poland or Lithuania which used the somewhat Polonized 'West Russian chancellery language' (7.23) containing буду + inf. frequently from *c*.1500, or in authors closely connected with the WSl. world, e.g. Peresvétov (first half of 16th c.), who spent several years in Bohemia and Poland, and Prince Kúrbsky, who fled to Lithuania in 1564. We may also note the evidence of Donatus's *Latin Grammar*, translated in the early years of the 16th c., which records, with terminological misconceptions: 2 причастия иземлются от слова дел[ь]наго (sc. the verb): настоящее яко *любящъ*, а грядущее яко *будетъ любити* (Lat. *amans, amaturus*).

There is thus little reason to doubt that this type of *impf* future, whatever support it may have had *within* living Russian, started as a *literary* importation, reaching Moscow from the West and more immediately from White Russia.[115] Where it occurs there are often other Polonisms, e.g. и язъ о томъ буду писати до государя своего (1558) (писать до is the Polish, not the Russian construction).

Conversely, there are at most doubtful examples in *Domostrój*

---

[113] The chief 14th c. texts—*Psałterz floriański, Psałterz puławski, Biblia królowej Zofii*—have 20 per cent or less *będę* + *l*-participle.

[114] It is found in early čakavic SCr. texts (where it may be native) but is displaced by the Balkan 'wish' future in the 16th c.

[115] Буду + inf. is reported sporadically in the Ukr. area from *c*.1350, no doubt as a Polonism. It remains in Ukr. as an alternative to type 1(*b*) above.

(1550s) where native procedures and vocabulary dominate: ино уже вдвое будетъ платити. The *Uloženie* of 1649, a conservative text in most respects, only employs the traditional уч(ь)ну of officialese. Kotoshíkhin (mid 17th c.) also only uses it rarely, following the practice of деловóй язы́к.

Perhaps the best chronological contrast is between Avvakúm (b. 1621) who uses no бýду (but the need for the future tense is small) and Pososhkóv (b. 1652) for whom бýду is normal.

Бýду + inf. appears to have become the *spoken* norm also about the middle of the 17th c.

The points of entry into general Russian usage are perhaps two:

(*a*) The existence, if only precarious, in the 16th c. of the future-perfect бýду + *l*-participle and, conceivably, the fact that parts of быть were otherwise the only auxiliaries (in the passive).

(*b*) More important, the widespread use of the sg. 3 бýдет in *impersonal* future sentences, with a dative of the interested person expressed or implied (i.e. the future form of the universal dat. + inf.), e.g. the dubious example from *Dom.* above and кому вами будет владѣти? 'who will own you?' (Песни Джемса, *с.* 1620). The transition to кто вами будет владеть? is small. The universality of бýду + inf. in all parts of Russia is evidently against it being a purely literary importation.

111 5. A future стану + *impf* inf. is recorded occasionally in Novg. texts of the 12th c., but is nowhere common till the 17th c. Ludolf defines the fut. as буду *vel* стану without further comment. It is still a living procedure but has never been completely grammaticalized as a neutral future; it retains a modal sense of *intention*, especially in negative phrases:

не станешь писать . . . (Grozny, 1576) 'if you won't write . . .';
из города в город винá по-прежнему возить не станут, но куды приедет, тут и купить будет[116] (Pososhkóv, *с.* 1724) 'they will not (have to) transport liquor from one town to another as heretofore . . .'.

The procedure was favoured by Avvakúm, perhaps being characteristic of his middle Volga dialect.

---

[116] Impersonal бýдет (since the inf. is *pf*): 'wherever [a person] happens to be, he [ему understood] will be able to buy [liquor] there'.

Imperative

112 The following early ESl. forms are attested:

		A1, 2	A3	B1, 2
Sg.	2	нес-и́	пиш-и́	мол-и́
	3	-и́	-и́	-и́
Du.	1	нес-ѣвѣ	пиш-и́вѣ	мол-и́вѣ
	2, 3	-ѣта[117]	-и́та	-и́та
Pl.	1	нес-ѣмъ	пиш-и́мъ	мол-и́мъ
	2	-ѣте	-и́те	-и́те

113 *Commentary*

1. The ChSl. forms are essentially the same but preserve stem palatalization, later removed in Russian: пьци́/R. пеки́, даждь, виждь (early ESl. дажь, later only дай). A complete paradigm is found at least in the verb *byti*: sg. 1 *bǫdĕmĭ*, 2, 3 *bǫdi*; du. 1 *bǫdĕvĕ*, 2 *bǫdĕta*, 3 *bǫdĕte*; pl. 1 *bǫdĕmŭ*, 2 *bǫdĕte*, 3 *bǫdǫ*.

2. The 1st and 3rd persons are optative or hortatory ('let us', 'may they'). The colloquial evolves other procedures. In the 12th–14th c. ать (cf. Czech *at'*) is the 3rd pers. marker: ате промьжю събою урядяте ся [= урядять] (1229) 'let them settle [the matter] between themselves'. It is replaced by пусть (subliterary пуска́й), imperatives of *pf* пусти́ть/*impf* пуска́ть 'let': а онъ пусть едеть ко Пскову (*c.*1464) 'let him come to Pskov'.

The pl. 1 may be said to persist in (pres.) идём 'let us go', more usually *pf* (fut.) напи́шем 'let us write', the small differences of form having been abandoned. Идём implies *two* people (I and thou), идёмте, with added pl. 2 ending, *more than two* (I and you, all of us). This colloquial procedure is recorded at latest in the 17th c.:

> да грѣнёмте бра́тцы
> въ я́ровы весе́лца (Песни Джемса, *c.*1620)

> 'let us bend to our oars (?of sycamore), boys . . .'
> (грѣнем < грѣ(б)нуть *pf*, inchoative of грести́ 'row').

Another colloquial procedure—no doubt more recent—is дава́йте + *impf* inf. (игра́ть) or *pf* fut. (сыгра́ем) 'let us play'.

ChSl. frequently has the Balkan да + present, still possible in Russian in solemn formulae:

---

[117] Here too (§98 above) ESl. has -та corresponding to OCS (ChSl.) -*te* in the 3rd pers.: идета на роту (*RP*, art. 37) 'let them both swear an oath'.

да при́дет цѣсар(е)ствие твое́ 'thy Kingdom come';
а Б[ог]ъ буди за тѣмь . . . да судить ему Б[ог]ъ (Mstislav's Deed,
c.1130) 'may God be . . . may God judge him . . .'.

3. In the remaining essential 2nd pers. forms (the dual also
disappearing) the minority type in pl. 2 -ѣте conforms to the
majority: неси́, неси́те. *Ostr.* already has приведите.

4. The full vowel -и- is retained only when stressed, or unstressed
after a difficult group of consonants (испо́лни). Otherwise и > ь,
or й after vowels: бу́дь(те), зна́й(те). Examples with reduction
are found from the 13th c.

5. The negative has no special forms or procedures. Some dialects have preserved the formula не моги́(те) + inf. (with моги́
restored from мози́), originally no doubt a strong expression ('don't
dare to . . .'). Current in ChSl.: не мози зазрѣти мнѣ . . . не
мозѣте кляти (colophon to *Ostr.*); не мози повѣдати никомуже
от братьи (*RPC s.a.* 1091) 'do not tell any of the brothers'.[118]

Infinitive and Supine

114   1. The *infinitive* in -ти is the dat. (or conceivably loc.) case of
an *ĭ*-stem verbal noun.

2. The ending -ти has only been preserved under stress: нести́,
ити́.[119] Conversely, some dialects have несть for нести́ *et sim.*

Reduction of -ти to -ть can be observed from the 13th c. Written
texts, whether ChSl. or not, tended to maintain -ти but the spoken
form was clearly -ть throughout the Muscovy period. *Domostrój*
has a high proportion of -ть; the second edition of the conservative
Uloženie of 1649 changes many -ти to -ть. The two forms are
frequently mixed in one and the same text, showing that -ть was
the spoken but -ти was considered the written norm, e.g. in
Vasili's correspondence with Ivan Grozny (1576): послать, писать,
сказать, говорить but спросити, солгати, окупати.

Traditional oral poetry preserves -ти for metrical reasons:

> да хо́четъ тере́мы лома́ти,
> меня́ хочетъ царе́вну пойма́ти
> и на У́стюжну на желе́зную отосла́ти . . .

(Песни Джемса, c.1620; a recent composition, since referring to the fall
of Borís Godunóv in 1605).

[118] This formula is still normal in coll. SCr. in the form *nèmōj(te)* = 'don't . . .'.
[119] In найти́, уйти́, etc. Reformed from the 14th c. as идти́ (итти́) after the pres.
stem. The subliterary итти́ть, with an extra normalized -ть, is fairly common from
the 17th to early 19th c.: не сойти́ться никогда́ (Lérmontov).

3. Velar stems have -чь (Type A1): бере́чь < берег-ти, печь < пек-ти, стричь < стриг-ти. Бечь (< бег-тй) survives in dialect but is replaced in the standard language by бежа́ть (< бег-ѣ-ти).

115　4. The *supine* is the verbal noun of intention; the form *-tŭ* is parallel to, if not identical with, the Lat. (acc.) *amātum*. It is regularly used after verbs of motion in early ESl., almost always (and properly) from *impf* verbs:[120]

да поидѣте княжитъ и володѣти [altered] нами (*RPC s.a.* 862) 'come and rule over us';

снидѣвѣся сама боротъ (ibid. 1022) 'let the two of us meet in (single) combat';

придоша половци первое на русьскую землю воеватъ (ibid. 1061) 'the Cumans came for the first time to make war on Russia';

а въ Новгородъ въсла .р̃. муж[ь] Новгородьць Мьстислав[а] проваживатъ из Новагорода (*Novg. Chr., s.a.* 1215) 'he sent 100 Novgorod citizens into Novgorod to remove Mstislav thence';

русину не звати латина на поле битъ ся (1229) 'a Russian may not challenge a foreigner to a duel'.

If the verb is transitive, the supine, as a noun, is followed by the gen.: идеть рыбъ ловитъ '(he) is going fishing' (i.e. 'for the catching of fish').

The supine was easily confused with the infinitive, which could have similar syntactical employment. In *Ostr.* we find: *idǫ položiti město*; *posŭla prizŭvati* (NB *pf* infinitives) but also correctly: *pride žena . . . počrětŭ vodý* '. . . to draw water' (R. поче́рпать).

The 1229 Treaty has: из Риги ехали на гочкыи берьго [= берегъ] тамо твердити миръ '. . . to make peace' (for твердитъ мира).

The supine was obsolete by the 15th c. Иду пахат is recorded from dialects but this may be a depalatalized infinitive (see §97 (*d*) above).

116 *Conditional*

OCS possessed a special conditional (presumably optative) tense of *byti*, viz. *bimĭ, bi, bi, bimŭ, biste, bǫ*, used with the *l*-participle of other verbs. This was already largely replaced in ChSl. by the aorist *byxŭ, by, by*, etc. No temporal distinctions are possible. ESl.

---

[120] As the result of an *intention* is only problematical and not actual the *pf* aspect is inappropriate. The same rule applies generally today with the infinitive.

has only the latter: аж быхъмъ что тако учинили (1229) 'if we
should do anything . . . '.

With the fairly early decadence of the aorist in ESl. the auxiliary
is reduced to an invariable particle (sg. 3) бы. There are examples
from the 13th c.: аще бы въ Турѣ [Tyre] быша силы были (1215),
where pl. 3 быша is still present but the extra бы shows the way
things are going. By the 14th c. we find аще бы слѣпи были
(1339). Full invariability is certain with the appearance of чтобы
'in order to' in the 14th c.:

а тыбъ ко мнѣ и впередъ о своемъ здоровьѣ отписывала . . . чтобы
мнѣ про то было вѣдомо (letter of Basil III to his wife Helen, c.1526–30).

Бы is early used to introduce uncertainty:

се убихъ Бориса; како бы убити Глѣба? (*RPC s.a.* 1015; later text)

and later as a marker of necessity or duty:

все бы было прибрано (*Dom.*) 'everything must be tidied away'.

For conditional clauses see 4.23 ff.

PARTICIPLES (VERBAL ADJECTIVES)

117   As with all adjectives a full 'short' and 'long' declension was, at
least theoretically, available. It is only necessary to show here the
peculiarities of the sg. and pl. NAG.

118 *Present Participle Active (p.p.a.)*

Commentary to Table XV

1. The suffix is *-ont/-ent-j-*, giving OCS *-ǫšt-/-ęšt-* (in ESl. spelling -ѫщ/-ущ- and -ащ-/-ящ-) but native ESl. *-uč'-/-jač'-* (-уч-/-яч-)
(1.19).

2. In addition to this important difference *consonantal roots*
(Type A1) have *ESl.* sg. masc./neut. nom. -a (неса, ида) but *ChSl.*
-ы (несы, иды).[121] The types зна́я, моля́, etc. are (nasals apart)
identical in both. As only a small minority of verbs had -a, it
disappears before analogical -я by the 15th c.: неся́, идя́ (and
неся́й, идя́й). Example: се язъ . . . пишу д[у]ш[е]вную грамоту
ида въ ворду (Ivan Kalitá, 1327–8) 'This is my last will and
testament [since I am] going to the Horde'.

3. The sg. fem. nom. is in *-ī* (§7 above). This too is early levelled
out: несучи(я) > несуча(я).

[121]   It is not certain whether this difference is phonological or morphological.

TABLE XV. The Present Participle Active

Early East Slav

		Short			Long		
		Masc.	Neut.	Fem.	Masc.	Neut.	Fem.
Sg.	N	неса	неса	несучи	несаи	несаи	несучия
	A	несучь	несуче	несучу (-чю)	N or G	несучее	несучую
	G	несуча (-чя)	несуча	несучѣ	несучего	несучего	несучеѣ
Pl.	N	несуче	несуча	несучѣ	несучеи (-ии)	несучая	несучѣѣ
	A	несучѣ	несуча	несучѣ	несучѣѣ	несучая	несучѣѣ
	G		несучь			несуч(и)ихъ	

OCS (ChSl.)

		Short		
		Masc.	Neut.	Fem.
Sg.	N	*nesy*	*nesy*	*nesǫšti*
	A	*nesǫštĭ*	*nesǫšte*	*nesǫštǫ*
	G	*nesǫšta*	*nesǫšta*	*nesǫštę*
Pl.	N	*nesǫšte*	*nesǫšta*	*nesǫštę*
	A	*nesǫštę*	*nesǫšta*	*nesǫštę*
	G		*nesǫštĭ*	

Similarly:

Early East Slav

		Short			Long		
		Masc.	Neut.	Fem.	Masc.	Neut.	Fem.
Sg.	N	зная	зная	знаючи	знаяи	знаяи	знаючия
		моля	моля	молячи	моляи	моляи	молячия
	A	знаючь	знаюче	знаючу (-чю)	N or G	знаючее	знаючую
		молячь	моляче	молячу	N or G	молячее	молячую
	G	знаюча	знаюча	знаючѣ	знаючего	знаючего	знаючеѣ
		моляча	моляча	молячѣ	молячего	молячего	молячеѣ

OCS (ChSl.)
Short

	Masc.	Neut.	Fem.
Sg. N	znaję	znaję	znajǫšti
A	znajǫštĭ	znajǫšte	znajǫštǫ
G	znajǫšta	znajǫšta	znajǫštę

4. The anomalous forms of the 'long' declension are superseded by regular formations on the oblique stem: знаяи > знаючий, знаючее, and the pl. NA loses gender distinctions as in all adjs.: знаючии, знаючая, знаючѣѣ > знаючие.

119 5. The oblique cases of the *short* declension were little used and disappeared *pari passu* with those of other adjectives. The *nom. forms,* singular and plural, in appositional use, alone remained in common (including colloquial) use, but from an early date tend towards *invariable* 'gerunds' (verbal adverbs),[122] abandoning gender agreement; the prevailing forms are sg. masc. and sg. fem. (or perhaps reformed pl. masc.) in -чи:

жены кланяются тако молвя (1282) (sg. masc. for pl. fem.);
приходячи, бѣгаючи, хотячи (*RPC s.a.* 907, 1054, 1093); but equally commonly платяче, стояче (ibid. 862, 1093).

The change to invariables in -я/-а or -ючи/-учи and -ячи/-ачи (much less common than -я/-а in Type B verbs) was complete by the 15th c.

6. Of the two types, that in -чи appears to be the more colloquial[123] and is still fairly common in the 18th c. It is noticeable that the forms in -чи/-че in *RPC* (as opposed to the ChSl. forms) are almost always from common colloquial verbs· идуче, воюючи, мимоходячи, and examples above. If ChSl. forms are used agreement is usually correct:

корсуняне, подъкопавше стѣну градьскую, крадуще сыплемую перьсть, и ношаху к собѣ въ градъ, сыплюще посредѣ града (*s.a.* 988) (pl. masc. nom. including the past p.a. подъкопавше).

Since the 18th c. the formal paradigm of the verb has preferred

---

[122] Vaillant prefers 'gerundive' (*gérondif*) but the function of the Russian form does not correspond exactly either to the Latin gerund or gerundive.
[123] In *NBG*, no. 9 (*c.* 1200) водя [not веда!] новую жену and добрѣ сътворя have a somewhat literary flavour, especially the second.

the type in -я with few exceptions: будучи 'being' (идучи, бдучи, живучи still possible in the 19th c.).

120   7. A number of invariable gerunds move away from the verb to become free adverbs, conjunctions, etc.: уже не говоря о + loc. 'not to mention'; кончая + instr. (and начиная от/с + gen.) 'ending/beginning with'; нехотя 'unwillingly'; походя 'as one goes along'; смотря по + dat. 'depending on'; несмотря на + acc. (learned невзирая на) 'despite'; судя по + dat. 'judging by' (NB gerund судя); хотя 'although'; не шутя 'in earnest'. So also some forms in -чи: крадучись 'stealthily'; жить припеваючи 'to live in clover'. The three positions лёжа, сидя, стоя are both adverbs and gerunds; the stress is, however, adverbial; similarly молча 'silently' but gerund молча́.

8. It has been suggested that certain colloquial pejorative nouns such as горемыка 'hapless person', пустомеля 'windbag', разиня 'scatter-brain', рёва 'noisy child', etc. are nominalized sg. masc. nom., preserving the older form -a in some cases.

121   9. The 'long' declension (no doubt rare in colloquial) was replaced in *literary* use by the corresponding *ChSl.* forms (very common in high texts): идущий, знающий, молящий. These forms predominate from the earliest texts but were in the nature of things rarely formed from verbs *not current in ChSl*. This situation remained till the middle of the 18th c. Lomonósov, in his normative *Grammar* (§43) took a cautious view of forming p.p.a. in -щий from exclusively Russian verbs. Usage has gone against him; the form has since then been fully integrated into the paradigm of the (literary) verb: all *impf* verbs form it freely (говорящий, присматривающий). In the reflexive the learned forms maintain -ся: читающийся, etc.; the native gerund has only -сь: решаясь.

122   10. Such native long forms as remain have become dissociated from the verb and are now pure adjs.: летучая мышь 'bat' (p.p.a. летящий '[actually] flying'; летучий 'able to fly'); бродячий музыкант 'strolling player'; висячий мост 'suspension bridge'; певучий 'sing-song'; могучий 'powerful' (p.p.a. могущий); колючий 'prickly'; падучая болезнь 'epilepsy'; стоячая вода 'stagnant water'; текучий 'liquid, mobile' (but текущий месяц 'the current month'); ходячая монета 'coin in circulation'; жгучий вопрос 'burning question'; горячий 'vehement' and горючее 'fuel' (p.p.a. горящий).

Some of these words do not correspond to normal participial

forms; there has clearly been extension of an adjectival category in -учий: плаку́чая и́ва 'weeping willow'. But горю́чий, лету́чий, тягу́чий, and others may belong to obsolete conjugations of the verbs reformed as горе́ть, лете́ть (лета́ть), and тяну́ть (p.p.a. горя́щий, летя́щий). There are (recent) derived nouns of the form плову́чий > плову́честь 'buoyancy'.

The 'long' native forms were not wholly extinct in the 17th c. Avvakúm writes лежа́чева по спинѣ уда́рилъ три́жды 'he struck (me) three times across the back as I lay there'. This might be interpreted as a Russianized лежа́щего, but the forms do appear in popular proverbs: лежа́чего не бьют = 'don't hit a man when he's down'.

11. The literary p.p.a. is now able to form adverbs on a small scale (recent): блестя́ще 'brilliantly', исчеза́юще ма́лое коли́чество (math.) 'infinitely small quantity'; вызыва́юще 'provocatively'. Other short forms are rare: я несве́дущ (в э́том) 'I am no expert'; он я́сен, све́тел, сверка́ющ (Herzen).

123   12. In the early ChSl. style of the chronicles 'continuous' tenses (of the English type) are not uncommon, e.g.

бяше около града [л]ѣсъ и боръ великъ, и бяху ловяще звѣрь . . . (*RPC ad init.*) 'there was about the settlement a great forest (where) they used to hunt';

бѣ бо тогда вода текущи въздолѣ горы киевския (ibid. 945) 'for there was at that time water flowing down the hill of Kiev';

и бѣ Ярославъ любя церковныя уставы (ibid. 1037), followed immediately by попы любяше по велику;

есть церкви та стоящи въ Корсунѣ градѣ (ibid. 988) 'this church is (still) standing in the city of Korsun''.

Similarly in OCS: *bě učę vŭ crŭkŭve* 'he was teaching in the synagogue' (− Gk. ἦν διδάσκων); *bǫdeši mlŭčę* 'you will be silent' (Gk. ἔσῃ σιωπῶν). Such procedures are unknown in any living Slav language. They seem to be an imitation of Greek in OCS. Phrases such as оже будеть кто его мьстя (*RP*, art. 1) hardly belong here; similarly бѣ Ярославъ любя can be translated 'Jaroslav was [a man] who loved . . .'.

24 *Past Participle Active (past p.a.)*

Exactly the same obtains here: only an adverbialized invariable form remained in living usage; all the rest is retained only in literary style from ChSl.

	Short			Long		
	Masc.	Neut.	Fem.	Masc.	Neut.	Fem.
Sg. N	несъ	несъ	несъши	несыи	несъшее	несъшия
	зна-въ	знавъ	знавъши	знавыи	знавъшее	знавъшия
A	несъшь	несъше	несъшу	N or G	несъшее	несъшую
	знавъшь	знавъше	знавъшу		знавъшее	знавъшую
G	несъша	as masc.	несъшѣ	несъшего	as masc.	несъшеѣ
	знавъша		знавъшѣ	знавъшего		знавъшеѣ
Pl. N	несъше	несъша	несъшѣ	несъшии	несъшая	несъшѣѣ
	знавъше	знавъша	знавъшѣ	знавъшии	знавъшая	знавъшѣѣ

The suffix is -ъш- (< -us-) after consonants, -въш- after vowels.
In the Second Conjugation OCS has the symmetrical formation sg.
masc. nom. *xval'ĭ* 'who praised', *pristǫpl'ĭ* 'having approached',
etc., to be considered archaisms in ChSl.

125   *Commentary*

1. The sg. masc. nom. знав, любив, etc. provides the invariable
gerund, with an alternative fem. нёсши, знáвши, люби́вши. The
latter is scarcely alive outside consonant stems (Type A1)—при-
нёсши, пришéдши—and even these are largely replaced by formations on the model of the *present* gerund—принеся́, войдя́ (принёс,
пришёд are quite extinct).[124] The ChSl. equivalent is in -ъше:
рек(ъ)ше 'having said'.

2. The past gerund is certainly as native a formation as the
present gerund; it is naturally almost always formed from *pf*
verbs:

аже кто ударить мечемь, не вынезъ его (*RP,* art. 23) 'if one person
    strikes (another) with a sword, without drawing it' (for выньзъ);
. . . а умреть не заплативъ (1229) '. . . and dies without having paid';
измавъ я вся посла исковавъ по своимъ городомъ (1215) 'having
    arrested them all (he) sent them in chains . . .';
и мы обыскавъ головника, выдали . . . (Pskov, *c.*1464) 'having sought
    out the murderer, we handed (him) over . . .'.

The establishment of an invariable form is complete by the 15th c.
Deverbalized forms (§120 above) are found in (нéсколько лет)
спустя́ 'later' and немнóго погодя́.

---

[124] Other difficult forms have been eliminated by adding -в to the infinitive stem:
взяв, сняв, начáв (for earlier and ChSl. възъмъ, съньмъ, начьнъ). Пришедъ
(пришод) and a few others were still current in the 17th c.

3. In verbs compounded with -ся the form in -ши has been preferred: помоли́вшись. This normalization is subsequent to the 17th c.; the *Uloženie* of 1649 still has не дождався указу *et sim*. In the long learned forms -ся is maintained: чита́вшийся (cf. §121 above).

4. The long forms have retained some literary use (cf. p.p.a. and 4.31).

There is a distinction between па́вший (literal) and purely ChSl. па́дший (metaphorical): па́дшая же́нщина. ChSl. is also усо́пший 'deceased' (< усну́ть, root *sйp*-).

126 The past p.a. in -*l*, perfect in function, is entirely affected to the cpd. perfect tenses, now a general preterite.

(i) Many old *l*-participles have become adjectives (see also §105 (*e*) above): уны́лый 'despondent'; та́лый снег 'melted snow (slush)'; обле́злый 'shabby'; окамене́лый 'petrified'.

(ii) Certain N. and W. dialects use formulae of the type он пришѐдши 'he has arrived', он вы́пивши 'he is drunk', thus re-establishing with the active participle (gerund) in -вш- the specifically perfect sense lost in пришёл, вы́пил. It is possible that this is due to the Baltic substrate (see Table XIX) since Lithuanian uses the corresponding participle with the verb 'to be' in the same contexts as the Slav participle in -*l*.

127 *Present Participle Passive (pres. p.p.)*

1. The characteristic is -*m*-. The short sg. masc. nom. is thus identical (stress differences apart) with the pres. pl. 1: зна́ем, моли́м (long зна́емый, люби́мый); exceptions are only a few consonant stems and anomalous verbs with connective vowel -*o*-: несо́м(ый), вѐдом(ый). The declension is regular adjectival. There is little evidence that this participle was a native ESl. form, apart from a few survivals. In the modern paradigm it is wholly a Slavonicism. Nor is it available from all verbs (*impf*): no verbs with consonant mutation form it (*пишемый). ChSl. example (*RPC s.a.* 1054): помроша бѣгаючи, Божьимь гнѣвомь гоними '. . . pursued by the wrath of God'. Apparently colloquial survivals, now adjectives, are люби́мый 'favourite', роди́мый 'own, native', and perhaps ла́комый 'tasty', (не)ви́димый '(in)visible'; also the forms in -ом-: свѐдом, (за)вѐдомо (adv.). Clearly learned are мни́мый 'imaginary'; весо́мый аргуме́нт 'a weighty argument';

иско́мое[125] (math.) 'the unknown quantity'; насеко́мое 'insect'; (мно́го)уважа́емый X. 'Dear X.' (in letters); derivative пито́мец 'nurseling'. Curious is есто́мые 'eatables' in *Dom.*, of unclear formation.

2. While comparatively little used as a verbal form, the type has been extended in literary vocabulary to provide (long) *adjectives*, usually negative, denoting (im)possibility. The formation is irrespective of aspect (a true *present* participle can only be formed from an *impf* verb): необита́емый 'uninhabited'; непромока́емый 'waterproof'; неисчерпа́емый 'inexhaustible'; обтека́емый (recent) 'streamlined'; необходи́мый 'unavoidable, necessary'; (не)осуществи́мый '(im)practicable'; (не)соизмери́мый '(in)commensurate'; непререка́емый 'incontrovertible'; невозврати́мый 'irretrievable'. Formations from obviously Russian verbs are not excluded: невыноси́мый 'unbearable'; непроходи́мый дура́к 'utter fool'.

There are models in OCS already, e.g. *nerazlǫčimŭ* 'inseparable'. Adverbs are occasionally possible: непроница́емо чёрный 'impenetrably black'.

128 *Past Participle Passive (p.p.p.)*

1. This is a necessary part of the transitive verb and outside ChSl. influence.

There are two types:

(*a*) in -*t*-, mainly from monosyllabic vowel-stems and verbs in -нуть (Types A2, A3α).

(*b*) the majority in -*n*- (-*an*-, -*en*-, -*jen*-): -несен, -писан, -делан, -пущен.

The type in -*t*- has been slightly extended in ESl. compared with OCS: native у-би́т-ый 'killed', OCS (ChSl.) у-биенъ; native откры́т-ый 'opened', ChSl. открове́н(ный) 'open, frank' (figurative).

2. P.p.p. in -ан are always stressed on the root: поте́рян(ный), сде́лан(ный), напи́сан(ный). Exceptions are Slavonicisms (apart from да́нный): жела́нный 'desired', избра́нный 'elect' (now usually и́збран(ный)), несказа́нный 'ineffable'.[126] Foreign words

---

[125] Plausibly a very ancient form before the establishment of the paradigm in *isk-j-* (pres. pl. 1 и́щем).

[126] Scarcely from R. сказа́ть 'say'; OCS (ChSl.) *sŭkazati* = 'explain': *sŭkaži namŭ pritŭčǫ* 'explain the parable to us'.

adapted with -ировать, -изовать often have or had alternative stress but the p.p.p. is preferably - óван-: бомбардировáть, -ирóван; инсценировáть 'produce', only инсценирóван(ный).

The stress of p.p.p. in -ен follows in almost all cases (as a rule of thumb)[127] the stress of the present (future) tense other than the sg. 1, but any palatalization in sg. 1 will also appear in the p.p.p. (-*jen*-):

>*pf* решить 'decide': решу́, реши́т; решён
>*pf* принести 'bring': при-несу́, -несёт; -нссён
>*pf* встре́тить 'meet': встре́чу, встре́тит; встре́чен
>*pf* разбуди́ть 'wake': раз-бужу́, -бу́дит; -бу́жен.

P.p.p. from ChSl. verbs now follow Russian phonology: возбуди́ть 'arouse', p.p.p. возбуждён(ный); победи́ть 'defeat', побеждён(ный). (У-)ви́денный is the only verb not to show the expected palatalization (sg. 1 ви́жу); but the ancient cpd. оби́деть 'insult' has оби́жен(ный). Occasionally there is differentiation: p.p.p. прибли́женный/now only adj. приближённый 'approximate'.

129   3. As an essential part of the predicate the p.p.p. appears in the short form and here preserves its original and correct spelling with one -н-: дан 'given', данó, данá, даны́; (при-)несён 'brought', -несенó, -несенá, -несены́.

As an attribute (long form) the spelling has been arbitrarily changed. Down to the 17th c. we still have predominantly въ разорёныхъ городáхъ, кóшеного сѣна, etc. But there was much confusion with adjectives in -(ь)ный from the same root, often virtually synonymous. Hence, by conflation укáзаный + укáзный (adj.) > укáзанный. Double -нн- (purely graphic; 2.27) begins to appear in the 16th c. (по преже писанному, *Dom.*) but is not fully regularized till the early 19th c.

4. The p.p.p. can theoretically be formed from either aspect but is now almost exclusively a form of the *pf* verb. Formerly *impf* p.p.p. were more freely formed and an aspectual difference is sometimes discernible: one can still write э́та кни́га пи́сана для

---

[127] Exceptions to the stress rule are rare and have arisen by mixed choices where there was a regional or other alternative in the present: standard are now e.g. клони́ть, -клóнит, -клонён; дели́ть, -де́лит, -делён; поручи́ть, -ру́чит, -ручён, but вручи́ть, -ручи́т, -ручён; and some others. Прину́дить and вы́нудить 'force, compel', both with native sg. 1 -нужу, both make p.p.p. in ChSl. form: принуждён (irregular stress), вы́нужден; the *impf* are both -нуждáть.

детéй 'this book has been written for children' (true perfect) in contrast to э́та кни́га напи́сана Чéховым 'this book was written by Chekhov' (equivalent to an aor. passive). The form is by no means extinct outside the passive tenses (i.e. as a near-adjective) and the perfect sense of *acquired state* is usually evident. The old spelling with one -н- is always retained: би́тый час 'a full hour'; бри́тое лицó '(clean-)shaven face' ('shaved' is вы́бритый); варёная ры́ба 'boiled fish'; вита́я лéстница 'spiral staircase'; вощёный пол 'waxed floor'; гружёные вагóны 'loaded wagons'; дéланый 'counterfeit'; дублёные кóжи 'tanned skins'; жáреное мя́со 'roast meat'; жжёная и́звесть 'slaked lime'; золочёный 'gilt, gilded'; калёное желéзо 'red-hot iron'; лóманая ли́ния 'dotted line'; мóлотый кóфе 'ground coffee'; морóженое 'an ice-cream'; рéзаный хлеб 'sliced loaf'; сушёные грибы́ 'dried mushrooms'; стри́женые вóлосы 'cropped hair'; учёный 'scholar'; хóленые рýки 'well-kept hands'; непрóшеный 'unsolicited', and numerous other negatives.

In the 16th–17th c. p.p.p. were more or less freely formed from *cpd. imperfectives* in a frequentative sense: дворя́не посы́ланы 'officers have been (repeatedly) sent'; а столникомъ . . . давано ис царские казны жалование (Kot.) 'a salary from the Treasury has been (regularly) paid . . .'; он распрашиванъ (1623) 'he has been questioned (several times)'.

This specific sense is not, however, always apparent; many such forms are no doubt due to the Polish fashions of the period (7.25); in Polish this participial formation is still normal. They have entirely disappeared from standard literary Russian.

130   5. Muscovite Russian also widely employed *impersonal* p.p.p. (neuter) from *intransitive* and *reflexive* verbs as well as transitive:

никому ни в чемъ не слыгивано [солгать *pf*], ни манено, ни пересрочено (*Dom.*, 16th c.);
а остатки [асс.] сверчено и связано (ibid.);
а с калмыками де у нихъ помиренось же (17th c.) 'peace has been made'.

The prevalence of this procedure in strongly colloquial texts (including Ivan Grozny's letters)[128] suggests that it was normal usage at that level, and indeed similar procedures are still widely recorded from N. and W. dialects: у него уехано = он уехал (usually *pluperfect*); всю картóшку съедено (N. dial.) 'all the

---

[128] А уж заехано, 4.82.

potatoes have been eaten'; у кота руку исцарапано (W. dial.) '(my) hand was scratched by the cat'; сижено 'we sat'; жито 'one has lived'.

But once again there may have been, at least in more literary contexts, some influence of Polish where compound passive tenses are avoided if the subject is *inanimate*. The following is a typical modern example: *Podatki* [acc. pl.] *nie tylko podwyższano ale także wydzierżawiano; uciekano się też do konfiskat* 'taxes were not only raised but also farmed out; recourse was had also to confiscations'. This procedure also disappeared from standard Russian after Peter the Great's reign. It persists in Ukrainian, perhaps as a Polonism.

131 6. A few ChSl. p.p.p. have been incorporated into Russian literary vocabulary as adjectives, e.g. совершённый (p.p.p. совершённый, 2.46), незабвенный 'unforgettable', обыкновенный 'ordinary, usual', вдохновенный 'inspired' (p.p.p. вдохновлён), дерзновенный 'insolent', откровенный 'frank' (p.p.p. открыт), надменный 'arrogant' (p.p.p. надутый). Difference in form is most conspicuous in verbs in -нуть (Type A2): согбенный 'bowed' (native p.p.p. согнутый 'bent').

Some participles from now intransitive verbs in Russian are either due to a change in rection or are from ChSl.: достигнутый 'attained' (достигнуть + gen.); пожертвованный 'donated' (otherwise жертвовать чем 'sacrifice'); неожиданный 'unexpected' (ожидать + gen.); желанный 'desired' (желать + gen.).

7. Russian has differentiated by stress certain p.p.p. segregated as adjectives: занятый 'occupied'/занятой 'busy'; развитый 'developed'/развитой 'mature' (short masc. развит and развит respectively).

132 *The Participles of* быть

These are all obviously ChSl. (except in its transitive cpds., e.g. p.p.p. забытый 'forgotten') but have achieved wide spoken use:

(*a*) p.p.a. сущий (the original sg. masc. nom. ESl. са(и), ChSl. сы(и) also occur). Now only metaphorical: он сущий дурак 'he is a perfect fool'. Many ChSl. derivatives: существо, существенный.

(*b*) *Future* будущий,[129] now an adj.: на будущей неделе 'next week'; в будущем 'in the future'.

---

[129] The unique fut. participle (буду is a *pf* tense); there are rare ChSl. alternatives, viz. на придущемь вѣцѣ (*RPC s.a.* 1068) 'in the life to come' (not an old form).

(*c*) Past p.a. бы́вший, from officialese: бы́вший секрета́рь 'former, ex-secretary'.

PASSIVE VOICE

133   1. On the evidence of OCS, CSl. had long abandoned any special passive (or middle) paradigm; the only passive *forms* were the indispensable p.p.p. and the pres. p.p. All Slav vernaculars untouched by education and literature avoid(ed) passive syntax as far as possible. It is still more natural and better in Russian to say э́ту кни́гу везде́ чита́ют than э́та кни́га везде́ чита́ется. Compare the text of Kotoshíkhin with the translation in 7.31.

If the passive is not be avoided, two procedures are possible and common in OCS (ChSl.):

(*a*) p.p.p. + appropriate part of auxiliary быть;
(*b*) a verb compounded with -ся (-*sę*).[130]

2. ChSl. and Slavonicized style continues the use of (*b*) as passive more or less irrespective of tense and aspect. It is highly doubtful that this procedure was ever native ESl. The more colloquial texts indicate that 'reflexive' passives were confined to *inanimate* subjects and the *impf* (continuous) tenses. In Russian кни́га пи́шется is normal but *кни́га написа́лась and *кни́га напи́шется are impossible; and ребёнок мо́ется = 'is washing (itself)', never 'is being washed'. Verbs that do allow a *pf* passive of this kind will be found to be Slavonicisms; only usage decides whether they are correct or not.

Altogether 'reflexive' forms as passives are shown to be largely literary by their relative rarity in, say, the colloquial parts of the *Novg. Chronicle*. The present pattern of usage is certainly not independent of ChSl. influence nor of W. European (French)

---

[130] As a verbal affix -ся has several uses. It will suffice to recall the other main ones here:

(i) true reflexive (internal *trans.*): (у)мы́ться 'wash (oneself)'; сади́ться 'seat oneself';

(ii) reciprocal: они́ ча́сто перепи́сываются 'they often correspond';

(iii) 'deponent' (internal *intrans.*, where ся may represent an earlier си, dat. of involvement): боя́ться 'fear'; намерева́ться 'intend' (*боя́ть, *намерева́ть do not exist).

(iv) impersonal (with dat. of involvement): мне хо́чется 'I want to'; мне не спи́тся 'I cannot sleep' (я хочу́, я не сплю equally possible but of different implication).

influence in the 18th–19th c. The language can thus make distinctions such as счита́ть себя́ + instr. 'to consider oneself', счита́ться 'to be considered' (by others).

3. Shades of meaning are obtainable at the literary level by substituting the habitual быва́ть for the auxiliary быть (быва́ет, быва́л прочи́тан) or the pres. p.p. for the p.p.r.: когда́ ру́сское иску́сство бы́ло гони́мо (Blok) '. . . was being persecuted'.

4. Ся only becomes fully bound to the verb form in the 17th c.; 16th c. texts still exhibit some freedom: сам назвался/ся сам назвал (same text, 1576).

134   5. The present-day paradigm is thus:

	Present	Past	Future
impf	кни́га пи́шется	писа́лась	бу́дет писа́ться
	is being written	was being written	will be (being) written
	is (always) written	used to be written	
pf	кни́га напи́сана	была́ напи́сана	бу́дет напи́сана
	has been written	was written	will be written
		had been written	will have been written

It should be specially noted that the conflation of aorist and perfect into a general preterite *does not take place* in the passive, where the present of the perfect кни́га (есть) напи́сана is still distinct. So in OCS: (aor.) *zatvoreny byšę dvĭri* 'the doors were closed' (action) but *juže dvĭri zatvoreny sǫtŭ* 'the doors have been closed, are closed' (state); and in ChSl.: не ходи, отьць ти умерлъ а братъ ти убиенъ от Святополка (*RPC s.a.* 1015) '. . . your brother has been killed by Svjatopolk' (with parallel active perfect).

Further examples of usage (ChSl. style):

яко же пишется (*RPC s.a.* 852) 'as is written';

си вси звахуться [imperf.] отъ Грекъ Великая Скуфь (ibid. 907) 'all these (people) were called by the Greeks "Great Scythia"';

пересѣчены быша грекы (ibid. 915) 'the Greeks were massacred';

написахомъ харатью сию, на неи же суть имяна наша написана (ibid. 945) 'we have written this document in which our names have been listed';

хранити все еже есть написана на неи (ibid.) 'to observe everything that is written in it';

и от тѣхъ заповѣдано обновити ветъхии миръ (ibid.) 'and (we) have been instructed by them to renew the former peace(-treaty)'.

In a colloquial text we find: аж бы миръ не ръздрушенъ былъ 'that the peace may not be broken'; аже будет(ь) холъпъ убитъ 'if a slave is murdered'; but аже кого уранять (pl. 3) 'if someone is wounded' (all 1229).

6. The extension of passive forms to the infinitive (быть сде́лан(ным)) and gerund (бу́дучи сде́ланным) is certainly literary only and recent.

7. It is therefore legitimate to say that though early ESl. had theoretically a complete passive system in practice its use was severely limited. Present usage has been formalized gradually under literary influences (ChSl. and Western).

VERBAL NOUN

135　1. In form the verbal noun adds -*ĭje* (ChSl. -ие, Russian -ье) to the short p.p.p., and is theoretically available from all verbs, trans. and intrans., *pf* and *impf*. Pure Russian forms are now relatively rare, usually from simple primary verbs and often with final stress: мытьё 'washing', шитьё 'sewing', дутьё 'glass-blowing', купа́нье 'bathing' (купа́ться); and frequently from verbs of sound, e.g. ка́рканье 'croaking', to which may be added the learned terms а́канье and цо́канье (Table XVII), etc. and derivatives of colloquial verbs in -ничать (< nouns in -ник), e.g. грима́сни-чанье 'pulling faces'. Many have passed from *action* to *concrete*: варе́нье 'jam', ку́шанье 'food, meal', вяза́нье '(piece of) knit-ting'. All the formations in -ание/-ение are on principle literary Slavonicisms: спасе́ние 'salvation', иссле́дование 'investigation', (раз)реше́ние 'solution', etc. Поня́тие 'idea' and понима́ние 'understanding' show the difference between the *pf* and *impf* verb. An artificial difference has also been established between (ChSl. spelling) воскресе́ние 'resurrection' and (R. spelling) вос-кресе́нье 'Sunday'.

Slavonicisms are particularly evident in the verbs in -нуть (ChSl. p.p.p. in -овен): исчезнове́ние 'disappearance', прикоснове́ние 'contact', мгнове́ние 'instant' (R. мигну́ть 'blink'), ка́мень преткнове́ния 'stumbling block'; also забве́ние 'oblivion' but R. забытье́ 'swoon' (both from забы́ть). Russian forms in -утье are no longer current (тяну́тье is still recorded in 1708).

As a now fully acclimatized derivative the noun in -ние is formed freely from purely Russian verbs: перепи́сывание 'copying (process)', выраже́ние 'expression'. A Russian spelling of these ChSl. words is quite frequent in early texts: не преимаи же ученья отъ Латынъ (*RPC s.a.* 988); начало княженья Ярославля (ibid. 1016). Conversely in the 1229 Treaty: аж товаръ перевезлъ без дѣржания 'that he may transport the goods without delay', the noun may well be colloquial. Forms in -нье are common in poetry for metrical convenience.

136   2. Verbal nouns from derived *impf* verbs denote the pure process and are common in technical language: отбе́ливание 'bleaching'; распознава́ние самолётов 'aircraft recognition'; при нава́ривании 'during the process of welding'. So in ChSl.: пострига́ние 'action of tonsuring' but пострише́ние 'the (whole) ceremony of tonsuring (and its result)'. But in ordinary usage one form commonly does duty for both, especially as many such words now indicate *state* rather than *action*, or are completely concretized: возмуще́ние (< воз-мути́ться and -муща́ться) 'indignation'; ChSl. одѣние/одѣяние 'dressing' > 'dress, clothes'; расте́ние 'plant'; зда́ние 'building'.

3. While the verbal noun in -нье is certainly native, the characteristic verbal nouns of Russian are either suffixless or with suffix -ка; the latter are rarely recorded before the 18th c. but are often preferred thereafter as technical terms: перепи́ска 'correspondence', ва́рка (пи́ва) 'brewing' (rather than варе́ние), стри́жка ове́ц 'sheep-shearing'. Modern vocabulary is thus rich in contrasts such as:

Native	ChSl.
сбор 'gathering, collection'	собра́ние 'collection' (concrete)
сбо́рка 'assembly'	собира́ние 'process of collecting'

and

Native	ChSl.
разворо́т 'turn'	развра́т 'depravity'
развёртка 'development'	развраще́ние 'corruption'.

4. It should be noted that the infinitive by itself was not used in the earlier language as the *subject* of a clause: this is the role of the verbal noun.[131] This usage becomes common under Western

[131] It was sufficiently verbal in OCS to take an object in the acc.: *o sŭbranii sŭborŭ.*

TABLE XVI. Summary of the Modern Verbal Paradigm

	Imperfective			Perfective		
	Process or habit	Participle	Gerund	Event	Participle	Gerund
Present	act. читáю I read, I am reading pass. читáется is (being) read	читáющий* (who is) reading читáющийся* (which is) being read	читáя (while) reading читáясь (while) being read	—	—	—
Future	act. бýду читáть I shall (be) read(ing) pass. бýдет читáться will be (being) read	—	—	прочитáю I shall read, I shall have read бýдет прочитан will be read	—	—
Past	act. читáл was reading, used to read pass. читáлся was being read, used to be read	читáвший* (who was) reading читáвшийся* (which was) being read	читáя (rare) having read читáвшись (rare) having been read	прочитáл read, have read, had read aor. был прочитан was read, had been read perf. прочитан has been read	прочитáвший* who read (прочитáвшийся*) (not always available) прочитанный read	прочитáв having read (прочитáвшись) (not always available)
Imperative	act. читáй! read! (go on reading!) pass. читáйся!	—	—	прочитáй! read!	—	—
Conditional	act. читáл бы would read	—	—	будь прочитáн! прочитáл бы would read, would have read	—	—
Infinitive	pas. читáлся бы act. читáть	—	—	был бы прочитан прочитáть быть прочитанным	—	—
Verbal noun	pass. читáться вы-читáние* 'subtraction'	—	—	чтéние* (from parallel verb честь/ прочéсть pf)	—	—

For considerations of aspect see also 4.83 ff. The starred forms are of ChSl. provenance.

influence in the 18th c. only. Proverbs, etc.—which may be old—can have the infinitive in a phraseological group, e.g. жизнь прожи́ть — не по́ле перейти́.

VERBS WITH VARIOUS ANOMALIES

137   1. Throughout Slav, сплю, спит 'sleep' (Type B1) has an unexplained infinitive спать.

2. Хоте́ть (early ESl. хотѣти and also х(ъ)тѣти) 'wish, want', apparently an old athematic verb reformed with a new infinitive of state. It had until the 17th c. a regular present of Type A3β, except for the original pl. 3 хотя́т(ь), with which goes a p.p.a. хотя́чий (> gerund хотя́): а вы хочете изъмерети гладомъ (*RPC s.a.* 946) 'you will (surely) die of starvation' (future, §109 above). Since then the pl. 1, 2 have submitted to the attraction of the pl. 3 and are now only хоти́м, хоти́те.

138   3. The CSl. verb *děti pf* (originally athematic?) has the following development of forms and senses:

(*a*)   OCS *děti pf* 'put', pres.-fut. *deždǫ* (< *ded-j-*, similar in form to *damĭ* < *dad-mĭ* (§91 above)).

The corresponding ESl. pres.-fut. (or pres.?) *děže*-survived until at least the 13th c.: камь [= камо] его хочеть, тамъ [= тамо] дѣжеть (1229), but the verb was reformed as *pf* деть, де́ну (on the model of стать, ста́ну), now mainly in cpds., e.g. оде́ть(ся) 'dress', заде́ть 'touch', with new *impf* дева́ть. Older *impf* дѣяти in ChSl. наде́яться 'hope, rely on', одея́ние 'clothes' (reduplicated stem in наде́жда 'hope' and оде́жда 'clothing').

(*b*)   Дѣяти *impf* 'do', replaced by the denominative дѣлати (де́лать) < *dělo* 'deed': что ся дѣсть по вѣремьнемь (1229 Treaty, *ad init.*), but also тако дѣлати руси у Ризѣ (ibid.).[132]

Де́ять(ся) is still present in R. dialects.

(*c*)   Дѣяти (дѣти) *impf* 'say': аще ли кто дѣеть вы (*RPC s.a.* 1078) 'if anyone says to you'. Obsolete in Russian (but Cz. *díti, dím,* etc.), having left behind only the coll. particle де(и) 'he says' (4.32 (1)) and its derivative де́скать (< де сказать?).

139   4. *The Verbs of Motion* in Slav have *two impf* forms, a *determinate* (actual motion in a specific direction) and an *indeterminate*

---

[132] Де́лать was relatively uncommon until recently. In the Muscovite period the normal verbs for 'to do' were твори́ть and чини́ть (5.46).

(motion in general or undirected). The ablaut relation is very ancient:

Det. *(Type A1)*	Indet. *(Type B1)*	
нести́	носи́ть	'carry' (on one's person)
вести́ (< вед-)	води́ть	'lead'
везти́	вози́ть	'carry' (in a vehicle)
брести́	броди́ть	'wade, pass'

To these must be added pairs with other newer relationships:

(intr.)	бежа́ть (*běg-ē-*)	бе́гать (*běg-ā-*)	'run'
	лезть	ла́зать (ла́зить)	'climb'
	лете́ть	лета́ть (лѣтати)	'fly'
	плыть	пла́вать	'swim, float' (i.e. move through water)
	ползти́	по́лзать	'crawl (about)'
(trans.)	гнать (гънати)	гоня́ть	'drive, chase'
	кати́ть	ката́ть	'roll (about)'
	тащи́ть	таска́ть	'drag (about)'

The above pattern is faithfully preserved in ESl.

Notes

(*a*) Бежа́ть replaces OCS or dial. бѣчь (*běg-ti*), from the present of which sg. 1 бегу́ and pl. 3 бегу́т remain.

(*b*) The older present of гнать was женю́, же́нет(ь) (common in ChSl.) < *gen-.[133] It has been replaced by гоню́, го́нит from an *indet.* *гони́ть, itself replaced by гоня́ть, гоня́ю (*gen-ti/gon-iti* : *nes-ti/nos-iti*).

(*c*) Лете́ть (летѣти) is a new infinitive (no other is recorded) with its regular present (Type B2) лечу́, лети́т; the original verb was probably athematic: Lith. has *lēkti*.

(*d*) The original sense of брести́/броди́ть is probably preserved in the noun брод 'ford', i.e. the verb indicated some difficulty in motion. The verb is usual for crossing rivers in the chronicles, side by side with перевозити 'ferry across'. The sense 'wander about' is later (whence бродя́га 'tramp'). In the 17th c. it is often little more than a synonym for идти́; so in Avvakúm: побрел один; я отбрел в дом свой. He also uses the already figurative на ум взбрело́ 'it came into my head'; с ума сбрёл 'went mad' (noun

---

[133] So still Ukr. гна́ти, pres. жену́.

сумасбро́д, also 17th c., still available side by side with the more learned сумасше́дший). These usages are wholly colloquial.

140   5. The determinate verbs of motion идти́ (or итти́, for ити́) 'go on foot, walk' and е́хать (ѣхати) 'go in a vehicle, travel' are highly irregular.

Both have a present with suffix -d-: иду́, ѣду (roots *ei-, *jā-).

The perfect participle of идти́ is from a different root *šĭd-: шьлъ, шьла > шёл, шла. This appears as *xod- in the corresponding indeterminate ходи́ть, no doubt by deprefixation (pri-s- > pri-x-, s > x after i, §58 (7) above).[134]

The -x- in the infinitive е́хать is obscure. OCS has jati and jaxati (ěxati), pres. jade-. Russian е́хать, е́ду is likewise the result of deprefixation, the CSl. rule being jā- initially, -ě- internally (cf. §94 above).

The corresponding indeterminate е́здить, е́зжу is altogether anomalous; it may be a denominative from езда́ but this does not explain much. Examples are rare before the 14th c.

It should be noted that in Muscovite Russian течь is widely used as a synonym of итти́ or бежа́ть. The original sense 'run' is found in OCS and still in SSl. (i.e. rapid motion, excluding flying). The Russian specialization to liquids ('run, flow') is recent and also present in the related causative точи́ть 'secrete'.

6. For the perfective-iteratives see 4.94.

---

[134] Ablaut forms *sed-/*sod-; cf. Gk. ὁδός 'way'.

4

SYNTAX

A full treatment of historical syntax is not attempted here. Attention is concentrated on the notable *continuity* of sentence structure with usually only revision of details.

TYPES OF SENTENCE (MAIN CLAUSE)

Nominal Sentence

1   Juxtaposition of subject and complement without expressed verb ('be' or the equivalent).

(*a*) The nominal sentence, at least for general statements, was perhaps normal in IE and CSl. Despite its frequency in Greek the insertion of естъ is common in OCS and even more so in later ChSl., but the traditional procedure is:

OCS: *duchŭ bo bŭdrŭ, a plŭtĭ nemoštĭna* 'the spirit is willing but the flesh is weak';
ChSl.: ибо все мы смертны (Vl. Mon., *RPC s.a.* 1096).

Cf. Lat. *ars longa, vita brevis*; *in vino veritas*.
Spoken Russian maintained the nominal sentence and extended it. The following (not wholly clear) example from Русская Правда may therefore be the normal usage of the early 11th c.: то тò ему за платежь, оже й били (art. 29). This norm is maintained: нъ къде с[вят]ая София, ту Новгородъ (1215). Modern: я студéнт; (pred. adj.) он бóлен; сегóдня жáрко; сад óколо дóма 'the garden is round the house' (but óколо дóма — сад 'there is a garden round the house').

(*b*) The same applies to the verbal participle: the absence of the copula (auxiliary) in both the active and passive perfect tense is recorded at latest from the early 12th c., perhaps from the 11th c.: Глѣбъ князь мѣрилъ мо[ре] по леду (1068; text no. 21); а язъ далъ рукою своею (*c.*1130; text no. 12), but also in the same text: а се я Всеволодъ далъ есмь блюдо серебрьно . . . велѣлъ есмь бити въ не (perhaps literary influence). Varlaam's Deed (*c.*1200)

188

has consistently въдале (= въдалъ), it being clear that this is the 1st person.

In the 1229 Treaty (text no. 18) the copula never appears with the *l*-participle but is present once in the perfect passive: ся грамота есть выдана . . . (surely a set formula rather than spoken usage). Modern usage: он убит; заседа́ние ко́нчено.

Whereas the copula disappeared (or was never colloquially present) in the 3rd persons syntactical clarity required its maintenance in certain cases in the 1st and 2nd persons. Ivan Grozny still writes in 1574: что писал еси, что по грехом взяли тебя в полон . . . (similarly in the reply: писал еси, государь, ко мне . . . (1576)). In the letter of 1576 we find phrases without copulas wherever there is no ambiguity: а того слова не говаривал, кое пора дей моя.

(*c*) We may conclude that as a general rule ESl. vernacular did not employ a copula *in any person* if the subject was expressed. In the verbal forms the alternatives were, as seen in the examples above, я дал or велел есмь. In course of time the pronouns prevailed. The presence of *both* is either formal (азъ есмь Аввакумъ протопопъ) or emphatic, especially where a contrast of subjects is involved: а се я Всеволодъ далъ есмь . . .

(*d*) In modern usage есть, and still more суть, is never truly colloquial. The following are the commonest contexts:

(i) existence (not a copula): Бог есть (= существу́ет). This is not a normal usage of OCS and earlier ChSl.;

(ii) mathematical or philosophical identity: x есть y; мысль изречённая есть ложь (Tyútchev);

(iii) as the positive of нет 'there is not' (§3 (3) below): есть таки́е . . . 'there are such people . . .', есть чем занима́ться 'there is plenty (for me) to do'.

Note. The есть of existence and/or position (и тут есть индиская страна (Af. Nik.)) finds a later synonym in the calque находи́ться < *se trouver* (5.40).

2   The verb име́ть 'have' also early lost ground in ESl.: a transitive construction was replaced by a *nominal sentence* of the type у меня́ большо́й сад.

The source of this idiom is disputed but there is some evidence for considering it of Finnic origin, generalized from N. dialects.[1]

[1] Veenker, pp. 118–19 (see Bibliography).

However, it does occur sporadically in OCS as an alternative to the dat. of possession (§47 below): *ašte bǫdetŭ u etera č[e]l[ově]ka 100 ovecĭ (Ass.,* Matt. 18: 12, translating Gk. γένηται + dat.). There are more numerous examples in 13th–14th c. ChSl. texts, but practically confined to family relationships: *ne běše u neju čęda* 'they had no children' (perhaps rather to be interpreted 'there were no children from them' (= of the marriage)).[2] This procedure has disappeared from Balkan usage but is enough to suggest that the idiom may not be wholly foreign in ESl. However, it does not appear at all in *RPC*, even in semi-colloquial speeches; there is only имѣю отрокъ своихъ 700 (*RPC s.a.* 1093). The following is doubtful (negative example): земла наша крещена . . . и нѣсть у насъ учителя (ibid. 898, reproducing earlier Cyrillo-Methodian texts; у нас = among us?)

Clear examples are present in Novg. texts at latest from the 13th c. (negative example): а иное грамоты у насъ нѣтуть (*c.*1260).

Имѣ́ть remained in ChSl. and the 'high style' generally and greatly increased from the 18th c. in imitation of French and German: имѣ́ть дѣ́ло с + instr. = *avoir affaire à*; имѣ́ю честь = *j'ai l'honneur*; имѣ́ть мѣ́сто = *avoir lieu* (5.40). (Не) имѣ́ется 'there is (not)' is wholly bookish. As a result of this contamination the modern rules stand as follows:

(*a*) concrete possession: у + gen. (native coll.);

(*b*) abstract objects: не имѣ́ю поня́тия;[3]

(*c*) non-personal subjects: пьѣ́са имѣ́ла большо́й успѣ́х;

(*b*) and (*c*) being literary only.

3 *Negative Sentences*

Throughout the history of Russian the following points apply without variation:

1. 'Не' is proclitic to the word which is logically negatived: я э́того не знал; не то я хотѣ́л сказа́ть; ка́ждый не с ней проведённый день. In a few instances there is recessive stress onto the proclitic: нé̮был, не была́, нé̮было, нé̮были (and sometimes нé̮дал and others).

2. Accompanying pronouns and adverbs must also be in the

---

[2] Cf. the common formula in *RPC*: въ се же лѣ́то родися Святославъ у Игоря.

[3] Cf. *RPC s.a.* 945: да не имѣ́ють власти зимовати у св. Мамы 'they shall not have the right . . .'.

negative form (ни-): нигдé нé было вѝдно никакóго огня́ 'no
light was visible anywhere'. The rare deviations from this rule may
be Germanisms in the 1229 Treaty and in Ludolf's *Grammar*
(1696): еще я никово пияново напоилъ (не missing: *ich habe
noch niemand voll getruncken*). The omission of не with the verb
in the presence of ни-forms is, however, quite common in OCS
and thence in ChSl., e.g.

николи же помышлю на страну вашю, ни сбираю вои (*RPC s.a.* 972);
ChSl.: идѣже ни червь ни тля тлитъ (AV, Matt. 6: 20) 'where neither
   moth nor rust doth corrupt'.

Soviet dialectologists have recorded the same occasionally in N.
dialects: никто ему велел.

3. With the obsolescence of имѣть the negative indicator of
possession becomes нет < *ne je tu(t)* (3.90 (*d*)(iv)), already present
in the 11th c.:

то вины ему в томь нѣтуть (*RP,* art. 23) 'he is not to blame for that';
наряда в ней нѣтъ (*RPC s.a.* 862).

4. A similar procedure is applied to pronouns and adverbs,
giving the elliptical modern нéгде сесть 'there is nowhere to sit',
нé с кем мне бы́ло совéтоваться 'there was no one to advise
me'. Recorded from the 16th c. but no doubt older: вы́работать
нел[ь]зя и не у кого; а взят[ь], государь, есть кому, а кормит[ь]
некому (both in 1576 letter to Ivan Grozny).

5. For gen. object in negative clauses see §41 below.

4 *Interrogative Sentences*

1. If no interrogative pronoun or adverb is present a question
has at all times been indicated by ли (enclitic to the word about
which the question is asked); correlative или:

завтракалъ ли ты?; крыло ли или ногу? (Ludolf, 1696) '(would you
prefer) a wing or a leg?'

2. Russian has created (like Latin) particles indicating the
expected reply, viz.

(*a*) рáзве[4] (Lat. *num*)—expected answer 'no' (the speaker does
not accept the apparent fact):

[4] A fully colloquialized Slavonicism; original sense 'except', e.g. in *RPC s.a.* 898:
не достоитъ никоторому языку имѣти букъвъ своихъ, развѣ еврѣи и грекъ и
латинъ.

ра́зве так по́здно? 'it can't be as late as that, can it?';
ра́зве он не зна́ет? 'surely he must know?';
ра́зве я старушо́нку уби́л? (Dost.) 'it wasn't I who killed the old woman, was it?'

(*b*) неуже́ли (Lat. *nōnne*), expecting the answer 'yes' (the speaker accepts the apparent fact):

неуже́ли вы ста́рше меня́? 'so you really are older than me?';
неуже́ли сего́дня у́тром мы пи́ли ко́фе в Москве́? (of a journey by air) 'to think that this morning we had our coffee in Moscow!'

Неуже́ли is thus often exclamatory.

There appear to be no early examples of either procedure in vernacular texts, though (не)ужели finds a similar use in ChSl.: не уже ли и свою м[а]т[е]рь укори съ мною 'did you not offend your own mother as well as me?'

Passive Constructions

5   1. To a considerable extent passive constructions have been, indeed have to be, avoided in Russian, throughout its history. They have been more abundantly used in the literary language than in speech, whether the former was ChSl. or the standard language of the 19th c. In the latter case the extension has been due to the influence of W. European languages, especially French.

Generally speaking, if subject and agent are both animate (within the extending meaning of this term, §41 below), a passive construction is frequently possible though perhaps not original;[5] if both are inanimate it is unnatural. Inanimate subjects are largely avoided in living speech but not in literary styles, e.g. его́ возвраще́ние бы́ло отло́жено 'his return was put off'.

6   2. *Reflexive* forms of passive sense belong exclusively to the *impf* aspect in living speech (there is no alternative in the true present). They are more widely employed in ChSl. (3.133 ff.). They are, however, rare in OCS outside the 3rd pers. sg. and pl. Such forms are sometimes ambiguous; e.g. да не ущитят ся щиты своими и да посѣчени будуть мечи своими (*RPC s.a.* 945). The second verb suggests that ущитят ся is also passive, not reflexive ('defend themselves').

7   The following examples illustrate the prevailing usage:

[5] Он был уби́т бра́том (for брат уби́(л) его́) may be an extension of он был уби́т мечо́м (inanimate agent).

(*a*) literary style:

Pres. inan.:

яко же пишет ся (*RPC s.a.* 852);

придоша близъ Руси идеже зоветь ся валъ половьчьскы (*Novg. Chr.*,
s.a. 1224) '. . . in the region (which is) called the Cuman Wall'.

Imperf. anim.:

си вси звахуть ся отъ Грекъ Великая Скуфь (*RPC s.a.* 907) 'all these
(peoples) were called by the Greeks "Great Scythia"'.

Aor. anim.:

пересѣчены быша Грекы (ibid. 915) 'the Greeks were massacred'.

Perfect inan.:

написахомъ харатью сию, на неи же суть имяна наша написана (ibid.
945) 'we made this document in which our names have been listed'.

Fut. inan.:

нашю землю д[ь]н[ь]сь от[ъ]яли, а ваша заутро възята будеть (*Novg.
Chr., s.a.* 1224) 'they have taken away our land today; tomorrow yours
will be taken'.

(*b*) colloquial style:

Anim.: аже будет[ь] холъпъ убитъ (1229 Treaty) 'if a slave has been
murdered'.

Inan.: аж бы миръ неръздрушенъ былъ (ibid.) 'that the peace may not
be broken'.

8   3. An *active* construction has always been necessary in such
sentences as меня́ всегда́ встреча́ет жена́ на вокза́ле 'I am always
met . . .'. If the agent is not specific the verb will be in the pl. 3
without pronoun; this still standard procedure is already established
in the 13th (very probably in the 11th) c.:

а видока два выведуть (*RP,* art. 29) 'and two witnesses are produced';
аже кого уранять (1229) 'if someone has been wounded'.

9   4. Vague *inanimate* agents are best expressed through a (neuter)
impersonal verb:

а въстала фуртовина на море да судно мен[ь]шое (acc.) разбило о
берег (Af. Nik., *c.*1470) 'a storm arose and our smaller boat was
wrecked on the shore';

теле́гу . . . дёрнуло, повали́ло и А.А. покати́лся под шоссе́ в кана́ву
— в спи́ну ему́ уда́рило тяжёлым мешко́м, завали́ло соло́мой
(A. Tolstoy).

10   5. In a passive sentence the agent, whether anim. or inan., stands
in the instr. at all times; от + gen. (animates) is a Slavonicism:[6]

> ChSl.: мы от рода рускаго . . . послании от Игоря . . . и от всякоя
> княжья и от всѣхъ людии руския земля; и от тѣхъ заповѣдано . . .
> (*RPC s.a.* 945).
> Mixed: аще кто диаволъмь наученъ и злымы ч[е]л[овѣ]кы наваженъ
> . . . (text no. 15, *c.*1200).

In some contexts the implication of от may be *from* (= in the
name of, representing) rather than *by*; this is still good usage.

Impersonal Sentences

11   Common at all times.

ChSl.: (при-)с-лучися + inf. 'it happened that'; не достоит
(подобает) 'it is not seemly'.

Modern: оказа́лось, что . . . 'it turned out that . . .'; про́сто
не ве́рится 'it is unbelievable'; меня́ тошни́т 'I feel sick'; and
commonly with a dat. of respect (§50 below): мне хоте́лось опя́ть
есть 'I felt hungry again'; мне ду́мается, что . . . 'it seems to me
that . . .'; мне не спи́тся 'I can't get to sleep' (cf. я хочу́, ду́маю,
не сплю of different implication).

With the omission of the copula in the pres. (§1 (*a*) above)
various adverbial phrases come to fulfil the function of an impers.
verb, notably на́до 'it is necessary, one must' (< надоб(ь)но <
loc. на добѣ 'at the right moment'; доба has been replaced in
Russian by пора́): (still with a subject) князю то не надобе;
латине то не надобѣ (1229) 'this does not concern the Prince (the
Europeans)'; modern: на́до ещё поду́мать об э́том 'this needs
further thought'. Similarly нельзя́ (3.29 *ad fin.*) 'one may not, one
cannot': здесь нельзя́ кури́ть.

TYPES OF SUBORDINATE CLAUSE

In general, form has been very stable, the changes bearing mainly
on the renewal or refinement of conjunctions.

---

[6] OCS has *ot* + gen. (possibly in imitation of Gk. ὑπό + gen.) mainly for
animates, otherwise instr.; Pol. also *od* + gen. for persons (apparently native),
otherwise *przez* + acc. Except as a Polonism че́рез (*przez* is a deformation of this
CSl. preposition) is never an *agent* in Russian: э́то бы́ло сде́лано через меня́ =
'through me' (not 'by me myself').

12 *Relative Clauses*

In early texts there is a clear contrast between ChSl. иже, еже, яже (anaphoric pronoun + же; 3.59) as a relative conjunction and various native procedures.

1. Only the neut. sg. еже is found in vernacular texts, where it appears to be a legal cliché for 'what, (all) that which':

и еже въ немь (Varlaam's Deed, text no. 15, *c*.1200) 'and everything on it';

еже ми отьць даялъ (*NBG*, no. 9, *c*.1200) 'what my father gave me';

еже было творити отроку моему, то самъ есмь створилъ (text no. 9, *c*.1100) 'whatever a retainer of mine had to do I (also) did myself'.

Cf. also понеже and занеже, §20 below.

13   2. Кто and что are used from very early times as relatives, especially after personal and demonstrative pronouns, as a rule кто following a vague antecedent, что a precise one:

у (= в) тѣхъ волости, кто сю свободу далъ (1229) 'in the territory of those who have granted this right';

ино тое пиво и медъ поимали наши люди, кому был Иване (nom.) виноватъ . . . (Pskov, *c*.1470) 'to whom Ivan was in debt'.

Деловóй язы́к uses что freely with any antecedent: сверх тѣх денег, что . . . отвезены и на Москвѣ плачены (17th c.); Борис Годунов, что былъ царемъ (Kot.).

Modern: все, комý не лень; нéкоторые из тех, с кем мы подружи́лись; я, что э́то уви́дел . . .; те, что . . . is subliterary: те, что остáлись.

14   3. Кто-то and что-то are sparingly represented in 13th c. texts, perhaps a regional variant: и всѣму латинескому языку, кто то у Русе (= в Руси) гостить 'and for all Westerners who trade in Russia'; всѣмь тѣмь, кто то на устоко (= в(о)сток) моря ходить; аже капь, чимь то весять, излъмльна будѣте (= будет)—all in the 1229 Treaty.

The formation is not surprising: it is paralleled in SSl. where Blg. кóйто, pl. кои́то (the normal relative conjunction) corresponds to SCr. *kòjī*. See also §16 below. It does not appear to be represented in modern R. dialects.

15   4. Котóрый,[7] like all *k*-forms, was originally interrogative with

---

[7] IE *kʷo-tero-* (Gk. πότερος): *koter-* (the expected form) is present in OCS side by side with *kotor-*. The form *kotór-* has no obvious explanation.

the sense 'which of two?' and, by extension, 'which in a series?' This usage is, of course, still available: кото́рый час?; кото́рый ты в кла́ссе? 'What is your position in your form?' So, in the 16th c.: и ты деи которое любишь, то ли кое уж жо[8] умерети, или то кое меж нас будет доброе дело? (1576) 'so (he said) which alternative do you prefer . . .?' Кото́рый was *never a relative conjunction* in OCS and ChSl. The generalized sense 'which (if any)?, whichever' is common to them and ESl. and from this the true relative can be traced developing in the latter:

даже который князь . . . (text no. 12, c.1130) 'if any prince . . .';

которыи вълъчанинъ възмьть латинескыи товаръ чересъ вълъкъ вѣсти (= вести) (1229) '(if any porter shall have undertaken to carry foreign goods over the portage';

а исъ тыхъ селъ, которая будеть за княгинею за Марьею села,[9] тѣ до ее живота (1356) 'the princess shall have for her lifetime those estates which she holds (at the time of my death)' (intermediate, semi-relative construction);

и съ тѣми селы которые тягли къ Костромѣ (1389)[10] (full relative);

. . . тыхъ людеи котории имали пиво (Pskov, c.1464) (full relative);

а которые говорили, те и бегали (1576) 'those who said so were the ones who fled'.

The relative use is thus established by the 14th c. The older 'if any' continued to be used in officialese down to the 17th c.

16 5. The simple кой existed at all times but is rare as a relative before the 15th c., after which it becomes characteristic of делово́й язы́к. It was much used by Pososhkо́v (c.1725) and survived in 18th–19th c. officialese. It had long ceased to be colloquial: всякая вещь, коя носит на себе царя нашего имя (Pos.).

17 6. The interrogative adjective како́й (каково́й)[11] 'of what kind?' often takes the place of the now more literary кото́рый: те кни́ги, каки́е на́до прочѐсть. This usage only becomes common after c.1700 (e.g. in Peter the Great's papers).

[8] Note кое = что (§16 below); уж жо (ужо́) = 'soon, by and by' (still present in dialect).

[9] Down to and including the 17th c. repetition of the antecedent is very common in administrative and legal language: прислали к нам . . . запись, по которой записи вы меж собою крест цѣловали; . . . к нѣкоему островy, на который остров вышед, нача горко плакати . . . (17th c.).

[10] Example from S. C. Gardiner in *WSJ* 8 (1960).

[11] As interrogatives no distinction initially; usage eventually decided for како́й long/како́в short (predicative) and similarly тако́й/тако́в. Каково́й was maintained in officialese but is now virtually obsolete.

Temporal Clauses

18   1. Future reference requires a fut. tense throughout the history
of Russian; an earlier fut.-perf. (3.107) is replaced by a *pf* future
(когда́ он придёт).

2. Когда́ 'when' is rare as a relative conj. before the 16th c.,
егда having remained at least at the literary level; ChSl. used егда,
внегда, and яко (= colloquial как).

Коли́ (also 'if', §25 below)[12] is common to both languages (only
interrogative in OCS). It is the normal conjunction in Ukr. and
WhR. and common in R. dialects but subliterary.

At the colloquial level как(о) is common from the Muscovite
period: како приде ся грамота, тако пришли ми . . . (*NBG*, no.
43, 14th c.) 'when this letter arrives . . .'; и как Василеи учал
гоняти сторожеи (1576); как привезли меня из монастыря
(Avvakúm, 1673). Whence как то́лько 'as soon as'.

3. 'While, until': ChSl. доньде(же)/доидеже (less often
доньжде(же)/доижде(же)) (*do-n-jde-že*) and донелѣ(же)/до-
нелиже (*do-n-jeli-že*, correlative to коли): донелѣ же са миръ
състоить (1130) 'as long as this world continues to exist'.

Доколѣ/доколи may be native but has been replaced by пока́
'while, as long as' (< по ка места, rare before the 17th c. but
evidently a very old formation) and пока́ не 'until': (modern)
подожди́те здесь, пока́ я не верну́сь. The confusion of time
and place is common in such conjunctions: temporal докуд(ов)а
(common) and докамест (rare) are used in 16th–17th c. делово́й
язы́к; similarly до тѣхъ местъ, что она похочетъ постричися
сама (Kot.) = modern до тех пор, как.

Перед тем как, до того как 'before' and после того как 'after'
are rather recent expansions, perhaps under Western influence
(Fr. *avant que, après que*).

Locative Clauses

19   It suffices to note that here too где (къде) 'where', etc. takes
over early in the living language from the relatives proper (ChSl.
maintains идеже < *jĭde-že*); in приде на холмъ, къде стояше
Перунъ (*RPC s.a.* 945) '(he) came to the hill where (the statue
of) Perun stood' къде no doubt comes from a recopying but no
precise dating is possible.

---

[12] коли игуменъ обѣдаеть (text no. 12, *c.*1130) can be translated 'if' or 'when'.

Causal Clauses (answering the question 'why?' = 'due to what cause?')

20   The normal conjunction is now потому́ что, correlative to почему́? (formerly also почто?), less often оттого́ что; the former appears in делово́й язы́к from *c.*1500, gradually replacing earlier зане(же) < *za-n-je-že*:

зане не знаеть у кого купивъ (*RP*) 'because he does not know from whom he bought (it)';

занеже без головника им[ъ] платити (ibid.) 'since they must (continue to) pay in the absence of the murderer';

зане ми здѣсе дѣлъ много (*NBG,* no. 43, 14th c.) 'because I am very busy here'.

By the 17th c. Kotoshíkhin's usage shows that потому́ что (also plain что) was normal in his language, занеже (also понеже) antiquated or 'high', and так как 'since' still unknown (from the late 18th c. only).

It should be noted that the ChSl. (enclitic) бо is co-ordinating rather than subordinating and is quite foreign to the vernacular: намъ бо достоить за нь Бога молити, понеже тѣмь Бога познахомъ (*RPC s.a.* 1015) 'for it behoves us . . . inasmuch as . . .'.

Я́ко = 'since' is wholly ChSl.

Clauses of Manner and Comparison

21   Conjunctions как 'as', так что 'in such a way that' (NB так чтобы 'in such a way as to, so that' is final, §22 below). Of special interest are the simile indicators of popular origin—бу́дто, то́чно, сло́вно—originally adverbs but then extended to clauses; modern examples:

он лежа́л бу́дто мёртвый;

он крича́л то́чно поме́шанный;

он так я́сно ви́дел своё село́, сло́вно шёл по его́ широ́кой у́лице '. . . as if he were walking down its broad street';

мину́ты две бы́ло ти́хо, то́чно обо́з усну́л (Chékhov) '. . . as if the caravan had fallen asleep'.

A more hypothetical comparison is introduced by как бу́дто бы 'as though'.

The ChSl. (OCS) equivalent of как(о) is я́коже: я́коже Ярославъ судилъ (*RP,* art. 2); я́коже имъ надобѣ (*RPC s.a.* 945).

Final Clauses (answering the question 'why?' = 'with what intention?')

22   There is here a clear distinction between native conjunctions based on что—mainly чтобы—and ChSl. да 'in order to'. Чтобы (and чтоб) as a bound unit appears in the 14th c. (for бы see 3.116):

а пишу вамъ се слово того дѣля, чтобы не перестала память . . . (1353).

Чтобы + inf. was regularized under Western influence in the 18th c. (Fr. *à fin de, pour*) to cases where there is no change of subject:

он приостановился чтóбы отдохнýть 'he paused to rest'.

The earlier procedure чтобы + dat. + inf. (with change of subject) became obsolete.

ChSl. да is usually constructed with the *pf* future, which might be called a present subjunctive (so currently in SCr.), but sometimes with the present:

тогда аще просить вои у насъ князь рускии да воюеть (*RPC s.a.* 945) 'if the Prince of Kiev asks for troops from us in order that he may wage war . . .'.

In later texts also дабы + pret., which persisted in 'high style' as a variant of чтобы.

All uses of да are quite foreign to ESl.

The 1229 Treaty has also аж бы, evidently W. dial., since WhR. (and Ukr.) still uses абы, perhaps retained under the influence of Pol. *aby*:

како ч[е]л[о]в[ѣ]ка то отплатити аж бы миръ неръздрушенъ былъ '. . . that the peace may not be broken'.

Conditional Clauses

23   1. A large number of conjunctions have been used in ESl. The typical ChSl. conjunction is аще 'if', widely used even in some otherwise relatively colloquial texts. Some instances are surely due to recopying, e.g. in Русская Правда:

аще ли утнеть руку и отпадеть рука (art. 23).

Аще is nearly universal in *RPC*, whatever the level of language.

2. The ESl. correspondent of аще is аче but this is not the commonest conjunction in the early period: predominant are аже and оже (of different origin):

ажь убьеть мужь мужа (*RP,* art. 1);
нъ оже будеть убилъ или в свадѣ или въ пиру явлено (ibid., art. 6);
аче будеть княжь мужь (ibid., art. 1).

In Русская Правда (and similar texts) a second dependent or contrasting if-clause is often introduced merely by ли:

познаеть ли надолзѣ . . . (art. 37) 'but if he later recognizes . . .';
не идешь ли а повежь ны (*Novg. Chr., s.a.* 1215) '(but) if you are not going to come let us know'.

24　　3. Оже disappears in the 14th, аже in the 15th c., аче probably as early as the 13th c. The new conjunctions of the Muscovite period are будет (буде) and тол(ь)ко. The former develops from a fut.-perf. used without expressed conjunction, as can be seen as early as the 13th c.:

а будѣть пьреже на неи не былъ (= было) сорома (1229) 'but if there has been no previous shameful conduct on her part'.

Буде(т) is typical of the деловóй язы́к of the 17th c., e.g. in Kotoshíkhin, and persists in Peter the Great's reign in conservative writers such as Pososhkóv:

а будет у которого отца или матери есть двѣ или три дочери дѣвицы (Kot.) 'if any parents have two or three unmarried daughters . . .';
а будет судное дело будет о бесчестии (ibid.) 'and if the lawsuit concerns a defamation . . .';
и буде кто и покусится межу заравнять (Pos.) 'and if anyone attempts to straighten a boundary-line . . .'.

Только is more characteristic of the 16th c.: it is common in *Domostrój*, but already absent from Kotoshíkhin:

тол[ь]ко деи не станешь писать (letter to Ivan Grozny, 1576) 'if you refuse to write (he said)';
и тол[ь]ко б не было такова слова и яз бы не дерзнул так писати . . . (ibid.) 'if such a statement had not been made I should not have dared to write so'.

The above examples indicate that буде(т) is confined to real positive conditions (it cannot be used with бы) and consequently только usual in hypothetical and negative ones.

25 4. Miscellaneous conjunctions of the Muscovite period:

(a) еже appears in the 16th c., more often in the strengthened form éжели. This may sometimes be a Slavonicism but the popularity of éжели in the 17th c. is certainly a Polonism (jeżeli); иже also occurs occasionally in Russian texts in imitation of Pol. iż. Éжели continued in certain styles of 18th c. writing but then went out of normal use.

(b) Колú (§18 (2) above) is a popular word fairly well represented in the 16th–17th c. and still present in dialect and subliterary colloquial:

коли еси сулил мену не по себе (Grozny, 1574) 'if you have promised an exchange not appropriate to your rank'.

26 5. Естьли (modern form éсли) is rare as a conjunction before the middle of the 17th c. though one must allow for loose colloquial usage earlier than that (есть ли . . ., будет ли . . . = 'should there be, if there are . . .').[13] At the literary level Polish influence seems certain (Pol. jeśli from the 15th c.) as the earliest examples are in the Westernized Peresvétov and Kúrbsky (7.21–2).

Если + inf. (éсли подýмать об éтом 'if one thinks about it') is recent but no parallel in W. European languages is evident.

6. Colloquial and country speech widely use когда and как as conditional conjunctions; also the hypothetical кабы́, which is not infrequent in proverbs: кабы стадо я пасла, разговору б припасла.

27 7. Hypothetical conditions include бы (б) which demands the pret. in -л and therefore can make no distinction of relative time:

éсли бы я знал об éтом 'if I knew (present)/if I had known (past) about this'.

This is inherent in the conditional tense at all times (3.116):

аж быхъмъ что тако учинили . . . (1229) 'if we should do anything . . (future).

Future reference requires a fut. tense at all times:

оже придеть кръвавъ муже (= мужь) на дворъ (RP, art. 29);
аче же и кръвавъ придеть и[ли] будеть самъ почалъ, а выступять послуси . . . (ibid.).

[13] Also the form ели (je + li), recorded in Novgorod as early as the 13th c. (NBG, no. 55).

The apodosis may be introduced by то, again at all times: аже кто ударить мечемь, не вынезъ его, или рукоятью, то 12 гр[и]вне продаже за обиду (*RP,* art. 23).

A and и are also used in this function down to the 17th c. (§82 below).

Concessive Clauses

28   General conjunction хотя́ (хоть) '(al)though', petrified pres. gerund of хотѣ́ть. Hypothetical statements include бы: хотя бы инъму кому виноватъ былъ русину (1229) 'even if he may be in debt to some other (Russian) person'.

The correlative conjunction is но: хотя и хму́рились то́нкие бро́ви, но в глаза́х выража́лось удово́льствие (L. Tolstoy).

Consecutive Clauses

29   Russian: так что from the 17th c.; then and earlier что often suffices.

ChSl.: яко with a clause or infinitive: яко по удольемъ крови (dat.) тещи (*RPC s.a.* 1019) 'so that the valleys ran with blood'.

Generalizing Clauses

30   Ни as a generalizing particle, as in кто-нибудь, etc., is apparently not well authenticated before the Muscovite period; the usage is foreign to OCS and other Slav languages but is scarcely likely to be so recent in ESl.: что ни говори́шь 'whatever one says'; кто бы то ни́ был 'whoever it may (have) be(en)'. In earlier language the plain pronoun suffices: и кого послаша и князь прия (1215) 'the Prince arrested whomever they sent'. By the 16th c. we find the modern usage established: а ково ни пошлю, и тот не доедет да воротится . . . (1576) (see this passage in §35 below).

31   *Alternative Construction of Subordinate Clauses with Participles or Gerunds*

This is common in literary style in *relative* and *temporal* clauses:

Relative:
вѣра же христианскаа, послѣжде явльши ся, больши первыа бысть . . . (text no. 4) 'but the Christian faith, which arose later . . .' (not a common OCS procedure);

(modern) Ники́тин, как всегда́ стоя́вший за стро́гость вообще́ . . . был
про́тив (L. Tolstoy) '. . . who was always on the side of severity'.

Temporal:

тъгда же учювъ Мьстислав[ъ] Мьстиславлиць зло то, въѣха въ
Новъгородъ . . . (1215) 'when M.M. learnt of this disaster . . .';

(modern) поговори́в об э́том, докури́в папиро́сы и допи́в чай, сена́торы
вы́шли в за́лу заседа́ний (L. Tolstoy).

Possible also in other types of clause except final:

Causal:

не зна́я э́то, он пришёл вчера́ 'he came yesterday since he did not know
this';

а нынѣ водя новую жену, а мнѣ не въдасть ничьтоже (*NBG,* no. 9,
c.1200) 'since (*or:* now that) he is taking a new wife he will give me no
portion'.

Conditional or concessive:

не получи́в разреше́ния 'if (*or:* although) one has not received permission'.

This procedure allows such sentences as the following:

се же Богъ показа на наказанье княземъ русьскым, да аще сии еще
сице же створять, се слышавше, ту же казнь приимуть, но и больши
сее, понеже, вѣдая се, сътворять тако же зло убийство (*RPC s.a.* 1019)
'. . . in order that, if they do such a thing again after hearing this, they
may receive the same punishment, or rather a greater one since they will
have committed as bad a murder although (despite the fact that) they
knew about this one'.

A gerund must refer specifically to the subject of the main clause.
'Hanging' gerunds are found in the looser syntax of the 17th c.,
e.g. жених и невѣста пришед в покой . . . снимают с них платье
(Kot.) This is equivalent to a ChSl. dative absolute (§49 below).
Hanging gerunds even increased in the 18th c. under French
influence but were soon stigmatized as incorrect, as indeed they
are since the gerund is by origin an appositional participle.
Lomonósov was categorical about this (*Grammar,* §532): . . .
многие въ противность сему пишутъ: идучи я въ школу,
встрѣтился со мною пріятель.

REPORTED OR INDIRECT SPEECH

32   1. Throughout the history of Russian (and in Slav generally) the
form of the main verb *has no effect* on the subordinate verb, which

retains as nearly as possible the form it would have had in a main clause. There is no 'sequence of tenses'.

The chronicles contain much reported speech. This is largely given in *oratio recta*, with or without an introductory яко (in imitation of Gk. ὅτι) or some part of the verb 'say'. Thus in the *Novg. Chronicle, s.a.* 1215:

и выеха на Ярослаль дворъ и цѣлова ч[ес]тьныи кр[ес]тъ, а новгородьци к нему, яко с нимь въ животъ и въ смерть; любо изищю му[жѣ] новгородьст[ѣи] волости, пакы ли а головою повалю за Новгородъ. 'And he rode out to Jaroslav's palace and took the oath (to them) and the people of Novgorod (likewise) to him, (saying) that (they would be) with him in life and in death. (And he said:) "I shall either recover these citizens of Novgorod or else lay down my life for Novgorod."'

And further on:

князь же Мьстиславъ створи вѣцѣ (= вѣче) на Ярослали дворѣ и поидемъ реч[е] поищемъ муж[ь] своихъ . . . 'And Prince Mstislav summoned an assembly at Jaroslav's palace and said: "Let us go and seek out our citizens . . ."'.

Similarly in higher style:

они же рѣша яко ходихомъ в болгары, смотрихомъ како ся покланяють въ храмѣ . . . (*RPC s.a.* 987) 'and they said: "we journeyed to the (Volga) Bulgars and observed their devotions in (their) temple . . ."'.

Lower styles may have R. како for яко, or оже (= ChSl. еже) which eventually becomes modern что:

и ту бы[сть] ему вѣсть . . . оже уже Ростиславъ идеть (*Hyp. s.a.* 1147) 'and the news reached him there that Rostislav was already on the march'.

The vernacular indicator of reported speech is де (дей) (< дѣет 'he says', 3.138 (*c*)), which has remained subliterary:

царь велел тебе говорити, только деи не станешь писать, и тебе деи уж же быти кажнену. 'The Khan has ordered (me) to tell you that if you refuse to write you will be executed forthwith.'

2. Preservation of the direct verbal form is of indefinite extension to anything which may be considered a person's words, expressed or not, i.e. after verbs of knowing, thinking, feeling, and the like. Thus after preterites:

он сказа́л, что придёт за́втра (direct: приду́);

я был увéрен, что им не удáстся 'I was certain that they would not succeed';

он чýвствовал, что что-то не лáдно 'he felt that something was wrong'.

33 3. Similarly, there is no special construction for indirect questions:

и не свѣмы, на н[е]б[ес]ѣ ли есмы были, ли на земли (*RPC s.a.* 987) 'we know not whether we have been in heaven or on earth';

modern: не знáю (не могý реши́ть), смешнó ли э́то, или печáльно; он спроси́л, все ли ужé вы́шли (direct: все ли ужé вы́шли?)

No exceptions to these syntactical procedures will be found in genuine Russian at any period. Indirect questions introduced by аще 'if' (in imitation of Gk. ἐάν or εἰ) are purely ChSl., nor did this procedure gain currency in the 18th c. in imitation of Fr. *si*.

WORD ORDER

34 1. Since Russian is a relatively highly inflected language (in modern European terms) word order is expressive rather than mandatory. Nevertheless there are, as in all languages, preferred orders (expressively neutral) of various components of a sentence. Moreover OCS—and early Russian ChSl. before the 'Second South Slav Influence' (7.19–20)—may be couched in very simple, straightforward sentences, modelled as it was as much on the unsophisticated popular Greek of the New Testament as on the Atticizing affectations of Byzantine literati. But there are wide differences; compare the colophon of *Ostr.*, a careful but at the same time unpretentious epilogue by the scribe of a grand codex, with Metropolitan Hilarion's *Sermon on the (Mosaic) Law and Grace*[14] (text no. 4), written a dozen years earlier as a public sermon on a great court occasion and intended to display all the literary potentialities of OCS. In the former will be noted the chiasmic balance of

самъ же Изяславъ кънязь правляаше столъ о[ть]ца своего Ярослава Кыевѣ· а брата своего столъ поручи правити близоку своему Остромиру Новѣгородѣ

and the initial position of the object in

Мънога же лѣт[а] даруи Б[ог]ъ сътяжавъшуму Еу[анге]лие се . . .

[14] The Old and the New Dispensation. Hence the matter is largely concerned with interpreting OT events as symbolic foreshadowing of the NT—a favourite Byzantine exercise, known as typology.

These small departures from the neutral order subject–verb–object, which we can posit for Slav in general and Russian in particular, are for *emphasis*.

A similar comparison may be made between the two contrasting portions of Vladímir Monomákh's *Admonition* (text no. 9)—the more artificial moral disquisition in ChSl. (with many quotations from the OT) and the much more colloquial account of his life.[15]

35 2. The emphatic positions are the initial and final, the initial position announcing the 'topic' of the sentence, as some linguists call it. But other considerations may rob these of any real emphasis. It is noticeable that in chronicle narrative the verb is frequently put first, stressing, but not greatly, the sequence of actions to be related; thus in *Novg. Chr., s.a.* 1176:

и постави (1) Всѣволодъ съ володимирьци и съ переяславъци противу его полкъ, и биша ся (2), и паде (3) обоихъ множьство много, и одолѣ (4) Всѣволодъ, и възврати ся (5) Мьстиславъ въ Новъгородъ, и не прияша (6) его Новгородьци нъ путь ему показаша . . .

The natural order of words can be judged from such artless texts as Vasili's letter to Ivan Grozny (1576), e.g.

И яз холоп твои, ходил по твоему государеву наказу; велено мне, государь, было и на Миюс ходити и на Молочные Воды язы́ков добывати, которые бы ведали царево умышленье, кое бы тебе, государю, безвестну не быти толко вестеи не будет ни от которых посылок. 'I went (there) in accordance with your royal command, (for your) orders were to go as far as (the river) Mius and Molochnyje Vody to capture informants such as would know the Khan's intentions, so that you should not remain in ignorance if no intelligence was to be had from any other sources.'

And he continues, with intentional emphasis:

И мне было, холопу твоему, посылати *неково*, а ково ни пошлю, и тот не доедет да воротится да приехав солжет . . . 'But there was no one I could send (on such a mission); anyone whom I sent would not (in fact) go that far but turn back and give a false account . . .'

36 3. *Mandatory* orders apply only to enclitics, which in early ESl.

---

[15] The order of a sentence such as 'Тура мя 2 метала на розѣхъ и с конемъ, олень мя одинъ болъ, а 2 лоси, одинъ ногами топталъ, а другыи рогома болъ . . .' is not so much a literary artifice as the 'list' technique (category–number–action); мя as an enclitic cannot stand anywhere except after the first independent word.

comprised же, ли (not consistently),[16] the 'short' acc. and dat. personal pronouns (3.55, 57), and a few Slavonicisms such as бо 'for'. To these must be added the somewhat later бы as the invariable hypothetical particle (3.116). Prepositions and не are, of course, proclitic to the word to which they apply. With the obsolescence of the short pronouns and the gradual attachment of ся to the verbal form (3.133 (4)) only же and ли remain. The present tense of быть was also frequently, though not necessarily, enclitic and this too is abandoned (писа́л еси rather than еси писал, etc.). The profusion of enclitics characteristic of SCr. thus disappeared in Russian and no rules are required for their ordering among themselves.[17]

37 4. A *preferred* order is to be expected as between adjectives and demonstratives and their noun. Toponymy suggests that, other things being equal, the adjective precedes its noun. From the earliest texts we always have: Нов(ъ)городъ, Выш(е)городъ (= acropolis), Новый Торгъ 'Newmarket', and later Вели́кие Лу́ки, Ни́жний Но́вгород. Similarly Вели́къ день 'Easter Sunday' and many other fixed pairs. Theoretically, of course, the 'long' adjective *must* precede since it incorporates a linking pronoun: *novo je vino* > но́вое вино́ (3.37). In freer association, however, it is clear that not all categories of adjectives behave alike and postposition became quite common. In the 1229 Treaty, which may be held to reflect the common usage of the time, we find (orthography normalized):

with adjs. in -ский: князь смоленский, владыка ризкий (= рижьский), but always латин(е)ский язык 'Westerners, Catholics' and готский берег 'Gotland', and пред смоленского князя, у полотского князя;

others: свободный человек, добрым людем (both fixed social terms), своего лучшего попа, перед русским послом, княжю холопу, русский гость, у (= в) русской земли; but суды серебреные.

Similarly in *Novg. Chr., s.a.* 1215: ядаху люди сосновую кору и лист липов и мох (no clear reason for the formal and positional contrast).

---

[16] Ли may be equivalent to или (e.g. in Русская Правда), cf. OCS *li bratriǫ li sestry*; early replaced in ChSl. as in Russian by или . . . или.

[17] e.g. SCr. *ȍn mu ga je dȁo* = Fr. *il le lui a donné* (different mandatory order). Note that all enclitics are liable to shortening: же > ж, ли > ль (14th–15th c.), -ся > -сь (14th c.), бы > б (16th c.).

As long as 'short' adjs. were still used attributively (§§70–2 below) in the nom. and acc. it was typical of Muscovite деловóй язы́к to place them after the noun, whereas 'long' ones still tended to precede. The distinction is surely artificial (no longer characteristic of living speech); postposition comes in all probability from the 'list' habit: eggs—large 6, medium 18, small 12. So in Ivan Kalitá's *Will* (1327–8):

далъ есмь с[ы]ну своему Семену 4 чепи золоты, 3 поясы золоты, 2 чаши золоты с женчуги, блюдце золото . . . 2 чума золота болшая, а исъ судовъ исъ серебрьныхъ да[лъ] есмь ему 3 блюда серебрьна . . .

With the relegation of short adjectives to predicative use only, postposition of the (long) adjective becomes rarer, except in ChSl. where it remained common. The order 'adj. + noun' is clearly normal but the opposite has never been excluded and finds much expressive use: он óчень ми́лый человéк (neutral)—он человéк óчень ми́лый (more emphatic). In later Muscovite times there is considerable evidence of the sort of distinction which still obtains in Polish—perhaps a Polish influence—where adjs. denoting permanent qualities normally precede but differentiating (specifying) adjs. follow (including possessives and ordinals): *złoty kubek, Białystok* but *sól kuchenna, dom boży, tom drugi*.

38　5. There was, and to a considerable extent still is, a similar freedom with demonstratives and pronominal adjs. in general. The OCS texts show that in some Slav dialects postposition of the *demonstratives* was very usual if not constant, so much so as to give rise to adverbs such as later OCS д(ь)несь < дьнь сь 'today', and to the regular attachment of тъ to its noun in spoken Bulgarian which led to its modern enclitic *article*. Forms such as рабо-тъ 'the servant', народо-сь 'this people' already occur sporadically in OCS manuscripts of the 11th c. on a par with other words with vocalized strong jers (2.14). The ESl. dialects surely inherited very similar habits. Дьньсь is evidently CSl. (Cz. *dnes*, SCr. *dànas*, R. dial. днесь). But development was not uniform and, except in N. Russia, preposition has become normal: днесь has been replaced by сегóдня. In the North the same procedure as in Bulgarian was initiated but stopped short of a grammaticalized system: рекáта 'the river' (3.67).

6. As regards adverbial complements it is usually preferred to state *time* before others: (modern) мы вчерá тудá éздили.

39 7. The practice of withholding the verb to the end of the clause (in particular a subordinate clause) is quite un-Russian. Though not without precedents in ChSl. it became fashionable in learned prose (and thence more generally) in the 17th–18th c. under the influence first of Latin and then of German, e.g. in Lomonósov:

меня долговременное въ российскомъ словѣ упражнение о томъ совершенно увѣряетъ (Российская грамматика (1755), Dedication).

The same is largely true of 'insets', as in the above example (долговременное . . . упражнение) or in Trediakóvsky:

Я во многихъ перебывалъ чюжестранныхъ краяхъ от того времени, какъ я съ вами разлучился (Езда в остров любви (1730), *ad init.*).

USE OF CASES

40 *Apposition*

Identical case is the rule at all times in гóрод Москвá, асс. гóрод Москвý, loc. в гóроде Москвé, and all similar situations. *The city of London* is impossible in Russian and did not even creep in under strong French influence in the 18th c. (*la ville de Paris*).

Genitive Case

41 1. *Genitive for Accusative: Animate and Inanimate*

(*a*) Any suitable verb may have a *partitive object* in the gen.:

дáйте мне водьí 'give me some water' (= Fr. *de l'eau*);
нарубѝть дров 'to cut some firewood'.

This usage is clear in OCS:

prijętŭ xlěba (John 21: 13) 'he took bread';
da . . . dastŭ imŭ života věčĭnaago (John 17: 2) 'give them (a part in) eternal life'.

The procedure is normal, both in OCS and ESl., without being obligatory, in sentences with a negative verb, presumably by extension of the partitive conception:

OCS (trans.):
ne tvoritŭ zakona 'he does not observe the law';

ESl. (intrans.):
а будѣтъ пьреже на ней не былъ (= было) сорома (1229) 'but if there

has been no previous stain on her character' (followed by: аже будѣте
пьрвѣе на неи съръмъ былъ);
или не будеть на немь знамения (*RP*, art. 29) 'but if there is no mark
on him'.

It can, though need not be, extended through an infinitive dependent on the negative verb: Я не люблю читáть таки́х книг (or
таки́е кни́ги).

Thus objects in the gen. were quite usual. Further, in the personal and other pronouns acc. and gen. were identical (мене/
меня, кого)[18]—how far back in CSl. this goes we cannot say—and
in the sg. declension of masc. nouns nom. and acc. were identical
(Table VI).

In view of the free order of words it became important to re-
establish a distinction between nom. and acc. in the case of *persons*,
specifically in the sg. masc. (in other contexts ambiguity could
scarcely arise):[19] it must be clear whether *Peter killed Paul* or *Paul
killed Peter*. In OCS such a personal object in the gen. is already
widespread if not *de rigueur*, i.e. probably a recently established
procedure: *uzrě Isusa idǫšta* '(he) saw Jesus coming', and already
extended to prepositional contexts: *vŭzrě na Petra*.

The same evolution takes place in ESl. Русская Правда has
practically no occasion to use *personal* nouns but we find:

ажь убьеть мужь мужа, то мьстити брату брата (*RP, ad init.*) 'if one
   freeman murders another, then a brother may avenge his brother . . .';
аже кто убиеть княжа мужа (ibid.).

In general, however, *category nouns* (animates) remain unchanged:

а оже уведеть чюжь холопъ любо робу (ibid.);
аще поиметь кто чюжь конь (ibid.);
пусти попъ безъ мира (*Novg. Chr., s.a.* 1215) 'he dismissed the priest
   without (making) peace'.

Many chronicle passages make clear this distinction between personal nouns and animates (person/category word), e.g.

посла къ нимъ сынъ свои Святослава;

---

[18] But not initially in the 3rd pers.: masc. sg. acc. *i*, gen. *jego* (3.59); pl. acc. *ję*,
ny, vy, early replaced by *ixŭ, nasŭ, vasŭ*.

[19] Neuters—nom. and acc. always identical (no persons); fem. sg. NA distinct,
except in the *i*-stems (few persons, but мать любит дочь is still theoretically
ambiguous); fem. pl. NA identical (unimportant); masc. pl. NA distinct to begin
with.

поиде Мьстиславъ на зять свои на Ярослава;

but the limits early became fluid and category nouns are more and more drawn in, provided they refer to *persons*, rarely if they refer to *animals*:

прислалъ въ Ригу своего лучьшего попа Ерьмея (1229);
новгородьци же . . . послаша Гюргя Иванковиця посадника и Степана Твьрдиславиця . . . (1215);
налѣзоша быкъ великъ и силенъ и повелѣ раздраждити быка . . . похвати быка рукою за бокъ (*RPC s.a.* 992—mixture of older and newer by later recopying down to the 14th c.);
привезлъ жеребца (Af. Nik., *c.*1470).

By the mid 17th c. acc. = gen. had become the rule for *all animates in the masc. sg.*; though exceptions will still be found: дать ему лутчей конь (1678).

Concurrently the procedure was being extended to masc. and fem. *plural* (these latter last of all) as the distinction was felt more and more appropriate to *animates as a whole*.[20] An early use of acc. = gen. in the (demonstrative) pronouns may have contributed:

Ярославъ же и тѣхъ не пус[ти] а гость новъгородьскыи в[ь]сь прия (1215);
аже будуть людие из ыное земль (= землѣ), тѣхъ посль (= после) вести (1229).

There is still no consistent rule in the 17th c.; the modern generalization is the work of the 18th c. Examples:

Acc.:
животину, лошади страдные и коровы и гуси и утки и свиньи и куры кормят (*Dom.*, 16th c.);
я веть (= ведь) за вдовы твои сталъ (Avv., 17th c.).

Gen.:
добывать языков (1576) (§35 above; perhaps to be classed as partitive).

Kotoshíkhin is rather conservative: лошади ихъ водити заказано (normal); взявъ у нихъ тѣхъ лошадей (rare).

Russian has gone further than other Slav languages in its interpretation of the category 'animate'. Ukr., WhR., and some R. dialects have stopped short at a stage comparable to Pol. 'personal gender', limiting acc. = gen. in the pl. to *humans*.

[20] The only neuters to be affected are Type 28 animates: pl. nom. ребя́та, AG ребя́т.

(*b*) There can be doubts about the limits of animacy: many would hesitate today over pl. acc. микро́бы or микро́бов. Some treat the masc. planets as anim., others do not: я уви́дел Марс/ Ма́рса.

At the colloquial level the following are normally treated as *animates*:

    (i) туз 'ace', AG туза́ (aligned with the 'animate' court cards—the rest are feminines in -ка);

    (ii) folk dances, e.g. отпля́сывать трепака́ 'to dance a trepak';

    (iii) kicks, slaps and the like administered to someone: дать кому́ тумака́ 'to give someone a cuff'.

Conversely, nouns in -тель, when extended beyond the literal animate category (of ChSl. origin; 5.18), are treated as *inanimate*, e.g. numerous recent technical terms such as указа́тель 'indicator, gauge', дви́гатель 'motor', мно́житель 'multiplier'.

Nouns denoting a *collection* of animates are never treated as animates, e.g. наро́д, полк.

Note that труп 'body, corpse' is inan. (= те́ло) but мертве́ц 'dead person, corpse' is still anim.: притащи́ли мертвеца́ (Pushkin).

42   (*c*) Remnants of the earlier state.

    (i) Very rare in the *masc. sg.*—only вы́йти за́муж 'get married'.

    (ii) Regular in the *pl.* (masc. and fem.) after the preposition в denoting entry into a category or class of persons: мы тебя въ прокля́тые положимъ (1502), and so modern

        вы́йти в лю́ди 'go out into the world';
        пойти́ в го́сти 'go off on a visit';
        избра́ть в депута́ты 'elect as deputy';
        он пошёл в лётчики 'he joined the Air Force';
        он её вы́брал в жёны 'he chose her as his wife' (no implication of polygamy!)

43   2. *Verbs Constructed with the Genitive*

    (*a*) Verbs of *fearing, avoiding* and the like take a gen. of ablatival origin: боя́ться соба́ки 'to be afraid of the dog'; береги́тесь воро́в 'beware of pickpockets'. So also страши́ться, остерега́ться, and others. Here too perhaps: а оному желѣти своихъ кунъ (*RP,* art. 37) 'and he must forgo his money'.

The ablatival gen. has declined in favour of от + gen. (which will be found sporadically in ChSl.): Олегъ ступился тѣхъ мѣстъ . . . Дмитрию (1381) (now only поступи́ться + instr. 'waive, forgo'); отшедше мира сего (ChSl.). In the 19th c. the plain gen. was still possible after бежа́ть in figurative sense: бежа́ть лжи 'to eschew falsehood'. The Slavonicism избежа́ть + gen. 'avoid' continues this usage, but otherwise only убежа́ть *pf* от + gen. 'run away from'.

(*b*) Verbs of *touching, attaining* and the like take a (partitive?) genitive. In modern usage до + gen. is often an alternative or has wholly superseded the plain gen.: дости́чь (дости́гнуть) *pf* це́ли 'to attain (achieve) one's goal' (so always in this sense); дости́г-нуть (до) верши́ны 'to reach the top'; каса́ться/косну́ться *pf* стены́ 'to touch the wall'; hence, figuratively, что каса́ется + gen. 'as concerns' (older English *touching*); держа́ться/приде́ржи-ваться (пре́жнего мне́ния) 'hold to' (but literal держа́ться за + acc. 'hold on to'); доби́ться *pf* своего́ 'to get one's own way'. In ChSl. a plain gen. is considerably more frequent with verbs compounded with до-, из-, and от-.

(*c*) Verbs of *goal* and *intention*: иска́ть 'seek' (also with acc. if the goal is sufficiently definite); тре́бовать 'demand, require' (Slavonicism); ждать, дожда́ться 'wait for'; ожида́ть 'expect'; хоте́ть, жела́ть 'desire'; жа́ждать 'thirst for' (Slavonicism); проси́ть 'ask for' (а онъ еще почялъ просити пива и меду (*c.*1464); modern проси́ть разреше́ния 'to ask for permission').

(*d*) In older language the gen. was common after many verbs of *perception*; it can no doubt be classed as partitive: посмотримъ бы́строго До́ну (*Zadonshchina*); даи ми г[осп]одь свѣта видить (*c.*1400); so with слу́шить 'listen' (still with слу́шаться 'obey'), гляде́ть 'look' (now only на + acc.; relic in того́ и гляди́ 'it looks as if . . .'). The construction was current at least till the time of Pushkin and is still not quite extinct in popular speech.

44   3. *Genitive of Possession*

Personal possession was normally expressed in OCS (ChSl.) and early ESl. by a possessive adjective (3.43), but the gen. had to be used if the possessor was accompanied by qualifier(s): братню сынови; княжь мужь (*RP*), but:

> Олегъ вниде въ градъ отца своего;
> столъ отьца своего Ярослава (*Ostr.*, colophon).

Mixed formulae are not uncommon:

Судъ Ярославль (adj.) Володимирица (*RP, ad init.*);
по отца моего животѣ по князя великого по Ивановѣ (adj.) (1388)
'after the death of my father, Grand Prince Ivan';
в брата твоего, князя Борисову (adj.) отчину мне не вступатися
(16th c.) 'I am not to take over the patrimony of your brother, Prince
Boris'.

Possession in the widest sense has always been expressed by
a gen.—if not otherwise avoided—and may be called simply a
dependent gen.: при закáте сóлнца 'at sunset'. Even so, an adj.
is often possible, sometimes preferable: лóндонские теáтры 'the
theatres of London'.

With increasing contact with Western languages *personal* possessive adjs. declined in cultivated speech, being replaced by genitives: дом сестры́ rather than сéстрин дом. The process starts in
the 17th c. and gathers strength in the 18th c.: Шемя́кин суд but
also о судѣ Шемяки (17th c.).

45 4. The plain gen. of *time* has declined: того лѣт[а], коли
Алъбрахтъ вл[а]д[ы]ка ризкии умьрлъ (1229). There remain:
сегóдня, трéтьего дня 'the day before yesterday', and dates of the
form пéрвого января́ 'on the first of January'.

5. The gen. of *comparison* (an original ablative, 3.1) is the
normal inherited construction; cf. лýчше всегó, всех (3.53), but
may be replaced by a clause with чем: лýчше, чем все другíе;
лýчше, чем я ожидáл (only so).

Dative Case

46 1. *Dative of Direction*

There is a distinction in early language between the plain dat.
after verbs of motion (implying complete process) and к + dat.
(implying 'up to, as far as'); confined to place-names and unknown
in OCS: Ольга приде Кыеву. Similarly in: и ходи Игорь ротѣ
(*RPC s.a.* 945) but also идета на роту (*RP,* art. 29) 'let them take
an oath'. The plain dat. is no longer possible; it survives disguised
in домóй 'homewards' (OCS *domovi*) and the rarer долóй: уйди́
с глаз долóй 'out of my sight!' (< *dolovi*, dat. of *dolŭ*; cf. OCS
loc. *dolu* or *dolě* 'below').

47   2. The *dative of possession* (with pronouns) is also extinct:

> отець ти умерлъ, а братъ ти убьенъ (*RPC s.a.* 1015).

The cliché и́мя ему́ (Ива́н) survived till recently. The dat. is still possible in Ukr.: брат йому (or його) не є вдома 'his brother is not in'. A dependent dat. (wider than the above), for Russian gen., is characteristic of ChSl.:

> образъ же закону и благодати — Агаръ и Сарра (text no. 4) 'Hagar and Sarah are symbols of the Law and Grace';
> и ту слезамъ пролитье бываетъ от вѣрныхъ ч[еловѣ]къ (Abbot Daniel, *c.*1108);
> женамъ глава мужь, а мужемъ князь, а княземъ Богъ (Dan. Zat.).

48   3. *Dative and Infinitive*

Normal at all stages of the language. Extremely common in Русская Правда and other legal texts:

> . . . то видока ему не искати, нъ платити ему продажю 3 гр[и]вн[ы] (*RP,* art. 29) '. . . he need not produce a witness but (the assailant) shall pay a fine of 3 grivnas'.

The dat. may still be carried over through an infinitive: гру́стно челове́ку быть одному́ среди́ мно́гих. Normal in earlier language: (ему) подобает быть трезву.

49   4. *Dative Absolute*

A subordinate clause—usually temporal but also others—may be expressed participially in the dat. The procedure is very common in OCS and thence in ChSl., so much so that temporal clauses are quite rare in the *RPC*. In default of any other sources it is not possible to be sure whether the construction was native to CSl. or an imitation of Gk. syntax. In view of the difference in case (Gk. *genitive absolute*; Lat. *ablative absolute* is irrelevant) it seems more likely that it was an adaptation of a native resource rather than wholly artificial.[21]

There is no good evidence that the procedure was native to ESl.; alleged traces of it in contemporary dialects are not convincing. It disappears as soon as ChSl. ceases to have any stylistic authority (18th c.) and never appears in делово́й язы́к. Examples:

> Изяславу же кънязу тогда прѣдрьжящу обѣ власти (*Ostr.,* colophon);
> Поляномъ же жившимъ особѣ по горамъ симъ . . . (*RPC, ad init.*);

---

[21] OHG also evolved a dat. absolute in imitation of Latin.

Намъ сущимъ по кѣльямъ почивающимъ по заутрени (*RPC s.a.* 1096) 'while we were in our cells resting after matins'.

It may be noted that Lomonósov in his *Grammar* (1755, §533) approved it as a resource for literary prose but considered it already obsolete and (with regret) impossible to revive.

50   5. *Verbs taking a Dative*

These are all by and large datives of respect parallel to к + dat. after nouns and adjs. (e.g. любóвь к сы́ну 'love for one's son', стрóгий, враждéбный к + dat. 'strict, hostile towards'): вреди́ть комý (Slavonicism) 'harm' (= причини́ть комý вред; OCS normally has acc. after this verb and so sometimes in early texts as a Slavonicism); (ото)мсти́ть 'take revenge on'; зави́довать 'envy'; мешáть 'hinder'; подражáть (Slavonicism) 'imitate'; слéдовать 'follow'; помóчь *pf* 'help'; рáдоваться 'be glad'; more recent втóрить 'play/sing second to'; аплоди́ровать 'applaud'; also the three Slavonicisms сопýтствовать 'accompany', соболéзновать 'condole with', содéйствовать 'promote'.

ChSl. has суди́ть + dat. of the person (acc. of the thing): да судить ему Б[ог]ъ (text no. 12) 'may God judge him'; Russian uses acc. for both.

Instrumental Case

51   1. For the passive agent see §10 above.

2. Instrumental of *time*: now only of the *seasons* (веснóй 'in the spring') and times of day (нóчью, днём, рáнним лéтним ýтром).

3. Instrumental of *direction*: always rather rare:

да входять в городъ одинѣми вороты (*RPC s.a.* 945) 'they shall enter the city by one (particular) gate';
modern: идти́ лéсом 'to go by way of the woods'.

Largely replaced by по, через, etc.

4. Instrumental of *respect* or *circumstance* (common at all times): изнемогоша голодомь 'they grew weak through starvation'; modern: тéлом си́льный, лицóм краси́вый (older лицемь красенъ), умóм гóрды; and of dimensions: ширинóй в 10 мéтров, рóстом (он рóстом с вас 'he is about your height'). The first example involves *cause*; in this usage the instr. is now usually replaced by от or из-за + gen.

5. Verbs taking the instr. are mainly the well-defined group of *directing, controlling,* etc.:

пра́вить,[22] управля́ть 'direct, govern';
заве́довать, руководи́ть 'manage, direct';
(за)владе́ть (Slavonicism) 'gain, have control over' (он хорошо́ владе́ет
    ру́сским языко́м);
облада́ть (Slavonicism) 'possess'.

The strength of this traditional construction is shown by the recent addition of кома́ндовать (кома́ндующий а́рмией 'army commander').

6. The constructions маха́ть (махну́ть *pf*) руко́й, повести́ плеча́ми 'shrug', дви́гать (дви́нуть *pf*) па́льцами, etc. may be held to be ordinary expressions of the instrument, e.g. 'to make a movement with the hand'. They are characteristic of all styles.

7. Miscellaneous: дорожи́ть 'value'; злоупотребля́ть 'misuse, abuse' (употребля́ть only with acc.); по́льзоваться 'make use of'.

52   8. *Predicative Instrumental*

In early ESl. as in OCS (ChSl.) the pred. instr. is rare, being narrowly confined to contexts with past tenses (occsionally fut.) of быть *pf* 'become' (change of state):

OCS:
sirotojǫ dětišti ne bǫdetŭ 'the child will not become an orphan';
turomŭ byvŭ 'having been changed into a bull';[23]
děvojǫ bo bě 'for she was a virgin' (rarer imperf. of *state*).

ChSl.:
бысть владыкою 'he became bishop';

and with an equivalent verb: самъ царемь ста (*Novg. Chr.*).

This instr. is neither obligatory nor strictly confined to such contexts in later texts; in particular it is extended to trans. verbs in the same general area:

ChSl.:
бысть самовластець русьстѣи земли (*RPC s.a.* 1036) 'he became sole
    ruler of Russia';
и да будеть рабъ . . . (ibid. 945);
бывъ преже игуменъ Печерьскому манастырю (ibid. 1094);

---

[22] Not in the senses 'straighten' and 'correct' (пра́вить ру́копись). ChSl. sometimes has acc. in the sense 'rule'.
[23] A. Vaillant, *Manuel du vieux slave*, vol. 1, p. 181.

и постави имъ игуменомь Варлама (ibid. 1051) 'and he appointed
Varlam their abbot';

бяше была черницею (ibid. 977) 'she had been formerly a nun' (state).

ESl.:

да не будеть Новыи Торгъ Новгородомъ, ни Новгородъ Торжькомъ
(1215) 'may Torzhók not become (a second) Novgorod nor Novgorod
(sink to the level of) Torzhók';

кто былъ ту, то будѣте (= будеть) послухъ (1229) 'let whoever was
present be witness (thereto)';

та два была послъмь у (= в) Ризѣ (1229) 'these two were appointed his
envoy(s) in Riga'.

This position changes very little in Muscovite texts until the 17th c.,
when the pred. instr. underwent rapid extension to most contexts
largely irrespective of verb and the distinction 'change of state'/
'state'. WhR. documents of the 15th–16th c. already used it widely:
from this chancellery language (7.23) it is conveyed to Moscow as
an indirect Polish influence.

There can be little doubt that this new syntactic fashion brought
about the final generalization of the pl. instr. in -ами (3.12), since
the older masc. pl. instr. -ы was identical with the pl. NA, and also
legitimized the use of 'long' adjs. as predicates (§71 below), since
'short' adjs. no longer had an instr. case. From then on we find:

(a) он был дóктором 'he was a doctor' (not 'became'). Nevertheless there is still a difference in that the above implies a change
of state at some moment; inherent qualities normally remain in the
nom. (он был англичáнин).

(b) With verbs of causing, becoming and the like (extended),
e.g. стать, сдéлаться, оказáться, a pred. instr. is now obligatory
if the predicate is a noun, facultative if it is an adj. The extension
to long adjs. appears to be rare before the later 18th c.:

older:

(он) учинился болен (Kot.) 'he made himself ill';

дом его совсем разорить и на несколько лет сотворить его пуст (acc.)
(Pos.).

newer:

дом оказáлся пусты́м (пуст and rarer пустóй are still possible);

побéда не былá сомни́тельною (Kar.).

(c) With verbs of motion and the like:

мы расстáлись больши́ми прия́телями (Púshkin);

(он) вернýлся в Россѝю англомáном (Turgénev).

(*d*) Extension to contexts where the verb is in the infinitive occurs fairly early, in the fut. rarely before the 18th c., in the imperative not complete in the modern standard—a pred. adj. must be in the short nom. (бýдьте так дóбры, любéзны).

In the context of the dat. + inf., however, a second dat. by attraction remained common in coll. language and is often found in proverbs and the like: комý быть повéшену, томý не утонýть. Cf. §48 above.

(*e*) With verbs of calling, naming, etc. the instr. appears from the 16th c. but a 'quotation' in the nom. always remains possible:

сдѣлаша градъ и нарекоша и (acc.) Новъгородъ (nom.) (*RPC, ad init.*);
сын боярскои полоняник, Ондраганом зовут (1576);
(modern) звáли её Настáсья Петрóвна.

Long adj. (cf. (*b*) above): Я думаю, что многие из наших сестр назовут меня нескромною (Kar.).

(*f*) In ChSl., compound predicates after transitive verbs normally show a double acc. (perhaps native Slav, perhaps an influence of Greek on OCS):

OCS: *obręštete mladenĭcĭ povitŭ ležęštĭ vŭ jaslexŭ* (Luke 2: 12).
ChSl.: видѣвъ ю добру сущю зѣло лицемь (*RPC s.a.* 955);
и Богъ неврѣжена мя съблюде (ibid. 1096).

The first example in (*e*) could also be so interpreted.

So in ESl.: ти дають Двину свободну (1229).

This procedure was still possible, with a participle only, in 19th c. literary style but the colloquial must have long abandoned it in favour of a clause with как:

нашёл егó у ворóт сидя́щего (Lérmontov);[24]
я вѝдел, как онѝ игрáли в тéннис (similarly я слы́шал, как онá игрáла на роя́ле).

(*g*) The instr. is never used for a predicate in nominal sentences (i.e. in the present tense): он — солдáт, maintaining earlier кто правыи купьць есть (1229) 'whoever is a genuine merchant'.

The occasional instr. is surely a Polonism.[25]

---

[24] Still a normal procedure in Polish: *widziałem go przechodzącego*.
[25] Polish, which maintains the copula, varies between nom. and instr. (commoner): *on jest żołnierzem/żołnierz*; *jestem Polką/Polka*.

53 *Locative Case*

1. In OCS and early ESl. a plain loc. is sufficient to indicate *place where* but is only normal with place-names:

самъ же Изяславъ кънязь правляаше столъ о[ть]ца своего Ярослава Кыевѣ, а брата своего столъ поручи правити близоку своему Остромиру Новѣгородѣ (*Ostr.*, colophon);
онъ же шедъ сѣде на столѣ Черниговѣ, Ярославу сущю Новѣгородѣ тогда (*RPC s.a.* 1024).

Such locatives have often become adverbs or prepositions, e.g. кро́ме (< кромѣ, loc. of крома́), среди́, ме́жду, сквозь (< *skvozě*); earlier горѣ, верху 'at the top'; and probably внѣ (cf. acc. вон).

2. Locative of time (especially seasons): зимѣ, лѣтѣ 'in the winter, summer'; той же вѣснѣ, той же осени. Here too perhaps нынѣ 'now'.

In both the above the plain loc. was obsolescent by the 13th and very rare after the 15th c., except for a few semi-adverbials (веснѣ, зимѣ in *Dom.*, 16th c.). Later copies of chronicles insert в (or на): а (в) Новѣгородѣ зло быс[ть] вельми (1215).

The temporal expressions tend to be replaced by the gen. (того лѣта, §45 (4) above) and finally by the instr. (ле́том, §51 (2) above).

The 1229 Treaty has у (= в) Ризѣ, у Смоленьскѣ consistently.

3. A few OCS verbs could be constructed with the loc., especially cpds. of при- (the prep. при takes the loc.):

cěsaristvě našemĭ g[ospod]i milostĭjǫ tvojejǫ priziri (*Kiev Fragments*) 'look with favour, O Lord, in your mercy on our realm'

but there appear to be no examples in ESl.

54 *Nominative and Infinitive*

The nom. case of a fem. sg. noun in -*a* (-*ja*) (other instances are very rare) as the apparent object of an inf. is regular, but not universal, from early times in some styles (especially as a legal cliché) down to the time of Peter the Great. Examples are numerous from the 13th c. but there are some in Русская Правда which may well belong to the original 11th c. text:

такова правда узяти русину у Ризѣ и на гочкомь березѣ (1229) 'a

Russian is to have the same right in Riga and Gotland' (but also: таку правду възяти русину . . .);

лучше бы ми вода пити въ дому твоемь, нежели медъ пити въ боярстѣмь дворѣ (Dan. Zat.);

продаяти ти дань своя Новгородцю (1304/5) (*i*-stem!);

и тому та вотчина выкупити (1550 Судебник) 'he shall redeem this estate';

как мукá сѣяти (*Dom*.; very common in this text);

а вѣлено имъ цѣна ставить всякимъ звѣрямъ (Kot., 17th c.);

сосѣдямъ тая же казнь чинить (Pos., *c*.1724);

у старостъ тѣхъ жителей взять сказка . . . (ibid.) 'procure a declaration from the local headmen . . .';

proverb: говори́ть пра́вда — потеря́ть дру́жба.

The focus of this evidently colloquial procedure is in NW dialects (specifically Novg.) where it still occurs. It is absent at a more literary level, e.g. from chronicle narratives and the formal wills of the Grand Princes of Moscow, and from C. and S. dialects except by extension of Muscovite legal and administrative clichés.

Its origin has been variously explained.[26] It was most probably originally an elliptical construction, stating the category word first irrespective of what follows. The beginnings are to be seen in the condensed phraseology of Русская Правда, e.g.

аже пьрьстъ утнеть кыи-любо, то 3 гр[и]вны продаже, а самому гривна кунъ (art. 23);

аже ударить мечемь, а не утнеть на см[е]рть, то 3 гр[и]вны, а самому гривна за рану (art. 29)

where (есть) платити 'is for payment' can be supplied.[27]

It has, however, been pointed out that a comparable construction is normal in Finnic[28] so that it may well have been supported, if not initiated, by the strongly bilingual milieu of the Novg. region. Further support perhaps came from the instability of declension in Northern dialects (6.22), where a nom./acc. developed in *a/ja*-stem nouns parallel to the nom./acc. identity in all other sg. nouns (only inanimates are in question): хочу́ пить холо́дная вода́; на́до вода́ носи́ть; на́, возьми́ верёвочка.

The nom. + inf. dies out in the early 18th c. as an anomaly, with the obsolescence of pre-Petrine legal language.

[26] See e.g. F. Cocron, *La Langue russe au XVIIme siècle*, pp. 54–8.

[27] Cf. Ger. *ist zu finden* (the inf. being the dat. of a verbal noun as in Slav.).

[28] Veenker, pp. 120 ff.; Kiparsky in *ZSP* 28 (1959).

PREPOSITIONS (INCLUDING VERBAL PREFIXES) (SELECTED)

The great majority of these are of CSl. stock. The following call for comment.

55 1. Вы- (prefix only), plausibly considered a Gmc. loan of Gothic date,[29] is characteristic of North Slav (WSl. and ESl.) only. The rare examples in OCS texts all point to origin or revision in a WSl. milieu (i.e. Moravia or Pannonia), e.g. *Ps. Sin. vyvrěšti, vygoniti/ vygŭnati, vyrinǫti.*

ESl. is thus able to develop a contrast *native* вы-/*learned* (SSl.) из-. Вы- monopolizes as usual the literal and concrete sense (spatial); ChSl. из- has various figurative uses (*spatial* из- is always a Slavonicism); *both* lead commonly to a construction with preposition из:

ESl.	*ChSl.*
выходи́ть из, вы́ход 'go/come out of', 'exit'	исходи́ть из/от, исхо́д 'proceed from', 'outcome'
вы́ключить электри́чество 'turn off the light'	исключи́ть из кружка́ 'exclude from the group'
вы́брать 'pick out, choose'	избра́ть 'elect'
он вы́нул[30] кни́гу из я́щика	

Native из- covers several well-defined areas, the most important being intensive or cumulative: изби́ть 'massacre', изно́шенный 'worn out' (of a garment, §94 below)—cf. поно́шенный 'second-hand'; не можаху пси из(ъ)ѣдати ч[е]л[о]в[ѣ]къ (*Novg. Chr.*, *s.a.* 1215) 'the dogs could not eat up (all) the corpses'.

56 2. Въз- and variants only appears as a *prefix* in ESl.; cf. OCS *blagodětĭ vŭz blagodětĭ* 'grace for grace' (AV) (i.e. one grace on/ after another), SCr. *uz* (*ŭz Dunav* 'up the Danube (upstream)'). A high proportion of cpds. with this prefix, particularly in the form воз-/вос- (2.31) are Slavonicisms, perhaps close on 500 words.

Main senses:

(*a*) inchoative (native also за-): восклú́кнуть *pf* 'exclaim' (cf. native вскрича́ть 'exclaim', закрича́ть 'start shouting'); воз-

---

[29] Gmc. *ūt* (Eng. *out*), the *t* falling before the initial consonant of the verb. The consistently initial stress in *pf* verbs (вы́нести) also recalls Ger. *áusnehmen*, perpetuating earlier Gmc. stress. Evidently this borrowed prefix originated in the *pf* aspect; derived imperfectives have normal stress (вы-носи́ть, -бира́ть). Вы́глядеть, a mid-19th c. calque of Ger. *áussehen*, is *imperfective*.

[30] Вы́нуть *pf*/вынима́ть for *вынять by attraction to verbs in -нуть.

любить *pf* 'fall in love with'; возникнуть *pf* 'arise, come into being'; воспламенить *pf* 'ignite', (fig.) 'inflame' (cf. native зажечь); возбудить *pf* 'arouse' (native разбудить 'rouse');

(*b*) 're-': возобновить *pf* 'renew'; восстановить *pf* 'restore'; воспоминания 'reminiscences, memoirs' (cf. native вспомнить *pf* 'remember')—in this sense often native пере- (§62 (9)(*c*) below); воздать *pf* 'render' (native отдать, передать).

The repartition of usage as between ChSl. and Russian, as will be seen, is by no means precise.

57 3. (*a*) За takes only acc. and instr. in ESl.; за + gen. 'during' is absent except in Ukr. (Pol. *za życia*, SCr. *za žìvòta* = R. при жизни). The latter is rare in OCS; it is occasionally to be found in ChSl. texts: за живота его (*RPC s.a.* 912) (sporadically also for из-за + gen.).

(*b*) A characteristic colloquial formation is seen in the type заспаться *pf* 'oversleep' (за = beyond (the normal)); so also застояться *pf* 'stand for too long', заизучать *pf* (trans.) 'study over-much'. Examples are available from the 16th c.: товар мои залежался (1569); заговориться (1582).

(*c*) For inchoative за- see (2) above.

(*d*) The idiom что за + (apparent) nom. is found as early as the 16th c.: не твоя б государская милость, и яз бы что за человек? (1576) 'but for your royal favour I should be a nobody'. It is highly improbable therefore that there is any direct connection with Ger. *was für ein . . .*, or even with Pol. *co za człowiek* (which could be a Germanism).

58 4. ESl. межю (du. loc.) and межи (sg. loc.) (межь) (also with prefix про-) were eventually ousted by ChSl. между at the literary level: аж бы промьжю нами бои былъ (1229) 'that there should be war between us'. *RPC* has predominantly межю + instr. but also промежю + gen., rarely между. Construction with the gen. has become unusual or subliterary: читать между строк 'to read between the lines'.[31] An acc. implying motion is also to be found, unknown today.

59 5. The cumulative на-, general in Slav (накопить *pf* 'amass', наделать (много) глупостей 'do a lot of silly things', набрать

---

[31] In composition usually между- (международный 'international'), but scientific language favours меж- (межзубный 'interdental', межпланетный 'interplanetary') and there are a few older Latin calques of the form междометие 'interjection'.

камне́й 'collect (enough) stones' (partitive gen., §41, 1(*a*) above)), is further developed in the coll. type нае́стъся 'eat one's fill', налюбова́ться 'admire to one's heart's content', but is scarcely new, having models in such OCS words as насы́титься *pf*/насыща́ться 'sate oneself', наслади́ться *pf*/наслажда́ться 'delight in'.

60   6. Низ- appears as a prefix in a few Slavonicisms only, e.g. низве́ргнуть *pf* 'overthrow', ниспосла́ть *pf* 'send down' (from on high), снисходи́ть к + dat. 'condescend to' (adj. снисходи́тельный).

61   7. (*a*) О + acc. 'in contact with' (as in о́коло) and о + loc. 'concerning' are current at all times, but as a prefix the value of о- is often hard to determine. It is the preferred prefix for perfectivizing intrans. verbs of (change of) state in -еть (-*ěti*): оробе́ть *pf* 'display timidity', окамене́ть *pf* 'turn to stone'; this is manifestly a wholly 'empty' prefix (*préfixe vide*, §86 below).

(*b*) The descriptive use of о + loc. (still normal in Polish) has virtually disappeared from literary usage, but survives in proverbs and the like: па́лка о двух конца́х = 'there are two ways of looking at anything'; ло́шадь о четырёх нога́х, да (и то) спотыка́ется = 'even Homer nods'.

8. For от after passive verbs see §10 above.

62   9. (*a*) Native пере- and ChSl. пре- (properly пръ-; CSl. *per- = Lat. *per*) were from early on specialized to different uses (neither exists except as a prefix in ESl.[32]); the Slavonicisms are exclusively metaphorical:

Native (spatial)	*ChSl.*
переступи́ть *pf* поро́г 'cross the threshold'	преступи́ть *pf* зако́н 'transgress the law'; преступле́ние 'crime'
переста́вить *pf* 'transpose'	преста́виться 'pass over, die' (calque of Gk. μετατίθεσθαι); преставле́ние 'decease' (formal word)
перегороди́ть *pf*/-гора́живать 'partition off'	прегради́ть *pf*/-гражда́ть путь 'bar the way'
переда́ть *pf* 'hand over, communicate'	преда́ть *pf* огню́ 'consign to the flames'; 'betray'

Similarly the Slavonicisms превзойти́ *pf* 'surpass'; преврати́ть

[32] OCS occasionally *prě* + instr. = *prědŭ* (probably a secondary development).

pf/-враща́ть 'transform'; презре́ть *pf*/-зира́ть 'despise'; пребыва́ть 'reside, be'; пресле́довать 'pursue, prosecute', and many more.

(*b*) The basic spatial sense is easily transferred to temporal: переночева́ть (= Lat. *pernoctare*).

(*c*) Native figurative senses not characteristic of ChSl. пре- are:

- (i) re-: переписа́ть *pf* 'rewrite'; перестро́ить 'reconstruct'.
- (ii) excess: перекупа́ться *pf* 'bathe (for) too long'; пересоли́ть *pf*/-са́ливать 'oversalt', of which the opposite is недо-: досыпа́ть недо́спанную ночь; недоумева́ть 'to be at a loss'; недостава́ть 'be lacking' (недоста́точно 'insufficient').

(*d*) With adjs. and adverbs ChSl. пре- was an intensive prefix at the literary level but is now antiquated: я вам премно́го обя́зан 'I am vastly obliged to you'; пренепри́ятное изве́стие 'most unpleasant news'. Fully colloquialized are прекра́сный 'beautiful' (simple now краси́вый), преле́стный 'lovely, exquisite'.

63 10. (*a*) ChSl. пред (OCS *prědŭ*), with acc. of motion or instr. of rest, is now virtually extinct in Russian as a preposition; it survived into the 19th c. in a few legal clichés, e.g. яви́ться пред суд 'appear in court'. Native пе́ред has lost the distinction of motion and rest, taking instr. in all contexts. The 1229 Treaty shows clearly the original distinction: (acc.) русину не звати латинеского на иного князя судъ, лише предъ (*sic*) смольнеского князя 'a Russian may not sue a foreigner in the court of any prince other than (that of) the Prince of Smolensk'; but (instr.) передъ судиями и передъ добрыми люд[ь]ми 'in the presence of . . .'.

(*b*) As a ChSl. verbal prefix пред- is usually temporal and in virtue of this *does not perfectivize a simple verb*: предви́деть 'foresee'; предчу́вствовать 'have a premonition'; предыду́щий 'preceding'; предстоя́ть 'lie ahead, be in store' (now only temporal but formerly also spatial, e.g. . . . отъ ангелъ, иже предстоять ему со страхомъ (*RPC s.a.* 1071) 'by the angels who stand before Him in fear'); but (cpd. verb) предупреди́ть *pf*/-упрежда́ть 'forestall, warn'; and *spatial* предста́вить *pf*/-ставля́ть 'present, introduce'. Предло́г 'preposition' and предме́т 'object' are Latin calques (5.35), as is no doubt also предписа́ть *pf* 'prescribe' (medical).

64   11. (*a*) По- is by far the commonest 'empty prefix' affected to the role of perfectivizing a simple verb (§86 below). Other special colloquial usages:

(i) limited action ('attenuative'): постоя́ть *pf* 'to stand for a time' (vague: exact length of time requires простоя́ть *pf*); поба́иваться *impf* 'be somewhat afraid of' (боя́ться);

(ii) sequence of like actions (plural subject): повыходи́ть 'come out one after another'; помере́ть *pf* 'die off' (in succession): а вожане помроша (1215); да ещо у них побили и поранили многих (1576) 'and even so (we) killed and wounded a lot of them'. Many such verbs are now subliterary.

(*b*) In the modern literary standard по + acc. is practically limited to the sense 'as far as': он стоя́л в воде́ по коле́ни 'he stood in the water up to his knees'; с января́ по март 'from January to March (inclusive)'. The sense 'in search of' is common in early texts, especially from Nóvgorod, and indeed appears to be predominantly a usage of the W. borderlands (it is still current in WhR. and Ukr.): новгородьци же останъке (nom.) живыхъ послаша Гюргя Иванковица посадника . . . по князя (*Novg. Chr.* 1215) 'the remnant of Novgorod citizens sent George Ivankovich the mayor . . . to fetch the prince' (perhaps simply 'to the prince', also a frequent usage, as in и не яша ся по то (ibid.) 'but they would not lend themselves to this'); (modern dial.) они́ ходи́ли в лес по грибы́ 'they went into the forest to look for (gather) mushrooms'.

A few relics of wider use remain in set phrases, e.g. spatial (nearer по + dat.): по ту сто́рону, по о́бе стороны́ (реки́) 'on the far side', 'on both banks (of the river)'.

(*c*) По (CSl. *pŏ*, Lat. *pŏ-situs*) has a (stressed) variant with long vowel па- (CSl. *pā*); in a few words this has developed a pejorative sense—'false', 'bogus': па́сека 'apiary', па́тока 'syrup' (postverbal nouns of сечь and течь); па́дуб 'holly'; па́сынок, па́дчерица 'step-son, -daughter'; perhaps also па́робок (па́рубок) 'lad' (Ukr. and some S. dial.), to which па́рень may belong, but the etymology is disputed. Па- also appears in OCS (ChSl.) па́губ-а, -ный 'ruin(ous)'.

65   12. Про is in modern usage chiefly a verbal prefix; its use as a preposition has been much restricted. Про 'concerning' has nearly

succumbed to o + loc.; про 'because of' is now only regional (про
то его князю не держати (1229) 'the Prince shall not detain him
on that account').

Specialized stressed form as prefix—пра-: OCS and ChSl.
праотьць 'forefather'; modern пра́дед 'great-grandfather'; learned
прароди́на, calque of Ger. *Urheimat*; индоевропе́йский праязы́к
'proto-IE language'.

13. As a prefix c (CSl. *sŭn*) appears in three forms referable
to the sense 'with' (c + instr.): native c-/co-, ChSl. co-, native and
ChSl. cy- (< *sǫ- < *sŭn + C-):

(*a*) ChSl. co- in сопоста́вить *pf* 'compare'; соедини́ть *pf* 'join,
combine'; соприкаса́ться 'be contiguous to'; соревнова́ться (all
constructed mainly or wholly with c + instr.); соболе́зновать
'commiserate with', соде́йствовать 'promote', сопу́тствовать
'accompany' (all with dat.).

(*b*) native: су́мерки (pl.) (ChSl. сумрак) 'twilight'; сугли́нок
'loam'; супе́рица 'rape-seed' (< ре́па 'turnip'); су́дорога 'cramp'
(2.50); су́тки (pl.) '24 hours' (< *sǫ-tŭki* = 'coincidence', cf.
наткну́ться *pf* 'strike against'); несура́зный 'absurd'.

ChSl.: супру́г 'spouse' (originally 'pair of animals harnessed
together'; native verb спряга́ть); сугу́бый 'double' (lit. 'folded
over'; native verb согну́ть *pf*/сгиба́ть); суста́в 'joint' (anat.).

The form сусе́д 'neighbour', normal in many Slav languages
including Ukr. and WhR., has been replaced in the literary standard by сосе́д but is still alive in dialect. Similarly супроти́в is now
subliterary, except in the technical term супроти́вный 'opposite'
(of leaves).

66 14. Через, ChSl. чрез, is a rare prefix in nouns and adjs. only:
native чересполо́сица 'strip farming'; чересчу́р (adv.) 'overmuch'
(dial. чур = 'limit, boundary', term still used in various children's
games); ChSl. чрезвыча́йный 'extraordinary'; чрезме́рный
'excessive, inordinate'.

67 15. From the 18th c. onwards various new 'phraseological' prepositions came into use, especially via officialese; some are modelled
on French. They take the gen.: всле́дствие, в результа́те 'as a
consequence of'; каса́тельно, относи́тельно 'concerning'; ввиду́
'in view of' (Fr. *en vue de*); насчёт 'in the matter of, about';
исключа́я 'excluding, except' (the original construction with acc.
as a pres. gerund has been replaced by gen., which has not happened with включа́я 'including'). Here also благодаря́ + dat.

'thanks to' (Fr. *grâce à*?; благодари́ть now takes the acc. but
sometimes the dat. in OCS); согла́сно + dat. or с + instr. 'in
accordance with', both Slavonicisms. Older is вме́сто 'instead of',
still usually in free association in the 17th c.: а посыла́ютъ въ ихъ
мѣсто ины́хъ (Kot.) 'and send others in their place'—modern
вме́сто них only.

68   16. Normal syntax now requires double expression of *prefix* and
preposition in many cases:

довести́ де́ло до конца́ 'complete the job';
вложи́ть всю свою́ ду́шу в рабо́ту 'put all one's heart into the work';
вдава́ться в подро́бности 'go into details';
заверну́ть за́ угол 'turn the corner';
наста́ивать на своём 'insist on one's own way';
подпа́сть под чьё-нибудь влия́ние 'come under someone's influence'.

Usage was freer in earlier language, and we can still have достига́ть
+ gen. (commoner) or до + gen., дозвони́ться + gen. or до +
gen. (or к + dat.) 'get an answer to one's ring'.

Conversely, the repetition of a *preposition* with several or all
members of a word group is now subliterary; it is very common in
the Muscovite period and still widespread in dialect:

а исъ портъ изъ моихъ . . . (1328);
при великомъ князѣ при Иванѣ Даниловичѣ (1381);
уже погании татарове на поля на наши наступаютъ (*Zadonshchina*);
да полѣзъ есми на судно на послово (Аf. Nik., 15th c.) 'so I transferred
     to the envoy's boat'.

69   17. All inherited true prepositions are proclitic. The traditional
pitch and stress pattern of proclitic and noun is best preserved in
SCr.; in ESl. it is better preserved in N. than S. dialects. Standard
literary examples: на́‿бе́рег, за́‿город, при́‿смерти, во́-время
(adv., but во вре́мя заседа́ния 'during the session'), как снег
на́‿голову 'out of the blue', со́‿смеху, взаше́й (вы́гнать) 'chuck
out' (ше́я 'neck'), за́муж(ем) 'married', и́з‿дому, and many others.

Two words appear also in early texts as *postpositions*, viz. ра́ди
'for the sake of' and дѣля (ChSl. also дѣльма) 'by reason of, for'.
In neither case is the etymology wholly clear. Ра́ди, perhaps a loan-
word (5.4), may have been originally confined to religious formulae
(ра́ди Бо́га) but was used more widely in the Muscovite period,
e.g. того ради 'therefore'. It has retained a limited use and its free

position. Дѣля (modern для) finally becomes the commoner and is now fully integrated into the prepositions (never postposited):

то зане к нимъ прикладываеть, того же дѣля имъ помогати головнику
   (*RP*, art. 5) '. . . in virtue of this they (shall) help the murderer';
царь деи тебя велел того для спросити, что . . . (1576) 'the Khan (he said) has ordered (me) to ask you because . . .'.

The earlier order is perpetuated in the Slavonicism богадѣльня 'almshouse'. Для has also limited its scope: it can no longer be resultative as in the above examples; для = из-за is still found in the 18th c.

SYNTACTICAL USE OF 'LONG' AND 'SHORT' ADJECTIVES

70 1. The 'long' adjective was the special or 'marked' form of the two—it is *determinate*, or better anaphoric, as its structure indicates (3.37), referring back to a fact already stated. This function is usually clear in OCS, as in the following (adjectival) participles:

prinesošę emu oslablenŭ žilami na odrě ležęštŭ . . . i reče oslablenumu . . . 'they brought a paralytic to him, lying on a bed . . . and he said to the paralytic . . .'.[33]

It follows that the long adj. is by nature *attributive* only, as well as determinate. All other uses of the adj. are the province of the 'short' nominal forms, viz.

(*a*) attributive *indeterminate*: новъ домъ 'a new house' (first statement of an attribute, new fact);

(*b*) predicative: домъ (есть) новъ 'the house is new';

(*c*) toponyms and the like which necessarily refer to something unique and therefore require no further determination:

Нов(ъ)городъ; cf. Eng. *Newmarket, Southwold, Whit(e)church*;
Велúкъ день 'Easter day';
велúкъ мостъ 'the great bridge' (at Nóvgorod);

and all *personal* possessives (3.43): сынъ Ярославль 'Jaroslav's son' (but always велúкий князь 'the Grand Prince', as opposed to all other princes).

The above categories define early ESl. usage: an attribute may be long or short according to context, a predicate may be only short.

---

[33] Matt. 9: 2 and parallel passages. Later versions: *razslablena . . . ležašta . . . razslablenomu*.

Taking Русская Правда as an example of 11th c. usage we find:

Прав[ь]да Русьская (title; later addition);

short:

аче будеть княжь мужь 'if he is a prince's official';

оже придеть кръвавъ муж[ь] на дворъ 'if a freeman covered with blood appears at the court';

пакы ли будеть что татебно купилъ въ търгу 'further, if (someone) has bought stolen goods in the market';

аже кто познаеть челядинъ свои украденъ 'if anyone recognizes a stolen slave of his';

long:

которая ли вьрвь начьнеть платити дикую виру 'if any commune shall be paying the communal fine' (sc. as defined above);

а кдѣ будеть конечнии тать 'and where the original thief is (found)'.

Similarly, in the 1229 Treaty: владыка ризкий 'the Bishop of Riga'; своего лучшего попа 'his best priest'; всему латинескому языку 'to all Westerners' (demonstratives necessarily involve determination).

With other verbs than 'be' the context may be called 'semi-predicative'; the adj., always following the noun, is invariably short:

а самъ приде сдравъ 'and he arrived safe and sound';

постави . . . Перуна древяна, а главу его сребрену, а усъ златъ (*RPC s.a.* 980) '(Vladímir) set up (a statue of) Perún of wood, with a head of silver and beard of gold';

а паропки да девочки ходят наги до семи лѣт (Af. Nik., 15th c.) 'and the little boys and girls go naked up to the age of seven'.

71   2. The two disruptive elements in this general situation were:

(*a*) early obsolescence of the *oblique cases* of short adjs. (3.48 ff.);

(*b*) early obsolescence of *short forms* in certain categories of adjs., in particular those in -ьск- (3.45).[34]

This meant on the one hand that the short forms were more and more specialized as predicates (nom. and acc. only, after the 17th c. only nom.) and on the other that the specific sense distinction between determinate and indeterminate attributes tended to be

---

[34] It should be noted that from the outset certain categories of adjs. had only determinate forms, notably those in -*īnjii* derived from adverbs (modern здѣшний, послѣдний, домашний, etc.).

obscured and was eventually lost, since short forms were no longer available from an adj. such as русский. *Short attributive* adjs. are rare throughout the Новгородские берестяные грамоты (*c.*1100–1500), which must reflect colloquial usage.

The loss of the attributive distinction is earlier than the moment when the short forms have to give up their unique function as predicates.

The situation in the Muscovite period is thus muddled. A few long predicates are found in the 16th c. but this is still exceptional: торгъ будетъ повол[ь]нои (nom.) (1588) 'trade will be free'.

With the rapid rise of the predicative instr. in the 17th c. (§52 above) a morphologically clear instr. form was required for adjs. too and this could only be supplied by the 'long' declension. This once established, it was a short step to the free admission of 'long' nominatives into the predicate also.

Thus the situation has reversed itself: in early ESl. the *long* forms had a single exclusive function, in the modern language the *short* forms have a single function, but not exclusive.

72   3. As between short and long adjs. as predicates at the present day the situation is fluid: the difference between дом нов 'the house is new' and дом но́вый 'the house is a new one' is stylistic or rhythmical rather than grammatical. It is sometimes true—depending on the adj.—that a short predicate connotes a *temporary* quality and a long predicate a *permanent* one, e.g. in

> он бо́лен 'he is ill' (sc. at the moment);
> он больно́й 'he is a sick man' (always);
> она́ до́брая 'she is a good woman';
> она́ добра́ 'she is good' (on this occasion)

(but больно́й could be claimed as a *noun*—'an invalid').

The *long instr.* may alternate, without perceptible distinction, with the *short nom.*: он оста́лся э́тим недово́лен *or* недово́льным (semi-predicative); cf. е́сли моя́ вы́ходка вам ка́жется смешна́ (Lerm.)/Инса́ров каза́лся им о́чень гро́зным (Turg.).

The loss of the distinction determinate/indeterminate in attributes—вели́к(ъ) мост(ъ) 'a great bridge'/вели́кий мост(ъ) 'the great bridge'—can hardly be called surprising in a language which did not develop articles designed to stress precisely this (the origin of *the* is similar—a worn-down demonstrative). Indeed no Slav language except SCr. maintains the distinction at all.

The only relic of the former state of affairs is to be found in a few petrified toponyms: Нóвгород, Белоóзеро (§70, type (c)).[35]

SYNTAX OF NUMERALS

73 1. The majority of modern European languages have taken the course of treating the cardinal numbers (sometimes excepting 'one' and with minor variations in a few other integers) as *indeclinable* numerical symbols. The Slav languages in general, and Russian in particular, did not make this simplification:[36] the syntax of numerals is involved, cumbersome, and full of anomalies. Indeed it is sometimes difficult to decide what 'part of speech' a numeral word is in Russian.

74 2. Taking the simple binomial 'number + noun', in the *oblique* cases there has been relatively little change (other than morphological): both stand in the case required by the context. For 1–4 this was the original state; 5 and above, originally *nouns* (3.75), were drawn into this pattern in the 15th–16th c.: о пятй книгъ (pl. gen.) > о пятй кнйгах. Only the higher numerals—тьíсяча, миллиóн, etc.—have remained pure nouns: тьíсяча душ, от тьíсячи душ, с тьíсячью (3.80) душ.

75 3. If the numerical expression is syntactically *nom.* or *acc.* quite different procedures apply. The loss of the dual (3.31, 3.42 (5)) and the extension of the distinction animate/inanimate (§41 above) required consequential changes.

The NA dual is reinterpreted as *sg. gen.*, differences of stress being usually removed (but see 3.32): два брáта, два бéрега (du. берегá, pl. бéреги (берези), later берегá), два слóва (pl. словá). This procedure was then in the Muscovite period *extended to 3 and 4*; the *morphological* interaction of 2–4 has been noted above (3.72–4): три рубля (1550); четыре алтына (1550). Plurals after 3 and 4 are still fairly common in the 16th c.: три годы (1576); probably more so with feminines since there was identity of form with the sg. gen. and stress difference is rarely indicated: за три

---

[35] Such cpds. can be found declined in both parts down to the end of the 14th c.: на Бѣлѣ озерѣ (1389). That the short instr. was an early loss (3.48) is confirmed by Новымъ городомъ (1368) (Новъмь городомь still c.1250).

[36] SCr., at the colloquial level, attempts some simplification with invariability of the number word, e.g. Sr̃bi svà trî (nom.) zákona (sg. gen.) for 'correct' Sr̃bi svîh (or svíjū) tríjū (gen.) zákōnā (pl. gen.) 'Serbs of all three faiths' (example from A. Meillet and A. Vaillant, *Grammaire de la langue serbo-croate* (Paris, 1924), p. 126). Russian mathematicians also use many invariable forms.

версты (версты́ sg. gen. or вёрсты pl. acc.?). Even in the 19th c. на все 4 сто́роны, за обе ру́ки, and others were still permissible.

In many dialects, however, and in WhR. and Ukr., the extension to 3 and 4 was not made or has remained incomplete, or the three genders do not behave alike;[37] typically inanimates and non-personal animates take pl. NA and this may be extended to 2 as well.

The numerals 5 and above continue to take the pl. gen.

Animacy. The order of extension in the nouns—sg. masc., pl. masc., pl. fem. (§41 above)—is generally followed in combination with numerals 2–4, with finally acc. = gen. in all cases. It should be noted, however, that 'classical' grammar makes a distinction between simple and cpd. numerals: (я уви́дел) четырёх студе́нтов, коро́в but (я уви́дел) два́дцать четы́ре студе́нта, коро́вы, *et sim.*

Modern colloquial blurs the distinction: я уви́дел четы́ре студе́нта is often said. Further, the *i*-stem type numerals 5 and above retain nom. = acc. even with animates: я купи́л пять соба́к; уби́ли пятьдеся́т челове́к.

For the cpd. decades and hundreds see 3.78 (ii) and 79.

As long as the *teens* were still phraseological cpds. (3.77) it was logical that agreement should be with the variable digit, viz. одна на десяте кннга; .в҃і. гр[и]внѣ (*RP,* art. 23) = двѣ на десяте гривнѣ (dual).

76   4. *Accompanying adjectives*

  (i) 2 (and о́ба) + dual adj. + dual noun;
  (ii) 3 and 4 + NA pl. adj. + NA pl. noun;
  (iii) 5 and above + gen. pl. adj. + gen. pl. noun.

(*a*) The change in the construction of (i) at no time induces an *adj. in the sg. gen.* (cp. SCr. *dvâ lépa kònja*). The pl. gen. of (iii) seeps back into 2–4 but is rivalled in 3 and 4 by the older pl. NA. It is to be expected that три ста́рые кни́ги (sg. gen. and pl. NA identical) would survive better. Standard 19th c. grammar preferred this in the fem. and also largely in the neut.; modern practice has tended to generalize the pl. gen.: два си́льных вола́ (always); две больши́х (less often больши́е) ко́мнаты; три

---

[37] Cf. SCr. 2–4 plus masc./neut. noun: sg. gen.; 2–4 plus fem. noun: pl. NA. This was the prevailing situation in Muscovite Russian.

ста́рых (less often ста́рые) кни́ги; пять но́вых домо́в.[38] In the
oblique cases all members of the numerical phrase agree in case.

(*b*) Adjectives standing outside the numerical expression are
normally, however, in the NA: все три бра́та, пе́рвые два часа́,
за после́дние три го́да, ка́ждые полчаса́. There is occasionally a
choice: це́лые 2 часа́ or це́лых 2 часа́. So also with 5 and above:
свои урочные пять лет (17th c.).

(*c*) Nominalized adjs., if animate, must stand in the pl. gen. if
masc./neut., in the NA if fem.:

animate: 2–4 ру́сских, портны́х; две го́рничные;
inanimate: (some variation): 3 моро́женых (neut.); 2–4 на́бережные or
   на́бережных (fem.).

77 5. In cpd. cardinals the last member decides the construction at
all times:[39]

> 21 день, 21 кни́га, 21 сло́во (gen. двадцати́ одного́ дня, etc);
> 21 ста́рая кни́га (loc. о двадцати́ одно́й ста́рой кни́ге);
> ты́сяча и одна́ ночь '1001 nights';
> два́дцать два челове́ка;
> со́рок пять мину́т.

6. *Pluralia tantum.*[40] As there is *no sg. gen.* available for use
after 2–4 in the NA it is necessary to have recourse to the collective
numerals (3.84):

> older: pl. NA трои сани 'three sledges';
> modern: тро́е сане́й (on the model мно́го люде́й).

In the oblique cases the collective forms are not obligatory and
are rarely used: двум (or двои́м) но́вым саня́м; по́сле двух (or
двои́х) су́ток (nom. дво́е су́ток).

Note. Collective numerals are now only correctly used otherwise
with *masc. animates* (or mixed groups) and in pronominal contexts:
че́тверо бра́тьев (дете́й) but три сестры́, пять сёл; он рабо́тал

---

[38] Postposited adjs. in the Muscovite period show similar variation: 3 двора
крестьянскихъ; двѣ пуговицы хрустальныхъ; четыре пуговицы серебряные.

[39] In mathematics 1 and 2 are always read as оди́н, два except for 1 in cpd.
fractions: одна́ (sc. це́лая) и две пя́тых (sc. ча́сти) = 1⅖.

[40] *Pluralia tantum* are numerous in most languages. Such are in Russian: лю́ди,
де́ти (used with different singulars); воро́та, я́сли, дрова́, обо́и, часы́, бели́ла,
черни́ла, сли́вки, щи; штаны́, но́жницы, ви́лы; по́хороны and the type имени́ны
'name-day'; опи́лки 'sawdust', вы́севки 'siftings', and other by-products of processes. Many of them never need to be enumerated.

за четверы́х 'he did the work of four'; нас бы́ло тро́е 'there were thrcc of us'; все тро́е верну́лись 'all three returned'.

7. Numerals have always been arranged in *descending order of magnitude*, with or without a connecting и or да: на тысячу да на триста да на шестьдесят да на четыре рубли (1501). The Germanic order integer + decade is not native: коли ся грамота п[и]сана, ишлъ былъ от р[о]ж[ес]тва г[оспод]ня до сего лѣта 1000 лѣт и 200 лѣт и 8 лѣт и 20 (1229 Treaty). The copyist was probably a German-speaking merchant resident in Smolensk; note also the foreign AD reckoning.

78   8. *Verbs in numerical phrases*. The original sequence та пять деревень сгорѣла (3.75 (i)) is replaced in Muscovite times by тѣ пять деревень сгорѣли; вся та пять лет погибла still occurs as an archaism in the 1720s (Pososhkóv).

A pl. verb naturally was regular with 3 and 4 and with 2 after the obsolescence of the dual.

The pl. remains predominant but a sg. neut. is frequent in the past tense especially if the verb precedes:

> все три ста́рые (or ста́рых) кни́ги сгоре́ли;
> сгоре́ло все три кни́ги.

The verb is always in the pl. with collective numerals.

9. *Ordinals*. Only the last member of a compound ordinal is declined: два́дцать пя́того февраля́ 'on 25 February'.

This procedure is sometimes now carried over colloquially into cpd. *cardinals*.

It is to be presumed that the above was true in earlier language but such numbers are rarely written out.

CO-ORDINATING CONJUNCTIONS

79   1. *Native* да 'and' (да 'in order to' is ChSl.: §22 above) is more colloquial than и. It is abundant in Muscovite делово́й язы́к and joins strictly parallel terms, less often clauses:

> а огород[ъ] всегды́ бы былъ за́мкнутъ да кому прика́зано, тот[ъ] бы его̀ всегды́ берёгъ (*Dom.*) 'your kitchen-garden must always be locked up and whoever is in charge must always guard it';
> по 3 голуби да по 3 воробьи (*RPC s.a.* 946) (see also the example in §77 (7) above);
> proverb: день да ночь — су́тки прочь;

Ива́н-да-Ма́рья 'heartsease' (wild pansy);

два да два (бу́дет) четы́ре '2 and 2 make 4';

он взял да (less often и or да и) . . . = 'he went and . . .' (of sudden or unreasonable actions): он взял да укра́л де́ньги 'he went and stole the money'.

Да can also be mildly adversative:

грустно гораздо да душе добро . . . (Avv., 17th c.) 'very unpleasant but good for the soul . . .'.

Да is, perhaps by chance, not recorded as 'yes' before the 15th c.

80 2. In early texts нъ (later но) is much more abundant in ChSl. than more or less colloquial contexts. However, there seems no good reason to doubt that it was native, having always been the strongest of the adversative conjunctions:

не едемъ на конѣхъ, ни пѣши идемъ, но понесѣте ны (асс.) въ лодьѣ (*RPC s.a.* 945) 'we (shall) not come either on horseback or on foot: rather, carry us in a boat';

не даите (sc. дань) козаромъ, но мнѣ даите (ibid. 885) 'do not pay (it) to the Khazars; pay it to me instead';

. . . тому людье не помагають, нъ самъ платить (*RP*, art. 8);

. . . и отложиша убиение за голову, нъ кунами ся выкупати (ibid., art. 2) 'and repealed the right of vendetta, but (decreed that) restitution is to be made in money' (late 11th c. addition in more literary style).

81 3. 'A' as a general connective covers, as in OCS, many shades of 'and' and 'but', normally implying some contrast (= Gk. δε); it rarely has the purely additive function of и and да:

отець ти умерлъ а братъ ти убьенъ (*RPC s.a.* 1015) 'your father has died and your brother has been murdered';

отроци Свѣньлъжи изодѣлися суть оружьемъ и порты, а мы нази (ibid. 945) 'Sveneld's men-at-arms have been fitted out with (new) weapons and clothing but we are (still) naked'.

'A' commonly introduces a new subject, at the beginning of a sentence or paragraph:

а о корсуньстѣи странѣ . . .; а о процѣ . . . (*RPC s.a.* 945) 'as regards the Crimea . . .; further . . .';

а едешь по корову, а вози 3 гривьнѣ (*NBG*, no. 8, 13th c.) 'and (if) you go to fetch the cow (then) take 3 grivnas (with you)'.

(It is possible that this 'a' sometimes stands for аже/аче 'if'.)

By Muscovite times а, да, and и are used indifferently in this function:

А шутил яз . . . и за тех изменников . . . да в твоеи же государеве грамоте (1576) (the last is stronger, as the же shows: 'moreover').

Very common in *Domostrój*:

а в жи́тницах бы у клю́чника бы́лъ бы вся́кой запа́съ . . . 'the steward must have stocks of everything in his storerooms' (§52);
а в погребе и на ле́дникех и на погрѣбицех хлѣбы и колачи́ . . .[41] (§54).

Similarly in Kotoshíkhin: а будетъ у которого отца . . .; и будетъ которая жена бываетъ противна . . .

The original sense of 'a' may well have been deictic (a! = lo!); the closely connected hortative function was retained in ать (3.113 (2)) and is also perceptible in plain 'a':

еже ми отьць даялъ . . . а то за нимь (*NBG*, no. 9) 'what my father gave me (as dowry?) . . . let that (remain) with him (sc. my husband?)'.

The deictic sense lies behind а то 'or else', following a negative imperative: не ходи́, а то я тебя́ накажу́ 'don't go; I shall punish you if you do'. (The synonymous не то corresponds rather to Eng. *otherwise*.)

82   4. The connective complementing most subordinate clauses is, from the earliest texts, то:

ажь убьеть мужь мужа, то мьстити брату брата . . . (*RP, ad init.*) 'if one freeman kills another (then) a brother may avenge his brother . . .'.

Reinforced form тоть: аже будѣте (= будет) русину платити латинескому, а не въсхъчеть платити, тоть латинескому просити дѣтского (1229) (cf. older Pol. *toć*).

From the 15th c. ино becomes characteristic in this role and plain и is equally possible:

а уж заехано ино было не по об'езному спати (1574) 'once you had got that far you shouldn't have been asleep on your reconnaissance';
и будетъ которая жена бываетъ противна . . . жалуетца сродичамъ своимъ, что онъ съ нею живетъ не въ совѣте и бьетъ и мучитъ, и тѣ сродичи на того человѣка бьютъ челомъ патриарху . . . (Kot.) '. . . and complains to her family that he is on bad terms with her and beats her and harasses her, (then) they prefer a complaint to the Patriarch against him . . .'.

[41] Stresses marked as in the manuscript.

Ино (и) disappears from cultivated use after the 17th c. but то has remained current.

ASPECT AND TENSE

83   There are only three *temporal* relations—present, past, future. Any finer distinctions which a verbal system may show, within a single voice or mood, are aspectual. Most European languages display aspect in this wide sense to a greater or lesser extent in their active finite 'tenses'. Aspect defines the mode or scope of the action (Ger. *Aktionsart*). Such distinctions may be made predominantly by morphological means, e.g. Ancient and Modern Greek, or analytically (by varying syntactical markers), as in English or spoken Arabic. Classical Greek, in the tradition of later IE, distinguished aspects by different verbal stems, each forming the particular repertoire of 'tenses' which it required. Later evolution or the crude convenience of grammarians conflates them into a single 'paradigm'.[42]

CSl. inherited the same basic mechanism, much changed in detail; thence it passed into all the living Slav languages. Owing to the fact that Latin was a language which made little capital of *aspect* but much of *relative time*, and that the categories and technical terms of the Latin grammarians became virtually the sole basis for the analysis of European languages down to the Renaissance and beyond, whether the language was descended from Latin or not, it is not surprising to find that, in the case of Russian, the fundamental importance of aspect was not clearly perceived nor put in proper theoretical perspective until very recently—after the pioneering grammatical work of Lomonósov in the middle of the 18th c. The word вид 'aspect' was not used by him. For more than two centuries, from the translation of the ever popular Latin Grammar of Donatus into Slav (16th c.),[43] Latin

---

[42] A typical case is the verb 'to be' in many IE languages, including English and Russian. The latter has associated in a suppletive paradigm

     (i) pres. stem only—*existence*: **es-* (ес-ть; reduced с-уть) (state);

     (ii) aor./inf. stem—*becoming*: **bhū-* (бы-ть; aor. бы-хъ) (perfective);

     (iii) newer imperf. of state: **bhu̯ē-* (imperf. бѣ-ахъ);

     (iv) special pres.-fut. with nasal infix (cf. 3.87, A2) and *-d* suffix: **bhū-n-d-* (fut. бу́ду, part. бу́дущий) (perfective).

[43] OB no. 46. Translated by the diplomat Dmitri Gerasimov (Tolmač = 'translator'), with all the material changed to a mixture of ChSl. and Russian. Thus it was not a handbook for learning *Latin* but a schema for describing Slav.

grammatical terminology was being adopted, mainly by calque
(5.26) and forced first on ChSl. and then on Russian. There was
little chance that the structure of the Russian (or ChSl.) verb would
be correctly analysed when the learned were intent on finding the
same categories as those present in Latin.[44]

84   Early ESl. shows much the same point of development as OCS.
Aspect is a quality of the verbal stem. The great majority of
inherited simple verbal stems were *durative* or 'imperfective'
(*impf*), i.e. indicated process or duration *in vacuo*. A few were
perfective, e.g. дать 'give', пасть 'fall', and the three verbs of
position стать, лечь, сесть, indicating only the event (the point of
change of state). The former were *present* stems, having a present
and imperfect (present in the past) tense only.[45] The latter could
not form a true present but only a punctual past (the so-called
aorist). A single verbal idea was usually compounded of two
aspectual stems—a present and an aor./inf. (3.87). The three verbs
of position display a triple aspectual range:

Pf (punctual)	Impf (durative)	State
стать (*stā-*) 'take up a standing position'[46]	(ста́вить)	стоя́ть (*stă-*) 'be in a standing position'
лечь (*lĕg-*) 'take up a lying position'	ложи́ть(ся) (*lŏg-*) 'process of laying/ lying'	лежа́ть (*lĕg-*) 'be in a lying position'
сѣсть (*sēd-*) 'take up a sitting position'	сади́ть(ся) (*sād-*) 'process of setting/ sitting'	сѣдѣти (later сидѣть) 'be in a sitting position'

85   Other aspectual differences (*Aktionsarten*) were evolved in CSl.
by more recent processes of derivation, either suffixation or prefixation, or as cpd. (analytical) formations. Thus in ESl.:

1. The *perfect* aspect (acquired state) was formed with appropriate tenses of быти + the perfect participle in -*l*:

present ('perfect' tense): есмь далъ (*pf*) or зналъ (*impf*);
past (pluperfect): бяхъ далъ, etc.,
future (future-perfect): буду далъ, etc.

[44] Similarly Ludolf (1696) does his best to fit in the Lat. ablative by the equivalents
instr. = *Ablativus Instrumentalis*, locative = *Ablativus*.
[45] The future may remain outside consideration for the moment. The forms of
the imperf. suggest a recent creation in late CSl.
[46] И се агг[е]лъ г[оспода]нь ста въ нихъ (Luke 2: 9).

2. The *habitual* aspect[47] was shown by a suffix -*va*-, later -*yva*- (extracted from бывати, the very common verb of habitual state—*by-va-* > *b-yva-*). This is essentially durative (*impf*) and therefore lacking an aorist.

3. Derived *perfectives*:

    (*a*) with suffix -*nu*-: кри́кнуть 'emit a (single) scream' (as opposed to process крича́ть (*krik-ěti*) 'emit a series of screams'). Usually called 'instantaneous' or 'semelfactive'. There is no true present tense;

    (*b*) by prefixation: возлюби́ть *pf* 'fall in love with' ('inchoative'—the beginning of a new state); разлюби́ть *pf* 'cease to love' ('terminative', indicating the end of a state).

4. Verbs of state (not process) with suffix -*ē*: име́ть 'be in possession of', горе́ть 'burn' (intrans.).

86   In primary *durative* and in *habitual* verbs there is no limitation of the process or state. In primary and derived *perfective* verbs limitation of the action is of the essence. It followed that prefixation, increasingly resorted to in the enlargement of vocabulary, tended more and more to be felt as imposing *perfectivization*.

That prefixed verbs are *pf* in the modern sense *cannot be assumed in early ESl*. Some prefixes, notably по- and о-, early acquired the purely grammatical role of markers of the perfective, no longer perceptibly modifying the sense of the verb (so-called 'empty prefixes'—*préfixes vides*).[48] Others, in particular strongly spatial prefixes, modified the sense but did not automatically change the aspect to perfective. This, incidentally, is the state of evolution at which Baltic languages such as Lithuanian have stopped. It is clear, for example, that in modern Russian течь is a durative and поте́чь an (inchoative) perfective, parallel to пойти́ 'set out', побежа́ть 'run off'. But in

изъ него же озера (Lake Il'men') потечеть Волховъ и въ течеть в озеро великое Нево (*RPC, ad init.*) 'the R. Volkhov rises in this lake and enters the great lake Nevo (Ládoga)'

потече́ть is a *habitual* present ('flows forth at all times'), as opposed to the *actual* present течеть ('is flowing at this moment' [sc. but

---

[47] Otherwise called *iterative* or *frequentative*. Terminology is fluid and often unsatisfactory.

[48] This does not apply, of course, to *all* uses of по- and о-.

does not always do so]). It is certainly not a *pf* future ('will start flowing') as it is today. Въте́четь shows the same lack of perfectivization in a spatial prefix; the parallelism ensures their significance.

87 The 'present tense' forms of inherited *pf* stems, e.g. да́мь, appear in ESl. from the outset as *futures*. The same logical shift was applied to all new derived perfectives. It is, of course, only contextually a future—a 'terminative' future since the *pf* characterizes exclusively real events[49]—and has not become one in SSl., where the 'wish' future (3.109) was applied to both aspects and the *pf* present may be called a kind of subjunctive. In Russian too it appears in proverbs and the like as a 'gnomic' present: сде́ланного не воро́тишь 'what's done cannot be undone'. Normal early usage: любо изищю муж[ѣ] новгородьстѣи волости пакы ли а головою повалю за Новъгородъ (1215) 'either I shall recover these citizens of Novgorod or else I shall lay down my life for Novgorod' (из- is here the native 'comprehensive' prefix).

88 ESl. retained for a time the imperfect and aorist tenses. In the nature of things the imperfect, being a durative tense, was formed predominantly from *impf* verbs, and conversely the aorist, being the tense of event in the past, from *pf* verbs. But the reverse cases were freely available and used to point special aspectual relations. For example:

(i) *impf* aorist:

въ томь вечерѣ перевозися Ярославъ съ вои . . . (*RPC s.a.* 1016). The *impf* stem implies a sequence of like actions constituting *one compound event*; перевезеся (Ярославъ же заутра . . . перевезеся, ibid.) would imply that all the troops were ferried over in a *single operation*.

This distinction is represented in modern Russian by the perfective-iteratives (§94 below).

(ii) *pf* imperfect:

аще кто умряше, творяху трызно (= тризну) надъ нимъ и по семь творяху кладу велику и възложахуть . . . (*RPC, ad init.*). The whole is a description of a recurring situation (творяху, etc.) but each death is a discrete event which leads to the habitual action.

[49] Hence an *impf* verb form is largely preferred in negative sentences (no real event) and in final infinitives (since an intention may not become a fact).

We translate therefore: '*whenever* a person died, they would . . . .
Later copies substitute умираше, the more usual *impf* imperfect.

Similarly: аще кто вылѣзяше ис хоромины, хотя видѣти, абье
уязвенъ будяше . . . и с того умираху (*RPC s.a.* 1092). (For
будяше see 3.90 (*c*).)

89   Spoken Russian abandoned the aorist and imperfect at an early
date (probably by *c.*1300—3.100 (*c*) and 102 (*e*)) and replaced
them by the perfect, automatically available in both aspects and of
easy formation in all verbs:

знаахъ > (есмь) знал; узнахъ > (есмь) узнал *pf*;
творяху > творили (суть); с(о)твориша > створили (суть) *pf*.

By this not unusual change the language sacrificed once and for all
the perfect aspect as a distinct category (except in the present
passive, 3.134). In doing so it inevitably also condemned the other
tenses of the perfect aspect to obsolescence: the pluperfect and
future-perfect die out in Muscovite times (3.106–7). There
remained then *no 'tenses of relative time'* from the Latin point of
view: all is reduced to fundamental present, past, and future in
two aspects:

	Present	*Past*	*Future*
impf (durative)	зна́ет (unchanged)	знал (conflating *impf* imperfect and perfect)	бу́ду знать (*impf* infinitive; the auxiliary is new—3.110)
pf	—	узна́л (conflating *pf* aorist, perfect, and pluperfect)	узна́ет (subsuming the fut.-perf.)

It should be noted also that the conditional (hypothetical) tense,
by its origin and structure (3.116), was incapable of showing relative
time.

With some indication from accompanying adverbs facts of relative time can still be indicated but not necessarily so in comparison
with English:

когда́ я вошёл, он уже́ уе́хал 'he had (already) left when I came in';
к концу́ бу́дущей неде́ли я зако́нчу чте́ние «Войны́ и Ми́ра»! 'by the
   end of next week I shall have finished reading *War and Peace*!';

он живёт в Ло́ндоне уже́ тре́тий год 'he has been living in London for over two years now'.

Slavonicized literary Russian naturally lagged behind speech, in particular maintaining the narrative aorist just as written French maintains the *passé défini*. The 18th c. was the battle-ground between the older and the living system.

The early ESl. verbal system finds its nearest modern parallel in the highly conservative Blg. verb, which has retained imperfect, aorist, and the perfect group, with all appropriate aspect distinctions (and moreover added the further complication of the tenses of 'renarration', perhaps under the influence of Ottoman Turkish from *c.*1400).[50]

It is untrue to assert that aspectual differences were only in process of definition in early ESl.: they are inescapably present in all verbal forms. It is their grammatical expression which has changed.

90   Given that the expression of aspect (mode of action) remained in Russian (as in most Slav languages) as more fundamental than that of temporal relations with respect to some fixed point (the main verb), it follows that the *aspectual indicators* became more strictly organized so that in all appropriate cases a perfective and an imperfective verb, complementing one another (as in the table above), provided all the required forms. In the evolution of Russian, therefore:

1. Prefixation of a *primary* verb creates, with relatively few exceptions, a *pf* verb, with or without change of sense.[51] The more fluid state of affairs which emerges from early texts disappears.

2. The exceptions to (1) are for the most part *Slavonicisms*, directly reflecting the earlier system or sometimes being younger Latin calques, e.g. принадлежа́ть *impf* + dat. 'belong to'; содержа́ть *impf* 'contain' (Lat. *continere*) (as verb of state not requiring a *pf*); the native verb is сдержа́ть *pf*/-де́рживать 'restrain'.

91   3. There is concurrent need to provide all the new derived

---

[50] A similar contrast can be seen as between two contemporary forms of SCr.: *spoken* Serbian, like Russian, has dropped aor. and imperf. in favour of one generalized preterite (ex-perfect); more conservative literary Croatian maintains aor. and imperf. and therefore the perfect as a separate category.

[51] Not to be confused with denominative *impf* verbs from *prefixed* nouns, e.g. ра́зум > разуме́ть 'understand'; наво́з > наво́зить 'manure'.

perfectives with an *impf* companion, without which there can be no present tense.

The older stratum of verbs in -ить and some others use the suffix *-já-* (less often *-á-*) with change of conjugation:

> да́ти *pf* 'give' > ChSl. and early ESl. дая́ти;
> реши́ть *pf* 'decide' > реша́ть (*-š-ja-*);
> ступи́ть *pf* 'step' > ступа́ть.

> Slavonicisms:
> соста́вить *pf* 'form' > составля́ть (*-v-ja-*);
> возврати́ться *pf* 'return' > возвраща́ться (*-t-ja-*).

ESl. has preferred the suffix -ыва-/-ива- (§85 (2) above), with more body and requiring in most cases no modification of the verbal stem:[52]

> переписа́ть *pf* 'copy' > перепи́сывать;
> отде́латься *pf* 'get rid of' > отде́лываться.

(There will be no **напи́сывать, *сде́лывать from the *pf* of the simple verb unless needed for some special sense.) The contrast here is well illustrated by the Slavonicism сопроводи́ть *pf*/-вожда́ть (*-d-ja-*) 'accompany', as against native вы́проводить *pf*/-ва́живать 'remove' (e.g. an unwanted guest).

There has been considerable hesitation as between the predominantly ChSl. and the native procedure; a few alternatives are still possible and a larger number are found in early texts—as many as three in съкупити *pf*/-купати, -купляти, -купливати. Examples:

соста́вить *pf*/составля́ть (Slavonicism) standard, but: сима же пришодъшема, начаста съставливати писмена (*RPC s.a.* 898);
(при)ба́вить *pf*/-бавля́ть standard, but при-/у-ба́вливать still in Pososh-kóv (*c*.1724);
изгото́вить *pf* 'prepare', изготовля́ть (lit.)/изгота́вливать (coll.);
останови́ть *pf* 'halt', остана́вливать standard/остановля́ть obs.;
наряди́ть *pf*/наряжа́ть 'detail, appoint' standard, but: сторожѣ сами наряживаите (*RPC s.a.* 1096) 'set the sentries yourselves'.

In *RPC, ad init.*, we find at a few lines' distance: но умыкиваху у воды дѣвиця . . . и ту умыкаху жены собѣ (perhaps different strata of recopying).

That the formation in -ыва- originally denoted specifically the *iterative* aspect can be seen not only from быва́ть 'be habitually'

---

[52] For the lengthening of stem vowel see 2.8.

(быть *pf* 'become' (entry into state)) but also from uncompounded verbs in -ывать, frequent in earlier times but now subliterary; they persist in dialect in the past tense only:[53]

а того слова не говаривал, кое пора деи моя (1576) 'I never said that it was time to be off' (a stronger negation than Grozny's так не говорят . . . да пора домов 1574);

Здесь ба́рин си́живал оди́н (Pushkin, EO, vii. 17) 'The master used to sit here all alone'.

In a few cases the difference of aspect is reduced in the infinitive to mere difference of stress:

засы́пать *pf* 'strew' (-сы́плю)/засыпа́ть (-сыпа́ю);
уре́зать *pf* 'cut down' (-ре́жу)/уреза́ть (-реза́ю) and уре́зывать.

The three verbs дать *pf,* стать *pf,* and знать (pres. зна́ю) formed new derivatives in -*va*-: дава́ть, става́ть, знава́ть (the last two now only in cpds.); the new inf. has come to be combined with the older pres. in -*j*-: даю́, -стаю́, -знаю́. In the latter case there is only a stress difference in the pres./fut.: узнаю́/узна́ю *pf.*

92   The sum of this regulative process is that verbs normally exist as *linked pairs.* Nevertheless this depends on the sense of the verb; there are many more isolated (unpaired) *impf* and *pf* verbs than might be thought. We may note the following categories:

1. *Pf* 'semelfactives' (R. однокра́тный глаго́л) in -нуть lacking a pres. tense (§85 (3)(*a*) above): она́ кри́кнула 'she screamed (once)'; крича́ть is a separate verb with (inchoative) perfectives закрича́ть and вскрича́ть, and a more or less neutral *pf* прокрича́ть.

2. The prefix по- signifying *discontinuous action* excludes perfectives:

он продолжа́л поку́ривать 'he continued smoking (at intervals)' (кури́ть = smoking continuously);
он посту́кивал по столу́ 'he tapped on the table from time to time'.

Also with при-: прихлёбывать 'sip'; припля́сывать 'skip'.

3. Many other special cases, e.g. заслу́живать *impf* only + gen. 'deserve', separate from заслужи́ть *pf*/-слу́живать + acc. 'earn'.

---

[53] The translator of Donatus pretends that these are equivalent to the Lat. pluperfect: любливах, -аше, -ал, -ахом, -асте, -аху—минувшее пресвершеное (NB imperfect endings except in the sg. 3).

4. There remain some verbs of *indifferent aspect*, some inherited from the more fluid state of late CSl., others created by usage:

бежа́ть 'run': basically *impf* but appears as *pf* sometimes in OCS. Modern usage allows *pf* in the sense 'flee, escape', e.g. он бежа́л из тюрьмы́ (= убежа́л); е́сли его́ не арестова́ть, он за́втра же бежи́т (*pf* fut.) but солда́ты ты́сячами бегу́т с фро́нта (pres.). So in *RPC*: а Святополкъ бѣжа (*pf*) . . . и бѣжащю ему (*impf*) '. . . during his flight' (*s.a.* 1019); Святополкъ же бѣжа (*pf*) в Ляхы (*s.a.* 1016);

жени́ться 'marry': я неда́вно жени́лся (*pf*); ожени́ть(ся) is not in normal lit. use and пожени́ться is only used of both parties;

роди́ть 'give birth to'/роди́ться 'be born': here a stress distinction has been introduced in the all-important preterite:

> *pf* роди́л(ся́), родила́(сь)
> *impf* роди́л(ся), роди́ла(сь)

There is also an *impf* рожда́ть (learned)/рожа́ть (coll.).

Variations of this kind are found also in веле́ть 'order' (p.p.p. ве́лено); казни́ть 'punish' (p.p.p. казнён but also pres. казни́т); ра́нить 'wound', минова́ть 'pass' (pres. ger. мину́я; but опа́сность минова́ла *pf* 'the danger is past'); отвеча́ть (*pf* if literal with recent alternative denominative отве́тить *pf*; *impf* if figurative—э́то не отвеча́ет мои́м ожида́ниям 'this does not come up to my expectations'); обеща́ть (Slavonicism) 'promise'. Прочита́ть, originally the *impf* of проче́сть is now the more usual *pf* of чита́ть, whereas счита́ть has remained *impf*.

The majority of verbs of indifferent aspect are to be found in the type in -ова́ть. This was originally an *impf* suffix, e.g. in купи́ть *pf*/купова́ть (so in OCS; replaced in Russian by покупа́ть). Uncertainty of aspect concerns the large number of recent foreign loan-words (18th c. onwards). As many of these were long words there was hesitation over adding a further prefix. In other words, modern verbs in -овать have not been fully integrated into the native binary aspect system. Examples (all *pf* and *impf*): атакова́ть, инсцени́ровать, модерниз(и́р)ова́ть, парализова́ть; but страхова́ть 'insure', *pf* застрахова́ть.

Usage alone decides whether атаку́ю may be both a pres. and a (*pf*) fut. and whether бу́ду атакова́ть is acceptable.

93 OCS and early ESl. купи́ть *pf*/купова́ть represents a type of linked pair which became exceptional in Russian. As an *impf* suffix

-*ova*- was replaced by -*yva*-/-*ïvu*-. SCr. has the mixed *zapisívati*/ pres. *zapìsujēm* regularly, and similarly Polish, though more recently and not quite completely. Relics of the former state in Russian are usually Slavonicisms; it is a case of two synonymous formations, e.g. за-, испо-ве́довать or -ве́дывать. In both verbs the ChSl. form in -овать is normal, but испове́довать 'confess' is of indifferent aspect and испове́дывать *impf* only, so there is a potential pair испове́доваться *pf*/испове́дываться 'make confession'.[54]

Traces of extinct variation can be seen in isolated forms such as неопису́емый 'indescribable' (there is now no *описовать); связу́ющее звено́ 'connecting link' (*связовать); испыту́ющий взгляд 'enquiring look' (*испытовать); сказу́емое 'predicate' (*сказовать). Cf. (ChSl.) *RPC s.a.* 912: показующе имъ истинную вѣру.

94 *The Perfective-Iteratives*

Some actions can only be completed or states reached by repeating a similar action a certain number of times. Russian is able to point the difference between the single operation and the sum of similar operations taken as a whole. It is necessary to start from two single verbs, the one indeterminate, the other determinate (occasionally *pf*), viz. those listed in 3.139–40 and such pairs as мета́ть/метну́ть *pf* 'fling', броса́ть/бро́сить *pf* 'throw', кида́ть/ки́нуть *pf* 'cast'.

Normal perfectives are formed from the determinates: навали́ть, раски́нуть, подтащи́ть (single operation). Perfective-iteratives are formed from the indeterminates: наваля́ть *pf*, раскида́ть *pf*, изъе́здить *pf* 'travel all over' (*изъе́хать not in use), износи́ть *pf* 'wear out', подтаска́ть *pf* (multiple operations). Imperfectives in this special sense are sometimes distinct (изна́шивать, изъе́зживать *not* *изъезжа́ть) but more often shared with the normal *pf* (нава́ливать, раски́дывать, подта́скивать).

Thus a verbal form may be *pf* in one sense and *impf* in another:

сходи́ть *impf*/сойти́ *pf* 'descend';
сходи́ть *pf* 'go and return'.

---

[54] Dostoievsky could still write (1877): Я пе́рвый стра́стно испове́дую э́то и всегда́ испове́дывал.

The procedure is ancient:

и поставиша скудельницу и наметаша полну (1215) 'and they made a communal grave and filled it full' (*pf* aor. parallel to поставиша);

яз всех перекусал же, все вдруг перепропали (1576) 'I dealt with them all; they all disappeared at once' (normal pair перекуси́ть *pf*/ перекусывать; the succession of like events is also stressed by the prefix пере- added to the normal *pf* пропа́сть);

тъгъда же Мьстиславъ, переброда ся Днѣпрь, прѣиде въ 1000 вои на сторожи татарскыя и побѣди я (1224) '. . . having ferried himself across the Dnepr' (several operations to get all 1000 men across).

Many *pf-it* will have a pl. or collective object: он оттаска́л (все) мешки́ 'he dragged all the sacks away'; оттащи́л may apply to one or more sacks but not too many for a single operation. The commonest prefixes are exemplified above.

95 *Verbs of Motion*

The determinate/indeterminate pairs (3.139) have been retained intact. Derived aspectual pairs are on the model нанести́ *pf*/ наноси́ть except for при-е́хать *pf*-езжа́ть (-е́здить only in *pf-it*), пере-плы́ть *pf*/-плыва́ть (-пла́вать only in the *pf-it* ис-/с-пла́вать), and -бега́ть (simple verb бе́гать).

There has been little change in usage. The 'there and back' sense of the indeterminates can be detected at an early date:

а въ вятичи ходихом по двѣ зимѣ (*RPC s.a.* 1096) 'we campaigned against the Vjatichi . . .' (sc. 'and returned home'; похо́д 'campaign');

он ездил в Чунар (Af. Nik., 15th c.) 'he made the journey to Junnar' (sc. 'and back'); but

иде Володимеръ на радимичи (*RPC s.a.* 984) 'Vladimir went to fight the Radimichi' (return not stressed);

поиде Ярополкъ на Олга 'Jaropolk set off to fight Oleg' (initial moment).

modern:

(я) хожу́ на по́чту 'I am just going round to the post office';

(с)бе́гай за до́ктором 'run and fetch the doctor' (sc. 'and return at once').

There are no 'neutral' perfectives of either form: пойти́ *pf*, etc., are inchoative, походи́ть *pf* 'to walk about for a time' and the like 'attenuative' (limiting in time; §64 above).

96 *Summary*

Aspect relations are now shown in Russian by *linked verbal pairs* forming a complementary paradigm joined by a common *present tense*. Each of the forms subsumes a number of aspects in the narrower sense (*Aktionsarten*), which can be grouped under the broader *grammatical* categories *pf/impf*:

perfective

primary: дать, пасть, etc.
cpd.: записа́ть, прочита́ть
semelfactive: толкну́ть,
    кри́кнуть
inchoative: закрича́ть, пойти́
terminative: отобе́дать,
    окамене́ть
pf-it: износи́ть

imperfective

primary: знать, люби́ть, нести́
derived cpds.: запи́сывать,
    прочи́тывать
iteratives: быва́ть,
    перепи́сываться
conatives: угова́ривать,
    отнима́ть ('try to persuade',
    'try to remove')[55]
indeterminate: носи́ть 'carry
    about'
factitive (causative): пои́ть
    'water' (trans.)
state: име́ть, стоя́ть, горе́ть
'faculty': ходи́ть 'be able to walk';
    чита́ть 'be able to read'.

97 The fundamental distinction *impf/pf* (the 'marked' member) as durative/punctual (process/event) and general (habitual)/particular is as clear in Ру́сская Пра́вда (11th c. usage) as it is today, witness the following passages:

(*a*) которая ли вьрвь начнеть платити (*impf*) дикую виру колико лѣт[ъ] заплатять (*pf*; some manuscripts заплатить *pf*) ту виру занеже безъ головника имъ платити (*impf*) (art. 4).

'If any commune shall be [in process of] paying a communal wergild they shall pay it off [terminal event] over a number of years (?however many years it may take) since they must continue paying [process] in the absence of the murderer.'

(*b*) оже придеть кръвавъ муже [= мужь] на дворъ, или синь, то видока ему не искати, нъ платити ему продажю 3 гр.; или не будеть на немь знамения, то привести ему видокъ . . . (art. 29).

'If a freeman arrives at the (prince's) court bloody or bruised, he need not produce a witness but (the assailant) shall pay a fine of 3 grivnas. But if there are no marks on him he must produce a witness . . .'

(придеть particular event; не искати general rule (absence of event); платити ему general rule; привести ему particular case).

---

[55] Process which may or may not lead to a successful (perfective) act.

(*c*) познает[ь] (*pf*) ли надолзѣ у кого купивъ (some manuscripts купилъ), то свое куны възметь (*pf*) и сему платити (*impf*) что у него (some manuscripts будеть) погыбло . . . (art. 37).

'If he later recognizes the person he bought (it) from he shall recover his money and (the seller) shall pay any loss'

(познаеть, възметь particular events; сему платити general rule).

Granted some uncertainties as to the aspectual value of some forms to a contemporary, there is nothing in these passages which conflicts with current usage.

5

VOCABULARY

The vocabulary of all languages is subject to continual change by all four arithmetical operations: *addition*—loan-words borrowed from other languages; *subtraction*—obsolescence of native words (e.g. *brougham, hansom, victoria, tilbury,* etc. when superseded by the *motor car*); *multiplication*—new derivatives from native words or acclimatized foreigners (e.g. *avail > available* (1451) > *availability* (1803)); and *division*—new senses of a word, subdivision or extension of its semantic field (e.g. *Sandwich* PN > *sandwich*—an item of food alleged to have been invented by Lord Sandwich). All these operations will appear in the following necessarily short sketch of Russian vocabulary but particularly the first, which illustrates the cultural, economic, and other connections of the country down the centuries. The contribution of ChSl. is at first in the field of addition, later of multiplication.

Words discussed are mainly those still in modern colloquial or literary use.

1   The IE core of CSl. vocabulary is still quite evident today by the most casual inspection of Russian, e.g. сын 'son', мать (gen. ма́тери) 'mother', брат 'brother', сестра́ 'sister', бровь 'brow', мышь 'mouse', дать 'give' (Lat. *dă-re*), мо́ре 'sea' (Lat. *măre*), дом 'house' (Lat. *dŏmus*), and many others almost as transparent.

Balto-Slav

2   The precise relationship of the *Baltic* and *Slav* language groups is still, and is likely to remain, a matter of argument (1.1). It is certain, from the circumstantial evidence of archaeology, toponymy, etc., that the speakers of both groups have lived in contiguity with one another for a very long time. Baltic and Slav are more nearly related than either is to any other IE language group. They share some important agreements with Germanic (not exclusively lexical), greater or at least now more visible in Baltic,[1] so that one must envisage a loose N. European cultural area in the Late Neolithic and early metal periods: Germanic, Baltic, and Slav share common terms for *gold* and *silver* (CSl. **zaltă*, **sĭrebră*; Latvian *zèlts*, Lith. *sidābras*)[2] but not for *copper* and *iron*. Other notable agreements are: *quorn*, Lith. *gìrna*, OCS *žrŭny*, R. жёрнов; *rye* (Ger. *Roggen*), *rugỹs*, рожь; *wax*, *vãškas*, воск; *delve*, *-dìlbti*, долби́ть; *thousand*, *túkstantis*, ты́сяча; *ale*, *alùs*, early ESl. *olŭ*.

3   By the time that copper and iron were in common use speakers of proto-Gmc. had joined a W. European cultural group (*iron*, Ger. *Eisen*, Lat. *aes/aer-*) and contacts with Balto-Slav appear to have ceased or been much reduced. The cultural ties of Baltic and Slav continued for they share the enigmatic *želězo* 'iron' = Lith. *geležìs*.

That Baltic and Slav had a considerable period of common development, if not in an organic sense at least at the level of close association, may be gauged from some very common words, peculiar to the two, whose formation has no exact parallel in any other IE language (though the root may be more widespread), e.g. OCS *rǫka*, R. рука́, Lith. *rankà* 'hand'; *noga*, нога́, *nagà* 'foot';[3] *glava*, голова́, *galvà* 'head'. Рука́ is now isolated in Slav but is at once explained by the cognate verb which Lithuanian has retained —*riñkti/renkù* 'grasp, pick up'. A like degree of exclusive similarity is found in more than a dozen terms for parts of the body, e.g. R. ве́ко 'eyelid', коле́но 'knee', ладо́нь (OCS *dlani*) 'palm', перст 'finger' (now only in derivatives), плоть 'flesh', те́ло 'body', ус 'face-hair', че́реп 'skull'; and in terms of the natural world, e.g. ли́па 'lime-tree' (*Tilia*), граб 'hornbeam' (*Carpinus*), лы́ко 'bast', оме́ла 'mistletoe', о́лово 'tin, lead',[4] рог 'horn', лёд 'ice', куна́ 'marten' (*Mustela*), звезда́ 'star'. Altogether there are some 300 such words more or less exclusive to the Balto-Slav vocabulary.

---

[1] Eng. *shall, should* = Lith. *skolà* 'debt', *skélti*; *help* = Lith. *šelpti* (neither now present in Slav). It must be remembered that the Baltic languages are known only from very recent times (16th c. onwards) but this is partly offset by exceptional conservatism.

[2] *Gold* from the colour (R. жёлтый/зо́лото), *silver* perhaps an Iranian word from the Caucasus region.

[3] Lith. *nagà* = 'hoof' ('foot' is *kója*) but OPr. *nage* apparently made the same semantic shift to 'foot (leg)'.

[4] R. о́лово 'tin', Pol. *ołowo* 'lead'; Lith. *álvas* 'tin', OPr. *alwis* 'lead'.

Iranian

4   The earliest visible outside influence of some importance on the
CSl. vocabulary, not shared by Baltic, is Iranian. It may well have
been the irruption of the Iranian Scythians into E. Europe *c.*700
BC which finally detached Slav from Baltic, having been hitherto
(as it has been put) an 'eccentric Baltic dialect'. At all events, after
*c.*500 BC Slav rapidly evolved its own peculiarities. For approximately a millennium, ending about AD 200, the steppe zone of
S. Russia was inhabited by semi-nomadic pastoralists of Iranian
speech, principally Scythians and Sarmatians. It is quite possible
that the 'Scythian farmers' of Herodotus (iv. 17–18) were Slavs
under their domination since pastoralists do not farm themselves
but appreciate having subjects who will provide them with the
products of agriculture. From this came a clear cultural influence
of Iranians on Slavs. Exact comparison is made difficult by the
fact that nothing of the extinct Scythian and Sarmatian languages
survives apart from some personal names in Greek sources and
some S. Russian toponymy (e.g. the great rivers Don, Dnepr, and
Dnestr), and that the branch of Iranian to which these peoples
probably belonged is poorly represented in Iranian languages still
spoken today. Nevertheless some two dozen CSl. words, all of
which are likely to be used frequently in religious language, show
close parallels in the earliest surviving Iranian religious texts (the
Avesta). They may have been for the most part not so much loan-
words as native words which acquired new senses in CSl. through
this cultural contact. They include (in OCS form): *blag-* 'good';
bogŭ 'god'; *kajati sę* (R. каяться, покаяние) 'repent'; *nebo* (usually
pl. *nebesa*) 'heaven' (a typical semantic agreement; cf. the still
literal Gk. νέφος, νεφέλη; Lat. *nebula*; Ger. *Nebel*); *slovo* 'word'
(cf. Gk. κλέϝος 'reputation, glory'); *sramŭ* 'shame' (present in
mod. Pers. *šarm*); *vatra* 'fire';[5] *věra* 'faith'; *xraniti* 'preserve'; *zŭlŭ*
'bad' (mod. Pers. *zūr*); *žrŭti*/pres. *žĭrǫ* 'sacrifice' (R. жертва,
жертвовать Slavonicisms); *radi* 'for the sake of' (4.69); and *raj*
'paradise' (Avestan *rāy-* 'happiness'; used in the original OCS
translations in pair with *adŭ* 'hell' from Gk. *Hades*). To these may
be added early ESl. *divŭ* 'bird of ill omen' (recorded in the Слово
о полку Игореве, text no. 14), parallel to Avestan *daēva* 'evil

---

[5] *Vatra* 'fire' (originally perhaps 'sacred fire' only, Avestan *ātar-*) is now only at
all usual in SCr., which also has CSl. **ăgnĭ* (R. огонь), cognate with Lat. *ignis*,
Lith. *ugnìs*.

spirit', with the pejorative sense introduced by the Zoroastrian religion, in contrast with the new *bogŭ* = Iranian *bhaga-*;[6] certain divine names such as *Svarog*; the specific sense of *svętŭ* (святóй) 'holy' (this shared with Lith. *šveñtas*, related to a native verb seen in Latvian *svinêt* 'celebrate a festival'); and a few other words of uncertain ancestry and date of borrowing into Slav, viz. R. топóр 'axe', сапóг 'boot', собáка (exclusively ESl.) 'dog'[7] (a special breed of pastoralists' sheep-dog?), and хмель 'hops' (**xŭmelĭ*; a *Wanderwort* which appears in Latin as *humulus*).

Gothic

5 In the 3rd–4th centuries AD the Iranian domination was brought to an end by a massive invasion of Germanic Goths from S. Sweden, who formed an 'empire' in a considerable part of the Slav lands between the Vistula and the Dnepr. From them came a new deposit of specifically *East Germanic* words in CSl. Southward migrations in both E. and W. Europe at this period brought Germanic peoples into contact with the Roman Empire, then at the zenith of its economic radiation. Mediterranean words thus for the first time began to reach the Slavs in their remote homeland, usually via Gothic. These include: (OCS) *vino* 'wine'; *kupiti* 'buy' (Goth. **kaupjan* < Lat. *caupō* 'trader'; Eng. *cheap* is cognate);[8] *kotĭlŭ* (R. котёл) 'cauldron, kettle'; *osĭlŭ* 'ass' (Lat. *asellus*); *dŭska* 'board' (Lat. *discus* < Gk.; other adaptations—Eng. *dish* (Ags.), *disc* and *desk* (learned), *dais* (via OFr.); Ger. *Tisch* 'table').

The Gothic influence affected more aspects of life than the Iranian. It included: (i) military words—*plŭkŭ* 'army' (R. полк, Eng. *folk*); *brŭnja* (броня́) 'armour'; *šlěmŭ* 'helmet'[9] (mod. R. 'crash-helmet' in the ChSl. form—the native form in ошеломи́ть 'stun'); *měčĭ* 'sword' (меч; there are other possibilities for this word); (ii) everyday objects: *bljudo* 'plate' (Goth. *biuþs* masc.; OCS also *bljudŭ* masc.); *stĭklo* 'glass'; *xlěbŭ* 'bread' (Goth. *hlaifs*

---

[6] Lithuanian has preserved the original IE sense *diēvas* 'god' (Gk. Ζεύς, Lat. *diuīnus*).

[7] CSl. *pĭsŭ*, retained in some other Sl. languages; R. пёс now only a technical term—'hound'.

[8] The older CSl. word *krĭnǫti* 'buy' (**kʷrī-*), with good parallels in Greek and elsewhere, evidently remained in use till early Christian times; it occurs in the 945 Treaty with Constantinople (text no. 1).

[9] Perhaps rather Germanic of the next stage (§6 below), since CSl. **šelmŭ* is more closely related to **helmaz* (W. Gmc.) than *hilms* (Goth.).

= Eng. *loaf*); *xlěvŭ* 'byɪe'; *xlŭmŭ* 'hill' (холм; cf. *Bornholm, Stockholm*); *xyzŭ* 'house' (Goth. *-hūs*; R. now only хижина 'hut'); (iii) verbs such as *-kusiti* 'bite' (*kausjan*); *lěčiti* 'cure, heal' (Goth. *leikeis* 'doctor', obs. Eng. *leech*); *xuliti* 'abuse' (OCS often 'blaspheme'); and perhaps *gotoviti* 'prepare' (**gataujan*);[10] (iv) abstracts: *duma* 'judgement, doom' (Goth. *dōms*); *lĭstĭ* 'deception' (R. лесть, льстить; mod. Ger. *List*); (v) adjectives: *xǫdogŭ* 'skilful' (Eng. *handy*; R. now only худо́жник 'craftsman, artist'); **tjud-* 'foreign'[11] (OCS *štuždĭ* > R. semi-Slavonicism чу́ждый 'alien'; native R. чужо́й 'other's'); *gorazdŭ* 'capable' (mod. R. has mainly adv. гора́здо); (vi) various: *ljudĭje* 'people' (mod. Ger. *Leute* which belongs to the Gmc. verb *liudan* 'grow'; cf. the native words наро́д and пле́мя derived from the idea of 'increase', as are also Gk. γένος and φῦλον and Lat. *natio*). R. верблю́д 'camel' is presumed to come via biblical usage from Goth. *ulbandus* 'ditto' and this plausibly from Gk. ἐλεφαντ-.[12] A few of the above words are considered by some scholars to be loans from Germanic before the Gothic period.

It is also generally admitted that certain Slav words which do not show the normal CSl. treatment of original aspirated and/or palatalized velars have been influenced by their Gothic parallels, notably: *gradŭ* (R. го́род) 'enclosure, fort'; *brěgŭ* 'slope, bank' (R. бе́рег, Ger. *Berg*); *gǫsĭ* 'goose';[13] and possibly also the verbal roots **leg-* (лежа́ть; Ger. *liegen*) and **mog-* (могу́ 'I can'; Ger. *mögen, mag*). A Germanic source, presumably Gothic, is also conceivable for *mlěko* 'milk' (молоко́; cf. OCS *mlěsti/mlĭzǫ* < **melg-*); *mŭnog-* 'much' (Goth. *manags*, Eng. *many*); *stado* 'flock, drove' (cf. Eng. *stud*; a neut. suffix *-do* is very rare in Sl.); the verbal root **wald-* 'have power' (OCS *vladěti*; Eng. *wield*) and others, but it is not always possible to determine when and from

---

[10] More certainly some other extinct words in *go-* which is clearly the Goth. prefix *ga-*.

[11] Goth. *þiuda* f. 'people'; Gmc. adj. *diut-isk-* > *deutsch*.

[12] OCS *velĭbǫdŭ*, influenced by вел(ик)ий and with dissimilation *l-l* > *r-l*.

[13] Thus Lith. *žąsìs* corresponds exactly to Lat. *(h)anser*, Gk. χήν, OHG *gans* (all **g'hans-*) as against Sl. *gǫsĭ*; similarly Sl. *gardŭ* (го́род/огоро́д, Lith. *gar̃das*) appears to have the Gmc. *g* of Goth. *gards* (**ghordh-* or **ghort-*) whereas R. dial. (о)зоро́д (Lith. *žárdas*) shows the regular reflex of **g'hordh-*. Variations in the IE velars are to be assumed so that it is impossible to be dogmatic about loans or influences. As the above examples show, *k, g, gh* of the 'centum' languages (here Gmc.) normally correspond to 'satem' *k', g', g'h* > CSl. *s, z* (Lith. *š, ž*) and *kʷ, gʷ, gʷh* to *k, g* > CSl. *k, g* (later palatalizations in CSl. apart).

whom they were borrowed if there is nothing specifically Gothic about their phonology. Even the direction of loan is in some cases uncertain, especially with words which are etymologically isolated in both language groups. A case in point is Sl. *skotŭ*/Gmc. *skatt-*, where the semantic evolution 'cattle' (R. скот) > '(movable) possessions' (mod. Ger. *Schatz* 'treasure') is perhaps the more likely (though E. Benveniste has argued the opposite for the parallel Lat. *pecu*/*pecūnia*).[14]

Other Germanic

6   The Gothic power dissolved at the end of the 4th c. AD under the onslaught of the Huns from Central Asia. Various parts of the Slav world now came into contact with other Germanic peoples, linguistically to be classed as *West Germanic*, in Central Europe. This stratum of loan-words covers the period *c.* AD 400–800. The majority probably date from the second half of this period after the Slavs had completed *c.* AD 600 their vast expansion which brought them to the Elbe in the west, the middle Danube, and almost all parts of the Balkan peninsula. Half a dozen Slav words in *-ędzĭ* derive from Germanic words in *-ing* (with Third Palatalization, 1.17), e.g. *kŭnędzĭ* 'prince' (*kuning-*); *vitędzĭ* 'freebooter' (perhaps from *Viking*); OCS *kladędzĭ* 'well' (**kalding-*; R. колóдец has changed the suffix); *skŭlędzĭ*/*skĭlędzĭ* 'shilling' (*skilling-*; in ESl. usually ChSl. склязь, now obsolete); *pěnędzĭ* 'penny' (*penning-*; still used in border towns of Russia such as Pskov in the 15th c.; still current in Polish as *pieniądz*). The *Russian Primary Chronicle* (*ad init.*) uses корлязи 'Franks' (= Carolingians), evidently a more learned word than корóль 'king'[15]—from the name of Charlemagne (**karl-jĭ*) and only later generalized to any foreign king—which has undergone the full ESl. phonetic development (*polnoglásie*, 1.22), after being handed on eastwards from one Slav dialect to another. There is a good case for considering the OCS suffixes *-ĭda*, *-znĭ*, and perhaps *-izna* as derived from Germanic models, no doubt in Moravia and Pannonia during the early translating period (1.2): *vražĭda* 'hostility' < Gmc. *wargiđa* (suffix *-eta*; CSl. has only *-ota*), then extended to *pravĭda* and *krivĭda* (these are the only three); *(ne)prijaznĭ*,

---

[14] *Le Vocabulaire des institutions indo-européennes* 1/i/4.
[15] Also королязи in Dan. Zat., but the text is unreliable.

žizni, bojazni, bolĕzni, kozni (mod. Russian has only pl. ко́зни 'intrigues'). All these words are Slavonicisms in Russian. But these suffixes hardly spread beyond the original nucleus of words. Far different were the fortunes of *-arjĭ* (perhaps from Goth. *-areis* but certainly from Germanic, where it was already a loan from Lat. *-ārius*), which was freely developed in some Slav languages though mainly learned in ESl.,[16] and above all of the adjectival *-ĭsk-*, now universal and common throughout Slav. *Rusĭskŭ* 'Russian' is a precisely parallel formation to *English*. But whether this suffix is native or a loan from Germanic is still a matter of controversy. We can probably add also *-mĕrŭ* as the second component of personal names, as in *Vladimĕrŭ*, ESl. *Volodimĕrŭ*, copying Gmc. *Waldemar* (Goth. *-mēr-s,* OHG *-māri*); *-mĕrŭ* was later altered to *-mirŭ* because a connection with *mĕr-* 'measure' seemed trivial, even if the original sense of *-mar* 'great' was no longer known.

Further Germanic words of this date adopted by some or most of the Slavs are: *plugŭ* '(a specific kind of) plough' (apparently a loan-word in Germanic also); *kapusta* 'cabbage' (ultimately from Latin); **mŭrky* 'carrot(s)' (морко́вь); **męty* 'mint' (мя́та); and *buky* 'letter' (бу́ква; 1.7)—the Slav fem. *ū*-stems (3.24) were the nearest equivalent to Gmc. fem. *ō*-stems. Finally CSl. **jĭstŭba* (R. изба́) is presumably to be ascribed to this period. It cannot derive directly from the prototype of mod. Ger. *Stube* and is better fitted to a Romance **estŭba* = **extūfa* (Fr. *étuve*), which then passed through some Germanic language. The original sense was 'stove', whence 'heated room' (изба́) and finally 'room' in general (SCr. *sòba*).

Turkic

7 After the downfall of the Goths the steppe zone of S. Russia was occupied by a succession of non-IE peoples speaking languages

---

[16] Biblical are врата́рь (Ps. 84: 10), мы́тарь 'publican'; learned—буква́рь, слова́рь, etc. (Eng. *-ary* is likewise learned: *bestiary, notary*); popular may be зна́харь 'quack', глуха́рь 'capercailzie'. Some words in -арь and almost all in -ап are much later borrowings from Polish (§30 (6) below). In this connection unusual is гонча́р 'potter' < гърньчаръ (2.18), recorded as early as 1219 (OCS has the standard *grŭnĭčar(j)ĭ*), so plausibly both native and not learned. An interesting case is Lat. *commerciārius* > **kŭrč(ĭ)marjĭ* (the intervening stages are obscure), from which was back-formed the noun *kŭrčma* 'tavern' (R. корчма́ obs., Pol. *karczma*).

of the Turkic (Altaic) family.[17] Ethnic and linguistic distinction between these peoples is often impossible since they were all more or less mobile, combining and recombining in shifting groups and federations; moreover there is little or no record of many of their languages, but the general type has been relatively stable and there are many modern forms to appeal to.

The broad succession is as follows:

(1) 375–453 (death of Attila): *Huns* dominated the steppes as far west as Hungary.

(2) 568: the *Avars* (early ESl. обре) settle in Hungary, forcing the Germanic Lombards out into N. Italy.

(3) 7th c.: 'steppe empire' of the *Bulgars* (the name is recorded from 480), soon splitting up. Some hordes entered E. Europe (Asparuch founded Bulgaria in 679), others remained under the new overlordship of the *Khazars* (early ESl. козаре), based on the lower Volga and N. Caucasus area.

(4) 8th–9th c.: heyday of the *Khazar* 'empire'. Their writ ran northwards as far as the 'Volga Bulgars' (of whom the Chuvash appear to be the modern descendants), one of the Bulgar splinter-groups which settled in the region about the confluence of Káma and Volga, and westwards as far as the more southerly ESl. tribes (including the Kiev area), who paid them tribute. The Khazars' wealth and power came from their control of the transit trade from C. Asia and the Islamic world. Part of their ruling and merchant class embraced Judaism and was literate.

(5) 10th–11th c.: decline of the Khazars, especially from 965, after the campaigns of Svjatosláv, Prince of Kiev. Arrival of the *Pechenégs* (Patzinak), following on the heels of the Magyars who had moved into Hungary in the 890s. The Pechenegs are first mentioned in *RPC s.a.* 968.

(6) 11–12th c.: domination of the steppes by the *Cumans* in succession to the Pechenegs (R. половцы < adj. полов- 'rufous, blond'; cf. Eng. *fallow*-deer). First mentioned in *RPC s.a.* 1054.[18] Dispersed by the Mongol invasion.

(7) 13th c. (first half): raids of the Mongols from C. Asia,

[17] With the exception of the Magyars, a Finno-Ugrian people from the Urál region, who drifted westwards in the 7th–9th c. On their way they absorbed a considerable Turkic component both in blood and language. There appear to be no Magyar loans into ESl. except possibly Ukr. and SR хáта 'hut' (mod. Magyar *ház*).

[18] A little of the Cuman dialect survives in the *Codex cumanicus* of the 13th c.

culminating in the destruction of Kiev in 1240 and the subjection of most of Russia. By this time only an insignificant part of the Mongol armies was Mongol in blood and speech; the administration of the Mongol empire was carried on largely in Turkic languages. The predominant dialect at the centre which administered Russia, Saraj (= encampment) on the lower Volga, was *Kipchak* (Qıpčaq), from which new Russian loans were most likely to come. It is sufficiently accurate to call the people and their language, as the Russians did, *Tatar*.

The 'Tatar yoke' was waning in the later 14th c. and was removed at the end of the 15th c.

8   We have here a thousand years of contacts, occasionally more or less intimate (e.g. the Avars and Slavs in C. Europe), usually loose and hostile. The Turkic tribes who settled in Europe were sooner or later absorbed, as for example the Bulgars into the Slavs of *Bulgaria*. In Russia the E. Slavs of the forest and parkland (лесостепь) zones had as yet no ability or ambition to colonize the steppes, but the steppe peoples made constant raids northwards, so that during the whole early history of Russia there was no well-defined southern frontier. This was the дикое поле, the no man's land between the sedentary Slavs and the nomads. In the conditions described it is rarely possible to ascribe a given ESl. loan-word from Turkic to a specific time and people. There is evidence for knowledge of the Pecheneg and Cuman dialects at Kiev and intermarriage was not unusual, especially with the Cumans. But appearance in texts is haphazard, as often as not long after the word was in local or even general use. The Turkic deposit in Russian is, in the nature of historical geography, far more prominent than in any other Slav language and is comparable to the Arabic deposit in Spanish with respect to other Romance languages. Among the earliest loan-words from Turkic may be put various now obsolete titles: *Kagan/Khagan* (the later *Khan* may be a contraction) which was certainly known to the Slavs from Avar times and even used by the early rulers of Kiev;[19] *tarkan/tarkhan* (recorded in Greek as Τάρχανος), which survives in the PN Tmutorokán' (on the Caucasian side of the Straits of Kerch; Gk. Ταμάταρχα) and Ástrakhan';[20] and *pašenog* ('governor, lieutenant'), recorded from

[19] 10th c.? (during and after the decline of the Khazars); still used by Hilarion in the 1040s (text no. 4), referring to Vladímir (d. 1015).

[20] See also 2.47 (2). It has been suggested that таракáн 'cockroach' is a form of this word.

Bulgaria and once, in garbled form, in the *Russian Primary Chronicle*.[21]

It is probable that the Khazar period, with its lively international trade, saw the first considerable intake of Turkic and other Asiatic words into ESl., among which may be suggested: телéга (телѣга) '(a particular kind of nomad's?) cart' (elsewhere only Blg. талига, which must be an old Bulgar word); вóйлок (earlier вóйлук) 'felt' (of which nomad tents were made; no early record); вьюк 'pack' (вью́чное живóтное 'pack animal'; earlier юкъ < Turkic *jük*; recorded from the 13th c.); толмáч 'interpreter' (no longer current in Russian but passed on westwards, e.g. Pol. *tłumaczyć* 'translate', Ger. *Dolmetsch(er)*); табýн 'drove' (of steppe horses); кочевáть 'lead a nomadic life' < Turkic *köč(mäk)* 'ditto'; and the earliest form of хозя́ин (? < Volga Bulgar *xoz'a*; no early record).

There are a number of such 'steppe words' in the Слово о полку Игореве, rare or unknown elsewhere, and therefore almost certainly inaccessible to a later falsifier: орътъма (ортьма) 'covering'; чага 'slave woman'. Such appearances underline the linguistic interpenetration along the southern frontier. Probably many such words of local usage never gained general currency.

9 The native ESl. word for the European horse was конь (grouped with комонь obs. and кобы́ла 'mare'). Лóшадь was borrowed surely for some particular breed of steppe horse. The source is Turkic *(a)laša* (perhaps < Mongol), in a Pecheneg or Volga Bulgar form, and recorded from 1103 by which time it had already acquired the possibly collective suffix -дь and false association with the adj. лош- 'bad' (current in SSl. but extinct in Russian).[22] It is worth noting that other equine terminology is also Turkic, e.g. аргамáк, мéрин, and many of the colours (мáсти), e.g. булáный 'sorrel'; игрéний 'skewbald'; кáрий 'chestnut' (now also applied to eye-colour; Turkic *kara* 'black'); саврáсый 'roan'; чáлый 'grey'; чубáрый 'piebald'.

10 Relatively early loans must also be: богаты́рь 'hero' (< Pers. *bahadur*, attracted to богат-); ватáга 'gang' (prob. < Chuvash); жéмчуг 'pearl(s)' (first rec. 1161 as женчугъ < Turkic *jünčü*,

---

[21] *s.a.* 945 (Treaty, *ad fin.*): надъ ручаемь конець пасынъчѣ бесѣды (possessive adj. of пашен(о)гъ, confused with пáсынок).

[22] See G. F. Odintsov in Этимология 1971. Лашá is recorded as late as 1489. There was also a neut. pl. лошáта (лошáта и волы (1305)). Ukrainian still has лошá (neut. type 28) and лошáк.

probably from Chinese); ковёр 'rug'; курга́н '(defensive) earth-
work', now 'burial mound, tumulus' (frequent in the chronicle
accounts of campaigns in the ди́кое по́ле); са́бля 'sabre' (the *short
curved* sword of the nomad horsemen as opposed to the *long
straight* меч of Europe and Islam);[23] саранча́ 'locust(s)'; степь
'steppe' (origin unknown); това́р 'trade goods' (originally, as in the
chronicles, 'baggage train, caravan');[24] хомя́к 'hamster';[25] шатёр
'tent' (ult. < Pers.). These are all words still alive in Russian; many
others are obsolete or present only in the dialects of the East and
South, e.g. (respectively) ропать 'mosque' and яр(у́га) 'ravine'.[26]

It is worth distinguishing those Turkic words which must have
reached ESl. from the Balkan Bulgars or other Near Eastern source
only *via the OCS texts* (10th–12th c.) but which of course could
have been familiar in some cases from other contacts: би́сер
'seed-pearls' (*büsür* < Ar. *busra(t)*, pl. *busur*); болва́н and куми́р
'idol, statue'; ка́пище '(heathen) shrine' (with added Slav suffix of
place -ище); ковче́г (ковьчегъ) '(Noah's) Ark'; сан 'rank, office';
чека́н- 'stamp' and черто́г 'hall, chamber' (ult. Pers.). Further R.
боя́ре and OCS (Balkan) *boljare* appear to be separate borrowings
of one Turkic prototype, later confused in Russia.

11 *Baltic*

To return a little in time. The loosening of the Gothic hegemony
over the Slavs (or a considerable part of them) from the end of the
4th c. AD was certainly one of the factors which set in train their
following rapid expansion. The East Slavs have in all probability
always been, geographically speaking, the eastern Slavs, i.e. those
settled in the east and north-east of the Slav праро́дина, south of
the Pripet basin and west of the lower Dnepr. Their direction of
expansion was northwards up the Dnepr valley and its left-bank
(eastern) tributaries. At this time Baltic peoples occupied all the
middle and upper Dnepr basin (see also 1.5 and Map no. 1), as

---

[23] *RPC, ad init.*: . . . оружьемь одиною стороною, рекше саблями, а сихъ
оружье обоюду остро, рекше мечь.

[24] Another form of this word is та́бор '(en)camp(ment)', borrowed from WSl.
or Magyar at a later date.

[25] *RPC, ad init.*: хомѣки и сусолы (mod. су́слик 'gopher'); full form хомѣсторъ
with new suffix -як.

[26] Ропать in *RPC s.a.* 987, no doubt borrowed from the Volga Bulgars (to whom
the passage refers) who had become Muslims in the early 10th c.; the ultimate
source is Arabic. Яру́га appears in the Слово о полку Игореве and is still present
in S. dialects.

the study of the hydronymy has shown; beyond them, to the north and east in the most heavily forested parts, there was a relatively sparse population of Finno-Ugrian tribes. Thus the ESl. expansion was from the outset into linguistically alien territories. The close association with Baltic speakers, formative at an earlier period (§§2–3 above), was now resumed in a more local form and must be taken into account in the interpretation of dialects (Chapter 6). But now the East Slavs appear as the dominant element (earlier it had been the Balts): there are many Slav loan-words into Baltic from this period onwards but few from Baltic into ESl. The best-authenticated are: (Lith.) *degùtas* > R. дёготь 'pitch, tar' (important forest product); *pākulos* > пáкля 'tow'; *gintāras* > янтáрь 'amber' (valuable product of the Baltic coast, traded as far as the Mediterranean world from the Bronze Age onwards); *káušas/ *kaušīnas* > ковш/кувшúн, vessels of particular shapes ('ladle'/ 'pitcher').

12 *Finnic*

The same applies to the Finnic dialects—few loan-words into ESl. of more than local significance (very abundant in N. dialects), many more in the reverse direction[27] (as also from Baltic into Finnic over a long period). The toponymy of North and East Central Russia has remained predominantly Finnic in its larger features, e.g. the rivers Невá and Мстá (Finnic 'black'); lake Il'men' (early ESl. Ил(ь)мѣрь < *Ilmajärv(i)*; Finnish *järvi* 'lake'); and many PN in -*ga* and -*da*, often still with Finnic initial stress: Лáдога, Онéга, Пúнега, Вóлогда, Вы́чегда. Finnic *salmi* ('strait') was used in the North sufficiently early to produce a *polnoglásie* form солóмя as well as сáлма. In the centre, whereas the river Окá appears to have a good IE ancestry (cf. Lat. *aqua* 'water'), Вóлга is probably Finnic and likewise Москвá, originally the name of the river on which the town stands (3.24 (*b*)(ii)). Finnic supplied words for the natural world of the Far North, few of which are, understandably, common literary words, but many more recently adopted into scientific language (18th–19th c.): векша (вѣкъша) '(species of) squirrel', adopted in early Nóvgorod as a unit of exchange in the fur trade, but both this and the more southerly and general Slav вéверица (cf. Pol. *wiewiórka*) have been replaced

---

[27] See also 2.7.

in standard Russian by бе́лка; ко́ндо́вый 'heartwood, solid' (<
konda 'fir');[28] лы́ва 'puddle (from melted snow)'—used by
Lomonósov but never accepted as literary; морж 'walrus'; не́рпа
'(species of) seal' (*Phoca vitulina*);[29] пурга́ 'blizzard'; ри́га 'thresh-
ing barn' (the town Riga is not connected); то́рос 'ice-hummock';
ту́ндра 'treeless Arctic zone'; тюле́нь 'seal' (now the general
word); я́гель 'reindeer moss' (*Cladonia rangiferina*).

13 *Scandinavian*

The northward push of the ESl. tribes did not reach the head of
the Gulf of Finland until the early 8th c. Not long after, new
contacts arose with the no less expansive Scandinavians, in this
case mainly Swedes. They opened up a trade route via Stáraja
Ládoga (on the southern shore of the lake), the Volga Bulgars,
and Khazaria to the Islamic world and later in the 9th c. a by then
more profitable route to the Black Sea and Constantinople via the
Dnepr valley. Nóvgorod and Smolénsk were the main stages on
the way to Kiev. Other Baltic rivers, especially the Dviná, provided shorter routes of penetration. Three names were applied to
these 'merchant adventurers': Русь, Варя́ги, and (more rarely)
Колбя́ги. To this day the nearest Finnic peoples call the Swedes
respectively *Rootsi* (Estonian) and *Ruotsi* (Finnish). Despite much
controversy this still remains the most probable source of the word
Русь,[30] though poorly authenticated in Scandinavia—a typical ESl.
fem. collective noun of the type widely applied to neighbouring
non-Slavs, e.g. Чудь 'Estonians', Весь 'Vepsians', Либь 'Livoni-
ans', Лопь 'Lapps', Сумь 'Finns' (Suomi), and others. Варя́г and
колбя́г were not so much ethnics as designations of members
of these merchant-warrior bands. The former was adopted in
Constantinople for the Scandinavian bodyguard of the Emperor
in the 10th–12th c. (Βάραγγοι).[31] The prototypes are Swedish
vāring-, kylfing-, without the no longer active Third Palatalization
(cf. *-ędzǐ, §6 above). The Scandinavians imposed their military and

---

[28] Blok, Двенадцать: Пальнём-ка пу́лей в Святую Русь — / В кондову́ю, / В
избяну́ю, / В толстоза́дую!

[29] Also но́рпа; not recorded before the 17th c.

[30] The phonetic difficulty can perhaps be surmounted by positing a form *Rōssi,
held to be likely in the Karelian type of dialect spoken in the main area of
Slav–Finnic–Scand. mixing, e.g. at Stáraja Ládoga.

[31] Though the Gk. initial stress is not decisive the original form was probably
Ва́ряг, to judge by a PN Ва́регово near Jaroslavl'; ва́режки 'mittens' may also be
relevant.

eventually political control over the East Slavs in the 9th–10th c.,
the term Русь first being applied to the ruling class at Kiev, then
geographically to the whole Kiev region and its inhabitants, and
finally to the country as a whole. But they were certainly never
numerous and, as in other W. European countries, soon adopted
the Slav language of the majority. Their cultural influence, to judge
by loan-words, was small. Expectedly, certain terms specific to
their military organization and customs figure in early texts but are
now obsolete: вира 'wergild' (perhaps only influenced by the
Scandinavian term since, as Русская Правда shows, vendetta was
current among the tribal Slavs too); гридь (*griði*) 'man-at-arms'
(whence the native derivative грид(ь)ница 'barracks'); стяг(ъ)
(*stang*) 'pennant'; ти(в)ун(ъ) 'steward' (*þjónn*, cognate with Scots
thane—continued in use in the WhR. area under Lithuanian rule);
ябедник (ябетьникъ), an official title (from **ambet-* 'work' (cf.
mod. Ger. *Amt*) with native suffix; the noun ябеда was back-
formed from this about the 15th c. and is still tenuously alive).
There was also a small contribution of terms connected with boats,
the Scandinavian ones being of quite different type from the Slav
river-craft: беть 'thwart' (*biti*, cf. French (of Normandy origin)
bitte); шнека 'longboat' (possibly still alive in dialects of the Far
North as шняка; Norse *snekkja*); and якорь 'anchor'. Apart from
these there are at most half a dozen living words: акула (*hákall*)
'shark'; кнут 'a *knotted* whip'; ларь (*lárr*) 'chest'; шёлк 'silk'; крюк
'hook' (*krókr* = Eng. *crook*); ящик 'box, drawer' (diminutive of
earlier яск(ъ), *askr*). Шёлк is not recorded before *c.*1300 but must
have a Germanic prototype and is plausibly connected with the
Scandinavians' Asiatic trade.

Scandinavian are also a number of personal names used by the
rulers of Kiev and other towns and then by Slavs of the upper
class: Олег (originally Олег?, 2.46 (6)) and Ольга (*Helgi, Helga*);
Игорь (*Ingvar*); Глеб (Глѣбъ < *Gudleifr*; Eng. surnames
Goodliffe, Godlee). They were soon abandoned as pagan to be
revived together with Slav pagan names (Владимир, Мстислав)
as 'romantic' in the 19th–20th c.[32]

The Scandinavians' international trade route, with terminal in

<hr />

[32] The 'Russian' signatories of the Treaty with Constantinople (945) are predominantly Scandinavian in their names. The first member of the ruling dynasty to be
known exclusively by a Slav name was Svjatosláv (d. 972). Nóvgorod people, in
view of their Baltic trade, continued to use more Scandinavian names, e.g. Якун
(*Haakon*).

Baghdad, is well illustrated by two words used by Nóvgorod merchants: ногáта, a 10th c. coin ($\frac{1}{20}$ *grivna*), from Arabic *naqd* (coin
of full weight, also 'cash'), and бéрковец from *bĭrkovĭskŭ* (sc.
pudŭ), the *pound* of Birka (Björkö), a great centre of trade and
exchange near Stockholm in the 10th c.

14 *Greek*

The organization of annual trading expeditions to Constantinople, the employment of Pусь in Byzantine service, and the
initiation (perhaps resumption) of Greek missionary activity at
Kiev by the end of the 10th c. brought the East Slavs into contact
with spoken Greek. Up to this time they knew Greek words only
indirectly via the OCS texts, e.g. стратиг(ъ) 'general'; such words
had no bearing on their daily life. Direct loans from spoken
Greek—very different from the artificial Atticizing literary Greek
which the Bulgarians were translating—now became possible.
Knowledge of Greek, whether vernacular or literary, was at no
time at all common in Russia; the quality of early translations made
in Kiev was often deplorable. Loan-words belong to trade, new
crafts exercised by imported craftsmen (e.g. architecture), increasing literacy. To the 10th–12th c. probably belong: грáмота 'writing,
written text' (Gk. neut. pl. γράμματα; 1.8); и́звесть 'lime'
(ἄσβεστος, deformed by 'popular etymology'); у́ксус 'vinegar'
(ὄξος); харатья́ 'parchment' (neut. pl. χαρτία;[33] the word is
already to be found in OCS as *xarŭtija* but is coupled with грáмота
in the 10th c. treaties); the obsolete оксами́т 'samite' (ἑξάμιτος)
and кубáра (κουμβάρι(ον) '(type of) boat'; noted in 945 Treaty).
The following are only recorded later but in most cases there is a
considerable probability of earlier oral transmission: ды́ня 'melon'
(14th c.; κυδώνιον); дьяк 'clerk' (διάκ(ον)ος—the learned form
was дьякон 'deacon'); кáторга 'penal servitude' (14th c.; τὰ
κάτεργα = 'the hulks'); кровáть 'bedstead' (15th c.); огурéц
'gherkin' (15th c.; ἀγγούρι(ον) with Slav dim. suffix); сáхар
'sugar' (14th c.); скамья́ 'bench' (13th c.; neut. pl. σκαμνία);[34]
тéрем 'women's apartments' (τέρεμνον; originally 'chamber' in
general); тетрáдь 'notebook' (τετράδι(ον));[35] фонáрь 'lantern'
(φανάρι(ον)).

[33] The oral transmission of this word is strongly suggested by the final stress in
Russian, since spoken Greek commonly has -ιά for learned -ία.   [34] See n. 33.
[35] Cf. Ital. *quaderno*, Fr. *cahier* < Lat. *quatern-*. Learned loan in OCS; status in
ESl. not necessarily the same.

Church Slavonic and Slavonicisms (ChSl. Loan-words in Russian)

15   OCS, reaching Russia from Bulgaria in the 10th c. (1.9–10), provided ESl. with virtually its whole Christian terminology and a large part of the vocabularies associated with religion and learning —ecclesiastical architecture, costume, and functions, for example: елéй '(olive) oil' < ἔλαιον (alternating, even in the Balkans, with олéй which would appear to be the colloquial form taken from Lat. *oleum*); епитрахи́ль 'stole'; панихи́да 'requiem' < παννυχίδα = 'all-night service'; просфорá 'communion wafer' < προσφορά (variously deformed in speech, partly to avoid non-Slav [f]); сáван 'shroud'; аналóй 'lectern' < ἀναλόγιον (both languages came to use more popular aphaeretic forms; R. налóй); and many others. Perhaps among the earliest to penetrate genuinely into the vernacular were the terms of the Church year, since the chronology of everyday life was reckoned not by dates but by festivals and saints'-days down to and even after Peter the Great's secular reformation. Thus the traditional pagan Slav names of the months, illustrating the climatic and agricultural calendar, gave way, except in the depths of the countryside, to the Latin–Greek terms which we also use, cf. *RPC s.a.* 1097: бѣ бо тогда мѣсяць груденъ, рекше ноябрь.[36]

16   Slavonicisms in Russian are abundantly illustrated throughout this book and need little further analysis here. A large number were absorbed into the usage of the literate class, far fewer into the speech of the peasantry. Thus although the *meaning* of маловѣр(ьнъ)—a calque (loan-translation) of ὀλιγόπιστης—was transparent even to a peasant it was likely to remain a literary word; conversely, благодари́ть 'thank' (= εὐχαριστεῖν), though not so obvious in its component parts, in course of time gained universal currency.

No exact chronology of the penetration of Slavonicisms has yet been worked out—indeed it is probably not recoverable in detail. But the starting-points are clear: the consistent ChSl. of Hilarion's *Sermon* (text no. 4) contrasting with the traditional ESl. language of customary law in Русская Правда. It is important to note that, in contrast to the situation in much of W. Europe, the legal language of medieval Russia remained in essentials vernacular, even if the parties concerned were churchmen or monasteries

---

[36] Ukrainian and Polish have retained the Slav terms in normal use or as alternatives; Ukr. грýдень and Pol. *grudzień* now = 'December', not 'November'.

(canon law had, of course, its own sphere). But lawyers are wedded to clichés and some ChSl. phrases soon found a place in legal documents of the more formal kind, usually formulae at the beginning or end. Such are the initial се азъ (from Mstisláv's Deed onwards) and various comminatory formulae, e.g. at the end of Varlaam's Deed (text no. 15): аще кто дияволъмь на[уч]енъ и злыми ч[е]л[о]в[ѣ]кы наваженъ цьто хочеть отяти . . . а буди ему противень с[вя]тыи сп[а]съ и въ сь вѣкъ и въ будущии. Here the centre of the phrase relapses into his normal Nóvgorod dialect. A few Slavonicisms likewise crept into Русская Правда, e.g. the widely used аще, but no doubt most are due to later revisions and recopyings; the earliest surviving manuscript (1282) is already two and a half centuries younger than the original.

The assimilation of ChSl. words can be better illustrated by *types* of words than individual cases, specifically by *prefixed* compounds and *suffixed* derivatives. Native ESl. did not lack either procedure but from the nature of the texts such words pullulated on every page of ChSl. For example:

17 Prefixes and first components of compounds:

(i) благо- (calquing Gk. εὐ-, e.g. благоро́дный = εὐγενής) is now an isolated Slavonicism in Russian, with its substantivized neut. adj. бла́го 'good, well-being'. About a hundred cpds. are listed in a modern dictionary, the great majority still confined to the religious or at least learned vocabulary.

Though the native equivalent болог- is not unattested[37] it is no longer present in the living language.

(ii) Another glance at the dictionary will show over 200 words in без-. Без is, of course, a native preposition but the majority of the earlier cpds. in без- were Slavonicisms. Once this model had been established, in written if not in spoken language, the procedure could be extended to native words, e.g. безоговóрочно 'unconditionally' (говори́ть is not ChSl.). Conversely, the negative prefix не- is largely but not exclusively native. The force of the two prefixes is admittedly not identical though virtual synonyms are to be found (безгра́мотный = негра́мотный 'illiterate').

(iii) The ChSl. prefixes пре- and пред- are sufficiently illustrated in 4.62–3 (see also Appendix, 33–4), and во-, воз-, со-, из- in

---

[37] There is a PN Бологóе near Tver′ (Kalínin) and бóлого, mainly as an adverb, was still attested in the 19th c. in N. dialects in that general area.

2.31, 4.55–6, 4.65. Whereas пре- and пред- are exclusively of ChSl. origin, во-, воз-, and со- can arise in certain native phonetic contexts, e.g. вобра́ть, сорва́ть, in which case they alternate with в-, с- (вбира́ть, срыва́ть). Thus во́здух 'atmosphere' and восто́к 'east' are at least influenced by ChSl.; вздух and всток exist in dialect in other senses. Из- also has its native uses distinct from ChSl. из- 'out of'.

18   Similarly with *suffixes*. The ChSl. contribution is somewhat less obvious. There is no reason to think that the CSl. suffixes -ость and -ство were absent from ESl. Both appear in the vernacular (dialect) vocabulary untouched by learned influence. But the great extension of these still productive suffixes took place at least partly under ChSl. influence. Иску́сство 'art' is clearly a Slavonicism (though not recorded in OCS); мастерство́ is a purely Russian creation from the loan-word ма́стер (§28 below). Similarly сво́йство 'attribute' is a Slavonicism contrasting with native свойство́ 'connection (by marriage)', which would appear to belong to the traditional vocabulary of the clan and 'great family'.[38] The variant -ствие is exclusively ChSl. and virtually unproductive on Russian soil. Yet even in this case a few words have reached everyday use, e.g. путеше́ствие 'journey' (but scarcely ше́ствие 'procession'), удово́льствие 'pleasure'.

In the case of -ость it may be said to be the preferred abstract suffix from the late 17th c.; creations are particularly numerous from the late 18th c. onwards. The number of derivatives in -ость actually recorded in OCS is small but enough to provide the model via ChSl. In this case, however, the extension may also be partly due to Polish, which had already developed by the 17th c. an extensive abstract vocabulary in -*ość*. At any rate -ость was at no time felt to be appropriate only to the words of the ChSl. stratum; native derivatives are clear, e.g. приверéдливость < привере́дливый 'fastidious'. But there can be uncertainty in particular cases: мо́лодость seems a natural derivative of молодо́й, and moreover in the native sense 'youthful' (the sense of млад- in OCS and ChSl. is confined to 'infancy'), but the word is not recorded before 1771 and could be a literary Russification of мла́дость. Finally, сме́ртность 'death-rate' and рожда́емость 'birth-rate'

---

[38] The form -ество nearly always indicates a Slavonicism: о́бщество, преиму́щество, челове́чество, вещество́.

can be taken as typical of the numerous recent technical 'neo-Slavonicisms'.

The suffix -ние of the verbal noun perpetuates ChSl. orthography in contrast to the rarer native -нье (2.33). The form is predominantly but not exclusively literary, providing the possibility of a noun of action from any *impf* verb; those from *pf* verbs are certainly Slavonicisms. Its literary nature is emphasized by the fact that the native formations such as враньё 'lying' are still often subliterary and that colloquial language often prefers a noun of process with suffix -ка or no suffix at all (i.e. suffix -ъ), e.g. сбор, сбо́рка 'collection, assembly' as against learned собра́ние, собира́ние. There may be a division in sense: перепи́ска 'correspondence', перепи́сывание '(act of) recopying'. See further 3.135–6.

Animate agent nouns in -тель are doubtfully native.[39] They have proved a useful resource taken from ChSl., some becoming quite colloquial, e.g. учи́тель, pl. роди́тели, писа́тель, люби́-тель. The type was particularly favoured during the Second South Slav Influence (15th–16th c.), which created several hundred. More important now are the numerous more recent inanimate neo-Slavonicisms, initiated by calques on Latin, e.g. указа́тель 'indicator' (see also 4.41). There are nearly 600 in the *Academy Dictionary*, of which less than 100 marked as ChSl. Derivatives in -тельный, -тельность, -тельство all belong to the Russian development of this suffix, scarcely before the 17th c. This also applies to the attachment of -тель to Russian roots, e.g. оберега́-тель, оборони́тельный.

The creation of neo-Slavonicisms is also exemplified in самодержа́вие 'autocracy'; *samodrŭžĭcĭ* and *samodrŭžiteli* both appear in OCS as calques of αὐτοκράτωρ. The title was adopted officially by Ivan IV in the 1550s in the former version; the abstract noun was created soon after. A similar case is драгоце́нный 'precious', found from the 16th c. but unrecorded in earlier ChSl., so plausibly a creation of that time.

To the suffix -ица as a *diminutive* (not as a feminine marker) the native correlative is -(ъ)ка, e.g. ChSl. рыбица/R. голо́вка. Likewise the corresponding masc. in -ьць (-ец): ChSl. градец (= SCr. *grádac*)/R. кружо́к; ChSl. венец (*věnĭcĭ*)/R. вено́к.

---

[39] Прия́тель is only secondarily and misleadingly in -тель: the essential part seems to correspond to (if not borrowed from) Gmc. *frijond-* (p.p.a.), whence Eng. *friend*. It is pan-Slav and certainly native. The verb is *prijati* + dat. 'be favourable to'.

19   It must not be assumed that all early Slavonicisms are immediately detectable by inspection in modern Russian: none of the phonetic criteria treated in Chapter 1 may be present. И́стина 'truth' is certainly taken from OCS,[40] as also кова́рный 'sly' (probably Moravian OCS since the noun *kovarjĭ* 'smith' is now only WSl.—elsewhere *kovalĭ* or *kovačĭ*); клевета́ 'slander' (revealed by the verb клевета́ть/клевещу́); доса́да 'vexation' (revealed by the verb досади́ть/досажда́ть—but there is always the possibility that the noun may be native and the verb a literary loan);[41] по́двиг 'feat'; о́браз 'form, image'; and many others. Вещь 'thing', now so commonplace, was rare in early ESl. usage and purely learned. The OCS senses were wide but included 'substance', the evolution of sense being thus rather similar to Eng. *matter* (what is the matter?). Finally, the derivatives of the stem доб- (удо́бный, подо́бие, etc.) are mostly Slavonicisms (for на́до < на добѣ, see 4.11), the noun до́ба '(right) moment' having disappeared early in ESl. (perhaps still present in dialect), though still current in other Slav languages.

The Period of the Tatar Yoke

20   То[мъ] же лѣ[тѣ] [1224] по грѣхомъ нашимъ придоша язы́ци незнаеми, ихже добрѣ никтоже не вѣсть, кто суть и отколе изидоша, и что язы́къ ихъ, и котораго племени суть, и что вѣра ихъ; а зовуть я татары, а инии гл[аголю]ть таурмены, а друзии печенѣзи . . . Б[ог]ъ единъ вѣсть кто суть и отколѣ изидоша.

So runs the *Novg. Chronicle*, freshly reporting the first big raid of the Mongol armies. The centre of gravity of the ESl. world had already been shifting for a century before this from Kiev and the South-West, too open to hostile incursions both from the steppe and from Europe, to the centre behind its protective screen of forests—safer but with more limited horizons both politically and culturally. However, the 'Kiev period' may be conventionally closed with the destruction of the city by the Tatars in 1240. From that date all Russia (with the partial exception of the Novgorod 'empire' in the North-West and Far North) came under Tatar

[40] The early Novg. commercial term истина 'capital, principal' may belong here. But derivatives of the adj. root *ist-* are present in R. dialects though much more widespread in SSl. (e.g. SCr. *ȉstī*).

[41] As also in the case of бедá 'misfortune', whose cpds. (победи́ть, бéдствие, etc.) are clearly Slavonicisms.

administration. The prostration of Russia encouraged the powers along the Baltic coast to grab what they could. The German town of Riga had been founded in 1200; the German knights set their sights at Pskov and Nóvgorod. During the 14th c. the still largely pagan Duchy of Lithuania absorbed Belorussia and much of the right-bank Ukraine. The new princely towns of the centre of Russia—Súzdal', Vladímir, Rostóv, Tver'—unlike Jaroslàv the Wise's Kiev in the 11th c., had little more than a local culture. Direct relations with the West were confined to the frontier towns (Pskov, Smolénsk, etc.) and the extreme South-West (independent Galicia); relations (especially ecclesiastical) with the Byzantine Empire and the Balkans were at times tenuous and hazardous but scarcely ever totally interrupted, even during the period of the Latin Empire (1204–63) when Emperor and Patriarch were in exile at Nicaea. Nóvgorod alone kept its maritime links with the West open via the Hanseatic network.

Tatar rule did not mean a total occupation of the country; it was more like the old nomad habit of living off sedentary peoples without mingling with them more than necessary. The capital of the Golden Horde was a long way away at Saráj on the lower Volga, well beyond the eastern limit of Russian settlement. Tatar troops and officials made their presence felt but were not permanently resident in strength. Thus the Tatar 'conquest' could have nothing comparable to the linguistic effects of the Norman conquest of England.

21 The accelerated intake of eastern words via Tatar is limited in the main to nouns of more or less concrete sense—words for new *realia* in Russian life imposed, adopted, or merely brought into view by political and economic dependence on an Asiatic power and Muslim culture. The leading culture languages of Islam—Arabic and Persian—were often the ultimate sources of these 'Tatar' words.

Writing his will in 1327–8 Ivan Kalitá (= 'purse'; the sobriquet is Tatar) begins: се язъ грѣшныи худыи рабъ Б[ож]ии Иван[ъ] пишу д[у]ш[е]вную грамоту ида въ ворду⁴² '. . . on my way to the (Golden) Horde'; there was no telling if he would come back alive. But to Saráj the Russian princes had to go to solicit

---

⁴² Mongol military term *ordu* taken as a fem. sg. acc., with the stress pattern órду, nom. орда́. Eng. *Horde* (16th c.) may have come via Polish.

their diploma of appointment (ярлы́к)[43] sealed with a vermilion (а́лый)[44] seal. There was in fact a considerable Russian colony resident at Saráj for much of the 14th c.

They had also to satisfy the Horde's tax-collector—баска́к (rec. from 1269). In the economic sphere we soon get (14th c.): казна́ 'treasury' and казначе́й 'treasurer';[45] тамга́ 'stamp, seal', whence тамо́жня 'customs-house'; and others. The Russian monetary system was partly renewed: native minting had ceased after the mid 11th c. The Asiatic ден(ь)га́ was now introduced, a *stamped* token (деньга́ and тамга́ are two versions of the same word, perhaps from different dialects), hence a coin of small value. By the 15th c. the pl. де́ньги 'money' replaced the by then regional and obsolescent ку́ны (Novg.) and пе́нязи (Pskov). The алты́н (= 6 *denga*) is also Tatar (recorded from 1375) but the later копе́йка (= 2 *denga*; first minted 1535) is not.[46]

Fashions changed; the terminology of clothing became markedly Asiatic: армя́к 'overcoat'; башма́к 'shoe' (16th c.); кафта́н '(men's) robe' (at first кавтанъ 15th c.; ult. from Persian); каблу́к 'heel'; калпа́к (колпа́к) and клобу́к 'headgear';[47] куша́к 'belt, sash' (16th c.); сарафа́н '(women's) robe'; хала́т 'robe (dressing-gown)'; чуло́к 'sock, stocking' (15th c.);[48] ю́бка 'skirt'. It is instructive to note that шу́ба 'fur coat' is a doublet of the last, both deriving ultimately from Ar. *jubba(t)*, which penetrated equally into W. European languages—Ital. *giubba*, Fr. *jupe*. The Russian versions are recorded from the 14th c. Юба (earliest form юпа) certainly came by an eastern route; шу́ба, despite the early date for a European loan, may derive from a MHG form—unlike юбка it is pan-Slav, but the details are obscure.

In adornment серьга́ 'ear-ring' replaces the older Germanic loan-word усеря́зь (Goth. *ausihriggs* = 'ear-ring'?) and other

[43] Tatar *yarlyq* (ult. from Mongol?), recorded from 1267; now usually dim. ярлычо́к 'label'.   [44] Turkic *al-*.

[45] Ar. *khazna(t)*; -чей represents the Turkic suffix of occupation -*či* (as in *çiftçi* 'farmer', *bostancı* 'gardener') which already features in a few OCS words, presumably from Bulgar: *kŭnigŭčii* 'bookman, *literatus*'; *samŭčii* 'official' (< *san*, §10 above).

[46] For пе́нязи see §6 above. Рубль is also native, perhaps a Novg. term (14th c.) soon adopted in Moscow where minting roubles began *c*.1450. Turkic *altyn* 'gold'; but this derivation is not quite uncontroversial, cf. *alty* 'six'.

[47] Two versions of the same word; one or both may belong to the earlier stratum of steppe words: the Karakalpak tribe (Black Caps) was settled south of Kiev before the Mongol incursions.

[48] Probably Chuvash (Volga Bulgar) *tšulga* interpreted as a dual.

words; бирюза́ 'turquoise' (1509) and изумру́д 'emerald' (1462) appear, both probably of Persian origin. The *pencil* каранда́ш (= 'black stone', i.e. graphite), *flat-iron* утю́г, *rhubarb* реве́нь (15th c.), and *brick* кирпи́ч are introduced. Tatar military and social organization are reflected in: бараба́н 'drum' (rec. 17th c. but may be older); карау́л 'guard' (1356); тюрьма́ 'prison' (*türmä; not* European); and ям 'post-station' (whence ямщи́к 'coachman, driver'). Persian provenance can be shown for: арбу́з 'water-melon' (grown on the lower Volga); бадья́ 'bucket'; балага́н 'booth, stall'; була́т 'steel'; десть 'quire' (of paper); мише́нь 'target' (14th c.; Pers. *nišān*); обезья́на 'monkey' (15th c.; deformed by 'popular etymology'); самши́т 'box' (*Buxus*); стака́н 'glass' (14th c. as *dŭstokanŭ*); and черда́к 'attic'; and Arabic provenance for: бакале́я 'delicatessen' (Ar. *baqqāl* 'grocer'); бахрома́ 'fringe' (cf. *makharramāt* = 'embroidery, lace'); наба́т 'tocsin' (*nawba(t)* = 'trumpet-call'); сунду́к 'trunk' (*ṣundūq*, ult. from Greek).

The following further words of interest may be noted: база́р (15th c.); барсу́к 'badger' (see also 6.55; the native term was язв-ик, -ец, still present in dialect); бары́ш 'profit' (1704, but certainly much older); жесть 'sheet iron'; изю́м 'raisins' (16th c.); каза́к 'Cossack' (rec. as козакъ 1395; Tat. *qazaq* = 'free(-man, -booter)'); камы́ш 'reed'; кинжа́л 'dagger'; нашаты́рь 'sal ammoniac' (16th c.) (Ar. *nušādir*); сурьма́ 'antimony' (*sürmä* = 'cosmetic'—its main use); тага́н 'trivet'; тума́н 'mist'; and шала́ш '(log) cabin'.[49]

The frequent Turkic suffixes *-aq, -uq, -yq* are conspicuous.

22 It must be remembered that the formal ending of the 'Tatar yoke' (1480) did not entail the drying up of such loans—quite the reverse. The Russian conquest of the Volga line by Ivan IV (destruction of the independent Khanate of Kazán' 1552, capture of Astrakhan' 1556) inaugurated the conquest of Siberia (Сиби́рь, name of a local Khanate east of the Ура́л) and large parts of Turkic-speaking Central Asia, and also in due course the annexation of the southern steppes and the Caucasus region (17th–19th c.). This imperial expansion has continued down to modern times. Some 16th c. loans may be specifically from the Kazán' dialect; sugges-tions are: киби́тка '(covered) cart' (originally 'tent'); колча́н 'quiver' (1589); мече́ть 'mosque' (1584) (ult. < Ar. *masjid*); сургу́ч

---

[49] We may add with a query слон 'elephant', appearing in ChSl. before the 15th c. (but not in OCS) < Turkic *a(r)slan* 'lion'.

'sealing-wax'; тюфя́к 'mattress'; чемода́н 'trunk'; чугу́н 'cast iron'; штаны́ pl. 'trousers' (6.55); and, more surprisingly, кады́к 'Adam's apple' and кула́к 'fist'. But after the 16th c. loan-words tend to be more local terms used by the Slav colonists, e.g. the picturesque Caucasian words used by Pushkin, Lermontov and Tolstoy. Many were eventually adopted in the 19th–20th c. as scientific terms, e.g. барха́н 'barchan' (crescent-shaped sand-dune in the C. Asian desert; from Kirghiz); тайга́ 'taiga, Siberian coniferous forest' (source language uncertain); бе́ркут 'imperial eagle'; канды́к 'dog's-tooth violet' (*Erythronium*); сайга́ 'saiga antelope'; керме́к 'sea-lavender' (*Limonium*; typical genus of the saline steppes).[50] They gained currency through the reports of the great scientific expeditions inaugurated in 1733.

It is hardly surprising that in the 15th–16th c. much Tatar blood was absorbed, even at the highest social level, by the Russification of Tatar noble families. Hence the many Tatar surnames, e.g. Акса́ков (*aqsaq* 'lame'), Ахма́тов (< Ar. *aḥmad*), Бердя́ев (= *Theodore* in Arabic), Булга́ков ('proud'?), Куту́зов (*qutuz* 'mad'), Огарёв (*oɣar* 'high'), Салтыко́в, Турге́нев (Mongol *türgen* 'hasty').[51] The Tatar language was quite well seen at court in the reign of Basil II and later.

This ready use of foreign words, against which there was no prejudice, can be well seen in Afanási Nikítin's account of his journey to India via the Caucasus and Persia in the years 1466–72,[52] when the descent of the Volga was still through hostile territory. He quotes Tatar phrases heard on the way: намъ кликали качма не бѣгаите (modern Ottoman Turkish neg. imperative *koşma* 'do not run') and many Indian words, mostly garbled, which caught his fancy, e.g. кичирис = 'kedgeree' (Anglo-Indian). The penetration is confirmed again in such idioms as ни бельме́са не понима́ет (Ottoman Turkish *bilmez* 'who does not know') and на свой салты́к 'in one's own way' (Tat. *salt-* 'order, method'). The quite frequent presence of Russian contingents serving in Tatar armies in Asia was another source of such colloquial phrases.

[50] In the Ivan–Vasili correspondence (1574–6) Ivan uses улу́с '(Crimean) village' and the latter в ка́домах 'idle' (never more than a dial. expression).

[51] It has been estimated that about 10 per cent of the 17th c. boyar families were of Tatar origin though not all bore Tatar names. Conversely some of the Tatar names are sobriquets given to native families.

[52] Best edn.: Хожение за три моря Аф. Никитина, ed. Grekova and Adrianova-Peretts (1948).

Finally we may note that tea was certainly used in Russia from 1638 but may well have been known earlier. The form чай is said to derive from a N. Chinese pronunciation via Tatar whereas the W. European *tea*, etc., came by the sea routes from a S. Chinese form. 'Caravan tea' was brought across Central Asia to Russia throughout the 18th–19th c.

23 The 'Second South Slav Influence'

It was not the practice of Islam to persecute the other faiths related to its own (Judaism, Christianity): ecclesiastical organization and religious practice were usually respected. The sanctions were economic—higher taxes, social disabilities. So also in Russia. The links of the Russian Church with the Patriarchate of Constantinople, the Balkan Orthodox churches, and the monastic republic of Mt. Athos were never deliberately cut by the overlords. The establishment of the Ottoman Turks in the Balkans from 1370 and their rapid conquest of nearly all Serbia and Bulgaria led to *closer* relations with the Balkan churches, of which actual emigration of Balkan churchmen to Russia was only a small part. From the late 14th c. Russia received a large new influx of Balkan religious texts. During the previous centuries ChSl. had been considerably Russified, just as the language of the Balkan churches had acquired a Serbian or Bulgarian cast. The differences were now brought home to the Russian and Balkan scholars and the latter were not slow to point out the departures of Russian usage from what they considered correct. The 14th c. saw a considerable literary renaissance in Balkan ChSl. The new style was now imposed on, indeed more or less willingly accepted by, the Russian church and monastic communities (see also 7.19). Its main impact was on higher literary style—artificial, elaborate and as far removed as possible from the language of everyday life. Living Russian was scarcely affected by what was essentially an alien fashion. Two things may be noted. First, the large artificial vocabulary created by this style had its period of prestige and gradually faded out. It was marked above all by love of elaborate compounds such as кокотоглашение 'cock-crow' and округлословие 'periphrasis'.[53]

[53] A proper chronological investigation of this vocabulary has still to be made, but the following calques (among many) probably belong: великоду́шный (μεγαλόψυχος), тщесла́вие (κενοδοξία), многообра́зный (πολύμορφος), законода́вец (νομοθέτης). There were many creations with first components благо-, бого-, веле-, все-, добро-, едино-, зло-, ино-, любо-, перво-, противу-, само-; and with second components -любие/-любец, -словие, -творение/ -творный.

Few of these proved useful in the long run. Some obsolescent OCS words were also revived, such as етеръ (3.64). Secondly, while the more extreme manifestations of this learned style were abandoned during the 17th c., certain elements of correctness persisted, for example the general acceptance thenceforward of ChSl. forms in -жд- which had been repugnant to Russian users of ChSl. in the Kiev period (2.19 (5)(ii)). Thus by late Muscovy times these forms were finally accepted as the norm: побѣженъ (*Novg. Minéi*, text no. 7; житие Нифонта, 1219) and осужаи disappear in favour of побеждён (победи́ть *pf*/-жда́ть), осужда́й (осуди́ть *pf*/ -жда́ть). Many Slavonicisms finally oust the native alternatives: прежде (earlier переже and hybrid преже);[54] вре́мя; ме́жду (мех-tenuously alive in cpds.); надё́жда and одё́жда (a few native derivatives—надё́жный, обнадё́жить; for examples of the mixed groups which resulted see also 1.19). With doublets the freer use of earlier centuries gave way to the modern idiomatic repartition of senses, e.g. in сторона́/страна́, коро́ткий/кра́ткий, переда́ть/ преда́ть. Such ChSl. words as преврати́ть (-враща́ть) 'turn', презре́ть (-зира́ть) 'despise', прекрати́ть (-краща́ть) 'discontinue', прерва́ть (-рыва́ть) 'interrupt', which had never had corresponding native forms in пере- were now readily demoted from ChSl. to neutral items of educated vocabulary.

24 *Baltic Trade*

While the central principalities bore the main brunt of the Tatar 'presence' and finally ridded themselves of it only by sacrificing their independence to Moscow, Nóvgorod had continued to go much her own way. Exporting, as she had done from the earliest times, the products of the northern forests and seas—wax, pitch, furs, dried fish, and later also tallow, cordage, flax and mast-timbers—she imported in exchange foreign cloth, metal goods, and sundry luxuries. There was in the city a resident 'Latin' merchant colony with its own (schismatic) church. Pskov and other frontier towns were also more or less loosely attached to the Baltic (Hanseatic) network. The main communications with Europe were in each case via the Baltic rivers and on by sea (cf. Smolénsk–Riga via the R. Dviná in the 1229 Treaty); overland trade via Poland appears to have started only in the later 15th c. and was never so important.

[54] Прежний remains a hybrid; fully native is опереди́ть *pf*/опережа́ть 'forestall'.

By these routes W. European words of limited range began to filter into common Russian usage. From the Baltic fisheries came сельдь 'herring' (recorded 1497), from relations with German Riga such titles as ратман 'town councillor'; мáстер, at first only as the title of the Grand Master of the German Knights (мастеръ божиихъ дворянъ, 1229), and пúскуп (= Lat. *episcopus*) applied to the Bishop of Riga (native епúскоп is from Greek).[55] Other trade words include: фунт 'pound' (a reimportation, perhaps as late as the 17th c.; first borrowed in respect of the Carolingian *pondus* as пуд; both words remained in use till metrication, the пуд being equivalent to 40 of the later фунт); дю́жина 'dozen'; крýжка 'mug'; имбúр 'ginger' (recorded in *Dom.*); купорóс 'vitriol' (ultimately from Lat. *cupri rosa*); прóба 'proof, trial'; стул 'chair' (14th c. at latest; not < Ger. *Stuhl* but Scand. *stóll*); сталь 'steel'. Here too may belong кóмната (rec. from Novg. in 1471), whose stress suggests a (direct) source in (Low) German rather than via Polish (cf. Ukr. кімнáта). The majority came from some form of Low German (Plattdeutsch), the speech of the Hanseatic capital Lübeck (where Nóvgorod maintained an office) and lingua franca of the Baltic trade. Few of the hundred or more such words in commercial use have retained their currency; many indeed are recorded relatively late (16th–17th c.), after the decline of the Hanse and the end of Nóvgorod's independence (1478)[56] but they belong to a current which had been flowing steadily from west to east for several centuries. The names of fabrics, such as еренга and карзай (later каразéя; both = Eng. *kersey*), have all become obsolete except for бáрхат 'velvet'. The beginnings of maritime terminology were also laid—at all times overwhelmingly foreign in Russian; but as Nóvgorod's exports were carried exclusively in foreign bottoms, this as yet hardly amounts to more than a few types of vessel: the Hanseatic *Kogge* appears as кóча (obs.); бáрка; бот (1564); and я́хта (1527)—all commanded by the pan-Baltic шкúпер 'skipper' (1566; Low German, not Dutch or Scandinavian).

We may also note in passing that the Black Sea trade, managed by the Genoese and other Italians, had a terminal in the Crimea

---

[55] Of clearly local usage are the following Germanisms in the 1229 Treaty: востокъ моря = 'Ostsee' (Baltic; not *east* to a Russian); орудие 'agreement, legal *instrument*'. We may note also the date given in AD reckoning, not adopted in Russia until the time of Peter the Great.

[56] The Hanseatic office in Nóvgorod was closed in 1494.

where Russian merchants were active in the late 13th–14th c. (сурожáне). This may have produced a few trade words and more local words used in the Mediterranean naval lingua franca (It. + Gk. + Turkish). A case in point is Afanási Nikítin's фуртовина 'storm', otherwise фуртуна < It. *fortuna*.

Medieval Learning

25   So far ChSl. has been considered principally as a *literary* language. It must be emphasized that it was also the language of learning, equivalent to Latin in the West, in so far as secular learning existed. The foundation for various technical vocabularies outside strictly ecclesiastical matters may be said to have been laid in the two *Anthologies* of 1073 and 1076 compiled for Svjatosláv (texts nos. 6 and 7), which contain excerpts from Greek writings not only of devotional and moral content but also of historical and 'scientific' interest. There is, for example, an article on mathematics (о количествѣ и о мѣремыихъ, 1073) providing some common terms already calqued by OCS on Greek, e.g. единьница (now единíца) 'unit'. Arithmetical computations of some complexity were, of course, required for the Church calendar, particularly to determine the date of Easter. The earliest surviving text dealing with such matters is Учение имже вѣдати человѣку числа всѣхъ лѣтъ by a Nóvgorod deacon Kirik (b. 1110). Calendrical terms have remained largely ChSl., e.g. the days of the week втóрник (3.83), средá, пя́тница.

Learning became more miscellaneous in the Muscovite period but scarcely more systematic. The Orthodox Church has been stigmatized as 'anti-intellectual' and there is some truth in this in comparison with W. Europe.[57] At any rate there was little enthusiasm for and originality in learned pursuits. Words were borrowed but little vocabulary was newly created in these fields. Philosophical and ethical vocabulary was wholly ChSl. Some interest, practical rather than theoretical, is shown in astronomy, geometry (surveying—книга большому чертежу, 1627), grammar and rhetoric, and medicine (especially in the form of herbals). In the first science квадрáт, эклíптика, and горизóнт(-áльный) appear fairly early. No mathematical textbook or primer, however, is known to antedate the 17th c.

[57] Astrology, for example, came under the ban of the Church (Стоглáв, 1551) and was never developed very far.

26 The famous Latin Grammar of Donatus was translated early in the 16th c. Here we find граматикия (later reformed) and a ChSl. terminology, still largely in use, calqued on the Latin terms which had themselves been calqued on the Greek: имя 'noun' (*nomen*); глагол 'verb' (*verbum* = ῥῆμα); падение (now падéж) 'case'; род 'gender'; уклонение (now склонéние) 'declension'; лицо 'person'; положительный 'positive', etc. The names of the cases are of the same vintage: именительный 'nominative'; звательный 'vocative'; винительный 'accusative'; родительный 'genitive'; дательный 'dative' (the Latin *ablative* was not needed and Slav instr. and loc. had no parallels; see 4.83 *ad fin.*).

27 Herbals (трáвник or лечéбник) were translated from the 15th c. from both Latin and German, and in the 17th c. from Polish.[58] Some Greek terms came through (from Galen) but the majority were now new words of W. European origin, e.g. гвоздúка 'clove, carnation'; миндáль (1534) 'almond' (? < Pol. *migdał*; but мигдаль is found much earlier, presumably direct from Greek); пастер-нáк 'parsnip' (*Pastinaca*); петрýшка 'parsley'; потáш 'potash'; селúтра 'saltpetre' (< *sal nitrum*); сулемá 'corrosive sublimate'; фиáлка 'violet'; шалфéй 'sage' (*Salvia*); шафрáн (1489) 'saffron'. Medicine also required дóктор (earliest form дохтур), in use at latest by the early 16th c.,[59] аптéка and аптéкарь (Polish loans replacing earlier Gk. апотека), and анатóмия (1698; probably earlier). Пульс (1516) is also an early loan.

28 Western vocabulary of the fine arts infiltrated at least from the time when Italian architects worked on the Kremlin in the last quarter of the 15th c. The Western архитектор (1627) tends to replace архитектон (from Greek) and the old OCS word зóдчий. Мáстер now means 'master-craftsman', which from the 16th c. might apply to armourers, gunsmiths, printers, and others.[60] Бумáга 'paper', known from 1414, came with the thing itself from Italy, perhaps via the Black Sea trade (§24 above *ad fin.*).

---

[58] H. Leeming (*SR*, Dec. 1963) has drawn attention to the Книга лекарская травник здешних и тамошних зелей польского языка, translated in the 17th c. He reckons that there were at least 1,000 medical and botanical words and the like taken into Russian by the end of the 17th c. from such works, of which a considerable proportion are still in use.

[59] Foreign doctors practised in Russia from this time. Thomas Korver, a Dutchman, was resident apothecary in Moscow in 1567, and an Englishman, Frencham or Frensham, *c.*1600. Mark Ridley was court physician in 1594–9.

[60] The first clock was installed in the Kremlin in 1404. Printing was started by Ivan IV in the 1550s but soon lapsed, to be revived more than fifty years later.

Several hundred foreign words of which there is no earlier record figure in the Русская торговая книга, compiled from the 1570s. Presumably not all were recent borrowings but the whole illustrates the constant widening of special vocabularies by loan-words. The Вести-Куранты (digests of current foreign news) prepared for Alekséj Mikhájlovich also contain many new borrowings. The stream was further swollen by the great increase in translation in the 16th–17th c. The often inexpert translators were officials of the Посóльский прикáз (office of foreign affairs, formally established in 1549) and perhaps other government offices. The majority do not seem to have been native Russians, at best natives of White Russia, more often Poles or Germans whose official task was to translate diplomatic correspondence in Latin,[61] German, and Polish. It is not always possible to determine the precise route of entry of a loan-word. The majority probably came via White Russia where the West Russian chancellery language had been long established (7.23). Relatively few words reveal a specifically Ukrainian form: the educated class in the Ukraine was either Polish or increasingly Polonized from 1569 (Union of Lublin).[62]

Polish

29 Polish loan-words arrived throughout the Muscovite centuries, two of the earliest being пýшка 'cannon'[63] and бунт (1400) 'revolt' (from German). But the main flood comes in the 17th c. after the Time of Troubles (1604–18), with the translation both of secular tales and of substantial learned and other texts such as the Велúкое Зерцáло (*c.*1677), a collection of edifying tales useful for sermon material—from the *Wielkie Zwierciadło Przykładów*, itself a translation of the *Speculum magnum exemplorum*.

Moreover, the lands lost to Russia from the 13th c. returned to Russian rule at various dates in the 17th c. and with them some elements of their Polonized vocabulary. Some 850 words of Polish provenance have been listed for this century. Some were naturally ephemeral, as будовáть 'build', влáсный 'own', and шкóда 'loss'.

---

[61] To Latin diplomatic correspondence is due the change from Русь to Рýсия (16th c.) on the general model of countries in -*ia*. It survives in Белорýссия but was superseded by the equally learned Россúя of Greek form (also 16th c.).

[62] A case in point is Латы́нь with no palatalization after *t* (Table XX (1)); but the adj. латúнский was maintained.

[63] Artillery appeared in Russia at the end of the 14th c. There was a пушечная изба (artillery department) at Moscow from *c.*1475.

A high proportion was already 'international', already borrowed
by Polish from German, Latin, or French. An obvious component is
military: атáка and атаковáть; вáхта 'watch'; вербовáть 'recruit';
карабúн 'carbine'; кýрок 'hammer (of a gun)'; мушкéт 'musket';
охрáна 'bodyguard' (Pol. *ochrona*, adapted to хранить); пóрох
'gunpowder' (a new sense modelled on Pol. *proch*; the native term
had been зелье); пýля 'ball' (1705 in this form; apparently a back-
formation from пýлька < Pol. *kulka*); рéкрут 'recruit'; рóта
'platoon'; сбрýя 'harness' (Pol. *zbroja*); солдáт; and the ranks
капитáн, полкóвник, сержáнт, etc. Many of these are used in the
translated Учение и хитрость ратного строения (1647), which,
however, still used the obsolescent рать 'army' rather than áрмия.
Командировáть is found as early as 1600, комáнда about a century
later.

But Polish loans cover a wider field than any previous imported
vocabulary, in particular new aspects of Western social and intellectual life. They include adjectives and verbs, abstract nouns as well
as concrete. Of particular note is свéтский 'social' (purely secular;
cf. 19th c. вы́сший свет), recorded in this sense in 1616 (Pol.
świecki). The following examples are broken down into rough
categories; some international words may be direct from Latin
rather than Polish, but less probably direct from German or French.
Many dates of introduction are very uncertain.

30   1. Politics and administration: áгéнт, áдрес, акт, áрéст, губéр-
ния and губернáтор, декрéт (1635), депутáт (1618), докумéнт,
импéрия and импeрáтор, канцелярия (1633), комúссия,
компáния, нáция, пáшпóрт (later пáспорт), пóдданство 'citizen-
ship' (пóддан(н)ый is earlier), полúтика, полúция, пóчта (1669)
(2.28), провúнция, ревизóр, револю́ция, реглáмент, секретáрь,
сенáтор, тúтул, трактáт 'treaty', штраф 'fine'.

    2. Concrete nouns: бáшня 'tower' (adaptation of *baszta*),
буты́лка (1694), ды́шло 'shaft',[64] зáмок 'castle' (*zamek*), карéта
and коля́ска 'carriage', крахмáл 'starch', кухáрка and кýхня
(native повáриха and повáрня, the latter still in Ludolf 1696),
лáмпа (but not лампáда, an ecclesiastical word from Greek),
линéйка 'ruler', машúна, монéта 'coin', скарб 'possessions',
тарéлка 'plate' (earlier тарѣль (1509) < *talerz*), трактúр 'inn',
фонтáн, шáпка 'cap' and шля́па 'hat' (doubtful; шáпка is recorded

[64] Ger. *Deichsel*; of paired shafts on either side of the draught-animal; the native
central shaft is оглóбля.

in 1327 and the Pol. form is *czapka*; шляпа is of German provenance but not current in Polish).

3. Abstract nouns: век 'century' (new sense; ChSl. вѣкъ = 'age, eternity'), идéя, интерéс, манéра, матéрия, мéтод(а), натýра, отвáга 'valour' (*odwaga*), пóвод 'cause' (other native senses), принцип (perhaps from German), причина 'reason' (причинить is older), секрéт, справедливость 'fairness', фигýра, фóрма, харáктер, цель 'aim' (Pol. *cel* < Ger. *Ziel*).

4. Verbs: достáть 'obtain'; поздрáвить 'congratulate' (almost certainly < Pol. *pozdrowić*, adapted to ChSl. здрáвие/здрáвствовать); публиковáть; рисовáть; дозвóлить and позвóлить 'permit' (cpds. of -волить incorporating Pol. prefix z-); стóить + acc. 'cost' (Polish stress).[65] Дозвóлить and дозволéние are common in the West Russian chancellery language.

5. Adjectives: вáжный 'important' (*ważny* < Ger. *Wage*), досконáльный 'thorough' (*doskonały*), зáйдлый 'inveterate', непристóйный 'indecent' (not directly related to a Russian verb), пóдлый 'base, common', публичный, скрóмный 'modest' (R. скорóм(ный) is not connected), специáльный, стрóгий 'strict' (*srogi*), фальшивый, учтивый 'polite' (*uczciwy*).

6. Professions, trades (almost all of German origin): áвтор (rec. 1611 but exceptional in the 17th c. in the literary sense), инженéр, кустáрь 'handicraftsman' (doubtful; the source is Ger. *Kunst(en)er*), лéкарь 'doctor', слéсарь 'locksmith', столя́р[66] 'joiner' (*stolarz*), фáктор 'agent'. Here too ры́нок 'market' (*rynek*) and я́рмарка 'fair'. Шáхта 'mine, pit' appears in the 16th c. (the Germans were the great mining experts throughout the Middle Ages).

7. Social: вéнзель 'monogram' (Pol. *węzeł* = ýзел), герб (1644) 'coat of arms, crest' (Pol. *herb* < Ger. *Erbe*), дáма 'lady', кавалéр 'gentleman', кáрты pl. 'playing-cards' (16th c.), коллéга 'colleague' (Polish type of masc. in -*a*; 3.2 (v)), конвéрт 'envelope' (doubtful; Fr. *couvert*—the -н- is unexplained), мéбель 'furniture', мещанин 'bourgeois' (Pol. *mieszczanin* < *miasto* 'town', the WSl. autonomous city of burghers; Pol. *gród* = гóрод only means 'fortress, castle'), музы́ка/музи́ка (so in 16th–17th c., finally—*c*.1800?—мýзыка),[67] обывáтель 'inhabitant', осóба 'per-

---

[65] Cf. earlier native *pf* стать: а стал ми во сто рублев (Af. Nik.).

[66] -ар/-яр points to Ukr. or WhR. transmission with depalatalized *r* (Table XX (12)).

[67] The earlier form was мусикия (< Greek).

sonage', поеди́нок 'duel' (*pojedynek*), ры́царь 'knight', табаке́рка 'snuff-box', та́нец '(Western) dance' (native folk-dance is пля́ска), фами́лия 'surname'. Here too духове́нство 'clergy' (as a social category) < Ger. *Geistlichkeit* via Polish.

8. Arts and learning: архитекту́ра, библиоте́ка (already probably existed in a Greek form), календа́рь, коме́дия (траге́дия seems to be direct from Latin), меха́ника, пункт (1698) (various senses), рели́гия, рису́нок 'drawing' (*rysunek*), табли́ца (math.) 'table', ци́фра 'figure' (= *cypher*), шко́ла 'school' (recorded as early as 1388 in a special sense, but only now does it supersede учи́лище).

9. Miscellaneous: Ве́нгрия 'Hungary' shows the Pol. nasal of *Węgier, Węgrzy* (early ESl. Угре); кро́лик 'rabbit';[68] the Polish verse-form *wierszy* was imitated in the later 17th c. in Russia (7.30 (*b*)) as ви́рши; шля́хта 'gentry' < *szlachta* (= Ger. *Geschlecht*; MHG *slahte*) lasted into the 18th c. especially in the title of the prestigious St Petersburg school for young gentlemen offering a complete Western education, the Сухопу́тный шляхе́тный ко́рпус (opened 1732).

31   The above examples make clear that Polish popularized the creation of verbs in -овать,[69] abstracts in -ость (§18 above), and abstract nouns of Latin type in -ия and -ция (па́ртия, на́ция, конститу́ция); the latter violated in their spelling if not in their pronunciation the by then depalatalized quality of Russian ц (2.38). Multiplication soon followed the use of the simple word, e.g. на́ция > национа́льный > национа́льность. For other formal and syntactical Polish influences see: е́сли (4.25–6); vocative (3.30); impersonal p.p.p. (3.130).

In the last years of Peter the Great's reign we find Pososhkóv in his tract Кни́га о ску́дости и о бога́тстве using a new Western vocabulary with a strong Polish component side by side with his traditional Russian legal and ChSl. literary vocabularies. Some of these Polonisms were already obsolescent. In addition to a number of military and administrative terms already listed above he uses: банке́т (perhaps < German or French); доспыта́цыя

---

[68] Pol. *królik* < Cz. *králík*, dim. of *král* 'king', calqued on MHG *küniklîn* < Lat. *cunīculus* ('coney'). The rabbit is a native of SW Europe and was hardly known in Russia before 1700.
[69] The Polish loans were either in -овать or -изовать; -ировать and -изировать come from Ger. *-ieren* and are mainly 19th c. creations.

= диспутáция (with adaptation to до- and пытáть); жáдный (Pol. *żaden* = Ger. *kein*: без жадныи причины); инстрýкция; интерéс; кóмпас (instrument; perhaps < German); манéр (русским манером, а не немецким; манéра is more obviously of Polish provenance); мизúрный 'wretched' (Pol. *mizerny*); нáгло in the Polish sense of *nagły* ('sudden'); натурáльный; ористокрáт (*sic*; the first known example of аристокрáт); персóна (сúльные or высóкие персóны); пошпорт (*sic*; already an *internal* pass without reference to its literal sense); прикро (Pol. *przykro* = неприятно); прóба; турбовáть 'harass' (and турбáцыя); фальш; шкóда 'damage'.

Peter the Great

32   Peter the Great's accession to power (1689) marks no more than an acceleration of the Western current which had long been flowing steadily. As can be seen from Polish loan-words listed above Russian society was poised for the kind of change which could not be brought about by the more or less casual diplomatic and commercial contacts with the outside world which had prevailed in the century 1550–1650.[70]

Linguistically more influential were the resident foreigners. The Foreign Concession (Немéцкая слободá) in Moscow was formally organized from 1652. It was here that the young Peter made friends with citizens of the Protestant countries, Dutch or German, and came to value their technical knowledge. Though a knowledge of Latin and Polish had become quite usual accomplishments in court circles from the reign of Alekséj Mikhájlovich[71] scarcely anyone as yet learned German or any other W. European language. From the time of Peter's first grand tour of Western Europe (1697–8) a broad programme of deliberate Westernization is inaugurated. Western knowledge must be acquired and exploited, Western social conventions imposed. Peter sent young Russians abroad to be trained in various useful arts (they did not always return). He recast the administration of Russia on Swedish and other European

---

[70] Thus, as far as England was concerned, the Muscovy Company of London was launched in 1553; Mark Ridley practised medicine at the Russian court 1594–9 (§27 above); Richard James was chaplain to a diplomatic mission negotiating in Moscow 1618–20. Both these men gathered valuable material on coll. Russian.

[71] Simeon Pólotsky taught them to his son Fëdor; he was also official instructor in Latin to the Foreign Office clerks (1664 onwards).

models: the necessary terminology was largely German, e.g. бурми́стр, магистра́т, сена́т, ра́туша (*Rathaus*), фиска́л. He commissioned translations of various technical manuals concerned directly or indirectly with the modernization of the armed forces—navigation, fortification, and the requisite applied mathematics. As an influential handbook we may take Magnitsky's Арифметика (1703) in which сумма and алгебра appear for the first time. Its Western origins are evident in the definition of arithmetic according to the terms of the *Trivium* and *Quadrivium*—пятая мудрость в семи великих мудростях.[72] The language is still ChSl. The translations ordered by Peter are naturally often awkward and tentative, not to say unintelligible, their authors having to create new terminologies for things which they sometimes only half understood themselves. Nevertheless such textbooks were necessarily used in his schools for mathematics and navigation in St Petersburg (1702) and the engineering and artillery schools opened in Moscow (1711–12). Aware of these difficulties Peter attempted to inculcate simplicity and intelligibility; the principle was, in his words, 'сенс [*sic!*] выразумев, на своем языке так писать, как внятнее может быть'. His ambassadors abroad who larded their dispatches with foreign words were rebuked. Even Prokopóvich, his ecclesiastical right-hand man, took this to heart and in his Первое учение отроком explained the Ten Commandments, Lord's Prayer, and Creed in more or less simple language. He voices the same strictures on the use of ChSl. for new secular purposes as Trediakóvsky was to make (7.42): с трудностью разумеется от человек и обученных, а простым невежам отнюдь недостизаемый есть.

Peter's ends were wholly practical and immediate. *Belles-lettres* did not come within his purview, nor under his régime did anyone have time for them; the language of literature stands still. Even the translation of Pufendorf which he commissioned (*De officio hominis et civis juxta legem naturalem*; not published till 1726) had a practical rather than intellectual purpose. But life was, superficially, secularized and 'modernized': new clothes (ту́фля or

---

[72] It should be further noted that Russia had used exclusively the Byzantine numerical system (1.39 ff.)—useless, like the Roman, for computation, which was done on the abacus (счёты). The Arabic numerals appear in the early 17th c. and tables of conversion are given in several primers and in the Учение и хитрость ратного строения (1647); they appear for the first time on coins in 1654. They were only officially adopted under Peter. The sign and name for 'zero' was thus new: ноль (or нуль).

ту́фель 'slipper'), new social habits (асамбле́я), new reckoning of time and calendar;[73] above all an enormous expansion of printing in the new secular alphabet (гражда́нский шрифт, 1708–10) which helps quickly to stabilize orthography. Зако́н is now applied to civil (human) law whereas it had previously been exclusively divine (in Russian schools down to 1917 Зако́н Бо́жий = 'divinity, scripture'). The formulae of politeness are partly renewed, as always with considerable social change. In 1696 Ludolf recorded the Muscovite set: чело́м бью (general formula of respect), пожа́луй 'please', спаси́бо 'thank you', здра́вствуй 'how do you do?', как тебя́ Бог милу́ет? 'how are you?', отпо́тчивай здоро́в 'good-night', прости́ 'goodbye'.[74]

33   We may observe the process of acclimatization of new words taking place under Peter's personal direction in a compilation (never published) Лексикон вокабулам новым по алфавиту—whose title cannot be said to accord with Peter's principles since а́збука was long established and сло́во simpler than the otiose вокабула. Peter made corrections to inadequate definitions in his own hand (italicized below):

бомба:[75] чиненое ядро великое *которыя мечют із мортироѳ*
вексель:[76] обмѣна денег *чрез писма*
генерал отютант [= адъютант]: есть менше генерала маеора *которой указы розносит словесныя от генерала командуещего* [*sic*].

A considerable proportion of the items in this dictionary has not stood the test of time, or at least not in the form first adopted.

New words pullulate in all Peter's larger administrative documents (often without explanation), e.g. the Генера́льный Регла́-

---

[73] The Western secular calendar came into force from 1 Jan. 1700 (NS 11 Jan.), displacing the Byzantine reckoning from the Creation with New Year on 1 Sept. The terms мину́та and секу́нда had long been known but only now entered everyday usage.

[74] Пожа́луй, now only an adverb ('perhaps') has been replaced by пожа́луйста [paža̍lstə]. The polite 2 pl. вы comes into general use in the early 18th c. from French (similarly, only too completely, in English from the Restoration); hence new, except at the most intimate level, здра́вствуйте, прости́те/проща́йте.

[75] Further military words of the time: патро́н (1699) 'cartridge'; ла́герь 'camp'; ло́зунг (1703) 'password'; мунди́р 'uniform' (ult. < Fr. *monture*); ранг 'rank'; штык 'bayonet' (< Pol. *sztych* < Ger.). The majority are now direct from German.

[76] Further economic words of the time: банк (1707), би́ржа (1705) '(stock) exchange' (no proper establishment of the institution before 1735); ка́сса; капита́л (1709); креди́т (1703); фа́брика (1705) (< Polish).

мент and Уста́в морско́й (1720, 1724), in which the following, among others, may have appeared in print for the first time: баллотирова́ть, биле́т, букси́рова́ть 'take in tow', журна́л, курс, лави́ровать 'tack', материа́л (матерья́л), по́мпа, профе́ссор, проце́нт, ра́диус, футля́р (< Ger. *Futteral*).

This huge intake of technical and other Western vocabulary must not be thought of as a written transmission only; much of it was oral through the experts recruited by Peter abroad and now working in Russian schools, shipyards, arsenals, etc.

34　As can be seen, Peter's reign is a Germanic-Protestant period linguistically. The main contributor was German. Swedish made hardly any contribution; Dutch and English dominated naval terminology but were otherwise rare. The above-deck terms of sailing vessels (sails, rigging, etc.) are said to be mainly taken from Dutch, as are also трюм 'hold' (Du. *in 't ruim*); ко́йка 'bunk, hammock'; га́вань (1697) 'port'; верфь (2.35) 'wharf, dockyard'; буй 'buoy'; матро́с (1694) 'sailor'; and дюйм 'inch' (= *thumb*).[77] The hull and interior use more terms of English origin; to these only very few can be added, viz. порт (1702) (probably English rather than German); ми́чман (1710) (< *midshipman*); and спирт 'alcohol, spirit' (a first or very early example in Pososhkо́v, *c*.1724). The new vocabulary of Peter's new fleet is illustrated by the Разговор адмирала с капитаном о команде (1724): the author, Naval Capt. K. N. Zо́tov, had been trained in England (1707–12).

German (and Latin) thenceforward never lost importance in the scientific and technical fields, whether on paper or through the experts who continued to be employed in Russia.[78] German at Court lasted well into the 1730s under Anne of Courland and her German entourage. But in that decade French asserts its primacy as the international language of diplomacy and culture, as happened to a greater or lesser degree in most W. European countries also. French became the mentor of an entirely renovated Russian literature and intellectual life.

---

[77] Dutch also are a number of trade-words, etc. of the time: абрико́с 'apricot'; апельси́н 'orange'; брю́ки 'breeches'; конто́ра 'office'; но́мер (ну́мер); and та́бель. Dutch ships had had the lion's share in the carrying trade to Russian Baltic outlets since the end of the 16th c.

[78] e.g. the Aberdonian Farquharson who was instructor at the Mathematical School in St Petersburg and prepared an edition of Euclid for translation into Russian (publ. 1739).

35   *The Early Eighteenth Century*

The development of scientific and technical vocabulary need not be followed further. It must suffice to note that Peter's founding of the Academy of Sciences in St Petersburg (Акадéмия наýк), with three sections Mathematics, Natural Science, and Humanities, paved the way for Russian contributions to international scholarship. It was only able to open its doors shortly after his death. Brilliant men were soon recruited, notably mathematicians such as L. Euler (in Russia 1727–41 and again later) and the Swiss brothers Bernouilli. From 1728 the Academy regularly issued its *Transactions*—in Latin, sometimes with summaries in Russian. We do not look to such eminent foreigners for much contribution to Russian vocabulary; Lomonósov was the first to write scientific papers in Russian a generation later (7.50). But printing and translating were important activities of the Academy and it was in the capacity of translator that one of its first Russian members— Trediakóvsky—achieved some renown. The value of the constant work of translation throughout the 18th c., full of experiments in acclimatizing or inventing words, cannot be gainsaid, but precise results from a comprehensive study are still wanting. Innovations in a learned work read by few might, however, become familiar to a wider readership through the literary periodicals of the 1740s onwards. Much of this vocabulary caused no difficulty, settling down as Russian adaptations of international Latin, sometimes direct but largely via already extant German or French versions. Calques also played some part but the use of only native material by calque was never elevated to a matter of principle and prestige.[79] Lomonósov's practice in this respect may be considered typical and judicious. Having Latin, German, and ChSl. equally at his command, he used on the one hand international автóграф (via Polish?), атмосфéра (not an exact synonym of вóздух), диáметр (already recorded 1720) rather than native поперéчник (used by Pososhkóv and still possible), горизóнт rather than небосклóн (which is literary rather than scientific); on the other hand the calques явлéние 'phenomenon' and предмéт = *objectum* and *subjectum* (Pol. *przedmiot* may have played a part).

[79] In his Арифметика Magnítsky gave the equivalents адитсие = считание (modern сложéние); сюстряксие = вынимание (mod. вычитáние); мюлтипли- касие = (у)множéние; дивизие = деловая/росчетная (mod. делéние), without specifically recommending his foreign transliterated terms. Native calques have here been preferred, with some modernization.

An important principle is to be seen here: in calquing, the word is likely to be *in ChSl. form*, if there is a choice, since ChSl. was, so to speak, the classical learned language of Russia corresponding to Latin, and still felt as such. This convention still largely obtains down to the present day, e.g. млекопита́ющие 'mammals' (late 18th c.); охлади́тель 'refrigerator' (19th c.); изда́ние 'edition', изда́тель 'publisher', and изда́тельство (18th c.) (calques of Latin or German).

36 *The Language of the Arts*[80]

With literature and the arts we turn away from Latin and German towards French and Italian. In the 16th–18th c. Italian was the main source of international terms in music, painting, and architecture. Italy and its language have never played an important part in Russian life; the Italian Renaissance is scarcely perceptible in its intellectual history. Only in the 17th c. did a trickle of Italian words begin to enter the language. Kurákin, Peter's ambassador to Venice, made газе́та familiar (1708);[81] карти́на 'picture' is of much the same date and perhaps the same provenance.

From the 1730s Italian theatre troupes came to Russia and Italian opera was first staged at Court in 1731.[82] All the imperial Directors of Music from that time were Italians. Both Kantemír and Trediakóvsky were competent in the language; it was one of the latter's tasks to provide Russian versions of the opera libretti. It can be assumed therefore that he acclimatized а́рия and other musical terms. The founding of the Academy of Arts (Акаде́мия худо́жеств) in 1757, with wholly foreign staff, ensured the primacy of Italian, side by side with French, in the world of the arts. The vocabularies are mixed: there are some French musical terms such as акко́рд 'chord'[83] and бемо́ль 'flat'; конце́рт 'concert(o)'[84] would seem to be from German, though first reaching print in Trediakóvsky. Nor were all older native words rejected: вая́тель 'sculptor'

---

[80] The foreign component in the establishment of all types of W. European artistic activity is attractively set forth in Ch. Marsden, *Palmyra of the North* (London, 1942).

[81] Venetian dial. *gazeta* = standard It. *gazzetta* (a small coin).

[82] The word о́пера is first casually used in 1697 but Staehlin finds it necessary to explain this strange new form of art in 1732 when opera and ballet became an established feature of the Court: Историческое описание театрального действия, которое называется *опера* (Спб-ские ведомости).

[83] This had appeared earlier in other than a musical sense.

[84] See n. 83.

has hardly survived in competition with скýльптор, скульптýра but худóжник 'artist' (§5 above) and живопи́сец 'painter' (ChSl. calque of Gk. ζωγράφος) are still very much alive.

37   In the spoken theatre Italian had little to offer. French was all-important, with a small contribution from German. French are актёр, актри́са, аплоди́ровать, грим(ирова́ть) 'make-up', роль—all current by the 1760s at latest; декора́ция 'set, scenery'; суфлёр 'prompter'; ре́плика 'cue'; pl. кули́сы 'wings'; and many others soon follow. A German source is evident for сце́на (at least in spelling),[85] генера́льная репети́ция 'dress rehearsal', теа́тр (already used in the time of Peter), and the later гастроли́ровать 'go on tour'. Here too a few native terms survived: де́йствие 'act' and явле́ние 'scene' have come down from the school dramas written in ChSl. in the 17th c. (7.30 (*a*)).

38 *The French Language*

French achieved undisputed pre-eminence in literature and the intellectual field (thought, criticism, history) from the accession of Elizabeth (1740). Everything French was worthy of imitation. This movement of taste was begun in the 1730s by Kantemír and Trediakóvsky, who had necessarily to be advocates both of the French literary genres new to Russia and of the indispensable classical background of French literature and literary theory—and this despite their totally different origins, status and education (7.41–2). Both faced—with indifferent success—the daunting task of combining living Russian, the literary and learned vocabulary of ChSl., and the essence of the European literary manner to form a new amalgam, to be the vehicle of a new Russian secular culture.

Kantemír found it expedient to ease the introduction of classical allusions and new words by providing explanatory notes to both his poems and translations (notably to that of Fontenelle's *De la pluralité des mondes*, publ. 1740):

  . . . *статуями, или столбами и другими зданиями мраморными;*
метафизика . . . которая рассуждает о сущем вообще и о свойствах
  души и духов;

---

[85] It is, of course, not unusual for a word to be borrowed from several sources, more or less contemporaneously, in several slightly different forms. In this case neither a *шена < Ital. *scena* nor a *сена < Fr. *scène* is recorded. Earlier, in the 17th c. 'school dramas', we sometimes find сень (from Latin?) as an alternative to native явление.

физика, или естествословие,[86] испытает состав мира;
слово руда значит *металл.*

Among new words in his writings are анатомист, логика, and
перук (later парик, < Fr. *perruque,* whence also Eng. *periwig,*
later *wig*). Stray Polonisms, at the end of their popularity, are still
present, e.g. наприклад = например (Pol. *na przykład*). As a
satirist he drew also on colloquialisms which the mature Neoclassi-
cal style was to eschew, e.g. in *Satire I* квас, с ума сошёл, чрезчур
(for pure R. чересчур), плюнь ему в рожу, врёт околесну,
докука, оплошный, пялить глаза, аза в глаза не знает. Creations
of his own may be понятие and наблюдение.

The Period 1730–60

39   Kantemír's contribution to the development of the language was
no doubt slight; his output was small and not printed till after
his early death (1744). Trediakóvsky (1703–69: 7.42 ff.), harshly
criticized, even mocked, by his contemporaries and subsequently,
yet left more mark on the new literary language than he is usually
given credit for. The same process of acclimatization is going
forward, especially in literary terminology: *версификация,* т. е.
способ сложения стихов.

His theoretical tract Новый и краткий способ к сложению
российских стихов (1735) is particularly rich in such neologisms:
поэт, поэзия, поэма (already in the restricted sense of a *narrative*
poem), просодия, тонический, рифма 'rhyme' (in his spelling
ріѳма), стиль.[87] To him also is due the excellent native equivalent
перенос for 'enjambment'. The tract was complemented by a verse
translation of Boileau's *Art poétique*—the password, as it were, to
the new literature.

His style, however, remains a jumble, both a lexical jumble and
a syntactical jumble. Cheek by jowl with Russian colloquialisms
such as перебывать 'travel about', забияка, час от часу, очюнь
(later очень, coming up in the 17th c. but still avoided by the
Classicists of the 18th c.), and нагохонек we find such heavy
Slavonicisms as воспоминовение, потщуся, отнележе. And there
is a perceptible aroma of officialese too (буде 'if', оный).

---

[86] A 'neo-Slavonicism' modelled on богословие 'theology'; now replaced by
естествознание or естествоведение.

[87] The first, French, borrowing; the German version штиль was used by Lomonósov but victory in the end fell to стиль.

40   Perhaps the most lasting achievement of Trediakóvsky's literary labours was not so much the invention of new words as the grafting of new European senses onto existing words. Thus in the 1730s вкус acquired at the hands of Kantemír and Trediakóvsky the aesthetic application of Fr. (*bon*) *goût*, just as Eng. *taste* had at the strongly Gallicized court of Charles II. The following appear to be due to Trediakóvsky: черта́ 'mark', now *trait* (*de visage*); нату́ра 'character', now (inanimate) 'Nature' (native приро́да has also maintained itself); персо́на 'personage' (§31 above), now *une personne* (*quelconque*); красота́ sg., now new pl. красо́ты = *les beautés*; сла́дкий 'sweet' (taste), now *doux* (of character). There are also many phraseological calques such as о́бщее ме́сто *lieu commun*; одни́м сло́вом *en un mot*; я ему́ обя́зан *je lui suis obligé*; по моему́ мне́нию *à mon avis*; со вре́менем *avec le temps*; and word calques such as находи́ться *se trouver* (мы нашли́сь бли́зко одного́ о́строва); беспоко́йство *inquiétude*; (время)препровожде́ние *passe-temps*; председа́тельствовать *présider*; скло́нность *penchant, inclination*; смягчи́ть *attendrir*; чувстви́тельный *sensible*; любо́вник *amant*; and other 'galant' terms; при-/от-су́тствовать *être présent/absent*; впечатле́ние *impression*. He also created many new abstract derivatives in -ость. Unsuccessful were the phraseological calques with име́ть *avoir* and чини́ть *faire* (causative), though име́ть ме́сто *avoir lieu* and име́ть честь *avoir l'honneur* persisted into the 19th c.; 'verbs of all work' are generally repugnant to Slav languages. The 'galant' words remained the darlings of the modish writers and only died with the death of sentimentalism (if it has ever died).

Starting in the enthusiasm of youth as a champion of the vernacular, Trediakóvsky ended as a defender of a highly Slavonicized literary language, at least in poetry, as exemplified in his Homeresque adaptation of Fénelon's *Télémaque* as Тилемахи́да (1766). It is described on the title-page as съ францу́зскія нестихосло́вныя рѣчи—an oblique way of indicating the indispensable term про́за which was already well established by 1762. The work abounds in lexical experiments of all kinds—archaic ChSl., Russian colloquialisms, Gallicisms, Polonisms—but it went virtually unread and was doubtfully the source of any useful neologisms.

41   Lomonósov (1711–65; 7.45 and 50), the great polymath of the mid 18th c., contributed to many fields of vocabulary, no doubt more to scientific than to literary, which went with his German and Latin rather than French formation. He introduced further international words such as баро́метр, термо́метр, and электри́чество, and invented calques such as преломле́ние 'refraction'. His grammatical terminology in his normative and influential Росси́йская Грамма́тика (1755) shows no great change from that of Smotrítsky (Грамматики словенския правильное синтагма, 1619; repr. Moscow, 1648), who shows no radical change from the Latin calques of Donatus (§26 above): настоя́щее 'present'; бу́дущее (also гряду́щсе) 'future'; повели́тельный 'imperative'; указа́тельный 'indicative'; страда́тельный 'passive' are still current today.[88] Lomonósov, however, prefers инфинити́в to such earlier attempts as неукончальный чин (Smotrítsky); and one notes particularly the absence of any term for verbal aspect (4.83 ff.)—вид being the satisfactory later choice.

Lomonósov was decisive where Trediakóẃsky vacillated. In О по́льзе книг церко́вных в росси́йском языке́ (1757) and other essays he clearly perceives and sets forth the desirable role of ChSl. in the new literary language in process of formation. The authority of Smotrítsky's *Grammar*, still widely assumed to be relevant to Russian, had to be removed. Lomonósov himself used the *Grammaire de Port-Royal* (1660) as a model of modern linguistic analysis. He never doubted that the basis, in virtually all matters of grammar (morphology), must be *contemporary spoken Russian*. ChSl. was indispensable as a reservoir of *vocabulary*, either existing or creatable; it could no longer be, on any terms, the basis of a *secular* literary language; indeed such a thing should never have been tried. Lomonósov's theory of vocabulary (the Three Styles) is quantitative, as befits a chemist and as arose from the facts of the situation. Future taste and practice had merely to draw the dividing lines at appropriate levels in the continuum of Russian vocabulary. It is refreshing also to find that he is clear that *usage*, not theory, is decisive in the long run: как во всей грамматике, так и в сем случае, одному употреблению повиноваться до́лжно (Полное собрание сочинений, vol. 7: Труды по филологии (Akad. Nauk, 1952), p. 84).

[88] Smotrítsky's 'eight parts of speech' (части слова) are: имя = *nomen*; мѣстоимение = *pronomen*; глагол = *verbum*; причастие = *participium*; нарѣчие = *adverbium*; предлог = *prepositio*; соуз (союз) = *conjunctio*; различие = *numerus*. Of these the *participle* and the *numeral* are no longer considered separate categories and the latter is now числи́тельное. The *adjective* (прилага́тельное) was considered by him, as still commonly, a subsection of the *noun* (*nomen adjectivum*).

42   The third member of the trio who were writing and polemicizing with one another in the formative period *c.*1740–65 was Sumarókov (1718–77; 7.46). Linguistically he was rather colourless and not very inventive but a few calques have been ascribed to him, e.g. переворо́т = *révolution*, предрассу́док = *préjugé*. Рассе́янный 'absent-minded' (if his) would appear to calque Ger. *zerstreut* rather than Fr. *distrait*. The highly successful (рас)тро́гать *toucher* and тро́гательный *touchant* are plausibly his contributions to the sentimental vocabulary. French phraseological calques are also fairly abundant.

43   To sum up the importance of these pioneers—the literary contribution of Kantemír was too slight and that of Trediakóvsky too contradictory and discredited to have much permanent effect on *usage*. In usage authority is all-important. This came in some measure from Sumarókov, who at least avoided all extremes, and principally from Lomonósov, limited in his literary scope but a model for the lesser lights as long as the 'high style' continued to retain any esteem. He was the one fully competent theoretician. He firmly relegated ChSl. to the role of *lexical resource*. The large number of Slavonicisms already in use, in some cases at the level of everyday speech, was of course now a permanent part of *Russian* vocabulary. Lomonósov certainly envisaged the further exploitation of this resource by the continued creation in literary and learned vocabulary of 'neo-Slavonicisms', as we have called them. From his time this became more and more rapid, just as 'Latin and Greek words' in Western scientific language, unknown either to Latin or Greek, continue to be formed in an unending stream down to the present day.

The Later Eighteenth Century

44   It would be unprofitable to pursue the intake of loan-words in the later 18th c. in detail; indeed no complete chronological investigation is yet available. Many neologisms at first ascribed to Karamzín, since they appear in his well-known works of the 1790s, have proved to have been in use at least a generation earlier. French continued to be the main source or model, but German increased towards the end of the century. This is a reflection of the fact that W. European literary movements and styles were by then reaching Russia with less and less time-lag.

English only appears as an influence in the background since most English literature still reached Russia via French translations (so Shakespeare, the influential journalism of Addison, etc., the early novelists, especially Sterne, and the Ossianic poems published by James Macpherson in the 1760s). There are few if any direct loans. It is impossible to decide, on present evidence, whether парк was taken direct from English, as Catherine the Great's enthusiasm for the new English landscape gardening and employment of the Scottish architect Cameron and others makes plausible, or from the French or German into which it had already been adopted. The Tsárskoe Seló gardens were remodelled as an English park in 1772.

A few more instances must suffice. French models are fairly clear for утончённый (*raffiné*) and развитие (*développement*) ascribed to Novikóv (1744–1818) and живописный (*pittoresque*), обстоятельство (*circonstance*), убийственный (*meurtrier*),[89] личность (*personnalité*), and неиссякáемый (*inépuisable*; неисчерпáемый is a more exact equivalent) ascribed to Karamzín (1766–1828). German models can be seen in образовáние 'education' (*Bildung*) (Novikóv) and самонадёжность, now самонадéянность (*Selbstvertrauen*) (Karamzín).

It goes without saying that the international suffixes -изм and -ист, and also Fr. *-age* (багáж, тирáж) and others, became prominent.

45 More important to the literary language in this period of intense activity were the two other sources of lexical increase. New derivatives, often 'neo-Slavonicisms', pullulate. The connection of the latter with ChSl. is, of course, merely formal (§35 above); they are Russian words from the moment of their creation. Novikóv introduced, for example, бýдущность 'future', изобретáтельность 'inventiveness', and непредвидимый 'unforeseeable'; Karamzín—промышленность 'industry', улучшéние 'improvement', влюблённость 'infatuation'. Secondly, words and idioms from the colloquial stratum which in the heyday of the 'high style' were rated as low and vulgar gain admittance to literature as taste and literary ideals and themes change.[90] *Pari passu* many

---

[89] The Slavonicism убийство had been current since the beginning of the literary tradition (native убóй now only 'slaughter' (of animals)).

[90] Karamzín could still object to пáрень 'lad' as irremediably vulgar in the context of his perhaps over-refined prose style. It is well known that the expansion of French literary vocabulary, especially poetic, which proscribed *vache* as too earthy and uncultured, did not really get under way till the time of Victor Hugo. Exactly the same objection was made to Pushkin's use of корóва in a poem.

Slavonicisms are abandoned or finally absorbed as *neutral* elements of the vocabulary. In other words the limits of vocabulary indicated in broad theoretical terms by Lomonósov were now subject to a practical working out. The changing limits can be followed up to a point in the dictionaries compiled in the later 18th–early 19th c., which understandably reflect a certain time-lag *vis-à-vis* actual usage. The Dictionary of the Russian Academy of 1789–94 may be said to reflect the outlook of Lomonósov's generation fairly accurately. By the time of its second edition (1806–22) at least 200 ChSl. words so marked in the first were felt to be more or less obsolete and conversely others (наедине́, е́ле, едва́, ра́зве) no longer merited that description: they had become part of the neutral literary vocabulary. As further examples of the changing balance may be instanced the following: Derzhávin was bold enough to use трущо́ба (in its original sense of 'thicket') but the earlier 19th c. still did not consider it a literary word; in the later 19th c. it reappears in prose with the new sense of 'slum'. Similarly захолу́стье 'remote place' from being a rare (dialect) word in the 18th c. had become a neutral literary word by the middle of the 19th c. Another aspect is the sorting out of near-synonyms: бы́стрый and ско́рый were not clearly delimited in the 18th c.; since then быстр- has become more specialized to rapid motion and скор- to relative time and motion (ско́ро 'soon', ско́рость 'speed'). The third 18th c. alternative бо́рзый disappeared except as a poetic word ('swift, fleet') and in the special term борза́я (a breed of dog).

46   The vernacular prose developed on the basis of Novikóv's journalism and the comedies and letters of Fonvízin and others achieved a consistent style at the hands of Karamzín (1790s) and finally, with further simplifications, in the tales of Pushkin. Colloquial говори́ть/сказа́ть have completely ousted ChSl. глаголати/рещи (он рек); only derivatives of the latter have remained in the literary vocabulary (изрече́ние, отре́чься, отрица́ть); де́лать prevails over both твори́ть (whose surviving derivatives are Slavonicisms with a religious background—творе́ц 'Creator', сотвори́ть 'create', тварь 'creature')[91] and the Muscovite (у)чини́ть (чини́ть now specialized as 'sharpen, mend'). These, and many similar cases, are enough to demonstrate that modern Russian prose, in other

---

[91] Тво́рческий 'creative' and тво́рчество *œuvre* have entered the vocabulary of literary criticism.

words the literary language, is not a Russianized ChSl. (as some have argued) but a vernacular much diversified with useful, indeed essential, ChSl. elements.

The same is not entirely true of poetry. It is possible here to speak of de-Slavonicization. Since there was no tradition of native lyric poetry it was natural that the 'high style' of Lomonósov's odes and the Slavonicized diction of the tragedies of Sumarókov and others set the tone for the bulk of the new poetry. 'Public' does not cede the primacy to 'personal' lyric poetry before the maturer works of Derzhávin. Here we find the first loosening-up of the poetic vocabulary—the use of 'low' words which would have been inconceivable a generation earlier. His poems of country life provide the best examples:

> Горшок горячих, добрых щей,
> Копчёный окорок под дымом;
> Обсаженный семьёй моей,
> Средь кóей сам я господином,[92]
> И тут-то вкусен мне обед!
>
> (Похвалá сéльской жúзни, 1798)

> Вдали тетеревéй глухое токованье
> (Евгéнию: жизнь Звáнская, 1807)

See also Приглашéние к обéду (1795).

Zhukóvsky and other poets of Alexander's reign continued the de-Slavonicization, much encouraged by their enthusiasm for German poetry.[93] The authority of a great poet—Pushkin—determined the balance of poetic vocabulary from the 1820s. The juvenilia apart, arbitrary Slavonicisms are virtually absent. Words of this stratum are either fully acclimatized elements of Russian vocabulary or used for special effect when the matter requires it (Прорóк; Монасты́рь на Казбéке;[94] parts of Мéдный всáдник), or (which is particularly telling) an object of gentle satire:

[92] A line out of style, including the very unusual pred. instr. in the present (4.52 (g)).

[93] This can be seen especially in Zhukóvsky's expert translations, e.g. of G. A. Bürger's *Lenore* (1773; tr. 1831). Contemporary English poetry has only a modest place (Moore, Byron). More important are his translations of Gray's *Elegy* (1750), both versions (1802, 1839) notably free from unnecessary Slavonicisms. But English *linguistic* influence is virtually nil.

[94] Прорóк: Перстáми лёгкими, как сон; Казбéк: Далёкий, вожделéнный брег! (брег = 'haven').

Мечты, мечты! где ваша сладость?
Где, вечная к ней рифма, младость?
(EO, vi. 44)

Colloquialisms and neologisms are introduced with the same tone:

Как говорится, машинально
(EO, iv. 17)

47 But poetry can be freer in its choices than prose. An element of the archaic is not necessarily an affectation. Older words, which in most cases had been common to Russian and ChSl., can remain as poetic variants. A case in point is various parts of the body: the colourless, everyday terms are not always the most suitable. Poetic language could still choose between вѣжда and вѣко 'eyelid', выя and шея 'neck', око/очи and глаз 'eye', ланита and щека 'cheek', лик and лицо 'face', перст and палец 'finger', уста pl. and рот (or губы) 'mouth, lips'.[95]

It should be noted, finally, that during this whole period of reassessment of Russian vocabulary writers (and lexicographers) proceeded by feel rather than exact knowledge. No distinction was made between real Slavonicisms, i.e. actual loan-words from ChSl. (e.g. вражда; an ESl. *ворожда is not attested, though ворог was present; see Appendix, no. 15), antiquated Russian words which coincided with ChSl. (e.g. сей, оный), and what are here termed 'neo-Slavonicisms'—the large and ever increasing number of Russian creations on ChSl. models, which had never been present in any form of ChSl. but arose from its processes of derivation and perpetuated some of its phonological peculiarities.

48 Standard Russian, therefore, from the time of its early 19th c. maturity, incorporated an enrichment of Slavonicisms, estimated by some at 10 per cent (a dubious figure, since too much depends on the criteria adopted) in four categories:

(i) ChSl. (usually OCS) words which have never had an ESl. equivalent;

(ii) ChSl. forms which have diverged in meaning from their ESl. equivalents and have given rise to the many mixed groups of derivatives in the Russian lexicon (see Appendix); страна, when

---

[95] Some derivatives of the older Russian terms remain in standard language, e.g. заочный; облик; напёрсток (2.45 (4)) 'thimble', перстень 'ring' and наперстянка 'foxglove'; наизусть. Cf. Eng. 'high-/lowbrow', 'browbeat' as against normal 'forehead'.

differentiated from сторонá, becomes a Russian word but a formal Slavonicism;

(iii) stylistic variants, frequent up to the end of the 18th c. but after that virtually confined to poetry;

(iv) the great bulk of 'neo-Slavonicisms'.

6

DIALECTS: THE BASIS OF THE MODERN STANDARD LANGUAGE

A 'language' is *at all times* a continuum of dialects. Various dialect features have been introduced above, especially in Chapters 2 and 3, where appropriate. The present chapter now reviews the ESl. dialects as a whole on a more precise geographical basis and with particular reference to the 'received standard'.

1   The history of the ESl. world has been one of constant territorial expansion from the early centuries AD down to the present day. Since the 16th c. Russian has been carried eastwards across the Volga and the Urál and is now spoken as a first or second language over a large part of Siberia and Central Asia. Siberian Russian dialects have been described, arising from the mixture of colonists from various parts of European Russia. Such recent colonial dialects are not of primary interest, but their formation repeats what had happened within European Russia on a smaller scale.

2   Archaeological and topographical evidence indicates with a high degree of certainty that the West (right-bank) Ukraine, eastwards as far as the Dnepr and northwards nearly to the R. Pripet (Припять), was part of the 'original' Slav speech-area (пра-ро́дина) and specifically that from which most, if not all, the ESl. tribes emerged. The first phase of expansion, down to *c.* AD 700, ending with the pattern of 'tribal' distribution fairly accurately recorded in the *Russian Primary Chronicle,*[1] embraced the middle and upper Dnepr valley and its main tributaries and reached as far

---

[1] *RPC, ad init.*; Map no. 2. These were, at least in part, no longer the tribes as they entered Russia, but, as some of the names show, new territorial divisions, e.g. Derevljáne, Dregoviči, Poljáne (men of the forest, fens, open country). The Slovéne of the Nóvgorod region preserved an old general name (§55 below, *s.v.*); Kriviči may be borrowed from Baltic.

north as the Nóvgorod region (L. Il'men'), a little way short of the
Gulf of Finland.

The incoming tribes no doubt brought slight dialectal differences
with them; others soon developed *in situ*, accentuated by different
substrates—Baltic speakers in the Dnepr river system and Finno-
Ugrian speakers over the whole of North and Central Russia.

3   The Kievan period saw a partial political unification and an
approximation to a standard form of *written* language, based on
ChSl. (below, Chapter 7, Section A), but no standard form of
spoken language was to be expected. Documentary evidence is
inadequate to give a tolerably complete picture but distinctions
between the spoken language of the South (political and cultural
centre—Kiev) and of the North (Nóvgorod) are discernible, some
of which at least were new. Written ChSl., though pronounced
more or less *à la russe* (1.12), naturally avoided on principle local
peculiarities, but only with partial success: there are Novgorodisms
even in *Ostr.* (2.49).

4   The whole of the Far North as far east as the Urál mountain
chain (and at some points beyond it) became Nóvgorod colonial
territory; its dialects derive from that of the small north-western
area about Nóvgorod. This expansion was especially vigorous in
the 12th–13th c. Not only the older toponymy of the North but
also the N. dial. vocabulary of the natural world and everyday life
is strongly permeated by Finnic loans (5.12). The colonists of the
Centre, between the upper Volga and the Oká, seem to have come
from every part: to the original Krivičí and Vjátiči were added
emigrants from the Kiev region and elsewhere. With the decline
of Kiev in the 12th c. and its rapid decadence from the time of the
Mongol incursions (early 13th c.) political and cultural primacy
passed to the new towns of the Centre—Rostóv, Súzdal', Vladímir.
It was the events of this period, which swept much of the Slav-
speaking population westwards and northwards off the exposed
southern lands, detached the extreme South-West (Galicia,
Volhynia) from the Russian political world, and finally fragmented
the never strongly unified Kiev polity into a multitude of local
princedoms (the so-called Appanage period[2]), which determined
the layout of dialects ancestral to the present-day dialect map.
Historical dialectology cannot claim to reconstruct the linguistic
situation further back than the 12th c.

[2] Уде́льный пери́од (уде́льные кня́жества).

Diagrammatic layout of dialect areas

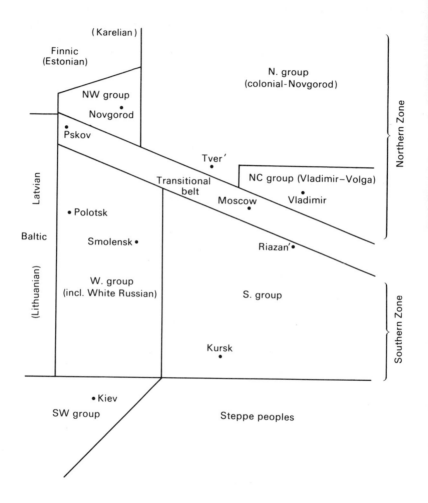

The towns are in their correct relative positions; the boundaries are merely schematic.

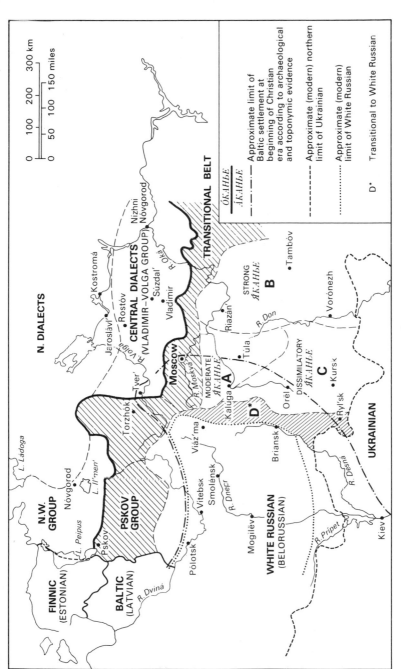

1. East Slav dialects

N. DIALECTS

CENTRAL DIALECTS
(VLADIMIR–VOLGA GROUP)

TRANSITIONAL BELT

N.W. GROUP

PSKOV GROUP

FINNIC
(ESTONIAN)

BALTIC
(LATVIAN)

WHITE RUSSIAN
(BELORUSSIAN)

UKRAINIAN

MODERATE
ЯКАНЬЕ **A**

STRONG
ЯКАНЬЕ **B**

DISSIMILATORY
ЯКАНЬЕ **C**

D*

ОКАНЬЕ
ЯКАНЬЕ — · — · — Approximate limit of Baltic settlement at beginning of Christian era according to archaeological and toponymic evidence

— — — — Approximate (modern) northern limit of Ukrainian

· · · · · · · · Approximate (modern) limit of White Russian

D* Transitional to White Russian

Moscow
R. Moskvá

L. Ládoga
L. Peipus
L. Il'men'
Nóvgorod
Pskov
Pólotsk
R. Dviná
Mogilëv
Vítebsk
Smolénsk
R. Dnepr
R. Pripet
Kiev
R. Desná
Briansk
Viáz'ma
Torzhók
Tver'
Jaroslávl'
Kostromá
Rostóv
Súzdal'
Vladímir
R. Vólga
Nízhni Nóvgorod
R. Oká
Riazán
Túla
Kaluga
Orël
Ryl'sk
Kursk
R. Don
Tambóv
Vorónezh

0   50   100   150 miles
0   100   200   300 km

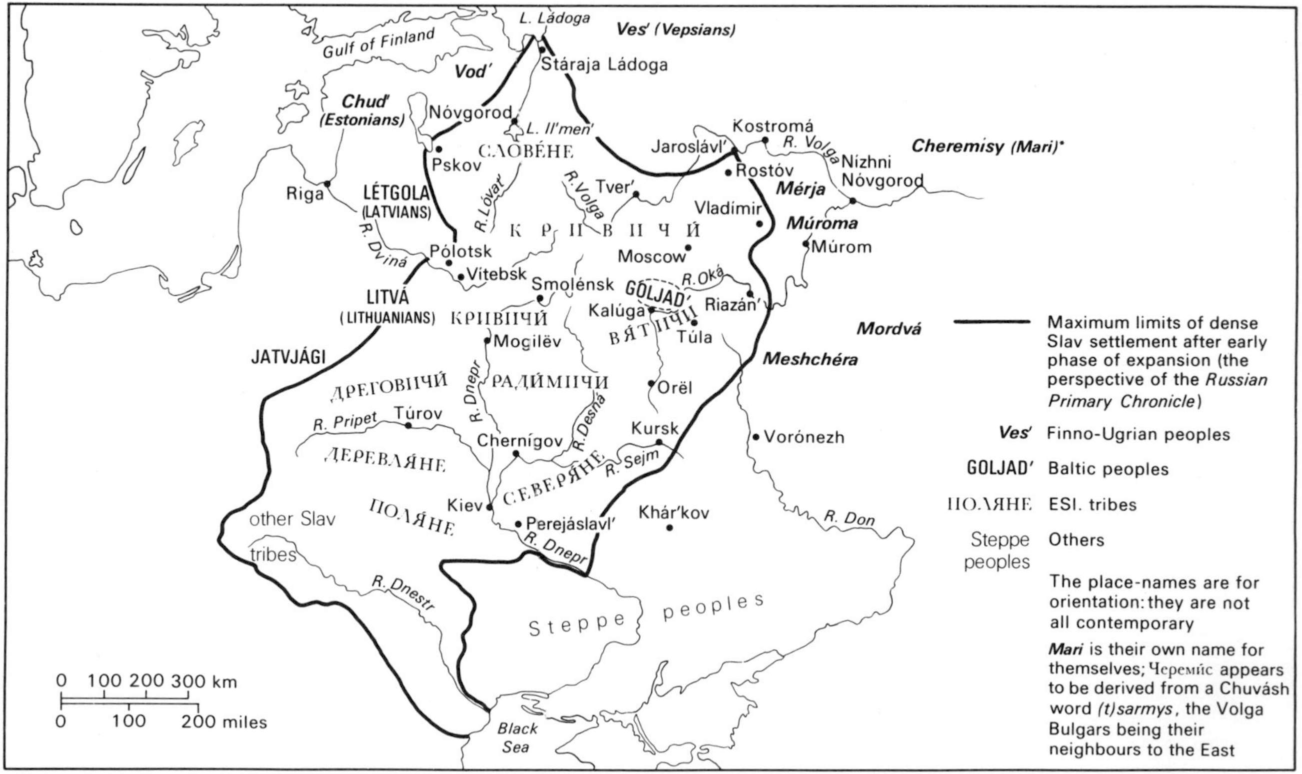
L. Ládoga
Ves′ (Vepsians)
Gulf of Finland
Stáraja Ládoga
Vod′
Chud′ (Estonians)
Nóvgorod
L. Il′men′
СЛОВЕ́НЕ
Pskov
Kostromá
R. Volga
Cheremisy (Mari)*
Jaroslávl′
Nízhni Nóvgorod
Rostóv
Riga
LÉTGOLA (LATVIANS)
R. Lóvat′
R. Volga
Tver′
Mérja
Vladímir
R. Dviná
К Р И В И Ч Й
Múroma
Múrom
Pólotsk
Moscow
Vítebsk
Smolénsk
GOLJAD′
R. Oká
Riazán′
LITVÁ (LITHUANIANS)
КРИВИЧИ
Kalúga
ВЯ́ТИЧИ
Túla
Mordvá
Mogilëv
JATVJÁGI
Meshchéra
ДРЕГОВИЧИ
R. Dnepr
РАДИ́МИЧИ
Orël
R. Pripet
Túrov
R. Desná
Kursk
Voronezh
Chernígov
ДЕРЕВЛЯ́НЕ
СЕВЕРЯ́НЕ
R. Sejm
Kiev
ПОЛЯ́НЕ
Khár′kov
R. Don
other Slav tribes
Perejáslavl′
R. Dnepr
R. Dnestr
Steppe peoples
0 100 200 300 km
0 100 200 miles
Black Sea
Maximum limits of dense Slav settlement after early phase of expansion (the perspective of the Russian Primary Chronicle)
Ves′ Finno-Ugrian peoples
GOLJAD′ Baltic peoples
ПОЛЯНЕ ESl. tribes
Steppe peoples Others
The place-names are for orientation: they are not all contemporary
Mari is their own name for themselves; Черемúс appears to be derived from a Chuvásh word (t)sarmys, the Volga Bulgars being their neighbours to the East

2. Early East Slav settlement

5   Even for the period *c.*1200–1400 evidence is very unequal. There is abundant material from Nóvgorod, relatively unaffected by the Mongol conquest, comparatively little from the 'new centre', and virtually none at all from what remained of the South for lack of any important centres in it other than Riazán'.[3] But it is clear that the present S. dial. area is to a considerable extent the result of *recolonization* southwards (less prominently eastwards) from the 16th c. (decline of Tatar power and rise of Moscow); in other words, the S. dialects are in part relatively recent colonial dialects, which eventually made contact with the expanding Ukrainian speech area (compare Maps 1 and 2). The sharp definition of the (South) Russian–Ukrainian language frontier, without transitional dialects, confirms this. No texts emanating from the S. dial. group proper are earlier than the 15th c.

Quite different is the *western* frontier, which is markedly indefinite: S. Russian dialect passes by gradations into typical White Russian (Belorussian) and the point at which the division is to be made is variously estimated according to the criteria used. The dividing line can be put a good deal to the west of that on Map 1, including Smolénsk on the Russian side. The expansion of the Lithuanian state from the 14th c., which reached eastwards to a point half-way between Smolénsk and Moscow, produced no closed frontier here; its *lingua franca* was not Lithuanian but Slavonic— the so-called West Russian Chancellery language (7.23). The Western and Southern dialect groups continued to form a single linguistic continuum.

6   Russian dialects can thus be divided crudely into a North and South group. Between them there arose a 'transitional belt', from the 13th c. onwards, characterized for the most part, but not exclusively, by the irruption of southern features into originally northern speech-areas. It must further be borne in mind that the population of Russia has been until recent times unusually mobile: apart from general expansion there have been various considerable displacements and deliberate resettlements, so that it is not surprising to find a detailed map spattered with 'islands' exhibiting dialect

---

[3] Present-day Riazán' is a new foundation further downstream (nearer Moscow). Literary works connected with Riazán' are the Повесть о разорении Рязани Батыем (1237, written *c.*1300?) and the Слово о куликовской битве (Задóнщина) (1378, written shortly after by Sofóni of Riazán'). They are irrelevant for knowledge of the local dialect.

TABLE XVII. Diagnostic Features of the Main Dialect Areas (modern state)

	Northern	Central (Vladimir–Volga)	Western	Southern
1	occlusive [g] (*k*/*g* paired)	occlusive [g] (*k*/*g* paired)	[ɣ] (*x*/ɣ paired)	[ɣ] (*x*/ɣ paired)
2	*v*/*f* (late)	*v*/*f*	/w/ (no /f/)	/w/ (no /f/)
3	цо́канье	*c*/*č'* distinguished	цо́канье (in part)	*c*/*č'* distinguished
4	final labials *depalatalized*	*not* depalatalized	*depalatalized*	*not* depalatalized
5	ѣ/е *distinguished*	ѣ/е *conflated* (late)	ѣ/е *conflated*	ѣ/е *conflated*
6	—	—	—	lengthening (diphthongization) of *e*/*o* before a lost jer
7	ёканье (unstressed [n'osú])	ёканье (limited)	я́канье (unstressed [n'asú])	я́канье
8	о́канье (unstressed [vodá])	о́канье	а́канье (unstressed [vadá])	а́канье
9	*vowel reductions* absent or limited	limited	prominent	prominent
10	assimilations *bm* > *m̃*, *dn* > *ñ*	—	(present in WhR.)	—
11	*intervocalic j* widely lost (vowel contractions)	occasionally lost	maintained	maintained
12	*verbal 3rd pers.* in -*t*	-*t*	-*t'*	-*t'*
13	AG меня́, тебя́, etc.	меня́/тебя́	мене́/тебе́	мене́/тебе́
14	DL тебе́, etc.	тебе́	тобе́	тобе́
15	demonstrative pronoun тот	тот	той (and variants)	той

	Northern	Central (Vladimir–Volga)	Western	Southern
16	pl. DI *conflated* in noun and adj.	no conflation	no conflation	no conflation
17	fem. sg. GLD *conflated* in noun	no conflation	*conflated*	no conflation
18	postposited 'article'	postposited 'article'	—	—
19	no confusions of gender	no confusions	no confusions	confusions *present*
20	nom. + inf. construction	absent	nom. + inf. construction	absent
21	—	—	'perfect' tense он ушовши or similar form	—

features characteristic of other quite distant areas. Nóvgorod dialect in the narrow sense altered considerably after the loss of independence (end of 15th c.) with the removal of much of its population in favour of new settlers from the centre.

7 While a basic contrast of the N. and S. dialects, respectively north and south of the Transitional belt, is adequate as a first approximation. Table XVII above presents some of the more important distinguishing features with reference also to the C. and W. groups. It is not to be assumed that these features are completely uniform over the areas indicated. The further element of *vocabulary* has not been included. It stands to reason that the working vocabulary of the northern regions will be considerably different from that of the southern if only through the factor of climate.[4] Considering the vast area of Russia, the differences between typical N. and S. dialects are by no means great and scarcely a barrier to comprehension.

[4] We may note the following, mainly agricultural, contrasting terms (N. dial. standing first): боронá/скородá 'harrow'; лéмех or лéмеш/сóшник 'ploughshare'; орáть/пахáть 'plough'; новинá or новь/целинá 'newly cultivated land' (Новь Turgénev, Целинá Shólokhov); пóжня/сеножáть 'stubble field'; плуг/сохá 'plough' (different types); стог/скирд(á) 'rick'; рúга/гумнó 'threshing-floor'; вéкша/бéлка 'squirrel'; кузнéц/ковáль 'smith' (family names Кузнецóв, Ковалёв); лáять/брехáть 'bark'.

ommentary to Table XVII

1. The whole of the North has the pair *k/g*, with local exceptions only in special contexts, e.g. [koɣda] (2.40), adj. masc. sg. gen. [-oɣo] (3.40) (and [mnoɣo] by extension). Today occlusive [g] includes the extreme northern edge of all the S. dial. area too. The exact boundary in earlier times cannot be reconstructed; almost certainly there has been some north to south extension of [g].

9 2. The pronunciation of Cyrillic в at a given time and place cannot always be inferred with certainty. Much of the North made the change *w > v*, in particular in final position, which was decisive for the further development of *f/f′* by devoicing (2.34): North—pl. fem. gen. [koróf], South—[karów]. The early symmetrical development of *v/v′* and *f/f′*, applied to all *w*, is characteristic of the C. group. Nóvgorod town seems to have made the change *w > v* relatively late; *f* remained marginal to the system here. /w/ is characteristic of Smolénsk (уздумал, у Ризѣ, 1229), Pskov (вдержал, 1460), and the whole WhR. area, as well as most of the South. The general rule is [v] before vowels but [w] before consonants and finally. Richard James (1618–20) apparently had a West Russian among his informants since he picked up *deuka* = девка and *βuixanat* = выгонять (*zautrakat* is ambiguous, §55 below).

10 3. Цо́канье is found in the earliest Nóvgorod documents.[5] The prevalent form was the conflation of *c′* and *č′* in *c′* (soft цо́канье). The reverse (чо́канье) occurs but is considerably rarer. Later changes produced hard цо́канье, e.g. at Nóvgorod itself, under the influence of the Moscow norm (§§49 ff. below) from the 16th c. Soft цо́канье is today in fact only characteristic of the remoter N. dialects. Hard чо́канье is found locally along the western borders in contact with WhR. hard *č*.

The C. group clearly distinguishes *c′/č′*, later *c/č′*. A few words with цо́канье have entered standard Russian vocabulary, notably цепь (цѣпь) 'chain': Ukr. has usually *čip-*, Polish only *czep-*, and чепь is still common in Moscow texts down to the 17th c.;[6] ца́пля 'heron': ча́пля in all the South (Ukr. PN Ча́плин), and *čap-* in all other Slav languages. Чапу́ра 'egret' (a white heron which does

---

[5] Despite other Novgorodisms there are *no* confusions of *c′/č′* in *Ostr*.

[6] Чепи золоты (Ivan Kalitá's Will, 1327–8). In a Pskov document of *c*.1465 искалъ на нихъ чепи золотои we must read цепи in conformity with the prevailing цо́канье (цего, ноць, боцекъ/бочекъ, and others).

not occur further north than the Black Sea coast and the Volga delta) preserves the original and southern form чап-.

11 4. Depalatalization (hardening) of *final* labials is fairly widespread in the Slav languages, the entire elimination of soft labials rather less so. Final hardening is characteristic of the Novg. area, much of the North, and of the western borderlands, eventually joining up with the same development in Ukrainian and Polish (*gołąb* = R. го́лубь).[7]

Case-forms in -*mĭ* (Tables VI and VIII) and pres. sg. 1 *damĭ*, etc. (3.91) passed to -*mŭ* at an early date *generally*, but otherwise the C. group does not depalatalize labials.

12 5. The raising and closing of ѣ (2.10) is general in N. dialects, but local rules differ in relation to stress and the quality of the following consonant (syllable). A common pattern is [ie] or [e] before *hard*, [i] before *soft* consonants: [xl′îep, o xl′ib′ε]. Nóvgorod shows [i] in most contexts from the 14th c.: к тоби́ (13th c.), на рики́ (14th c.), роздили́ло (*c.*1440) (see also §62 below). From Pskov southwards there was early identity or near-conflation of ѣ/e, e.g. in the Smolénsk Treaty of 1229. In the C. group ѣ/e conflated relatively late, not before the 15th c. (Table XVIII below).

Northern и < ѣ does not appear in any standard Russian words; some with a special regional application are sometimes met, e.g. си́верко 'cold Arctic wind'.[8]

13 6. The 'compensatory lengthening' of e/o before a lost jer is characteristic of many S. dialects and of all the Ukr. area. For the further stages in Ukrainian see Table XX (2) below. In S. dialects the pronunciation remained [e:]/[o:] (commonly transcribed *ê*/*ô*) or became diphthongal [ie]/[uo]: [nûos] < *nosŭ*, [naruód]. Such dialects are thus 'seven-vowel' dialects as opposed to the predominantly 'five-vowel' dialects of the West and North.[9] The C. group shows some presence of *ê*/*ô* (*ê* may also come from late preserved ѣ), no doubt a Southern feature, but they did not persist in Moscow and are therefore absent from the modern standard.

14 7–9. *Unstressed vowels.* By and large the whole N. dial. area preserves the quality of vowels *irrespective of stress*, the further north the more so. In contrast none of the S. dialects possesses five

[7] It is reported that there are a few small areas in the Vólogda region (N. dial.) where virtually all final consonants are depalatalized: ого́н, де́вят, е́хат. Ludolf's девать, десать, ѣхать (*Grammar*, 1696) are personal or typographical errors.

[8] Richard James (1618–20) recorded *siẞer, snigom* from informants at Archangel.

[9] *y* (ы) and *ə* not counted separately, since determined positionally.

distinct unstressed vowels. There has been a process of *reduction*. Reduction, as usually defined, implies not only change of vowel timbre but also a literal reduction of the number of unstressed vowels in the system by *raising* (which may include centring). It follows on the one hand that the vowels which by nature cannot be perceptibly reduced are /i/ and /u/ since they are the highest (R. верхнего подъёма)—they can only be eliminated altogether; and on the other hand that processes of reduction will certainly involve /a/ as being the lowest and most open. There will thus be left in some systems *three* unstressed vowels only—/i/, /u/, and /ə/. This is commonly the case in East Bulgarian: *e > i, o > u, a > ə*; който is pronounced [kuitu]. The English words *reduction* and *séparate* illustrate these principles: (i) in [rɪ'dʌkʃən] *e* is reduced to /i/; the original syllable [ʃi] is lost by total reduction (elimination) of the high vowel; the *o* of the final syllable is reduced to [ə]; (ii) reduction or elimination of all post-tonic vowels: ['sɛpərət], ['sɛprɪt], or ['sɛprət]. Such reductions are a commonplace in languages with strong word stress (English, German, Bulgarian, Russian); they are absent or very limited in those where stress is light since secondary to some other factor controlling word rhythm (French, Czech, Serbo-Croat).

It is evident that after the fall of the weak jers—itself a manifestation of reduction—word stress continued to strengthen in Russian and reduction of unstressed vowels began (or rather continued) according to the general pattern

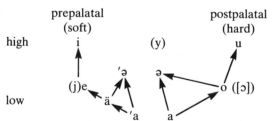

No one Russian dialect has the simple reduction pattern *i/u/ə*. There are limited areas of иканье in the South (несу́ > [n'isu]) and limited areas of у́канье in the North (одному́ > [udnomu]).[10] In standard pronunciation *ä* is commonly reduced all the way to [i] (пяти́ [p'it'i]) and any vowel not in the high range may be

[10] The earliest recorded example is given as угоро́д (1665) but its appearance in spelling is sure to have been much delayed.

reduced to əʹʹə after the stress. But written and etymologically correct воробей is pronounced [vərabʹéj]. *Reduction alone* may produce [vurubʹéj] or [vərəbʹéj] or some combination of these, but not the actual [vərabʹéj]. Nor can reduction produce [nʹasú] from несу. Thus part, *but only part*, of the observed vowel changes is due to reduction.

15 The genesis of S. dial. áканье and яканье is still disputed. They may be defined as the lack of unstressed *o/e* which appear as sounds close to *a/ja*: вода [vada], несу [nʹasu]. The quality of this unstressed /a/ varies somewhat with context, region, social level, etc. One reflex determined by experimental phonetics is [ʌ], which is typically about half-way between [ɔ] and [a]—lower and more central than [ɔ]. But many good speakers use almost identical vowels (length apart) in, say, вода.

We shall maintain the transcription [a] in conformity with the conventional terms áканье/яканье. The changes *o > a* and *je > ja* (ʹe > ʹa) are of a diametrically opposite kind to reduction. Whatever the precise timbre of the original vowel and its replacement they involve a *lowering and opening* of the pair *o/e*. Moreover in analysing this phenomenon we must also take ёканье into account (2.42–4), which it is misleading to treat in isolation.

16 To account for S. dial. [vadá], [nʹasú] we must start further back in time. There is abundant evidence that late CSl. (early Christian centuries) lacked 'typical' *o* and *e*: ō̆ and ā̆ had fallen together as a long or short vowel of intermediate timbre (improbably a true diphthong), for which perhaps Shevelov's transcription ₒā̆ is the most convenient, i.e. ā̆ with a postpalatal on-glide. Similarly *(j)ē̆* can be subsumed under ₑā̆, i.e. ā̆ with a prepalatal on-glide. About the 8th c. AD the *short* pair closed somewhat: ₒă > ŏ, ₑă > (j)ĕ. This is the stage recorded in OCS, with ŏ, (j)ĕ, ā, jā/(j)ē.[11] The majority of Slav dialects made a similar change at roughly the same time; but local factors might disturb this development.

The ESl. tribes were colonizers of Baltic- and Finnic-speaking lands. Precisely in the middle Dnepr valley, from Kiev northwards, they mingled intimately with Baltic-speakers, some of whom remained as relict islands in a Slav sea for several centuries.[12]

[11] The Glagolitic alphabet did not provide separate symbols for etymological *jā* and *ē* (i.e. ₑā). This reveals the closeness of their phonetic structure. See also 2.10.

[12] Notably the Голядь (Lith. *Galindai*), on the middle Oká to the north of Kalúga. *Galindai* means the same as *Ukrainians*—those on the border (from the Baltic point of view).

In Baltic the evolution of the above vowels had been different: $\ŏ$ and $\ă$ had conflated in $\ă$, $\ō$ and $\ā$ in $\ō$ (with various later reflexes); $\ĕ$ was very open and often alternates dialectally with $\ă$ (Lith. *ēzeras/ āzeras* 'lake'), while $\ē$ was, and still is, much more close. Thus the Slav tribes who settled in areas of Baltic speech from *c.* AD 400, under conditions of widespread bilingualism, found support for their $_o\ă$, $_e\ă$ in Baltic and *were inhibited from making a total change* to $\ŏ/(j)\ĕ$. The *stressed* pair, somewhat clearer, made the change but *unstressed* $_o\ă/_e\ă$ remained—as а́канье and я́канье. There is nothing surprising therefore in the fact that in the Ukraine (extreme SW dial.), outside Baltic influence, the whole normal Slav evolution took place, and likewise among the most northerly tribes whose substrate was not Baltic but Finnic (see Map no. 1). А́канье and я́канье are absent from all Ukr. and N. Russian dialects. The following correspondences are therefore to be expected theoretically between the then Central, Baltic-influenced, dialects and the extreme North and South:

CSl.	Baltic	Central		N. and SW
		unstressed	stressed	
$\ă$ ($_o\ă$)	$\ă$	$\ă$	$\ŏ$	$\ŏ$
$\ĕ$ ($_e\ă$)	ie, ia	$_e\ă > {}'a$	$_e\ŏ > {}'o$	$_e\ŏ > {}'o$

In other words, where we find а́канье we should expect also я́канье, and where we find о́канье we should also expect ёканье ($'e > {}'o$). This is precisely the pattern of the ESl. dialects. A. Vaillant was among the first to advocate this view but the implications needed further study (§§36 ff. below).

17　10. The labial assimilation $bm > \tilde{m}$ and dental assimilation $dn > \tilde{n}$ are characteristic of the North-West (Novg.) and extend southwards into the Western group. They would not appear to be very early (15th–16th c.?) but evidence is scarce: обма́н [oṁan], одна́ [oña], сты́дно [styño]. An assimilation $wl > \bar{l}$ (if this is what the spelling represents) is found a good deal earlier at Nóvgorod: дъчерь мьстиславлю; нарослаль дворъ (1215).

18　11. Loss of intervocalic *j* is widespread but not universal in the North. The most usual are *-aje-, -aja- > -ā-*: pres. sg. 2, 3 знаш, знат (or зна); добра = добрая. Others are more sporadic, e.g. моего́ [movo].

Contraction also occurs in the C. dialects immediately to the North of Moscow, but was probably never characteristic of Moscow

town dialect. The earliest example noted in a Moscow text is
сказываш (1433). However, fem. patronymics have the widespread—and correct—allegro form Андре́вна < Андре́евна,
Никола́вна < Никола́евна (the corresponding masc. eliminate
-ов-/-ев-: Серге́ич < Серге́евич, Семёныч < Семёнович).

19 12. *Verbal termination -t/-t′ (3rd pers. sg. and pl.).* The S.
dialects have preserved early ESl. *-t′* in general. The focus of hard
-t seems to have been Nóvgorod, where examples are recorded in
the 13th c. Hard *-t* is not clearly present in Moscow until the later
14th c. The reason for this non-phonetic change has been discussed
in 3.97 (*d*).

The areas where this final *-t/-t′* is wholly or partly missing (more
often absent in the sg. 3 than pl. 3) are small but interesting in
view of the fact that the ESl. branch is now alone in maintaining
it (with some exceptions in Bulgarian). Loss of *-t* is commonest in
the North-West (Pskov, Novg. to Onéga) and in a few central S.
dialects; there would appear to be no connection between these
two areas.

On the evidence of the colophon to *Ostr.* a sg. 3 without *-t* was
not unknown to Novg. dialect in the middle of the 11th c.: да иже
горазнѣе сего напише. But this may be a scribal error or imperfect
abbreviation.

20 13–14. The pronominal gen. in *-я* is exclusively Northern; it
is presumed to be analogous to the *jo*-stem nouns, e.g. коня́
(Table VI, Type 17). Almost every permutation of the stems теб-/
тоб- is represented in dialect; S. dialect tends to generalize the
stem тоб-, N. dialect the stem теб-. Literary texts tend to follow
ChSl. (OCS DL *tebě*, instr. *tobojǫ*) and thus confuse the issue as
to what was the colloquial norm, at Moscow in particular.

21 15. The reinforcement of the original ESl. demonstrative pronoun тъ took two directions: either sg. nom. той (тый, тей),
whence тое, тая, and pl. nom. тии, тая, тые; or тот (< тътъ),
without change in the other forms. The type той is not characteristic
of the North though it reaches Nóvgorod (introduced from further
south), and is absent from the C. group. Examples:

тая правда (Smolénsk, 1229)
тей Иволтъ ⎫
тое пиво ⎬ (Pskov, 1463/5)
тую же ночь ⎭
(but also тотъ Иволтъ).

Сей is apparently much more widespread than сесь (< сьсь) and became also the literary norm under ChSl. influence (see also 3.61).

22 16–17. Conflation of the pl. DI in N. dialects is very general and extends to the (long) adjectives, where indeed it may have originated.[13] The form is commonly -м, less often -мы or -ма, rarely -ми. The confusion of the sg. GDL in fem. nouns is more morphological than phonological (though local ѣ > и may also enter into it) and is bound up with the establishment of a new symmetry between 'hard' and 'soft' declensions on various possible patterns (3.4 ff.). If we take point 20 below also into account an inan. fem. noun in -a may be reduced in N. dialects to a three-form sg. and a four-form pl.:

> sg. NA водá, GDL водьı́ or водé, instr. водóй
> pl. NA вóды, gen. вод, DI вóдам, loc. вóдах

This is nearly identical to the schema of the (inan.) *ĭ*-stems, e.g. ночь—a stable type.

There are thus some signs that declension was more precarious in the N. dialects (excluding the C. group) but this is still far from a collapse of declension such as took place in Bulgarian: this would have required also phonetic confusion of the endings and precisely in the North the quality of the vowels was little affected by stress pattern.

23 18. It does not seem likely therefore that the postposited 'article' of the North was a reaction to case confusion (it is not primarily that in Bulgarian either). Distinct forms are only common in the nom. and acc.:

sg. nom.	(дом)-от	(селó)-то	(водá)-та
acc.			(водý)-ту[14]
pl. NA	-те (-тѣ)	-та	-те (-тѣ)

For other cases an enclitic -то may be used.

This article is found in the C. group immediately to the North of Moscow but gained no standing there.

24 19. The prevalence of neut. pl. NA of masc. type (óкны) and also fem. pl. nom. of the masc. type in -á (лошадя́, степя́) points

---

[13] An early example is даруи Боже молящимися (*c.*1400).
[14] Enclitic stress: вóду, нá воду, водý-ту.

to a certain weakness in *gender* distinctions in the South, but nowhere is the neut. eliminated altogether (the neut. was lost in Lithuanian and in the evolution of the Romance languages from Latin). It is clear that where there is áканье and vowel reduction fem. and neut. forms will in many contexts become indistinguishable. These incipient gender confusions were part of the S. dial. current flowing into Moscow in the Muscovite period. There was for a long time hesitation in literary usage between e.g. меня́ло 'money-changer' (original suffix) and меня́ла ('common' noun type, where fem. suffixes are numerous; 3.2), the latter prevailing. Similarly, Ukr. personal names in -ко, transmitted to the centre via S. dialects, were for some time spelt indifferently -ко/-ка and often declined as *fem.* in accordance with the latter (sg. gen. Дорошéнки even in the 19th c.).[15] The increasingly regular neut. pl. in -ки (from the 17th c.) also belongs at least partly to this confusion (я́блоко, pl. я́блоки; see also 3.19 (2)).

Neut. plurals of the type óкны were characteristic of Moscow town speech. They will be found in literary works down to the generation of Pushkin, especially if the author or his character is a native Muscovite, e.g. in Gribojédov.

25 20. *Nom. + inf. construction*. See also 4.54 (with examples). This procedure seems to have originated in the North-West (Novg.) and spread thence southwards (e.g. to Smolénsk) and into Muscovite legal and administrative style. There is no good evidence that it was native to the S. dialects, where occasional examples are clearly due to importation from Moscow. It is probably an effect of the Finnic (Estonian) substratum at Nóvgorod since there is a parallel construction in that language.

26 21. In many north-western and western areas он ушовши (or a variant of this) replaces он ушёл in its original *perfect* aspectual sense. It is to be presumed that the procedure arose with the decadence of the aor. and impf. and the consequent demotion of ушёл to an all-purpose preterite.

Vowel Systems of the North and South

In the light of the relevant points above, the vowel systems of the North and South can be characterized as follows:

[15] Ukrainian declines them as masc. Nowadays they are usually treated as indeclinable in Russian.

27   1. N. dialects (all dialects north of the Transitional belt): five-vowel system, *stressed and unstressed*.

(*a*) *Stressed* ѣ and o may become more or less diphthongal: ѣ́ [ē] > [ie], with commonly further development [i] (2.10); ó > [uo]: [dwu͡or] = двор, [voru͡ona] = воро́на.[16] This northern labialization has crept into a few standard words with initial *vo-* < *uo-*: во́семь 'eight' (ChSl. осмь), ѣ́отчина '(inherited) estate' (< *otьčina*), навостри́ть у́ши 'prick one's ears' (adj. dial. востёр, WhR. во́стры).

(*b*) *Unstressed* vowels generally maintain their timbre: reductions are limited both in type and geographical area. These are:

(i) *'a* (especially < *ä* < *ę*) > *'e*: тяну́ [t'enu], пряду́ [pr'edu] (stressed зять [z'et'], взяли [v'z'el'i] also widespread but not in the NC group).

(ii) *o* > *u* (у́канье): most often in syllables other than the pretonic, e.g. сторона́ [sturona], but also locally [kuru͡ova], [xuru͡oš-], [vurub'ej].[17] This reduction is commonest in the NC group and in areas to the north colonized from there.

(iii) Alternatively *o* > *ə* in similar patterns: [gəłová].

(iv) True и́канье is not found but unstressed ѣ > [i] occurs, as well as the more general *stressed* ѣ > [i]: в рѣкѣ́ [wr'ek'ɛ or wr'ik'ɛ or wr'ik'i].

(*c*) Unstressed ёканье is general but *'o* > *'e* before *soft* consonants is more usual: несу́ [n'osu] but неси́ [n'es'i]. This ёканье locally embraces also unstressed ѣ: [w‿l'osú], [gn'ozdó], [r'oká] (notably in the NC group).

28   2. S. dialects (S. and W. groups, i.e. all dialects south of the Transitional belt, including WhR., but not Ukr.): five or seven *stressed* vowels, *less than five*, typically three, *unstressed* (*i, u, a*).[18] All these dialects have а́канье but there are notable differences in the patterns of я́канье which serve as diagnostic features. These differences are surely relatively recent. The main variants are:

29   (*a*) Strong   я́канье: characteristic of the eastern half of the S.

---

[16] This strong labialization of *o* only takes place when the vowel originally had rising pitch (cf. 1.24); otherwise [gorot] = го́род *et sim.* and new o < ъ is unaffected, e.g. in кусо́к.

[17] Richard James (1618–20) transcribed *smytri, myrskoi, radyst,* i.e. [smutri] = смотри́, etc., from one of his N. dial. informants.

[18] [ə] and [e] arise from reduction and are not counted separately.

dial. area. (Pretonic) ['a] is maintained in all contexts, e.g. at Riazan' нясу́, нясе́ш, нясе́ть, нясе́м, нясе́те, нясу́ть.

(b) Dissimilatory яканье (several subtypes): most of the W. dialects, and the south-west of the S. dial. area.

Note. Both (a) and (b) are represented in the WhR. dialects.

(c) Moderate яканье (уме́ренное яканье) is found everywhere to the immediate south and west of Moscow and has overrun (b) from the north, forming a hybrid area which includes the important town of Orël. The dialect map strongly suggests that moderate яканье is itself a hybrid produced by a southward extension of N. dial. speakers overrunning (b).

(d) Assimilatory яканье: rare in a pure form; clearly secondary to (a).

30 Most Soviet dialectologists proceed from the assumption that some form of (b) is the primitive form of яканье, especially that of the extreme South-West (Обоянский тип). If the view outlined above (§16) is correct, strong яканье (a) was the original state:

а́канье: [vadá], [vad'έ]; [baradá];
яканье: [n'asú], [n'as'í]; [b'ar'óza], [s'aɫó].

This pattern is typical of Riazán', the one place of importance southwards from Moscow at an early date, but also of Túla, further west, where it forms a small island in 'moderate' territory. It is to be observed that 'strong' яканье is now found further east than the area of Baltic influence which is claimed to have given rise to it (Map no. 1); it is by no means unusual for an archaic feature to be preserved in a peripheral area more remote from influences for change.[19]

31 Types (b) and (c) can be derived without difficulty from 'strong' яканье:

---

[19] An influence tending to produce а́канье in a bilingual situation with the local Finnic people (Mordvá) has been suggested for the Riazán' area (see G. J. Stipa in *ZslPh* 37 (1974)). It cannot be ruled out that two different substrates may have inhibited $a > o$ in two different areas but the link with яканье does not emerge clearly from the suggestion. (The PN Ряза́нь is a recent яканье spelling for Резан-, deriving from the Finnic Erzä people of that area, a part of the Mordvá.)

It is worth noting that а́канье ($o > a$ in certain contexts) is also found in certain Blg. dialects (Rhodope), and in certain dialects in S. Serbia and Montenegro where Albanians form a high proportion of the population, e.g. [ćavek] for standard SCr. *čòvek*. The reason for the former is not clear but the latter is clearly parallel to the Baltic–Slav symbiosis in Russia with Alb. a = Slav o. See I. Popović, *Geschichte der serbokroatischen Sprache* (Wiesbaden, 1960), p. 575.

(i) Dissimilatory яканье preserves unstressed ′a except before syllables containing a:

[n′asú], [n′as′í], [s′astrý];
but [n′esłá], [s′estrá] (or [n′isłá], [s′istrá]).

(ii) Moderate яканье preserves unstressed ′a except before all soft consonants:

[n′asú], [n′asłá], [s′astrý];
but [n′es′í], [s′estrɛ́], [s′el′ɛ́] (or [n′is′í], etc.).

This pattern is essentially *assimilatory*. The rare 'assimilatory' яканье is the reverse, preserving ′a only before syllables containing a: [n′asłá], [s′astrá] but [n′esú] or [n′isú], etc.

32 The subsequent *reductions* are clearly superimposed on the áканье/яканье patterns, viz.

(i) ′a > ′e > i (éканье and íканье), as noted above. The areas of consistent éканье and íканье are relatively small and scattered.

(ii) a > ə: various patterns are found: [bəradá], [bərədá], [barədá]. Most commonly the pretonic syllable is maintained relatively strong and clear [bəradá]. A dissimilatory type is recorded with ə appearing only before syllables containing a: [vadój] but [vədá], [nə‿vad′ɛ́]; [snəxá] but [marózu], [damój]. This goes with dissimilatory яканье as a rule. Here and there reduction may be strong enough to lead to the loss of a syllable, e.g. [pəxran′il′i] = похоронíли.

Chronological Evidence for áканье

33 1. The statement 'поскольку аканье является результатом редукции гласных, трудно предположить . . . редукцию гласных полного образования при сохранении в то же время слабых редуцированных' (Borkovski and Kuznetsov, Историческая грамматика русского языка, p. 142) implies that *all* changes in the timbre of unstressed vowels are to be considered as following, more or less immediately, on the loss of the weak jers, i.e. as starting not much earlier than 1200. This is certainly true of the *reductions* as defined above. There is indeed no documentary evidence of áканье or яканье at a date *before* the fall of the weak jers. They will appear, of course, as sporadic misspellings made either by an а́кающий or by an о́кающий hearing something unfamiliar from the lips of an а́кающий. Discounting some doubtful cases,[20] the earliest certain examples are found in a Moscow copy of the Gospels dated 1339: въ апустѣвшии земли; се и есть дивна (for о-пуст-, дивно). There is no credible explanation of these except an actual pronunciation [a] (or [ə]) normal to the copyist.

After these we may cite:

алкгердъ for Олге́рд (Smolénsk, 1359; WhR. кг = [g], г = [ɣ]);
гади́на, Маскву́ (Pskov, 1383);
Бро/ашев[ая], Шаго/атью (Moscow, c.1389)

—telling examples, since it is precisely in obscure place-names of unclear etymology that mistakes will be made (the correct forms are Брошева́я, Ша́готь).[21] Further: Анофреи for Ону́фрий (Pólotsk, 1399).

Most striking are the hypercorrections found before the end of the 14th c., e.g. in the Си́йское ева́нгелие (1393), considered to be a copy made in Moscow from a Ukrainian manuscript, that is, one in which there could not be any а́канье: за́пода, полога́еть, привя́зоно (side by side with взра́давашася and others). Hypercorrections will only be made by an а́кающий who is aware that the literary norm frequently has *o* for his native *a* but is not sufficiently educated to know where. In this case the confusion is clearly aural, i.e. the result of dictation, not copying.

34   2. *Smolénsk* certainly lies within the original а́канье area. Yet the 1229 Treaty (text no. 18) contains *no mistakes* that can be attributed to а́канье or я́канье, despite its other orthographical failings and the virtual lack of any ChSl. influence. This is held to be strong evidence that neither was present in Smolénsk speech in the 13th c. and, by inference, before the fall of the jers. There is no trace of а́канье either in one of the few early manuscripts from Riazán', a ко́рмчая of c.1284; it appears abundantly in later texts (15th–16th c.): кабылу, носильства = насильство, на = но, спи́сак, дона́ = дана́, скоза́л, etc.

Against the evidential value of the above it has always to be remembered that from the beginning, orthography was based on

[20] The spelling манастырь is found very early side by side with монастырь and is due to variations in Greek (cf. SCr. *mằnastīr*).
[21] Similarly the frequent variation Ра́донеж (correct)/Ра́данеж.

ChSl. which recognizes neither áканье, яканье, nor ёканье and strictly avoids them as vulgar and no part of cultivated written language, and that the majority of early documents are either frankly ChSl. or strongly imbued with it, or if neither, at any rate written by men educated in the ChSl. rules and standards as the only proper *written* procedures. It is no more surprising to find no early examples of áканье than of ёканье, though admittedly the latter are not entirely lacking (2.43). Moreover, the two most active cultural centres of early Russia—Kiev and Nóvgorod—both lay outside the áкающий area (and have remained óкающий to the present day), as did also the towns of the new centre (7.15). Thus neither tradition nor local habits favoured the admission of these features into a written text. Nor were there any cultural centres of importance in the areas where áканье/яканье were or became characteristic, which greatly reduces the likelihood of their presence in texts. Any kind of departure from the ChSl. norm only becomes likely and visible with the wide diffusion of writing among scribes who have an imperfect mastery of ChSl. The early Novg. deviations are due precisely to this. Nor is it unusual for a dialect text to reflect *some* local features but not others in an apparently arbitrary way: a case in point is the 'chancellery language' of the Lithuanian state (7.23) which ignores certain WhR. features certainly present during its long period of use (14th–16th c.), including áканье (except towards the end).

As a further parallel we may adduce the fact that an Englishman of limited education whose speech lacks the initial aspirate *h* will nevertheless write it (in *horse, have,* etc.), since he has been taught so to spell at an elementary stage and told that 'dropping one's h's' is vulgar. Hypercorrections will result, such as *hover* for *over*.

35 3. It is argued that in dialects with dissimilatory яканье the timbre of the pretonic vowel is determined by the following stressed vowel but that no difference is made between original pretonic syllables and those that became so through the loss of a jer: яканье cannot therefore be older than this loss. Further, that some types of dissimilatory яканье show different treatments before new *ê* and *ô* (§13 above) and original *e/o*: [s'ałô], [w s'al'ê] but [zə s'iłom] (Обоянский тип). The objections disappear if it is posited that all adjustments to a pattern of strong яканье—that is, all reductions —certainly took place after the fall of the jers.

General Theory of the Evolution of Unstressed Vowels

The chronological sequence of all the phenomena concerning unstressed vowels discussed above may be resumed as follows (N. = later area of NR dialects in the broadest sense (NW, N., and NC groups), S. = later area of SR and WR dialects (old Baltic area); SW = later area of Ukr.):

36   1. *Eighth–Ninth Centuries* (c.*800?*)

(*a*) $_o\breve{a} > o$ generally in Slav and specifically in ESl. in the North and South-West but not in the South (old Baltic area): here *stressed* $_o\breve{a} > o$ but *unstressed* $_o\breve{a} > a$ (§16 above);

(*b*) inversion took place in SSl. and WSl., *polnoglásie* in ESl. (1.22–3).

In both cases the change took place not later than the early 9th c. since both are fully established in the dialect of SS Cyril and Methodios (b. 826/7 and 815 respectively) and incorporated regularly in OCS. The changes may, of course, have been a little later in the ESl. area than in the Balkans; they were no doubt more or less contemporaneous.

Results in ESl.: CSl. *$g_o\breve{a}tw_o\bar{a}$ (Lith. *galvà*) > N. and SW *gołowá*, S. *gaławá*.

37   2. *Late Ninth–Early Tenth Centuries?*

$_e\breve{a} > _eo$ in the North in all contexts; $_e\breve{a}$ remains in the South if *unstressed*, $> _eo$ if *stressed*. Development in South-West unclear ($_e\breve{a} > _eo$ only in part?)

Results: CSl. *$b_earz_o\bar{a}$ (Lith. *béržas* [$b_e$aržas]) > N. $b_eor_eóza$, S. $b_ear_eóza$; N. $n_eós(t)ŭ/n_eoslá$ (perfect)/$n_eosí$ (imperative), S. $n_eós(t)ŭ/n_easlá/n_easí$; N. $s_rotó/w\underset{\smile}{s}_eolě$, S. $s_eató/w\underset{\smile}{s}_ealě$.

38   3. *Tenth Century*

(*a*) After old palatal(ized) consonants (2.5)—*š'*, *ž'*, *č'* (including *š'č'*), etc.—the on-glide is merged into the palatalization. We get: N. and SW *ž'oná*, *š'č'oká*, S. *ž'aná*, *š'č'aká*.

This stage is reflected sporadically in Kievan texts (ChSl. in the main) shortly after 1050 and clearly represents the already established spoken norm on a par with other vernacular and even local traits (e.g. 3 sg. -ть) which infiltrated into ChSl. where orthography raised no difficulties and the standard of ChSl. accomplishment was not too high.

In the South-West (Ukr.) *žoná*, *ščoká*, etc. have *remained*, but
there has been considerable later rearrangement: nouns generalize
o (*žoná*, *žoni*, etc.), verbs (pres. tense) generalize *e*.

(*b*) Before fully or semi-palatalized (semi-soft) consonants
stressed *ₑo* > *e*: *š'estĭ* (not **š'ostĭ*). Initial *je-* > *jo-/ja-* as in (*a*) but
the *j-* soon disappeared, probably as a result of sentence context: N.
and SW *jomú/jogó*, *jod'ínŭ*, *josₑótrŭ*, *józₑoro*; S. *jad'ínŭ*, *jasₑótrŭ*,
józₑara, finally *od'ínŭ*, *osₑótrŭ*, *ózₑoro/ad'ínŭ*, *asₑótrŭ*, *ózₑara*; *jomú/
jogó* remain since *j-* is the root (Ukr. now йомý, йогó). There are
irregularities in this development which cannot all be satisfactorily
explained (1.29).

39   4. *Tenth Century*

CSl. *ę* > ESl. *ä* > *'a* with full palatalization (2.9):

$$*rędŭ > *rädŭ > r'adŭ;$$
$$*pętĭ > *pätĭ > p'ätĭ.$$

40   5. *Tenth–Eleventh Centuries*

Full palatalization extended to all consonants but the velars
before *e* and *i* (2.16), catalysed by (4) above and the merging of
existing pairs such as *ni/n'i*, *si/s'i* (2.5): *ₑo* > *'o* as in (3)(*a*).[22]

Results: N. *b'or'óza*; *n'ósŭ/n'ostá/n'os'í*; *s'ołó/wₛs'ol'ě*; *m'ódŭ*;
búd'omŭ; S. *b'är'óza*; *n'ósŭ/n'astá/n'äs'í*; *s'ałó/wₛs'äl'ě*.

Full palatalization *does not take place in the South-West (Ukr.)*
with eventual total depalatalization before *e* and *i* (Table XX
below); therefore in Ukrainian no further ёканье appears beyond
those established in (3) above.

41   6. *Eleventh–Twelfth Centuries*

(*a*) Loss of the *weak* and vocalization of the *strong* jers; *new*
e < ь treated as hitherto (2.43): *lĭnŭ* > *l'en* > *l'on*.

(*b*) In syllables before the pretonic, with its special status (cf.
§53 below), *C'oC'/C'äC'* (< *C'aC'*) revert to *C'eC'*; there are
thus normally no *sequences* of unstressed syllables with ёканье or
яканье and the loss of a jer is irrelevant to the phonetic shape:

---

[22] A much later example may be seen in *Theodore* (Gk. Θεόδωρος) > Фёдор
([fₑo-] > [f'o-]). There are many examples in Romance, e.g. *tₑo* > *t'o* in Lat.
lintéolu(m) > *lintjólu (with change of stress) > It. *lenzuolo*.

CSl. *$w_eart_ean_uá$ > N. *$w'or'ot'onó$ > $v'er'et'onó$, S. *$w'är'ät'anó$ > $v'er'et'anó$.

There are some irregularities in WhR., e.g трапятáцца (R. трепетáть), верацянó (веретенó).

7. *Thirteenth–Fourteenth Centuries*

Hardening of *š*, *ž* and other adjustments consequent on the loss of the jers (2.37 ff.): ежь [jež'] > еж [još] (C'eC' > C'oC).

43 ### 8. *Thirteenth Century and Later*

Reductions, especially in the South (S. and W. dialects), some of which may have been initiated earlier; they cannot be precisely dated:

N. *gołowá* > *gołová*, locally *gułová, gəłová* (§27 (1)(*b*) above);
S. *gaławá* > *γałavá* > *γəłavá* (WhR. *γałavá*);
SW *gołowá* > *γołová* > *hołová* (no reduction in Ukr.).

Northern:
b'or'óza/b'er'óza;
n'osú; *n'os/n'osłá*; *n'es'í* (*n'os'í* now rare);
s'ołó/v̯ s'el'é, *v'osná/k̯ y'es'n'é* (now much more frequent than *v̯ s'ol'é, k̯ y'os'n'é*).

B'er'óza, n'es'í, etc. may be considered not so much a reduction as an extension of C'eC' to a pretonic syllable.

Southern (S. and W. dialect) éканье and íканье patterns of reduction:

b'är'óza > *b'er'óza* (*b'ir'óza*);
n'asú; *n'os, n'asłá*; *n'as'í* (strong яканье);
n'asú; *n'os, n'asłá*; *n'es'í/n'is'í* (moderate яканье);
n'asú; *n'os, n'esłá/n'isłá*; *n'as'í* ('dissimilatory' pattern);
n'esú/n'isú; *n'os, n'asłá*; *n'es'í/n'is'í* ('assimilatory' pattern).

Notes

(i) In the North, *n'osú*; *n'os/n'osłá*; *n'es'í* is equivalent to moderate яканье of which it may be the source (§29 (*c*) above). There is clearly no phonetic motive for the development of the 'dissimilatory' and 'assimilatory' patterns of the South.

(ii) In the South, 'dissimilatory' may stand as a phonetic description but 'assimilatory' as commonly conceived is misleading: *n'asłá* is original.

44 9. *Absence of* еканье *(S. dialect)*

Total absence of ёканье appears to be unknown but it is reported that in the strong яканье dialect of the Riazan' area ё now occurs only in some masc. noun forms of the soft decl. which are manifestly analogical to the hard decl. and no doubt recent: канём after сталóм, канёк after кусóк.

If this statement is correct the absence of ё in нёс, мёд, and the like is not easy to account for. In a dialect in which there are no unstressed e analogical levellings can only go a very short distance, e.g. pl. 1 (pres. tense) [n′as′ém] is quite intelligible in the context of S. dial. sg. 3 [n′as′ét′], pl. 2 [n′as′ét′e]—the contrary, therefore, of the standard levelling несёте after the other pres. forms with N. dial. depalatalization of the final consonant (2.45 (3)).

In the case of ё < ь (2.42–3) it is conceivable that the 'law' ceased to operate in this area earlier than elsewhere, giving лен < льнъ, not лён.

The matter requires further investigation.

45 10. *Treatment of* ѣ

In those dialects which early conflated e/ѣ the latter will follow the fortunes of e, viz. S. dial. pѣкá [r′aká]; WhR. [raká] (Table XX (12)). In the North, *stressed* ѣ normally remained distinct (Table XVII (5) above) but *unstressed* ѣ may be treated as e: [r′oká]/[r′ɛká] according to dialect, pl. gen. [r′ɛk]/[r′ik] but never *[r′ok]; sg. loc. [v r′ek′ɛ]/[v r′ik′ɛ] but never *[v r′ok′ɛ].

46 11. *Moscow Standard*

(*a*) This is essentially that of a NC dialect as to ёканье with a further move towards éканье, viz. ё is strictly confined to *stressed* C′eC; all *unstressed* C′eC and all C′eC′ have e: несý, несёш(ь) (late hardening), несёт (late hardening), несём, несёте (very late analogical form contrary to the rule), несýт; нёс, неслá, etc.

(*b*) No яканье forms are admitted.

(*c*) Though pёкá is common in NC dialects, e/ѣ conflated too late in Moscow for this extension except by occasional analogy (2.45 (2)).

(*d*) Absence of ё after stress is a natural product of reduction: бýдет, бýдем (бýдёт, бýдём still present in some N. dialects).

(*e*) For áканье rules see §53 below.

47   12. *Summary*

While part of the above must remain speculative in its details
the three important pieces of evidence which combine to suggest
the proposed sequence of events are:

(*a*) Point 3—early recording of *o* after old palatalized consonants;

(*b*) the still extant forms N. dial. бёрёза/S. dial. бярёза in
polnoglásie, which can scarcely be explained as recent innovations;

(*c*) post-tonic (unstressed) ёканье in many parts of the North
(бу́дёт, бу́дём), which again is improbably an analogical innovation.

The patterns of unstressed front vowels are today quite complicated: there has been much adjustment, hybridization, analogy. It
is manifestly improbable that the original pattern(s) were as complex as would be required for basing all development on a comparatively late 'dissimilatory' яканье. The reflexes of *o/a* are so stable
that they reveal nothing about the chronology.

The Dialect of Moscow

48   Moscow lies in the Transitional belt. There can be little doubt
that the original dialect of the region was of the NC type
(Rostóv–Súzdal'). The place is first mentioned in 1147, an unimportant domain given by Alexander Nevsky to his youngest son
Daniíl.[23] During the 13th c. more and more а́кающие from the
South took refuge in the safer lands north of the R. Oká and soon
became an element in the population of Moscow, especially after
its partial destruction by the Mongols in 1238. The same effect was
no doubt produced by the Lithuanian expansion in the next century:
W. dial. speakers, also а́кающие, would move east towards
Moscow, by then the political centre for defence on all fronts. At
its greatest extent the Lithuanian state included Smolénsk and
lands to its east to within 200 km of Moscow. Thus а́кающие
became a substantial part of Moscow's population from an early
date. These movements were an important factor in the creation

---

[23] Moscow lies just about on the boundary of the old Baltic area (Map no. 1),
so its region cannot be definitely excluded from the possible original а́канье area
(in our sense). But this seems unlikely; the population of the new settlement and
expanding town surely came mainly from the Rostóv–Súzdal' area. Even if the
environs were а́кающий the *town dialect* was of NC type. The southern elements
are intrusions from nearer or further away. The pressure of S. dialects on Muscovite
speech habits is visible throughout the Muscovite period (early 14th–17th c.).

of the Transitional belt: the Transitional dialects can be shown to be Northern with intrusions of Southern traits, though there may be some exceptions at the extreme ends of the belt. The process can be followed further in space and time: Tver', 150 km north-west of Moscow, was eventually absorbed into the Transitional belt; áканье begins to appear in its documents from *c.* 1450 (хадѝла, стóраны, катóрава).

49   The speech of Moscow became a *Northern dialect incorporating certain Southern features*. A balance seems to have been reached in the 16th c. By then the standards of Moscow had become the standards of Russia, as one part after another came under the political control and administrative tentacles of the Tsars. In writing we have the more or less uniform деловóй (or прикáзный) язы́к (especially in the 17th c.—7.24); in speech we have the hybrid pronunciation of Moscow town, which has imposed itself as the cultured, literary standard.

50   With reference to Table XVII the repartition of N. and S. features in the *modern standard* appears in Table XVIII (omitting some irrelevant secondary points).

51   Moscow dialect, of the NC type, specifically derived from the Rostóv–Súzdal' subtype, thus ended up with a curious balance of N. and S. features. It *accepted* certain S. original features or innovations (notably points 8 and 9) but refused others (e.g. points 1, 2, 19). Similarly it accepted certain N. *innovations* (points 12, 13, 14) but refused others (points 11, 16, 17, 18[24]). Other points are not so clear-cut. As regards point 7 it struck its own balance but could be said to agree with *both*, since there are dialects with complete or nearly complete (unstressed) éканье in both North and South, though not necessarily directly influential on Moscow habits. By and large Moscow *consonantism* has remained Northern, whereas its *vocalism* has acquired a Southern cast. Its *morphology* is also in the main Northern, but characteristic of the conservative Vladímir–Vólga group, not of the wider North: all categories are maintained clear-cut (maximum number of hard/soft consonantal pairs; no confusion of cases; no confusion of genders). In sum, Moscow dialect is far removed from a specific *NW dialect*, the Nóvgorod type.

---

[24] Though the 'article' is present in NC dialects to the immediate north of Moscow, there is no evidence that it was ever characteristic of Moscow itself and therefore later eliminated by S. influence. This may be held to be improbable.

TABLE XVIII. Characteristics of Moscow Language

N. dialect (especially NC group)		Moscow (modern literary standard)		S. dialect (the W. group largely agrees)
1	[g]	⟷	[g]	[ɣ/h]
2	v/f (w/v in NW)	⟷	v/f	/w/ (v in some contexts, but no f)
3	c/č′ distinguished (NC) but цóканье in NW and much of the N.	⟷	c/č′ distinguished	⟷ c/č′ distinguished
4	final labials not depalatalized (NC) but depalatalized in NW and much of the N.	⟷	not depalatalized	⟷ not depalatalized
5	reflexes of e/ѣ wholly or partly distinct		e/ѣ conflated[25] (relatively late)	⟷ e/ѣ conflated
7	ёканье (unstressed) (complete or partial)		NEITHER	яканье
8	óканье		áканье	⟷ áканье
9	limited vowel reductions		prominent vowel reductions	⟷ prominent vowel reductions
11	intervocalic j lost (in part)		intervocalic j kept	⟷ intervocalic j kept
12	verbal 3rd pers. in -t (or absent)	⟷	in -t	in -t′
13	gen. меня́, тебя́	⟷	меня́, тебя́	мене́, тебе́
14	LD тебé	⟷	тебé	тобé
15	demonstrative type тот	⟷	тот	various (той predominantly in W.)
16	noun pl. DI conflated		no conflation	⟷ no conflation
17	noun sg. fem. GLD conflated		no conflation	⟷ no conflation
18	postposited 'article'		no article	⟷ no article
19	no confusions of gender	⟷	no confusions of gender	confusions of gender

[25] With the consistent rule [CɛC]/[CeC′]; see 2.10.

52　　The most noteworthy feature of Moscow pronunciation is, of course, áканье. In contrast one might say that я́канье was positively discouraged. Though there is much *orthographic* confusion of e/ѣ/я it does not seem that a *pronunciation* [n'asú], still less [r'aká] (< pѣká), was ever widespread, though there are a few examples of я́канье spelling in the 13th c.: яго́, ви́дям. A generalized éканье was early established, with a tendency to S. и́канье [n'isú], still present in standard pronunciation.

Áканье was present in Moscow as early as the 14th c. It does not follow that it was as yet 'good' pronunciation—probably not. It can be observed spreading in non-literary texts of the 15th c. By the 16th c. it was evidently becoming 'respectable'. Ivan Grozny himself writes in a letter which keeps close to the colloquial (1574): в Олексине. He can have been in no doubt that the correct form was Алéксин.[26] Vasili Grjaznoj replies (1576) with Офонáсей, прямáя служби́шко (pl. neut.), and розгодáл (гадáть).[27] These are few but they reveal the presence of áканье in cultivated speech. Likewise there is sporadic áканье in the more colloquial parts of *Domostrój* (mid 16th c.): всякое жита, паря́дня, and others.

By the 17th c. áканье spellings have become a commonplace in everyday documents, including the letters and papers of Alekséj Mikhájlovich himself and his court: хорашó, сóкалы, ани́, абрóшныхъ (= оброчных). This continues down to the papers of Peter the Great: даговóр(ъ), аѳице́ру (= офицеру), дажидáюсь караблéй (1693); взять вѣдамасть караблямъ (1697).

Áканье was thus 'good' pronunciation by, at latest, the beginning of the 17th c. That it imposed itself from below, socially speaking, after a considerable period of incubation, is highly probable and a frequently observed phenomenon in linguistic change. It is noteworthy that Alekséj Mikhájlovich legislated for the validity of áканье in legal documents (1675): Будет кто в челобитье своем напишет . . ., не зная правописания, вместо о — а, или вместо а — о . . . по природе тех городов, где кто родился и по обыкностям своим говорить и писать извык, того в бесчестье не ставить. The norm of прикáзный (делово́й) язы́к, as propagated from Moscow, was of course óкающий.

---

[26] Strictly speaking this only proves that his secretary was áкающий.
[27] Also нагáй for modern standard ногáй but this was a foreign name probably variable in any case.

53 *The Modern Standard*

The rules governing unstressed vowels now stand as follows:

1. (*a*) áканье is applied to all unstressed *o*;
   (*b*) all such unstressed *a* except the pretonic may be further reduced to [ə], unless the *a* is in absolute initial position;[28]
   (*c*) the quality of an absolutely final *a* will depend on the need to avoid morphological ambiguity: stage diction, and indeed careful speech as a whole, avoids reduction. Examples:

   сковорода́, асс. ско́вороду [skəvərada, skovərədu]
   свобо́дная [svabodnəjə]
   ду́мала [duməɫa *or* duməɫə]
   оборо́на [abaronə]
   окорока́ [akərəka]
   о́лово; gen. о́лова [oɫəvə; oɫəva *or* oɫəvə]

   An original *a*, if not pretonic, is commonly reduced too: старики́ [stər'ik'i]. The normally unstressed verbal affix -ся is pronounced [sə] (depalatalized).

   (*d*) All vowels except the highest row (и, ы, у) tend towards [ə] after the stress: ста́рое = ста́рая [starəjə], вы́работать [vyrəbətət'].[29]

Thus the fall in intensity and clarity is abrupt after the stress whereas the approach to the stress is gradual:

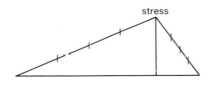

освободи́тельного
[asvəbad'it'əl'nəvə]

---

[28] Maintaining the CSl. rule against initial ъ, which took epenthetic *w*: *ŭn > wŭ(n) > въ; *ŭp- 'cry' > wŭpiti > ChSl. вопи́ть. Reduction of initial *a > ə is recorded sporadically in modern dialect.

[29] Until relatively recently analogical spellings of the type се́рцо, инозе́мцов (following кольцо́, купцо́в) were not uncommon but the pronunciation was surely always [-сə], [-сəf]. Such spellings survive in a few family names, e.g. Звеги́нцов.

54   2. There is no яканье. Unstressed e/ѣ and я are reduced along
the normal line ($> e$) $> i$, there being no absolute standard on this
point: a ($\ddot{a}$) $> i$ is usual, e may scarcely move at all. Examples:

> тяну́ [t′inu] ([t′enu] is N. dial., §27 (1)(*b*) above);
> река́ (рѣка) [r′eka *or* r′ika];
> намерева́ться [nəm′ir′ivačə];
> пятьдеся́т [p′id′is′at];
> часы́ [č′isy].

After depalatalized *š*, *ž*, *c* a pretonic reduced vowel will be of
the type /y/: шага́м [šygam], цена́ [cyna] (but now increasingly
[žará] *et sim*.). Reduction therefore clearly preceded depalatalization.

It has been claimed that the final stage of и́канье did not achieve
the status of 'good' pronunciation until quite recently—the end of
the 18th c. The evidence is rather conflicting. И́канье is not
uncommonly noted in 17th c. documents (Питру́шка). But the
popular prints (лубо́чные карти́ны) of the 18th c., which broadly
reflect colloquial pronunciation, show no и́канье whereas е́канье
and, of course, а́канье are commonplace. Their geographical origin
is, however, not always determinable.

It should be noted that the transference of the capital from
Moscow to St Petersburg at the beginning of the 18th c. had
virtually no effect on standard pronunciation, though [š′č′] was
apparently preferred to [š′] (2.39).

False Orthography

55   The accepted spelling of a number of words is etymologically
wrong. Generally speaking the 18th c. restored orthography to
sensible rules after the laxness of the 17th c. The perpetuated
mistakes therefore mostly affect isolated words without clear
affinities. The most usual are:

барсу́к 'badger': earlier борсукъ (Ukr. and Pol. *borsuk*)—a Turkic
   loan-word. The animal is much commoner in S. than in N.
   Russia.

pl. бразды́ 'reins': this is in fact an instance of false ChSl. Early
   ESl. бръзда́ > брозда́. Lomonósov still wrote звучи́т брозда́ми
   (1750) but the word was wholly poetic and 'looked better' in
   high style as бразды́, as if corresponding to R. *борозды.

забо́та 'care': abstract noun of the verb зоба́ть (dial. зоба́ться

= забо́титься). Not so much an а́канье spelling as a false *rapprochement* to the prefix за-. A similar case is the frequent but transitory (17th c.) начева́ть for ночева́ть 'pass the night'.[30]

за́втрак 'lunch': from за-утр-ъкъ: заутрокавше (*RPC s.a.* 1095); завтрок(ать) frequent in 16th c. No doubt influenced by за́втра and/or the suffix -ак.

заря́ 'sunrise, sunset': earlier зоря́; sg. acc. зо́рю (and зарю́), pl. nom. зо́ри (cf. stressed роз-, unstressed раз-, 1.25). Etymology unclear; the word varies between *za-/zo-* throughout Slav, including OCS *zarja/zorja*. ESl. generalized *zo-* (so also SCr. *zòra*, acc. *zòru*); озари́ть is a Slavonicism. But cf. also за́рево.

кавы́чки 'inverted commas': appears to belong with заковы́ка.

кала́ч 'roll': колачь in *Dom.* Derivative of кол(ес)о.

карака́тица 'cuttle-fish, squid': a *polnoglásie* word, viz. adj. *korok-at-* 'many-legged' (type бородат- 'bearded'). Bulgarian has кракатица, agreeing with its normal word крак 'leg' (in ESl. only о́корок 'ham'). The animal is southern (Black Sea, etc.), so a *rapprochement* with Turkic *kara* 'black' (ink, sepia) is likely.

карма́н 'pocket': not native and source uncertain; корман(ъ) occurs in 14th c. Novg. and Pskov texts but is not certainly the prototype.

карта́вить 'speak with a burr': ?earlier корта́вый (на Ивана на кортавого, Pskov *c.*1465).

каса́тка 'house-martin': probably belongs to коса́ in allusion to the forked tail. So also каса́тик/коса́тик 'iris, flag' from the falcate leaves. There are a number of other similar cases in the names of less familiar animals and plants.

крапи́ва 'nettle': earlier кропи́ва and so widely throughout Slav, the original form being supposedly *kopriva* (SCr. *kòpriva*, PN *Kòprīvnīk*). The form кропи́ва is still sometimes used by botanists.

ладо́нь 'palm of the hand': deformation of *dolon'* (Ukrainian has долоня); the *polnoglásie* is confirmed by OCS *dlani*.

лапша́ 'shovel': also лопша́, related to лопа́та 'spade'; SCr. and Czech confirm [lo-].

ла́сковый 'affectionate': hypercorrection for ла́скавый (suffix -ав-); Pol. *łaskawy*.

о́вод 'gadfly': earlier óvad(й) and so in other Sl. languages.

---

[30] So also Polikarpov (*Leksikon*, 1704) начлѣгъ/нащлѣгъ for ночлег, attracted to на-.

о́стов 'skeleton, shell': apparently for остав(ъ) (= оста́тки).

панёва 'skirt': OCS, Balkan, and Ukr. *ponjava*; so also in early ESl. texts, but the garment was typical of S. Russia (а́канье area).

паро́м 'ferry': for поро́м (*polnoglásie*); so in early texts and still in Ukrainian.

пола́та (more often pl. пола́ти): equally often пала́та, whence пала́тка 'tent, marquee'. This loan-word is in fact variable from the outset (cf. монасты́рь, §33 above, n. 20). OCS has normally *polata* < Lat. *pălātium* via Greek.

раки́та 'willow':[31] Ukr. роки́та, Pol. *rokita*—a typical W. dial. word, the 'Pripet marshes' being in Pol. *Rokitno Błoto*. The correct form роки́та is found in N. dialect.

славя́не 'Slavs': a learned form of слове́не; OCS and early ESl. use the derivative *slověnĭskŭ językŭ* for the Slavs as a whole and for their as yet undifferentiated language, e.g. *RPC, ad init.*: се бо токмо слове́нескъ языкъ в Руси. Not so much an а́канье spelling as a false *rapprochement* with сла́ва.

стака́н 'tumbler, glass': recorded from the 14th c. as дъстъканъ/достоканъ; from Persian via Turkic. N. dialect still has стока́н.

тарова́тый 'sly': dial. also торова́тый; the root is that of тере́ть/то́рная доро́га.

штаны́ 'trousers': appears to be based on a Turkic *ičton* (> *išton*) (5.22). First rec. in Mark Ridley *c.*1599 as стани, then in R. James (*c.*1620) as *stanie*.

For раз- and рабо́та see 1.25.

Personal names such as Авдо́тья, Алёна have adopted an а́канье spelling, perhaps influenced by Алексе́й and others; the sources are Ἐυδοκία, Ἑλένη (1.29). The reverse effect—Офона́сей for Афана́сий—seems to be due to the almost complete lack of native words with initial *a*-. Some surnames appear to be in S. dial. form, e.g. Валу́ев, if from волу́й.

Here may be noted also the confusion of the unstressed suffixes -ла/-ло and -ка/-ко (§24 above), evident from the 17th c.; derived surnames in -кин and -ков have an arbitrary distribution, often going against the normal rule -ка > -кин, -к(о) > -ков, e.g. ба́тюшка/Ба́тюшков.

---

[31] The three common words for 'willow'—и́ва, раки́та, ве́рба—are affected, but not exclusively, to different species, the difference being vital in basket-making, etc. Раки́та is on principle *Salix fragilis* or *viminalis*. In literary usage ве́рба has ChSl. overtones (ве́рбное воскресе́нье 'Palm Sunday').

56   Mistakes in prepalatal vowels are less frequent:

ветчина́ 'ham': known from the 16th c. (*Dom.*) in the forms ветчина and ветшина and frequently contrasted with свежина́ 'fresh meat'. Ве́тхий may thus be the true source; alternatively a 'popular etymology' for *вядчина, parallel to вя́леное (мя́со) 'dried'.

десна́ 'gum': earlier дясна with well-authenticated nasal (Pol. *dziąsło*, dial. *dziąsna*).

ресни́ца 'eyelash': earlier рясни́ца and so in ChSl. The surname Рясни́цын may still exist.

снето́к 'smelt': a N. dial. word usually so spelt, for снято́к.

тетива́ 'bowstring': earlier тятива́ with well-authenticated nasal (?*te-m-p-* or *ten-t-*).

я́стреб 'hawk': earlier ястрябъ (Pol. *jastrząb*). Similarly ле́бедь 'swan' < ле́бядь (1.24).

за́яц 'hare': -яц is correct on the evidence of Pol. *zając* but mod. gen. за́йца shows re-formation as *за́ец, perhaps rather a substitution of suffix.

For Ряза́нь see §30 above, n. 19.

57   The type of а́канье described above, together with the reduction of all unstressed vowels except *i/y* and *u* (the original *long* vowels of the highest range), has been the received standard since the early 19th c. But it should be noted that 18th c. poetry, especially the 'high style' odes, was conceived as more ChSl. than Russian and declaimed (or read) according to the norms of ChSl. pronunciation. The main points were: no а́канье; little or no reduction of unstressed vowels; [ɣ] for [g] (2.40); [′e] for [′o] (2.46); little palatalization before *e*, fuller palatalization before ѣ = [ie]: [boɣat]; [mɛt] = мёд; [bɛrɛx], [br′i͡ex] = брѣг. We may suppose that these conventions were observed by Pushkin in 1816 when reciting his prize poem before Derzhávin at the Lycée.

58   New foreign loan-words are generally subject to the normal rules but there is a good deal of minor variation, particularly in the avoidance of и́канье: температу́ра [t′emp′e-] or [tɛmp′e-], less often [t′imp′i-]. There are very few exceptions to а́канье: at least until recently [poét], [poéma] were preferred, following *poète*, *poème,* and the same applies, or may apply, to other more or less international French words, e.g. оте́ль [otel′], консоме́ [konsomɛ].

History of Stress

59   Few early manuscripts indicate stress, whether ChSl. or not. The subject bristles with difficulties and cannot be fully treated here. The available evidence has been brought together and analysed by V. Kiparsky, *Der Wortakzent der russischen Schriftsprache* (1962) and V. V. Kolesov, История русского ударения (именная акцентуация в древнерусском языке) (1972). Notable stressed texts (at least in part) are:

(i) ChSl.: 11th c.—*Nóvgorod Minéi* (text no. 8); Житиé Кондрáта; Синáйский патерúк. 14th c.—*New Testament* of Metropolitan Alekséj. By this date the numerous differences between the traditional ChSl. norm and spoken Russian demanded guidance for the reader. ChSl. stress was further codified in the 17th c. Bible.

(ii) Russian: 16th c.—*Domostrój*.

A glance at the Толкóвый слóварь живóго великорýсского языкá by V. Dal' (1st edn. 1863–6) reveals the considerable variation in stress patterns in different parts of Russia at a time when the speech of the countryside was still largely unaffected by literary or urban norms. In broad terms:

1. the N. dial. area is conservative, preserving the majority of original mobile stress patterns in the nouns and also such contrasts as по грязи/в грязú (3.6) and the recessive stress rhythm нá голову, зá морем. Conversely it may abandon mobile stress in the pres. tense of second conj. verbs: люблю́, лю́бишь, лю́бит;

2. the S. dial. area shows a tendency to iron out mobility in fem. nouns (e.g. sg. acc. рукý, ногý) but not in the verbs, e.g. дарúть: дарю́, дóришь, дóрит (cf. older Muscovite norm платúть, плачý, плóтит—still not wholly extinct), but N. dial. дарю́, дарúшь, дарúт (standard).

60   There were only a few inherited mobile stress patterns in the nouns. Others have been created more or less recently by hybridization. Nouns have moved by analogical or other obscure causes from one pattern to another, and the process still goes on. The early 18th c. loan-word бал 'dance, ball', as an immigrant, had fixed stress at first. By the early 19th c. it followed the pattern бал, бáла . . .; бáлы, балóв . . .; it now has pl. балы́, балóв . . . Another, earlier, loan спи́на 'back' has become спинá with a similarly artificial mobile stress (acc. спи́ну, зá спину; pl. спи́ны);

so also гу́ба > губа́, стру́на > струна́, and others. Лист, мост, плод, след all appear to have been root-stressed in early ESl. (as theory demands); they now have sg. gen. листа́, плода́, следа́, with мо́ста́ still variable. There is no unique 'correct' stress pattern for such a common word as река́—several (regional) alternatives are accepted. The surname Ивано́в—the commonest of all, according to Unbegaun's statistics[32]—varies between Ива́нов (to be expected on the basis of Ива́н, Ива́на) and the 'smarter' Ивано́в.

The following points may be noted:

1. Final stressed jers were never treated as strong. As they weakened, their stress passed to the preceding syllable, hence the pattern боб, боба́; коро́ль, короля́; кусо́к, куска́, *et sim.*

2. Rearrangements of stress evidently took place in the 'long' adj. but the details are obscure. It is possible that the family names Дурново́ and Сухово́ are relics of original end-stress in the oblique cases (cf. still его́, кого́, того́).

3. In the pres. tense of verbs of Type A1 and some B1 (3.87) the end-stress of e.g. pl. 1, 2 *nesemú/nesemó, neseté* has been preserved in Ukrainian but replaced in Russian by 'columnar' stress: несу́ . . . несём, несёте, несу́т.

61 *Two Important Dialects*

The dialect of *Nóvgorod* and its immediate environs is the only one whose characteristics can be followed continuously from the beginning of the literate period to the present day. Its main characteristics are therefore resumed below to emphasize its distance from the Moscow norm.

It is instructive also to compare with it that of Pskov, only some 180 km to the south-west and expectedly under Novg. influence even when politically independent.

62 *Nóvgorod Dialect*

Several features were already well established in the 11th c. (nos. 1, 2, and 5, perhaps also 7), the rest by *c.*1300:

1. цо́канье (§10 above); ньмного ѡсподинь [= господине voc.] ржи на твою цасть. два овина. цьтвьрти (*NBG,* no. 23, 15th c.); цоловѣкъ (*NBG,* no. 43, late 14th c.);

---

[32] *Russian Surnames* (1972), p. 412.

2. secondary *polnoglásie* (2.49): attested in *Ostr.* (1056–7) and *Novg. Minéi* (1095–6)—пьрьва, жьрьтву, гъръдыню;

3. stressed ѣ > [i] (§12 above): говорѣ с нѣми сама (*NBG,* no. 131, 14th c.) shows ignorant hypercorrection (ѣ for real и); ѣ may, of course, represent [ie] (with either component predominating) rather than [i]. Parallel diphthongization of some stressed o as [uo] (§27 (1)(*a*) above);

4. final e/o for a lost jer (*graphic*, not phonetic, peculiarity): се въдале варламе (text no. 15, *c.*1200);

5. pretonic ёканье consistently maintained (2.43–4);

6. reduction of unstressed vowels unusual, except for pretonic я > е: тяни́, тяну́ [t′en′i, t′enu], presumably by extension from general *stressed* C′äC′ > C′eC′ [z′et′, v′z′él′i];

7. verbal 3rd pers. sg. and pl. in -*t* or nil (3.97 (*d*));

8. assimilations producing the long consonants *l̃, m̃, ñ* (§17 above);

9. local vocabulary, including the following: испра́ва 'investigation', купчи́на 'merchant', оби́лье 'corn', о́дерень (2.49), по́жня 'stubble field', поса́дник 'mayor'.

63 *Pskov Dialect*

The area shares a considerable *Finnic* substratum with Nóvgorod but also has a *Baltic* component. It is properly placed at the extreme north-western end of the Transitional belt. Plausibly some at least of the Pskov-group dialects would now have been WhR. dialects but for the infusion of Northern traits from Nóvgorod. Typical Pskov dialect has:

1. а́канье and 'strong' я́канье (§29 (*a*) above) in its essentials. Newer types of я́канье (dissimilatory in WhR., 'moderate' in other W. dialects) now separate it from other areas with strong я́канье. Not all agree that these features are original in the dialect;

2. no /f/; /w/ finally and at junctions ([drow, ɫawka]). Initial *u*-also > *w*- before consonants: вдержалъ (1465) (= удержа́л);

3. verbal 3rd pers. in -*t′* (WhR. preserves -*t′* in the evolved form -*c′*: Table XX (17)).

Novg. features are:

4. цо́канье: цего, ноць, боцекъ/бочекъ (gen. pl.) (1465);

5. presence of [ie] and [uo] (§27 (1)(*a*) above), but not ѣ > и. Novg. point 4 also occurs sporadically.

Individual features:

6. *tl/dl*, preserved longer than in most of ESl.,[33] changed in limited contexts under Baltic influence into *kl/gl* (CSl. **ardlă* = Lith. *árklas*): привегли; перечóк < -чеклъ < -четлъ (standard -чёл); жереглó (2.50) = standard жéрло;

7. Pskov is one of the few small areas of шепелявость in Russia, i.e. where the pairs *š'/s'*, *ž'/z'* are not distinguished, as in Polish *mazurzenie* which is probably likewise due to the Baltic substratum in E. Poland. In the document of 1465: залуютсѧ/жалуютсѧ, отсталошь, пéнежи (= пенязи); по пск[овск]ои послине (= пошлине). The pronunciation is [s']/[z']. Цóканье can be subsumed as a parallel development [tš'] > [ts']. Шепелявость is also found in some W. dialects, perhaps by spread from the Pskov area;

8. pl. 1 personal pronoun ны for мы (after нам, нас?), unrecorded elsewhere in Russia.

Ukrainian and White Russian (Belorussian) compared with (Great)[34] Russian

64 The 'unity' of the West branch and South branch of the Slav languages can easily be called in question, though the objections depend largely on chronological definition. 'Unity', that is, a continuum of closely related dialects, is too narrow a concept in their case. Nevertheless in both branches there are some common innovations not shared with the other groups. The isoglosses of the late CSl. period—the period of migration and break-up—make a quite complex geographical picture.

In the case of the ESl. branch the 'unity' is scarcely questionable. That WhR. is no more than one dialect of the ESl. continuum, still clearly allied to the modern SR dialects, which underwent some not very profound separate development from a relatively late date when under Lithuanian (later Polish) rule, can hardly be gainsaid. Without this political, but only partially linguistic, separation from the Muscovite state WhR. would today be a SR dialect of the type adumbrated in the Smolénsk Treaty of 1229.

---

[33] SSl. and ESl. are opposed to WSl. in simplifying *tl/dl* > *l*: CSl. **mydlo*: SCr. *mȉlo*, R. мы́ло but Pol. *mydło*, Cz. *mýdlo*; CSl. **pletlŭ*, **pletla*: R. плёл, плелá but Pol. *plótł*, *plotła*, Cz. *pletl*, *pletla* (the final *l* is no longer pronounced in *plótł*, *pletl*).

[34] Великору́сский, a term now in use again among *philologists* but which was formerly used in a political and geographical sense in contrast to малоросси́йский 'Little Russian' (= Ukrainian).

TABLE XIX. The Evolution of East Slav: Diagrammatic Summary

see Map no. 2	Southern tribes (Poljáne (Kiev area), Derevljáne,?Severjáne; other tribes further S. and SW)	Central tribes (W.: Radímiči, Drěgoviči; E.: Vjátiči)		Northern tribes (Slověne (Novgorod area), Kriviči)		
	substratum *negligible*	substratum *Baltic*		substratum *Finnic* (and some Baltic)		
Kiev period	dials. of the SW and Kiev–Polesie	W. dials.[b] (e.g. Smolénsk)	S. dials.[b] (e.g. Riazán')	NW dials. (Novgorod) ↓ NC dials.← (Vladímir–Vólga group)[d]	↘ — N. dials.	
*c.*1200	↓	↓		↓		
	Ukrainian← —[a] →White Russian (Belorussian)	SR dials.		Moscow town dial. (Transitional belt) Moscow standard (*c.*1500)	NR dials.	
*c.*1700	↓	↓	↓	↓	↓	
	modern literary Ukr.	modern literary WhR.	SR dials.	R. modern literary standard	NR dials.	

[a] The boundary between Ukr. and WhR. now lies in the ancient territory of the Drěgoviči ('fenmen' of the Pripet basin); there has been mutual interaction over a long period between N. Ukr. and S. WhR. which hardly affects the two standard languages.

[b] Typical WhR. coincides approximately with the territory of the земля́ по́лоцкая; the земля́ смоле́нская became transitional between this and the SR dialects formed in the земля́ черни́говская. For approximate boundaries *c.*1100 see K. V. Gorshkova, Историческая диалектология русского языка (1972), p. 62.

[c] For the Lithuanian chancellery language see 7.23.

[d] The population probably included some (Central) Vjátiči and some (Northern) Kriviči, with further intakes from other areas, including the Kiev region. The Moscow dialect belongs more narrowly to the Rostóv–Súzdal' group.

65   The case of Ukrainian is not so clear. The dialects ancestral to modern Ukrainian (or most of them) were indubitably ESl. dialects since Ukrainian as a whole shared the fundamental ESl. innovations of the immediate pre-literate centuries, e.g. *polnoglásie* and the reflexes of the CSl. nasals (1.21), and continued to share at least some ESl. developments down to the 13th c., notably the general treatment of the jers and the generalization of the fem. pl. endings -ах, -ам, -ами. But there are signs of individual development from the 10th c. (§§37 ff. above). After *c.*1300 the Ukr. area pursued a divergent path, divorced from further typical Great Russian developments, as part of the Lithuanian–Polish political and cultural sphere.

66 It is generally assumed that the speech of Kiev in the early literate centuries was a dialect of the Ukr. group, to wit óкающий, but there is *no direct evidence of this*. Early texts emanating from Kiev, none wholly vernacular in any case, merely reflect the óкающий norm of OCS (ChSl.). The assumption relies perhaps too heavily on modern linguistic boundaries. However that may be, when a term such as 'proto-Ukrainian' is applied to Kievan texts it must not be held to imply a distinct linguistic area only loosely attached to ESl.: Ukrainian does not show features which attach it more closely to any other Slav language (Polish, Slovak, even SCr.) than to ESl., nor can it be said to constitute a type of its own separate from the East, South, and West groups.

67 Some features of both Ukr. and WhR. were no doubt present as dial. differences *ab initio* (even dating from the pre-literate period), e.g. the treatment of /g/ (2.40). Some differences of fundamental vocabulary which are shared by Ukr. and WhR. in contrast to Great Russian have also been detected, apart from those due to later Pol. influence on both.

In sum, the separation of Ukr. and WhR. from Russian is largely due to historical circumstances. If they had remained parts of the Russian political world throughout they might still be properly classed as R. dialects, however distinct. In any case the distinction of *dialect* and *language* is not an absolute one and *not a purely linguistic one*. Yorkshire speech, though abundantly distinct, has remained a dialect with respect to standard English. On the other hand some would class Scots English, very different both in phonology and lexicon, as a separate language since Scotland was politically independent and had its own literary tradition down to the beginning of the 18th c. A *dialect* earns the name of *language vis-à-vis* other dialects of the continuum by being raised to the dignity of literary or other conventional use.

68 To cope with their innovations the following contrasts to Russian have been incorporated into their relatively recently codified *orthographies*:

(i) Ukr. и = [y] (nearer Pol. than R. [y]), i = [i] (< *ě, o*), ï = [ji] (e.g. in своїм), e = [ɛ], є = [je].

(ii) WhR. incorporates а́канье and я́канье into the orthography: галава́, чалаве́к, бяро́за,[35] бяда́. Special symbol ў for *w* < *ł, v*; i for R. и throughout. (Hard) э used internally: чэсць (R. честь), цэп.

Below are set out the more important distinctions.

TABLE XX. Distinguishing Features of Ukrainian and White Russian (Belorussian)

	Ukrainian (some examples are taken from OB 32 (1378) and OB 34 (1398))	White Russian (standard; the NE dials. have remained closer to the SR type, the SW dials. have common developments with N. Ukr. dials.)	References and remarks
1	Palatalization lost before *e* and *i*; consequently *i* and *y* merge. The *Galician-Volhynian Chronicle* (ending 1292) shows clearly the conflation of *i/y*; cf. also тиса́чю (1378), кымъ (1398) (modern ким). Loss of palatalization before *e* was apparently complete only later than these examples.	Palatalization maintained before *e* and *i* as in Great Russian	2.16 and §40 above

[35] человѣкъ: e > я by я́канье (Table XX, point 5) but ч then depalatalized; o > a by а́канье; ѣ > e (point 3); берёза: e > я by я́канье; e > ё but p then depalatalized.

	Ukrainian	White Russian	References and remarks
2	*e* and *o* in a new clo-sed syllable > *ē̆, ō̆* and by various diph-thongal stages > [i] ('compensatory lengthening'); *ē̆* is early revealed by the spelling ѣ, *ō̆* less often distinguished: будѣть, камѣнь (late 12th c.). Inter-mediate stages diffi-cult to indicate in the Cyrillic alphabet are represented by своѥмъ, грошювъ, божьюмъ (sg. loc.), чтюнъ (p.p.p.) (1378 and 1398). Modern: конь > кінь, ледъ > лід, полночь > північ [piwnič], носъ > ніс, несъ (pret.) > ніс. 　　*Note.* New *e/o* < ь/ъ are *not* leng-thened: сон, пес, день	As in Great Russian	§13 above
3	ѣ > [i] from 12th c.: *sněgŭ* > сніг [s′n′ix]; причистоѣ (1378; prefix прѣ-). Many dials. have [ie] stressed/[e] un-stressed	ѣ/e early conflated (ѣ then included in 4 below)	§12 above

	Ukrainian	White Russian	References and remarks
4	Ёканье only after original palatals (2.43) and usually pretonic: шо́стий, жона́, його́ (but до ньо́го), чоловік	Ёканье on SR models; зялёны, бяро́за, нёс (i.e. *stressed* syllables only)	§§38 and 46 (11)(*a*) above
5	No а́канье or я́канье and only sporadic vowel reduction ([birú], [vudá] occur). A few words, e.g. хазя́їн, гара́зд, have presumably been adopted from SR dial.	А́канье and я́канье present with some vowel reductions (general agreement with SR dial. but the post-tonic reduction *u* > *ə* ([própəsk]) is individual as also the (normally) lack of reduction in *polnoglásie*: [ɣaɫavá] not *[ɣəɫavá])	§§14 ff. and 29 above
6	Reflex of unstressed CSъC is блиха́, крива́вий	Reflex of unstressed CSъC is блыха́, крыва́вы	2.48 (3)(ii)
7	*Stressed o* > *u* widespread but not universal or standard: торгу́вля (1378)	Unknown	Unknown in Russian
8	*g* > *h* ([ɦ], voiced pharyngeal)	*g* > *ɣ* or *h* (the spelling кг for foreign plosive [g] is recorded from the 14th c.)	2.40–1
9	No /f/; [w] general and always before consonants and finally: жив [žyw], пра́вда [prawda]	No /f/; [w]/[v] as in Ukr. or SR dial.: дау́но́, кроу́, зяу́ну́ў = R. давно́, кровь, зевну́л	2.34; §9 above

	Ukrainian	White Russian	References and remarks
10	[ł] > [w] finally in pret. and in some other contexts: вів [viw] = R. вёл; вовк [vowk]	[ł] > [w] as in Ukr. (written ў): воўк, тóўсты, чытáў, зяўнýў	[ł] stable in most R. dial.
11	Final (and occasionally other) labials depalatalized: гóлуб, сíм 'seven', степ	Variable but usually as in Ukr.: гóлуб, сем	§11 above
12	[r'] partly depalatalized: терати (1398); тепéр; but sg. gen. мóря, рябúй	r' > r in all contexts: бярóза, ракá (< рѣка)	r/r' maintained in Russian
13	Final consonants (including those of internal closed syllables) *not* devoiced: [hólub], [knyžka]	Devoicing as in Great Russian	2.24 and 2.34–5
14	Velar palatalizations preserved in declension: хоньци (dat. of хонька) (1378); на дорóзі	Velar palatalizations preserved in declension: на парóзе (R. порóге), sg. fem. DL руцэ́	3.29
15	*Hard č* and *soft c',* but also č', c in certain limited contexts	Hard č and c (the former clearly recorded from the 15th c.). For new c' see 17 below	2.38
16	*(z)d + j* > [dž] and [ždž] mainly in 2nd conj. verb forms: ходжý, розпоря́дження; їжджу [jiždžu] = R. éзжу	As Ukr.: гляджý, саджý; éжджу; also ураджай (R. урожáй)	Absent in Russian

	Ukrainian	White Russian	References and remarks
17	Absent	New [dz′]/[c′] < *dj*, *tj* and *d/t* + front vowel (similar but not identical with Pol. reflexes and perhaps derived thence): дзеці = R. дéти; дзéсяць; ляцéць = летéть. Established by the 14th c.	Absent in Russian
18	Long (double) consonants from new contiguity of C + *j* (< Cь*j*) (15th c.): знання́, столíття (= R. -ние/нье, -тие/ тье); нíччю [niččju] = R. нóчью. Does not apply to labials	Similar long consonants: збóжжа, жыццё, пыта́нне, вясéлле	2.33 (virtually all R. dials. preserve Cь*j*)
19	Absent	Assimilation *dn* > *ń*, *bm* > *ṁ*: сягóння = R. сегóдня	Table XVII (10)
20	Vocative case retained	Vocative case retained	3.30
21	Adoption of *u*-stem endings in *o*-stem declension different from R. norm, e.g. dat. -ові/-еві preserved (Иванови, зᴀтеви, 1378) and often extended to loc.	Some differences from R. norm	3.14 ff.
22	Absent	Neut. pl. NA in -ы: сяло́, pl. сёлы	§24 above
23	Short forms of adj. decl. virtually eliminated; masc. sg. nom. in -ий	Short forms of adj. virtually eliminated; masc. sg. nom. in -ы	3.48

	Ukrainian	White Russian	References and remarks
24	Adj. suffix -*n's'k*- by progressive palatalization (written -нськ-)	Adj. suffix -*nsk*-/-*n'sk*- corresponding to -*n*/-*n'* in the noun	Russian has -*nsk*- by regressive depalatalization (2.26)
25	3rd pers. pres. tense in -ть (*nil* in 3 sg. of 1st conj.)	3rd pers. pres. tense in -ць (*nil* in 3 sg. of 1st conj.)	3.97 (*d*)
26	1 pl. pres. tense and imperative in -*mo* (not recorded early but scarcely a late innovation; cf. SCr. -*mo*). Some dialects have -*me*	As in Great Russian (Ukr. type only in SW dial.)	3.96 (*b*)
27	*Impf* fut. with suffixed -иму etc. (the R. type буду + inf. is also used). Not recorded early but scarcely an innovation	буду + inf. (Ukr. type only in SW dial.)	3.108 ff.
28	Infinitive in -ти, pres. gerund in -чи (p.p.a. virtually extinct)	Infinitive in -ць, pres. gerund in -чы (p.p.a. virtually extinct)	3.114, 118–19
29	Numerals 2–4 constructed with nom. pl. (i.e. early ESl. construction of 3–4 retained and extended to 2)	As Ukr.	4.75
30	Anim./inan. distinction not extended beyond *persons* in the pl.: гна́ти коро́ви	May be extended to all animates: даіць каро́ў = R. до́йть коро́в	4.41

7

SPOKEN LANGUAGE AND WRITTEN LANGUAGES

A. The Kievan Period to c.1250

1 A literary language, in the strict sense of the term,[1] is a conventional medium for the expression of 'literature' and, as such, is as much a dialect of the language as any of its other regional or social variants. Unlike a dialect it is artificial: it is a conscious selection from the whole resources of the language, based (normally) on the usage of one region and one class—though rarely wholly and exclusively on one—those for whom the literature is being written. 'Correct' grammar and 'good' usage are correct and good for a few at a certain place and moment but only by convention for many over a larger area and a longer time.

2 A language may thus in the course of its history give rise to several different literary dialects. If, however, the quality of an early literature is sufficiently high and the prestige of the early normative writers correspondingly great, the great part of their linguistic conventions may remain standard almost indefinitely— provided there is no profound revolution in the structure of the language itself—whatever the subsequent history of the *spoken* language. Thus literary Italian is still essentially the eclectic language of Florentine Dante and other 14th c. writers; no new universal standard stood a chance of arising later on the basis of the dialect, say, of Milan, Naples, or Venice, however successfully used from time to time by purveyors of a more local literature.

3 Political and cultural centres may change; the literary standard of a language does not necessarily change with them. Thus in the case of Polish the first important (secular) literature was written during the late Renaissance (15th–16th c.) in Cracow, the political and cultural centre of that time, yet this literary dialect preserved,

---

[1] It should be noted that Soviet linguists generally only make a distinction between *spoken* and *written* forms of Russian: any form whatever put into writing belongs to 'литерату́рный язы́к'.

apparently deliberately, not a few linguistic features of earlier cultural centres (Gniezno, Poznań) of different dialect, to which evidently some prestige attached. The Renaissance literature of Cracow was printed; the conventions adopted by the Cracow writers and printers thus acquired a strongly normative role for the future. The transference of the capital to Warsaw in the 18th c.—in a quite different dialect area once more, and moreover one with no past prestige—has been scarcely reflected in the modern standard literary dialect.

4   The written literature enjoyed by a cultured class, unlike the oral 'literature' of a peasantry, is not necessarily composed in some form of vernacular language contemporary with the writers and first readers: it may be composed in an imported language of exceptional prestige. Such was the use of Latin at certain periods in certain W. European countries. Such was also the case of the ESl. world. During the course of the 10th c. OCS was introduced from Bulgaria (1.10), bearing all the prestige of the sacred language of Christian texts and of the active Bulgarian cultural centres, above all the capital Preslàv. The linguistic differences between this SSl. dialect (already subjected to literary convention) and the vernacular of the ESl. world have been examined in Chapter 1. They were not considerable, though examples from each extreme (e.g. texts nos. 2 and 4) appear superficially to be widely different. OCS arrived in Kiev as a *ready-made written language* for sacred and wider literary purposes (1.13). It was subjected from the outset to some Russification of details; no more than this was needed. No one expects a written style[2] to be identical with speech. For a Kievan to say сторона́ but write страна́ became as natural as for an educated Englishman to say (informal) *can't, don't, I'll* but write (formal) *cannot, do not, I shall*. Further, OCS provided the orthography for writing all forms of ESl.—an invaluable normative role which has continued throughout the centuries with only changes in detail (1.10; 1.39 ff.). Foreign though OCS might be, it was scarcely felt as such: both it and Kiev speech were *slověnĭskŭ jazykŭ*.

5   In the ESl. world so recently drawn into the Christian commonwealth and still in great part to be evangelized (a process that was

---

[2] OCS (ChSl.) in Russia was always essentially a written language, though of course sung and recited in church but otherwise spoken only to a limited degree and in special circumstances.

to go on for many centuries) it is no surprise to find that OCS quickly established itself as a literary and learned language. Education for a long time hardly reached outside the Church and the ruling class. So much of importance to be learnt and absorbed came through the mediation of OCS that the need for an independent *literature* in some form of the native speech was not strongly felt. The converse is also true: precisely because of the very close relationship of these two forms of *slověnĭskŭ jazykŭ* there was little or no impulse in Russia to press the pure vernacular into the service of the Church: ChSl. fulfilled all needs. In Latin-using European countries many of the earliest surviving original compositions in the vernacular are religious in content and bear witness to an ambition to endow the vernacular with a literary status side by side with Latin. Such, for instance, are the *Vie de S. Alexis* in France (mid 11th c.) and the *Heliand* epic in Saxon Germany (9th c.).

6   Thus on principle the *spoken language in its pure form* was only used in Russia for non-literary purposes. The language of any piece of writing depended strictly on its purpose and genre. We may single out the following main genres appropriate to the *literary language*:

1. Liturgical texts and the like: the exclusive province of OCS, to begin with copied from (usually) Bulgarian manuscripts with every good intention of preserving the sacred text accurately but in fact subject from the outset to limited Russification, which may even include regional features, e.g. the Novgorodisms in *Ostr.* and the *Novg. Minéi* (2.49; 3.97 (*d*); 6.62).

2. Other genres closely connected with the Church and its teachings: on principle in OCS (soon ChSl.) but may contain occasional ESl. words and forms and regularly such for native *realia* having no equivalent in OCS, viz. personal and place-names, some concrete objects. Here come:

(*a*) Sermons: a typical example, for an important and solemn occasion, fortunately survives in Metropolitan Hilarion's *Sermon on the [Mosaic] Law and Grace* (text no. 4) which admirably illustrates the cultivation of OCS in Russia in the 11th c. Hilarion knows that he can count on a high level of Christian learning, and therefore knowledge of OCS, among his Court audience.[3] Parts of the text are his own, parts adapted from much-used Greek originals.

(b) Hagiography and allied genres: the models are mainly Byzantine, whether direct or via Bulgaria. The genre title is, of course, OCS—житиé (2.33). Typical original compositions are: *The Life of St Theodosius, The Story of Boris and Gleb.* Here also may be included such works as *The Virgin Mary's journey through Hell* (Хождéние Богорóдицы по мýкам, translated in the 12th c.) and the *Paterikón* of the Cave Monastery in Kiev (Киево-печéрский патерѝк, compiled early 13th–late 15th c.).

(c) Learned works: favourite passages culled from Greek theological, moral, historical and scientific works, either copied from Bulgarian translations or newly translated in Kiev. The Избóрник Святослáва (*Anthology*) of 1073 is such a copy; the Избóрник of 1076 contains sections apparently specially translated for it in Kiev. Here too such works as the Физиóлог, whose textual history is uncertain (the earliest surviving copy is of the 15th c.), the *Pilgrimage of Abbot Daniel to the Holy Land* (Хождéние игýмена Даниѝла), referring to the years 1106–8—a travelogue in form but most of the matter belongs to the sphere of the sacred; and the *Alexandria*—legends of Alexander the Great considered as history and therefore in learned language.[4] All of these contain sporadic rather than regular vernacular linguistic features; where the alternatives are clear, the infiltration of ESl. forms into the 1076 *Anthology* has been estimated as varying between one tenth and one twentieth.

7 *Non-literary texts* are wholly or largely independent of ChSl. but may contain a certain proportion of borrowed Slavonicisms. Of major importance are:

(i) Рýсская Прáвда (text no. 2), the core of which is ESl. customary law, probably reduced to writing in the 1020s and well preserved, with later additions, in a conservative copy of 1282. An

---

[3] Не къ невѣдущимъ бо пишетъ, но преизлиха насыщщем ся сладости книжныя 'for [this] is written not for the ignorant (= uneducated) but for those abundantly nourished with the sweets of (Christian) literature'. Пишетъ = пишетъ ся (passive), following a still-current Gk. usage (mod. αὐτή ἡ λέξη ἔτσι γράφει 'this word is spelt so').

[4] Date of translation from Greek unknown; there are several versions.

invaluable source of native legal and social vocabulary and, within its limitations, syntax. Art. 2, added in the period of the Triumvirate (1054–93), shows the sort of Slavonicism which it became natural to employ on occasion: убиение, съвъкупивъше ся.

(ii) A comparison of the Deeds of Gift made respectively by Prince Mstisláv c.1130 to St George's Monastery at Nóvgorod (founded 1119) and by a certain Nóvgorod monk Varlaam c.1200 to St Saviour's Monastery (his own foundation, 1192) shows that ChSl. was not, and by and large never became, the medium for administrative and legal documents in the way that Latin had a considerable (but not exclusive) place in these areas in much of the West. In Varlaam's Deed ChSl. only appears in the final formula of commination, that is, in an accepted cliché, and even there not consistently. Mstisláv's Deed, as emanating from the central authority, exhibits more of the literary influence of ChSl. in both vocabulary and syntax. It is, one may say with confidence, a typical example of the fertilization of the spoken by the literary language and a convincing blend of the two. We may presume that this deed was not alone in using a more or less uniform conventional style. It would be an exceptional document which contained not a single ChSl. word or expression.

(iii) Diplomatic documents. The original linguistic form of the three Treaties with Constantinople, which appear (not necessarily in extenso) in RPC under the years 912, 945, 972 (text no. 1) is a matter of controversy. They cannot as they stand be taken as direct evidence of 10th c. linguistic practice. All things considered it seems most probable that the framework—which follows the set practice of Greek diplomatic documents—was in OCS, long familiar to the imperial chancellery from its dealings with Bulgaria and already employing a number of Greek calques (e.g. рав[ь]но = ἴσον 'true copy'), but that the reported speeches of the Kievan delegations may have been recorded in more or less native form. More important for linguistic history are the treaties made with Baltic powers in the earlier 13th c. The 1229 Treaty between the Prince of Smolénsk, Riga (the German base), and Gotland (the Swedish entrepôt) (text no. 18) is couched wholly in the everyday commercial language of the time. See further 5.24.

8   Between these two poles there is a large area where ChSl. and the vernacular can meet and elaborate a fruitful mixture. There is association, but not free association since under all conditions matter determines language. This hybrid style, or rather group of styles, is best represented in *historical writing*.

Almost all the Byzantine historians used by the Bulgarians wrote in a 'high' archaizing form of Greek. This was readily translated by them into OCS. *Past* history thus came to Russia under the wing of religion and a 'high' style, for past history was the record of God's purpose in creating the world and man and of the fulfilment of that purpose in the Christian Church and Empire. Such knowledge was part of the Christian and intellectual apprenticeship of a newly converted people, as necessary as the historical books of the Bible to a Jew. *Contemporary* history was another matter—annals concerned the doings and sayings of people living or recently alive; no general import could be read into them.

A composite work like the *Russian Primary Chronicle* (Повесть временныхъ лѣтъ)[5] illustrates the consequent automatic changes of language with matter. The résumé of past history, including such matters of vital moment to Russians as the mission of SS Constantine and Methodios to Moravia, is in ChSl. (and not all new work). Local tales of the 9th–10th c. deriving from oral tradition, whether Slav or Scandinavian, are in a more or less popular language. Narrative is more formal than reported speech; but the language of reported speech varies with person: princes normally speak a more bookish language than commoners, especially on formal occasions. The story of a miracle will be in a language closer to pure ChSl. than that of a military campaign; a matter of national importance will always be in a higher style than one of local interest only.

9 We may cite as examples (orthography slightly simplified):

1. *Russian Primary Chronicle*[6]

   (*a*) formal narrative:

И нача княжити Володимеръ въ Киевѣ единъ, и постави кумиры на холму внѣ двора теремнаго: Перуна древяна, а главу его сребрену, а усъ златъ, и Хърса, Дажьбога, и Стрибога и Симарьгла и Мокошь. И жряху имъ, наричюще я богы, и привожаху сыны своя и дъщери и жряху бѣсомъ, и оскверняху землю требами своими. И осквернися

---

[5] Usually translated *Tale of Bygone Years* (on the assumption that the title applies primarily to the introductory past history) but perhaps rather *Record of the Passing Years*, i.e. simply annals.

[6] Texts after Повесть временныхъ лет, ed. V. P. Adrianova-Peretts (1950).

кровьми земля руска и холмо-тъ. Но преблагии Богъ не хотя смерти грѣшникомъ, на томъ холмѣ нынѣ церкви стоить, святаго Василья есть, якоже послѣди скажемъ. Мы же на преднее въз[в]ратимся. (*s.a.* 980)

(*b*) speech:

. . . и приде к ним Игоревичь Давыдъ и рече к ним: «на что мя есте привабили? Осе есмъ. Кому до мене обида?» И отвѣща ему Володимеръ: «Ты еси прислалъ к нам: хочю, братья, прити к вам, и пожаловати ся своея обиды. Да се еси пришелъ и сѣдишь с братьею своею на одином коврѣ: то чему не жалуешься? До кого ти нас жалоба?» (*s.a.* 1100)

2. *First Novgorod Chronicle*

(*a*) local disaster—vernacular (OB no. 24(iii)):

. . . а Новѣгородѣ зло быс[ть] вельми: кадь ржи купляхуть по 10 гр[и]в[ь]нъ, а овса по 3 гр[и]внѣ, а рѣпѣ возъ по 2 гр[и]вьнѣ; ядяху люди сосновую кору и листъ липовъ и мохъ. О горѣ тъгда братье бяше: дѣти свое даяхуть одьрень, и поставиша скудельницю и наметаша полну. О горѣ бяше: по търгу трупие, по улицямъ трупие, по полю трупие; не можаху пси изѣдати ч[е]л[о]в[ѣ]къ. А Вожане помроша, а останъке разиде ся; и тако по грѣхомъ нашимъ разиде ся власть наша и градъ нашь. (*s.a.* 1215)

(*b*) national disaster (the first Mongol raid)—sustained ChSl. (OB no. 23(iv)):

Том[ъ] же лѣт[ѣ] по грѣхомъ нашимъ придоша языци незнаеми, их же добрѣ никто же не вѣсть, кто суть и отколе изидоша, и что языкъ ихъ, и котораго племене суть, и что вѣра ихъ; а зовуть я татары, а инии гл[аголю]ть таурмены, а друзии печенѣзи; инии же гл[аголю]ть яко же се суть о них же Мефодии патомьскыи еп[и]с[ко]пъ съвѣдѣтельствуеть, яко си суть ишли ис пустыня етриевьскыя, суще межи въстокомъ и сѣверомъ, тако бо Мефодии гл[аголе]ть, яко скончанию врѣменъ явити с[я] тѣмъ, яже загна Гедеонъ, и поплѣнять всю землю, от въстокъ до Ефранта, и от Тигръ до Поньскаго моря, кромѣ Ефиопия; Б[ог]ъ единъ вѣсть кто суть и отколѣ изидоша. Прѣмудрии муж[и] вѣдять я добрѣ, кто книгы разумѣеть; мы же ихъ не вѣмы, кто суть, нъ сде въписахомъ о нихъ памяти ради рускыхъ кн[я]зь, и бѣды яже быс[ть] от нихъ имъ. (*s.a.* 1224)

10   A particular illustration of the contrast in linguistic levels is afforded by the *Admonition* or *Instruction* (Поучение) of Vladímir Monomákh, inserted into *RPC* arbitrarily under the year 1096 but probably written between 1100 and 1118. The first part, a moral exhortation to his family, is in 'high' style with many quotations from the Psalter and Wisdom books; the second, a short autobiography concerned wholly with concrete events, is in vernacular language.[7] The distinction, as always, is not absolute but the principle of such a distinction continued to be observed for many centuries (see §21 below).

11 Chronicle narrative points to the creation of a new conventional literary language to be used by all writers (in appropriate contexts), as does Mstisláv's Deed to an embryonic administrative koine for the whole country. It was precisely in narrative that cross-fertilization was most probable; it was the matrix for the adoption of many ChSl. words into ESl. written and spoken usage and provided the impulse for the extension of ESl. vocabulary on ChSl. models. It also imposed some syntactical sophistication.

This possible goal of a standard literary language was never quite achieved. The unity of the ESl. world was always precarious; Nóvgorod had always been separatist. There was no longer even nominal unity after the death of Vladímir Monomákh (1125). By this date Kiev was already losing its importance to the towns of the 'new centre' (§15 below).

12 How much of early Kievan literature, the literature of Court and cultured society, may have been lost we do not know. The absence of lyric and narrative poetry is at least remarkable. Religious verse in OCS (ChSl.), partly translated, partly imitated from the Greek, was a notable part of many liturgical texts but it followed the alien syllabic principle of Byzantine hymns and had no points of contact with native oral poetry, which was certainly abundant. The so-called былины, collected in N. Russia mainly in the 19th c. from the oral recitation of the peasantry, give some idea of what such Kievan poetry may have been like since their *form* (metre) and some of the matter in all probability goes back in its essentials to Kievan times; on the other hand the *language*, though highly traditional, has been equally certainly renewed throughout the many centuries of oral transmission, preserving (as in the language of Homer) archaic forms and clichés metrically too difficult to replace.

---

[7] e.g. голову си розбихъ дважды и руцѣ и нозѣ свои вередихъ . . . се бо мя выгналъ из города отца моего. (Slavonicism бо; the Slavonicism вредúть has now replaced native вередить.)

The *Tale of Igor's Campaign* (Слóво о полкý Ѝгореве), presumably written shortly after the event described (1185), is often held to show that oral did develop into literary poetry and, by implication, that the latter was a flourishing genre. This is too frail a structure. Borrowings from, or rather sophisticated imitations of, oral poetry are manifest in the Слово but it is at most rhetorical prose, sometimes falling into rhythmic elements but having no overall metrical scheme. The faulty transmission of the text (text no. 14), not all of which is likely to belong to the end of the 12th c., does not allow any firm conclusions about its original linguistic form, but it is worth noting that it displays a similar mixture of native and ChSl. alternative forms (e.g. соловей/славий), without apparent contextual motivation, to that of chronicle narrative in general and specifically of the narratives of the same events given in the *Hypatian Chronicle s.a.* 1185 and the *Laurentian Chronicle* (continuation of *RPC*) *s.a.* 1186. If any larger corpus of cultivated poetry did exist we should expect its language to be not dissimilar to that of the Слово as we have it, but less uneven; some of the Slavonicisms in our text probably date from the 16th c. and after.

But there must be grave doubts about this supposed marriage of Christian court and pre-Christian oral tradition. In a recently converted country—and Russia was a country still in process of conversion—the Church must disapprove of any literature redolent of the past and may be partly successful in suppressing or destroying it. But it cannot suppress ordinary human impulses indefinitely; sooner or later, if the voice is strong enough, secular poetry will assert itself. One cannot therefore believe that the absence of early lyric and narrative poetry (normal in most young literatures)[8] can be charged against a censorious Church unusually efficient in its campaign of suppression. Rather, if the seed germinated in the 12th c., the seedling then withered in the 13th c. This was an irreparable loss to the continued cultivation of Russian as a literary medium. Nor can we be certain that the educated class provided the patronage, stimulus, and audience without which there will be no artistic development in that particular genre.

13   A significant product, outside historical writing, of late Kievan times is the *Petition* or *Lament* of Daniíl (Моление Даниила Заточника), written probably not long after 1200. The text as we

[8] Over eighty narrative poems (some of epic length) *survive* from the early period of French.

have it suggests the same social context as the Слово—a small 'court' with some book culture but not cut off, as medieval life rarely was, from the countryside and its speech and traditions. We find in it the same rhetorical prose tending in places to a stricter rhythmic organization, a mixture of ChSl. and native forms the stylistic reason for which (if part of the original text) is not always apparent. But this text too has suffered at the hands of later editors and copyists; it was certainly Slavonicized in the 16th–17th c.

However that may be, the work is little more than a rather self-conscious parade of learning. The linguistic resources are there but the high and low elements cannot be said to be integrated into a style, that is, a consistent linguistic medium applicable to many subjects. Some 'strophes' are predominantly vernacular, others, as the following, consist wholly of biblical quotations and paraphrase, especially from the Psalms:

> Княже мои, господине!
> Помяни мя во княжении своемъ,[9]
> Яко азъ рабъ твои и сынъ рабы твоя![10]
> Вижю,[11] господине, вся человѣкы,
> Яко солнцемъ, грѣеми милостию твоею;
> Точию азъ единъ, яко трава въ застѣни израстущи,
> На нюже ни солнце сияетъ, ни дождь идетъ;
> Тако азъ хожю во т[ь]мѣ,
> Отлученъ день и нощь свѣта очию твоею.
> Тѣмъ, господине, приклони ухо твое
> Во глаголы устъ моихъ[12]
> И отъ всѣхъ скорбеи моихъ избави мя![13]

Popular proverbs stand cheek by jowl with such passages, e.g. Ни птица во птицахъ сычь, / Ни въ звѣрѣхъ зверь ежь, / Ни рыба въ рыбахъ ракъ . . .; на холопѣ порты дороги.[14]

Was there here a *littérature courtoise* in the making? If so, no further development followed that has come down to us.

[9] Luke 23: 42.
[10] Ps. 116: 16 = Wis. Sol. 9: 5.
[11] With хожю below, the only Russian form (to be expected: 1.19) in a passage wholly ChSl. in vocabulary and syntax.
[12] Ps. 54: 2 and elsewhere.
[13] Ps. 119: 153 and elsewhere.
[14] *Polnoglásie* and other Russian forms have usually been preserved in these. There are also clear signs of N. dial. vocabulary, e.g. обѝлие (= cereals), керста́ (< Finnic), чемерѝца, лы́чьница (= лапоть), дивья́ (adv. = хорошо́, still known from some NW dialects).

14   In terms of *use of language* we may surely assert that the most
successful Kievan genre, and the most promising for the future,
was historical prose narrative in which a native style was well on
the way to maturity, having absorbed much, especially in syntactical
handling, from ChSl. For (as in many Western countries) a vernacular standard was born in the monasteries in the ambit of ecclesiastical interests and needs. Hagiography also displays much competent
writing in ChSl., but the leading churchmen's ChSl. style tends to
ponderousness rather than elegance (Hilarion, Clement of Túrov).
Yet it was difficult to prevent ChSl. from dominating the vernacular
in their association. There were no other models than what ChSl.
had brought in; no stimulus from elsewhere—indeed not necessary,
but desirable[15]—despite the far-flung political connections of the
Kievan world (Scandinavia, the WSl. world, even France and
England),[16] certainly not from Greek literature, where Russian
interest was concentrated on the Christian 'classics' and ignored
contemporary writing, which in any case despised and avoided the
living language. The vernacular had become an element in literary
expression but the religious structure of society inhibited a fuller
independence from ChSl.

B. The Period of Fragmentation, c.1200–1400

15   After the death of Vladímir Monomákh (1125) the fragile unity
of the Kievan realm dissolved. New economic and cultural centres
—Rostóv, Súzdal', Vladímir (founded by Vladímir Monomákh a
few years after 1100)—took over the lead, in a different dialect
area (see Map no. 1). Nóvgorod, with its subarctic empire and
valuable Baltic trade outlets, asserted its independence with its
own peculiar political constitution. The onslaught of the Mongols
(1224–40), followed by the consolidation of their overlordship, led
if not to a marked decline, at least to a cultural and economic
standstill. Even before their invasion the unit had become the petty
princedom (кня́жество), each ruler often at loggerheads with his
neighbour, all impotent at first before the rulers of the Golden
Horde. Fragmentation and rivalry can be a stimulus to cultural

---

[15] The stimulus of Latin literature was always at the elbow of W. European
writers.

[16] Vladímir Monomákh mentions that his father, Vsévolod, son of Jaroslár the
Wise, knew five foreign languages.

advance; but to have this (as in Italy and Germany) there must be abundant economic resources and an adequate intellectual formation. Neither of these requirements was fulfilled in Russia at that time.

There was no marked break, however, in the continuity of the literary tradition. The conventions of chronicle writing, in particular, were handed on to the 'new centre', to now independent Galicia in the extreme South-West, and were already well established and vigorously cultivated at Nóvgorod. Uniformity of language is preserved on principle at the higher level in ChSl. and therefore in such genres as it was appropriate to. We may instance: (*a*) the *Life of St Nifont* (manuscript of 1219 from Rostóv), a typical житиé which seems to have been translated direct from Greek about that date; the ChSl. appropriate to hagiography contains a small admixture of vernacular features; (*b*) the *Life of Alexander Nevsky* (d. 1263), more a житиé than a historical record, employing the more formal end of the spectrum of chronicle language; (*c*) Повесть о разорении Батыем Рязани (written not long after the event, 1237), in a similar linguistic register. The prestige of ChSl. was in no way lowered. But with the passing of time the language tended to be less accurately written and with less literary skill, which points to lower standards of education in monasteries and anywhere else that book-learning could be got. But at the lower level regional traits of the living language became more pronounced. This was not a time when *a generally accepted vernacular literary norm*, however compounded with ChSl., could arise (or be maintained if it had existed) in default of the overwhelming literary authority of some Dante. Concurrently, spoken Russian was rapidly drawing away from its passable agreement with ChSl.: the latter maintained all the jers in its conventional pronunciation (2.31) and the aor. and imperf. tenses which had clearly disappeared from speech by about 1250, if not earlier. *This divergence could only increase with time.*

16   The best surviving literary work of this period comes from Nóvgorod. As the many hundreds of texts recovered during archaeological excavations show (text no. 16), there had been from an early date a considerable quantity of everyday, non-literary, writing in this self-governing community of merchants, and in the local dialect. This substructure can be felt in the best passages of the Nóvgorod chronicles, especially in the 13th c. Differentiation of language according to matter is quite strict: local history is told in popular language with only that minimal recourse to Slavonicisms which represents their adoption as a normal component of cultivated speech and writing. Matters of wider importance are couched in a far higher style. Reproduced above (§9 (2)) are the story of the great famine of 1215 (local) and the account of the coming of the Mongols in 1224 (national). Both are competent, if not highly polished, pieces of prose. It is important to bear in mind that even the colloquial passages are not in *pure* Nóvgorod dialect but in a locally coloured form of the earlier Kievan semi-standard language. It is not known when traditional (oral) Nóvgorod stories (e.g. Садко, новгородский гость) were first given literary shape; they are only known from much later.

The 13th and 14th centuries thus only produced regional literature in so far as the living language was used. ChSl. alone commanded a general literary authority. The commercial centres in the western borderlands apart (Pskov, Pólotsk, Smolénsk), all the centres of major importance were in the óкающий area (see Map no. 1). The Ukraine and White Russia (the latter áкающий) pass out of the control of any Russian prince, being absorbed by Lithuania and Poland;[17] they must henceforward be counted out of any account of the development of spoken or literary Russian until the 17th c. (§§25 ff. below). There were constant close relations between Nóvgorod and the new centre—indeed the latter and Nóvgorod were economically dependent on one another—but each kept to its own local speech and variety of administrative language. It was impossible to foresee during this period of fragmentation and somewhat beyond where a new dominating linguistic authority might arise, coupled or not with political dominance.

C. The Muscovy Period, c.1350–1600

17   The political rise of Moscow was rapid in the 14th c. It emerged as a geographically well-placed centre for organizing first defence against the Tatars and soon the offensive against them. This was coupled in the far-sighted policy of the princes of Moscow with the

---

[17] The Lithuanian expansion began with the annexation of Pólotsk in 1250. Gediminas (1316–41) absorbed White Russia, Algirdas took Smolénsk (1357) and Kiev (1362). Lithuanian union with Poland started effectively from 1386, from which time the Lithuanian ruling class became Catholic and Polonized.

reuniting of all the independent princedoms under one rule—that of Moscow. Both these objectives had been attained by 1500: the power of the Golden Horde was shaken at Кулико́во по́ле in 1380[18] and collapsed altogether during the following century; the independence of the largest and wealthiest province, the republic of Nóvgorod, perhaps Moscow's only serious rival for hegemony, was extinguished by 1489. By 1500 Imperial Moscow had been born.

During the two centuries of Moscow's rise to greatness spoken Russian had drawn rapidly away from the theoretically unchanging ChSl. norm. The intimate association between the two which had been possible and fruitful in Kiev times became increasingly difficult and artificial; they ceased to appear to contemporaries as mere stylistic variants. The high Muscovy period, 15th–16th c., became a time of *prevalent bilingualism*: written ChSl. is used for all serious literary purposes—and accessible more and more only to the best-educated—the vernacular for more trivial matter and for administrative and legal documents of all kinds. *The literary cultivation of the vernacular* is almost abandoned.

18 A number of factors during the confused centuries ending *c.*1500 had worked together to produce and accentuate this bilingualism.

In the first place, the political ascendancy of Moscow was reinforced by the fall of Constantinople to the Ottoman Turks in 1453. The Byzantine Empire, as the history books had taught the Russians since their conversion, was the embodiment of God's purpose towards mankind. If Constantinople could no longer lead the Christian world—the true Christian world, for the Western schismatics went their own way—then Moscow as the one Orthodox power independent of the Turks must take over the leadership. Theory and practice were brought into harmony by the marriage of Zoe (Sophia in Russia), a niece of the last Byzantine emperor, to the Grand Prince of Moscow in 1456. The title of *tsar* (emperor) was cautiously used from this time, though not officially till the

---

[18] The work celebrating this victory, usually known as *Zadónshchina*, was written shortly after the event but once again the transmission of the text is too uncertain for firm linguistic conclusions (see the edition by R. Jakobson and D. S. Worth, *SPR* 51). Vernacular forms (e.g. вы́ѣдеть, перелетѣ́ша) are capriciously intermingled with ChSl.; the *l*-preterite alternates with the aor.; in some cases vernacular vocabulary seems to be archaistic stylization rather than contemporary usage (комонь, лукоморье), but there are also new Asiatic words (калантырь, байдана, катуна). There is no sign of a new literary style in the making.

reign of Ivan IV. Small wonder, then, if Moscow abandoned the Kievan tradition of historical writing and wrote only high-style imperial history, however contemporary the matter. While Nóvgorod and its sister-city Pskov continued to the end of their independence to compile local annals in a locally coloured vernacular language,[19] the official or semi-official chronicles of Moscow give virtually no place to the living language, culminating in the heavy ChSl. of the Степе́нная кни́га (*Book of Degrees, c.*1563), a glorification and justification of the Moscow dynasty as the champion of unity and Orthodoxy. The same is true (unfortunately) of the Повесть о взятии Царьграда, written shortly after 1453 by a Russian eyewitness of the events. This 'grand manner' in historiography continued in works dealing with the next phase in Muscovite expansion, e.g. in the Сказание о взятии царства Казани, written in the 1560s. In particular one notes that the lament of the Princess of Kazan′, which as a stylized oral плач might be expected to preserve some features at least of popular poetry, is no longer comparable with the princess's lament in the Сло́во о полку́ И́гореве but linguistically indistinguishable from the rest of the ChSl. text.

19 In the second place, the Balkan Orthodox spiritual and cultural renaissance of the 14th c. was soon propagated to Russia, partly through the presence of Russians in the important Balkan ecclesiastical centres (Tǎrnovo, Athos) and partly through the somewhat later arrival of Balkan men of learning in Russia in the face of ever-increasing Turkish pressure (almost the whole of Serbia and Bulgaria had been conquered by 1400). This 'Second South Slav Influence' affected not only literature but also the other arts. In the visual arts it was notably beneficial;[20] in linguistic matters this is open to grave doubt. Not only did these eminent men reinforce a preoccupation with ChSl. which was indeed the international medium of the Slav Orthodox world and as such of great value, but they imported into Russia their own variant of the language. This they not unnaturally believed to be superior to ChSl. as then cultivated in Russia. It was more correct in some respects. But they were largely unaware of the Balkan peculiarities of their own practice—a long way already from OCS—and they succeeded in

---

[19] See the *Pskov Chronicle, s.a.* 1510, the account of its final loss of independence.
[20] Consult D. S. Likhachëv, Культура Руси времени Андрея Рублева и Епифания премудрого (1962).

imposing at the same time an eccentric orthography (1.42) and their own highly artificial literary style which copied the elaborate Greek style of the time (Athonite–Hesychast), itself far removed from vernacular Greek. ChSl. liturgical texts were 'Byzantinized' —brought nearer to the Greek—as became evident later, in the 17th c., when this Moscow ChSl. was confronted by the 'Latinized' ChSl. of Kiev and the western borderlands. During the century 1350–1450 new translations of the Psalter and the New Testament reached Russia from the Balkans, thus setting the seal on this Byzantinization. Learned work on the texts was further pursued in Russia by Maksím the Greek (1480–1556).

Taken as a whole there is nothing unreasonable, even unexpected, in this 'influence': on the one hand the Balkans had scholars to spare just at the moment when Moscow urgently needed new texts;[21] on the other, there had been no clear and unassailable standard in the use of ChSl. in Russia for a long time and native translating activity appears to have ceased with the Mongol conquest (1240). Monks from the Russian monastery on Athos would recommend the standards of the Balkan scholars with which they were already familiar. Finally Moscow's pretensions to lead the Orthodox world, especially after 1453, naturally encouraged the adoption of what appeared to be the best contemporary practice. But as a result ChSl. in its more literary aspects (outside the liturgical) enclosed itself in a world of its own, the preserve of learned men who took no interest in, indeed despised the vernacular, and, if foreigners, were not familiar with it.

20   Epifáni the Wise (the very epithet премудрый is a warning), who died about 1420, gave the movement its models in his Lives of St Stephen of Perm' (d. 1396) and St Sérgij of Rádonezh (d. 1392). Such rhetorical decoration and deliberate avoidance of the concrete and of any reflection of contemporary life continues in hagiography and similar pieces well into the 17th c. The pernicious influence of this style and these literary principles must be held responsible for the denaturing of such a story of popular origin as *Peter and Fevronia,* which in its 16th c. ChSl. form has lost all the immediacy of an oral tale and not acquired in the process either some new formal balance or narrative competence. We may be

---

[21] The Tatar general Tokhtamýsh destroyed much of Moscow in 1382; survival of earlier manuscripts has been very small. There followed a flood of Balkan (predominantly Bulgarian) manuscripts to replace the losses.

sure that the market-place audience, the right judge of story-telling, would have rejected it out of hand.[22] Vanity and narrow-mindedness have always been—and there are many examples—the hallmark of such a learned literature: its practitioners soon assert that there can be no other kind of literature. There is a fatal narrowing of what is 'worthy of literary treatment'. The vernacular, and all that comes within its orbit, is rejected as 'unworthy', the spoken language as 'corrupt'. How can colloquial Russian not be corrupt when it no longer uses the aorist and imperfect, and on so many points of grammar and pronunciation no longer coincides with the revered models of the past?

In short, the Second South Slav Influence turned attention away from the cultivation of the vernacular as a literary medium and itself became for the uninitiated very much what Latin was at the same time to a simple Westerner. An unbridgeable gulf had opened between the ChSl. and Russian languages and writing in them. The fruitful co-operation of Kiev times was over; there was no longer any fertile middle ground.

All that can be said in favour of this recrudescence of a high ChSl. style, whatever its merits in its own restricted literary field, is that it did in the long run promote the adoption of useful Slavonicisms in the general vocabulary of cultivated Russians. But few if any of these were those favoured by or specifically invented for its stylistic needs. It is to this period that belongs rather the final adoption as standard of many correct ChSl. forms in place of the semi-Russianized ones which had long been current, e.g. прежде, replacing both переже and преже, and other forms in -жд- (побеждён ousts побежен); the choice between alternatives (время, no longer веремя); and the sorting out of usage between such doublets as сторонá/странá.

But this is also the time of the arbitrary Slavonicization of many earlier works on recopying—an activity which the linguist can only deplore.

21   The private letters of Basil III (1505–33) and Ivan IV (1533–84) show that a quite natural and, within its limits, acceptable vernacular prose style existed, but it existed *below the level of acknowledged literature*. The contrast is well illustrated in the writings of Ivan Grozny himself. His letters to the *oprichnik* Vasili, held prisoner in the Crimea, and the latter's replies (1574–6) are in the vigorous

[22] It was immensely popular; at least 150 manuscripts survive in various forms.

Russian such as was spoken at Court—a little rough but almost without affectations. The following will serve as a sample:

А что сказываешьс[я] великой человек — ино что по грехом моим учинилос[ь], и нам того как утаити?, что отца нашего и наши князи и бояре нам учали изменяти, и мы и вас, страдников, приближали, хотячи от вас службы и правды. А помянул бы ти свое величество и отца своего в Олексине — ино таковы и в станицах езживали, а ты в станице у Пенинского был мало что не в охотникех с собаками, и прежние твои были у ростовских владык служили. И мы того не запираемся, что ты у нас в приближенье был. И мы для приближенья твоего тысячи две рублев дадим, а доселева такие по пятидесят рублев бывали; а ста тысяч опричь государеи ни на ком окупу не емлют, а опричь государеи таких окупов ни на ком не дают.[23]

But Ivan's correspondence with the renegade Prince Kurbsky (1563–4 and 1577–9), conceived as political propaganda and intended for publication, is couched in the rhetorical 'high style', displaying a wealth of learning and syntactical elaboration. It purports to be 'literature'. So is Kurbsky's own *History* (История о великом князе московском, 1576–8).[24]

The same contrast is to be seen within the *Domostrój* (or *The Book of Household Management*), compiled (it is thought) in the early 16th c. and extant in a mid-century copy and many later ones. It continues the tradition of Vladímir Monomákh's *Instruction* (§10 above): the first part of *Domostrój,* dealing with matters of religion and morals, the education of children, etc., is in a high style; the second part, dealing with the practical considerations of running a household as an economic unit, is in almost pure everyday language. The writer, of course, only considered the first part 'literature'. The relative lack of cultivation of the vernacular is shown in the primitive and slapdash syntax of the second part.[25] The wealth of concrete vocabulary, covering matters and objects not normally

[23] 1574; spelling and punctuation as given in OB no. 59.

[24] It has been estimated that Kurbsky's language is about 80 per cent ChSl./20 per cent vernacular, and much the same for Ivan. The following features in Kurbsky's usage may be noted: аз, not я; иже, not который; infin. in -ти, rarely -ть; *č/šč* and *ž/žd* variable; few *polnoglasie* forms; 2–4 constructed with the nom. pl.; some use of the fut. with буду; frequent masc. pl. nom. in -ове (no doubt a Polonism); much Western vocabulary, i.e. Polish words used throughout the Polish–Ukrainian–White Russian area.

[25] e.g. careless anacolutha: чтóбы в огород[ъ] собáки ни свиньи, ни куромъ ни гусемъ ни уткамъ и вся́ко [*sic*] житнѣ взоитѝ не имуть (§45).

figuring in 'literature', is of the greatest linguistic value.[26] The prevailing strict principle 'ChSl. for literature, vernacular for needs of daily life' is carried out in this composite work, among other indicators, by an almost exact repartition between пре- in the first half and пере- in the second.

22   Two other writers of the Muscovy period deserve mention as indicative of the linguistic scene. Afanási Nikítin, a merchant of Tver' (still an independent princedom), made in the years 1466–72 a journey down the old trade route via the Volga and Persia to India. He kept an intermittent record of his travels. The text opens with some formality, as appropriate to the solemnity of the undertaking and of its ecclesiastical and princely blessing. After a few lines he lapses in mid-sentence from the bookish aorist поидох into the vernacular preterite, and from then on, except for special reasons, the vernacular prevails. There are some residual Slavonicisms of the indifferent sort (§24 below): на плещѣ, 1,000 златыхъ, кто хощет поити, власы, нощь. Though loose in syntax—the prevailing sin of the unschooled writer—Afanási's account is vivid and concrete. Unfortunately, he died on the return journey before reaching home, so never worked up from his jottings a final and perhaps more careful text. However that may be, travel was not, or no longer, a subject for 'literature';[27] Afanási recognizes this implicitly in his vernacular diary.

Secondly, the works of Ivan Peresvétov, in particular his Сказание о Магмете-Салтане (i.e. Ivan IV, c.1547), illustrate the sources of the Western current about to enter Muscovite life and language. A gentleman from the Lithuanian lands, he spent his early life in military and political service in Poland and Bohemia, both of which countries had by then flourishing vernacular literatures. In the service of Ivan IV from c.1539, Peresvétov writes in the current Muscovite деловóй язы́к but with a greater stiffening of Slavonicisms such as was characteristic of the chancellery language of Lithuania, to suit his serious, at least semi-literary purpose as a political publicist. It was through such men, in their speaking or writing, that Polonisms and other Western features

[26] In addition the value of the earliest manuscript is enhanced by the fact that the text is partially stressed.

[27] Abbot Daniil's account of his pilgrimage (text no. 11) and several other similar works, having a religious and edifying intention, belonged to the literary sphere of ChSl.

insinuated themselves into Muscovite usage. Attention has been drawn in particular to the continuous future бу́ду + inf. (3.110).

23 The chancellery language of Lithuania (*Westrussische Kanzleisprache*)—the делово́й язы́к of those parts—was of considerable importance as a link in the 14th–15th c., particularly the later half. It has been noted (6.5) that the S. and W. dialects of (Great) Russian form a simple continuum; there has never been any sharp linguistic frontier, however sharp the political frontier, between what is now designated White Russia and the centre of Muscovy. The administrative language of the Lithuanian state was thus a parallel formation to that taking shape in the areas ruled by Moscow: the basis was in each case (as it always had been) vernacular Russian. Some features of WhR. and Ukr. were admitted, but nothing which was too eccentric to the traditional style of written Russian.[28] Of course, some of the more pronounced distinctive traits of these two new languages had not yet or only recently arisen, e.g. WhR. *c'/dz'* (Table XX (17)). There was a considerable admixture of ChSl. and in course of time more and more Polonisms in the working vocabulary, many of which have remained in Ukr. and WhR.; we may instance: дозволе́нье; змо́ва 'agreement' (= Muscovite сго́вор, later догово́р); шко́да (5.29); лист 'letter' (as in Polish); скарб; во́длуг (= Pol. *według*) 'according to'; и́нший 'other'; неха́й = Muscovite пусть; личба́ 'number'; ле́пший 'better'; ма́етность 'property'; ужива́ть 'use'. This style of language had no literary pretensions though it did on occasion serve for more elevated purposes.

24 The делово́й язы́к—administrative language—of Muscovy must be considered its most important linguistic creation. The imposition of central rule was virtually complete by 1500; regional language as a written medium (e.g. at Nóvgorod or Pskov) rapidly fades out thereafter. For the first time there was a universal linguistic norm, a koine, based on the spoken usage of Moscow itself and spread to all parts of the expanding empire by the penetration of its administrative tentacles. Smolénsk came in in 1514 and Riazán', the troublesome southern town which had on occasion been in alliance with the Tatars, in 1521. All important centres at least

---

[28] Usually the following were present: в = [w]; г = [ɣ]; *ě = e*; *ë* after old palatals whether stressed or not (2.43); *r'* depalatalized; verbal 3rd pers. present in *-t'*; infin. in *-ti*; demonstrative pronoun той (3.61; Table XVII (15)); continuous fut. бу́ду + inf.

more or less conform to this standard in writing. As the population of Moscow was, and probably always had been, very mixed (6.48), the norm in pronunciation and grammar mixed Northern and Southern features and this had the virtue of not being too strange to a speaker of any dialect. The normative role of делово́й язы́к was considerable, though of course only relative.[29] Many alternative forms circulating hitherto (as is frequently the case in derived vocabulary) soon disappear in favour of Moscow's preference, e.g. the modern standard дождли́вый supersedes дожди́вый, дожде́вный, and possibly others. If they have survived at all, then only in dialect; a standard language does not usually allow itself the luxury of too many synonyms of this kind. The grammar and vocabulary of делово́й язы́к is predominantly vernacular. Slavonicisms in the vocabulary (apart from special cases) are chiefly those which were already in common spoken use, e.g. возвраща́ться, сохраня́ть, здра́вствовать, содержа́ть, and several verbs in пре-; plus a number of auxiliary words such as паки 'again', вел(ь)ми 'very', вкупѣ 'together', зѣло 'very', дондеже 'until', развѣ 'except'; and a few words still in more or less 'free alternation' (no distinction of sense or style), e.g. свеча/свеща, голова/глава, молодой/младой, пред/перед (preposition), един-/один-. This repertoire continues without much change into the 17th c. Many Slavonicisms in -ость and -ние were likewise in process of becoming neutral and colloquial. In the case of the technical and jargon words of the administrative documents, their future life will naturally depend on the permanence of the thing or concept denoted: дере́вня 'hamlet without a church', волоки́та 'delay' (now = 'red tape'), прика́зчик (usually spelt прика́щик) and распи́ска/расписа́ться are still with us; подья́чий 'clerk' and про́тивень 'copy' have been replaced. It is worth noting also that new colloquial terms for various parts of the body gained their universal currency in this language: глаз replaces о́ко, па́лец—перст, рот—уста́; the older words, shared by the earlier vernacular and ChSl., are more and more felt as Slavonicisms and end up in the 18th–19th c. as poetic words of archaic flavour (5.47). This imperial koine of the 16th–17th c. was originally, as has been noted, the town dialect of Moscow. It incorporated a few regional words and

---

[29] A few regionalisms persisted down to c.1600, e.g. pres. pl. 1 of быть: есмя (Novg. and North), есмо (Smolénsk and West generally), есме (Moscow), есми (Pólotsk), есмы (occasional).

expressions, some from the long-influential commercial language of Nóvgorod, some from the motley population of the town itself. It was from the latter in all probability that áканье emerged as the standard pronunciation (6.33–5). The vocabulary covered the needs of administrators, lawyers, merchants, craftsmen, and the like. There was less contribution from the countryside—the peasantry proper. But of course it did not remain for long identical with the colloquial even of Moscow town: like all administrative language it soon became riddled with clichés and conservative, while living speech inexorably moved on.

An administrative language cannot be expected to be a good breeding-ground for a literary dialect. Nevertheless деловóй язы́к, at least in its earlier manifestations, was close to the living language and could, given zealous cultivation, have provided a medium for a more popular literature. But the mirage of ChSl. as the only possible literary language continued to deflect men's minds from the development of their own vernacular for intellectual and artistic purposes.

D. *The Muscovy Period: the Seventeenth Century*

25   The seventeenth century shows us a still highly traditional Orthodox society but one in which increasingly close links with Europe, sought or unsought, were beginning to exert an unsettling effect. The Polish 'intervention' and ephemeral presence in Moscow (1605–10) was a concrete manifestation of that west–east intellectual current which had already been flowing fitfully in the previous century (5.24 ff.). The current now gathered strength. Specifically, the 17th c. is the time of maximum Polish cultural and linguistic impact on Muscovy; the role of Poland was predominantly that of middleman, passing on elements of W. European culture. It has been noted (5.28) that this current had two branches, the one passing through the Ukraine, the other through White Russia. As subjects of the Polish state, chiefly as peasantry under respectively Polish and Polonized Lithuanian gentry, their inhabitants used a more and more Polonized vocabulary. Both these regions were reabsorbed into the Russian empire from the middle of the 17th c. with a consequent increase of their influence on Muscovite life and affairs. In the case of the Ukraine one might speak rather of the reactivation of a link that had virtually snapped early in the

15th c. when that region was finally severed both politically and ecclesiastically from Moscow.[30]

26   There were important schools in these lands, in particular at Kiev, where the Catholic–Latin–Polish tradition met and mingled superficially with the Orthodox. Much of the earliest Cyrillic printing (after Ivan IV's ephemeral experiments in Moscow in the 1550s, not revived till the 1630s) was being done in these non-Polish parts of the Polish state.[31] This is natural since the Orthodox faith and Church was constantly on the defensive against established, sometimes militant, Catholicism and there was a consequent need among the clergy for better education in ChSl.—which had admittedly fallen to a low level—and a reliable supply of bibles and service-books. By the beginning of the 17th c. ChSl. had everywhere—whether in Moscow, Kiev, or Vilna—to be acquired with much study, and therefore a codification of ChSl. grammar became for the first time in its ESl. history an urgent desideratum. The most influential *grammar* was that of Meléti Smotrítsky of Vilna (1578–1633), published there in 1619 and republished with revisions in Moscow in 1648 and subsequently. Berýnda's *Dictionary* (Kiev, 1627) attempted to bridge the gap between ChSl. and ESl. vocabulary; on a smaller scale the Лексис of Zizáni (Лаврéнтий Зизаний; Vilna, 1596) listed a total of over a thousand ChSl. words reckoned 'difficult' by that time.

27   Smotrítsky had, of course, no interest in codifying *spoken* Russian (or WhR.). This, as frequently happens, was first done by a foreigner, the Dutchman H. W. Ludolf, who published his *Grammatica russica* in Oxford in 1696. He clearly realized, and stated in his preface, that (even at that date) an educated Muscovite spoke one language but wrote—for any serious literary purpose as then conceived—in another, Church Slavonic. Slavonicisms in Russian are by and large correctly distinguished by him. The great value of this pioneering work is its record of late 17th c. Russian

[30] The Orthodox population of the Ukraine and White Russia became the exclusive responsibility of the Metropolitan of Kiev, independent of, sometimes hostile towards, the Metropolitan of Moscow (Patriarch from 1589).

[31] Bible: Ostróg, 1581; dictionary: P. Berýnda (Памва Берында), Лексикон славеноросский (Kiev, 1627); primers: from that of Ivan Fëdorov, L'vov, 1574; main centres: Vilno (Vilna), Ostróg, Évje, Kutéjno, Mogilëv, Kiev. The primers do not contain much grammar, their purpose being elementary literacy—the alphabet, leading up to some prayers, the Creed, the Ten Commandments, passages from the Psalms, Proverbs, etc.

morphology and everyday vocabulary, principally, it would appear, that of the merchant and petty official class in Moscow.[32]

28 Smotrítsky's *Grammar* was not of high scholarly quality. It contains much that is arbitrary, indeed spurious, in its grammatical norms. But taken as a whole this new and relatively intensive cultivation of ChSl. in the old borderlands produced, if not a new species, at least a distinct variety of ChSl. Especially in Kiev the Polish–Latin background made itself felt since Kievan Orthodox schools had adopted the widespread and highly successful Jesuit scholastic methods applied to Latin in Catholic Europe. Kievan ChSl. (as it may be called) thus became suspect to conservative Muscovites whose liturgical texts had followed the Balkan tradition and had again been recently 'corrected' by direct recourse to sound Orthodox Greek texts in the church reforms of Patriarch Níkon (1652–8). A typical product was Nikon's Bible, still the standard version, carefully printed with the traditional stresses since these by then often differed from those of current speech.

29 The root of the trouble, however, did not lie in relatively minor linguistic differences between Kiev and Moscow. It was that Kievan ChSl., again in imitation of Latin, had pretensions to establish itself as a medium for certain genres of *secular literature*. Though the scope of ChSl. writing had, as we have seen, tended to widen with passage of time since its arrival in Russia, the language had always been withheld on principle from anything that was deemed a purely secular use. To attempt now, in the 17th c., to write, say, amatory verse in ChSl. was not merely an imprudence but impiety, a complete misconception of its proper role. And in any case doomed to failure: love poems are never written in a dead language. This secularizing ChSl. (not identical with the liturgical ChSl.) did, however, succeed in introducing two new genres of literature to Moscow:

30 (*a*) *The stage play*. Directly imitated from the Jesuit 'school drama'. The first was produced at Court in 1672. The subjects were biblical, the intention moral edification, so that ChSl. was not in itself an inappropriate vehicle. But in practice the dialogue was so stilted and artificial as to defeat any dramatic intentions which the

---

[32] Ed. B. Unbegaun, Oxford, 1959. There are grave shortcomings in the orthography (which can be discounted), due partly to his own imperfect ear and partly to the novelty of Cyrillic printing in England—the type had to be obtained from Holland.

author may have had. Further, the same language often spills over into the humorous interludes (интермéдии), played between the acts of the serious drama, which could only retain their character as contrasts and satirical comments on contemporary life by being spoken in the vernacular. A joke in ChSl. is hardly credible.

(*b*) *Verse.* Native verse, as we have seen, had never raised itself above the oral tradition. The ChSl. verse, as cultivated notably by Simeon Pólotsky (1629–80), a Kiev-educated monk who became tutor to the imperial family, had no native roots. It followed the rules of Polish syllabic *wierszy* (Russified as вúрши) and as such was an artificial imposition on the Russian language, devoid of potentialities for the future. For Polish, like French, is a language of light, fixed stress, so word-stress is not an element of the metrical *form* but part of the rhythmic manipulation of the poet. In deference to Polish penultimate stress rhymes had to be 'feminine' (disyllabic) and were therefore bound to rely to a monotonous degree on identical grammatical forms. A couple of lines of Pólotsky's Вертоград многоцветный is enough to illustrate the flatness of the result:

> Во первых всякий купец усердно желáет
> Малоценно да купит, драго да продáет.[33]

This poetry eschews the Russian vernacular in all its characteristic phonetic and morphological traits. It betrays its origin through certain elements of *Ukrainian* pronunciation, accepted as part of the conventions: since in Ukrainian и and ы had merged they were deemed to make good rhymes (Кудри/пудры), as also could и and ѣ (the latter having become [i] in standard Ukrainian— Table XX (3)): лиху/утѣху.

In short, the whole of this secular literature in ChSl. was a learned game. Its practitioners deliberately held aloof from contemporary Russian life. It is, if we like, Russian Baroque, a pale copy at many removes from that of Western Europe. It is perhaps a merit that it did begin to familiarize the tiny circle for which it was intended with the Classical component of European Renaissance and Baroque literature, as for example in Pólotsky's Орелъ россий- ский (*c.*1667). The fuller development of this comes only in the 18th c.

31   If we turn to the use of the vernacular in 17th c. writing we can

---

[33] Russian продаёт or продáст; the latter would be properly parallel to купит.

detect the stirrings, as yet only half-conscious, of a new vitality
below the scholarly exercises. The vast quantity of делово́й язы́к,
often now called прика́зный язы́к—the written language of the
government offices (nobody spoke it)—continues as before as a
subliterary medium and is well exemplified in the tract on the
society and government of Muscovy written by the renegade civil
servant Gregory Kotoshíkhin (1630–67).

Russian in morphology and vocabulary (always excepting Slavonicisms already in everyday use), it falls below what can be
accepted as literary in its syntax: his sentences perpetuate the
snakes of legal language, intended to obviate any possible ambiguity but in fact often obscuring the sense of a plain statement by
their complexity or lack of coherence. An example:

И будет такие люди бывают бол[ь]ны ненарочным дѣлом, и*а* ихъ,
осмотря, от службы отставливаютъ,*b* а посылаютъ въ их мѣсто иных;
а будет у осмотру позна́ют, что учинился боленъ*c* нарочнымъ дѣлом,
хотя избыть того, чтоб с тѣмъ человѣком не быть, с кѣмъ ему велено,*d*
и*a* такого человѣка с тѣмъ человѣком посылаютъ бол[ь]ного, доколе
обможетця, а будет умретъ, или к самому времяни, к которому будетъ
надобен, не обможетця, и*a* въ его мѣсто посылаютъ иныхъ, а ево имя
запишут, хотя и болен был, однако с тѣмъ человѣкомъ, с кѣмъ
велено,*d* посылан*e* и был . . .*34*

Every literate person, of course, still learnt ChSl. at least to an
elementary stage, for this was the matter of his reading primer
(§26 n. 31). But the increasingly strong Western social and literary influences were slowly making it more obvious that no new
(Western-style) literature could take ChSl. as its basis. Where to
find a style for these new genres in the abyss between делово́й
язы́к and ChSl.? This intractable linguistic problem is responsible

34 О России в царствование Алексея Михайловича, ch. 4, sect. 14. The original
form of the text is meticulously reproduced with commentary by A. Pennington,
Oxford, 1980.
Notes: (*a*) и = то (4.82); (*b*) pure Russian form; now usually отставля́ть (the
more ChSl. form: 4.91); (*c*) the preceding pl. такие люди has been forgotten; pred.
instr. not yet obligatory (4.52); (*d*) sc. служить or similar; (*e*) Polish type of *impf*
p.p.p., fashionable at this time (3.129 (4)).
Translation: 'If such people are genuinely ill they are excused service after a
medical examination and others are sent in their stead. But if the examination
shows that [the man in question] made himself ill deliberately in order to avoid
serving with the person with whom he had been ordered to serve, he is appointed
to go, ill as he is, until such time as he recovers. If he dies or does not recover by
the time he is needed others are sent in his stead but his name is officially included
in the list as having accompanied the said person despite the fact that he was ill.'

for the lack of direction and sense of style in most contemporary writing. The traditional exists side by side with the innovating without producing a new compound. Nor are the goals of literature at all clear.

32   An increasingly secular outlook and intention is to be seen in two types of literary activity: historical writing and fiction.

1. Historical annals had, in Russia as in the West, for many centuries been compiled by monks and other churchmen, best placed to be informed of events and to comment on them. In the 17th c., historical records are virtually for the first time made by others. The Летописная книга (or Повесть от прежних лет) attributed to Prince I. M. Katyrév-Rostóvski (*c.*1626) is a layman's account of the Смута ('Time of Troubles', 1604–13). The language is certainly still ChSl. in its essentials—the aor. and imperf. as narrative tenses are still there, as also the dat. absolute (4.49)—but no longer the very rigid 'high style' of official historiography (§18 above). The living language is never far below the surface. The same may be said of the biographies of the 17th c., which still belong essentially to the hagiographical tradition, recording as they do the lives of 'holy women', but written of lay people by lay members of their own families. The Повесть о святой и праведной матери Иулиании Лазаревской (d. 1604) still employs the aor. and imperf. narrative tenses and the dual; the Житие боярыни Морозовой, Княгини Урусовой и Марьи Даниловой (after 1672) cautiously admits a few colloquial elements. History meets the traditional genre of the воинская повесть in Fëdor Poróshin's Повесть об азовском осадном сидении (events of 1637–41).[35] This eyewitness account in fairly pure деловóй язы́к (with some traditional bookish and some 'folklore' elements) should be contrasted with the eyewitness account of the fall of Constantinople (§18 above).

33   2. Secular fiction begins to blossom. Promoted by the considerable activity in translating Western tales, usually via Polish, a motley collection of tales now reaches written form and a new reading public, with roots in traditional oral stories, religious legends, and popular satire. This is, or should have been, the growing point of a Russian prose style neither wedded to деловóй

---

[35] The two accounts of the taking of Azóv by the Don Cossacks in 1637 and of the subsequent Turkish siege (1641) were combined into one narrative towards the end of the 17th c.

язы́к nor full of ChSl. pretensions. A generally accepted norm of language just fails to emerge. Perhaps the material was too heterogeneous; certainly the anonymous authors had as yet no clear artistic aims. Among these stories there are some which are well told and unpretentious, keeping close to popular material and language (Фрол Скобе́ев, Карп Суту́лов); others, especially those with a moral purpose, affect a more bookish style (Са́вва Гру́дцын). The Court patronized, as we have seen, an artificial ChSl. literature; the composers and readers of these tales belonged to a lower social stratum (minor clergy, officials, merchants, etc.) with less inflated literary standards. Even so, the popular satire that came to be written down is not uniformly in popular language, as a comparison of the language of Шемя́кин суд with the almost pure colloquial of Ерш Ершо́вич will show.

However, it is clear that a 'literary feeling' is in the making. Both ChSl. (for the first time) as something antiquated and affected and the administrative language as something humdrum and cliché-ridden became objects of *parody*. Some of the Slavonicisms in Карп Суту́лов are satirical in intention; the satire Слу́жба кабаку́ (or Пра́здник каба́цких яры́жек, before 1666) is directed specifically at the clergy and their language. In the latter, colloquial, not to say vulgar, words keep deliberately intruding on 'serious' ChSl. There could be no clearer indication of an incipient linguistic revolution. In the more serious tales too it is fair to say that the ChSl. element is present more by tradition than conviction. Its use has become automatic and lifeless; it is either an archaism which the author has not the courage to shrug off or the vanity of the semi-literate.

34   Further, in contrast to the stilted Court poetry, the native poetic tradition shows signs of emerging into 'literature', though not yet strongly enough to receive much artistic development. Perhaps the most interesting piece is the По́весть о Го́ре-Злоча́стии (probably mid 17th c.), anchored firmly in oral metre[36] and vernacular language but not innocent of Slavonicisms appropriate to its moral purpose:

> И в тот час у быстри́ реки
> Скочи Горе из-за ка́мени,

---

[36] The same metre as that of the были́ны later collected in N. Russia (§12 above): the stresses produce an approximately dactylic rhythm, usually with a strong anacrusis. There is no rhyme.

Босо-наго, нет на Горе ни ни́точки,
Еще лычком Горе подпоя́сано,
Богатырским голосом восклика́ло: . . .

The chance inclusion of half a dozen short oral poems in Richard
James's notebook (1619–20) bears witness to the vitality of the
popular poetic spirit which kept up a running commentary on
contemporary events. One of them, on the return of Patriarch
Filarét to Moscow, can only just have been composed (summer
1619). Another is a well-conceived lament (плач) put in the mouth
of Ksénia Godunóva.[37]

35　Towering above all these adumbrations of a new secular literature in the vernacular, which had yet to find its feet and discipline
itself (the patronage which demands quality was lacking), stands
Archpriest Avvakúm's *Autobiography*. He makes his own linguistic
position clear at the outset. He did not set out to be 'literary'—quite
the reverse. For him literature meant, understandably in the 1670s,
the secularized ChSl. productions of Pólotsky and his like, which
is anathema to him as a wrong use of the excellent and sacred church
language, and moreover now tainted by its heretical Catholic
background picked up in Kiev and other Western centres.

He says: аще что реченно просто, и [= то] вы, Господа ради,
чтущии и слышащии, не позазрите просторечию нашему, понеже люблю свой русской природной язык, виршами фило-
софскими не обык речи красить . . . The вирши философские
are precisely what Pólotsky was then writing at Court—Polish-
inspired verse with all the learned tricks of Jesuit education in
rhetoric. Просторе́чие is ordinary colloquial Russian (nowadays
the technical sense is 'subliterary colloquial'). The sentence quoted
is not pure просторе́чие. It was to be expected that the earlier
parts of his narrative, which deal with his calling as a priest and
quarrels with the ecclesiastical authorities—solemn matters which
call for some elevation of style—should be in a mixed language.
Aorist and imperfect are used as narrative tenses, though not
consistently. But thereafter, when he embarks on the story of his
harsh Siberian exile, living Russian prevails. ChSl. appears only in
strongly motivated contexts or as biblical quotations. Thus:

Он со шпагою стоит и дрожит, начал мне говорить: поп ли ты, или

---

[37] The Slavonicism преставле́ние 'demise' is not out of place in juxtaposition to
such colloquial forms as ба́тюшков and ма́тушкин.

роспоп? И *аз отвещал: аз есмь Аввакум протопоп*; говори, что тебе дело до меня?

ог

И аз ему малое писанейце написал, сице начало: «Человече! Убойся Бога, седящаго на херувимех и призирающаго в без[д]ны, его же трепещут небесныя силы и вся тварь со человеки, един ты презираешь и неудобство показуешь», и прочая; там многонько писано, и послал к нему.

The text of the note is all quotation or near-quotation from ChSl., intended to put the fear of God into Pashkóv. There emerges from this a clear realization on his part that the two languages have different functions and cannot be *arbitrarily* mixed, as in so many of the stylistically hesitant stories of the time.

Avvakúm's descriptive talent and syntactical control (the importance of which can scarcely be exaggerated) show that, however modest the aims—and the work was only intended for the simple souls who became his adherents in his opposition to the established Church—genuine literary talent is needed to impose a universally acceptable literary norm. Provided that other circumstances are favourable; unfortunately, in Avvakúm's case they were not: the writings of the leader of the schismatics were ignored and this outstanding model of simple prose was thus without effect on the following generations.

As a final example of his narrative technique—rapid, economical, idiomatic—the following may serve:

Посем привезли в Брацкий острог и в тюр[ь]му кинули, соломки дали. И сидел до Филипова поста в студёной башне; там зима в те поры живет, да Бог грел и без платья. Что собачка в соломке лежу: коли накормят, коли нет. Мышей много было, я их скуфьёю бил и батожка не дадут дурачки. Всё на брюхе лежал: спина гнила. Блох да вшей было много. Хотел на Пашкова кричать: прости!, да сила Божия возбранила — велено терпеть. Перевел меня в теплую избу, и я тут с аманатами и с собаками жил скован зиму всю. А жена с дет[ь]ми вёрст с двадцать была сослана от меня. Баба её Ксенья мучила зиму ту всю — лаяла да укоряла. Сын Иван — невелик был — прибрёл ко мне побывать после Христова Рождества, и Пашков велел кинуть в студёную тюр[ь]му, где я сидел: начевал милой и замёрз было тут. И наутро опять велел к матери протолкать. Я его и не видал. Приволокся к матери — руки и ноги ознобил.

Prose of this simplicity, directness, and vigour is not found again for a century and more.

E. *The Eighteenth Century and Beyond*

36   The reforms of Peter the Great finally undermined the prestige of ChSl. as the one and only medium for serious literature. It was a privileged position which—quite apart from its proper liturgical use—it had enjoyed unquestioned for far too long and moreover not really lived up to; literature in ChSl. might have been better appreciated if the language had been more carefully cultivated (as Latin had been in the West) by its practitioners and their level of literary technique had been higher. As it was, by the end of the 17th c. the self-esteem of ChSl. was no longer justified and its condescension towards the vernacular, as the corrupt medium of everyday intercourse quite incapable of elevation to a literary medium, was merely the common argument of those who have a vested interest in perpetuating what they have laboriously learnt but who lack genuine talent and imagination. There is, of course, no validity in this argument: any language can become a fine literary vehicle given suitable cultivation, technical skill, intellectual control. We must agree with the great philologist A. Meillet that 'la persistance des langues religieuses devenues langues littéraires devient à la longue une gêne'.[38]

37   It was easy to condemn the past; it was hard to build a new literary future. The whole first quarter of the 18th c.—to the death of Peter in 1725 and even a little beyond—is a virtual blank in literary progress. Peter's accelerated Westernizing, in the face of much passive resistance,[39] kept everyone too busy to cultivate the graces of social life. There was no court in any sense understood in the West, nor any notable provincial centres of culture. The city of Moscow abruptly lost its primacy; St Petersburg arose on uninhabited marshes with a population drafted in from all over Russia. Peter himself might encourage 'assemblies' (5.32) but such things did not in themselves create a class of patrons in literature and the arts. Those few of the great families (Golítsyn, for example)

---

[38] *Aperçu de l'histoire de la langue grecque* (3rd edn., 1930), p. 120.

[39] Cf. Pososhkóv, Книга о скудости и о богатстве, ch. 3: пособников по его желанию не много, он на гору аще и сам-десят тянет, а под гору милионы тянут, то како дело его споро будет?

which had taken considerable steps towards a serious assimilation of Western culture in the later 17th c. were under Peter in a precarious position. Peter's policies were limited wholly to the utilitarian.

38   Literary production during his reign continued in a small way in established forms without any notable linguistic change (newly borrowed words apart): more tales, inspired or not by Western models (Гисто́рия о росси́йском матро́се Васи́лии Корио́тском may be taken as typical);[40] further edifying 'school drama'. It is hardly surprising that the townsman Pososhkóv's tract Кни́га о ску́дости и о бога́тстве, completed in 1724, is so conservative in language and style that it might have been written a couple of generations earlier. His only concession to the contemporaneity of the social and economic problems which he is discussing is the unavoidable use of a number of new Petrine military and administrative terms (5.31).

39   That literary production was at a low ebb is, however, the less important side of the picture. Peter's policy, no less utilitarian in language than in other matters, brings us to a permanent and irreversible linguistic divide. His reform of the alphabet (1.43) both reduced the repertoire of letters and simplified their shapes to suit the rapid expansion of *printing* and of the bureaucracy. As finally promulgated in 1708–10 the new *secular alphabet* (гражда́нский шрифт; NB Slavonicism + Westernism) did not take simplification to its logical conclusion but it was sufficient to relegate (as intended) the superseded alphabet to specifically *ecclesiastical* use. Though one cannot speak of a direct attack on the Church and its language, its administration was secularized (establishment of a ministry—the Holy Synod—1721) and the pretensions of ChSl. to establish itself in various *secular* genres of literature was, if not quite dealt a quick mortal blow (for the problem lingered on throughout the 18th c.), at least put in a new light. The morphology of spoken Russian had in all important respects reached what is now the accepted standard—though not, of course, in detail—by the end of the 17th c. The extension of printing itself usually leads rapidly to the imposition of a written norm, both in spelling and in grammar—though nothing ever quite stands still in language. Thus the

---

[40] In this tale the new foreign loan-words фрунт, маршировать, вексель, пароль, термин, etc. stand side by side with such archaisms as овамо, понеже, живяше (imperf.), всташа (aor.) and the dat. abs.

Westernized stratum of Russian society, emerging from the time of Peter and seeking a new Western-type literature in Russian, faced the problem, felt but not capable of clear definition or solution in the 17th c., *what is to be a new literary norm of Russian above* деловóй язы́к *but below ChSl.?* (§31 above *ad fin.*).

40   Peter's own practice in his voluminous papers is to use as simple and direct a colloquial language as possible, essentially of course деловóй язы́к (since he was no literary man) but shedding some of its syntactical cumbersomeness. This was also his directive to his envoys abroad and administrators generally (see also 5.32). His intentions are perhaps best seen in the Вéдомости, compiled and published under his eye from 1703. They are, of course, in 'officialese', with a good deal of unnatural word order and syntax of the Kotoshíkhin type, but unnecessary Slavonicisms are on the whole avoided. New and unfamiliar loan-words are glossed by Russian equivalents, e.g.

Нынешняго августа [1704] в 9 день славный и крепкий город Нарва (Руıодев) с Б[о]жиею помощию воинством бл[а]гочестивейшаго н[а]шего Г[о]с[у]даря взят в три четверти часа приступом, хотя неприятель подкопом наших некую часть и подорвал, однакожь салдатов тем устрашить не мог, потом в другую старую крепость неприятель вбежал и бил шамад (здачу) да бы окорд (договор) или хотя бы пардон (м[и]л[о]сть) получить, но салдаты наши того и слышать нехотели, и в тот час, и во оную крепость ворвались, а потом и в самый замок, где неприятелю такой трактамент (подчивание) учинили, что и младенцев не много на сей свет пустили.

Perhaps the best examples of an emergent natural style are to be found in the book of Western etiquette published in 1719 as Ю́ности честнóе зерцáло (a Slavonicism: R. зéркало) and in the autobiography of Prince B. I. Kurákin (completed *c.*1706), a prominent military and political figure of the time. Neither is self-consciously 'literary' in intention. From the former:

Руки твои да не лежат долго на талерке, ногами везде не мотай; когда тебе пить, не утирай губ рукою, но полотенцом, и не пий, пока еще пищи не проглотил. Не облизывай перстов, и не грызи костей, но обрежь ножем.[41]

From the second:

---

[41] Residual Slavonicisms да and пий; перст for пáлец must be considered rather archaic by this date; for талерка see 5.30 (2).

... в седьмой день, в самом безпамятстве, людям своим велел принесть воды, самой холодной со льдом, ушат, а сам лег на постелю и велел себя поливать в таком самом жару, аж покаместь пришел в безпамятство и заснул. И заснув, пробудился от великого холоду и озяб: и потом велел себя положить к печи и окутать. И пришел в великой пот и спал чуть не целые сутки.

The Pioneers of a New Literature and Literary Language (c.1730–60)

41   For the generation which grew up about the time of Peter's death the Russian past was almost irrelevant. A whole new conception of literature, new techniques, new genres had to be acclimatized to complement all the other aspects of Westernization. This required the hammering out of a new literary language.

To begin with there were, as always, compromises. It could hardly be expected that Prokopóvich (1681–1736), Peter's propagandist in ecclesiastical affairs and political theory, steeped in the linguistic theory and practice of the Kiev schools, would be an innovator in language since the genres which he cultivated were the school drama, the sermon on important national occasions, the political tract, and syllabic poetry in ChSl. His funeral sermon for Peter shows the extent of his 'modernization': it hardly goes beyond an unintegrated medley of ChSl., some vernacular elements, and new Western vocabulary characteristic of 17th c. tales. Similarly in his Слово похвальное о флоте российском:

Продолжает Бог радости твоя, о Россие, и данная тебе благополучия новыми и новыми благополучии дополняет. Тот год прошол без виктории твоея, в который не понудил тебе неприятель обнажить оружия. Аки бы рещи: тогда нам жатва не была, когда они не сеяли. Не воспоминая преждних, в прошлом году, когда крыемое долго соссд наших немиролюбие яве откровенно стало, кия плоды пожал мечь российский видели мы с радостию, видели они с великим своим плачем и стенанием. Лето нынешнее было, по видимому, в нечаянии новых славы прибылей, понеже корабельный флот, смотрением политическим удержан, из гавани не выходил. И се над чаяние прилетает к нам 6-го дня июня весть радостная щастливаго наших воев действия с немалою неприятеля утратою. Еще же ведомость тая, почитай, говорити не перестала, и се летит другая и гласит нам викторию, в 27 день иулия полученную. Се уже пред очима нашима и плоды ея довольнии; взятии фрегаты, и воинство, и аммуница, честный и богатый плен. Продолжает воистинну и умножает Бог радости твоя, о Россие!

The strong influence of Latin syntax can be discerned behind this style of ChSl. We should remember that Prokopóvich wrote an elaborate *De arte poeticā* in Latin dealing exclusively with Latin poetry.

A different compromise is to be seen in the work of A. D. Kantemír (1708–44). With a thorough Western Classical education,[42] he cultivated the verse satire on Latin and French models and initiated the translation of Classical authors and French literature (Horace, Boileau, Montesquieu's *Lettres persanes*). Though a thoroughgoing acclimatizer of the *matter* of Western literature he surprisingly made little approach to its *manner* but continued to use the syllabic verse of 17th c. ChSl. Court poetry. His language, as befits satire, has a strong colloquial bias (5.38 *ad fin.*), but mixed with many more or less arbitrary Slavonicisms. The metre obliges him to an unnatural syntax which cannot be excused as corresponding to the free word-order of, say, Horace's odes. Though enjoying some *succès d'estime*, the *Satires*, written from 1729, were not printed till 1762; by that time a new Russian poetry was sailing before the wind on quite a different course. Technically and formally Kantemír's *Satires* were a dead end.

42   Trediakóvsky (1703–69) is a typical man of two worlds. The son of a priest, his education began under Jesuits in provincial Astrakhan' and continued at the most Westernized school in Moscow—the Slavo-Greco-Latin Academy. Trediakóvsky was granted three years of study and literary formation in Paris (1727–30). He, rather than Kantemír, stands at the head of the intelligentsia of the new Russian literature, that is to say, those who recommend and interpret alien ideas to their fellow countrymen. Hence in Trediakóvsky too, and in many writers to follow, the running commentary of theory and justification which accompanied their literary productions. He had returned to Russia in 1730 full of enthusiasm for French *galant* literature. He understood the unsuitability of ChSl. or a heavily Slavonicized style for literature of this kind, and in this context his disparagement of the literary qualities and value of ChSl. was wholly justified.

But Trediakóvsky did not move in high circles, either in France

---

[42] The Kantemirs were a Phanariot family which rose to high office under the Porte in Moldavia, whence they crossed into Russia after Peter's disastrous campaign on the R. Prut in 1711. His father had written a notable *History of the Ottoman Empire* in Latin.

or Russia. He no doubt appreciated that a court and men of education and taste were the indispensable patrons of literature and the other arts; he realized also that the French literary language was to be defined as the consensus of good usage among such speakers—far indeed from the colloquial of the Paris streets or the patois of the countryside, but still a *particular selection of the contemporary spoken language.* It is doubtful that he was fully aware of the immense sophistication of this literary French and of the long period of cultivation which had gone into its making. Working as a translator and literary factotum at the Academy of Sciences he naturally looked round for comparable patrons and a comparable consensus of good usage. Alas, there was no Versailles; Russia could boast of few men of culture. The nursery training of Юности честное зерцало (§40 above) was still needed. The founding of a school for the turning out of young gentlemen was still a few years in the future: the Сухопу́тный шляхе́тный ко́рпус opened in St Petersburg in 1732, and the social and literary effect of its education could not be perceptible before the 1740s. He had failed to realize that in his country there was as yet no accepted usage of an educated class, no *volgare illustre* (to use Dante's term)[43] into which he could translate such a polished work as Paul Tallemant's *Voyage à l'isle de l'amour* (1663). Certainly it was not to be found at the Germanized court of the Empress Anne of Courland. Nor had he the sheer literary talent to invent and impose such a linguistic norm himself. In the nature of things his practice was inadequate to his aspirations.

43 Езда́ в о́стров любви́ was thus a very unwise choice (1730). The Preface makes his theoretical intentions clear: ChSl., into which some might have expected him to translate the work, was now imperfectly understood by the layman, harsh and inflexible, and wholly unsuited to a work of manifestly secular content. So far, so good. But he asks us to believe: не изво́льте погне́ваться (буде вы еще глубокосло́вныя держи́тесь славенщи́зны),[44] что я ону́ю не славе́нским языко́м перевел, но почти самым простым русским словом, то есть каковым мы меж собою говорим.

His vocabulary hovers uneasily between genuine colloquial

---

[43] *De vulgari eloquentia*, I. xvii. 1; in full *vulgare illustre, cardinale, aulicum et curiale*, terms covering the conception of a 'received standard' based on the usage of the cultivated class.

[44] A Polonism: cf. Pol. *polszczyzna* = 'the Polish language', *et sim.*

(очюнь = очень), the officialese of an article in the Вѣдомости, Gallicisms, and (recognized or unrecognized) Slavonicisms. Thus:

Сіе еще умножитъ настоящее мое нещастіе, ежели мнѣ надобно будетъ возновить въ памяти моей то, которое уже прошло, и также сіе не имѣетъ какъ возрастить мою болѣзнь, ежели мнѣ надлежитъ мыслить о оныхъ роскошахъ, отъ которыхъ мнѣ не осталось какъ гор[ь]кое токмо воспоминовеніе. Однако я уповаю, что сіе мнѣ имѣетъ быть къ великому моему утѣшенію, ежели я учиню вамъ наилучшему отъ моихъ друговъ вѣденіе о моихъ печалѣхъ и о моихъ веселіяхъ, ибо печал[ь]ная жалоба не малую чинитъ пользу зло-частнымъ.

It is hardly necessary to point out the artificialities of this passage, in particular such forced Gallicisms as учиню . . . вѣденіе (= *faire le récit*) and the curious не имѣетъ какъ возрастить мою болѣзнь (= *c'est accroître ma douleur que de . . .*).

All the trouble lies in the почти́: the spirit was willing but the flesh was weak. Trediakóvsky was a timid innovator whether in orthography (1.43), versification, or language.[45] Above all he fails in the one essential to which apparently he had not given much thought—syntax. Artificial word-order—inserts, keeping back the verb to the end of the clause or sentence (4.39)—removes all feeling of natural language (. . . каковымъ мы межъ собою говоримъ) and merely serves to underline the cumbersome Slavonicisms which were an inheritance from Baroque word-play.

This proved to be the limit of his approach to the spoken language. As time went on this official translator of Italian opera libretti relapsed into the practice and defence of a highly Slavonicized style.

44 Trediakóvsky's stylistic failures were to be expected: no one can create a new literary language *de toutes pièces* overnight. Though he did not die till 1769, the middle decades of the century belong to Lomonósov (1711–65) and Sumarókov (1718–77). The new genres, with their grading in the hierarchy of French literary theory, dominate the scene, from epic and ode at the summit, through tragedy and the various forms of lyric poetry, to satire and other humble genres. It was no doubt inevitable that at this moment the

---

[45] Timid also towards the text which he professed to admire: *je vis venir une femme toute nue fort belle* . . . becomes я увидел, что один человек прямо к нам шол, весьма статен собою и весь нагохонек . . . and so throughout, in the masculine.

higher genres would exert an irresistible fascination: their successful cultivation would prove the validity of the new literature not only in Russian but in Western eyes too. Lomonósov produces the models in the ode (from 1739—poetry for public occasions), Sumarókov in tragedy[46] (from Хорев, 1747) and the short lyric poem. A new educated readership is in process of formation to patronize and appreciate all these things. Prose for the moment takes second place—unfortunate, perhaps, since only in that could an all-purpose norm of literary language find general acceptance. But that this was the essential desideratum is, if nowhere stated in so many words, implicit in the pronouncements of both these authors.

45 Lomonósov's theoretical standpoint has been touched on in 5.41 above. It may be summarized as follows from the statements of his Риторика (1744, revised 1748) and Российская грамматика (1755):

1. Let us be clear what is (contemporary) Russian *grammar* (especially morphology) and what is Church Slavonic. The two must no longer be allowed to mix: no one can write naturally half in one language and half in another.[47] The dividing line was not in fact clear and neat at all points. Lomonósov himself finds it difficult to decide whether to 'allow' hybrids such as говорящий—a ChSl. p.p.a. from a Russian verb absent from ChSl. In this case, since literary Russian was to find the p.p.a. useful (spoken Russian had abandoned it except as an adj.), the ChSl. form has remained embedded in the paradigm of the Russian verb and all feeling that the form was not appropriate to purely Russian verbs soon disappeared.

Lomonósov's *Grammar* was *normative*, based on observation rather than theory, and stood the test of time till well into the 19th c.

2. ChSl. and Russian have a large common stock of vocabulary, most of it of CSl. inheritance. Further, Russian has adopted many Slavonicisms over the centuries which must now be accounted normal Russian words (e.g. время, надежда, вопрос). The 'middle style' (roughly Sumarókov's domain) should use this common stock of words with a judicious admixture of Slavonicisms. The 'low' style (which neither he nor Sumarókov was much concerned with

---

[46] Tragedy was not, in strict theory, a 'high' genre but inevitably gravitated in that direction since it was used for political and moral debate.

[47] Cf. Pushkin's remark quoted in §59 below, *ad fin*.

in practical literary activity) will avoid virtually all Slavonicisms. The 'high' style will use Slavonicisms liberally, including new words formed on ChSl. models, with one important proviso: all such Slavonicisms must be immediately intelligible in Russian terms. Any ChSl. word, or worse still obsolete OCS word, which is too obscure must now be dropped as an otiose archaism; he instances абие 'at once'.

The theory of the 'three styles' lays no claim to originality: it is just the adaptation of French literary theory to the Russian situation.

The effect of his teaching was to cut out the extreme top and bottom of the vocabulary range from literary use. Subsequent writers interpreted his general prescription differently in respect of particular words: the demotion and promotion of words is a natural phenomenon. It is much to Lomonósov's credit that he was aware of the essential need for a neutral, 'middle' (prose) style, though he did not practise it himself: в сем штиле до́лжно наблюдать всевозможную равность, которая особливо тем теряется, когда речение славенское положено будет подле российского простонародного . . .

46   Such general prescriptions, however sound, can only point the way, to await the usage of a master hand. Neither Lomonósov nor Sumarókov was a master hand; they were competent craftsmen. Sumarókov's education at the Сухопу́тный шляхе́тный ко́рпус left him well grounded in French, German, and Italian but weak in the Classics and ChSl. He was often reprimanded by Lomonósov and Trediakóvsky for solecisms which he committed in the latter. His reply was the Вздо́рные О́ды in which he made fun of Lomonósov's 'high style' pomposity. Indeed the 'grand manner' is exceedingly difficult to sustain without sometimes falling into bombast or bathos. Even if he felt it incumbent on him to use нощь and дщерь in his tragedies, Sumarókov had little use for ChSl. His lyric poetry, though formally an important advance, revolves for the most part in the dreary, small world of rococo myrtles and roses. His positive merit was to seize and insist on the French virtues of clarity and simplicity, not only in vocabulary but also in syntax, the weakest part of Lomonósov's normative work. Most important of all, he and Lomonósov acclimatized a new iambic metrical structure which, though no less an importation (this time from German poetry) than the Polish syllabic ви́рши of the 17th c., did not contradict the natural rhythms of Russian and was quite as suitable to a language of strong stress as the predominantly trochaic or dactylic rhythms of popular oral poetry hesitantly put forward as a model by Trediakóvsky.[48]

At this point we must separate the development of poetry from that of prose. Their basic requirements are different, both in syntax and vocabulary.

Poetry in the Later Eighteenth and Early Nineteenth Centuries

47   No assiduous Russian pupil can be blamed in the middle of the 18th c. for not realizing that the 'high style' was on its way out in the country of its origin and therefore hardly a profitable model. Such was the prestige of Lomonósov's odes that the last formal compositions of this kind were written as late as on the accession of Alexander I in 1801. The epigones during the whole of Catherine the Great's reign made no advance in poetic language and technique, indeed for the most part handled the 'high style' with less finesse than Lomonósov himself. We should, however, not forget that, even amid the collapsing structure of the 'high style' the epic still beckoned as the pinnacle of literary achievement. French critics acknowledged with some shame that no French epic stood where it should on this pinnacle, the best available being (hélas!) Voltaire's *Henriade* (1724). But nothing could alter the theory, repeated by Trediakóvsky in the Preface to his pseudo-epic Тилемахи́да[49] (1766): кра́йний верх, вене́ц и преде́л высо́ким произведе́ниям ра́зума челове́ческого. The pinnacle was scaled in 1779 by another competent craftsman, M. M. Heráskov, in his Россия́да. Bringing to bear on the task a thorough literary preparation (Classical and Italian epic, Klopstock's *Messias* (1748–73), and even *Paradise Lost* in translation) as well as historical sources such as the Исто́рия о каза́нском ца́рстве (written *c.*1564–5), Heráskov manipulated the high style with considerable virtuosity, and remained wedded to it in all his most serious works (including two *Bildungsromane* in prose) right down to the end of the century.

---

[48] It is to be noted that the French Alexandrine, a *syllabic* metre, inevitably turned in Russia, as also in England, into the 'heroic couplet', a metre founded on stress.

[49] A retelling of Fénelon's prose *Avantures de Télémaque* (1699) in Russian 'hexameters' (thus bringing it nearer to seeming like a sequel to the *Odyssey*).

Thus it is not difficult to feel that much of this effort had been wasted, that many of these works of prestige so patiently gestated were in fact stillborn. There is some truth in this: a large proportion of high-style poetry is mere 'verse', turned out according to rules and thus making none of the large demands that poetry should make on form and language. Yet the mere bulk of poetic production in the second half of the 18th c. must be accounted as a positive good: practice makes perfect. Russian, no less than other European literatures, had then to work its way out of the 'high style' (almost as soon as it had espoused it), to cede the stage to the individual lyric voice and to find the language for the private, as opposed to the public, poem—an especially hard task, perhaps, in that there was *no strong tradition of lyric poetry* inherited from earlier periods of the language.

48   Sumarókov's poetic practice had pointed the way. Derzhávin, the first considerable poet with an individual voice, showed in the last two decades of the century that poetic language had to be both *de-Slavonicized* and opened to the living idiom—in other words, poetry too had to find a 'middle style' extensible both upwards and downwards at need. His ode Фелѝца (1782) is an ode only in name: neither the form nor the language belong to the 'high style'. Derzhávin's touch is still uncertain but we can clearly see that from then on Slavonicisms in poetic language can only be *either* those which were an accepted and already often unnoticed element of general vocabulary *or* poetic vocabulary (in contrast to prose), there being usually and quite properly in poetry a verbal component of the archaic or learned, always provided that it contributes to the genuine needs of expression. The principle was already formulated by Aristotle who held that poetry must mix ταπεινὰ ὀνόματα (ordinary, commonplace words) with ξενικά (rare, exotic).[50] An acceptable balance continued to be hammered out by the poets of 1800–20 but there is still in them too often a residue of Slavonicisms which are no more than 'poetic licence', that is, technical failures in face of a difficulty (usually rhythmic), which weakly falls back on, say, an unmotivated брег because берег will not fit the verse.

Such are still present in Pushkin's Руслáн и Людмѝла (1817–20) and other early work. The Pushkinian balance was not achieved only by de-Slavonicization. In his Бáсни (from 1806) Krylóv showed how a stylized colloquial could be the vehicle for charming

[50] *Poetics*, xxii.

poetry and reanimated Sumarókov's insistence on natural simplicity and clarity. Indeed the *fable* in the tradition of La Fontaine—a satirical or ironical comment on human nature—had been one of the successful 'lower' genres of 18th c. poetry. In Pushkin's mature poetic style the language is finally brought into harmony with the matter: the hard core is living Russian—the refined colloquial, the *volgare illustre*; the Slavonicisms achieve their effect by being thus thrown into higher relief when deliberate poetic intention requires them (5.46).

Prose in the Later Eighteenth and Early Nineteenth Centuries

49   Antoine Meillet wrote: 'Il n'y a guère de langue . . . qui ne serve à quelque poésie; mais seule une langue d'une civilisation arrivée à un haut niveau de culture intellectuelle comporte une prose.'[51] The best literary achievements of the Kiev period had been in narrative prose (§§14 and 16 above). Thereafter the cultivation of vernacular prose had been neglected. Conditions for the creation of a new secular prose style did not become wholly favourable again until the reign of Catherine the Great, when there was a court in the full sense of the term, a more uniform education of 'polite society' with some intellectual interests and artistic taste. As recently as the 1730s Trediakóvsky had come to grief on the absence of this. Consciously or unconsciously, all writers not wholly wedded to the most Slavonicized high style were looking for a 'middle style', flexible, suitable for all subjects, and, as Dryden put it in a similar situation, 'capable of elevation when required'. The incubus both of деловóй язы́к, with its inescapable legal mustiness and pseudo-pedantry of semi-educated clerks, and of ChSl. prose, with its tendency to heaviness and convolution (reinforced in the 17th–18th c. by the influence of learned Latin and perhaps to a small extent German prose) had to be thrown off.

The chief variable in poetry is vocabulary: syntax takes second place. In prose, conversely, the chief problem of the new writers was *syntax*; 'middle' vocabulary had been well defined by Lomonósov and always allowed some variation with matter and individual taste.

50   Lomonósov wrote no imaginative prose. His various important scientific papers and critical essays of the fifties are a notable

[51] *Aperçu de l'histoire de la langue grecque* (3rd edn., 1930), p. 218.

advance in handling Russian[52]—indeed the use of Russian for such purposes instead of ChSl. or Latin was in itself a notable advance. But the Latin and German superstratum of his scientific education is still too much in evidence:

Великая часть Физики, и полезнейшая роду человеческому наука есть Медицина, которая чрез познание свойств тела человеческого достигает причины нарушенного здравия, и употребляя приличные к исправлению оного средства, часто удрученных болезнью почти из гроба восставляет.[53]

The growing-point has to be looked for elsewhere—in *comedy* and the *literary periodical*.

51   1. *Comedy*, at the lower end of the spectrum of genres, positively requires (if not in verse) the natural rhythms and vocabulary of conversation. Sumarókov again stands at the beginning with his Опекýн (1765). But especially influential were the two comedies of D. Fonvízin—Бригадúр (1769) and Недóросль (1783)—in which the speech of the characters is nicely graded, from household serf to intellectual from the capital. Fonvízin's object (among other things) is to ridicule the stilted periods of the *raisonneurs*, still giving off an odour of ChSl., the vulgarisms of the provincial gentry who did not yet belong to 'polite society' and spoke virtually the same language as their own peasants, and the excesses of Gallomania among those (especially young people) whose Westernized education was wholly superficial. Contemporaries, it is recorded, were amazed that a literary work could be so 'realistic'. For it had never been tried before; language according to character and social class was the antithesis of the uniformly elevated diction of the high style. The extremes of language, including the Gallomania of the *petits-maîtres*, were a nuisance rather than a danger. Putting them aside, we are left with that neutral, 'middle' style on which the comedy is carried. The contribution of comedy to the establishment of the modern literary language was far greater than that of the pious copies of French tragedies. To the plays must be added Fonvízin's Пúсьма из Фрáнции . . . (1777–8), which deserve to be considered as one of the first achievements of sustained new prose (see example below).

52   2. The *journalism* of Catherine's reign, partly satirical, partly

[52] e.g. Слóво о пóльзе хúмии (1751); Слóво о пóльзе книг церкóвных (1757).
[53] An example of his private correspondence is given below, §53 (i).

informative and edifying in intention, but in any case demanding an easy flow and easy reading, was even more decisive in the acquiring of a nice control of syntax and an ability to match expressive devices to the subject-matter. The central figure is the unassuming Novikóv (1744–1818) whose zeal in publishing new and translated works[54] (1777–92) made the essential models accessible to an ever-expanding readership, to those for whom ChSl. was a closed book and to those who did not read foreign languages.

Though the origins of literary journalism were at least partly English—the *Spectator* and its congeners—knowledge of English was a rare accomplishment; English exerted virtually no influence, syntactical or lexical. The all-important influence was French: French *contes*, essays, works of historical and political scholarship imposed themselves—and not only in Russia—as the best models of 18th c. prose, in respect of lucidity, concision, and logical structure.

Novikóv made no theoretical statements about language but he clearly saw that the 'middle style' must rest on good spoken usage—neither too popular nor too Frenchified. Thus he parodies and satirizes, as occasion demands, both the 'high style' and officialese and that просторе́чие which (as Lomonósov also indicated) must remain below the level of cultivated society and educated usage.

Other contributors to this formation of a 'middle style' prose were M. Chulkóv (Приго́жая повари́ха (1770)—a picaresque story owing something to Richardson) and Krylóv in his По́чта ду́хов (1789), continuing the matter and manner of the *Spectator* already exploited by Novikóv. All that was now required to establish it was the stamp of a greater literary and linguistic imagination.

53 We may pause a moment to compare three extracts:

(i) A private letter of Lomonósov (1753), not intended for publication; vernacular basis with awkward touches of formality:

Обучаясь в Спасских школах, имел я со всех сторон отвращающиеся от наук пресильные стремления, которые в тогдашние лета почти неопределенную силу имели. С одной стороны, отец, никогда детей кроме меня не имея, говорил, что я, будучи один, его оставил, оставил все довольство (по тамошнему состоянию), которое он для меня кровавым потом нажил и которое после его смерти чужие расхитят.

[54] Outstanding works of French, German, English, and Italian literature and some Classics.

С другой стороны, несказанная бедность: имея один алтын в день жалованья, нельзя было иметь на пропитание в день больше как на денежку хлеба и на денежку квасу, прочее на бумагу, на обувь и другие нужды. Таким образом жил я пять лет и наук не оставил.

(ii) Novikóv, Живопи́сец, pt. 1 (1772); gently satirical imaginary correspondence—a deliberately subliterary colloquial:

Эй, сынок, спохватись! Не сыграй над собою шутки: вить [= ведь] недалеко великий пост, попоститься мне немудрено; Петербург не за горами, я и сам могу к тебе приехать. Ну, сын, я теперь тебя в последний раз прощаю по просьбе твоей матери; а ежели бы не она, так уж б я дал себя знать. Я бы и ее не послушался, ежели бы она не была больна при смерти. Только смотри, впредь берегись . . .

(iii) Fonvízin, Пи́сьма из Фра́нции (1777–8); careful prose intended for publication:

Я думал сперва, что Франция, по рассказам, земной рай; но ошибся жестоко. Все люди, и славны бубны за горами. Удивиться до́лжно, друг мой сестрица, какие здесь невежды. Дворянство, особливо, ни уха, ни рыла не знает. Многие в первый раз слышат, что есть на свете Россия и что мы говорим в России языком особенным, нежели они. Человеческое воображение постигнуть не может, как при таком множестве способов к просвещению здешняя земля полнёхонька невеждами. Со мною вседневно случаются такие сцены, что мы катаемся со смеху.

54 After the spadework had been done the master hand made its appearance in the 1790s in Karamzín's *contes*. Karamzín (1766–1828) was accused, in both cases with some justice, of too Frenchified a style and, when his work could be looked back on, too narrow a linguistic basis—a 'salon' style lacking breadth and fresh air. But both shortcomings were natural in the heyday of Sentimentalism, which Russian writers embraced as uncritically as all other Western literary movements. At all events Karamzín was a stylist, the stylist of *bon goût*, who handled Russian with flexibility and musicality and was at once recognized as superior to his predecessors.[55] His stories, *Reisebilder* (Пи́сьма ру́сского путеше́ственника, 1791–2) and *History of the Russian state* (Исто́рия госуда́рства росси́йского, from 1816, in a deliberately more elevated style echoing the early chronicles) were the nourishment of the young Pushkin, who in his turn stripped away the sentimental

[55] 'Вопрос, чья проза лучшая в нашей литературе. Ответ — Карамзина. Это еще похвала небольшая' (Pushkin, 1822).

trappings, revivified the vocabulary, moving out of the four walls of the salon into the Russian countryside, and produced models of the simplest and starkest prose. The art of narrative—a *syntactical art*—had been fully learnt.

A passage from Óстров Бóрнгольм will illustrate Karamzín's style:

Сердце все еще билось у меня от страшных сновидений, и кровь моя не переставала вольноваться. Я вступил в темную аллею, под кров шумящих дубов, и с некоторым благоговением углубился в мрак ее. Мысль о друидах возбудилась в душе моей, и мне казалось, что я приближаюсь к тому святилищу, где хранятся все таинства и все ужасы их богослужения. Наконец, сия длинная аллея привела меня к розмаринным кустам, за коими возвышался песчаной холм. Мне хотелось взойти на вершину его, чтобы оттуда при свете ясной луны взглянуть на картину моря и острова . . .

55   Without 'society' in the best sense there can be no literary standard. In the generation of Karamzín Russian reaches that mature stage when not merely is the linguistic usage of 'polite society' the basis of the literary dialect but conversely the speech of polite society models itself on the literary dialect. The true function of a literary language is then fully apparent: it not only transcends all other forms of native speech, regional and social: it is also the speech of all educated people. From this time onwards the Russian literary language and educated speech evolve together.

We must, of course, not forget that it was only a numerically minute upper class that had been Westernized from the late 17th c. The literary language of the 18th c. and beyond is for its exclusive benefit. The illiterate peasantry remained virtually untouched by a century of radical change and the 'middle class' (merchants and the like), which was not yet in Russia a solid stratum rising in economic and social importance, was also highly conservative in its speech, as a comparison of the language recorded by Ludolf in 1696 with the almost sociological record made by Ostróvsky in some of his plays in the middle of the 19th c. shows.

Thus the social habits of the educated class will decide just how wide a vocabulary its literary language needs or will tolerate. It can be argued that the narrowness of French literary (especially poetic) vocabulary in the 17th–18th c. (as defined by the *Dictionnaire de l'Académie*) reflects the fact that (among other factors) the landed class was by and large more cut off from the life of its peasantry than in England and Russia. The examples given above and the frequent remarks of Pushkin[56] show clearly that modern Russian prose—if anyone doubted it—drew vitality from a level which the high style had stigmatized as 'low' (but not 'vulgar').

56   By the end of the 18th c. the high style had lost all credibility. Thenceforward higher and lower styles, as in European literature generally, were specially coloured variants of the middle style for special purposes.

The diehard rearguard was, however, not unexpectedly to hand. At the turn of the century Admiral Shishkóv could attack Karamzín and his school not only on the grounds of excessive adulation of all things French (which is unpatriotic)[57] but also on the principle that the literary language of Russia should be ChSl., or at least highly Slavonicized, *in perpetuo*. He stubbornly maintained that ChSl. (славе́нский язы́к) and Russian were one single language, a belief which one would have thought had already been refuted once and for all by Lomonósov with proper technical demonstration. But his case illustrates the tenacity of the feeling that any literature worth the name could only be written in the tongue which had been sacred from the outset and further hallowed by so many centuries. In other words, he saw the new 'middle' style of purely secular literature as destroying the proper hierarchical contrast between serious and trivial. It was his view of *literature* which was obsolescent: his view of language followed from that. The original importation of OCS had been a great boon to the Russians in that they received a ready-made literary language which was close enough to their own vernacular to be no barrier to intellectual advance or to an open and stimulating association of the two. This, as we have seen, had long ceased to be actual. Shishkóv could not see that by the 18th c. ChSl. was a tired idiom, with no vitality for the future, and a positive encumbrance in the new intellectual climate of Russia. The purist always resists change and 'progress', which admittedly can never be proved to be progress at the time.

---

[56] e.g. 'Не худо нам иногда прислушиваться к московским просвирням. Они говорят удивительно чистым и правильным языком' (1830).

[57] Shishkóv therefore advocated the replacement of all foreign loan-words by native creations, suggesting for example мокроступы for кало́ши (< Fr. *galoche*). Such people are naturally only up in arms against *contemporary* loan-words, not the unassailable ones already embedded in the language which are largely unrecognized by them and go unheeded.

Conclusion

57   If we look back at these developments the question naturally arises: what is the nature of the link between the writing of the late 17th c. and that which got under way in the 1730s? A complete break is out of the question; such a thing does not happen, for language flows on from generation to generation and is always present to a writer in some of its many forms. But if we put Pososhkóv's Кни́га о ску́дости и о бога́тстве, completed in 1724, side by side with Trediakóvsky's Езда́ в о́стров любви́, completed and published only six years later, we are aware of a linguistic abyss. The link is tenuous. From 1730 literary directions and aspirations were so wholly different from anything which existed before Peter that none of the new writers was looking backwards into the Russian past for models either of style or content. Trediakóvsky's expressed contempt for ChSl. is only one manifestation of this. Interest in the Russian past was not absent: V. N. Tatíshchev (1686–1752) stands out as the first considerable lay historian with an adequate command of the medieval sources;[58] Novikóv initiated the publication of medieval texts (Дре́вняя росси́йская вивлиофи́ка, from 1773). But this was scholarly, not literary work. Tatíshchev's language is almost to be bracketed with that of Pososhkóv. Imaginative literature had its gaze firmly fixed on foreign models—French and to a lesser extent German and Classical. The new language for a new literature had to be created by a painful process of trial and error. As late as 1831 Pushkin, as well read as anyone of his generation both in foreign literatures and in the Russian past, could write: Слове́сность наша, кажется, не старее Ломоно́сова и чрезвычайно еще ограничена. Whatever merits he acknowledged in the Сло́во о полку́ И́гореве and other medieval works, 'literature' (слове́сность) meant for him the productions of the preceding hundred years in the European manner. Russia had attached itself to a different cultural tradition.

The 18th c. was thus necessarily a century of linguistic as well as literary experiment. Concurrently the past had to be divested of its authority (de-Slavonicization) and the authority of the vernacular principle established. Preoccupation with the high style, which imposed itself at this critical moment for reasons of theory and prestige, served only to retard the process of finding the right

---

[58] История российская с самых древнейших времен, not published in his lifetime.

balance. Its main merit was to stimulate *cultivation*. The *métier* of author, so conspicuously lacking in the Muscovite period, comes into being. Trediakóvsky and the other pioneers seize on what is to hand—colloquial idiom, moribund Slavonicisms, the clichés of administrative language, foreign words and phrases—but it is beyond their power to fashion a new standard in the span of one generation. Only in this piecemeal way is 18th c. literary language linked to the past; a broad tradition could not flow through from the one world to the other.

58   The literary languages of Russia in their historical sequence are therefore as follows:

1. The *first literary language* (outside the pure ecclesiastical use of OCS) was a fertile *association and blend* of OCS and native elements, variable according to matter. Unfortunately, a more or less stable and unitary society barely lasted long enough to impose that degree of conventional linguistic uniformity which is the touchstone of a cultivated literary dialect. Internal disintegration and the Mongol conquest brought its development to an end.

2. The *second literary language*, of the Muscovite period, was a refurbished ChSl. and in its more extreme forms confined to a very small body of practitioners. The Second South Slav Influence emphasized the *dissociation* of ChSl. from living Russian which itself had undergone far-reaching changes in the 13th–14th c. In the nature of things a compromise language becomes virtually impossible to achieve and when attempted falls behind the best practice of Kievan times. Vernacular, or predominantly vernacular, writing exists only below the strictly literary level. The subliterary administrative language is based on Moscow dialect.

3. The 18th c. is the time of transition to a secularized society with entirely new literary ideals and needs. The 'secular ChSl.' of the 17th c. and the high style of the 18th c. were both retarding factors in the search for a new standard based on the living language. By the beginning of the 19th c. this had been hammered out with considerable help from foreign models. This was the *third literary language* of Russia—the modern standard. Though the capital is now at St Petersburg the dialect basis does not sensibly change (6.53–4).

4. The *modern standard* is:

   (*a*) almost wholly Russian in *morphology* (the p.p.a. is an exception—3.121);

(*b*) predominantly Russian in *syntax*, a leaven of ChSl. and foreign procedures affecting detail rather than substance;

(*c*) largely Russian in *vocabulary*. The ChSl. component (which could no more be dispensed with than the Latin component in English, whether direct or via French) comprises:

(i) Slavonicisms which descended into everyday speech throughout many centuries (страна́, вре́мя, вопро́с, благодари́ть) and are fully acclimatized in Russian;

(ii) literary Slavonicisms, many quite neutral elements of the vocabulary, others confined to the more learned styles;

(iii) 'neo-Slavonicisms', unknown to ChSl., created and still being created to provide intellectual and technical vocabulary.

59   Among Pushkin's *obiter dicta* we find remarks which reveal his awareness of the evolution summarized above. It was indeed largely his taste and judicious ear which set the seal on that choice of vocabulary which thenceforward was recognized as that of the standard literary dialect. On the one hand he wrote (letter of 1836): писать еди́нственно языко́м разгово́рпым зна́чит не знать языка́; that is to say, he recognized that a ChSl. component was indispensable in a cultivated literary style. And on the other hand (in a fragment of 1834): убеди́лись ли мы, что славе́нский язы́к [ChSl.] не есть язы́к ру́сский и что мы не мо́жем сме́шивать их своенра́вно? With one well-chosen Slavonicism—*arbitrarily*—he puts his finger unerringly on the crux of the matter: for so long there had been *arbitrary* mixtures of ChSl. and the vernacular, the one or the other preponderating. When the mixture ceased to be arbitrary, in the practice of Pushkin and his contemporaries, the modern standard literary language could be considered mature.

APPENDIX

Illustrations of the *polnoglásie* and non-*polnoglásie* (Church Slavonic) forms in Russian word-groups

	Russian	Church Slavonic	Notes
1.	бе́рег 'bank' на́бережная 'quay' береговóй 'coastal'	прибре́жный 'coastal'	брег is still possible as a poetic variant only
2.	бере́чь, берегу́ 'guard' бе́режный 'careful'	пренебре́чь *pf* + instr. 'neglect' небре́жный 'careless'	
3.	береди́ть 'irritate'	бред 'delirium' бре́дить 'rave'	obscure: neither брѣд nor брёд attested
4.	бере́менная 'pregnant' забере́менеть *pf* 'become pregnant'	бре́мя 'burden' обремени́тельный 'onerous'	WhR. бярэ́мя 'armful'
5.	PN Бологóе (5.17) (otherwise extinct)	бла́го 'good' (óбщее бла́го 'common weal') благодари́ть 'thank' благополу́чно 'safely', and all cpds. in благо- поблáжка 'indulgence'	благóй 'crazy' and блажи́ть 'act crazily' belong to the colloquial and might be of different origin but the semantic shift Lat. *benedictus* (= ChSl. блаже́нный) > Fr. *benêt* 'simpleton' is notably parallel
6.	борóться 'struggle' оборóна 'defence'	брани́ть 'scold' брáнное слóво 'swear-word' возбрани́ть *pf* 'prohibit' (cf. Fr. *défendre*)	
7.	dial. бóрошно 'rye meal'	брáшно 'food'	Virtually extinct in both forms
8.	ве́ред 'boil' привере́дливый 'fastidious'	вред 'harm' вреди́ть + dat. 'damage'	береди́ть (No. 3) perhaps from об(в)ереди́ть by deprefixation
9.	(веремя in use till Muscovite period); *verem-* still in Ukr. and WhR.	вре́мя 'time' вре́менный 'temporary'	
10.	dial. вере́тье 'sacking'	вре́тище 'sackcloth'	Virtually extinct in both forms

	Russian	Church Slavonic	Notes
11.	волóга (dial. only) отволóжить *pf* (-волáживать) 'moisten'	влáга 'moisture' влáжный 'moist' увлажни́ть *pf* (-ня́ть) 'moisten'	Root virtually extinct in R. form. Modern science uses the ChSl. forms; отволóжить is an ancient tech. term of various crafts
12.	Волóдя, Всéволод вóлость 'administrative district' (obs. since 1917)	завладéть *pf* + instr. 'seize' власть 'power' влады́ка 'bishop' (title) преобладáть 'prevail' óбласть 'province'	Волóдя is familiar form of Влади́мир (early ESl. Володимѣръ). Володѣти/владѣти and волость/власть are stylistic synonyms in numerous passages of *RPC*
13.	волóчь/волочи́ть 'drag, pull' вóлок 'portage' оболóчка 'cover, membrane' dial. óболоко 'cloud' нáволока/нáволочка 'pillow-slip' прóволока 'wire' заволóчь *pf* (-волáкивать) 'obscure'	влачи́ть(ся) 'drag' (in a few set phrases) óблако (earlier óблак) 'cloud' влечь 'draw' при-/от-влéчь *pf* (-влекáть) 'attract/distract' увлечéние 'enthusiasm'	Two ablaut forms of this root (**welk-/*wolk-*) which fall together in ESl. (1.22)
14.	вóлос 'hair' светло-/темно-волóсый 'fair-/dark-haired'	власяни́ца 'hair shirt'	ChSl. form virtually extinct
15.	вóрог 'foe' (obs., dial., and Ukr.) ворожи́ть 'tell fortunes' ворожбá 'divination'	враг 'enemy' враждéбный 'hostile'	тъ есть ворогъ нама (*RPC s.a.* 1095) (in reported speech)
16.	вóрот(ни́к) 'collar' ворóта pl. 'gate' вороти́ть *pf* 'bring back' ворóчать глазáми 'to roll one's eyes' наоборóт 'on the contrary' поворóт 'turning-point' веретенó 'spindle'	возврати́ться *pf* (-вращáться) 'return' обрати́ть *pf* (-ращáть) 'turn' (fixed phrases) обрáтно 'back(wards)' пре-/раз-врати́ть *pf* разврáт 'depravity'	Roots **wert-/*wort-*, and also **wr̥t-* (ESl. **wĭrt-*) in R. вертéть, and its derivatives ('turn, revolve') воротися Смолиньску (*RPC s.a.* 1095), but возвратиться much commoner and early adopted into the colloquial
17.	головá 'head' (Fr. *tête*) головнáя боль 'headache' изголóвье 'bedside'	главá 'head, chief' (Fr. *chef*) глáвный 'chief' заглáвие 'heading, title'	Typical case of semantic differentiation into a doublet

Russian	Church Slavonic	Notes
18. го́лос 'voice' голосова́ть 'vote' голосовы́е свя́зки 'vocal chords' разноголо́сица 'dissent, discordance'	во́зглас 'exclamation' гласи́ть 'run' (of a text) огласи́ть *pf* (-глаша́ть) 'proclaim, divulge' полногла́сие (1.22) разногла́сие 'disagreement, discrepancy'	The simple noun глас now only possible as a poetic Slavonicism
19. го́род 'town' (orig. 'fort') горожа́нин 'townsman' и́згородь 'fence, hedge' огоро́д 'garden' за-/от-городи́ть *pf* (-гора́живать) 'fence in/off' перегоро́дка 'partition'	(-)град 'city' (now only in PN) граждани́н 'citizen' огради́ть *pf* (-гра-жда́ть) 'protect' за-/пре-гради́ть *pf* 'obstruct, block'	сдѣлаша градъ и нарекоша й Новъгородъ (*RPC, ad init.*)
20. де́рево 'tree' деревя́нный 'wooden'	дре́вко 'shaft, flagstaff' древе́сный у́голь 'charcoal' древеси́на 'timber'	
21. доро́га 'road, way' подоро́жник 'plantain' придоро́жный 'wayside'	подража́ть + dat. 'imitate'	The etymology of подража́ть is still debatable; surviving senses in SSl. are more specialized: SCr. *drȁga* = 'defile'
22. дорого́й 'dear' дорожи́ть + instr. 'value' (вз)дорожа́ть 'rise in price'	драгоце́нный 'precious' дража́йшая полови́на 'better half' (i.e. 'wife')	
23. dial. же́реб(ей) 'lot' жеребьёвка 'casting of lots'	жре́бий 'lot'	
24. здоро́вый 'healthy' здоро́вье 'health' здоро́ваться 'greet' оздорови́ть *pf* (-вля́ть) 'clean up, improve' (living conditions, etc.) не поздоро́вится ему́ 'much good will it do him'	здра́вый смысл 'common sense' здра́вствуйте! (formula of greeting) поздра́вить *pf* (-вля́ть) 'congratulate'	
25. зо́лото 'gold' золото́й 'gold(en)'		зла́то only as poetic Slavonicism

Russian	Church Slavonic	Notes
(вы́)золоти́ть 'gild' (золочёный 'gilded') золотни́к old measure of weight (1/96 lb) золоту́ха 'scrofula'	позлати́ть *pf* (-ща́ть) 'gild' (nearly obs.)	ChSl. forms nearly extinct except for a few cpds. in злато-
26. зо́рок dial. only; cf. зо́ркий 'sharp-sighted', from *zür-k-* (also in близору́кий < близозо́ркий 'short-sighted')	зрачо́к 'pupil' (of the eye) при́зрак 'phantom' прозра́чный 'transparent'	The derivatives of the verb зреть 'see' (*zĭr-), e.g. зре́ние 'vision', зри́тель 'spectator', презре́ть *pf* (-зира́ть) 'despise', are Slavonicisms though the simple verb may well have been native ESl.
27. коло́ть 'stab, split' заколо́ть *pf* (-ка́лывать) 'stab' (*polnoglásie* only in the infinitive)	закла́ть 'sacrifice' закла́ние 'immolation'	колоти́ть 'batter, pound' may be another derivative of the same root
28. коро́ткий 'short' о-/у-короти́ть *pf* (-кора́чивать) 'shorten' коро́че 'shorter'	кра́ткий 'brief' сократи́ть *pf* (-краща́ть) 'curtail, reduce' сокраще́ние 'abbreviation' кратча́йший путь 'shortest route' прекрати́ть *pf* (-краща́ть) 'break off, discontinue'	крат- in кра́тный 'divisible' and многокра́тный 'multiple' is an unconnected root; only in ChSl. form
29. молодо́й 'young' моло́же 'younger' смо́лоду 'from one's youth' (по)молоде́ть 'appear younger'	младе́нец 'infant' мла́дший 'younger'	comparative моло́дший still found in 15th–16th c.
30. молоко́ 'milk' молоча́й 'spurge' моло́чная кислота́ 'lactic acid'	млекопита́ющие pl. 'mammals' мле́чный путь 'Milky Way'	
31. моро́ка 'darkness' (fig.) о́бморок 'swoon, faint'	мрак 'gloom' мра́чный 'sombre' помрачи́ть *pf* (-а́ть) 'obscure'	су́мрак 'dusk' is now less usual than native су́мерки (pl.) from another form of the root (verb ме́ркнуть)
32. норови́ть 'strive, aim at' челове́к с но́ровом 'difficult person'	нра́виться + dat. 'please' нра́вы pl. 'manners,	The nouns not clearly distinguished in the initial period: норовы

APPENDIX

Russian	Church Slavonic	Notes
приноровить *pf* (-норá-вливать) 'fit, adapt' сноро́вка 'knack'	morals' нравоуче́ние 'admonition'	поганьския (*RPC s.a.* 955); кождо свой нравъ (ibid., *ad init.*)
33. пере-, e.g. in переста́ть *pf* (-стáвать) 'cease' переда́ть *pf* (-дáвать) 'hand over'	пре-, e.g. in беспреста́нно 'incessantly' преда́ть *pf* 'betray'	
34. перед 'in front of' пере́дник 'pinafore' пере́дний 'fore-, front' вперёд 'forwards' впереди́ 'ahead' опереди́ть *pf* (-жáть) 'outstrip'	пре́жде 'before' пре́жний 'former' prefix пред- (4.63) пре́док 'ancestor' впредь 'in future' предупреди́ть *pf* (-ждáть) 'warn'	перед specialized largely to *space*, пред- to *time*
35. поперёк 'across' попере́чник 'diameter' пере́чить + dat. 'contradict' (fig.)	вопреки́ 'in spite of' прекосло́вить + dat. 'contradict'	
36. по́лымя (dial. form) 'flame' (only in из огня́ да в по́лымя = 'out of the frying-pan into the fire')	пла́мя 'flame' воспламени́ть 'ignite, inflame'	
37. поло́н 'captivity' полони́ть *pf* 'take captive' (both virtually obs.)	плени́ть 'captivate, charm' взять в плен 'take captive' пле́нник 'prisoner of war'	
38. поро́жний 'empty' опоро́жнить *pf* (-порáжнивать or -порожня́ть) 'empty, drain'	пра́здный 'idle' пра́здник 'holiday' (от)пра́здновать 'celebrate' упраздни́ть *pf* (-ня́ть) 'abolish, cancel'	OCS *prazdinŭ*
39. по́рох 'powder' поро́ша 'new snow' зубно́й порошо́к 'tooth-powder' запороши́ть *pf* (-порáшивать) 'powder'	прах 'dust' (fig.) вертопра́х 'frivolous person'	разби́ть в пух и прах 'rout'
40. середи́на 'middle'	(по)среди́ 'in the midst of' среда́ (1) 'milieu'; (2) 'Wednesday' сре́дний 'mean, average'	

Russian	Church Slavonic	Notes
	cpds. in средне-, e.g. средневекóвье 'Middle Ages' срéдство 'means' сосредотóчить *pf* (-тóчивать) 'concentrate' непосрéдственно 'directly'	
41. сморóдина '(black) currants'	смрад 'stench'	Another form of the root in смердéть 'stink'
42. сóлод 'malt' солóдка 'liquorice'	сдáдкий 'sweet' (cpds. in сладо-) сластёна 'sweet-tooth' (по)сластить 'sweeten' насладиться *pf* + instr. (-слаждáться) 'enjoy, delight in'	
43. сорóчка 'shirt, blouse' (for сóрок '40' see 3.78 (iii))	срачица 'shirt' (as part of vestments)	
44. (dial. only) сóром 'genitalia'	срам 'shame' о-/по-срамить *pf* (-срамлять) 'disgrace'	
45. стóрож 'watchman' насторожить *pf* (-сторáживать) ýши 'prick up one's ears' осторóжный 'careful'	стрáжа 'guard'	Different ablaut in the verb стерéчь, стерегý
46. сторонá 'side, direction' (по)сторониться 'stand aside' сторóнник 'adherent' посторóнний 'outside, extraneous'	странá 'country' страница 'page' стрáнный 'strange' стрáнствовать 'wander' устранить *pf* (-нять) 'remove, eliminate' прострáнство 'space' распространить *pf* 'spread, extend' иностáнный 'foreign'	стрáны свéта '(cardinal) points' preserves older sense
47. теребить 'pull, pester'	трéба 'rite' трéбовать 'demand' употребить *pf* (-треблять) 'use' потрéбность 'need' до вострéбования 'to be called for'	Semantic connection no longer evident. Original sense of теребить was apparently 'assart'

APPENDIX

Russian	Church Slavonic	Notes

48. хóлод 'cold'
холóдный 'cold'
холоди́льник 'refrigerator'
холоднокрóвный 'cold-blooded' (sc. animals)
захолодéть *pf* 'grow cold'

прохлáдный 'cool'
cpds. in хладно-, e.g. хладнокрóвный 'cool' (fig.)
(хладнокрóвие 'sang-froid')
охлаждéние 'cooling'
охлади́тель 'refrigerator, coolant'

49. хорóбрый (dial. only and Ukr.) 'brave'; but here may belong хорóший 'good' with substitution of the 'diminutive' or familiar suffix -š- as in Сáша, Алёша

хрáбрый 'brave'

50. хорóмы pl. 'mansion, barn'

храм 'temple'

51. пóхороны pl. 'funeral'
за-/с-херони́ть *pf* 'bury'

охрáна 'protection'
сохрани́ть *pf* (-ня́ть) 'preserve'
предохрани́ть *pf* 'protect'

52. черевики (Ukr.) 'leather boots' (< черево 'hide, skin' obs.)

чрéво 'womb'
чревáтый 'pregnant' (also fig.)

cf. *RPC s.a.* 1019: черево твое толстое 'paunch'

53. череда́ 'turn, sequence'
чередовáть 'alternate'
óчередь 'queue, turn'

учреди́ть *pf* (-чреждáть) 'found, establish'
учреждéние 'institution'

54. чéрез 'through, across'
чересчýр 'too (much)'
чересполóсица 'strip-cultivation'

чрезвычáйно 'extraordinarily'
чрезмéрный 'excessive'

55. шелóм (obs. or poetic) 'helmet'
ошеломи́ть *pf* (-мля́ть) 'stun'

шлем 'crash-helmet'

56. There is little or no evidence of ESl. equivalents for the following Slavonicisms: брак 'matrimony' (etymology uncertain; may not be *bor-kǔ* 'taking', formed as зна-къ); глагóл 'verb' (глаголати = говорить); злáки pl. 'grass' (*Gramineae*).[1] Трéзвый 'sober' (dial. терёзвый, тверёзый, and other forms) and член 'member' (расчлени́ть *pf* 'dismember'; early ESl. and Ukr. čelen-) now exist only in ChSl. form in the literary standard.

[1] But perhaps from *zlō-k-*; cf. Gk. χλω-ρός.

401

APPENDIX

57.   The following are the most usual Russian words which now exist or have always
existed in ESl. form only; the high proportion of concrete Russian *realia* will be
observed: берёза 'birch'; болóто 'marsh'; бородá 'beard'; бороздá 'furrow';
боронá 'harrow'; вéрес(к) 'heather' (*Calluna*); воробéй 'sparrow'; вóрон 'raven'
and ворóна 'crow'; гóлод 'hunger'; горóх 'peas'; долотó 'chisel'; жереб-éц/-ёнок
'stallion, foal'; жóлоб 'gutter'; колóда 'log'; колóдец 'well' (5.6); кóлокол 'bell';
кóлос 'ear' (of corn); корóва 'cow'; корóль 'king' (королéва 'queen' but also
formerly крáля 'queen' (in cards)); мерёж(к)а 'net'; мóлот 'hammer'; морóз
'frost'; моросúт 'it is drizzling' (мóрось); нéрест 'spawning season'; пáпоротник
'fern'; полóвый 'blond' (Пóловцы 'Cumans', 5.7 (6)); полоскáть 'rinse'; полотнó
'linen' (полотéнце 'towel'); плáтье 'dress' is not connected); порóг 'threshold';
поросёнок 'pigling'; скоморóх 'minstrel, clown';[2] соловéй 'nightingale'; солóма
'straw'; сорóка 'magpie'; толóчь 'pound' (толокнó 'oatmeal'); торокá pl. 'straps'
(part of harness); торопúться 'hurry' (расторóпный 'prompt'); хвóрост 'brushwood'; холóп 'slave, serf'; холостóй 'single, bachelor'; чéреп 'skull' (черепáха
'tortoise').

The following infinitives should also be noted: колóть (pres. колю́; OCS *klati*/
koljǫ); -мерéть (-мру; *mrěti/mĭrǫ*); молóть (мелю́; *mlěti/meljǫ*); полóть (полю́
after колю́; *plěti/plěvǫ*; *plěvelŭ* 'weeds, "tares"'); терéть (тру; *trŭti*, i.e. **tr̥ti/tĭrǫ*).

---

[2] Etymology unknown; Pol. had *skomroszny*.

402

REGISTER OF RUSSIAN WORDS
TREATED IN CHAPTER 5

Reference is to section; † denotes a now obsolete
or narrowly 'historical' word

абрикос 34, n. 77
автограф 35
áвтор 30 (6)
áгéнт 30 (1)
áдрес 30 (1)
áзбука 33
аккóрд 36
Аксáков 22
акт 30 (1)
актёр 37
актрѝса 37
акýла 13
áлгебра 32
† алтьн 21
áлый 21
аналóй 15
† анатомѝст 38
анатóмия 27
апельсѝн 34, n. 77
аплодѝровать 37
аптéка(рь) 27
арбýз 21
аргамáк 9
áрéст 30 (1)
аристокрáт 31
áрмия 29
армяк 21
архитéктор 28
архитектýра 30 (8)
† асамблéя 32
атáка 29
атмосфéра 35
Ахмáтов 22

багáж 44
бадья 21
базáр 21
бакалéя 21
балагáн 21
баллотѝровáть 33

банк 33, n. 76
банкéт 31
барабáн 21
бáрка 24
барóметр 41
барсýк 21
бархáн 22
бáрхат 24
барьш 21
† баскáк 21
бахромá 21
башмáк 21
бáшня 30 (2)
бедá 19, n. 41
без 17
бéлка 12
Белорýссия 28, n. 61
бельмéс 22
бемóль 36
Бердяев 22
бéрег 5
† бéрковец 13
бéркут 22
беспокóйство 40
беть 13
библиотéка 30 (8)
билéт 33
бѝржа 33, n. 76
бирюзá 21
бѝсер 10
блáго- 4, 17
благодарѝть 16
блюдо 5
бог 4
богатьрь 10
божéственность 40
болвáн 10
болéзнь 6
бóмба 33
бóрзый 45

бот 24
боязнь 6
боя́ре *pl.* 10
брат 1
бровь 1
броня́ 5
брюки *pl.* 34, n. 77
† будовáть 29
бýдущее 41
бýдущность 45
буй 34
бýква 6
буквáрь 6, n. 16
буксѝровáть 33
булáный 9
† булáт 21
Булгáков 22
бумáга 28
бунт 29
бурмѝстр 32
бутьлка 30 (2)
бьстрый 45

вáжный 30 (5)
† варяг 13
ватáга 10
вáхта 29
ваятель 36
† вéверица 12
вéжда 47
век 30 (3)
вéко 3, 47
вéксель 33
† вéкша 12
великодýшный 23,
 n. 53
Вéнгрия 30 (9)
венéц/венóк 18
вéнзель 30 (7)
вéра 4

верблю́д 5
вербова́ть 29
верфь 34
вещество́ 18, n. 38
вещь 19
вид 41
вини́тельный 26
вино́ 5
† ви́ра 13
† ви́рши *pl.* 30 (9)
вкус 40
владе́ть 5
Влади́мир 6, 13
† вла́сный 29
влюблённость 45
во́здух 17
во́йлок 8
Во́лга 12
Во́логда 12
воск 2
восто́к 17
впечатле́ние 40
вражда́ 6, 47
враньё 18
врата́рь 6, n. 16
вре́мя 23
времяпрепровожде́-
  ние 40
вто́рник 25
Вы́чегда 12
† вы́я 47
вьюк 8

га́вань 34
газе́та 36
гастроли́ровать 37
гвозди́ка 27
герб 30 (7)
глаго́л 26
глаз 47
Глеб 13
глуха́рь 6, n. 16
говори́ть 17, 46
голова́ 3
гонча́р 6, n. 16
гора́зд(о) 5
горизо́нт 25, 35
го́род 5
гото́в(ить) 5
граб 3
гра́мота 14
† гридь 13
грим(ирова́ть) 37

гряду́щее 41
губе́рния 30 (1)
гусь 5

да́ма 30 (7)
да́тельный 26
дать 1
дёготь 11
де́йствие 37
декора́ция 37
декре́т 30 (1)
де́лать 46
де́ньги *pl.* 21
депута́т 30 (1)
десть 21
диа́метр 35
† див 4
диспута́ция 31
† до́ба 19
дозво́лить 30 (4)
до́ктор 27
докуме́нт 30 (1)
долби́ть 2
дом 1
доса́да 19
доска́ 5
доскона́льный 30 (5)
доста́ть 30 (4)
драгоце́нный 18
ду́ма 5
духове́нство 30 (7)
ды́ня 14
ды́шло 30 (2)
дьяк 14
дья́кон (диакон) 14
дю́жина 24
дюйм 34

едва́ 45
едини́ца 25
е́ле 45
еле́й 15
епитрахи́ль 15
-ество 18, n. 38

† жа́дный 31
желе́зо 3
же́мчуг 10
жёрнов 2
же́ртва 4
жесть 21
живопи́сец 36
живопи́сный 44

жизнь 6
журна́л 33

забия́ка 39
зако́н 32
за́мок 30 (2)
зао́чный 47, n. 95
захолу́стье 45
зая́длый 30 (5)
зва́тельный 26
звезда́ 3
здра́вствуй(те) 32
зло (зол) 4
зна́харь 6, n. 16
зо́лото 2

И́горь 13
игре́ний 9
иде́я 30 (3)
из- 17
изба́ 6
и́звесть 14
изда́тель(ство) 35
изобрета́тельность 45
-изовать 31
изрече́ние 46
изумру́д 21
изю́м 21
Ильме́нь 12
имби́р 24
имени́тельный 26
име́ть 40
импе́рия 30 (1)
и́мя 26
инжене́р 30 (6)
инстру́кция 31
интере́с 30 (3), 31
инфинити́в 41
-ировать 31
иску́сство 18
и́стина 19
-ица 18

-ка 19
каблу́к 21
кавале́р 30 (7)
† кага́н 8
кады́к 22
каза́к 21
казна́(чей) 21
календа́рь 30 (8)
† калпа́к 21
камы́ш 21

канды́к 22
канцеля́рия 30 (1)
капита́л 33, n. 76
капита́н 29
† ка́пище 10
капу́ста 6
караби́н 29
каранда́ш 21
карау́л 21
каре́та 30 (2)
ка́рий 9
карти́на 36
ка́рты pl. 30 (7)
ка́сса 33, n. 76
ка́торга 14
кафта́н 21
ка́яться 4
квадра́т 25
квас 38
керме́к 22
киби́тка 22
кинжа́л 21
кирпи́ч 21
† кичири́с 22
клевета́ 19
клобу́к 21
кнут 13
князь 6
кобы́ла 9
кова́рный 19
ковёр 10
ковче́г 10
ковш 11
ко́зни pl. 6
ко́йка 34
† колбя́г 13
коле́но 3
колле́га 30 (7)
коло́дец 6
колпа́к 21
колча́н 22
коля́ска 30 (2)
командирова́ть 29
коме́дия 30 (8)
коми́ссия 30 (1)
ко́мната 24
† комонь 9
компа́ния 30 (1)
ко́мпас 31
конве́рт 30 (7)
ко́ндо́вый 12
конститу́ция 31
конто́ра 34, n. 77

конь 9
копе́йка 21
† корля́зи pl. 6
коро́ль 6
† корчма́ 6, n. 16
котёл 5
кочева́ть 8
красота́ 40
крахма́л 30 (2)
кре́ди́т 33, n. 76
крова́ть 14
кро́лик 30 (9)
кру́жка 24
крюк 13
† куба́ра 14
кувши́н 11
кула́к 22
кули́сы pl. 37
куми́р 10
куна́ 3, 21
купи́ть 5
купоро́с 24
курга́н 10
ку́рок 29
курс 33
-куси́ть 5
куста́рь 30 (6)
Куту́зов 22
куха́рка 30 (2)
ку́хня 30 (2)
куша́к 21

лави́ровать 33
ла́герь 33, n. 75
Ла́дога 12
ладо́нь 3
ла́мпа 30 (2)
лампа́да 30 (2)
лани́та 47
ларь 13
Латы́нь 28, n. 62
лёд 3
лежа́ть 5
ле́карь 30 (6)
лесть 5
лечи́ть 5
† Либь 13
лик 47
лине́йка 30 (2)
ли́па 3
лицо́ 26, 47
ли́чность 44
ло́гика 38

ло́зунг 33, n. 75
† Лопь 13
ло́шадь 9
лы́ва 12
лы́ко 3
люби́тель 18
любо́вник 40
лю́ди pl. 5

магистра́т 32
мане́р(а) 30 (3), 31
ма́стер 24, 28
мастерство́ 18
материа́л 33
мате́рия 30 (3)
матро́с 34
мать 1
маши́на 30 (2)
ме́бель 30 (7)
ме́жду 23
ме́рин 9
ме́тод 30 (3)
меха́ника 30 (8)
меч 5, 10
мече́ть 22
мещани́н 30 (7)
† мизи́рный 31
минда́ль 27
мину́та 32, n. 73
ми́чман 34
мише́нь 21
мла́дость 18
млекопита́ющие
pl. 35
мног- 5
многообра́зный 23,
n. 53
могу́ 5
мо́лодость 18
молоко́ 5
монѣ́та 30 (2)
мо́ре 1
морж 12
морко́вь 6
Москва́ 12
Мста 12
Мстисла́в 13
му́зыка 30 (7)
мунди́р 33, n. 75
мушке́т 29
мы́тарь 6, n. 16
мышь 1
мя́та 6

набáт 21
наблюдéние 38
нáгло 31
надéжда 23
нáдо 19
наединé 45
наизýсть 47, n. 95
налóй 15
напёрсток 47, n. 95
наперстя́нка 47, n. 95
† наприклáд 38
настоя́щее 41
натýра 30 (3), 40
натурáльный 31
находи́ться 40
нáция 30 (1), 31
нашатьíрь 21
не- 17
нéбо 4
небосклóн 35
Невá 12
неиссякáемый 44
непредви́димый 45
непристóйный 30 (5)
неприя́знь 6
нéрпа 12
-ние (-нье) 18
ногá 3
† ногáта 13
ноль (нуль) 32, n. 72
нóмер 34, n. 77

обезья́на 21
оберегáтель 18
óблик 47, n. 95
оборони́тель(ный) 18
óбраз 19
образовáние 44
обстоя́тельство 44
óбщество 18, n. 38
обывáтель 30 (7)
обя́зан 40
-овать 31
Огарёв 22
оглóбля 29, n. 64
огóнь 4, n. 5
огорóд 5, n. 13
огурéц 14
одéжда 23
Окá 12
óко 47
† ол (olŭ) 2

Олéг 13
олéй 15
óлово 3
Óльга 13
омéла 3
Онéга 12
óный 47
óпера 36, n. 82
опереди́ть 23, n. 54
ордá 21, n. 42
осёл 5
осóба 30 (7)
-ость 18, 31, 40
отвáга 30 (3)
отрицáть,
    отрéчься 46
отсýтствовать 40
охлади́тель 35
охрáна 29
óчень (очюнь) 39
ошеломи́ть 5

падéж 25
пáкля 11
пáлец 47
панихи́да 15
пáрень 45, n. 90
парк 44
пáртия 31
пáспорт (пашпорт) 30
    (1), 31
пастернáк 27
патрóн 33, n. 75
† пéнязь 6, 21
перебывáть 39
переворóт 42
перенóс 39
перепи́ска 18
персóна 31, 40
перст 3, 47
пéрстень 47, n. 95
† перýк 38
пёс 4, n. 7
петрýшка 27
Пи́нега 12
писáтель 18
плоть 3
плуг 6
пля́ска 30 (7)
повари́ха 30 (2)
повáрня 30 (2)
повели́тельный 41

пóвод 30 (3)
пóдвиг 19
пóдданство 30 (1)
пóдлый 30 (5)
подóбие 19
поеди́нок 30 (7)
пожáлуй(ста) 32
позвóлить 30 (4)
поздрáвить 30 (4)
поли́тика 30 (1)
поли́ция 30 (1)
полк 5
полкóвник 29
Пóловцы pl. 7
положи́тельный 26
пóмпа 33
поня́тие 38
пóрох 29
порт 34
потáш 27
пóчта 30 (1)
поэ́т 39
прáвда 6
пре- 17
преврати́ть 23
пред- 17
предмéт 35
предрассýдок 42
председáтельство-
    вать 40
прéжде 23
прéжний 23, n. 54
презрéть 23
преимýщество 18,
    n. 38
прекрати́ть 23
преломлéние 41
прервáть 23
привередли́вый 18
† прикро 31
при́нцип 30 (3)
прирóда 40
присýтствовать 40
причи́на 30 (3)
прия́тель 18, n. 39
прóба 24, 31
прови́нция 30 (1)
прóза 40
промьíшленность 45
просóдия 39
просфорá 15
профéссор 33
процéнт 33

публикова́ть 30 (4)
публи́чный 30 (5)
пуд 24
пульс 27
пу́ля 29
пункт 30 (8)
пурга́ 12
путеше́ствие 18
пу́шка 29
пя́тница 25

ра́ди 4
ра́диус 33
ра́зве 45
развитие 44
рай 4
ранг 33, n. 75
рассе́янный 42
растро́гать 42
†ратман 24
†ра́туша 32
†рать 29
реве́нь 21
ревизо́р 30 (1)
револю́ция 30 (1)
регла́мент 30 (1)
ре́крут 29
рели́гия 30 (8)
ре́плика 37
ри́га 12
рисова́ть 30 (4)
рису́нок 30 (8)
ри́фма 39
рог 3
род 26
роди́тели *pl.* 18
роди́тельный 26
рожда́емость 18
рожь 2
роль 37
Росси́я 28, n. 61
рот 47
ро́та 29
рубль 21, n. 46
рука́ 3
ру́сский 6
Русь 13, 28, n. 61
ры́нок 30 (6)
ры́царь 30 (7)

са́бля 10
са́ван 15
савра́сый 9

сайга́ 22
салты́к 22
Салтыко́в 22
самодержа́вие 18
самонаде́янность 44
самши́т 21
сан 10
сапо́г 4
саранча́ 10
†сарафа́н 21
са́хар 14
сбо́р(ка) 18
сбру́я 29
све́тский 29
сво́йство 18
свят- 4
сей 47
секре́т 30 (3)
секрета́рь 30 (1)
секу́нда 32, n. 73
сели́тра 27
сельдь 24
сена́т 32
сена́тор 30 (1)
серебро́ 2
сержа́нт 29
серьга́ 21
сестра́ 1
Сиби́рь 22
сказа́ть 46
скамья́ 14
скарб 30 (2)
скло́нность 40
скором- 30 (5)
ско́рый 45
скот 5
скро́мный 30 (5)
ску́льптор 36
сла́дкий 40
сле́сарь 30 (6)
слова́рь 6, n. 16
сло́во 4
слон 21, n. 49
сме́ртность 18
смягчи́ть 40
соба́ка 4
соб(и)ра́ние 18
солда́т 29
†соломя́ 12
спаси́бо 32
специа́льный 30 (5)
спирт 34
справедли́вость 30 (3)

срам 4
среда́ 25
ста́до 5
стака́н 21
сталь 24
-ствие 18
-ство 18
стекло́ 5
степь 10
стиль 39
сто́ить 30 (4)
столя́р 30 (6)
страда́тельный 41
страна́ 47
стро́гий 30 (5)
стул 24
†стяг 13
сулема́ 27
су́мма 32
сунду́к 21
сургу́ч 22
сурьма́ 21
суфлёр 37
сце́на 37
сын 1

табаке́рка 30 (7)
та́бель 34, n. 77
табли́ца 30 (8)
та́бор 10, n. 24
табу́н 8
тага́н 21
тайга́ 22
†тамга́ 21
тамо́жня 21
та́нец 30 (7)
тарака́н 8, n. 20
таре́лка 30 (2)
†таркан 8
тварь 46
творе́ц, твори́ть 46
тво́рческий, тво́рчес-
  тво 46
теа́тр 37
теле́га 8
те́ло 3
-тель 18
те́рем 14
термо́метр 41
тетра́дь 14
ти(в)у́н 13
тира́ж 44
ти́тул 30 (1)

407

REGISTER OF RUSSIAN WORDS

товáр 10
†толмáч 8
тонúческий 39
топóр 4
тóрос 12
трагéдия 30 (8)
трактáт 30 (1)
трактúр 30 (2)
трóгательный 42
трóгать 42
трущóба 45
трюм 34
тумáн 21
тýндра 12
†турбовáть 31
Тургéнев 22
тýфля 32
тщеслáвие 23, n. 53
тьíсяча 2
тюлéнь 12
тюрьмá 21
тюфя́к 22

убúйственный 44
удóбный 19
удовóльствие 18
указáтель 18
указáтельный 41
ýксус 14
улýс 22, n. 50
улучшéние 45
ус 3
устá *pl.* 47
утончённый 44
утю́г 21
учúлище 30 (8)
учúтель 18

фáбрика 33, n. 76
фáктор 30 (6)
фальш 31
фальшúвый 30 (5)
фамúлия 30 (7)

фиáлка 27
фигýра 30 (3)
†фискáл 32
фонáрь 14
фонтáн 30 (2)
фóрма 30 (3)
фунт 24
†фуртовина 24
футля́р 33

халáт 21
харáктер 30 (3)
харатья́ 14
хáта 7, n. 17
хúжина 5
хлеб 5
хлев 5
хмель 4
хозя́ин 8
холм 5
хомя́к 10
хранúть 4
худóжник 5, 36
хулúть 5

цúфра 30 (8)

чай 22
чáлый 9
чекáн- 10
человéчество 18, n. 38
чемодáн 22
чердáк 21
чéреп 3
чертá 40
чертóг 10
чинúть 40, 46
чубáрый 9
чувствúтельный 40
чугýн 22
†Чудь 13
чýждый 5

чужóй 5
чулóк 21

шалáш 21
шалфéй 27
шáпка 30 (2)
шатёр 10
шафрáн 27
шáхта 30 (6)
шёлк 13
шéя 47
шкúпер 24
†шкóда 29, 31
шкóла 30 (8)
шлем 5
шля́па 30 (2)
†шля́хта 30 (9)
†шнека (шняка́) 13
штаны́ *pl.* 22
штраф(овáть) 30 (1)
штык 33, n. 75
шýба 21

щекá 47

эклúптика 25
электрúчество 41

юбка 21

я́бедник 13
явлéние 35, 37
я́гель 12
я́корь 13
ям(щúк) 21
янтáрь 11
яр(ýга) 10
ярлы́к 21
я́рмарка 30 (6)
я́хта 24
я́щик 13

408